XI'AN

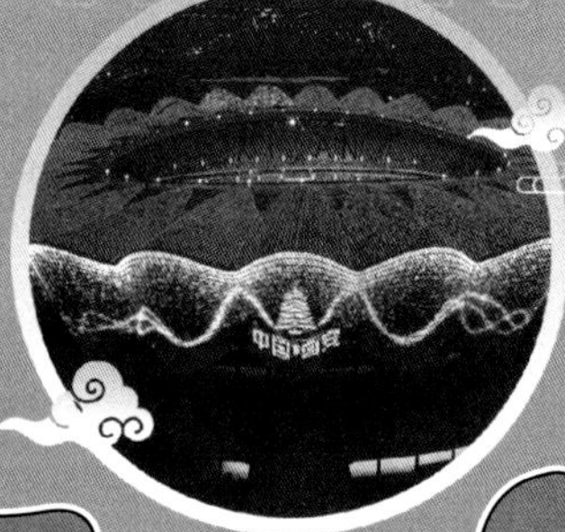

西安统计年鉴 2021

STATISTICAL YEARBOOK

中英文对照 Chinese/English

中国统计出版社
China Statistics Press

西安市统计局
XI'AN MUNICIPAL BUREAU OF STATISTICS
国家统计局西安调查队
NBS SURVEY OFFICE IN XI'AN

图书在版编目（CIP）数据

西安统计年鉴. 2021 = Xi'an Statistical Yearbook 2021 : 汉英对照 / 西安市统计局, 国家统计局西安调查队编. -- 北京 : 中国统计出版社, 2021.9
ISBN 978-7-5037-9561-9

Ⅰ. ①西… Ⅱ. ①西… ②国… Ⅲ. ①统计资料－西安－2021－年鉴－汉、英 Ⅳ. ①C832.411-54

中国版本图书馆CIP数据核字(2021)第139605号

西安统计年鉴—2021

作　　者/ 西安市统计局 国家统计局西安调查队
责任编辑/ 钟 钰
装帧设计/ 西安乐成品牌策划设计有限公司
出版发行/ 中国统计出版社有限公司
地　　址/ 北京市丰台区西三环南路甲6号
邮政编码/ 100073
电　　话/ 邮购（010）63376909 书店（010）68783171
网　　址/ http://www.zgtjcbs.com
印　　刷/ 西安第一印刷厂
经　　销/ 新华书店
开　　本/ 890mm×1240mm 1/16
字　　数/ 1098千字
印　　张/ 44.5 彩页1.25
版　　别/ 2021年9月第1版
版　　次/ 2021年9月第1次印刷
定　　价/ 260.00元 Price: 260.00yuan(RMB)

本书附同版本CD-ROM一张，光盘内容以书面文字为准。
如有印装差错，由本社发行部调换。

《西安统计年鉴—2021》编辑部

XI'AN STATISTICAL YEARBOOK 2021

EDITORLAL STAFF

编者说明

一、《西安统计年鉴—2021》系统收录了全市、区县及开发区2020年经济、社会各方面统计数据，以及重要历史年份主要统计数据，是一部全面记载西安市国民经济和社会发展情况的大型连续性统计文献资料和重要工具书。

二、本年鉴正文内容分为二十二个篇章：（一）综合；（二）基本单位；（三）国民经济核算；（四）人口、从业人员与职工工资；（五）固定资产投资；（六）财政；（七）物价指数；（八）人民生活；（九）城市公用事业；（十）环境保护；（十一）农业；（十二）工业；（十三）能源；（十四）建筑业；（十五）运输、邮电和信息化；（十六）国内贸易；（十七）对外经济贸易和旅游；（十八）规模以上服务业；（十九）金融业；（二十）教育和科技；（二十一）文化、体育、卫生、社会福利和其他；（二十二）企业调查。同时，为方便读者使用，各篇章前设有简要说明和主要统计指标，对本篇章的主要内容、资料来源以及历史变动情况予以简要概述，篇末附有《主要统计指标解释》。

三、本年鉴统计资料的统计标准，按当时国家统计制度执行，有关指标的涵义、口径、范围、计算方法等，在不同时期可能有所不同，使用时请注意。如国民经济行业分类按GB/T4754—2017标准执行。

四、为便于国内外读者查阅，本年鉴全部内容均采用中英文对照编辑。

五、本年鉴中，国民经济核算部分的2018年数据为全国第四次经济普查数据，2003-2017年数据为第四次经济普查修订数据；工业部分的2018年数据为第四次经济普查数据；国内贸易部分的1993-2017年为第四次经济普查修订数据；农业部分的2007-2017年农林牧渔业总产值、产量等和2013-2017年畜产品等为依据第三次农业普查调整后数据；2011-2019年常住人口及相关指标数据为依据第七次全国人口普查修订数据；固定资产投资数据主要为增长速度等相对指标数据；科技数据（除部门数据）、创新活动为2019年数据。

六、数据口径：本年鉴中2017年起全市数据中，基本单位、国民经济核算、农业（除个别指标）、工业、建筑业、国内贸易、服务业、能源、固定资产投资、常住人口、从业人员和职工工资、信息化、企业调查、城市公用事业（除城市公共交通部分等）、财政、教育、文化、卫生、社会福利和行政区划等指标数据包含西咸新区；2018年起人民生活、利用外资等指标包含西咸新区；2019年起证券、气象等指标包含西咸新区；2020年起水资源相关指标包含西咸新区。物价指数（除部分指标）、运输邮电、环境保护、对外贸易和旅游（除部分指标）、银行和保险、体育、户籍人口、土地面积等指标数据为西安原口径（不包含西咸新区咸阳片区）或不包含西咸新区数据，具体情况见表下附注。

七、本年鉴中的部分指标合计数或相对数由于单位取舍不同产生的计算误差均未作机械调整。

八、本年鉴所使用的计量单位均依据2020年相关统计报表制度。

九、本年鉴使用的符号说明："…"表示数据不足本表最小单位；"空白"表示该项统计指标无数据或数据不详；"#"表示其中项；"*"表示另有注解。

感谢社会各界长期以来对《西安统计年鉴》的广泛关注和大力支持。为进一步做好工作，更好地为广大读者服务，希望社会各界提出宝贵意见。

PREFACE

I. *Xi'an Statistical Yearbook 2021* is a periodical statistic yearbook which record economic and social development of Xi'an all-around in 2020 and some selected data series in historical important years. With its features of comprehensive and intensive information, this practically provides data covering the situation of social and economic developments in Xi'an.

II. The book contains twenty-two parts, 1.General Survey; 2.Basic Unit; 3.National Economic Account; 4.Population, Employment and Wages; 5.Investment in Fixed Assets; 6.Government Finance; 7.Price Indices; 8.People's Livelihood; 9.Urban Public Utilities; 10.Environmental Protection; 11.Agriculture; 12.Industry; 13.Energy; 14.Construction; 15.Transportation, Post and Informatization; 16.Domestic Trade; 17.Foreign Trade; 18. Service Industry; 19.Financial Intermediation; 20.Education, Science and Technology; 21.Culture, Sports, Public Health, Social Welfare and Other Social Activities; 22.Enterprises Investigation. Meanwhile, for the convenience of the reader, a brief explanation and major statistical indicators are provided before each chapter, the main contents, sources and historical changes of this chapter are briefly summarized. The final part is accompanied by the interpretation of major statistical indicators.

III. The data of various years in conformity to the statistical standards prescribed by national statistical system of the time. The meaning, scope and calculating method of indicators may have some difference in different periods, which readers must pay attention to. For example, national industries classification is carried out according to standard GB/T4754-2017.

IV. For the convenience of being consulted by foreigners, the book is Chinese-English bilingual edition.

V. In this yearbook, the data of 2018 at the part of National Economic Accounting and Industry is the results of Fourth National Economic Census, the data from 2003 to 2017 at the part of National Economic Account have adjusted by Fourth National Economic Census. The data of industry in 2018 is revised for The Fourth National Economic Census; The domestic trade part of 1993 to 2017 is based on the adjusted data of The Fourth National Economic Census. The agricultural output, the total output value, output of agriculture, forestry, animal husbandry and fishery in 2007 to 2017 and the livestock products and aquatic products in 2013 to 2017 are based on the adjusted data of the third agricultural census. The data of permanent population and related indicators from 2011 to 2019 are the revised data of the seventh national population census.The per capita disposable income of urban residents and rural residents is revised based on the new caliber innovation activities in 2019; Fixed asset investment data are mainly relative indicator data such as growth rate.

VI. Statistical scope: in this yearbook, the data from 2017 about the basic unit, the national economic accounting, agriculture, industry, construction industry, domestic trade, services, energy, investment in fixed assets, labor wages, informatization, enterprise survey, urban public utilities, finance, education, culture, health and social welfare contains Xixian New District. Since 2018, the indicators such as people's living and utilization of foreign capital include Xixian New District. Since 2019, the indicators such as securities and meteorology include Xixian New District.Since 2020,the indicatiors such as water resources are include Xixian New District. The price index (except for individual indicators), transportation, post and telecommunications, environmental protection, foreign trade and tourism (except for some indicators), Banking and Insurance, sports, household registration, land area and other indicators are Xi'an original caliber data or does not include Xixian New District. See the notes under the table for details.

VII. Statistical discrepancies due to rounding are not adjusted automatically in this yearbook.

VIII. Unit of measurement is used in this yearbook according to 2020 statistics system.

Ⅸ. Explanations on symbols used in this yearbook:

"..." indicates the data is less than the minimum unit in this table;

(Blank) indicates the data not available;

\# indicates the items of the total;

* indicates some other explanatory note.

Here we would like to express our sincere thanks to the people for their concerning and support to the Xi'an statistical yearbook. In order to do better and provide better service to readers, we hope that the whole society fields can propose constructive advices.

地区生产总值（亿元）

Gross Domestic Product (100 million yuan)

地区生产总值指数（以上年为100）

Indices of Gross Domestic Product (preceding year = 100)

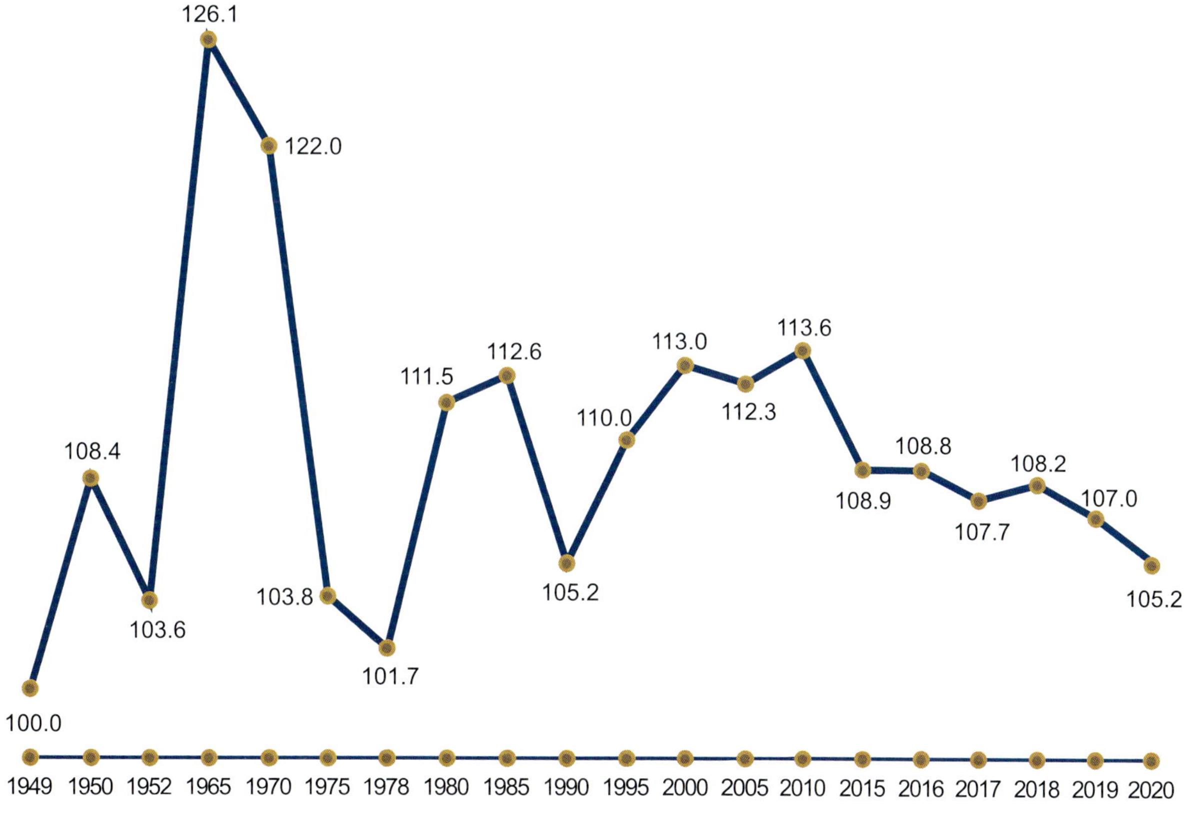

地区生产总值构成（%）

Composition of Gross Domestic Product (%)

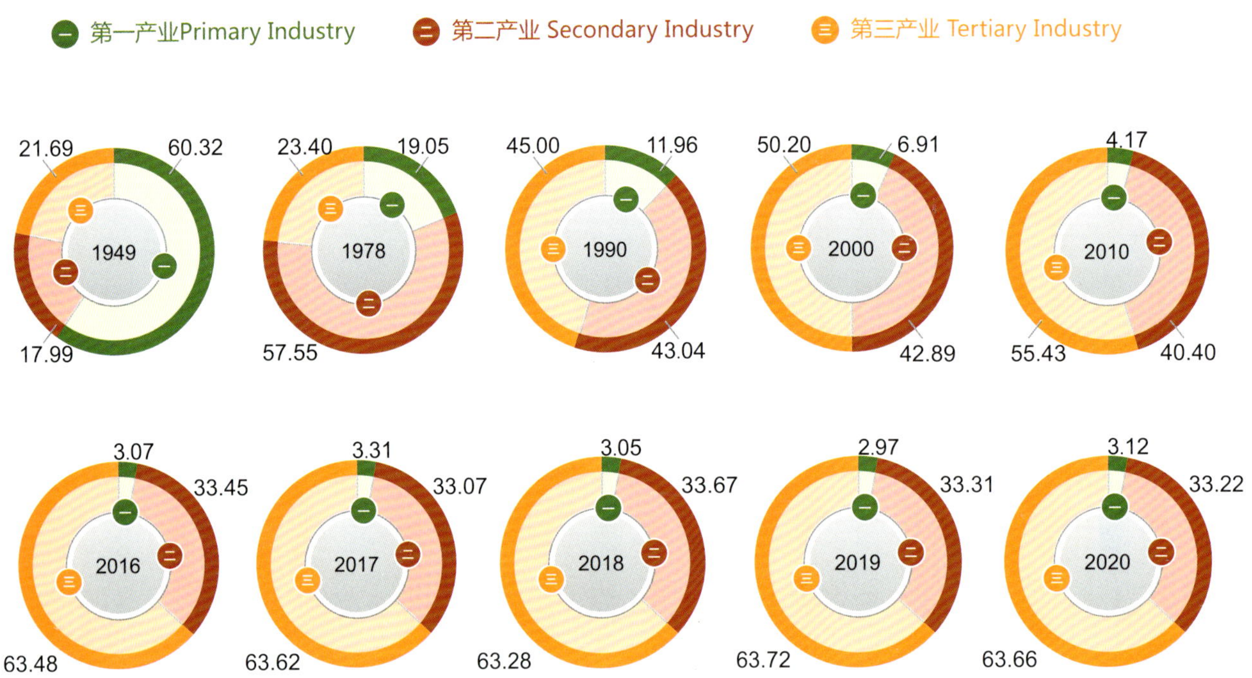

人均GDP（元/人）

Per Capita GDP(yuan/person)

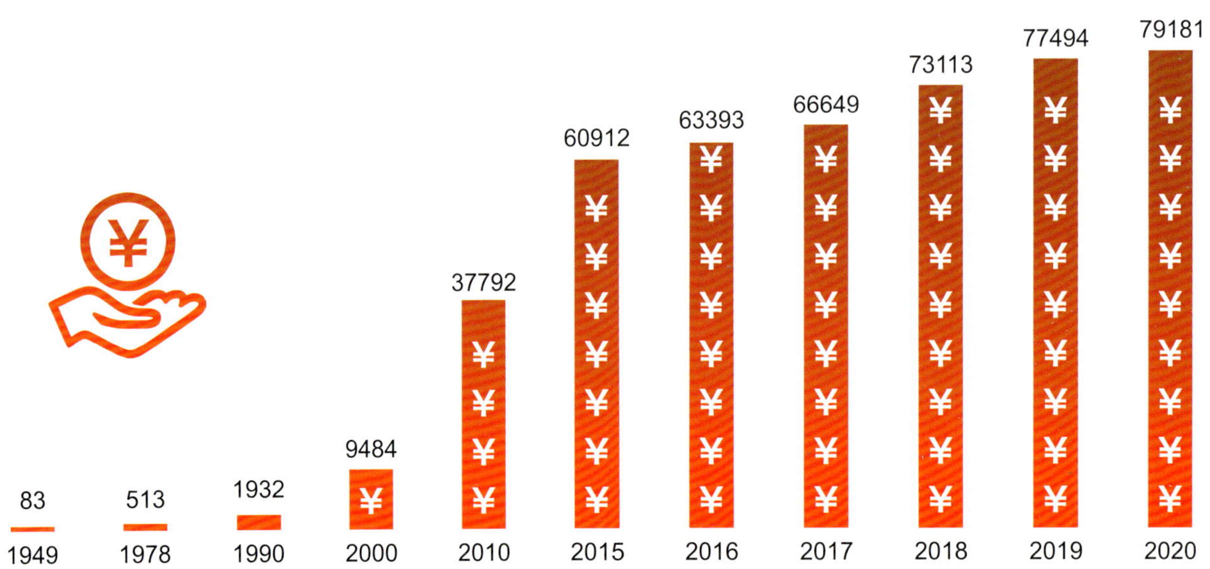

年末常住人口（万人）

Year-end Permanent Population(10 000 persons)

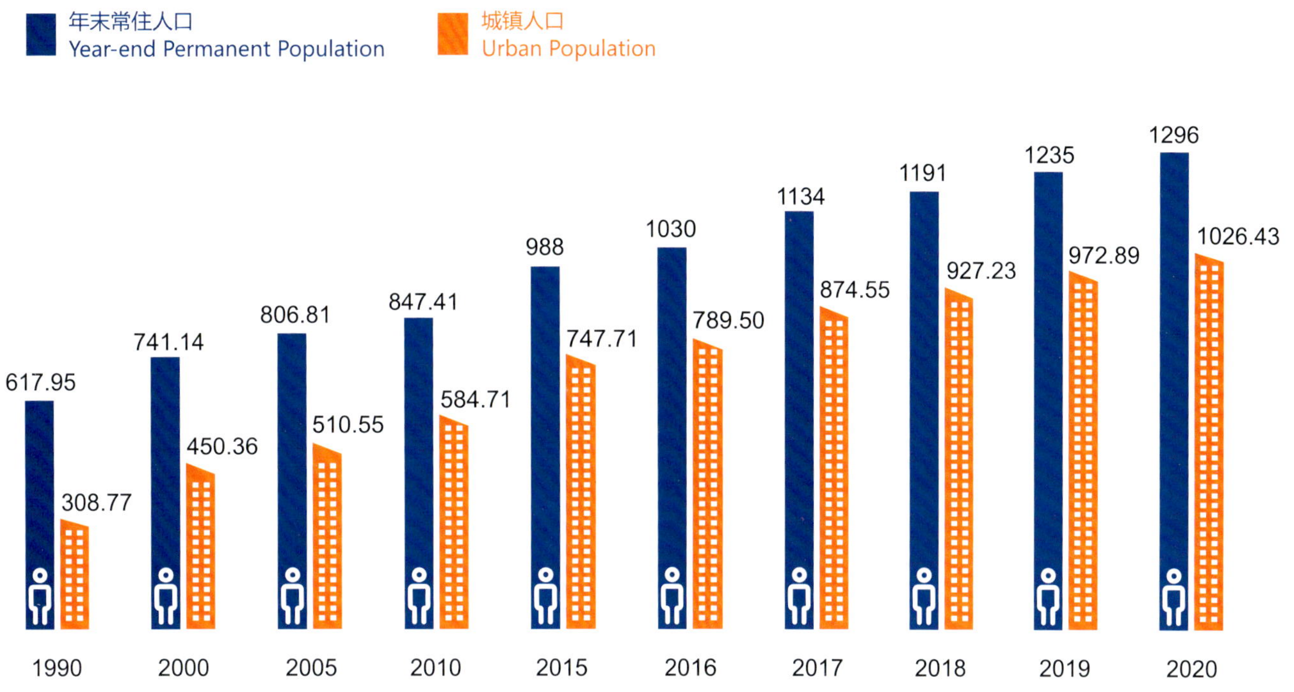

全社会从业人员（万人）

Social Workers(10 000 persons)

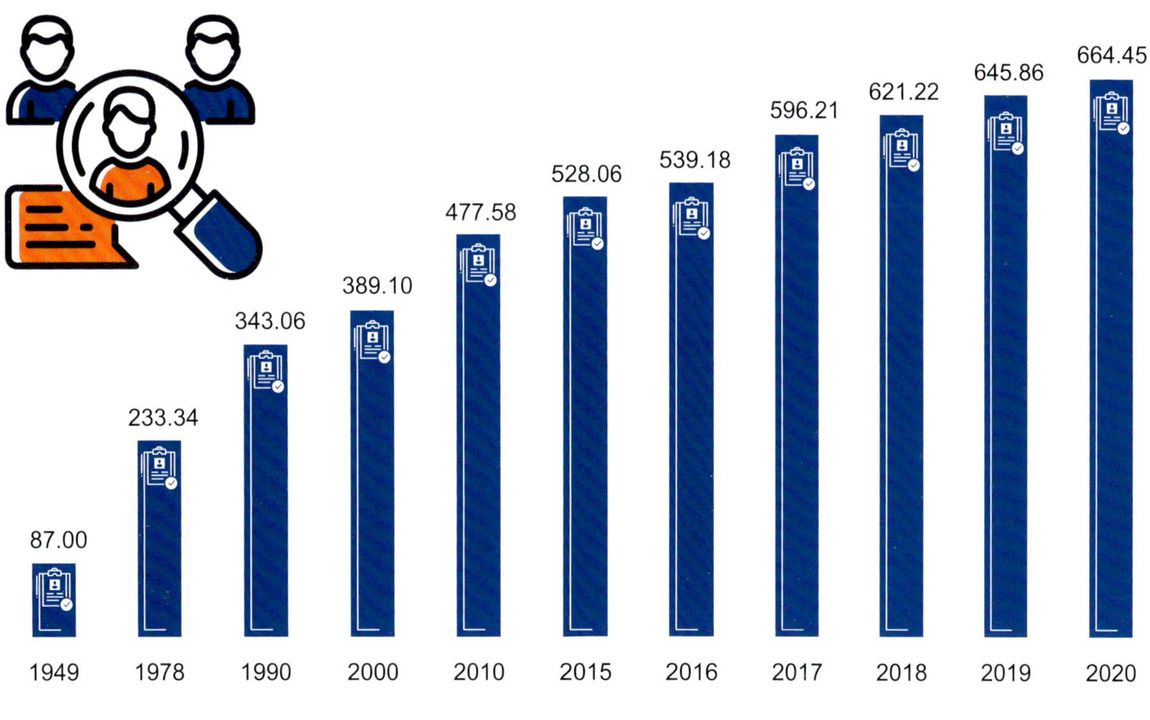

固定资产投资增长速度（%）

Growth Rate of Investment in Fixed Assets（%）

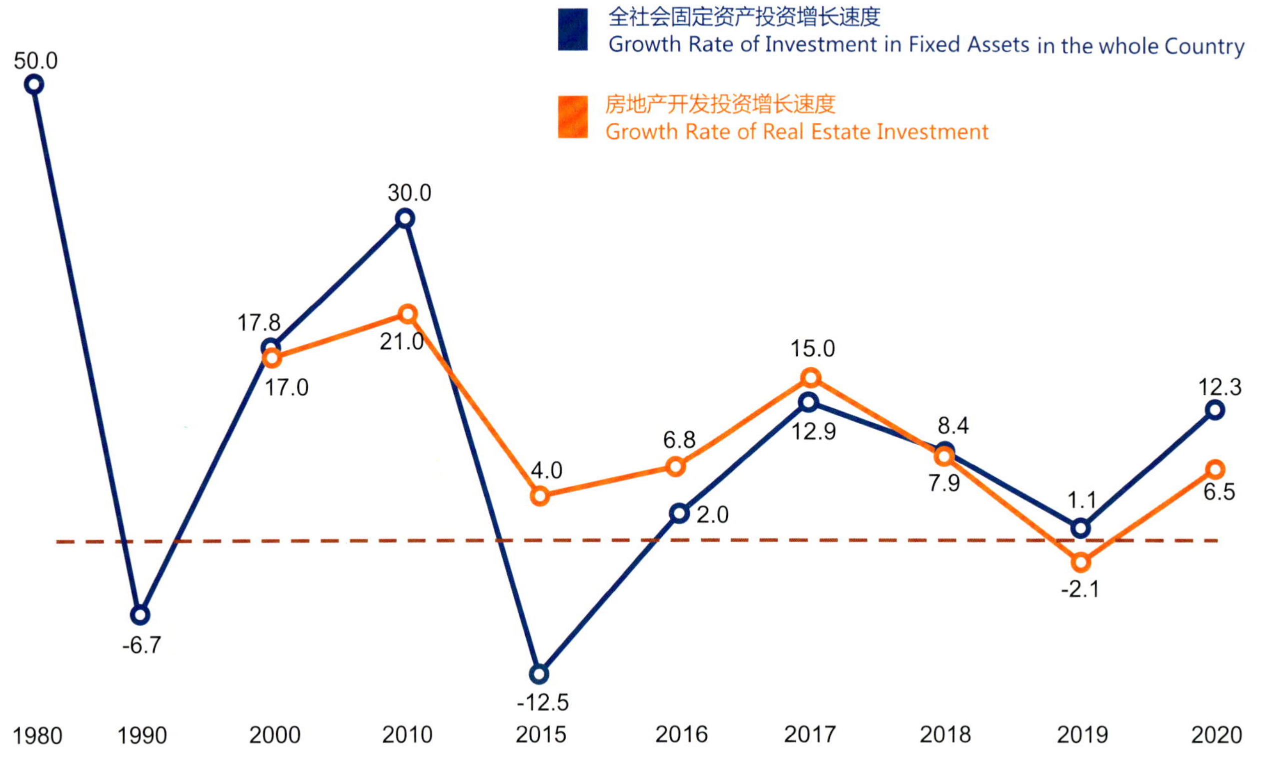

商品房销售面积（万平方米）

Floor Space of Commercialized Buildings Sold(10 000 sq.m)

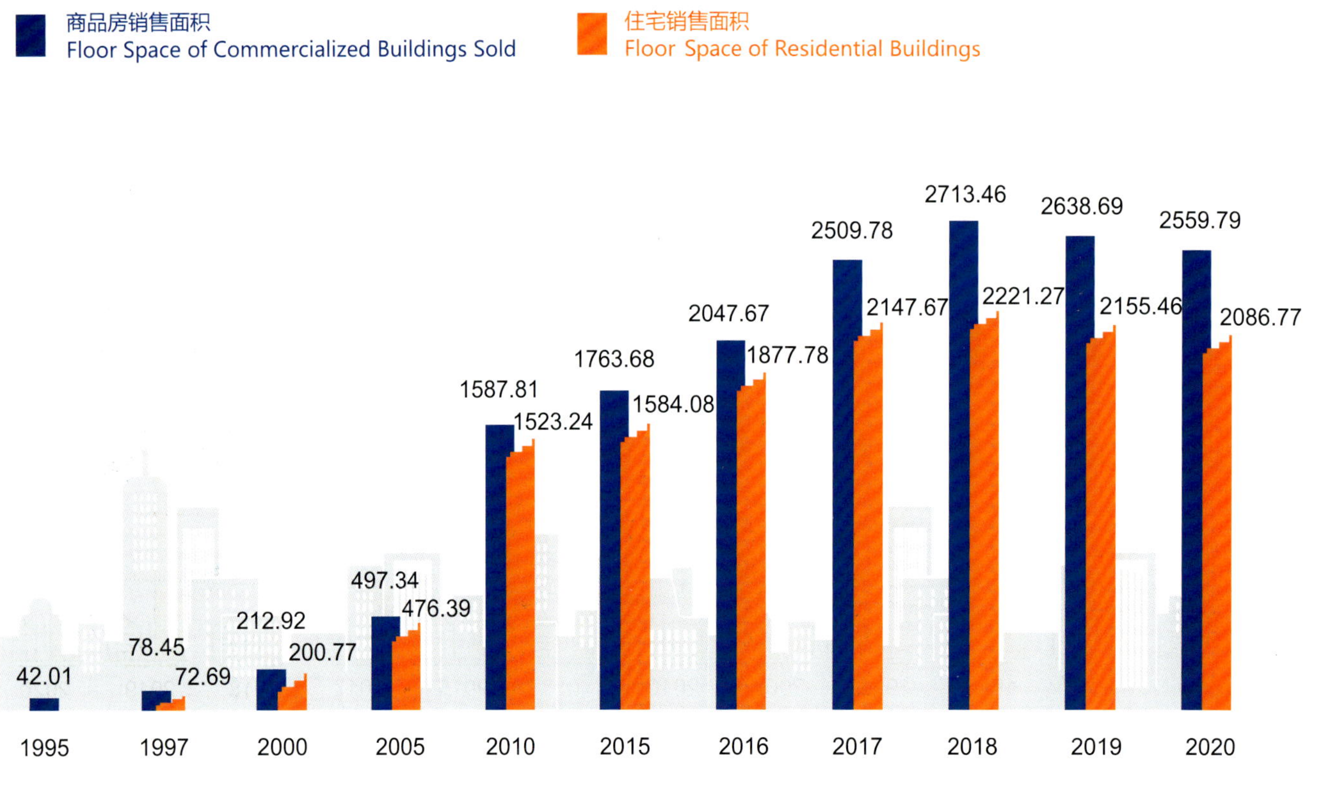

农林牧渔业总产值（亿元）

Gross Output Value of Farming,Forestry,
Animal Husbandry and Fishery (100 million yuan)

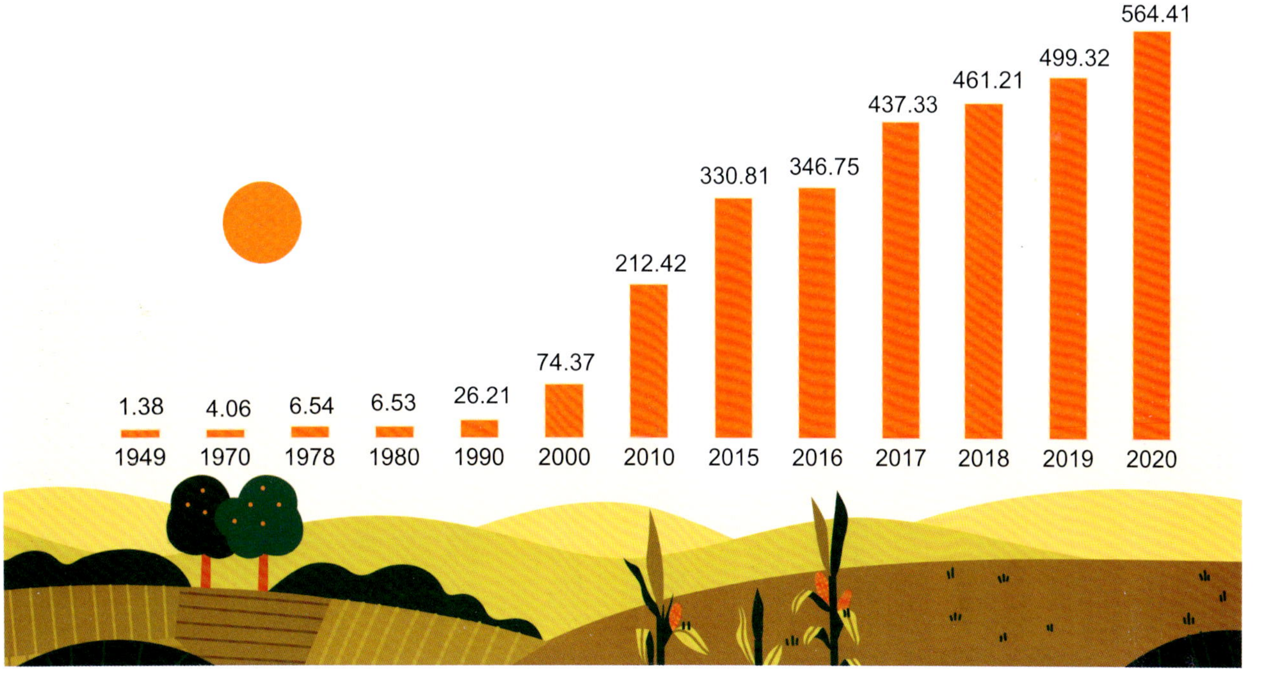

粮食产量（万吨）

Grain Product(10 000 tons)

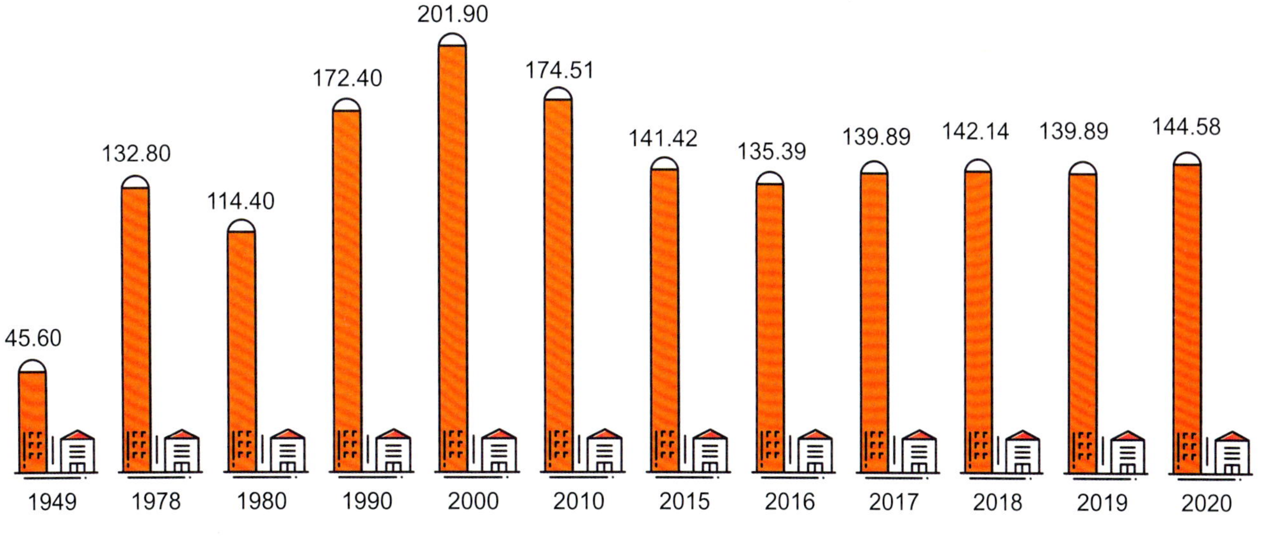

蔬菜产量（万吨）
Vegetables Product(10 000 tons)

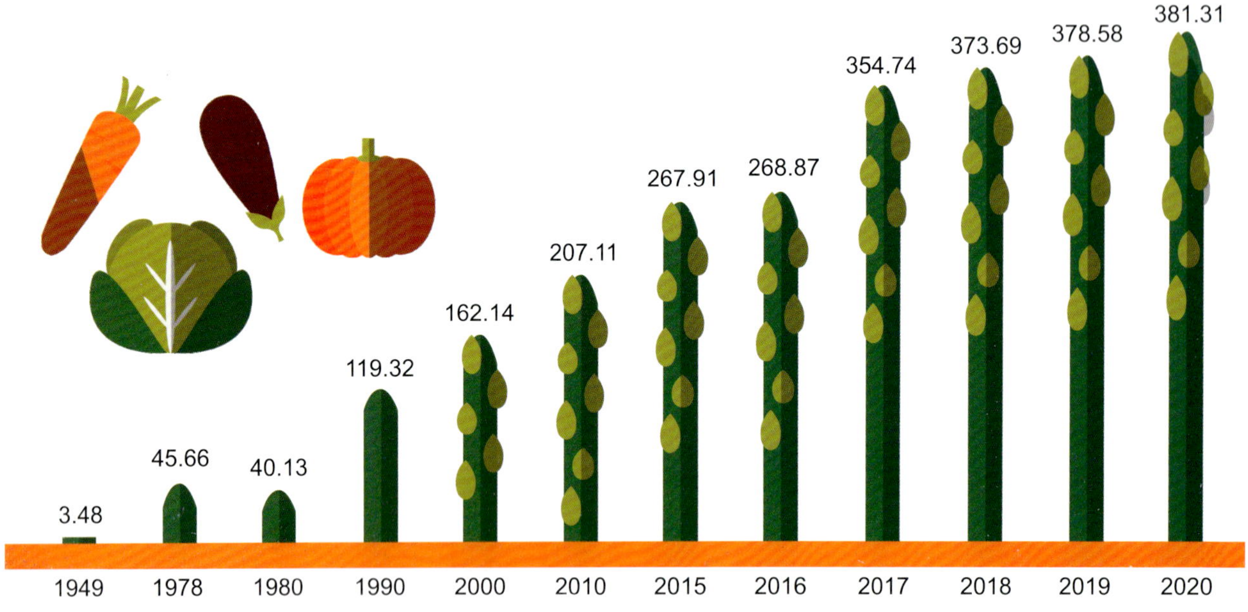

规模以上工业企业主要产品产量
Major Output of Industrial Products Enterprises Above Designated Size

汽车（万辆）
Motor Vehicle(10 000 units)

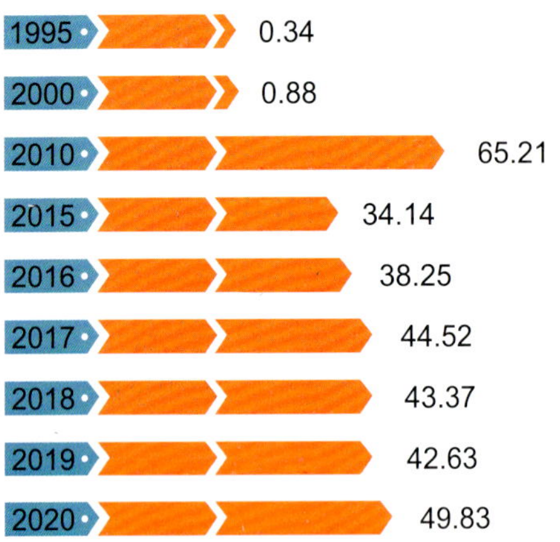

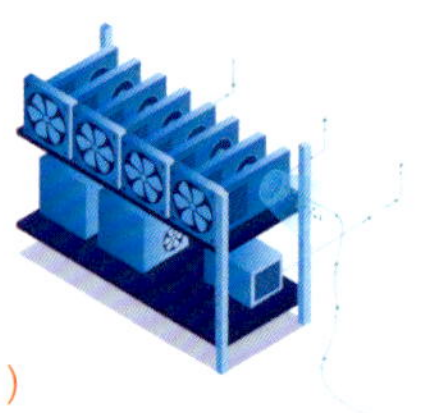

变压器（万千伏安）
Transformer (10 000 kva)

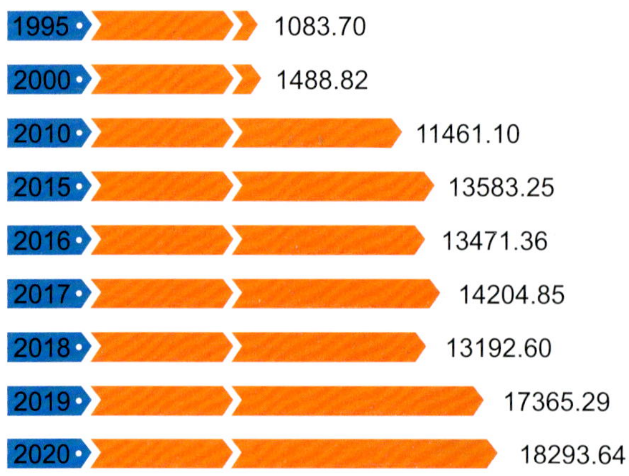

交通
Traffic

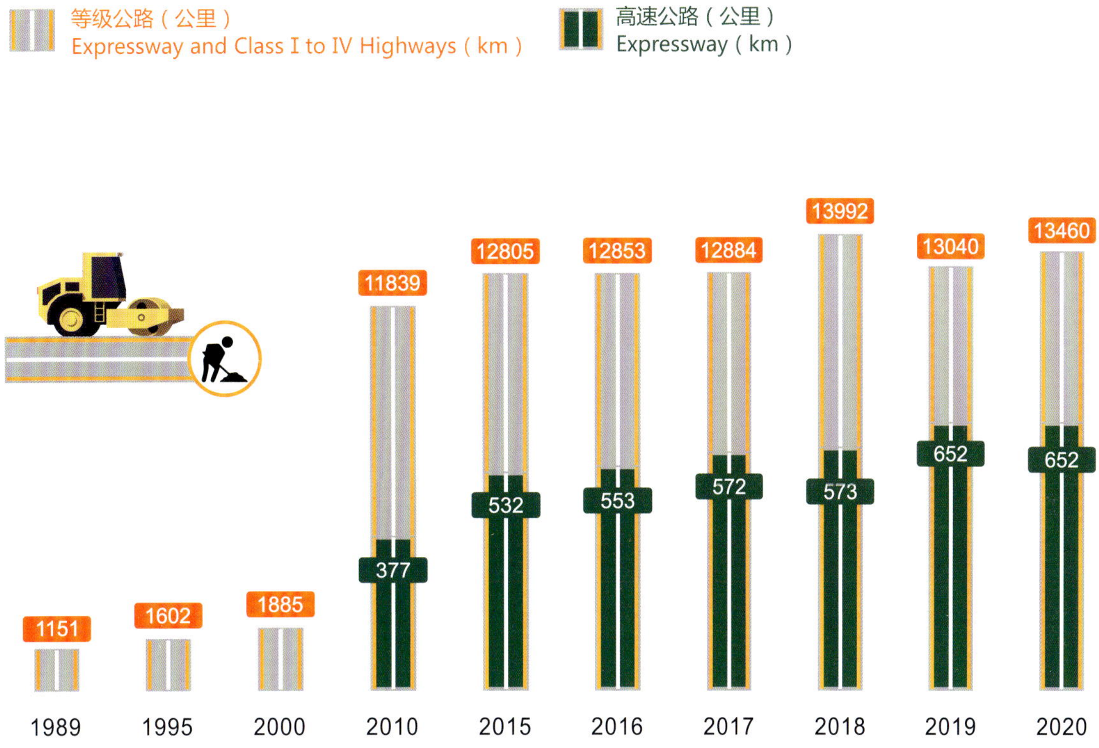

全社会车辆数（万辆）
Possession of Civil Vehicles(10 000 units)

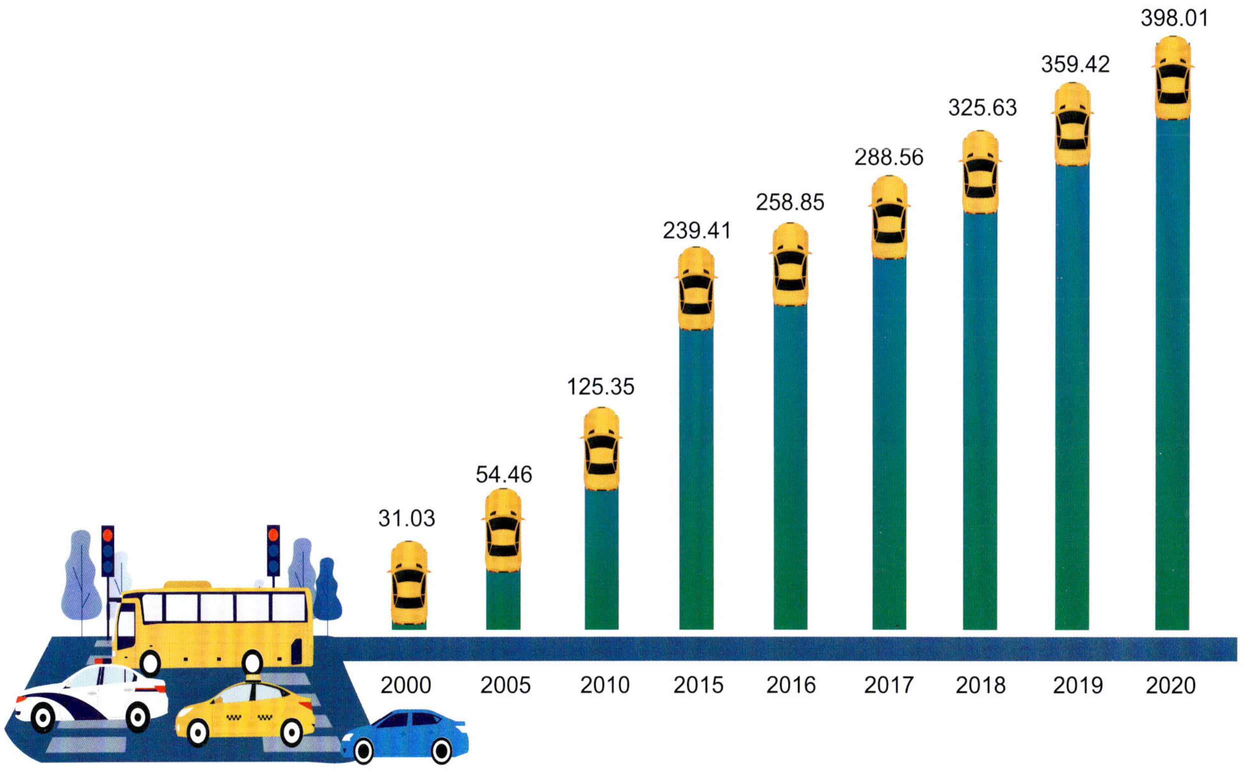

社会消费品零售总额（亿元）

Total Retail Sales of Consumer Goods(100 million yuan)

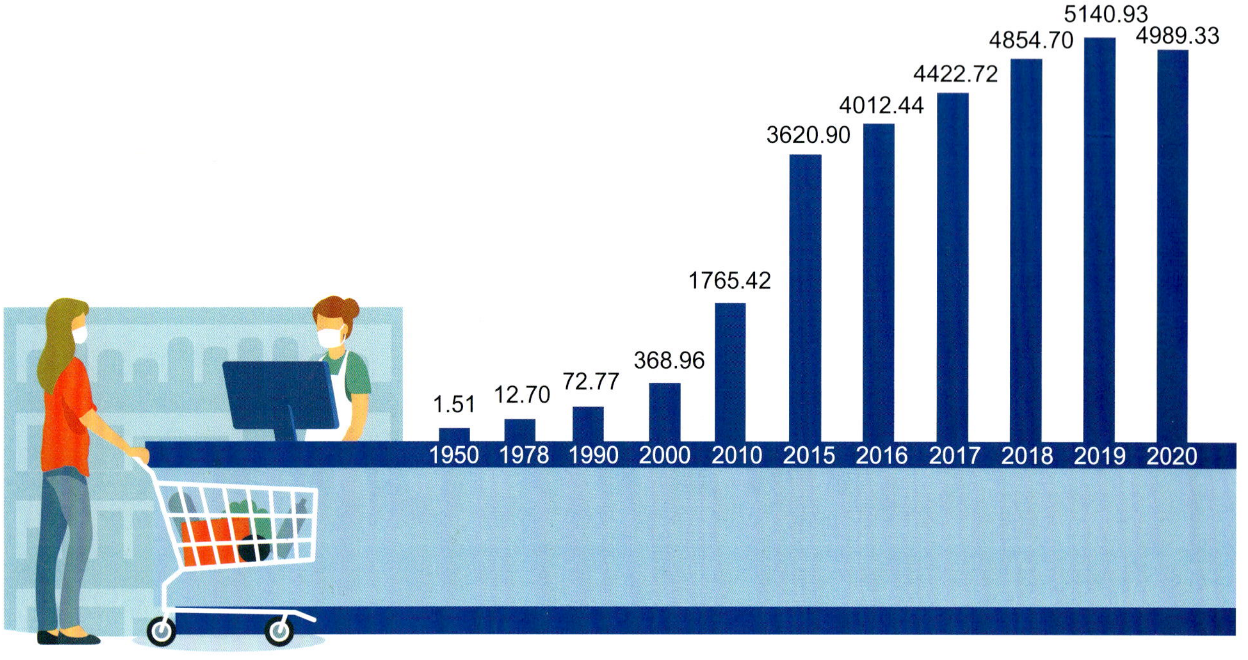

实际利用外资（亿美元）

Actual Utilized Foreign Investments(USD 100 million)

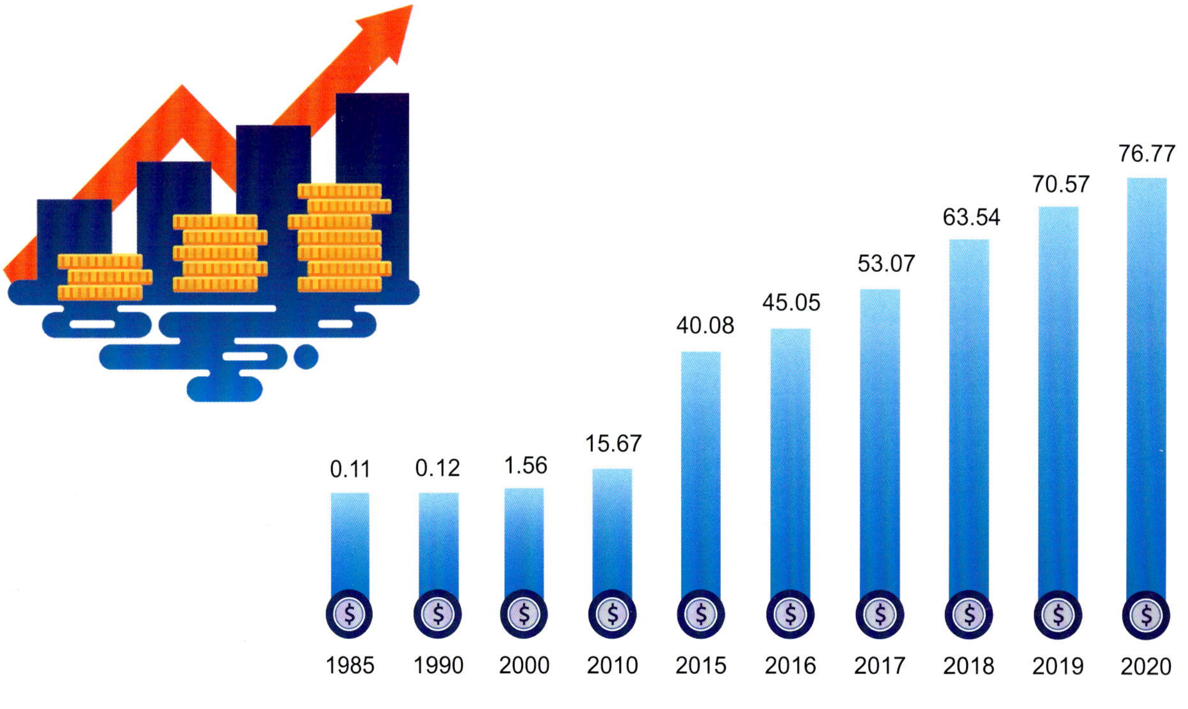

进出口总值

Total Value of Imports and Exports

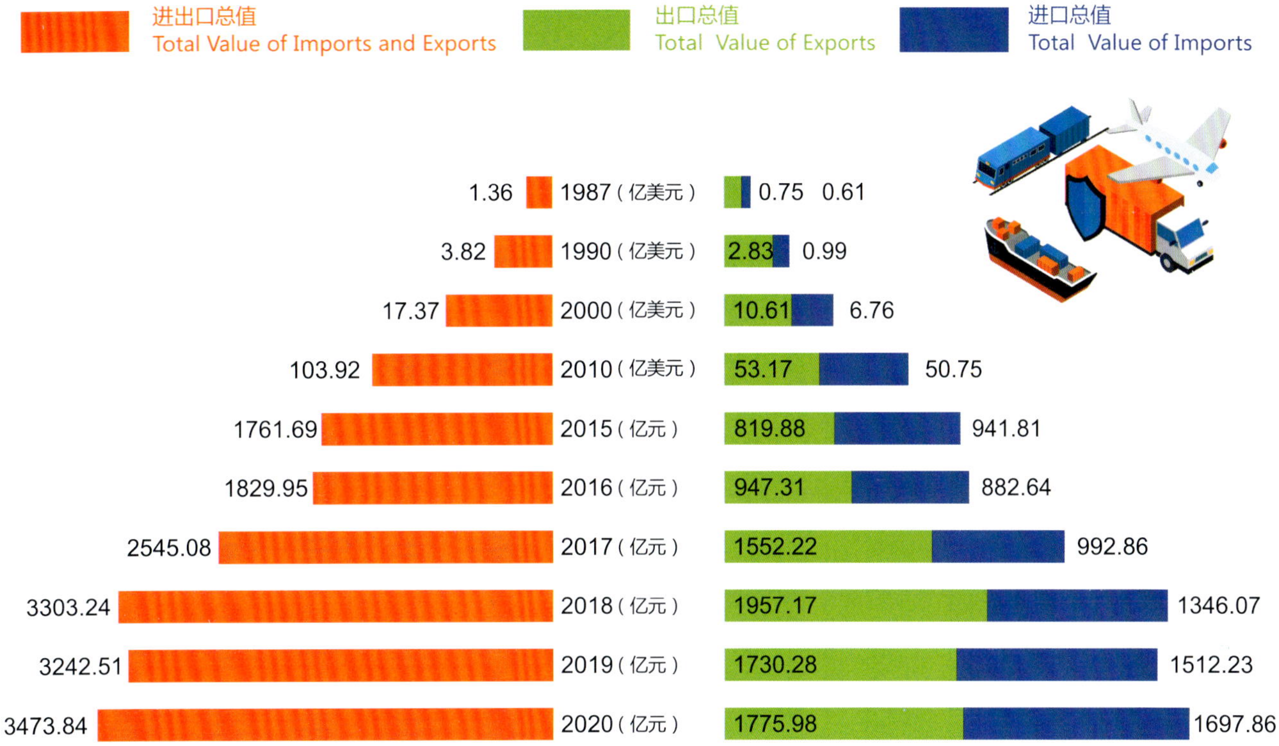

旅游人数及收入

Number of Tourists and Tourism Earnings

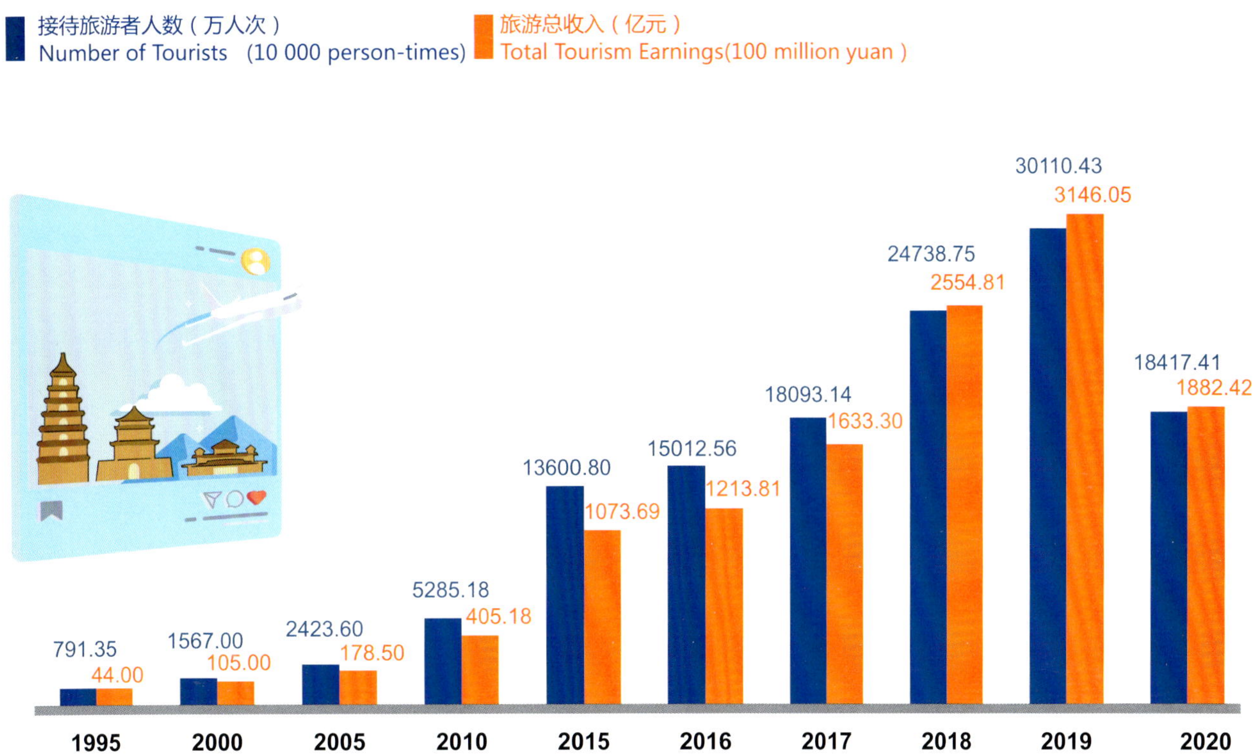

财政收支（亿元）

Government Revenue and Expenditure(100 million yuan)

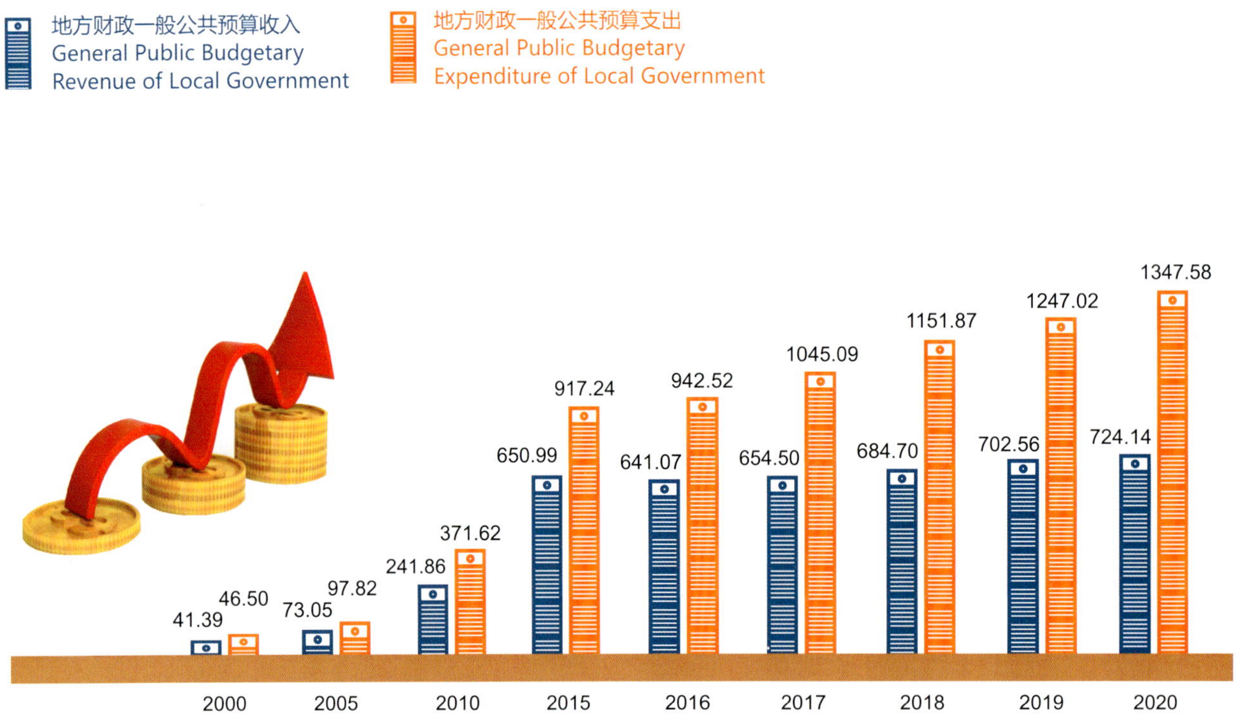

金融机构人民币存贷款年末余额（亿元）

Year-end Deposits and Loans in Financial Institutions (100 million yuan)

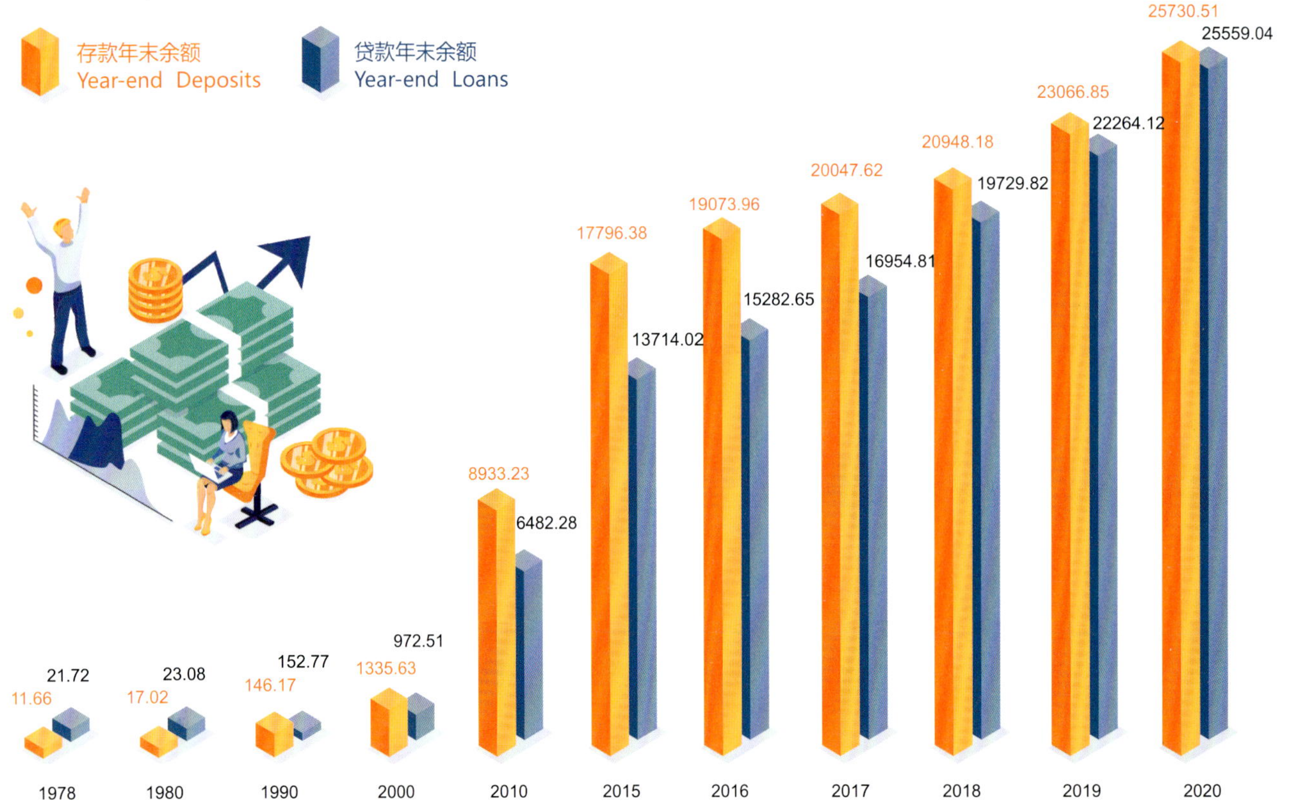

城市公共运营车辆（辆）
City Operating Vehicles(unit)

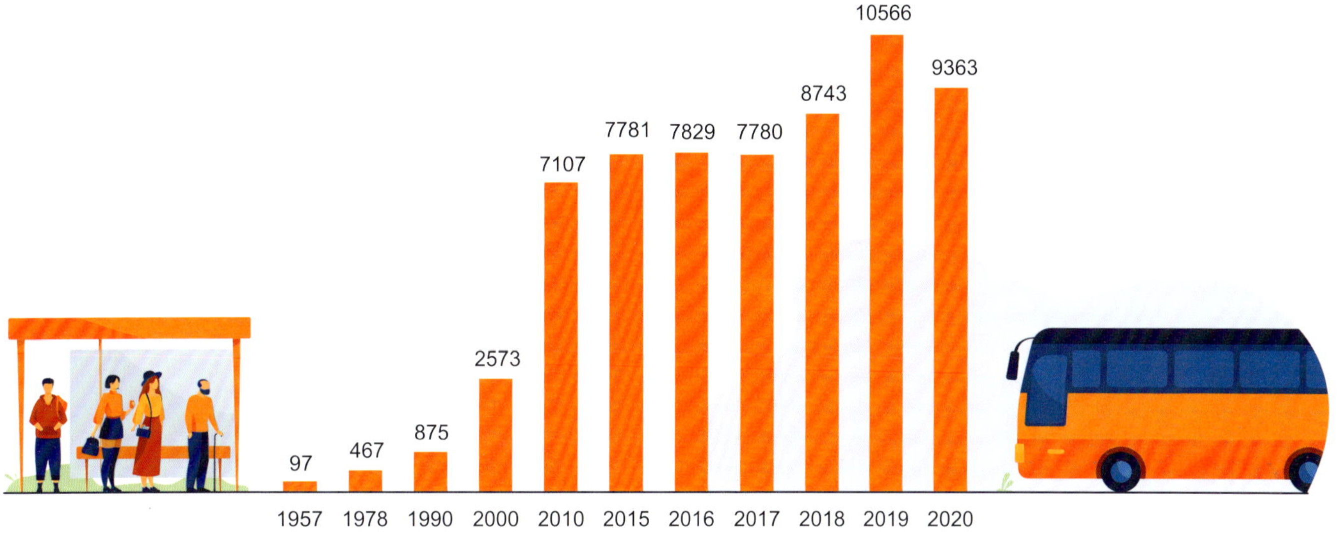

天然气供气总量（万立方米）
Total Natural Gas Supply(10 000 cu.m)

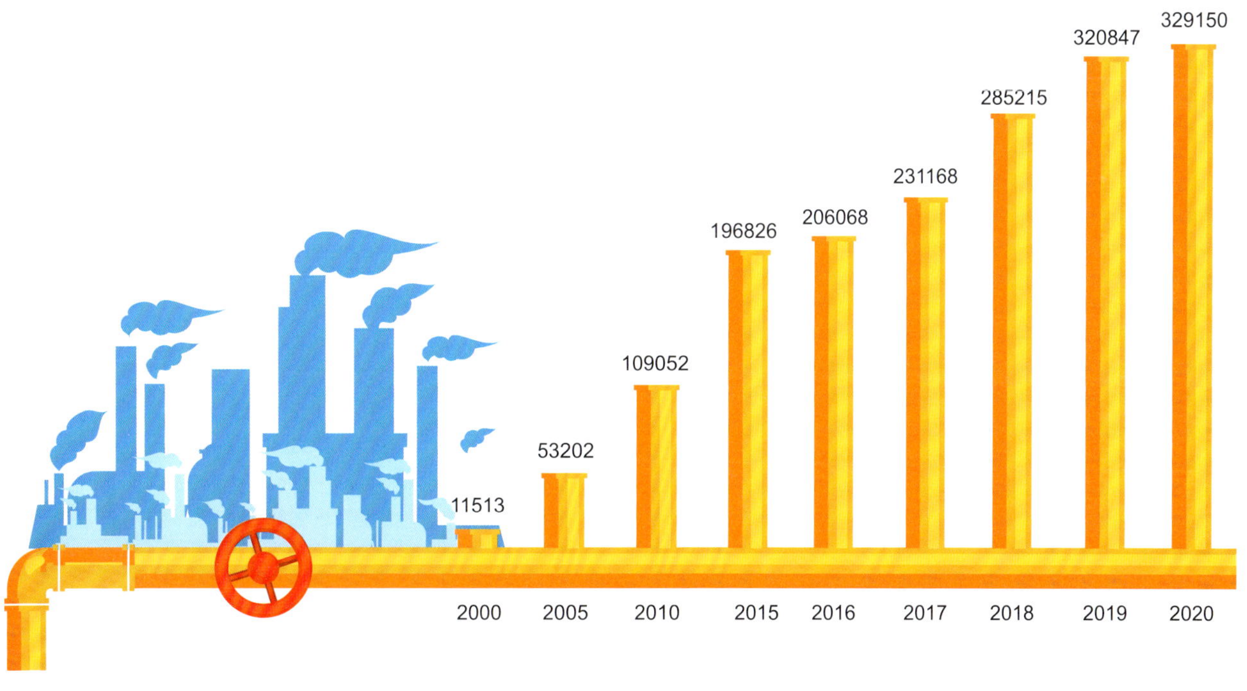

绿地面积（公顷）

Green Area（hectare）

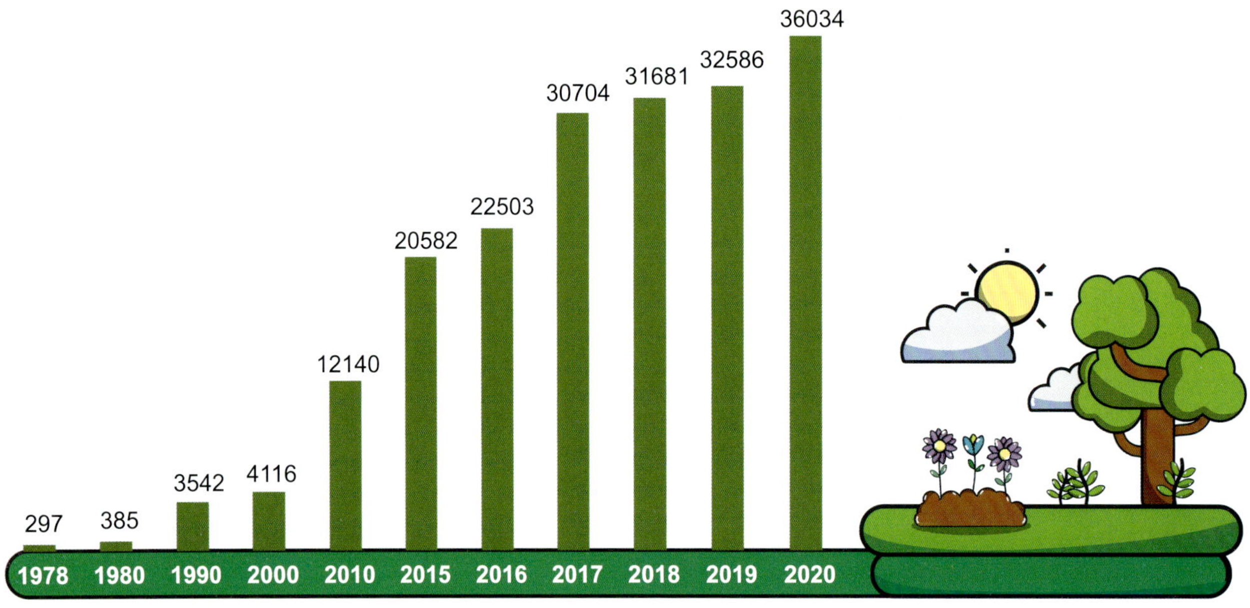

普通教育在校学生（万人）

Total Enrollment of Regular Education（10 000 persons）

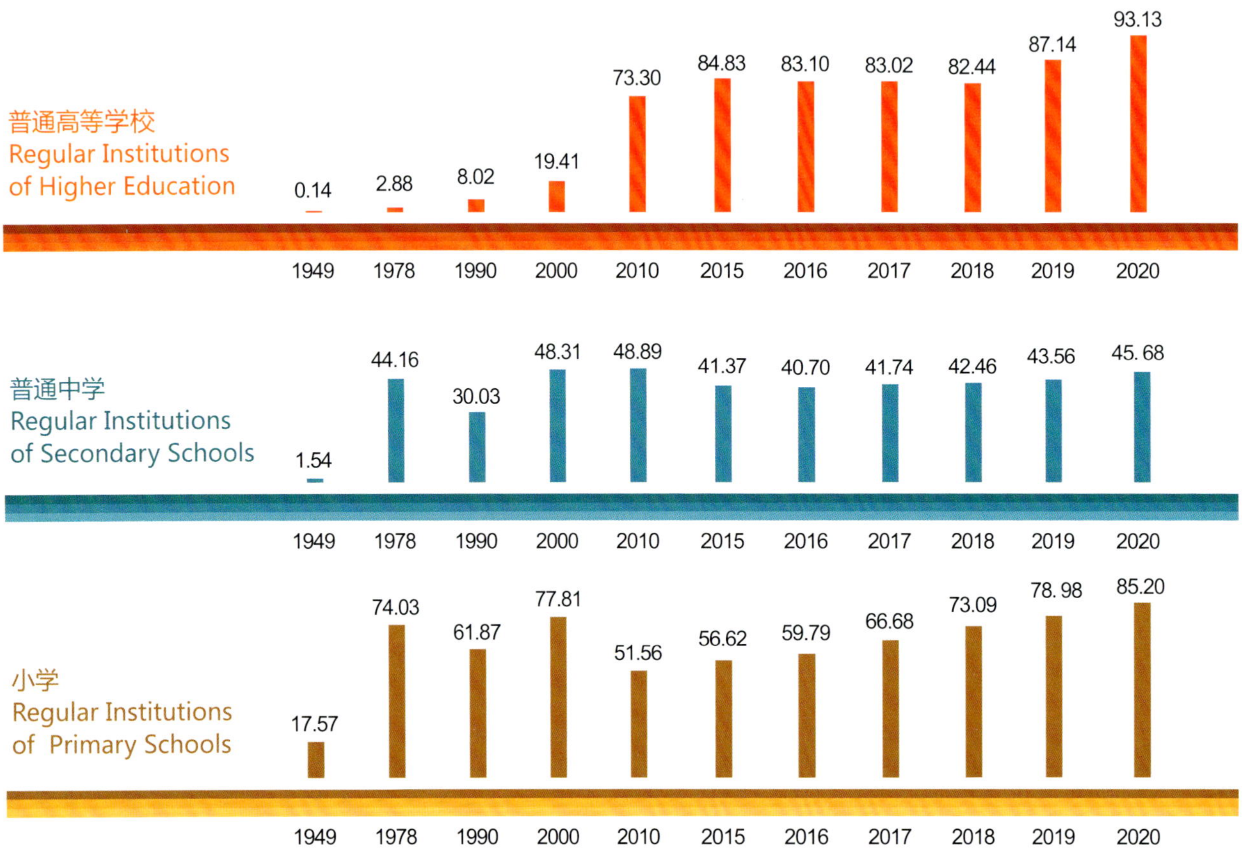

专任教师（万人）

Full-time Teachers (10 000 persons)

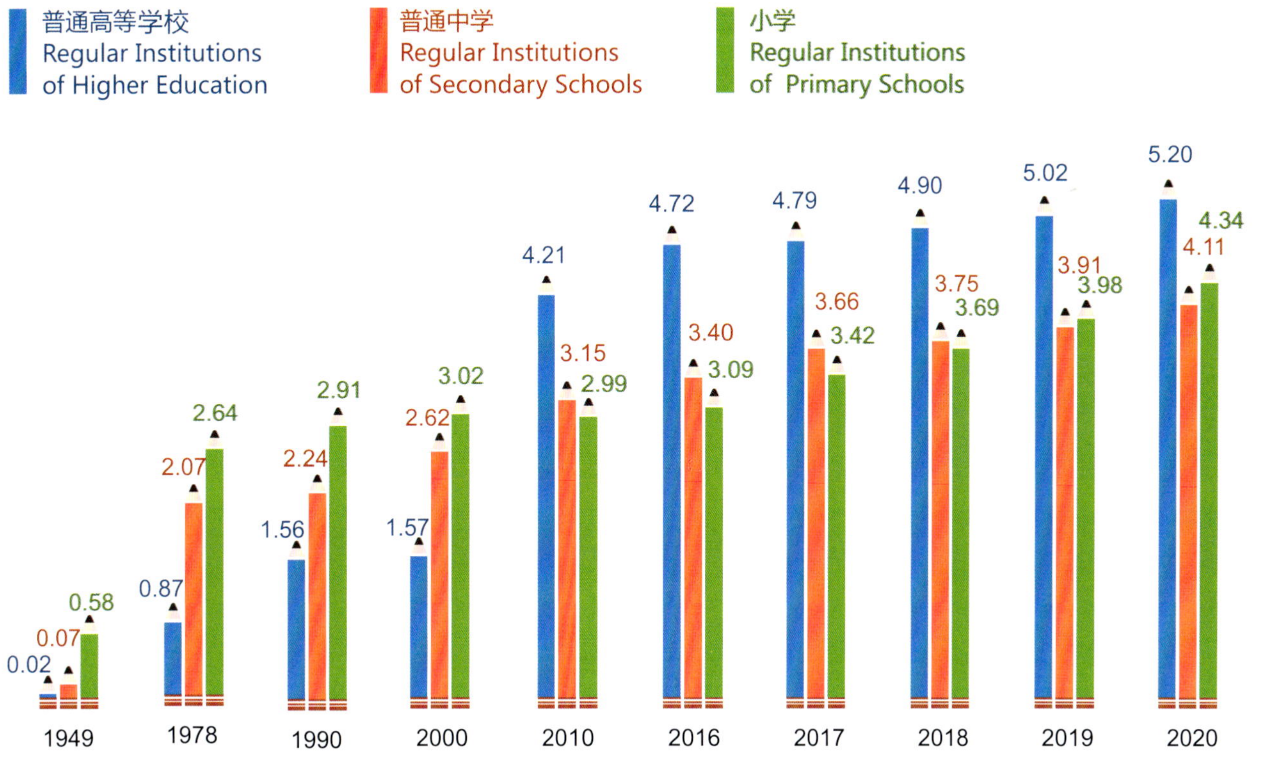

价格指数（以上年价格为100）

Price Indices(the price of preceding year=100)

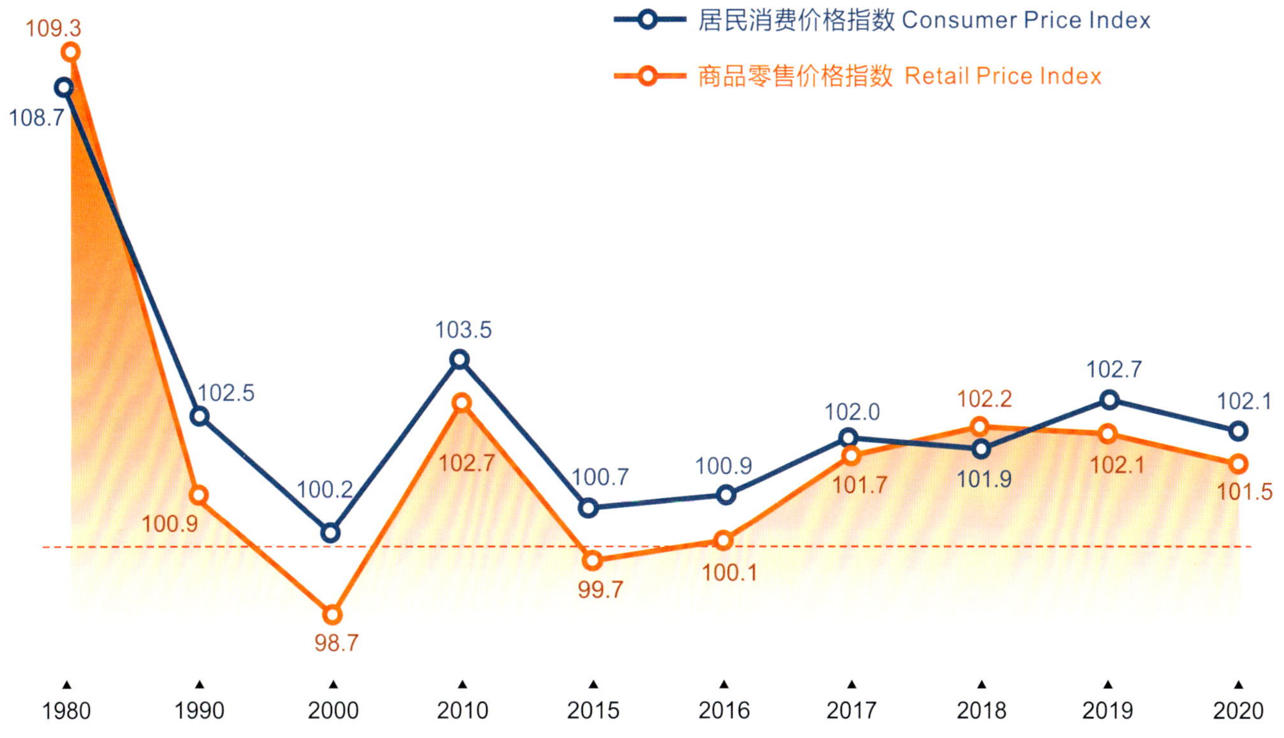

目　　录

CONTENTS

一、综　　合

GENERAL SURVEY

二、基本单位

BASIC UNIT

三、国民经济核算

NATIONAL ECONOMIC ACCOUNTS

四、人口、从业人员与职工工资

POPULATION, EMPLOYMENT AND WAGES

五、固定资产投资

INVESTMENT IN FIXED ASSETS

六、财　政

GOVERNMENT FINANCE

七、物价指数

PRICE INDICES

八、人民生活

PEOPLE'S LIVELIHOOD

九、城市公用事业

URBAN PUBLIC UTILITIES

十、环境保护

ENVIRONMENT PROTECTION

十一、农　业
AGRICULTURE

十二、工　业
INDUSTRY

十三、能　源

ENERGY

十四、建筑业

CONSTRUCTION

十五、运输邮电和信息化

TRANSPORT，POSTAL TELECOMMUNICATION SERVICE AND INFORMATIZATION

十六、国内贸易

DOMESTIC TRADE

十七、对外经济贸易和旅游

FOREIGN TRADE AND ECONOMIC COOPERATION TOURISM

十八、规模以上服务业

SERVICE INDUSTRY ABOVE DESIGNATED SIZE

十九、金融业

FINANCIAL INTERMEDIATION

二十、教育和科技

EDUCATION，SCIENCE AND TECHNOLOGY

二十一、文化、体育、卫生、社会福利和其他
CULTURE, SPORTS, PUBLIC HEALTH, SOCIAL WELFARE INSTITUTIONS AND OTHER SOCIAL ACTIVITIES

二十二、企业调查

ENTERPRISES INVESTIGATION

西安市2020年国民经济和社会发展统计公报[1]

西安市统计局　国家统计局西安调查队

2021年3月18日

2020年，面对新冠肺炎疫情严重冲击和复杂严峻的国内外环境，在以习近平同志为核心的党中央坚强领导下，西安市认真贯彻落实习近平总书记来陕考察重要讲话精神，统筹推进疫情防控和经济社会发展，扎实做好“六稳”工作，全面落实“六保”任务，以十项重点工作率先突破，有效推动生产生活秩序恢复，经济运行快速恢复，发展质量稳步提升，民生福祉持续增进，社会事业繁荣发展，生态环境整体改善，全面建成小康社会取得决定性成就，“十三五”圆满收官。

一、综合[2]

根据市（区）生产总值统一核算结果，全年地区生产总值[3]（GDP）10020.39亿元，比上年增长5.2%。其中，第一产业增加值312.75亿元，增长3.0%；第二产业增加值3328.27亿元，增长7.4%；第三产业增加值6379.37亿元，增长4.2%。三次产业构成为3.1：33.2：63.7。全市万元GDP能耗[4]比上年下降7%以上。非公经济增加值占GDP比重53.1%。

图1：2016-2020年生产总值及其增长速度

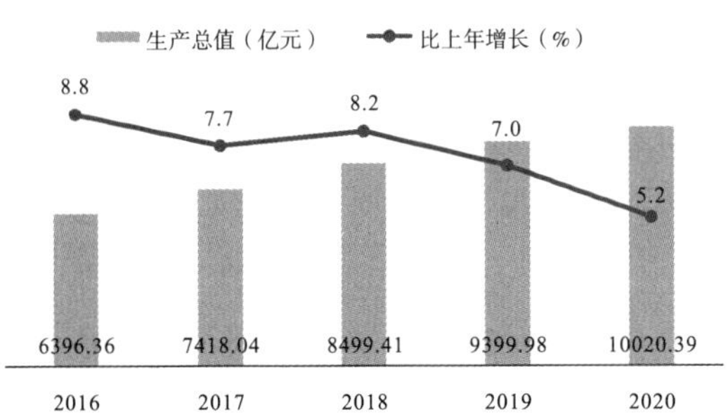

注：2019年生产总值及其分项为最终核实数。

图2：2020年三次产业增加值占生产总值比重（%）

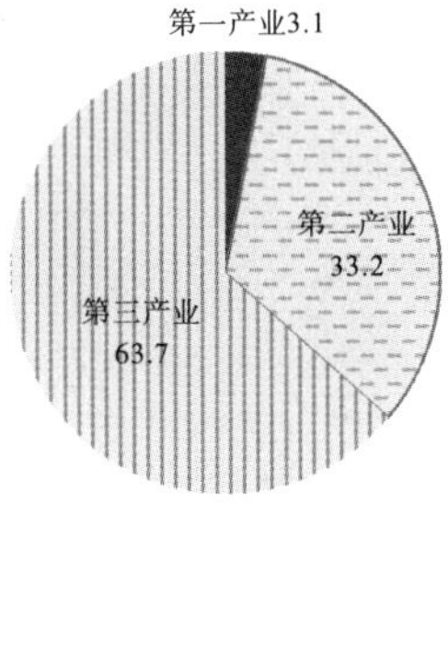

全年居民消费价格比上年上涨2.1%，其中，食品烟酒价格上涨6.1%。商品零售价格上涨1.5%。工业生产者出厂价格上涨0.2%，工业生产者购进价格上涨0.4%。新建商品住宅销售价格上涨8.9%。

图3：2020年居民消费价格月度涨跌幅度（%）

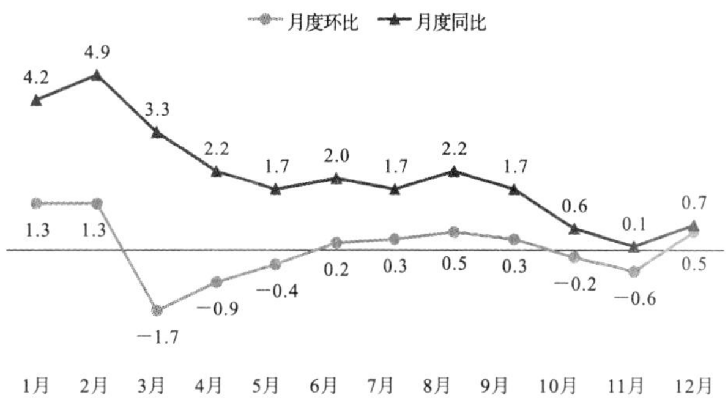

表1：2020年居民消费价格比上年涨跌幅度

指标	涨跌幅度（%）
居民消费价格	2.1
其中：食品烟酒	6.1
衣着	0.4
居住	-0.4
生活用品及服务	0.6
交通和通信	-1.7
教育文化和娱乐	2.5
医疗保健	-0.2
其他用品和服务	5.7

全年新增城镇就业15.31万人，城镇失业人员再就业5.38万人。年末城镇登记失业率为3.64%。

新产业新业态新模式逆势成长。全年规模以上工业[5]中，战略性新兴产业[6]总产值比上年增长13.3%，占规模以上工业总产值的比重为46.9%；高技术制造业[7]总产值增长23.4%，占规模以上工业总产值的比重为32.4%。全年规模以上服务业[8]中，高技术服务业企业营业收入比上年增长12.4%。全年高技术产业投资[9]比上年增长25.9%。全年光纤产量732.05万千米，比上年增长29.7%；集成电路圆片产量205.90万片，增长43.7%；太阳能电池产量148.25万千瓦，增长6.0倍。全年限额以上企业（单位）中，网上商品零售额[10]592.75亿元，占限额以上消费品零售额的23.6%，比上年提高6.7个百分点；比上年增长37.1%。全年新登记市场主体[11]44.92万户，日均登记1227户，年末累计登记各类市场主体达242.98万户。

二、农业

全年粮食种植面积408.15万亩，比上年下降0.4%；蔬菜种植面积109.45万亩，增长1.6%；瓜果种植面积14.36万亩，下降2.5%；油料种植面积5.20万亩，增长11.7%；棉花种植面积0.08万亩，下降35.0%。

全年粮食产量144.58万吨，比上年增长3.4%，其中，夏粮产量72.58万吨，增长2.8%；秋粮产量72.00万吨，增长3.9%。肉类产量4.56万吨，下降11.4%；奶类产量14.03万吨，增长13.4%；禽蛋产量5.22万吨，下降3.0%；蔬菜产量381.31万吨，增长0.7%；园林水果产量100.93万吨，增长3.9%。

图4：2016-2020年粮食产量（万吨）

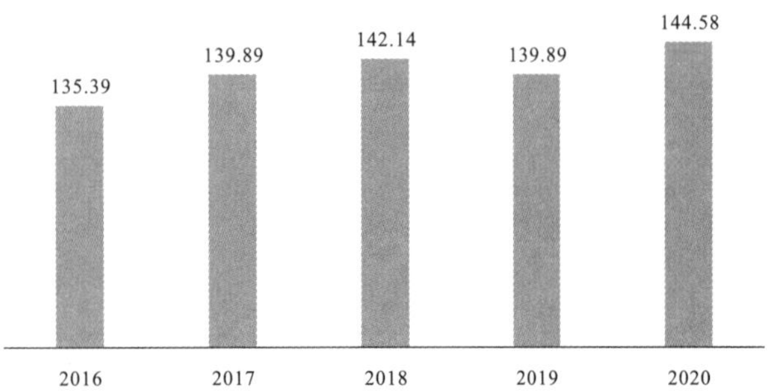

表2：2020年主要农产品产量及其增长速度

产品名称	单位	产量	比上年增长（%）
粮食	万吨	144.58	3.4
蔬菜	万吨	381.31	0.7
园林水果	万吨	100.93	3.9
肉类	万吨	4.56	-11.4
#猪肉	万吨	2.85	-15.1
奶类	万吨	14.03	13.4
禽蛋	万吨	5.22	-3.0
猪年末存栏数	万头	30.13	1.6
牛年末存栏数	万头	5.25	1.8
羊年末存栏数	万只	7.26	1.0
家禽年末存栏数	万只	641.63	-0.3

三、工业和建筑业

全年全部工业增加值1828.59亿元，比上年增长5.8%。规模以上工业增加值增长7.0%。规模以上工业总产值增长2.6%，其中，轻工业产值下降26.9%，重工业产值增长8.7%。

图5：2016-2020年全部工业增加值及其增长速度

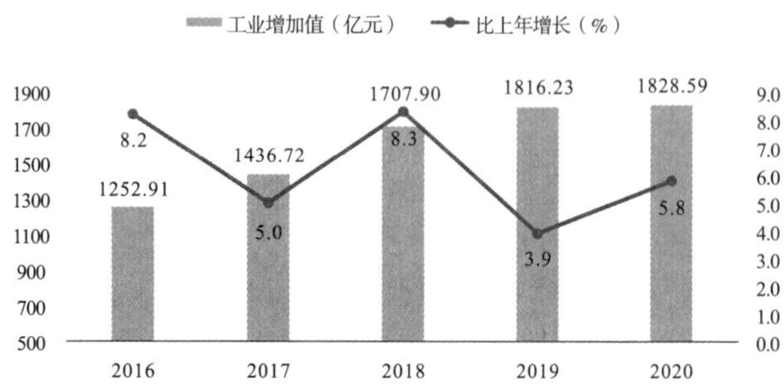

全年规模以上工业中，装备制造业[12]产值增长14.9%，占规模以上工业总产值的比重为70.4%。其中，计算机、通信和其他电子设备制造业增长42.0%，电气机械和器材制造业增长18.4%，汽车制造业增长9.5%，金属制品业增长1.3%，铁路、船舶、航空航天和其他运输设备制造业下降30.5%，仪器仪表制造业下降32.6%，通用设备制造业下降3.0%，专用设备制造业下降8.7%。

表3：2020年工业主要行业产值增长速度

行业名称	比上年增长（%）
规模以上工业总产值	2.6
#装备制造业	14.9
#战略性新兴产业	13.3
#高技术制造业	23.4
主要行业	
汽车制造业	9.5
铁路、船舶、航空航天和其他运输设备制造业	-30.5
电气机械和器材制造业	18.4
计算机、通信和其他电子设备制造业	42.0
医药制造业	-13.4
电力、热力生产和供应业	0.6

表4：2020年主要工业产品产量及其增长速度

产品名称	单位	产量	比上年增长（%）
发电量	亿千瓦小时	154.29	3.6
饮料	万吨	162.56	-21.5
小麦粉	万吨	64.49	47.6
饲料	万吨	93.97	26.5
乳制品	万吨	60.42	-16.8
中成药	万吨	1.19	-4.7
汽车用发动机	万千瓦	595.44	52.9
交流电动机	万千瓦	241.22	-7.7
变压器	万千伏安	18293.64	5.3
汽车	万辆	49.82	16.9
其中：载货汽车	万辆	24.39	26.8
轿车	万辆	10.11	-28.5
运动型多用途乘用车（SUV）	万辆	15.33	65.6
新能源汽车	万辆	5.95	-36.3
单晶硅	万千克	163.86	-7.1
电力电缆	万千米	19.15	3.4
光纤	万千米	732.05	29.7
光缆	万芯千米	912.52	34.8
锂离子电池	万只	2068.00	17.4
智能手机	万台	1699.74	48.9
电子元件	亿只	45.19	-3.0
集成电路圆片	万片	205.90	43.7
3D打印设备	台	206.00	19.1
太阳能电池	万千瓦	148.25	599.6

规模以上工业企业营业收入6255.80亿元，比上年增长4.7%。实现利润总额436.00亿元，增长46.9%。

全年全社会建筑业增加值1547.44亿元，比上年增长9.3%。全市具有资质等级的总承包和专业承包建筑业企业完成建筑业总产值5124.37亿元，增长13.5%，其中，国有及国有控股企业产值4002.19亿元，增长15.4%。所有资质等级企业签订合同额14107.37亿元，增长11.3%。

四、服务业

全年批发和零售业增加值795.83亿元，比上年增长1.8%；交通运输、仓储和邮政业增加值353.59亿元，增长0.8%；住宿和餐饮业增加值159.97亿元，下降16.6%；金融业增加值1069.98亿元，增长6.9%；房地产业增加值849.84亿元，增长0.8%；其他服务业增加值3069.00亿元，增长6.8%。全年规模以上服务业企业营业收入3179.93亿元，比上年增长5.1%。

全年货物运输总量25712.81万吨，比上年增长5.6%；货物运输周转量502.69亿吨公里，增长5.1%。旅客运输总量14337.59万人次，下降45.5%；旅客运输周转量231.46亿人公里，下降40.3%。国际（地区）航线92条，境外航班通航架次5524架。年末全市机动车保有量398.01万辆，比上年末增长10.7%。其中，私人汽车保有量360.50万辆，增长11.2%。

表5：2020年客货运输量及其增长速度

指标	单位	绝对数	比上年增长（%）
货物运输总量	万吨	25712.81	5.6
公路	万吨	25204.00	5.7
铁路	万吨	471.18	-3.3
民航	万吨	37.63	-1.5
旅客运输总量	万人次	14337.59	-45.5
公路	万人次	7485.60	-50.9
铁路	万人次	3744.60	-40.9
民航	万人次	3107.39	-34.2

全年邮政业务总收入91.25亿元，比上年增长14.9%。邮政行业全年完成邮政函件业务901.54万件，包裹业务26.28万件；快递业务量6.71亿件，快递业务收入75.71亿元。全年电信业务总收入154.71亿元，比上年增长5.6%。年末移动电话用户1792.82万户，固定互联网宽带接入用户[13]480.05万户。

五、国内贸易

全年社会消费品零售总额[14]4989.33亿元，比上年下降2.9%。其中，限额以上企业（单位）消费品零售额[15]2512.61亿元，下降1.3%。在限额以上企业（单位）中，按经营地统计，城镇消费品零售额2507.93亿元，下降1.3%；乡村消费品零售额4.69亿元，下降30.3%。按消费形态统计，商品零售2418.67亿元，下降0.4%；餐饮收入93.94亿元，下降20.7%。

图6：2016-2020年社会消费品零售总额（亿元）

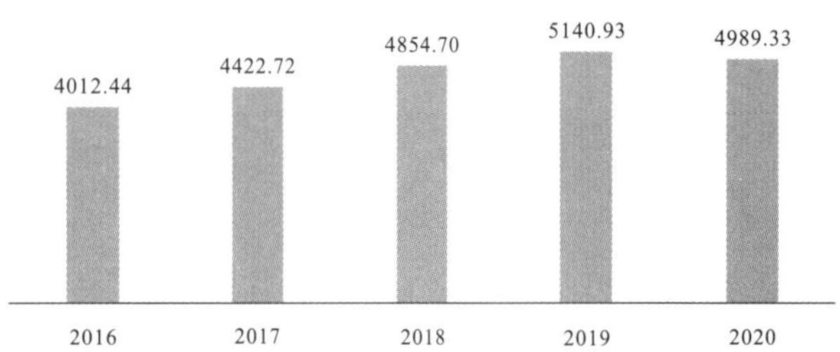

在限额以上企业（单位）商品零售额中，粮油、食品类零售额比上年下降0.5%，服装、鞋帽、针纺织品类下降0.4%，化妆品类增长14.0%，金银珠宝类增长9.8%，日用品类下降8.7%，体育、娱乐用品类下降9.0%，书报杂志类增长10.7%，家用电器和音像器材类增长8.6%，文化办公用品类增长32.8%，通讯器材类增长25.5%，石油及制品类下降8.1%，建筑及装潢材料类增长49.3%，汽车类下降5.0%。

六、固定资产投资

全年全社会固定资产投资比上年增长12.3%。其中，固定资产投资（不含农户）增长12.8%，农户投资下降25.0%。

在固定资产投资（不含农户）中，第一产业投资比上年下降43.6%；第二产业投资增长15.5%，其中，工业投资增长15.2%；第三产业投资增长12.8%。民间固定资产投资[16]比上年增长7.7%，基础设施投资[17]增长5.5%，文化产业投资增长2.9%。

表6：2020年分行业固定资产投资（不含农户）增长速度（%）

行业	比上年增长
固定资产投资（不含农户）	12.8
农、林、牧、渔业	-40.7
采矿业	-10.8
制造业	13.5
电力、热力、燃气及水的生产和供应业	27.3
建筑业	-56.3
批发和零售业	-60.5
交通运输、仓储和邮政业	9.9
住宿和餐饮业	22.8
信息传输、软件和信息技术服务业	29.6
金融业	145.1
房地产业[18]	12.5
租赁和商务服务业	24.9
科学研究和技术服务业	31.7
水利、环境和公共设施管理业	0.7
居民服务和其他服务业	-85.6
教育	135.2
卫生和社会工作	30.2
文化、体育和娱乐业	39.4
公共管理和社会组织	-34.4

全年房地产开发投资比上年增长6.5%。其中，住宅投资下降1.3%，办公楼投资增长19.0%，商业营业用房投资增长21.1%。商品房销售面积2559.79万平方米，下降3.0%。年末商品房待售面积149.51万平方米，比上年末下降26.2%。

七、对外经济

全年进出口总值3473.80亿元，比上年增长7.2%。其中，出口总值1776.00亿元，增长2.6%；进口总值1697.80亿元，增长12.3%。对“一带一路”沿线国家进出口546.20亿元，增长33.0%。

图7：2016-2020年进出口总值及其增长速度

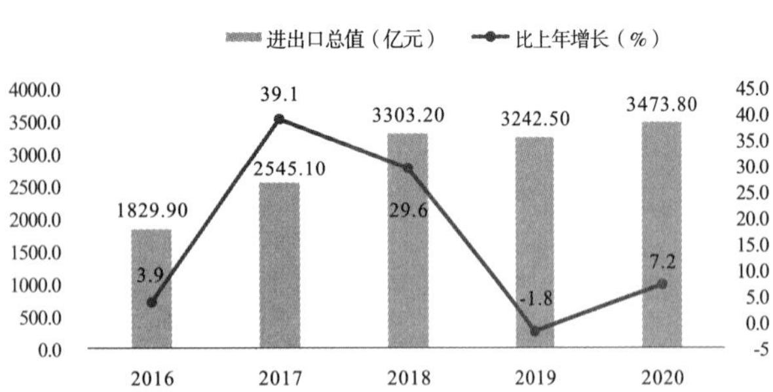

在进出口总值中，加工贸易进出口2094.50亿元，增长3.1%，占进出口总值的60.3%；一般贸易进出口744.30亿元，增长13.2%，占进出口总值的21.4%。

主要进口商品中，机电产品进口1327.80亿元，增长8.6%。主要出口商品中，机电产品出口1624.40亿元，增长2.0%；农产品出口21.70亿元，增长16.3%；基本有机化学品出口13.90亿元，增长2.0%。

全年实际使用外资76.77亿美元，比上年增长8.8%。

图8：2016-2020年实际使用外资（亿美元）

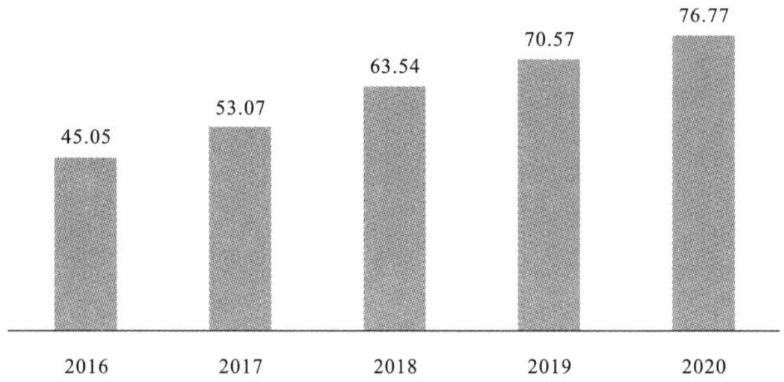

八、财政金融

全年全市财政一般公共预算收入724.13亿元，比上年增长3.1%，其中，税收收入571.60亿元，下降1.6%。全年全市财政一般公共预算支出1352.69亿元，比上年增长8.5%。

图9：2016-2020年财政一般公共预算收入（亿元）

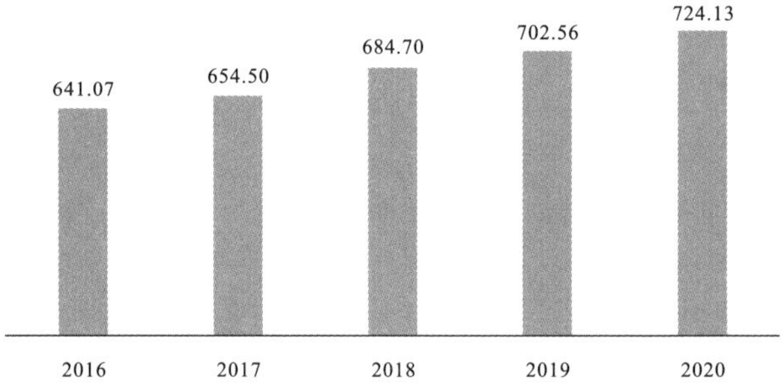

注：2016-2019年数据为决算数，2020年为快报数。

年末全市金融机构本外币存款余额26045.87亿元，比上年末增长11.6%；人民币存款余额25730.51亿元，增长11.5%，其中，住户存款余额10913.05亿元，增长14.2%。金融机构本外币贷款余额25792.89亿元，增长15.0%；人民币贷款余额25559.04亿元，增长14.8%。

全年证券市场各类证券交易总额58526.64亿元，比上年增长29.4%。年末全市拥有境内上市公司42家，比上年新增5家，总股本648.05亿股，总市值10794.33亿元。

年末全市共有保险机构67家。全年保费收入550.77亿元，比上年增长5.3%。全年赔款给付支出158.79亿元，比上年增长11.5%。

九、居民收入消费和社会保障

据城乡一体化住户调查，全年全市居民人均可支配收入35783元，比上年增长5.0%。其中，城镇居民人均可支配收入43713元，增长4.5%；农村居民人均可支配收入15749元，增长8.0%。城乡居民收入比为2.78，比上年缩小0.09。

城镇居民人均可支配收入中，工资性收入26145元，比上年增长1.0%；经营净收入2734元，增长0.7%；

财产净收入4633元，增长11.2%；转移净收入10201元，增长12.3%。

农村居民人均可支配收入中，工资性收入9226元，比上年增长5.4%；经营净收入2652元，增长9.8%；财产净收入379元，增长16.1%；转移净收入3492元，增长12.9%。

图10：2020年城镇居民人均可支配收入构成（%）

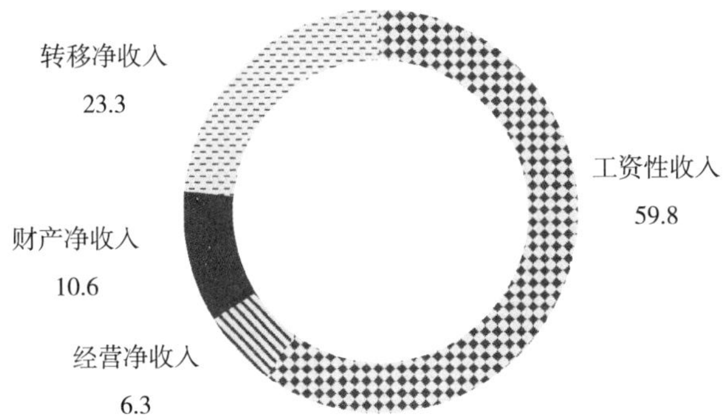

图11：2020年农村居民人均可支配收入构成（%）

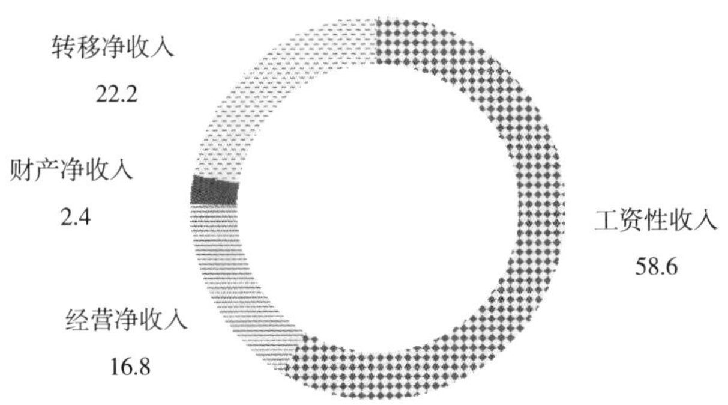

全年全市居民人均消费支出22168元，比上年下降6.4%。其中，城镇居民人均消费支出25813元，下降8.3%；农村居民人均消费支出12958元，增长3.2%。

剩余建档立卡贫困户5304户8533人全部脱贫，周至县顺利通过国家普查和第三方评估，高标准打赢脱贫攻坚战。

年末全市城乡居民医疗保险参保人数684.04万人，城镇职工基本医疗保险（含生育保险）参保人数378.60万人。基本养老保险参保人数768.98万人，其中，城镇企业职工养老保险参保人数486.93万人。失业保险参保人数240.75万人，工伤保险参保人数280.19万人。

全市提供住宿的养老机构168个，床位2.90万张，年末收养人数1.20万人。年末城市低保对象1.40万户、2.04万人，发放低保金1.61亿元；农村低保对象2.83万户、7.69万人，发放低保金4.16亿元。7221人享受农村特困人员救助供养，发放供养金1.49亿元。

十、科技、教育、文化、卫生健康和体育

年末全市国家级高新技术企业5234家，比上年增加1561家。全年技术市场合同交易额1648.56亿元。截至2020年11月末，全市专利申请量68353件，其中，发明专利申请量31376件；专利授权量41387件，其中，发明专利授权量10083件。

全市普通高等学校（本专科）63所，在校学生76.49万人，毕业生19.36万人。研究生培养机构43所，在校学生14.80万人，毕业生3.34万人。普通中学495所，在校学生45.68万人，毕业生13.89万人。小学1172所，在校学生85.20万人，毕业生10.75万人。

全市博物馆（不含私营）133座，各级别文物保护单位432处。公共图书馆14个，市级群众艺术馆1个，文化馆14个。图书馆总藏量达2646千册件，比上年增长8.5%。电视及广播人口覆盖率均达到100%。全年举办各类会展活动188个，其中，举办国际性会展活动8个，全国性会展活动42个；全年参展参会人数138万人次。

年末全市共有各类卫生机构7130个，其中，医院359个，社区卫生服务中心（站）262个，卫生院117个。各类卫生技术人员11.77万人，其中，执业（助理）医师4.07万人。各类卫生机构床位7.50万张。

图12：2016-2020年年末医疗卫生机构及技术人员数

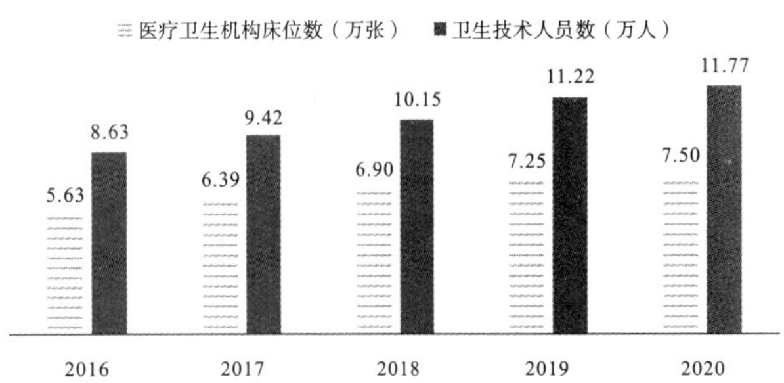

全年举办各类群众体育展示表演和竞赛活动共计400项次，体育社团举办和承办体育赛事300项次，其中，国际性和全国性赛事23项次。新建村级农民体育健身工程124个。全市新增社会体育指导员1888名。培养输送运动员参加国际、国内各项比赛获得金牌18枚、银牌18枚、铜牌17枚[19]。

十一、资源、环境和应急管理

全年各类建设用地供应量7.69万亩，其中，供应保障性住房建设用地0.45万亩。

全年空气质量优良天数250天，比上年增加25天。环境空气中二氧化硫年平均浓度为8微克/立方米，比上年下降11.1%；二氧化氮年平均浓度为41微克/立方米，下降14.6%；颗粒物（PM10）年平均浓度为88微克/立方米，下降8.3%；颗粒物（PM2.5）年平均浓度为51微克/立方米，下降10.5%。城市主要饮用水源水质达标率为100%。区域环境噪声等效声级均值为55.8分贝，道路交通噪声等效声级均值为69.4分贝。

全年发生各类生产安全事故227起、死亡177人。其中，道路运输事故180起、死亡123人；工矿商贸事故45起、死亡53人；农机事故2起、死亡1人。

注释：

[1]本公报中2020年数据为初步统计数。部分数据因四舍五入的原因，存在着分项与合计不等的情况。

[2]2020年开展第七次全国人口普查，相关数据拟于2021年发布，具体时间由国家统计局统一安排，公报中不再单独发布人口和就业人员相关数据。

[3]生产总值、三次产业及相关行业增加值绝对数按现价计算，增长速度按不变价格计算。2016–2017年生产总值及相关行业增加值为第四次全国经济普查修订结果，2018年为第四次全国经济普查数据，2019年为最终核实数据。

[4]万元GDP能耗按2015年价格计算。

[5]规模以上工业统计标准为年主营业务收入2000万元及以上的工业法人单位。

[6]工业战略性新兴产业包括新一代信息技术产业，高端装备制造产业，新材料产业，生物产业，新能源汽车产业，新能源产业，节能环保产业七大产业中的工业相关行业。

[7]高技术制造业包括医药制造业，航空、航天器及设备制造业，电子及通信设备制造业，计算机及办公设备制造业，医疗仪器设备及仪器仪表制造业，信息化学品制造业。

[8]规模以上服务业统计范围包括：年营业收入2000万元及以上的交通运输、仓储和邮政业，信息传输、软件和信息技术服务业，水利、环境和公共设施管理业，卫生行业法人单位；年营业收入1000万元及以上的房地产业（不含房地产开发经营），租赁和商务服务业，科学研究和技术服务业，教育行业法人单位；年营业收入500万元及以上的居民服务、修理和其他服务业，文化、体育和娱乐业，社会工作行业法人单位。

[9]高技术产业投资包括医药制造、航空航天器及设备制造等六大类高技术制造业投资和信息服务、电子商务服务等九大类高技术服务业投资。

[10]网上商品零售额是指企业（单位）通过公共网络交易平台（包括自建网站和第三方平台）取得订单，售给个人、社会集团非生产、非经营用的实物商品金额（含增值税），付款可以在网上进行，也可以在网下进行。公共网络包括计算机互联网、移动互联网等。

[11]市场主体为截至2020年12月25日数据。

[12]装备制造业包括金属制品业，通用设备制造业，专用设备制造业，汽车制造业，铁路、船舶、航空航天和其他运输设备制造业，电气机械和器材制造业，计算机、通信和其他电子设备制造业，仪器仪表制造业。

[13]固定互联网宽带接入用户是指报告期末在电信企业登记注册，通过xDSL、FTTx+LAN、FTTH/0以及其他宽带接入方式和普通专线接入公众互联网的用户。

[14]根据第四次全国经济普查结果及有关制度规定，对2016–2019年社会消费品零售总额数据进行了修订。

[15]限额以上企业（单位）消费品零售额的统计标准为年主营业务收入2000万元及以上的批发业企业（单位）、500万元及以上的零售业企业（单位）、200万元及以上的住宿和餐饮业企业（单位）。

[16]民间固定资产投资是指具有集体、私营、个人性质的内资企事业单位以及由其控股（包括绝对控股和相对控股）的调查单位建造或购置固定资产的投资。

[17]基础设施投资包括电力、热力、燃气及水的生产和供应业，交通运输、邮政业，电信、广播电视和卫星传输服务业，互联网和相关服务业，水利、环境和公共设施管理业投资。

[18]房地产业投资除房地产开发投资外，还包括建设单位自建房屋以及物业管理、中介服务和其他房地产投资。

[19]受新型冠状病毒肺炎疫情影响，2020年国际级体育赛事大幅减少，全市运动员参加国际比赛获奖牌数比往年有所减少。

数据口径：

本公报中2020年进出口、交通运输、电信、环境监测、低保、农村特困人员救助供养、文化等指标数据为西安原口径数据，未包含西咸的咸阳片区；居民人均可支配收入及消费支出、就业、市场主体、财政、实际使用外资、机动车保有量、邮政、证券、会展、科技、专利、教育、体育、卫生、社会服务机构、建设用地、安全生产、生产总值、农业、工业、建筑业、固定资产投资、国内贸易等指标数据为包含西咸新区数据。物价数据中，2020年居民消费价格、商品零售价格、新建商品住宅销售价格为西安原口径数据，工业生产者出厂价格、工业生产者购进价格为包含西咸新区数据。金融数据中，保险保费、金融机构数、存贷款数据为西安原口径数据，未包含西咸的咸阳片区；证券数据为包含西咸新区数据。社会保障数据中，城镇企业职工养老保险参保人数为西安原口径数据，医疗保险、失业保险、工伤保险参保人数为包含西咸新区数据。

资料来源：

本公报中粮食产量、畜禽产量、物价、居民收入及消费支出数据来自国家统计局西安调查队；城镇新增就业、登记失业率、社会保障数据来自西安市人力资源和社会保障局；市场主体、专利数据来自市市场监管局；财政数据来自市财政局；进出口数据来自西安海关；实际使用外资数据来自市投资合作局；公共图书馆、群众艺术馆、文化馆、广播、电视数据来自市文化旅游局；博物馆数据来自市文物局；客货运输数据来自市交通运输局；机动车数据来自市公安局；邮政业务数据来自市邮政管理局；电信业务数据来自中国移动西安分公司、中国电信西安分公司、中国联通西安分公司；金融数据来自中国人民银行西安分行营业管理部；证券、保险数据来自市金融工作局；教育数据来自市教育局；科技数据来自市科学技术局；会展数据来自市商务局；体育数据来自市体育局；医疗保险数据来自市医疗保障局；卫生数据来自市卫生健康委员会；社会服务、低保、农村特困人员救助供养数据来自市民政局；建设用地数据来自市自然资源和规划局；环境监测数据来自市生态环境局；安全生产数据来自市应急管理局；其他数据均来自市统计局。

Statistical Communique of Xi'an City On 2020 National Economic and Social Development[1]

Xi'an Municipal Bureau of Statistics and NBS Survey Office in Xi'an

Mar.18th.2021

In 2020, Facing the severe impact of novel coronavirus pneumonia epidemic and the complicated and severe domestic and international environment, Under the strong leadership of the CPC Central Committee with Comrade Xi Jinping as the core, Xi'an conscientiously implemented the spirit of the important speech delivered by General Secretary Jin Ping during his visit to Shaanxi, Make overall plans to promote epidemic prevention and control and economic and social development, Do a solid job of "six stability", We fully implemented the "Six Guarantees" tasks, took the lead in breaking through ten key tasks, effectively promoted the restoration of production and living order, the rapid recovery of economic operation, the steady improvement of development quality, the continuous improvement of people's livelihood and well-being, the prosperity and development of social undertakings, and the overall improvement of the ecological environment. Decisive achievements were made in building a well-off society in an all-round way, and the 13th Five-Year Plan ended successfully.

I. General Outlook[2]

According to the unified accounting results of the city (district) GDP, annual gross domestic product[3] GDP reached 10020.39 billion yuan, an increase of 5.2% over the previous year. Of this, the added value of the primary industry reached 312.75 billion yuan, up 3.0%;The added value of the secondary industry was 3328.27 billion yuan, up 7.4%;The added value of the tertiary industry reached 6379.37billion yuan, up 4.2%.The three industries constitute 3.1 ∶ 33.2 ∶ 63.7. The city's energy consumption per 10000 yuan GDP[4] decreased by more than 7% over the previous year. The added value of the non-public sector accounting for 53.1% of GDP.

Table 1 GDP and its growth rate from 2016 to 2020

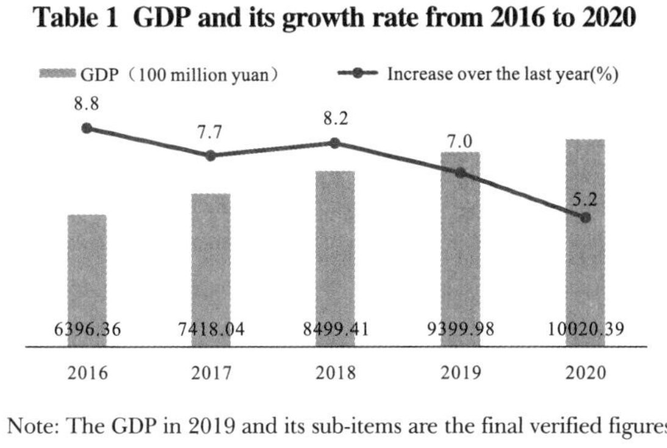

Note: The GDP in 2019 and its sub-items are the final verified figures.

Table 2 Proportion of added value of three industries to GDP in 2020 (%)

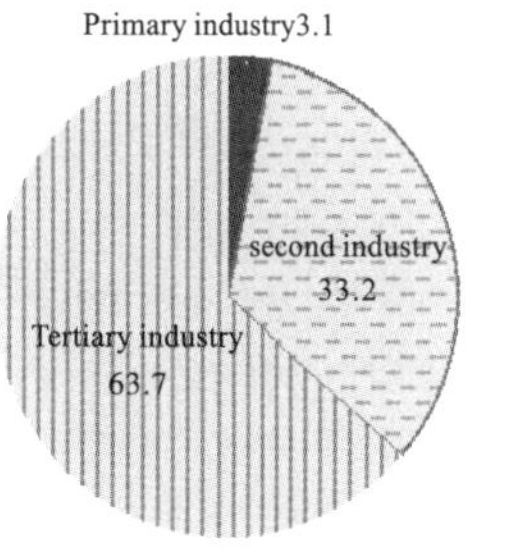

The consumer price index rose by 2.1%, of which the prices of food, tobacco and alcohol rose by 6.1%. Retail prices rose 1.5%. Producer prices rose by 0.2% and producer prices rose by 0.4%. New residential sales prices rose 8.9%.

Table 3 The Rate of Increase and Decrease of CPI in 2020 (%)

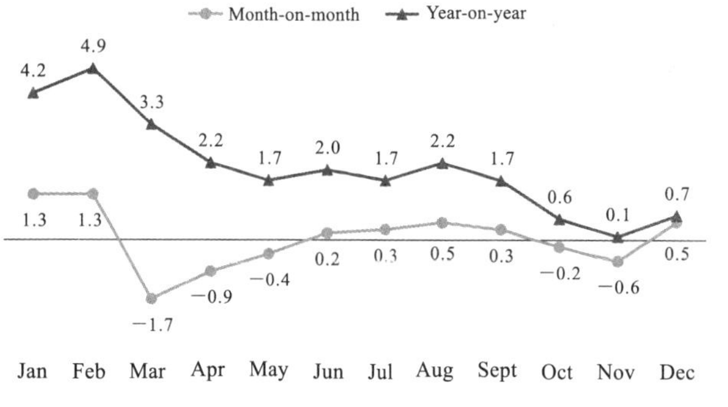

Sheet 1 Increase and decrease rate of consumer price ratio in 2020

Item	Rise or fall（%）
Consumer price Index	2.1
Food alcohol and tobacco	6.1
dress	0.4
live	-0.4
Articles and services for daily use	0.6
Transportation and Communications	-1.7
Education, culture and entertainment	2.5
Health care	-0.2
Other supplies and services	5.7

A total of 153100 urban jobs were created, and 53800 unemployed urban workers were re-employed. The registered urban unemployment rate was 3.64% at the end of the year.

New industries, new formats and new models are growing against the trend. Above the annual scale of the industry[5], strategic emerging industries[6], the total output value increased by 13.3% over the previous year, accounting for 46.9% of the total industrial output value. The total output value of high-tech manufacturing industry[7] increased by 23.4%, accounting for 32.4% of industries above the industrial scale. Annual scale above the service sector[8],the operating revenue of high-tech service enterprises up 12.4% over the previous year. The annual investment in high-tech industries[9] increased by 25.9% over the previous year. The annual optical fiber output was 7.3205 million kilometers, an increase of 29.7% over the previous year; The output of integrated circuit wafers was 2.059 million, an increase of 43.7%; The output of solar cells was 1,482,500 kilowatts, an increase of 6.0 times. Among the enterprises (units) above designated size in the whole year, the retail sales of online goods[10] was 59.275 billion yuan, accounting for 23.6% of the retail sales of consumer goods above designated size, an increase of 6.7 percentage points over the previous year; It increased by 37.1% over the previous year. In the whole year, there were 449,200 newly registered market entities[11], with an average daily registration of 1,227. At the end of the year, a total of 2,429,800 market entities were registered.

II. Agriculture

The total area planted with grain was 4,081,500 mu, down 0.4% from the previous year. The vegetable planting area was 1.0945 million mu, up 1.6%. Melon and fruit planting area 143,600 mu, down 2.5%;Oil planting area of 52,000 mu, up 11.7%;Cotton planting area of 800 mu, an increase of 35%.

Grain output for the whole year was 1.44580 million tons, up 3.4% from the previous year, including 725,800 tons for summer grain , up 2.8% ;And 720,000 tons for autumn grain, up 3.9%. The meat output was 45,600 tons, down 11.4%; The milk output was 140,300 tons, an increase of 13.4%; The output of eggs was 52,200 tons, down 3.0%; Vegetable output reached 3,813,100 tons, up 0.7%; The output of garden fruits was 1,009,300 tons, an increase of 3.9%.

Table 4 Grain output from 2016 to 2020 (10,000 tons)

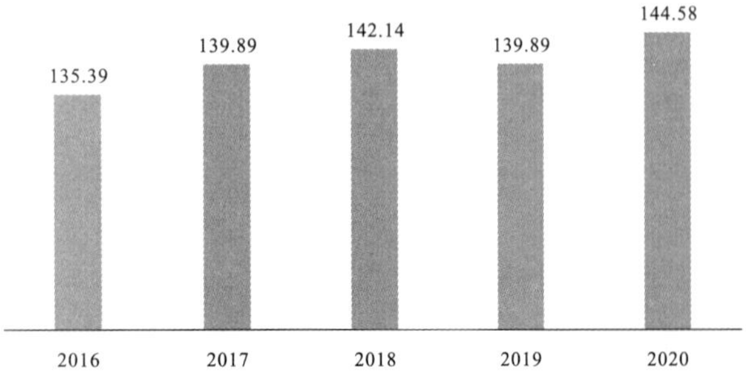

Sheet 2 The main Product of Agriculture Production in 2020

Name of Product	Units	Output	Increase over the last year (%)
Grain	10,000 tons	144.58	3.4
Vegetable	10,000 tons	381.31	0.7
Fruit	10,000 tons	100.93	3.9
Meat	10,000 tons	4.56	-11.4
# Pork	10,000 tons	2.85	-15.1
Milk	10,000 tons	14.03	13.4
Poultry egg	10,000 tons	5.22	-3.0
Year-end Pig on hand	10,000 head	30.13	1.6
Year-end Ox on hand	10,000 head	5.25	1.8
Year-end Sheep on hand	10,000 head	7.26	1.0
Year-end Fowl on hand	10,000 head	641.63	-0.3

III. Industry and Construction

The total added value of industry reached 182.859 billion yuan, an increase of 5.8% over the previous year. Above scale industry added value increased by 7.0% . The total output value of industrial enterprises above designated size increased by 2.6%, among them, the added value of light industry fell by 26.9% , while that of heavy industry rose by 8.7% .

Table 5 Total industrial added value and its growth rate from 2016 to 2020(%)

Among the above-scale industries in the whole year, the output value of equipment manufacturing industry[12] increased by 14.9%, accounting for 70.4% of the total output value of above-scale industries. Among them, computers, communications and other electronic equipment manufacturing growth 42.0%, electrical machinery and equipment manufacturing industry to grow 18.4%, automobile manufacturing industry increased by 9.5%, metal products industry increased by 1.3%, railway, shipbuilding, aerospace and other transportation equipment manufacturing industry increases 30.5%, the instrumentation manufacturing industry fell by 32.6%, general equipment manufacturing growth 3.0%, special equipment manufacturing growth 8.7%.

Sheet 3 Growth rate of output value of major industrial industries in 2020

Industry name	Increase over the last year (%)
Gross output value of industrial enterprises above designated size	2.6
# Equipment manufacturing industry	14.9
# Strategic emerging industries	13.3
# High-tech manufacturing industry	23.4
Major industries	
Automobile manufacturing industry	9.5
Railway, ship, aerospace and other transportation equipment manufacturing industry	-30.5
Electrical machinery and equipment manufacturing industry	18.4
Computer, communication and other electronic equipment manufacturing industry	42.0
Pharmaceutical manufacturing industry	-13.4
Electricity and heat production and supply industry	0.6

Sheet 4 Output and growth rate of main industrial products in 2020

Name of Product	Units	Output	Increase over the last year(%)
Electricity	100 million kilo watt-hour	154.29	3.6
Soft Drink	10,000 tons	162.56	-21.5
Wheat Meal	10,000 tons	64.49	47.6
Feed	10,000 tons	93.97	26.5
Dairy	10,000 tons	60.42	-16.8
Chinese Patent Medicine	10,000 tons	1.19	-4.7
Automobile Engine	10,000 Kilowatt	595.44	52.9
AC Motors	10,000 Kilowatt	241.22	-7.7
Transformer	10,000 kilovolt amperes	18293.64	5.3
Motor Vehicle	10,000 units	49.82	16.9
Among them: Truck	10,000 units	24.39	26.8
Car	10,000 units	10.11	-28.5
Sports Utility Vehicle	10,000 units	15.33	65.6
New Energy Vehicle	10,000 units	5.95	-36.3
Monocrystalline Silicon	10,000kg	163.86	-7.1
Electric Cable	10,000km	19.15	3.4
Optical Fiber	10,000km	732.05	29.7
Optical Cable	10,000 core kilometers	912.52	34.8
Lithium Ion Battery	10,000 units	2068.00	17.4
Smart Phone	10,000 units	1699.74	48.9
Electronic Component	100,000,000 units	45.19	-3.0
Integrated Circuit Chip	10,000 chips	205.90	43.7
3D printing equipment	1 unit	206.00	19.1
Solar cell	10,000 Kilowatt	148.25	599.6

The main business income of industrial enterprises above designated size reached 625.58 billion yuan, up 4.7% over the previous year. The total profit reached 43.6 billion yuan, down 46.9%.

The added value of the construction industry reached 154.744 billion yuan, an increase of 9.3% over the previous year. The total output value of general contracting and specialized contracting construction enterprises with qualification grades reached 512.437 billion yuan, up 13.5%, among which the output value of state-owned and state-holding enterprises was 400.219billion yuan, up 15.4%. The value of contracts signed by enterprises of all levels of qualification reached 1410.737 billion yuan, up 11.3%.

IV. Service Industry

The added value of wholesale and retail businesses amounted to 79.583 billion yuan, an increase of 1.8% over the previous year. Transportation, warehousing and postal services added 35.359 billion yuan, up 0.8%;The added value of the accommodation and catering industry reached 15.997 billion yuan, up 16.6%;The added value of the financial sector reached 106.998 billion yuan, up 6.9%;The added value of the real estate industry reached 84.984 billion yuan, up 0.8%;The added value of other services is 306.9 billion yuan, up 6.8%.The annual operating income of service enterprises above designated size was 317.993 billion yuan, an increase of 5.1% over the previous year.

Cargo transport totaled 257.1281 million tons last year, an increase of 5.6% over the previous year. Cargo transport turnover reached 50.269 billion ton-km, up 5.1%. The total number of passenger trips reached 143.3759 million, down 45.5%; Passenger traffic amounted to 23.146 billion passenger-km, down 40.3%. There were 92 international (regional) routes and 5524 overseas flights. At the end of the year, the number of motor vehicles in the city was 3980100 an increase of 10.7% over that at the end of the previous year. Among them, the number of private car PARC reached 3605000, up 11.2%.

Sheet 5 Passenger and freight transportation volume and its growth rate in 2020

Indicators	Units	Absolute number	Increase over the last year (%)
Total cargo transportation	10,000 tons	25712.81	5.6
Highway	10,000 tons	25204.00	5.7
Railway			
Civil aviation	10,000 tons	471.18	-3.3
Total passenger	10,000 tons	37.63	-1.5
transport	10,000 person-times	14337.59	-45.5
Highway	10,000 person-times	7485.60	-50.9
Railway	10,000 person-times	3744.60	-40.9
Civil aviation	10,000 person-times	3107.39	-34.2

The total revenue of postal services reached 9.125 billion yuan, up 14.9% over the previous year. The postal industry completed 9,015,400 postal mail businesses and 262,800 parcel businesses throughout the year; The express delivery business volume is 671 million pieces, and the express delivery business income is 7.571 billion yuan. The total revenue of telecom business reached 15.471 billion yuan, up 5.6%. By the end of the year, there were 17.9282 million mobile phone users, as well as fixed Internet broadband access users[13] 4.8005 million households.

V. Domestic trade

The total retail sales of consumer goods[14] was 498.933 billion yuan, down 6.0% over the previous year. Among them, the quota above enterprises (units) retail sales of consumer goods[15] was 251.261 billion yuan ,down 0.2%. According to local statistics, the retail sales of consumer goods in urban areas reached 250.793 billion yuan, down 1.3%. Rural retail sales of consumer goods was 469 million yuan, down 30.3%. According to consumption patterns, retail sales of goods was 241.867 billion yuan, down 0.4%; Food and beverage revenue was 9.394 billion yuan, down 20.7%.

Table 6 Total retail sales of social consumer goods from 2016 to 2020 (100 million yuan)

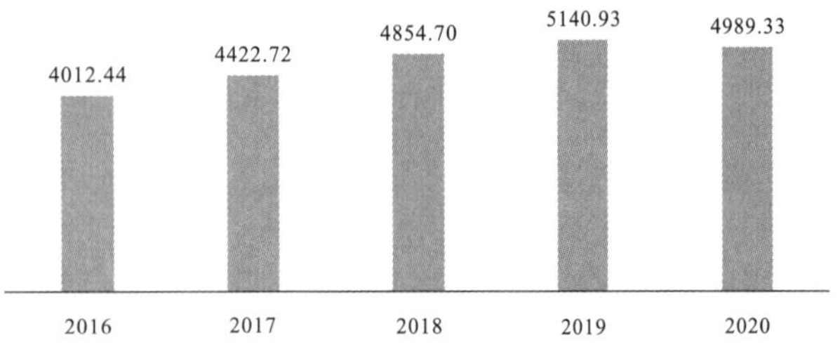

In the above designated enterprises (units) the retail sales of goods, grain and oil, food, retail sales down 0.5% over the previous year, a 0.4% drop in clothing, shoes and hats, the needle, textiles, cosmetics class increased by 14.0%, 9.8% gold and silver jewelry, daily necessities down 8.7% in the class, sports and entertainment products down 8.7%, books, newspapers and magazines increased by 10.7%, household appliances and audio-visual equipment increased by 8.6%, cultural office supplies increased by 32.8%,25.5% growth communications equipment class, oil and products down 8.1%, building and decoration materials increased by 49.3%, a 5.0% drop in motor vehicles.

VI. Investment in Fixed Assets

Investment in fixed assets rose by 12.3% over the previous year. Of this, fixed asset investment (excluding rural households) rose by 12.8%, while investment by farmers decreased by 25.0%.

In fixed asset investment (excluding rural households), investment in the primary industry decreased by 43.6% compared with the previous year. Investment in the secondary industry increased by 15.5%, of which industrial investment increased by 15.2%. Investment in the tertiary industry increased by 12.8%. Private investment in fixed assets[16] increased by 7.7% over the previous year, infrastructure investment[17] increased by 5.5%, and cultural industry investment increased by 2.9%.

Sheet 6 Growth rate of fixed assets investment by industry (excluding farmers) in 2020

Industries	Growth rate(%)
Investment Fixed Assets (excluding farmers)	12.8
Agriculture, Forestry, Animal husbandry and Fishery	-40.7
The Mining Industry	-10.8
Manufacturing	13.5
Production and Supply of Electricity, Heat, Gas and Water	27.3
The Construction Industry	-56.3
Wholesale and Retail	-60.5
Transportation, Warehousing and Postal Services	9.9
Accommodation and Catering	22.8
Information Transmission, Software and Information Technology Services	29.6
The FinancialSector	145.1
The Real Estate Industry[18]	12.5
Leasing and Business Services	24.9
Scientific Research and Technical Services	31.7
Water, Environmental and Public utility Management Industries	0.7
Residential Services and Other Services	-85.6
Education	135.2
Health and Social Work	30.2
Culture, Sports and Entertainment	39.4
Public Administration and Social Organization	-34.4

Investment in real estate development increased by 6.5% over the previous year. Investment in residential buildings decreased by 1.3%, investment in office buildings fell by 19.0%, and investment in commercial buildings increased by 21.1%. The sales area of commercial housing was 25.5979 million square meters, down 3.0%. At the end of the year, the area of commercial housing for sale was 1,495,100 square meters, down 26.2% from the end of the previous year.

VII. Foreign Economic Relation

Imports and exports totaled 347.38 billion yuan, up 7.2% from the previous year. Among them, exports reached 177.6 billion yuan, up 2.6%; Imports reached 169.78 billion yuan, up 12.3%. Import and export to countries along the "the belt and road initiative" reached 54.62 billion yuan, an increase of 33.0%.

Table 7 Total Value of Import and Export of Goods and the Growth Rates 2016 to 2020

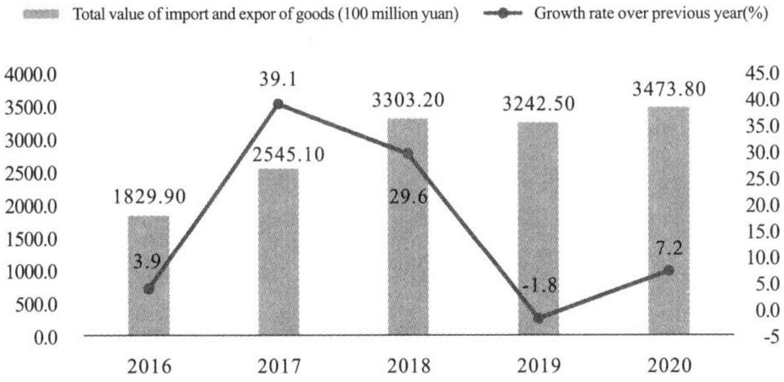

Of the total value of imports and exports, processing trade totaled 209.45 billion yuan, up 3.1% and accounting for 60.3% of the total value. Imports and exports in general trade totaled 74.43 billion yuan, up 13.2% and accounting for 21.4% of the total value of imports and exports.

The main imports included mechanical and electrical products, which reached 132.78 billion yuan, up 8.6%; The main exports were mechanical and electrical products, which totaled 162.44 billion yuan, up 2.0%; the export of agricultural products reached 2.17 billion yuan, up 16.3%; the export of organic chemicals came to 1.39 billion yuan, up 2.0%. The actual use of foreign capital reached 7.677 billion US dollars, an increase of 8.8% over the previous year.

Table 8 Actual use of foreign capital from 2016 to 2020 (US $100 million)

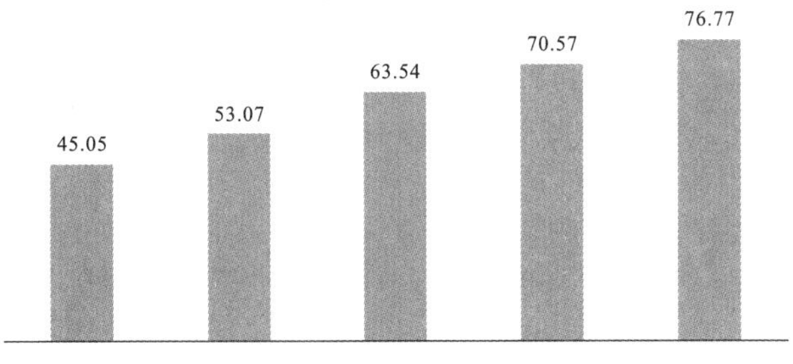

VIII. Financial

In the whole year, general public budget revenue in Xi' an was 72.413 billion yuan, an increase of 3.1% over the previous year, of which the tax revenue was 57.16 billion yuan, a decrease of 1.6%. In the whole year, the general public budget expenditure of the whole city was 135.269 billion yuan, an increase of 8.5% over the previous year.

Table 9 General public budget revenue from 2016 to 2020 (100 million yuan)

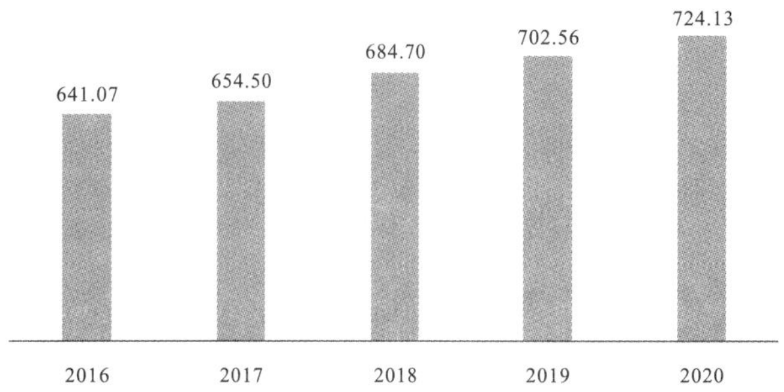

Note: The data from 2016 to 2019 are final accounts, and the data from 2020 are express reports.

At the end of the year, the balance of local and foreign currency deposits of financial institutions in Xi' an was 2604.587 billion yuan, an increase of 11.6% over that at the end of the previous year. The deposit balance of RMB was 2573.051 billion yuan, up by 11.5%, among which, the household deposit balance was 1091.305 billion yuan, up by 14.2%. The balance of domestic and foreign currency loans of financial institutions was 2579.289 billion yuan, up 15%. The balance of RMB loans is 2555.904 billion yuan, up 14.8%.

All kinds of securities traded on the stock market totaled 5852.664 billion yuan last year, an increase of 29.4% over the previous year. At the end of the year, the city had 42 domestic listed companies, 5 more than the previous year, The total listed capital is 64.805 billion shares and the total market value is 1079.433 billion yuan.

At the end of the year, there were 67 insurance institutions in the city. The annual premium income was 55.077 billion yuan, an increase of 5.3% over the previous year. The government paid 15.879 billion yuan in reparations, an increase of 11.5% over the previous year.

IX. Residents' income, consumption and social security

According to the household survey of urban-rural integration, the per capita disposable income of residents in the whole city was 35,783 yuan, an increase of 5.0% over the previous year. Among them, the per capita disposable income of urban residents was 43,713 yuan, an increase of 4.5%; The per capita disposable income of rural residents was 15,749 yuan, an increase of 8.0%. The income ratio of urban and rural residents was 2.78, which was 0.09 smaller than that of the previous year.

Among the per capita disposable income of urban residents, the wage income was 26,145 yuan, an increase of 1.0% over the previous year; The net operating income was 2,734 yuan, an increase of 0.7%; The net property income was 4,633 yuan, an increase of 11.2%; The net transfer income was 10,201 yuan, an increase of 12.3%.

Among the per capita disposable income of rural residents, the wage income was 9,226 yuan, an increase of

5.4% over the previous year; The net operating income was 2,652 yuan, an increase of 9.8%; The net property income was 379 yuan, an increase of 16.1%; The net transfer income was 3,492 yuan, an increase of 12.9%.

Table 10 Composition of per capita disposable income of urban residents in 2020 (%)

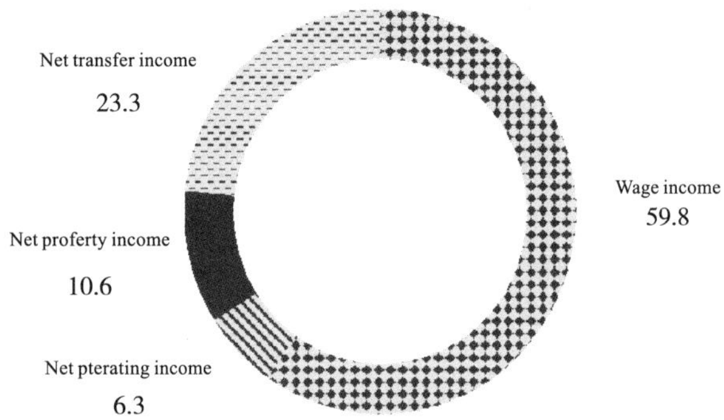

Table 11 Composition of per capita disposable income of rural residents in 2020 (%)

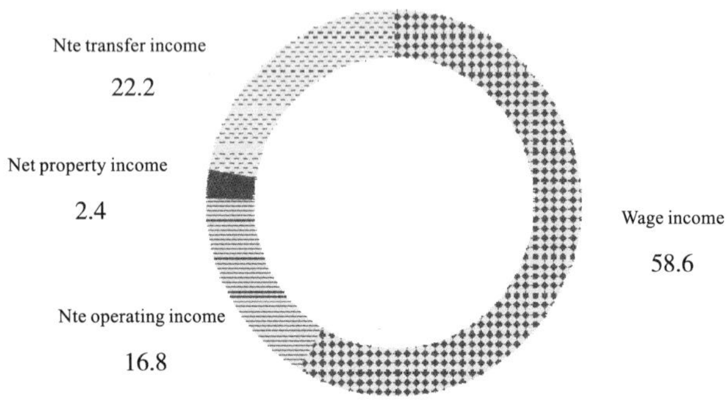

In the whole year, the per capita consumption expenditure of residents in the whole city was 22,168 yuan, down 6.4% from the previous year. Among them, the per capita consumption expenditure of urban residents was 25,813 yuan, down 8.3%; The per capita consumption expenditure of rural residents was 12,958 yuan, an increase of 3.2%.

The remaining 5,304 poor households with 8,533 people were all lifted out of poverty. Zhouzhi County successfully passed the national census and third-party evaluation, and won the tough fight against poverty with high standards.

At the end of the year, the number of urban and rural residents participating in medical insurance was 6,840,400, and the number of urban workers participating in basic medical insurance (including maternity insurance) was 3,786,000. There are 7,689,800 people participating in basic old-age insurance, of which 4,869,300 are participating in old-age insurance for urban enterprise employees. There are 2,407,500 people participating in unemployment insurance and 2,801,900 people participating in industrial injury insurance.

There are 168 old-age care institutions providing accommodation in the city, with 29,000 beds and 12,000 adoptions at the end of the year. At the end of the year, there were 14,000 urban subsistence allowances and 20,400 people, and 161 million yuan of subsistence allowances were paid; There are 28,300 rural minimum living allowances and 76,900 people, and 416 million yuan of minimum living allowances are paid. 7,221 people enjoyed assistance and support for poor people in rural areas, and paid 149 million yuan of support funds.

X.Science and technology, education, culture, health and sports

At the end of the year, there were 5,234 state-level high-tech enterprises, an increase of 1,561 over the previous year. The annual contract transaction volume of technology market is 164.856 billion yuan. By the end of November 2020, there were 68,353 patent applications in the city, including 31,376 invention patent applications; There are 41,387 patents granted, including 10,083 invention patents granted.

There are 63 colleges and universities in Xi' an, with 764,900 students and 193,600 graduates. There are 43 postgraduate training institutions with 148,000 students and 33,400 graduates. There are 495 ordinary middle schools with 456,800 students and 138,900 graduates. There are 1,172 primary schools with 852,000 students and 107,500 graduates.

The city has 133 museums (excluding private ones) and 432 cultural relic protection units at all levels. There are 14 public libraries, 1 municipal mass art gallery, and 14 cultural centers. The total collection of the library reached 2,646 thousand copies, an increase of 8.5% over the previous year. Both television and radio coverage reached 100%.188 exhibition events were held throughout the year, 8 of which were international events and 42 national exhibition activities. The annual number of participants reached 1.38million.

By the end of the year, there were 7130 health institutions of all kinds in the city, among which 359 were hospitals, 262 were community health service centers (stations) and 117 were health centers. There were 117700 health technicians of all kinds, including 40700 practicing doctors (including assistant doctors. There are 75000 beds in various health institutions.

Table 12 Number of medical and health institutions and technical personnel at the end of 2016 to 2020

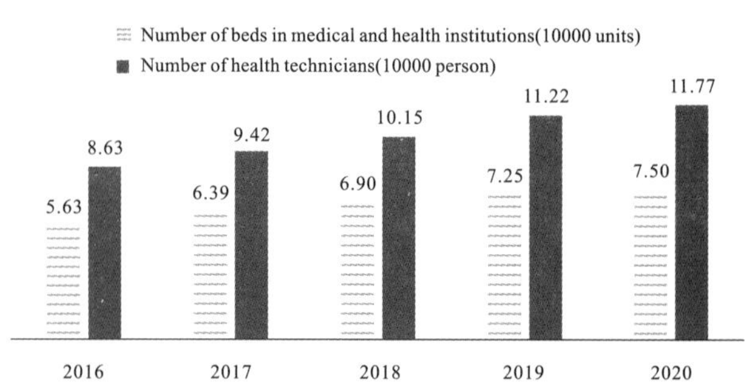

A total of 400 mass sports exhibitions and competitions were held throughout the year, and 300 sports events were held or organized by sports associations, among which 23 were international and national events. 124 new village-level farmers' physical fitness projects were built. The city's new social sports instructors 1888.Our city trains and trains athletes to participate in international and domestic competitions and win 18 Gold medals, 18 Silver medals and 17 Bronze medals[19].

XI. Resources, Environment and Emergency Management

The annual supply of various construction land is 76,900 mu, including 4,500 mu of affordable housing construction land.

There are 250 days with good air quality throughout the year, an increase of 25 days over the previous year. The average annual concentration of SO_2 in the ambient air was 8 $\mu g/m^3$, down 11.1% from the previous year and that of nitrogen dioxide was 41 $\mu g/m^3$, down 14.6%.The average annual concentration of particulate matter (PM10) was 88 $\mu g/m^3$, down 8.3% and that of particulate matter (PM2.5) was 51 $\mu g/m^3$, down 10.5%.The water quality of centralized drinking water source in the whole city reaches the standard rate of 100%.The average equivalent sound level of regional environmental noise is 55.8 dB, and the average equivalent sound level of road traffic noise is 69.4 dB.

There were 227 production safety accidents and 177 deaths. Among them, there were 180 traffic and storage accidents, with 123 deaths;45 industrial, mining and trade accidents, 33 deaths;2 farming, forestry, animal husbandry and fishery accident, 1 death.

Notes:

[1] The 2020 data in this communique are preliminary statistics. Some of the data is rounded, there is a breakdown and total unequal.

[2] The seventh national census will be held in 2020, and the relevant data will be released in 2021. The specific time will be uniformly arranged by the National Bureau of Statistics, and the relevant data of population and employed persons will no longer be released separately in the bulletin.

[3] The absolute value-added value of GDP, tertiary industries and related industries is calculated at current prices, and the growth rate is calculated at constant prices. The GDP in 2016 to 2017 and the added value of related industries are the revised results of the fourth national economic census, the data of the fourth national economic census in 2018 and the final verified data in 2019.

[4] Energy consumption per 10,000 yuan of GDP is calculated at the price in 2015.

[5] The statistical standards for industries above the scale are industrial legal entities with annual main business income of 20 million yuan or more.

[6] Industrial strategic emerging industries include new generation information technology industry, high-end equipment manufacturing industry, new materials industry, biological industry, new energy automobile industry, new energy industry, energy conservation and environmental protection industry.

[7] High-tech manufacturing includes pharmaceutical manufacturing, aviation, spacecraft and equipment manufacturing, electronic and communication equipment manufacturing, computer and office equipment manufacturing, medical instrument equipment and instrumentation manufacturing, and information chemicals manufacturing.

[8] The statistical scope of service industries above designated size includes: transportation, warehousing and postal services, information transmission, software and information technology services, water conservancy, environment and public facilities management, and health industry legal entities with annual operating income of 20 million yuan or more; Real estate industry (excluding real estate development and operation), leasing and business services, scientific research and technical services, and education industry legal entities with annual operating income of 10 million yuan or more; Legal entities in residential service, repair and other service industries, culture, sports and entertainment industries, and social work industries with annual operating income of 5 million yuan or more.

[9] High-tech industry investment includes six categories of high-tech manufacturing investment, such as pharmaceutical manufacturing, aerospace and equipment manufacturing, and nine categories of high-tech service investment, such as information services and e-commerce services.

[10] Retail sales of online goods refer to the amount of physical goods (including VALUE-ADDED tax) sold to individuals and social groups for non-production and non-business use through public online trading platforms (including self-built websites and third-party platforms) that enterprises (units) obtain orders from. Payment can be made online or offline. Public network includes computer Internet, mobile Internet and so on.

[11] The main body of the market is the data as of December 25th, 2020.

[12] Equipment manufacturing industry includes metal products industry, general equipment manufacturing industry, special equipment manufacturing industry, automobile manufacturing industry, railway, ship, aerospace and other transportation equipment manufacturing industry, electrical machinery and equipment manufacturing industry, computer, communication and other electronic equipment manufacturing industry, and instrumentation manufacturing industry.

[13] Fixed Internet broadband access users refer to

those who are registered with telecommunications enterprises at the end of the reporting period and access the public Internet through xDSL, FTTx+LAN, FTTH/0 and other broadband access methods and ordinary dedicated lines.

[14] According to the results of the fourth national economic census and relevant system regulations, the data of total retail sales of social consumer goods from 2016 to 2019 were revised.

[15] The statistical standards of retail sales of consumer goods for enterprises above designated size are wholesale enterprises (units) with annual main business income of 20 million yuan or above, retail sales enterprises (units) with annual retail sales of 5 million yuan or above, and accommodation and catering enterprises (units) with annual sales of 2 million yuan or above.

[16] Private fixed assets investment refers to the investment in the construction or purchase of fixed assets by domestic funded enterprises and institutions with the nature of collective, private and individual, and the survey units that are controlled by them (including absolute holding and relative holding).

[17] Infrastructure investment includes the production and supply of electricity, heat, gas and water, transportation, postal services, telecommunications, radio and television and satellite transmission services, Internet and related services, water conservancy, environment and public facilities management.

[18] In addition to real estate development investment, real estate investment also includes self-built houses by construction units, property management, intermediary services and other real estate investment.

[19] Affected by the epidemic situation in novel coronavirus pneumonia, the number of international sports events will be greatly reduced in 2020, and the number of medals won by athletes in our city in international competitions will be reduced compared with previous years.

Data calibres: The 2020 import and export, transportation, telecommunications, environmental monitoring , subsistence allowances, assistance and support for rural destitute people, culture and other index data in this communique are the original calibres of Xi 'an, excluding Xianyang district of Xi Xian; Indicators such as per capita disposable income and consumption expenditure, employment, market players, finance, actual use of foreign capital, number of motor vehicles, postal services, securities, exhibitions, science and technology, patents, education, sports, health, social service institutions, construction land, safe production, GDP, agriculture, industry, construction industry, investment in fixed assets and domestic trade include the data of Xixian New Area. Among the price data, consumer price, retail price and sales price of new commercial housing in 2020 are the original data of Xi 'an, while producer price and industrial producer purchase price include the data of Xi Xian New Area. Among the financial data, the insurance premium and financial institutions are the original data of Xi 'an, excluding Xianyang district of Xi Xian. The number of securities data include the data of Xi Xian New Area. Among the social security data, the number of urban enterprise employees participating in endowment insurance is the original data of Xi'an, and the number of medical insurance, unemployment insurance and industrial injury insurance includes the data of Xixian New District.

Source: Grain output, livestock and poultry output, price and per capita disposable income data in this communique are from the Xi 'an Survey Team of the National Bureau of Statistics; New urban employment, registered unemployment rate and social security data are from Xi 'an Human Resources and Social Security Bureau; Market entities and patent data are from mBAS; The financial data are from the municipal Finance Bureau; Import and export data from Xi 'an Customs; Data on utilization of foreign capital came from municipal Investment cooperation Bureau; Museum data comes from the Municipal Cultural Relics Bureau; Passenger and freight transportation data comes from the Municipal Transportation Bureau; Motor vehicle data comes from the Municipal Public Security Bureau; The postal service data are from the municipal Postal administration; The telecom business data came from Xi 'an Branch of China Mobile, Xi 'an Branch of China Telecom and Xi 'an Branch of China Unicom. The monetary and financial data are from the Operation Management Department of Xi 'an Branch of the People's Bank of China. The data of securities and insurance are from the Municipal Finance Work Bureau; The education data came from the municipal Education Bureau; The science and technology data are from the municipal Science and Technology Bureau; Exhibition data from municipal Bureau of Commerce; The sports data are from the municipal Sports Bureau; Health data from the municipal Health and Health Commission; Data on social services, subsistence allowances and assistance and support for people in extreme poverty in rural areas are from the Civil Affairs Bureau; The construction land data comes from the Municipal Natural Resources and Planning Bureau; Environmental monitoring data from municipal Bureau of Ecology and Environment; The safety production data comes from the municipal Emergency management Bureau; Other data are from the municipal Bureau of Statistics.

1 综 合

GENERAL SURVEY

资料整理：李　芬
Data management：Li Fen
数据审核：边可为
Data audit：Bian Kewei

第一部分　综合

一、简要说明

本章资料主要包括西安市行政区划、自然地理、自然资源、气象、国民经济和社会发展等综合资料，由西安市统计局综合处根据局内各专业处及有关部门统计资料进行整理和编辑。

二、主要指标

地区生产总值（亿元）	10020.39	比上年增长	5.2%
农林牧渔业总产值（亿元）	564.41	比上年增长	3.2%
全社会固定资产投资额（亿元）	-	比上年增长	12.3%
社会消费品零售总额（亿元）	4989.33	比上年下降	2.9%
财政一般公共预算收入（亿元）	724.14	比上年增长	3.1%
财政一般公共预算支出（亿元）	1347.58	比上年增长	8.1%
进出口总值（亿元）	3473.84	比上年增长	7.1%
城镇常住居民人均可支配收入（元）	43713	比上年增长	4.5%
农村常住居民人均可支配收入（元）	15749	比上年增长	8.0%

1　GENERAL SURVEY

Ⅰ.Brief Introduction

This chapter consists of mainly unified data of administrative divisions, natural geography, natural resources, meteorology, national economy and social development of Xi'an city. It is compiled by Integration Division according to the reported data from other divisions of the Xi'an Bureau of Statistics and other departments of the municipal government.

Ⅱ. Major Indicators

		Increase over Preceding Year
Gross Domestic Product (100 mil. Yuan)	10020.39	5.2%
Gross Output Value of Farming, Forestry, Animal, Husbandry and Fishery (100 mil. Yuan)	564.41	3.2%
Total Investment In Fixed Assets (100 mil. Yuan)	-	12.3%
Total Retail Sales of Consumer Goods (100 mil. Yuan)	4989.33	-2.9%
Government General Public Budgetary Revenue (100 mil. Yuan)	724.14	3.1%
Government General Public Budgetary Expenditures (100 mil. Yuan)	1347.58	8.1%
Total Value of Imports and Exports (RMB 100 mil.Yuan)	3473.84	7.1%
Per Capita Annual Disposable Income of Urban Households (Yuan)	43713	4.5%
Per Capita Annual Disposable Income of Rural Households (Yuan)	15749	8.0%

1-1 行政区划（2020年）

Administrative Division（2020）

单位：个 (unit)

地 区	Region	乡镇及街道办 Township and Urban Subdistrict Office	镇数 Town	街道办事处 Urban Subdistrict Office	村民委员会 Villagers' Committee	社区居委会 Neighbourhood Committee
西安市	**Xi'an**	**187**	**42**	**145**	**1990**	**1260**
新城区	Xincheng	9		9		101
碑林区	Beilin	8		8		98
莲湖区	Lianhu	9		9		131
灞桥区	Baqiao	9		9	76	68
未央区	Weiyang	10		10	50	201
雁塔区	Yanta	10		10	42	145
阎良区	Yanliang	7		7	73	30
临潼区	Lintong	23		23	226	45
长安区	Chang'an	21		21	232	88
高陵区	Gaoling	7		7	86	29
鄠邑区	Huyi	13		13	193	18
蓝田县	Lantian	19	18	1	337	11
周至县	Zhouzhi	20	19	1	237	16
西咸新区	Xixian	22	5	17	254	148

注：本表数据来源市民政局。2020年基层社会组织全市数（村委会、社区居委会）统计口径包含7个开发区（高新区村委会156个、城市居委会70个；经开区城市居委会11个；浐灞生态区城市居委会10个；曲江新区城市居委会15个；航天基地城市居委会9个；航空基地城市居委会2个；港务区村委会28个、城市居委会14个）

1-2 土地面积和常住人口密度（2020年）

Statistics on Land Area and Density of Permanent Population（2020）

地　区	Region	土地面积 绝对数（平方公里） Absolute Value (sq.km)	Area 比重（%） Proportion (%)	常住人口（万人） Total of Permanent Population (10 000 persons)	常住人口密度（人/平方公里） Density of Permanent Population (person/sq.km)
西安市	**Xi 'an**	**10096.81**	**100.0**	**1296**	
市区	**Urban**	**5145.66**	**51.0**	**1060.6**	
新城区	Xincheng	30.13	0.3	61.8	20513
碑林区	Beilin	23.37	0.2	75.8	32429
莲湖区	Lianhu	38.32	0.4	101.9	26589
灞桥区	Baqiao	324.50	3.2	102.1	3146
未央区	Weiyang	264.41	2.6	155.6	
雁塔区	Yanta	151.44	1.5	204.9	13531
阎良区	Yanliang	244.55	2.4	30.3	1239
临潼区	Lintong	915.97	9.1	67.6	738
长安区	Chang'an	1588.53	15.7	158.7	
高陵区	Gaoling	285.03	2.8	44.2	1551
鄠邑区	Huyi	1279.42	12.7	57.7	
二县	**Two Counties**	**4951.15**	**49.0**	**104.9**	**212**
蓝田县	Lantian	2005.95	19.9	49.2	245
周至县	Zhouzhi	2945.20	29.2	55.7	189
西咸新区	**Xixian**			**130.5**	

注：1.本表土地面积数据来源市自然资源和规划局，为西安原口径数据。表中土地面积数据为2018年数据。
2.全市常住人口数据包含西咸新区。
3.由于全市、市区及相关区县常住人口包含西咸新区，土地面积为原口径，暂不计算人口密度。

1-3 自然状况和资源（2020年）

Nature Conditions and Resources（2020）

指　标	Item	2020
一、自然状况	**Nature Conditions**	
土地总面积（平方公里）	Total Land Area (sq.km)	10096.81
#市区面积	Urban Area	5145.66
气候（市区）	Climate (Urban)	
年平均气温（℃）	Average Annual Temperature (℃)	15.2
年降水量（毫米）	Total Annual Precipitation (mm)	648.4
日照总时数（小时）	Total Sunshine Time (hour)	1700.6
平均风速（米/秒）	Average Wind-speed (m/sec.)	2.1
二、自然资源	**Natural Resources**	
林业用地面积（千公顷）	Area of Forestry (1 000 hectare)	480.49
全市水面面积（万亩）	Whole Water Area (10 000 mu)	0.17
水资源总量（亿立方米）	Total Water Resource (100 million cu.m)	26.78
#天然地表水资源总量	Total Savageness Surface Water Resource	22.76
地下水资源总量（亿立方米）	Total Underground Water Resource (100 million cu.m)	11.60

注：1.全市水面面积包括湖泊、水库、鱼塘、城市段河流面积等。水面面积数据为新增水面面积。
2.本表数据来源市气象局、自然资源和规划局、水务局等。
3.本表水资源总量等水务局相关指标数据含西咸新区，其他指标数据均为西安原口径数据。
4.本表林业用地面积数据为2018年调整数据。土地面积为2018年数据。

1–4 气象情况（2020年）

Climate Condition（2020）

地 区	Region	平均气温（℃）Average Temperature（℃）	日照时数（小时）Sunshine Time (hour)	降水天数（天）Raining days (day)	年降水量（毫米）Total Annual Precipitation (mm)	平均风速（米/秒）Average Wind-speed (m/second)
市 区	Urban	15.2	1700.6	96	648.4	2.1
灞桥区	Baqiao	13.7		114	629.9	1.5
阎良区	Yanliang	14.7		117	820.6	0.9
临潼区	Lintong	14.9	1764.4	98	703.6	1.7
长安区	Chang'an	13.7	1917.4	119	642.7	1.2
高陵区	Gaoling	14.5	2257.4	94	611.8	1.8
鄠邑区	Huyi	14.4	1942.7	116	670.5	1.6
蓝田县	Lantian	13.6	2827.5	108	714.5	1.5
周至县	Zhouzhi	13.9	1858.4	115	847.8	1.5
西咸新区	Xixian	14.2		100	712.0	1.9

注：本表数据来源市气象局；灞桥区、阎良区、西咸新区为区域气象站，无日照监测资料。下同。

1–5 市区及远郊区县各月平均气温（2020年）

Average Temperature of Xi'an and the Districts and Outer Suburban of Each Month（2020）

单位：℃ （℃）

月 份	Month	市区 Urban	灞桥区 Baqiao	阎良区 Yanliang	临潼区 Lintong	长安区 Chang'an	高陵区 Gaoling	鄠邑区 Huyi	蓝田县 Lantian	周至县 Zhouzhi	西咸新区 Xixian
一月	January	2.4	1.9	1.4	2.0	1.0	1.6	1.7	0.8	1.5	1.4
二月	February	6.2	5.3	5.0	5.7	4.4	5.0	5.3	4.1	5.0	4.6
三月	March	12.6	10.7	11.0	12.2	10.5	11.5	11.4	10.3	11.1	11.1
四月	April	16.4	14.5	15.0	16.3	14.5	15.3	15.2	14.4	14.9	15.0
五月	May	23.0	23.1	23.1	22.7	21.1	22.0	22.1	21.0	21.7	21.6
六月	June	24.8	22.7	24.6	24.9	23.6	24.8	24.3	23.8	23.9	24.2
七月	July	25.7	23.4	26.0	25.4	24.5	25.8	25.0	24.6	24.3	25.2
八月	August	25.4	23.2	25.1	25.1	24.4	25.1	24.7	24.6	24.0	24.7
九月	September	21.8	20.1	21.7	21.2	20.3	21.2	20.9	20.7	20.0	21.1
十月	October	13.6	11.6	13.5	13.4	12.4	13.5	13.0	12.1	12.4	12.8
十一月	November	9.4	7.7	9.2	9.0	7.5	8.6	8.4	7.4	7.7	8.5
十二月	December	1.1	-0.3	0.4	0.7	0.2	-0.1	0.7	-0.9	0.6	0.2

注：本表数据来源于市气象局。

1-6 市区及远郊区县各月日照时数（2020年）

Sunshine Duration of Xi'an and the Districts and Outer Suburban of Each Month（2020）

单位：小时 (hour)

月 份	Month	市区 Urban	临潼区 Lintong	长安区 Chang'an	高陵区 Gaoling	鄠邑区 Huyi	蓝田县 Lantian	周至县 Zhouzhi
一月	January	83.7	86.6	146.6	88.6	67.9	149.7	78.2
二月	February	172.6	174.6	227.8	169.3	161.6	210.4	186.9
三月	March	164.9	174.2	271.6	241.0	160.8	260.9	273.9
四月	April	186.1	195.5	240.8	292.2	206.1	282.0	235.6
五月	May	232.7	218.7	233.0	341.6	344.5	334.5	236.1
六月	June	140.9	139.1	130.9	271.0	276.0	263.6	145.9
七月	July	143.3	147.3	146.5	223.0	205.5	294.0	157.6
八月	August	147.1	154.6	132.6	152.9	129.9	286.9	131.3
九月	September	161.1	169.3	132.8	173.1	142.0	237.8	149.4
十月	October	69.2	74.5	62.4	81.0	62.5	150.7	68.2
十一月	November	110.1	123.6	99.1	128.0	100.6	182.9	106.8
十二月	December	88.9	106.4	93.3	95.7	85.3	174.1	88.5

注：本表数据来源市气象局。

1-7 市区及远郊区县各月降水天数（2020年）

Precipitation Days of Xi'an and the Districts and Outer Suburban of Each Month（2020）

单位：天 (day)

月 份	Month	市区 Urban	灞桥区 Baqiao	阎良区 Yanliang	临潼区 Lintong	长安区 Chang'an	高陵区 Gaoling	鄠邑区 Huyi	蓝田县 Lantian	周至县 Zhouzhi	西咸新区 Xixian
一月	January	4	14	6	8	9	6	9	11	7	5
二月	February	4	5	4	5	4	3	7	5	4	3
三月	March	4	6	4	5	10	3	6	6	10	5
四月	April	4	5	4	4	4	4	4	3	5	3
五月	May	4	5	8	5	8	6	8	6	5	6
六月	June	14	10	15	11	12	10	10	12	10	13
七月	July	13	14	20	15	14	13	14	13	14	15
八月	August	14	15	21	14	15	16	17	15	19	16
九月	September	9	10	7	8	9	9	9	9	8	7
十月	October	15	16	14	14	18	14	18	15	19	16
十一月	November	9	9	12	7	10	8	9	9	8	9
十二月	December	2	5	2	2	6	2	5	4	6	2

注：本表数据来源市气象局。

1-8 市区及远郊区县各月降水量（2020年）

Amount of Precipitation of Xi'an and the Districts and Outer Suburban of Each Month (2020)

单位：毫米 (mm)

月份	Month	市区 Urban	灞桥区 Baqiao	阎良区 Yanliang	临潼区 Lintong	长安区 Chang'an	高陵区 Gaoling	鄠邑区 Huyi	蓝田县 Lantian	周至县 Zhouzhi	西咸新区 Xixian
一月	January	3.2	3.2	7.6	3.8	9.5	5.6	6.5	9.6	5.7	6.3
二月	February	7.2	12.6	6.5	11.7	13.1	7.3	10.4	10.2	10.6	10.1
三月	March	16.5	24.5	13.2	17.5	27.4	12.5	19.6	22.3	16.9	20.7
四月	April	8.3	10.0	7.2	8.6	14.5	5.7	11.2	9.3	8.1	8.0
五月	May	81.5	59.4	51.6	69.9	46.0	35.9	62.2	56.4	79.2	55.9
六月	June	158.6	118.5	189.0	106.9	123.5	138.5	150.0	144.2	217.2	141.2
七月	July	104.5	120.7	133.4	133.3	96.4	106.3	107.9	129.9	135.2	99.2
八月	August	116.6	100.6	211.0	157.2	110.9	154.3	123.0	150.2	226.6	220.6
九月	September	37.8	43.3	41.2	48.1	46.7	35.3	46.6	49.0	49.7	38.4
十月	October	68.6	74.7	94.2	86.4	91.7	65.1	90.4	92.3	80.3	67.2
十一月	November	42.9	60.7	52.1	56.0	54.5	43.2	37.4	31.8	13.0	40.3
十二月	December	2.7	1.7	13.6	4.2	8.5	2.1	5.3	9.3	5.3	4.1

注：本表数据来源市气象局。

1-9 市区及远郊区县各月平均风速（2020年）

Average Wind Velocity of Xi'an and the Districts and Outer Suburban Districts (2020)

单位：米/秒 (m/s)

月份	Month	市区 Urban	灞桥区 Baqiao	阎良区 Yanliang	临潼区 Lintong	长安区 Chang'an	高陵区 Gaoling	鄠邑区 Huyi	蓝田县 Lantian	周至县 Zhouzhi	西咸新区 Xixian
一月	January	1.7	1.3	1.0	1.4	1.2	1.4	1.3	1.2	1.2	1.6
二月	February	2.1	1.7	1.1	1.8	1.5	2.0	1.7	1.7	1.6	1.9
三月	March	2.2	2.0	1.2	1.7	1.4	2.0	1.9	1.6	1.8	2.2
四月	April	2.2	1.7	0.9	1.9	1.2	1.9	1.7	1.6	1.7	2.0
五月	May	2.4	2.0	0.9	2.0	1.3	2.2	2.0	1.8	1.9	2.2
六月	June	2.1	1.5	0.9	1.8	1.2	1.8	1.7	1.6	1.7	1.9
七月	July	2.3	1.0	0.8	1.7	1.1	2.1	1.4	1.4	1.4	2.0
八月	August	2.4	1.6	0.9	2.0	1.2	2.0	1.7	1.6	1.6	2.2
九月	September	2.1	1.2	0.8	1.6	1.0	1.7	1.4	1.4	1.2	1.8
十月	October	1.6	1.4	0.6	1.5	1.0	1.4	1.4	1.2	1.2	1.5
十一月	November	2.2	1.8	0.8	1.7	1.3	1.8	1.6	1.4	1.4	1.8
十二月	December	1.7	1.3	0.9	1.5	1.3	1.4	1.4	1.2	1.3	1.5

注：本表数据来源市气象局。

1-10 主要年份国有土地使用权出让、划拨情况

The Transfer and Allocation of State-Owned Land Use Right in Representative Years

项　　目	Item	2010	2013	2014	2015	2016	2017	2018	2019	2020
国有土地使用权出让	**Lease of the Use Right of State-owned Land**									
出让地块(宗)	Land leased (item)	386	550	506	416	457	397	387	540	619
协议	Agreement	173	90	109	72	82	69	79	116	117
招标	Invitation for Bid	3								
拍卖	Auction	11					25	203	171	89
挂牌交易	Listed Transaction	199	460	397	344	375	303	105	253	413
出让面积（公顷）	Area of Totally Leased Land (hectare)	1364	2195	1789	1294	1599	1736	1623	2157	2812
土地使用权出让总收入（万元）	**Total Revenue from Leasing of the Use Right(10 000 yuan)**	**358098**	**292945**	**183901**	**109116**	**2832632**	**3988818**	**5738433**	**8221571**	**12462600**
国有土地使用权划拨	**Administrative Allocation of the Use Right of State-owned Land**									
划拨地块（宗）	Land Allocated (item)	108	234	152	141	132	130	116	205	167
划拨面积（公顷）	Area of Land Allocated(hectare)	1027	1986	1739	1209	1135	1411	3099	4605	2312

注：1.本表数据来自市自然资源和规划局。
2.2016年起土地使用权出让总收入，包括协议出让和招拍挂出让收入。
3.2019年起包含西咸新区。

1-11 主要年份国民经济和社会发展总量与速度指标

指 标	Item	总量指标 Total quantity index 1995	2000	2005	2010
人口与就业	**Population and Employment**				
人口	**Population**				
年底户籍总人口（万人）	Population at the Year-end （10 000 persons）	648.21	688.01	741.73	782.73
城镇人口	Urban Population	255.71	285.79	333.14	374.64
乡村人口	Rural Population	392.50	402.22	408.59	408.09
男性人口	Male Population	334.75	355.18	382.02	398.80
女性人口	Female Population	313.46	332.83	359.71	383.93
就业	**Employment**				
全社会从业人员数（万人）	Employment（10 000 persons）	372.60	389.10	415.83	477.58
#全部单位在岗职工人数	Number of Employed Staff and Workers	141.17	109.62	119.73	130.70
城镇登记失业人数（万人）	Registered Unemployed in Urban Areas（10 000 persons）	5.92	3.85	8.45	10.46
宏观经济	**Macroeconomic Indicator**				
国民经济核算（亿元）	**National Accounts（100 mil. yuan）**				
地区生产总值（亿元）	Gross Domestic Product（100 mil. yuan）	330.35	646.13	1294.05	3195.05
第一产业	Primary Industry	41.40	44.65	66.01	133.22
第二产业	Secondary Industry	135.33	277.13	511.19	1290.93
第三产业	Tertiary Industry	153.62	324.35	716.86	1770.89
工业	Industry	112.50	218.44	393.51	875.97
建筑业	Construction	22.83	58.69	117.68	414.96
固定资产投资	**Investment in Fixed Assets**				
全社会固定资产投资总额（亿元）	Total Investment in Fixed Assets（100 mil. yuan）	103.42	232.37	835.10	3250.56
按类别分：	By classification:				
固定资产投资（不含农户）	Investment in Fixed Assets （excluding farmers）	88.50	203.01	776.33	3104.92
#房地产开发投资	Real Estate Investment	21.65	51.85	225.23	842.34
农户投资	Farmer Investment	14.92	29.36	58.77	145.64
按经济成分划分：	By Economic Component				
国有单位	State-owned	69.08	159.60	373.70	1348.76
集体单位	Collective-Owned	9.78	14.65	59.23	326.44
个体经济	Self-employed Individual	11.13	24.40	79.04	54.73
其他经济	Other	13.43	33.72	323.13	1520.63
财政	**Public Finance**				
地方财政一般公共预算收入（亿元）	General Public Budgetary Revenue of Local Government （100 mil. yuan）	18.21	41.39	73.05	241.86
地方财政一般公共预算支出（亿元）	General Public Budgetary Expenditure of Local Government （100 mil. yuan）	18.42	46.50	97.82	371.62
物价指数（上年=100）	**Price Indices（preceding year=100）**				
商品零售价格指数	Retail Price Index	114.6	98.7	99.7	102.7
居民消费价格指数	Consumer Price Index	117.0	100.2	100.3	103.5
工业生产者出厂价格指数	Producer Price Indices （PPI） for Manufactured Goods	110.8	99.4	103.9	102.3
利用外资	**Utilization of Foreign Capital**				
利用外资签定协议额（万美元）	Amount of Foreign Capital for Utilization Through Signed Contracts or Agreements（USD 10 000）	28956	54123	121499	119689
外商实际直接投资额（万美元）	Amount of Foreign Capital Actually Utilized （USD 10 000）	18653	15633	57113	156653

注：1.国民经济核算2003—2017年为全国第四次经济普查修订数据。2018年为全国第四次经济普查数据。2019年为最终核算数，2020年为初步核算数。本部分其他相关数据也进行了相应调整。
2.2009年及以前年份财政收支为一般预算收支与基金预算收支之和。部分历史年份数据有所修订。
3.由于2010年固定资产投资起报点的变化，指数和平均增长速度为可比口径计算。
4.2015年，市公安局提供户籍人口分类为“城镇人口”和“乡村人口”，2015年之前，分类为“非农业人口”和“农业人口”；2020年城镇人口和乡村人口暂缺。

Total and Speed Index of National Economy and Social Development in Representative Years

				速度指标（%）				Indices and Growth Rates（%）		
2015	2018	2019	2020	指数（2020比以下各年）（2020 as percentage of the following years）				平均增长速度 Average Annual Growth Rate		
				2005	2010	2015	2019	2006-2010	2011-2015	2016-2020
815.66	922.82	956.74	977.97	131.8	124.8	119.8	102.2	1.1	0.8	3.7
545.95	639.62	668.57						2.4	7.8	
269.71	283.20	288.17						…	-7.9	
412.23	461.51	477.13	486.50	127.4	122.0	118.0	102.0	0.9	0.7	3.4
403.43	461.31	479.61	491.47	136.6	128.1	121.9	102.5	1.3	1.0	4.0
528.06	621.22	645.86	664.45	148.1	128.9	116.7	102.9	2.8	2.0	3.1
181.86	181.76	192.14	197.11	162.3	148.7	106.8	102.6	1.8	6.8	1.3
10.74	12.48	12.52	13.58	160.5	129.8	126.3	108.5	4.4	0.5	4.8
5932.86	8499.41	9399.98	10020.39	457.4	238.9	142.8	105.2	13.9	10.9	7.4
191.91	258.98	279.13	312.75	205.0	153.9	120.4	103.0	5.9	5.0	3.8
2070.47	2861.86	3130.80	3328.27	393.5	218.7	137.6	107.4	12.5	9.7	6.6
3670.48	5378.56	5990.06	6379.37	533.3	260.0	147.2	104.2	15.5	12.1	8.0
1242.18	1707.90	1816.23	1828.59	348.9	211.7	135.2	105.8	10.5	9.4	6.2
857.40	1210.79	1370.63	1547.44	549.2	237.7	142.4	109.3	18.2	10.8	7.3
5165.98				1107.1	284.5	141.8	112.3	31.2	14.9	7.2
5086.93				1211.5	302.9	144.5	112.8	31.9	15.9	7.6
1831.67				1123.8	300.4	138.1	106.5	30.2	16.8	6.7
79.05				106.1	42.8	78.8	75.0	19.9	-11.5	-4.7
1826.62				997.8	276.5	161.8	114.5	29.3	11.3	10.1
158.14				80.4	14.6	23.8	48.9	40.7	-9.4	-25.0
80.47								-7.1	13.2	
3100.75				1406.4	298.9	116.4	111.1	36.6	20.7	3.1
650.99	684.70	702.56	724.14	1340.3	401.5	143.0	103.1	27.3	22.9	7.4
917.24	1151.87	1247.02	1347.58	1344.2	353.5	142.0	108.1	30.6	20.0	7.3
99.7	102.2	102.1	101.5					2.5	1.7	1.5
100.7	101.9	102.7	102.1					3.1	2.6	1.9
98.5	101.1	101.6	100.2					2.2	0.1	0.2
193684	475508	196410	735596	301.8	306.3	189.5	374.5	-0.3	10.1	13.6
400833	635370	705738	767702	1290.6	470.6	183.9	108.8	22.4	20.7	13.0

5.2015年，国家取消了城乡投资分组，“农户投资”2014年之前为原来的“农村投资”。
6.由于2017年部分指标包含有西咸新区数据,速度指标为同口径计算数据。
7.本表数据2020年数据口径情况详见总说明和相关章节表下注释。
8.农业部分数据依据三农普数据对2007-2017进行了修订。畜牧业数据2013-2017年为三农普修订数据。下同。
9.投资有关数据2018年起为相对数据，与投资总量相关的指标，暂不计算。下同。
10.全部单位在岗职工人数统计范围为城镇非私营单位。

1-11 续表1

指 标	Item	总量指标 Total quantity index 1995	2000	2005	2010
产 业	**Industry**				
农业	**Agriculture**				
农林牧渔业总产值（亿元）	Gross Output Value of Farming，Forestry, Animal Husbandry and Fishery（100 mil yuan）	75.46	74.37	106.54	212.42
主要农产品产量（万吨）	Output of Major Farm Products（10 000 tons）				
粮 食	Grain	175.30	201.90	205.50	174.51
奶 类	Milk				
蔬 菜	Vegetables	133.60	162.14	195.70	207.11
水 果	Fruits	24.10	34.36	51.29	66.11
肉 类	Meat				
水产品	Aquatic Products	0.85	1.14	0.94	1.19
工业	**Industry**				
规模以上工业企业主要经济指标（亿元）	Main Economic Indicators of Industrial Enterprises above Designated Size（100 mil yuan）				
资产总计	Total Assets		958.05	1503.85	3592.13
主营业务收入	Revenue from Principal Business		420.42	980.97	3011.19
利润总额	Profits		16.11	28.72	245.37
从业人员年平均人数（万人）	Annual Average Employees（10 000 persons）		43.25	37.92	47.11
主要工业产品产量	Output of Major Industrial Products				
布（亿米）	Cloth（100 mil.m）	3.03	2.48	2.70	2.38
机制纸及纸板（万吨）	Machine-Made Paper（10 000ton）	36.44	5.47	22.19	49.60
发电量（亿千瓦时）	Electricity（100 million kwh）	22.00	19.00	48.00	96.94
钢材（万吨）	Steel Products（10 000ton）	31.44	10.00	24.02	110.77
汽车（万辆）	Motor Vehicle（10 000 units）	0.30	0.90	4.10	65.21
建筑业	**Construction**				
建筑业企业从业人数（人）	Number of Employed Persons（person）		136718	158311	539000
建筑业总产值（亿元）	Gross Output Value（100 mil. yuan）	42.55	105.93	326.65	1334.00
房屋建筑施工面积（万平方米）	Floor Space of Buildings under Construction（10 000 sq.m）	601.70	793.30	1801.20	4592.57
房屋建筑竣工面积（万平方米）	Floor Space of Buildings Completed（10 000 sq.m）	177.15	336.80	569.01	1391.91

注：1.规模以上工业2018年为全国第四次经济普查数据。
2.由于2010年规模以上工业起报点的变化，指数和平均增长速度为可比口径计算。

continued 1

2015	2018	2019	2020	速度指标（%） Indices and Growth Rates（%） 指数（2020比以下各年）（2020 as percentage of the following years） 2005	2010	2015	2019	平均增长速度 Average Annual Growth Rate 2006-2010	2011-2015	2016-2020
330.81	461.21	499.32	564.41	222.4	159.2	121.7	103.2	6.8	5.5	4.0
141.42	142.14	139.89	144.58	84.4	78.3	95.9	103.4	1.5	-4.0	-0.8
7.68	11.52	12.37	14.03	142.2	94.8	94.1	113.4	8.5	0.1	-1.2
267.91	373.69	378.58	381.31	194.1	150.1	114.2	100.7	5.3	5.6	2.7
73.33	89.15	97.18	100.93	245.4	148.6	119.7	103.9	10.6	4.4	3.7
7.21	5.45	5.14	4.56	69.2	92.2	78.1	88.7	-5.6	3.4	-4.8
1.42	1.35	1.36	1.13	120.2	94.9	79.6	83.1	5.7	3.6	-4.5
6740.26	8409.16	9449.95	10638.17	721.7	302.0	160.9	112.6	19.0	13.4	10.0
4374.11	6055.58	6483.80	6650.76	640.8	208.9	143.7	102.6	25.1	7.8	7.5
206.88	399.52	325.60	466.63	1401.3	164.1	194.6	143.3	53.6	-3.4	14.2
50.59	51.87	49.75	50.16	121.5	97.8	91.1	100.8	4.4	1.4	-1.8
1.04	1.28	1.21	0.99	36.8	41.8	95.6	82.1	-2.5	-15.3	-0.9
12.22	15.39	11.38	4.22	12.9	5.8	23.4	37.0	17.5	-24.4	-25.2
158.68	172.76	155.00	154.27	286.8	142.0	86.7	103.6	15.1	10.4	-2.8
37.03	33.40	31.47	39.99	281.1	61.0	182.4	119.3	35.8	-19.7	12.8
34.14	43.37	42.63	49.83	1214.9	76.5	145.9	116.9	73.9	-12.1	7.8
596245	740351	835995	867328	540.7	158.9	143.6	103.7	27.8	2.0	7.5
2650.41	3925.72	4514.38	5124.37	1563.7	382.9	192.8	113.5	41.0	14.7	14.0
11979.16	15855.39	17174.05	20218.75	1102.4	432.2	165.8	117.7	20.6	21.1	10.6
2712.01	2755.17	2726.28	3486.09	574.9	235.0	120.6	127.9	19.6	14.3	3.8

1-11 续表2

指 标	Item	总量指标 Total quantity index			
		1995	2000	2005	2010
交通运输	**Transportation**				
货运量（万吨）	Freight Traffic（10 000 tons）	9590	6999	12051	34323
铁 路	Railways	3317	3101	540	706
公 路	Highways	6268	3890	11505	33610
民用航空	Civil Aviation	5	8	6	7
客运量（万人次）	Passenger Traffic（10 000 persons-times）	9069	8068	10479	30294
铁 路	Railways	2678	2130	1796	2781
公 路	Highways	6128	5578	8294	26536
民用航空	Civil Aviation	263	360	389	977
邮电通信业	**Post and Telecommunication Services**				
邮电业务总量（亿元）	Total Business Revenue（100 mil. yuan）	7.65	46.16	132.04	323.11
函 件（万件）	Number of Letters Delivered（10 000 pieces）	14647	8230	9526	8176
本地电话局用交换机容量（万门）	Capacity of Local Office Telephone Exchanges（10 000 line）	58.30	204.80	457.30	449.00
本地电话年末用户（万户）	Local fixed telephone end users （million）	29.95	124.26	321.48	261.77
城市电话用户	Urban Telephone Subscribers	29.11	107.24	271.40	228.26
乡村电话用户	Rural Telephone Subscribers	0.84	17.02	50.08	33.50
移动电话用户（万户）	Number of Mobile Telephone Subscribers（10 000 subscribers）		73.10	419.96	1423.08
互联网年末宽带用户（万户）	Number of Subscribers of Intemet Services（10 000 subscribers）			33.93	146.18
国内贸易	**Domestic Trade**				
社会消费品零售总额（亿元）	Total Retail Sales of Consumer Goods（100 mil. yuan）	188.35	368.96	698.37	1765.42
对外经济贸易	**Foreign Trade**				
进出口总值（万美元）	Total Value of Exports and Imports（USD 10 000）	137510	173696	390146	1039273
出口总值	Exports	110163	106062	263441	531729
进口总值	Imports	27347	67634	126705	507544
旅游	**Tourism**				
旅游者人数（万人次）	Number of Tourists（10 000 persons）	791.35	1567.00	2423.60	5285.18
旅游总收入（亿元）	Earnings from Tourism （10 000yuan）	44.00	105.00	178.50	405.18
金融业	**Financial Intermediation**				
金融机构（不含外资）人民币存款余额（亿元）	Balance of Deposits in Domestic Funded Financial Institutions （100 mil. yuan）	359.51	1335.63	3599.70	8863.36
金融机构（不含外资）人民币贷款余额（亿元）	Balance of Loans in Domestic Funded Financial Institutions （100 mil. yuan）	334.50	972.52	2158.10	6420.72
保险公司保费收入（亿元）	Insurance premium income （100 million Yuan）	4.70	13.58	44.94	129.38
保险公司赔款及付给金额（亿元）	Indemnity Insurance and Amount Paid（100 million yuan）	1.70	1.39	9.50	26.39

注：1.2006年铁路数据按新口径统计；2018年起铁路数据为西铁局西安口径数据。
2.2006年国际互联网络用户改为互联网宽带用户。
3.1993—2017年社会消费品零售总额为全国第四次经济普查修订数据。本部分其他相关数据也进行了相应调整。
4.2014年起，海关不发布进出口美元口径数据，为了数据可持续性，使用年均汇率折算为美元口径。

continued 2

2015	2018	2019	2020	速度指标（%） Indices and Growth Rates（%） 指数（2020比以下各年）（2020 as percentage of the following years） 2005	2010	2015	2019	平均增长速度 Average Annual Growth Rate 2006-2010	2011-2015	2016-2020
46270	26219	27426	25713				93.8	23.3		
848	497	487	471				96.7	5.5		
45401	25691	26901	25204				93.7	23.9		
21	31	38	38				100.0	3.1		
26904	26057	26315	14338				54.5	23.7		
3982	6037	6332	3745				59.1	9.1		
19625	15555	15261	7486				49.1	26.2		
3297	4465	4722	3107				65.8	20.2		
331.53	739.53	1421.70	1721.55	1304.1	533.0	519.3	121.1	19.6	0.5	39.0
1707	1081	1028	902	9.4	11.1	52.9	87.7	-3.0	-26.9	-12.0
145.10								-0.4	-20.2	
292.08	262.28	250.08	238.95	74.3	91.2	81.7	95.5	-4.0	2.2	-4.0
261.44	237.78	229.46	219.78	80.9	96.2	84.0	95.8	-3.4	2.8	-3.4
30.63	24.50	20.62	19.17	38.4	57.3	62.7	93.0	-7.7	-1.8	-8.9
1767.00	1858.09	1711.36	1704.47	405.8	119.8	96.4	99.6	27.6	4.4	-0.7
289.97	392.48	438.65	479.24	1414.0	328.2	165.5	109.3	33.9	14.7	10.6
3620.90	4854.70	5140.93	4989.33	745.1	297.8	146.7	97.1	20.4	15.4	8.0
2828479	4991748	4700323	5036454	1291.7	484.9	178.2	107.2	21.6	39.6	12.2
1316350	2957605	2508203	2574853	977.1	484.1	195.5	102.7	15.1	35.3	14.3
1512129	2034142	2192120	2461601	1944.1	485.4	162.9	112.3	32.0	43.9	10.3
13600.80	24738.75	30110.43	18417.41	760.2	348.5	135.4	61.2	21.6	37.0	6.2
1073.69	2554.81	3146.05	1882.42	1054.3	464.4	175.2	59.8	15.1	38.4	11.9
17682.94	20811.95	22891.88	25600.53	711.3	288.9	144.9	111.8	19.7	14.8	7.7
13604.89	19610.88	22135.23	25456.70	1179.2	396.4	187.1	115.0	24.4	16.2	13.3
263.02	478.56	522.85	550.43	1225.7	425.7	209.4	105.3	23.6	15.2	15.9
87.62	130.82	141.42	157.75	1659.6	597.3	180.0	111.5	24.8	27.1	12.5

1-11 续表3

指　标	Item	总量指标 Total quantity index 1995	2000	2005	2010
教育、科技、文化	**Education, Science and Technology and Culture**				
教育	**Education**				
专任教师数（人）	Full-time Teachers（person）				
#普通高等学校	Institutions of Higher Education	15914	15679	29498	42098
普通中等专业学校	Regular Specialized Secondary Schools	2533	3172	2130	1845
普通中学	Regular Middle Schools	21984	26230	31094	31506
小　学	Primary Schools	30270	30215	29647	29944
在校学生数（万人）	Students Enrollment（10 000 person）				
#普通高等学校	Institutions of Higher Education	11.67	19.41	53.06	73.30
普通中等专业学校	Regular Specialized Secondary Schools	3.74	6.02	6.16	6.75
普通中学	Regular Schools	32.32	48.31	55.74	48.89
小　学	Primary Schools	79.36	77.81	60.47	51.56
科技	**Science and Technology**				
国家级高新技术企业数（个）	Hi-tech Enterprises（unit）				827
企事业单位累计授权专利数（件）	Accumulated patents awarded（unit）	3164	6139	11670	31999
文化	**Cultural**				
图书馆总藏量（千册件）	Total Collections in Library（1000 Volume-time）	2830	3214	3671	4465
文化馆、站（个）	Cultural Centers or Stations（unit）	201	251	192	197
电视节目制作时间（时：分）	Time for TV Programs Production（hour）	5738	11871	27377	29626
家庭、生活、环境	**Family, People's Livelihood and Environment**				
家庭	**Family**				
家庭总户数（户籍人口）（万户）	Total Number of Households（10 000 household）	171.25	187.08	203.04	226.71
城镇常住居民平均每户家庭人口（人）	Average Household Size in Urban Areas（person）	3.88	2.99	2.93	2.81
农村常住居民平均每户家庭人口（人）	Average Household Size in Rural Areas（person）	4.60	4.30	4.22	3.94
婚姻	**Marriages and Divorces**				
结婚（对）	Number of Marriages（couple）	47236	46415	49962	83645
离婚（对）	Number of Divorces（couple）	4296	5161	12747	19060
居住	**Housing**				
城镇居民人均现住房建筑面积（平方米）	Per Capita Building Area of Urban Residents（sq.m）	13.05	14.82	16.38	28.70
农村居民人均现住房建筑面积（平方米）	Per Capita Building Area of Rural Residents（sq.m）	21.77	28.31	36.73	66.73

注：1.2008年及以前图书馆总藏量为图书馆藏书量。
2.2005年以前城镇居民人均现住房总建筑面积为城镇人均住房使用面积。
3.2014年城乡居民人均住房面积为城乡住户调查一体化改革后新口径数据，与往年不可比。
4.结婚和离婚对数2018年数据含西咸新区与往年不可比，增速暂不计算。

continued 3

2015	2018	2019	2020	速度指标（%） Indices and Growth Rates（%）						
				指数（2020比以下各年）（2020 as percentage of the following years）				平均增长速度 Average Annual Growth Rate		
				2005	2010	2015	2019	2006-2010	2011-2015	2016-2020
47768	49018	50236	51996	176.3	123.5	108.9	103.5	7.4	2.6	1.7
1228	958	918	970	45.6	52.5	79.0	105.7	-2.8	-7.8	-4.6
33014	37539	39143	41133	124.5	122.8	117.2	105.1	0.3	0.9	3.2
28748	36878	39836	43423	135.1	133.6	140.9	109.0	0.2	-1.1	7.1
84.83	82.44	87.14	93.13	175.6	127.1	109.8	106.9	6.7	3.0	1.9
3.47	2.48	2.79	3.02	48.9	44.7	86.9	108.2	1.9	-12.5	-2.8
41.37	42.46	43.56	45.68	78.9	90.0	106.5	104.9	-2.6	-3.3	1.3
56.62	73.09	78.98	85.20	133.4	156.6	142.5	107.9	-3.1	1.9	7.3
1316	2620	3673	5212		629.9	396.0	141.9		9.7	31.7
103910	206703	240826	286233	2454.6	895.1	275.6	118.9	22.4	26.6	22.5
6522	7711	8012	7977	217.5	178.9	122.4	99.6	4.0	7.9	4.1
199	202	202	204	95.6	93.3	92.4	101.0	0.6	0.2	-1.6
43563	45731	58427	30016	109.6	101.3	69.0	51.4	1.6	8.0	-7.2
253.13	290.41	300.95	310.59	152.8	137.0	122.7	103.2	2.2	2.2	4.2
2.80	2.80	2.80	2.80	95.6	99.6	100.0	100.0	-0.8	-0.1	
3.60	3.70	3.70	3.50	83.0	88.9	97.2	94.6	-1.6	-1.8	-0.6
80790	93007	87315	75887				86.9	10.9	-0.7	
22748	42034	45329	41785				92.2	8.4	3.6	
32.10	34.40	34.80	34.90			108.8	100.3	11.9		1.7
50.70	51.40	49.10	50.20			98.9	102.2	12.7		-0.2

1-11 续表4

指 标	Item	总量指标 Total quantity index 1995	2000	2005	2010
生活	**People's Livelihood**				
城镇居民人均可支配收入（元）	Per Capita Annual Disposable Income of Urban Households （yuan）	4153	6364	9628	22244
农村居民人均可支配收入（元）	Per Capita Annual Disposable Income of Rural Residents（yuan）	1353	2344	3460	7750
住户存款（亿元）	Household deposits（100 mil. yuan）	291.46	675.83	1716.76	3641.09
工资	**Wages**				
在岗职工工资总额（亿元）	The Gross Salary of Workers （100 mil. yuan）	67.23	101.68	211.14	501.76
城镇非私营单位从业人员年平均工资（元）	Aunual Average Wage of Stuff and Workers in Urban Non-privite Enterprises（yuan）	4763	9179	17728	37870
卫生	**Health Care**				
医院、卫生院（个）	Number of Hospitals（unit）	368	426	479	412
执业（助理）医师（人）	Licensed （Assistant） Doctors （person）	18846	18750	17730	18763
医院、卫生院床位数（张）	Number of Hospital Beds（unit）	28265	28697	30087	36796
市政建设	**City Construction**				
自来水供应量（万立方米）	Volume of Tap Water Supply（10 000 cu.m）	35885	30273	35776	41089
自来水供水管道长度（公里）	Length of Water Supply Pipelines（km）	1066	2237	2315	2416
城市天然气供气总量 （万立方米）	Volume of Natural Gas Supply in Urban Areas （10 000 cu.m）	8419	11513	53202	109052
城市公共运营车辆（辆）	Total Number of Public Buses and Trolley Buses（unit）	977	2573	4762	7107
道路长度（公里）	Length of Paved Roads（km）	835	975	1382	2662
绿地面积（公顷）	Areas of Green Land（hectare）	5603	4116	4867	12140
环境、灾害	**Environment and Disaster**				
工业废水排放量（万吨）	Volume of Waste Water up to the Standard for Discharge（10 000 tons）	12479	9145	16969	13840
火灾发生数（起）	Number of Fire Disasters（case）	426	1040	2664	1825
火灾事故损失额（万元）	Fire Loss（10 000 yuan）	742	472	1566	2224
交通事故发生数（起）	Number of Traffic Accidents（case）	3065	4099	4903	2323
交通事故损失额（万元）	Loss of Traffic Accidents（10 000 yuan）	1103	1116	2024	737

注：1.城镇非私营单位从业人员年平均工资2012年前为城镇非私营单位在岗职工年平均工资。
2.2014年及以后城乡居民人均收入为新口径数据。2013年及以前“农村居民人均可支配收入”为“农村居民人均纯收入”。依据2018年新口径对2017年城乡居民收入进行了衔接，其他年份不可比。
3.部门对住户存款部分历史年代数据进行了修订。2015年之前住户存款为储蓄存款。
4.市政建设大部分指标2017年起包含西咸新区，与以前年份不可比，故不计算相关增速指标。

continued 4

2015	2018	2019	2020	速度指标（%） 指数（2020比以下各年）（2020 as percentage of the following years） 2005	2010	2015	2019	Indices and Growth Rates（%） 平均增长速度 Average Annual Growth Rate 2006-2010	2011-2015	2016-2020
33188	38729	41850	43713	574.9	248.8	141.9	104.5	18.2	15.1	7.2
14072	13286	14588	15749	692.5	309.3	152.0	108.0	17.5	15.3	8.7
6571.18	8360.33	9553.29	10913.05	636.2	300.0	166.2	114.2	13.3	12.5	10.7
1202.01	1622.72	1903.84	2081.05	952.1	400.8	167.3	109.3	18.9	19.1	10.8
60557	83821	92359	99315	563.0	263.6	164.8	107.5	16.4	9.8	10.5
395	462	477	476	89.1	103.6	108.2	99.8	-3.0	-0.8	1.6
26626	33776	38469	40714	221.7	209.3	147.5	105.8	1.1	7.3	8.1
51345	65552	69107	68426	217.2	177.5	127.2	99.0	4.1	6.9	4.9
56055	90394	75392	76944				102.1	2.8	6.4	
4371	4960	4977	5991				120.4	0.9	12.6	
196826	285215	320847	329150				102.6	15.4	12.5	
7781	8743	10566	9363	196.8	131.8	120.4	88.6	8.3	1.8	3.8
3571	4712	5142	5284				102.8	14.0	6.1	
20582	31681	32586	36034				110.6	20.1	11.1	
5204	4163	3914	2998	18.6	22.7	60.3	76.6	-4.0	-17.8	-9.6
2590	2066	1871	3034	113.9	166.4	117.1	162.2	-7.3	7.3	3.2
2402	1783	1887	2387	152.7	107.4	99.4	126.5	7.3	1.5	-0.1
2392	3153	2973	2835	57.8	122.1	118.5	95.4	-13.9	0.6	3.5
1470	2191	1809	1738	85.8	235.9	118.2	96.1	-18.3	14.8	3.4

1-12 主要年份国民经济和社会发展结构指标

单位：%

指　　标	Item	1995	2000	2005
人口与就业	**Population and Employment**			
人　口	**Population**			
城乡结构	Structure			
城镇人口	Urban Population	39.45	41.54	44.91
乡村人口	Rural Population	60.55	58.46	55.09
性别结构	Sexual Structure			
男	Male	51.64	51.62	51.50
女	Female	48.36	48.38	48.50
就　业	**Employment**			
全社会从业人员产业结构	Industrial Structure of the Whole Society			
第一产业	Primary Industry	41.17	37.78	32.78
第二产业	Secondary Industry	29.43	27.57	27.46
第三产业	Tertiary Industry	29.40	34.65	39.76
宏观经济	**Macro Economy**			
国民经济核算	**National Accounting**			
地区生产总值产业结构	Industrial Structure of GDP			
第一产业	Primary Industry	12.53	6.91	5.10
第二产业	Secondary Industry	40.97	42.89	39.50
第三产业	Tertiary Industry	46.50	50.20	55.40
投　资	**Investment**			
全社会固定资产投资结构	Structure of Total Investment in Fixed Assets			
报表种类结构	By classification			
固定资产投资（不含农户）	Investment in Fixed Assets (excluding farmers)	85.57	87.36	92.96
#房地产开发投资	Real Estate Investment	20.93	22.31	27.00
农户投资	Farmer Investment	14.43	12.64	7.04
经济成分结构	Registion Status Composition			
国有经济	State-owned Enterprises Investment	66.79	68.68	44.75
集体经济	Collective-owned Enterprises Investment	9.46	6.30	7.09
个体经济	Self-employed Individual	10.76	10.50	9.46
其他经济	Other	12.99	14.51	38.69
财　政	**Government Finance**			
财政收入结构	Structure of Government Revenue			
中　央	Central Government		31.94	58.30
地　方	Local Governments		68.06	41.70

注：1.2015年，市公安局提供户籍人口分类为“城镇人口”和“乡村人口”，2015年之前，分类为“非农业人口”和“农业人口”。
　　2.本表2008年以后财政收入结构中地方指地方财政一般公共预算收入。

Structural Indicators of National Economic and Social Development in Representative Years

(%)

2010	2013	2014	2015	2016	2017	2018	2019	2020
47.86	50.79	51.29	66.93	66.94	67.12	69.31	69.88	
52.14	49.21	48.71	33.07	33.06	32.88	30.69	30.12	
50.95	50.66	50.59	50.54	50.49	50.29	50.01	49.87	49.75
49.05	49.34	49.41	49.46	49.51	49.71	49.99	50.13	50.25
25.65	20.81	19.71	20.39	19.50	18.98	16.30	15.70	15.05
29.65	28.55	28.49	24.53	23.72	22.73	24.79	25.48	23.45
44.70	50.64	51.80	55.08	56.78	58.29	58.91	58.83	61.50
4.17	3.68	3.44	3.23	3.07	3.31	3.05	2.97	3.12
40.40	39.24	38.59	34.90	33.45	33.07	33.67	33.31	33.22
55.43	57.08	57.97	61.87	63.48	63.62	63.28	63.72	63.66
95.52	97.03	96.25	98.47	98.18	98.77			
25.91	31.08	29.84	35.46	37.67	30.88			
4.48	2.97	3.75	1.53	1.52	1.23			
41.49	34.49	32.46	35.36	44.92	54.62			
10.04	4.28	3.44	3.06	2.93	2.03			
1.68	1.64	1.41	1.56	1.57	1.24			
46.78	59.58	62.69	60.02	50.58	42.10			
37.28	30.80	29.61	28.94	31.68	35.63	39.86	40.83	39.89
47.36	55.60	57.25	58.39	56.45	47.96	46.88	45.80	46.98

1-12 续表1

单位：%

指 标	Item	1995	2000	2005
产 业	**Industry**			
农 业	**Agriculture**			
农林牧渔业总产值结构	Structure of Gross Output Value of Farming, Forestry,Animal Husbandry and Fishery			
农 业	Farming	68.03	69.23	61.69
林 业	Forestry	0.96	1.14	1.23
牧 业	Animal Husbandry	30.29	28.58	30.96
渔 业	Fishery	0.72	1.05	0.69
农林牧渔专业及辅助性活动	Farming,Forestry,Animal Husbandry and Fishery			5.43
建筑业	**Construction**			
建筑业总产值结构	Structure of Gross Output Value of Construction Industry			
房屋建筑业	Building Construction	12.84	9.28	34.05
土木工程建筑业	Civil Engineering Construction	86.27	88.50	56.59
建筑安装业	Installation of Construction			
建筑装饰和其他建筑业	Decoration and others	0.89	2.22	9.36
交通运输业	**Transportation**			
客运量结构	Structure of Passenger Traffic			
铁 路	Railways	29.53	26.40	17.14
公 路	Highways	67.57	69.14	79.15
民 航	Civil Aviation	2.90	4.46	3.71
货运量结构	Structure of Freight Traffic			
铁 路	Railways	34.59	44.30	26.92
公 路	Highways	65.36	55.58	73.04
民 航	Civil Aviation	0.05	0.12	0.04
国内贸易	**Domestic Trade**			
社会消费品零售总额结构	Composition of Retail Sales of Consumer Goods			
城 镇	Urban Area	88.95	87.99	90.17
农 村	Rural Area	11.05	12.01	9.83
教育文化、卫生、人民生活	**Education and Culture，Health Care，People's Livelihood**			
教 育	**Education**			
在校学生结构	Structure of Student Enrollment			
#普通高等学校	Institutions of Higher Education	8.81	12.44	28.48
普通中等专业学校	Regular Specialized Secondary Schools	2.84	3.84	3.33
普通中学	Regular Schools	24.55	30.93	29.89
小 学	Primary Schools	59.91	49.89	32.45

continued 1

(%)

2010	2013	2014	2015	2016	2017	2018	2019	2020
65.40	66.66	67.95	68.06	68.00	68.81	70.04	69.97	69.53
1.26	2.62	2.69	2.96	2.95	3.10	3.67	3.70	4.18
25.35	21.22	19.60	18.54	17.93	16.67	14.74	14.56	15.06
0.60	0.74	0.74	0.59	0.57	0.52	0.57	0.44	0.33
7.39	8.75	9.02	9.85	10.56	10.90	10.98	11.33	10.90
24.63	43.03	41.58	38.41	36.69	36.64	37.73	39.84	39.49
68.61	47.86	49.43	51.84	53.63	54.13	54.84	52.80	53.49
4.39	5.86	5.32	5.91	6.61	6.30	4.88	4.79	4.42
2.37	3.25	3.67	3.84	3.07	2.93	2.55	2.56	2.60
9.18	8.02	13.65	14.80	17.74	18.53	23.17	24.06	26.12
87.59	85.18	74.97	72.95	66.63	64.24	59.70	57.99	52.21
3.23	6.80	11.38	12.25	15.63	17.24	17.14	17.94	21.67
2.06	1.71	2.14	1.83	3.58	3.90	1.90	1.78	1.83
97.92	98.25	97.81	98.12	96.32	96.00	97.99	98.09	98.02
0.02	0.04	0.05	0.05	0.10	0.10	0.12	0.14	0.15
96.00	96.89	96.85	96.70	96.61	96.43	98.05	98.02	97.84
4.00	3.11	3.15	3.30	3.39	3.57	1.95	1.98	2.16
32.60	33.09	33.16	32.78	31.38	29.13	27.52	27.44	27.81
3.02	1.84	1.58	1.34	1.17	0.96	0.83	0.88	0.90
21.74	17.26	16.53	16.00	15.37	14.65	14.18	13.72	13.64
22.95	20.51	20.88	21.88	22.58	23.40	24.40	24.87	25.44

1-12 续表2

单位：%

指　　标	Item	1995	2000	2005
专任教师结构	Structure of Full-time Teachers			
#普通高等学校	Institutions of Higher Education	21.25	19.89	29.93
普通中等专业学校	Regular Specialized Secondary Schools	3.38	4.02	2.16
普通中学	Regular Middle Schools	29.37	33.21	31.55
小 学	Primary Schools	40.41	38.34	30.08
人民生活	**People's Livelihood**			
城镇居民消费结构	Consumption Structure of Urban Residents			
食品烟酒	Food,Tobacco and Alcohol	44.68	36.46	37.04
衣 着	Clothing	12.67	8.13	9.03
居 住	Residence	6.49	11.23	9.10
生活用品及服务	Living Articles and Services	13.75	11.33	4.73
交通和通信	Transport and Communication Services	5.58	6.93	9.67
教育文化娱乐	Recreation, Education and Culture Services	9.05	13.74	17.18
医疗保健	Medical and Health Care Services	3.27	7.23	9.45
其他用品和服务	Other Commodities and Services	4.51	4.95	3.80
农村居民消费结构	Consumption Structure of Rural Residents			
食品烟酒	Food,Tobacco and Alcohol	50.31	36.63	36.34
衣 着	Clothing	8.39	6.65	6.11
居 住	Residence	5.92	21.41	17.76
生活用品及服务	Living Articles and Services	5.17	5.47	5.11
交通和通信	Transport and Communication Services	8.09	4.21	8.19
教育文化娱乐	Recreation, Education and Culture Services	18.53	14.49	16.15
医疗保健	Medical and Health Care Services	1.78	6.93	8.19
其他用品和服务	Other Commodities and Services	1.81	4.21	2.15
卫　生	**Health Care**			
卫生技术人员结构	Medical Technical Personnel by Types			
执业（助理）医师	Licensed（Assistant） Doctors	45.42	44.82	41.96
注册护士	Registered Nurses	32.68	34.29	33.14
药　师	Junior Paramedics	8.78	8.31	7.30
技　师	Technicians	5.21	5.21	5.33
其　他	Others	7.91	7.37	12.27

注：2014年及以后为城乡住户调查一体化改革后数据，居民消费结构与2014年之前不可比。

continued 2

(%)

2010	2013	2014	2015	2016	2017	2018	2019	2020
32.47	33.91	33.87	34.52	32.63	30.90	30.74	29.97	29.13
1.42	1.08	0.97	0.89	0.84	0.64	0.60	0.55	0.54
24.30	22.95	23.62	23.86	23.50	23.58	23.54	23.35	23.04
23.10	21.49	20.57	20.52	21.41	22.03	23.13	23.76	24.33
31.29	32.44	29.21	29.59	29.26	29.44	27.08	26.80	28.08
11.11	12.02	9.09	8.78	8.22	8.12	7.91	7.65	6.65
9.33	7.82	17.89	17.78	17.87	17.84	20.01	21.00	24.21
7.56	7.80	7.21	7.42	7.59	7.57	7.86	7.26	7.16
12.06	14.01	14.16	13.31	13.67	13.00	11.74	11.85	11.21
14.66	14.17	12.60	12.48	12.29	12.61	13.93	13.69	10.60
9.50	7.99	7.32	7.92	8.14	8.28	8.97	8.95	9.80
4.49	3.76	2.53	2.72	2.96	3.15	2.50	2.79	2.30
32.54	32.96	29.93	28.18	26.86	27.27	24.43	25.45	27.98
6.55	7.87	7.44	7.12	6.65	6.50	5.94	6.25	6.09
24.41	19.82	21.99	23.28	23.38	23.54	23.60	23.10	24.25
6.53	7.76	6.97	6.60	7.59	7.85	7.67	7.22	5.81
8.45	9.86	10.66	10.70	10.76	10.69	11.71	11.85	12.59
11.20	10.56	10.26	11.68	11.86	11.90	13.26	13.15	11.41
8.54	8.41	11.07	10.68	11.17	10.47	12.05	11.46	10.37
1.78	2.77	1.68	1.76	1.73	1.79	1.34	1.51	1.51
33.16	33.58	32.66	32.69	32.30	32.71	33.28	34.27	34.60
40.01	42.13	42.28	42.74	43.50	44.15	45.77	46.22	46.18
5.36	4.99	4.88	4.86	4.72	4.54	4.36	4.20	4.09
8.11	5.75	5.63	5.76	5.86	5.94	5.95	5.91	5.94
13.36	13.55	14.56	13.97	13.62	12.66	10.64	9.40	9.19

1-13 主要年份国民经济和社会发展比例和效益指标

指　　标	Item	1995
人口与就业	**Population and Employment**	
人口	**Population**	
出生率（‰）	Birth Rate（‰）	11.95
死亡率（‰）	Death Rate（‰）	4.98
自然增长率（‰）	Natural Growth Rate（‰）	6.79
就业	**Employment**	
就业者负担人口	Dependency Ratio	1.7
三次产业就业者比例	Employment Ratio by Type of Industry	
（以第一产业为100）	（Employment in primary industry=100）	
第一产业	Primary Industry	100
第二产业	Secondary Industry	71.5
第三产业	Tertiary Industry	71.4
城镇登记失业率（%）	Unemployment Rate in Urban Areas（%）	3.1
宏观经济	**Macro Economy**	
国民经济核算	**National Accounting**	
三次产业增加值比例	Ratio of Value-added by Type of Industry	
（以第一产业为100）	（Employment in primary industry=100）	
第一产业	Primary Industry	100
第二产业	Secondary Industry	326.9
第三产业	Tertiary Industry	371.1
全社会劳动生产率（元／人）	Overall Labor Productivity（yuan/person）	8963
第一产业	Primary Industry	2698
第二产业	Secondary Industry	12404
第三产业	Tertiary Industry	14488
人均地区生产总值（元）	Per Capita GDP（yuan）	5131
固定资产投资	**Investment in Fixed Assets**	
全社会固定资产投资相当于地区生产总值比例（%）	Proportion of Investment in fixed Assets to GDP（%）	31.3
房屋建筑面积竣工率（%）	Rate of Floor Space of Buildings Completed in Construction（%）	33.4
固定资产交付使用率（%）	Rate of Fixed Assets Completed in Capital Construction and Put into Use（%）	70.7
建设项目建成投产率（%）	Rate of Projects Completed in Capital Construction and Put into Use（%）	43.7
财政	**Finance**	
财政总收入相当于地区生产总值比例（%）	Proportion of Government Revenue to GDP（%）	5.5
一般公共预算支出相当于地区生产总值比例(%)	Proportion of Government General Public Budgeary Expenditures to GDP（%）	5.6
利用外资	**Utilization of Foreign Capital**	
外商实际直接投资额相当于利用外资协议金额比例（%）	Proportion of Foreign Capital Actually Used to Total Amount of Foreign Capital for Utilization by Signed Contracts or Agreements（%）	64.4

注：本表财政收入数据2009年及以前为一般预算财政收入和基金收入之和。依据部门历史年份修订结果对财政相关数据进行了重新计算。本表涉及常住人口计算的指标数据依据第七次全国人口普查数据进行了修订。

Proportions of National Economic and Social Development and Benefit Index in Representative Years

2000	2005	2010	2011	2012	2013	2014	2015	2016	2017	2018	2019	2020
13.07	9.58	9.73	9.71	10.13	9.57	10.11	10.15	11.54	12.62	12.47	12.32	
5.96	5.16	5.34	5.38	5.57	5.37	5.47	5.51	5.40	5.42	5.48	5.53	
7.11	4.42	4.39	4.33	4.56	4.20	4.64	4.64	6.14	7.20	6.99	6.79	
1.8	1.8	1.8	1.8	1.8	1.8	1.8	1.8	1.9	1.9	1.9	1.9	1.9
100	100	100	100	100	100	100	100	100	100	100	100	100
73.0	83.8	124.0	125.0	141.3	137.2	144.6	120.3	121.7	119.7	152.1	162.3	155.9
91.7	121.3	183.3	184.7	206.5	243.3	262.9	270.1	291.3	307.1	361.4	374.8	408.8
3.4	4.3	4.2	3.9	3.5	3.4	3.4	3.4	3.3	3.3	3.3	3.3	3.6
100	100	100	100	100	100	100	100	100	100	100	100	100
620.7	774.4	969.0	916.6	953.3	1066.0	1123.5	1078.9	1087.9	1000.1	1105.1	1121.6	1064.2
726.4	1086.0	1329.3	1275.5	1359.5	1550.4	1687.5	1912.6	2064.6	1924.4	2076.8	2146.0	2039.8
16367	31356	67973	77893	86490	94907	104867	111837	119867	130668	139628	148372	152946
2960	4747	11129	13883	15351	16204	17783	18045	18483	22470	24156	27552	31067
25443	45258	93218	102201	110093	124045	141911	147176	166245	186251	197683	196560	207770
24024	44611	83586	96232	106847	111886	118682	129488	136009	144404	150770	160613	161790
9484	16158	37792	43723	48530	53624	58829	60912	63393	66649	73113	77494	79181
36.0	64.5	101.7	88.3	97.1	103.5	105.9	87.1	81.2	101.9			
42.0	28.1	6.9	10.0	8.7	13.2	11.4	6.8	9.9	11.2	6.4	6.3	4.9
74.0	52.8	38.4	40.4	42.4	37.1	42.5	40.3	38.3	43.4	26.9	33.6	37.2
44.2	54.2	53.9	54.9	56.1	56.1	62.5	61.0	64.6	62.4	36.3	55.3	42.0
9.5	12.7	16.0	17.1	17.2	18.2	18.3	18.8	17.8	18.4	17.2	16.3	15.4
7.2	7.6	11.6	13.0	13.7	14.7	14.7	15.5	14.7	14.1	13.6	13.3	13.4
28.9	47.0	130.9	167.0	68.8	124.3	145.0	207.0	441.2	114.1	133.6	359.3	104.4

1-13 续表1

指　　标	Item	1995
能　　源	**Energy**	
单位生产总值能耗降低率（%）	Decreasing Rate of Energy Consumption per Unit GDP（%）	
产　　业	**Industries**	
农业	**Agriculture**	
每个农林牧渔业劳动力农产品	Output of Farm Products per Farming,Forestry,Animal	
生产量（公斤）	Husbandry and Fishery Husbandry and Fishery Laborer（kg）	
粮食	Grain	1150
蔬菜	Vegetables	877
禽蛋	Poultry Eggs	
肉类	Meat	
水产品	Aquatic Products	6
每公顷播种面积农产品产量（公斤）	Output of Farm Crops per Hectare of Sown Area（kg）	
粮食	Grain	3806
油料	Oil-bearing Crops	1753
蔬菜	Vegetables	34800
工业	**Industrial**	
规模以上工业企业经济效益	**Economic Benefit of Industrial Enterprises above Designated Size**	
总资产贡献率（%）	Ratio of Total Assets to Industrial Output Value（%）	
资产负债率（%）	Assets-Liability Ratio（%）	
流动资产周转次数（次/年）	Rate of Annual Turnover Working Capitals（times/year）	
成本费用利润率（%）	Ratio of Profits to Cost（%）	
产品销售率（%）	Proportion of Industrial Products Sold（%）	
全员劳动生产率（元/人）	Overall Labor Productivity（yuan/person）	
建筑业	**Construction**	
技术装备率(元/人)	Value of Machinery per Laborer（yuan/person）	5990
产值利润率（%）	Ratio of Per-tax Profits to Gross Output Value（%）	3.5
全员劳动生产率（元/人）	Overall Labor Productivity（yuan/person）	37689
（按总产值计算）	（in terms of gross output value per employee）	
邮电通信业	**Post and Communication Services**	
电话普及率（含移动电话）（部/百人）	Access to Telephones, National（include mobilphone）（set/100 persons）	7.9
移动电话普及率（部/百人）	Access to Mobilphones（set/100 persons）	0.5

continued 1

2000	2005	2010	2011	2012	2013	2014	2015	2016	2017	2018	2019	2020
		2.06	3.56	3.51	3.57	5.89	3.20	3.83	4.61	5.99	4.78	7.52
1382	1493	1497	1438	1480	1398	1276	1346	1323	1267	1456	1430	1469
1110	1421	1777	1844	2012	2249	2338	2549	2628	3214	3827	3870	3874
					45	43	49	61	48	54	55	53
					61	64	69	67	53	56	53	46
8	7	10	10	12	13	13	14	13	13	14	14	11
4342	4796	4682	4772	4949	4886	4831	5132	5052	4947	5082	5122	5313
1526	1821	1950	2027	1992	1948	1519	2099	1408	2173	2180	2157	2135
37797	35231	39798	40668	42990	45271	38085	48711	39152	50851	52027	52717	52258
	8.4	12.2	8.6	7.7	8.5	7.4	5.7	6.4	7.2	7.3	5.4	6.1
65.0	65.0	57.6	57.7	59.4	59.5	59.7	57.3	55.7	53.0	54.8	53.9	55.2
1.0	1.3	1.7	1.5	1.5	1.5	1.4	1.3	1.3	1.4	1.3	1.2	1.1
4.2	3.1	8.8	5.2	4.5	5.2	5.2	4.8	6.0	6.6	6.7	5.1	7.1
97.1	97.5	97.1	97.4	96.7	95.7	94.9	94.5	96.0	97.3	96.2	94.0	93.0
29496	82815	188483	194105	230032	264324	275288	268182	277240	294393			
6805	13332	9461	28669	12216	10339		12712	14193	10051	10005	7964	7562
3.4	4.8	4.4	4.4	2.8	2.6	2.3	2.3	3.1	2.8	3.0	2.5	3.0
74347	206337	321340	334172	479232	354419	347000	406962	422421	411690	457700	467200	497600
31.2	100.0	199.0	212.5	231.4	264.9	242.9	208.4	196.5	187.6	178.0	158.8	150.0
10.6	56.6	168.0	182.0	197.3	230.8	211.0	178.8	168.9	163.5	156.0	138.6	131.5

1-13 续表2

指 标	Item	1995
国内贸易	**Domestic Trade**	
人均批发零售和住宿餐饮业消费品零售额（元）	Per Capita Retail Sales of Wholesale,Retail Trade and Accommodation Catering Trade （yuan）	1997
对外经济贸易	**Foreign Trade**	
进出口总额相当于地区生产总值比例（%）	Proportion of Total Imports & Exports to GDP（%）	34.76
旅游	**Tourism**	
每一游客花费（元）	Expenditure per International Tourist（yuan）	556
金融业	**Finance and Insurance**	
金融机构存款相当于地区生产总值比例（%）	Bank Deposits as Percentage of GDP（%）	108.83
金融机构贷款相当于地区生产总值比例（%）	Bank Loans as Percentage of GDP（%）	101.26
教育、科技、文化	**Education, Science and Technology and Culture**	
教育	**Education**	
毕业率（%）	Graduation Rate（%）	
小学	Primary Schools	
初中	Junior Schools	
学校教师负担系数	Student-teacher Ratio	
高等学校	Colleges and Universities	6.83
中等学校	Secondary Schools	14.42
小学	Primary Schools	26.22
文化	**Culture**	
每百万人有艺术表演团体（个）	Number of Troupes per Million Persons（unit）	3.39
每百万人有公共图书馆（个）	Number of Public Libraries per Million Persons（unit）	2.31
家庭、生活、环境	**Family, People's Livelihood and Environment**	
家庭	**Family**	
城市居民家庭	Urban Households	
平均每一劳动力负担人口（人）	Persons supported by Each Laborer （person）	1.8
农村居民家庭	Rural Households	
平均每一劳动力负担人口（人）	Persons supported by Each Laborer （person）	1.6
卫生	**Health Care**	
每万人医院数（个）	Number of Hospitals per 10 000 Persons（unit）	0.60
每万人医生数（人）	Number of Doctors per 10 000 Persons（person）	29.10
每万人医院床位数（张）	Number of Hospital Beds per 10 000 Persons（unit）	43.60
市政建设	**City Construction**	
城市自来水普及率（%）	Percentage of Households with Access to Tap Water（%）	
城市用气普及率（%）	Percentage of Households with Access to Tap Gas （%）	
人均公园绿地面积（平方米）	Per Capita Public Green Areas (sq.m)	3.80

continued 2

2000	2005	2010	2011	2012	2013	2014	2015	2016	2017	2018	2019	2020
4122	9160	20882	24751	28106	31336	34571	37176	39767	40875	41761	42382	39426
22.25	24.79	21.54	20.94	18.72	22.11	27.47	29.69	28.61	34.31	38.86	34.49	34.67
645	737	767	797	820	801	792	789	809	903	1033	1045	1022
206.71	278.17	277.41	272.99	275.61	275.51	270.11	298.05	296.38	268.85	244.86	243.53	255.48
150.51	166.77	200.96	197.70	195.86	200.19	207.57	229.31	237.00	226.90	230.73	235.48	254.05
		100.4	100.2	100.2	99.8	99.6	99.6	99.8	99.8	100.0	99.8	100.0
		99.7	100.6	98.7	99.3	99.9	98.3	98.7	98.3	100.0	99.0	99.9
12.38	17.99	17.41	17.92	18.15	18.05	18.27	17.76	17.62	17.33	16.82	17.35	17.91
17.84	18.47	17.78	16.91	16.43	15.07	14.01	13.88	13.05	12.78	13.10	13.06	12.89
25.75	20.38	17.22	18.06	17.15	17.66	18.94	19.94	11.98	11.42	11.31	11.13	11.11
3.20	2.56	1.53	3.38	2.08	1.92	1.88	1.82	1.75	1.59	1.51	1.46	1.39
2.18	2.02	1.77	1.69	1.64	1.60	1.56	1.32	1.26	1.15	1.09	1.05	1.08
2.2	2.1	1.9	1.8	1.9	1.8	1.3	1.3	1.3	1.3	1.3	1.3	1.3
1.6	1.6	1.5	1.5	1.5	1.5	1.4	1.4	1.4	1.4	1.5	1.6	1.5
0.57	0.59	0.49	0.41	0.41	0.41	0.40	0.40	0.38	0.40	0.39	0.39	0.37
25.30	21.98	22.14	24.30	25.22	25.52	25.85	26.95	27.05	27.18	28.36	31.15	31.42
38.72	37.29	43.42	42.01	44.40	47.21	49.04	51.97	51.46	53.36	55.04	55.96	52.80
98.95	99.00	98.77	99.95	100	100	100	100	100	99.25	97.85	98.27	98.67
81.51	91.30	97.02	97.46	98.19	98.68	98.71	98.79	98.89	96.07	99.90	99.96	99.87
5.12	5.63	9.11	9.89	10.22	10.70	11.22	11.47	11.61	12.04	9.97	9.97	11.79

1-14 主要年份平均每天主要社会经济活动

指　　标	Item	1995	2000
一、每天创造的财富	**Daily Production**		
地区生产总值（万元）	Gross Domestic Product（10 000 yuan）	9050.7	17702.2
第一产业	Primary Industry	1134.3	1223.3
第二产业	Secondary Industry	3707.7	7592.6
第三产业	Tertiary Industry	4208.8	8886.3
工业	Industry	3082.2	5984.7
建筑业	Construction	625.5	1608.0
批发和零售业	Wholesale and Retail Trade	909.6	1804.7
交通运输、仓储和邮政业	Transport, Storage, Post & Telecommunication Services	674.0	1178.4
住宿和餐饮业	Hotels and Catering Services		505.8
财政总收入（万元）	Total Government Revenue（10 000 yuan）	498.8	1686.8
财政一般公共预算支出（万元）	Government General Public Budgetary Expenditures（10 000 yuan）	504.7	1274.0
粮食（吨）	Grain（ton）	4801	5532
奶类（吨）	Milk（ton）		
蔬菜（吨）	Vegetables（ton）	3660	4442
肉类（吨）	Meat（ton）		
水产品（吨）	Aquatic Products（ton）	23	31
布（万米）	Cloth（10 000 m）	83	77
发电量（万千瓦小时）	Electricity（10 000 kwh）	610	534
钢材（吨）	Steel（ton）	861	274
汽车（辆）	Motor Vehicle（unit）	8	25
二、每天消费量	**Daily National Consumption**		
社会消费品零售总额（万元）	Total Retail Sales of Consumer Goods（10 000 yuan）	5160	10108
三、每天其他经济活动	**Other Daily Economic Activities**		
竣工住宅面积（平方米）	Floor Space of Buildings Completed（sq.m）	6927	14930
货运量（万吨）	Freight Traffic（10 000 tons）	26.3	19.2
客运量（万人次）	Passenger Traffic（10 000 person-times）	24.8	22.1
邮电业务总量（万元）	Business Volume of Postal and Telecommunications Services（10 000 yuan）	209.6	1264.7
进出口总值（万美元）	Total Value of Imports and Exports（USD 10 000）	110.2	475.9
出口值	Exports	82.5	290.6
进口值	Imports	27.7	185.3
外商实际直接投资额（万美元）	Foreign Capital Actually Used（USD 10 000）	51.1	42.8
旅游者人数（人次）	Number of Tourists（person-time）	21681	42932
四、每天人口变动和婚姻	**Daily Population Changes and Marriages**		
出 生（人）	Births（person）	211	247
死 亡（人）	Deaths（person）	88	113
结 婚（对）	Marriages（couple）	129	129
离 婚（对）	Divorces（couple）	12	14

注：本表财政收入数据2009年及以前为一般预算财政收入和基金收入之和。依据部门历史年份修订结果对财政相关数据进行了重新计算。

Major Social and Economic Activities Per Day in Representative Years

2005	2010	2013	2014	2015	2016	2017	2018	2019	2020
35453.4	87535.6	135896.7	152794.0	162544.1	175242.7	203234.0	232860.5	257533.7	274531.2
1808.5	3649.9	5002.7	5248.8	5257.8	5387.9	6719.5	7095.3	7647.4	8568.5
14005.2	35367.9	53331.0	58970.7	56725.2	58616.2	67203.3	78407.1	85775.3	91185.5
19640.0	48517.5	77563.0	88574.5	100561.1	111238.6	129311.2	147357.8	164111.2	174777.3
10781.1	23999.2	34745.8	38000.8	34032.3	34326.3	39362.2	46791.8	49759.7	50098.4
3224.1	11368.8	19138.1	21688.8	23490.4	25206.8	28694.2	33172.3	37551.5	42395.6
3823.8	9026.8	14034.5	15131.8	16146.0	16413.2	17903.8	19429.0	21594.2	21803.6
1619.7	3679.2	5335.1	5803.6	6565.2	7366.8	8151.8	8674.8	9535.1	9687.4
1303.8	2628.2	3315.1	3448.2	3887.1	3927.1	4204.1	4498.4	5142.2	4382.7
4489.6	13991.5	24733.3	27936.7	30547.4	31114.5	37389.3	40010.7	42024.4	42232.9
2680.0	10181.4	19994.8	22453.2	25129.9	25822.5	28632.6	31558.1	34164.9	36920.0
5631	4781	4156	3857	3875	3709	3833	3894	3833	3961
		202	222	210	217	319	316	339	384
5362	5674	6683	7065	7340	7366	9719	10238	10372	10447
		181	194	198	188	161	149	141	125
26	33	39	39	39	37	38	37	37	31
74	65	38	33	29	33	35	35	33	27
1316	2656	5055	4920	4347	4411	4842	4733	4247	4227
658	3035	1488	1175	1015	1203	1504	915	862	1096
112	1787	1156	1027	935	1048	1220	1188	1168	1365
19133	48368	79414	89790	99203	109930	121170	133005	140847	136694
16400	12287	23014	40078	22632	36472	36683			
33.0	94.0	137.3	115.2	126.8	65.4	69.9	71.8	75.1	70.4
28.7	83.0	104.9	70.5	73.7	64.9	66.5	71.4	72.1	39.3
3617.7	8852.3	6793.0	8016.4	9083.1	10496.2	12050.7	20261.1	38950.7	47165.8
1068.9	2847.3	4927.5	6833.5	7749.3	7547.9	10327.4	13676.0	12877.6	13798.5
721.8	1456.8	2322.8	3276.7	3606.4	3907.3	6298.6	8103.0	6871.8	7054.4
347.1	1390.5	2604.7	3556.8	4142.8	3640.6	4028.8	5573.0	6005.8	6744.1
156.5	429.2	857.5	1014.5	1098.2	1234.2	1453.9	1740.7	1933.5	2103.3
66400	144799	277534	328767	372625	411303	495702	677774	824943	504587
210	225	225	238	241	277	330	335	341	
63	124	126	129	131	130	142	147	153	
137	229	244	250	221	212	194	255	239	208
35	52	56	60	62	70	79	115	124	114

1-15 各区县国民经济和社会发展主要指标（2020年）

指 标	Item	新城区 Xincheng	碑林区 Beilin	莲湖区 Lianhu
一、年底总人口（常住人口）（万人）	Population at the Year-end Permanent population(10 000 persons)	61.8	75.8	101.9
二、地区生产总值（亿元）	Gross Domestic Product（100 mil. yuan）	579.05	1060.47	814.95
第一产业	Primary Industry			
第二产业	Secondary Industry	164.41	256.13	276.99
第三产业	Tertiary Industry	414.64	804.34	537.96
三、全社会固定资产投资增长速度（%）	The growth rate of Total Investment in Fixed Assets（%）	13.0	4.7	2.9
固定资产投资（不含农户）增长速度	The growth rate of Investment in Fixed Assets （excluding farmers）	13.0	4.7	2.9
#房地产开发投资增长速度	The growth rate of Real Estate	-28.6	-24.1	-45.2
四、财政一般公共预算收入（万元）	General Public Budgetary Revenue（10 000 yuan）	184949	332924	347614
财政一般公共预算支出（万元）	General Public Budgetary Expenditure（10 000 yuan）	353718	311093	414568
五、农林牧渔业总产值（万元）	Gross Output Value of Farming，Forestry Animal Husbandry and Fishery(10 000 yuan)			
主要农产品产量（万吨）	Output of Major Farm Products（10 000 tons）			
粮食	Grain			
蔬菜	Vegetables			
瓜果	Melon and Fruit			
肉类(吨)	Meat （Ton）			
奶类(吨)	Milk （Ton）			
六、规模以上工业企业营业收入（亿元）	Business Revenue of Industrial Enterprises above Designated Size（100 mil. yuan）	376.78	28.49	429.54
七、建筑业	Construction			
房屋建筑施工面积（万平方米）	Floor Space of Buildings under Construction （10 000 sq.m）	605.38	6074.85	2863.14
房屋建筑竣工面积（万平方米）	Floor Space of Buildings Completed（100 mil. yuan）	94.24	1136.54	471.84
八、社会消费品零售总额（亿元）	Total Retail Sales of Consumer Goods （100 mil. yuan）	252.50	556.00	482.37
九、城镇居民人均可支配收入（元）	Per Capita Annual Disposable Income of Urban Households（yuan）	48208	47977	47995
农村居民人均可支配收入（元）	Per Capita Disposable Income of Rural Households （yuan）			
十、医疗机构数（个）	Number of Health Care Institutions（unit）	296	452	436
卫生技术人员（人）	Number of Medical Technical Personnel （person）	13436	15321	13708
床位数（张）	Number of Beds（unit）	8114	9297	9175

Major Indicators of National Economy and Social Development by Region（2020）

灞桥区 Baqiao	未央区 Weiyang	雁塔区 Yanta	阎良区 Yanliang	临潼区 Lintong	长安区 Chang'an	高陵区 Gaoling	鄠邑区 Huyi	蓝田县 Lantian	周至县 Zhouzhi	西咸新区 Xixian
102.1	155.6	204.9	30.3	67.6	158.7	44.2	57.7	49.2	55.7	130.5
542.06	1319.43	2510.72	249.10	252.53	1136.25	374.49	233.61	142.96	139.44	612.50
18.94	1.61		32.42	41.37	32.76	30.84	31.10	32.38	40.39	50.93
157.90	580.10	575.78	85.67	63.55	604.96	203.49	96.94	22.11	12.35	204.70
365.22	737.72	1934.94	131.01	147.61	498.53	140.16	105.57	88.47	86.70	356.87
10.0	21.1	9.2	9.8	-5.2	31.1	-6.1	28.6	-36.4	31.8	11.2
10.3	21.2	9.2	10.7	-3.4	31.7	-5.8	34.0	-37.1	50.1	11.5
-2.8	27.8	22.5	-20.6	-34.1	-2.2	-17.0	-30.0	-46.2	13.7	11.3
186308	302293	378509	71021	132693	202109	125061	78825	29102	23206	839989
371532	371215	350047	209821	465366	493565	280141	386977	444261	428194	1339388
342532	28476		557053	770480	561784	601632	547410	588042	719245	927485
2.40	0.01		11.93	34.65	16.66	12.48	20.04	17.89	12.48	16.05
9.98	0.83		75.98	53.97	20.08	63.09	30.17	11.80	22.92	92.50
0.24	0.03		27.14	6.34	3.83	0.74	5.03	2.78	0.14	2.83
906			2605	11714	4164	3484	6095	7022	6778	2827
3951			23363	68654	5574	11205	6706	12812	4112	3914
166.06	913.78	700.82	302.59	311.05	1724.90	1072.96	424.38	50.77	21.60	374.48
489.82	5480.63	2993.58	39.71	82.40	225.97	79.58	68.50	21.63	8.51	1185.06
11.70	762.56	529.11	7.72	19.54	132.95	39.14	26.83	10.97	1.12	241.85
516.66	909.49	1144.40	37.22	55.09	232.46	177.86	41.25	39.20	34.33	510.51
40328	44628	48685	40631	30810	42051	38794	24788	23893	22407	25270
17969			15808	14659	15928	16370	13632	14731	13137	14027
431	556	671	186	515	603	233	433	585	485	744
5084	12153	18113	2669	3718	8687	3223	4459	2577	3079	4031
3284	6832	9289	1935	3135	6950	2979	3152	2162	2285	2804

主要统计指标解释

行政区划 指国家对行政区域的划分。根据有关法规规定，我国的行政区域划分如下：（1）全国分为省、自治区、直辖市；（2）省、自治区分为自治州、县、自治县、市；（3）自治州分为县、自治县、市；（4）县、自治县分为乡、民族乡、镇；（5）直辖市和较大的市分为区、县；（6）国家在必要时设立的特别行政区。

气候 指地球与大气之间长期能量交换与质量交换所形成的一种自然环境状态，它是多种因素综合作用的结果。气候既是人类生活和生产的环境要素之一，又是供给人类生活和生产的重要资源。气温、降水、湿度等气象要素的多年平均值是用来描述一个地区气候状况的主要参数，而各种气象要素某年、某月的平均值（或总量）则可以反映出该时期天气气候状况的重要特征。

自然资源 指人类可以直接从自然界获得，并用于生产和生活的物质资源。自然资源一般可以分成可再生资源和非再生资源两大类。可再生资源指在较短时间内可以再生、可以循环利用的资源，包括土地资源、水资源、气候资源、生物资源和海洋资源等。非再生资源指在使用后不能再生的资源，包括矿产资源和地热能源。

土地资源 土地指陆地的表层部分，它主要由岩石、岩石的风化物和土壤构成。土地资源按利用类型可以分为农用地、建筑用地和未利用地。农用地包括耕地、园地、林地、牧草地和水面。建筑用地包括居民点及工矿用地、交通用地和水利设施用地。未利用地指农用地和建筑用地以外的土地，包括滩涂、荒漠、戈壁、冰川和石山等。

耕地面积 指经过开垦用以种植农作物并经常进行耕耘的土地面积。包括种有作物的土地面积、休闲地、新开荒地和抛荒未满三年的土地面积。

森林面积 指由乔木树种构成，郁闭度0.2以上（含0.2）的林地或冠幅宽度10米以上的林带的面积，即有林地面积。森林面积包括天然起源和人工起源的针叶林面积、阔叶林面积、针阔混交林面积和竹林面积，不包括灌木林地面积和疏林地面积。

林业用地面积 指生长乔木、竹类、灌木、沿海红树林等林木的土地面积，包括有林地、灌木林、疏林地、未成林造林地、迹地、苗圃等。

水资源总量 指评价区内降水形成的地表和地下产水总量，即地表产流量与降水入渗补给地下水量之和，不包括过境水量。

地表水资源量 指评价区内河流、湖泊、冰川等地表水体中可以逐年更新的动态水量，即当地天然河川径流量。

地下水资源量 指评价区内降水和地表水对饱水岩土层的补给量，包括降水入渗补给量和河道、湖库、渠系、渠灌田间等地表水体的入渗补给量。

气温 指空气的温度，我国一般以摄氏度（℃）为单位表示。气象观测的温度表是放在离地面约1.5米处通风良好的百叶箱里测量的，因此，通常说的气温指的是离地面1.5米处百叶箱中的温度。其统计计算方法为：

月平均气温是将全月各日的平均气温相加，除以该月的天数而得。

年平均气温是将12个月的月平均气温累加后除以12而得。

降水量 指从天空降落到地面的液态或固态（经融化后）水，未经蒸发、渗透、流失而在地面上积聚的深度。其统计计算方法为：

月降水量是将全月各日的降水量累加而得。

年降水量是将12个月的月降水量累加而得。

日照时数 指太阳实际照射地面的时间。其统计方法与降水量相同。

平均增长速度 平均增长速度表明社会经济现象在一个较长的时期内逐期平均增长变化的程度，它不能根据各个环比增长速度直接求得，但与平均发展速度之间存在着一定的数量关系：平均增长速度 = 平均发展速度 - 1。

平均发展速度 是一种根据环比发展速度计算的序时平均数,由于各时期对比的基础不同，所以计算平均发展速度不能采用一般的序时平均数的计算方法，计算方法分为水平法和累计法。水平法，又称几何平均法，即将环比发展速度按连乘法用几何平均数公式计算。累计法，也称方程法，根据一段时期内各年发展水平总和与基期水平的关系，列出方程式计算平均发展速度。水平法着重考虑最后一年所达到的发展水平；累计法着重考虑整个时期累计发展水平的总量。

本年鉴内所列的平均增长速度，均用“水平法”计算。从某年到某年平均增长速度的年份，均不包括基期年在内。如建国六十年以来的平均增长速度是以1949年为基期计算的，则写为1950-2009年平均增长速度，其余类推。

Explanatory Notes on Main Statistical Indicators

Divisions of Administrative Areas refers to the division of administrative areas by the State. The relative laws stipulate that (1)the whole country is divided into provinces, autonomous regions and municipalities directly under the Central Government;(2)provinces and autonomous regions are further divided into autonomous prefectures, counties, autonomous counties and cities; (3)autonomous prefectures are further divided into counties, autonomous counties and cities; (4)counties and autonomous counties are further divided into townships, ethnic townships and towns; (5)municipalities directly under the Central Government and large cities are divided into districts and counties, (6)the State shall, when necessary, establish special administrative regions.

Climate refers to the natural environmental status formed by the long-term exchange of energy and mass between the earth and the atmosphere, and is the result of interaction of many factors. Climate is both one of the environment factors and also the important resources for living and production activities of the human being. The average values across several years of meteorological factors such as temperature, rainfall and humidity are used as important parameters to describe the climate of a region, while the average values (or total values)of a given year or month of meteorological factors reflect the key characteristics of climate for that period of time.

Natural Resources refer to material resources that could be obtained from the nature by human being and used for production and living. Natural resources in general can be classified as renewable resources and non-renewable resources. Renewable resources refer to resources that could be renewed and recycled during a relatively short period of time, including land resource, water resource, climate resource, biology resource and marine resource. Non-renewable resources include resources that could not be renewed, such as minerals and geothermal resource.

Land Resource Land refers to the surface of the earth, consisting of mainly rocks and its whethering and earth. Land resource can be classified, by its utilization, as land for agriculture, land for construction and unused land. Land for agriculture includes cultivated land, plantation land, forestland, grassland and waters. Land for construction includes land for residential purpose, for manufacturing and mining, for transportation and for water-conservancy projects. Unused land refers to land other than land for agriculture and.construction, including beaches, deserts, Gobi, glaciers and rock mountains.

Area of Cultivated Land refers to area of land reclaimed for the regular cultivation of various farm crops, including crop-cover land, fallow, newly reclaimed land and land laid idle for less than 3 years.

Forest Area refers to the area of trees and bamboo grow with canopy density above 0.2, the area of shrubby tree according to regulations of the government, the area of forest land inside farm land and the area of trees planted by the side of villages, farm houses and along roads and rivers.

Area of Afforested Land refers to area for land for trees bamboo, bushes and mangrove, including forest-covered land, bush-covered land, sparse forest land, land planned for afforestation and nurseries of young trees.

Total Water Resources refers to total volume of water resources measured as run-off for surface water from rainfall and recharge for groundwater in a given area, excluding transit water.

Surface Water Resources refers to total renewable resources which exist in rivers, lakes, glaciers and other collectors from rainfall and are measured as run-off of rivers.

Groundwater Resources refers to replenishment of aquifers with rainfall and surface water.

Temperature refers to the air temperature. China uses centigrade as the unit. The thermometry used for weather observation is put in a breezy shutter, which is 1.5 meters high from the ground. Therefore, the commonly used temperature refers to the temperature in the breezy shutter 1.5 meters away from the ground. The calculation method is as follows:

Monthly average temperature is the summation of average daily temperature of one month divided by the actual days of that particular month.

Annual average temperature is the summation of monthly average of a year divided by 12 months.

Volume of Precipitation refers to the deepness of liquid state or solid state (thawed)water falling from the sky to the ground that has not been evaporated, infiltrated or run off. The calculation method is as follows:

Monthly precipitation is the summation of daily precipitation of a month.

Annual precipitation is the summation of 12 months precipitation of a year.

Sunshine Hours refer to the actual hours of sun irradiating the earth. The calculation method is the same as that of the precipitation.

Average Annual Growth Rate shows the average growth rate of social and economic development during a longer period. It can not be directly calculated by chain based growth rate. The relation is:

Average Annual Growth Rate=Average Speed of Development - 1

Average speed of development is the time series average of speed which calculated by chain based.Because the reference bases during the different periods are not same, average speed of development can not be calculated by the general method. Level approach and accumulative approach for calculating average speed of development rate are applied. The "level approach" , or the method of calculating the geometric average, is derived by the formula of geometric average of the chain-based speeds of development, or comparing the level of the last year of the interval with that of the beginning year; the other is called the "accumulative approach" or the "algebraic average" , "equation" method, which is derived by the summation of the actual figure of each year in the interval divided by the figure in the base year. The level approach focuses on the level of the last year, while the accumulative approach emphasizes the aggregate development in the duration.

The average annual growth rates listed in the Yearbook are calculated by the level approach except for the growth rate of investment in fixed assets. The base year is not listed in the duration for which average annual growth rates are computed. For instance, the average annual growth rate of the 60 years since 1949 is shown as the average annual growth rate of 1950 to 2009 without showing the base year 1949.

2 基本单位

BASIC UNIT

资料整理：张　奇　张　斌
Data management：Zhang Qi　Zhang Bin
数据审核：曾文元
Data audit：Zeng　Wenyuan

第二部分　基本单位

一、简要说明

本章资料主要包括法人单位、产业活动单位和企业一套表调查单位数等资料，由西安市统计局普查中心提供。本年统计年鉴一套表调查单位数为年报数，使用时请注意。

二、主要指标

指标	数值		增长
法人单位数（个）	290366	比上年增长	13.9%
产业活动单位数（个）	312010	比上年增长	13.1%
规模以上工业企业数（个）	1634	比上年增长	2.3%
限额以上批发零售住宿餐饮业企业数（个）	2916	比上年增长	9.5%
资质内建筑业企业数（个）	1361	比上年增长	5.7%
房地产开发经营企业数（个）	1208	比上年增长	8.3%
规模以上服务业企业数（个）	2222	比上年增长	7.1%

2　BASIC UNIT

Ⅰ.Brief Introduction

This chapter consists of unified data of enterprises and industrial active unites and investigation unit in "Enterprises Data in One sheet", provided by census center of Xi'an Municipal Bureau of statistics . Data of "Enterprises Data in One Sheet" in this Yearbook Reserch the number of annual reports, please note that when used.

Ⅱ.Major Indicators

		Increase over Preceding Year
Number of Enterprises (unit)	290366	13.9%
Number of Industrial Active Units (unit)	312010	13.1%
Number of Industrial Enterprises above Designed Size (unit)	1634	2.3%
Number of Enterprises about Wholesale、Retail、Accommodation and Catering above Designed Size (unit)	2916	9.5%
Number of Qualified Construction Enterprises (unit)	1361	5.7%
Number of Real Estate Development Enterprises (unit)	1208	8.3%
Number of service Enterprises above Designed Size (unit)	2222	7.1%

2-1 按登记注册类型分法人单位数（2020年）

Impersonal Entities by Status of Registion（2020）

单位：个 (unit)

分 组	Classify	法人单位数 Number of Enterprises	企业 Enterprises
总 计	**Total**	**290366**	**269338**
#非公有制企业法人	Non-public corporate	264456	264456
按登记注册类型分	**Grouped by Status of Registion**		
（一）内资	Domestic Funded Enterprises	289123	268095
国有	State-owned Enterprises	6278	914
集体	Collective-owned Enterprises	1806	1017
股份合作	Cooperative Enterprises	186	162
联营	Joint Ownership Enterprises	72	34
国有联营	State Joint Ownership Enterprises	8	5
集体联营	Collective Joint Ownership Enterprises	32	17
国有与集体联营	Joint State-collective Ownership Enterprises	6	5
其他联营	Other Joint Ownership Enterprises	26	7
有限责任公司	Limited Liability Corporations	13865	13772
国有独资公司	State Sole Funded Corporations	617	617
其他有限责任公司	Other Limited Liability Corporations	13248	13155
股份有限公司	Share-holding Corporations Limited	647	644
私营	Private Enterprises	251126	249891
私营独资	Private-funded Enterprises	5125	4471
私营合伙	Private Partnership Enterprises	1398	1190
私营有限责任公司	Private Limited Liability Corporations	243350	242981
私营股份有限公司	Private Share-holding Corporations Ltd.	1253	1249
其他	Other Domestic Funded Enterprises	15143	1661
（二）港澳台商投资	Enterprises with Funds from Hong Kong, Macao and Taiwan	465	465
与港澳台商合资经营	Joint-venture with Funds from Hong Kong,Macao and Taiwan	121	121
与港澳台商合作经营	Cooperative Enterprises with Funds from Hong Kong Macao and Taiwan	8	8
港澳台商独资	Enterprises with Sole Investment from Hong Kong Macao and Taiwan	223	223
港澳台商投资股份有限公司	Share-holding Corporations Ltd. with funds from Hong Kong, Macao & Taiwan	10	10
其他港澳台商投资	Other Enterprises with Funds from Hong Kong, Macao and Taiwan	103	103
（三）外商投资	Foreign Funded Enterprises	778	778
中外合资经营	Sino-foreign Joint Ventures	249	249
中外合作经营	Sino-Foreign Cooperation Enterprises	5	5
外资企业	Foreign Owned Enterprises	463	463
外商投资股份有限公司	Limited Company Funded by Foreign Investment	28	28
其他外商投资	Other Foreign Funded Enterprises	33	33

2-2 按国民经济行业分法人单位数（2020年）

Impersonal Entities by Industry of the National Economy（2020）

单位：个 (unit)

分 组	Classify	法人单位数 Number of Enterprises	企业 Enterprises
总 计	**Total**	**290366**	**269338**
（一）农、林、牧、渔业	Agriculture,Forestry,Animal Husbandry and Fishery	5656	2088
农业	Farming	2429	808
林业	Forestry	833	300
畜牧业	Animal Husbandry	1209	500
渔业	Fishery	40	20
农、林、牧、渔专业及辅助性活动	Agriculture, Forestry, Animal husbandry, Fishery and Auxiliary Activities	1145	460
（二）采矿业	Mining	210	210
煤炭开采和洗选业	Mining and Washing of Coal	6	6
石油和天然气开采业	Extraction of Petroleum and Natural Gas	10	10
黑色金属矿采选业	Mining of Ferrous Metal Ores	7	7
有色金属矿采选业	Mining of Non-ferrous Metal Ores	8	8
非金属矿采选业	Mining and Processing of Nonmetal Ores	80	80
开采专业及辅助性活动	Mining Professional and Auxiliary Activities	86	86
其他采矿业	Mining of Other Ores	13	13
（三）制造业	Manufacturing	19175	19136
农副食品加工业	Processing of Food from Agricultural Products	554	534
食品制造业	Manufacture of Foods	562	560
酒、饮料和精制茶制造业	Manufacture of Beverages	274	273
烟草制品业	Manufacture of Tobacco	6	6
纺织业	Manufacture of Textile	145	143
纺织服装、服饰业	Manufacture of Textile Wearing Apparel	207	204
皮革、毛皮、羽毛及其制品和制鞋业	Manufacture of Leather, Fur,Feather and Related Products and Footware	21	20
木材加工和木、竹、藤、棕、草制品业	Timber Processing,Bamboo,Cane,Palm Fiber and Straw Products	430	427
家具制造业	Manufacture of Furniture	610	610
造纸及纸制品业	Manufacture of Paper and Paper Products	403	403
印刷和记录媒介复制业	Printing,Reproduction of Recording Media	652	652
文教、工美、体育和娱乐用品制造业	Manufacture of Articles For Culture,Education and Sport Activities	329	327

2-2 续表1 continued 1

单位：个 (unit)

分组	Classify	法人单位数 Number of Enterprises	企业 Enterprises
石油加工、炼焦和核燃料加工业	Processing of Petroleum, Coking,Processing of Nuclear Fuel	63	63
化学原料和化学制品制造业	Manufacture of Raw Chemical Materials and Chemical Products	857	857
医药制造业	Manufacture of Medicines	324	324
化学纤维制造业	Manufacture of Chemical Fibers	15	15
橡胶和塑料制品业	Manufacture of Rubber and Manufacture of Plastics	565	565
非金属矿物制品业	Manufacture of Non-metallic Mineral Products	1596	1595
黑色金属冶炼和压延加工业	Smelting and Pressing of Ferrous Metals	158	158
有色金属冶炼和压延加工业	Smelting and Pressing of Non-ferrous Metals	188	188
金属制品业	Manufacture of Metal Products	1591	1591
通用设备制造业	Manufacture of General Purpose Machinery	2709	2709
专用设备制造业	Manufacture of Special Equipment	1862	1861
汽车制造业	Manufacture of Motor Vehicle	317	317
铁路、船舶、航空航天和其他运输设备制造业	Railways,Shipbuilding,Aerospace and Other Transportation Equipment Manufacturing Industry	406	406
电气机械和器材制造业	Manufacture of Electric Equipment and Machinery	1437	1437
计算机、通信和其他电子设备制造业	Manufacture of Communication Equipment,Computers and other Electronic Equipment	1195	1194
仪器仪表制造业	Manufacture of Measuring Instruments and Machinery	761	761
其他制造业	Other Manufacturing	131	131
废弃资源综合利用	Recycling and Disposal of Waste	102	102
金属制品、机械和设备修理业	Metal Products,Machinery and Equipment Repair Industry	705	703
（四）电力、热力、燃气及水的生产供应业	Production and Distribution of Electricity,Heat ,Gas and Water	631	625
电力、热力生产和供应业	Production and Supply of Electric Power and Heat Power	374	371
燃气生产和供应业	Gas mining and supplying industry	82	81
水的生产和供应业	Production and Supply of Water	175	173
（五）建筑业	Construction Industry	41776	41776
房屋建筑业	Construction of Building	9835	9835
土木工程建筑业	Civil Engineering	11188	11188
建筑安装业	Architectural Installation	5812	5812
建筑装饰、装修和其他建筑业	Architectural Decoration and Other Construction	14941	14941
（六）批发和零售业	Wholesale and Retail Trades	86556	84080
批发业	Wholesale Trade	45558	43475

2–2 续表2 continued 2

单位：个 (unit)

分 组	Classify	法人单位数 Number of Enterprises	企业 Enterprises
零售业	Retail Trade	40998	40605
（七）交通运输、仓储和邮政业	Traffic, Transport, Storage and Post	5515	5222
铁路运输业	Transport Via Railway	14	14
道路运输业	Transport Via Road	3707	3682
水上运输业	Water Transport	53	53
航空运输业	Air Transport	79	78
管道运输业	Transport Via Pipeline	3	3
多式联运和运输代理业	Multimodal Transport and Transportation Agency	616	616
装卸搬运和仓储业	Loading,Unloading,portage,storge and management of Land industry	886	620
邮政业	Post	157	156
（八）住宿和餐饮业	Hotels and Catering Services	5853	5852
住宿业	Hotels	2102	2101
餐饮业	Catering Services	3751	3751
（九）信息传输、软件和信息技术服务业	Information Transmission, Software and Information Technology	19305	19272
电信、广播电视和卫星传输服务	Telecom & Other Information Transmission Services	753	752
互联网和相关服务	Internet and Relevant Services	3176	3168
软件和信息技术服务	Software Industry	15376	15352
（十）金融业	Financial Intermediation	1434	1430
货币金融服务	Monetary and Financial Services	515	513
资本市场服务	Capital Market Services	423	422
保险业	Insurance	191	191
其他金融业	Other Financial Intermediation	305	304
（十一）房地产业	Real Estate	13459	13447
房地产业	Real Estate	13459	13447
（十二） 租赁和商务服务业	Leasing and Business Services	38280	37395
租赁业	Leasing	3710	3705
商务服务业	Business Services	34570	33690
（十三）科学研究和技术服务业	Scientific Research, Technical Sevice	19929	19292
研究与试验发展	Research and Experimental Development	2513	2423
专业技术服务业	Professional Technical Services	11954	11726
科技推广和应用服务业	Services of Science and Technology Exchanges and Promotion	5462	5143

2-2 续表3 continued 3

单位：个 (unit)

分组	Classify	法人单位数 Number of Enterprises	企业 Enterprises
（十四）水利、环境和公共设施管理业	Management of Water Conservancy, Environment and Public Facilities	2254	2068
水利管理业	Management of Water Conservancy	145	70
生态保护和环境治理业	Environmental Management	330	303
公共设施管理业	Management of Public Facilities	1411	1337
土地管理业	Lang management	368	358
（十五）居民服务、修理和其他服务业	Services to Households and Other Services	6964	6901
居民服务业	Services to Households	2770	2720
机动车、电子产品和日用产品修理业	The Repair Service Industry for Motor Vehicle、Electronic	3101	3099
其他服务业	Other Services	1093	1082
（十六）教育	Education	6129	2241
教育	Education	6129	2241
（十七）卫生和社会工作	Health, Social Security	2869	1194
卫生	Health	2398	1089
社会工作	Social Work	471	105
（十八）文化、体育和娱乐业	Culture, Sports and Entertainment	7504	7109
新闻和出版业	Journalism and Publishing Activities	206	182
广播、电视、电影和录音制作业	Broadcasting,Movies,Television and Audiovisual Activities	1540	1526
文化艺术业	Cultural and Art Activities	1821	1549
体育	Sports Activities	774	725
娱乐业	Entertainment	3163	3127
（十九）公共管理、社会保障和社会组织	Public Management and Social Organizaion	6867	
中国共产党机关	Organs of Communist Party of China	179	
国家机构	Government Agencies	1786	
人民政协、民主党派	People's Political Consultative Conference and Democratic Parties	21	
社会保障	Social Security	57	
群众团体、社会团体和其他成员组织	Mass organizations、Social Groups and other members of the organization	1748	
基层群众自治组织及其他组织	Autonomous Organizations at the Grassroots Level and other Organizations	3076	
（二十）国际组织	International Organizations		
国际组织	International Organizations		

2-3　各区县法人单位数（2020年）

Impersonal Entities by Region and Development Zone（2020）

单位：个　　(unit)

区　县	Region	法人单位数 Number of Enterprises	企业 Enterprises
总　计	**Total**	**290366**	**269338**
新城区	Xincheng	11825	11113
碑林区	Beilin	25152	24185
莲湖区	Lianhu	22912	21945
灞桥区	Baqiao	17207	16282
未央区	Weiyang	57051	56048
雁塔区	Yanta	81996	80513
阎良区	Yanliang	4363	3679
临潼区	Lintong	6001	4273
长安区	Chang'an	15808	13985
高陵区	Gaoling	5823	4833
鄠邑区	Huyi	8777	6270
蓝田县	Lantian	5260	3479
周至县	Zhouzhi	7437	3632
西咸新区	Xixian	20754	19101

注：西安市行政区不包含西咸新区单位数，西咸新区单位数按统计局代码汇总。

2-4　按登记注册类型分产业活动单位数（2020年）

Industrial Active Units by Status of Registion（2020）

单位：个　　　　(unit)

分　组	Classify	产业活动单位数 Number of Industrial Active Units	企业 Enterprises
总计	**Total**	**312010**	**289046**
按登记注册类型分	Grouped by Status of Registion		
（一）内资	Domestic Funded Enterprises	308903	285939
国有	State-owned Enterprises	8679	1625
集体	Collective-owned Enterprises	2122	1209
股份合作	Cooperative Enterprises	255	231
联营	Joint Ownership Enterprises	82	44
国有联营	State Joint Ownership Enterprises	11	8
集体联营	Collective Joint Ownership Enterprises	34	19
国有与集体联营	Joint State-collective Ownership Enterprises	8	7
其他联营	Other Joint Ownership Enterprises	29	10
有限责任公司	Limited Liability Corporations	16969	16876
国有独资公司	State Sole Funded Corporations	753	753
其他有限责任公司	Other Limited Liability Corporations	16216	16123
股份有限公司	Share-holding Corporations Limited	2719	2716
私营	Private Enterprises	262792	261552
私营独资	Private-funded Enterprises	5243	4586
私营合伙	Private Partnership Enterprises	1437	1228
私营有限责任公司	Private Limited Liability Corporations	254577	254207
私营股份有限公司	Private Share-holding Corporations Ltd.	1535	1531
其他	Other Enterprises	15285	1686

2-4 续表 continued

单位：个 (unit)

分 组	Classify	产业活动单位数 Number of Industrial Active Units	企业 Enterprises
（二）港澳台商投资	Enterprises with Funds from Hong Kong,Macao and Taiwan	830	830
与港澳台商合资经营	Joint-venture with Funds from Hong Kong,Macao and Taiwan	153	153
与港澳台商合作经营	Cooperative Enterprises with Funds from Hong Kong Macao and Taiwan	12	12
港澳台商独资	Enterprises with Sole Investment from Hong Kong Macao and Taiwan	452	452
港澳台商投资股份有限公司	Share-holding Corporations Ltd. with funds from Hong Kong, Macao & Taiwan	54	54
其他港澳台商投资	Other Enterprises with Funds from Hong Kong,Macao and Taiwan	159	159
（三）外商投资	Foreign Funded Enterprises	2277	2277
中外合资经营	Sino-foreign Joint Ventures	354	354
中外合作经营	Sino-Foreign Cooperation Enterprises	8	8
外资企业	Foreign Owned Enterprises	1612	1612
外商投资股份有限公司	Limited Company Funded by Foreign Investment	176	176
其他外商投资	Other Foreign Funded Enterprises	127	127

2-5 按国民经济行业分产业活动单位数（2020年）

Industrial Active Units by Industry of the National Economy（2020）

单位：个 (unit)

分　组	Classify	产业活动单位数 Number of Industrial Active Units	企业 Enterprises
总　计	**Total**	**312010**	**289046**
（一）农、林、牧、渔业	Agriculture,Forestry,Animal Husbandry and Fishery	5714	2102
农业	Farming	2436	815
林业	Forestry	834	300
畜牧业	Animal Husbandry	1211	501
渔业	Fishery	41	21
农、林、牧、渔专业及辅助性活动	Agriculture, Forestry, Animal husbandry, Fishery and Auxiliary Activities	1192	465
（二）采矿业	Mining	221	221
煤炭开采和洗选业	Mining and Washing of Coal	6	6
石油和天然气开采业	Extraction of Petroleum and Natural Gas	12	12
黑色金属矿采选业	Mining of Ferrous Metal Ores	7	7
有色金属矿采选业	Mining of Non-ferrous Metal Ores	9	9
非金属矿采选业	Mining and Processing of Nonmetal Ores	80	80
开采专业及辅助性活动	Mining Professional and Auxiliary Activities	94	94
其他采矿业	Mining of Other Ores	13	13
（三）制造业	Manufacturing	19747	19707
农副食品加工业	Processing of Food from Agricultural Products	576	555
食品制造业	Manufacture of Foods	593	591
酒、饮料和精制茶制造业	Manufacture of Beverages	284	283
烟草制品业	Manufacture of Tobacco	6	6
纺织业	Manufacture of Textile	150	148
纺织服装、服饰业	Manufacture of Textile Wearing Apparel	218	215
皮革、毛皮、羽毛及其制品和制鞋业	Manufacture of Leather, Fur,Feather and Related Products and Footware	23	22
木材加工和木、竹、藤、棕、草制品业	Timber Processing,Bamboo,Cane,Palm Fiber and Straw Products	437	434
家具制造业	Manufacture of Furniture	624	624
造纸及纸制品业	Manufacture of Paper and Paper Products	414	414
印刷和记录媒介复制业	Printing,Reproduction of Recording Media	670	670
文教、工美、体育和娱乐用品制造业	Manufacture of Articles For Culture,Education and Sport Activities	334	332

2-5 续表1 continued 1

单位：个 (unit)

分组	Classify	产业活动单位数 Number of Industrial Active Units	企业 Enterprises
石油加工、炼焦和核燃料加工业	Processing of Petroleum, Coking,Processing of Nuclear Fuel	65	65
化学原料和化学制品制造业	Manufacture of Raw Chemical Materials and Chemical Products	885	885
医药制造业	Manufacture of Medicines	343	343
化学纤维制造业	Manufacture of Chemical Fibers	15	15
橡胶和塑料制品业	Manufacture of Rubber and Manufacture of Plastics	584	584
非金属矿物制品业	Manufacture of Non-metallic Mineral Products	1662	1661
黑色金属冶炼和压延加工业	Smelting and Pressing of Ferrous Metals	160	160
有色金属冶炼和压延加工业	Smelting and Pressing of Non-ferrous Metals	190	190
金属制品业	Manufacture of Metal Products	1632	1632
通用设备制造业	Manufacture of General Purpose Machinery	2764	2764
专用设备制造业	Manufacture of Special Equipment	1910	1909
汽车制造业	Manufacture of Motor Vehicle	332	332
铁路、船舶、航空航天和其他运输设备制造业	Railways,Shipbuilding,Aerospace and Other Transportation Equipment Manufacturing Industry	414	414
电气机械和器材制造业	Manufacture of Electric Equipment and Machinery	1489	1489
计算机、通信和其他电子设备制造业	Manufacture of Communication Equipment,Computers and other Electronic Equipment	1220	1219
仪器仪表制造业	Manufacture of Measuring Instruments and Machinery	781	781
其他制造业	Other Manufacturing	138	138
废弃资源综合利用	Recycling and Disposal of Waste	102	102
金属制品、机械和设备修理业	Metal Products,Machinery and Equipment Repair Industry	732	730
（四）电力、热力、燃气及水的生产供应业	Production and Distribution of Electricity,Heat ,Gas and Water	723	714
电力、热力生产和供应业	Production and Supply of Electric Power and Heat Power	432	426
燃气生产和供应业	Gas mining and supplying industry	102	101
水的生产和供应业	Production and Supply of Water	189	187
（五）建筑业	Construction	42846	42846
房屋建筑业	Construction of Building	10181	10181
土木工程建筑业	Civil Engineering	11443	11443
建筑安装业	Architectural Installation	6004	6004
建筑装饰、装修和其他建筑业	Architectural Decoration and Other Construction	15218	15218
（六）批发和零售业	Wholesale and Retail Trades	93846	91365
批发业	Wholesale Trade	46620	44534

2-5 续表2 continued 2

单位：个 (unit)

分 组	Classify	产业活动单位数 Number of Industrial Active Units	企业 Enterprises
零售业	Retail Trade	47226	46831
（七）交通运输、仓储和邮政业	Traffic, Transport, Storage and Post	6307	6003
铁路运输业	Transport Via Railway	36	36
道路运输业	Transport Via Road	4046	4010
水上运输业	Water Transport	54	54
航空运输业	Air Transport	98	97
管道运输业	Transport Via Pipeline	6	6
多式联运和运输代理业	Multimodal Transport and Transportation Agency	753	753
装卸搬运和仓储业	Loading,Unloading,portage,storge and management of Land industry	924	658
邮政业	Post	390	389
（八）住宿和餐饮业	Hotels and Catering Services	6984	6982
住宿业	Hotels	2311	2310
餐饮业	Catering Services	4673	4672
（九）信息传输、软件和信息技术服务业	Information Transmission, Software and Information Technology	20159	20124
电信、广播电视和卫星传输服务	Telecom & Other Information Transmission Services	1008	1006
互联网和相关服务	Internet and Relevant Services	3271	3262
软件和信息技术服务	Software Industry	15880	15856
（十）金融业	Financial Intermediation	3961	3951
货币金融服务	Monetary and Financial Services	2102	2094
资本市场服务	Capital Market Services	641	640
保险业	Insurance	859	859
其他金融业	Other Financial Intermediation	359	358
（十一）房地产业	Real Estate	14696	14684
房地产业	Real Estate	14696	14684
（十二） 租赁和商务服务业	Leasing and Business Services	40441	39512
租赁业	Leasing	3877	3872
商务服务业	Business Services	36564	35640
（十三）科学研究和技术服务业	Scientific Research, Technical Sevice	20901	20212
研究与试验发展	Research and Experimental Development	2575	2484
专业技术服务业	Professional Technical Services	12670	12404
科技推广和应用服务业	Services of Science and Technology Exchanges and Promotion	5656	5324

2-5 续表3 continued 3

单位：个 (unit)

分组	Classify	产业活动单位数 Number of Industrial Active Units	企业 Enterprises
（十四）水利、环境和公共设施管理业	Management of Water Conservancy, Environment and Public Facilities	2378	2148
水利管理业	Management of Water Conservancy	170	76
生态保护和环境治理业	Environmental Management	344	311
公共设施管理业	Management of Public Facilities	1477	1388
土地管理业	Lang management	387	373
（十五）居民服务、修理和其他服务业	Services to Households and Other Services	7339	7270
居民服务业	Services to Households	2937	2884
机动车、电子产品和日用产品修理业	The Repair Service Industry for Motor Vehicle、Electronic	3275	3273
其他服务业	Other Services	1127	1113
（十六）教育	Education	6865	2484
教育	Education	6865	2484
（十七）卫生和社会工作	Health, Social Security	3095	1346
卫生	Health	2617	1239
社会工作	Social	478	107
（十八）文化、体育和娱乐业	Culture, Sports and Entertainment	7803	7375
新闻和出版业	Journalism and Publishing Activities	214	188
广播、电视、电影和录音制作业	Broadcasting,Movies,Television and Audiovisual Activities	1602	1587
文化艺术业	Cultural and Art Activities	1877	1577
体育	Sports Activities	852	803
娱乐业	Entertainment	3258	3220
（十九）公共管理、社会保障和社会组织	Public Management and Social Organizaion	7984	
中国共产党机关	Organs of Communist Party of China	183	
国家机构	Government Agencies	2839	
人民政协、民主党派	People's Political Consultative Conference and Democratic Parties	21	
社会保障	Social Security	68	
群众团体、社会团体和其他成员组织	Mass organizations、Social Groups and other members of the organization	1765	
基层群众自治组织及其他组织	Autonomous Organizations at the Grassroots Level and other Organizations	3108	
（二十）国际组织	International Organizations		
国际组织	International Organizations		

2-6 各区县产业活动单位数（2020年）

Industrial Active Units by Region and Development Zone（2020）

单位：个 (unit)

区 县	Region	产业活动单位数 Number of Industrial Active Units	企业 Enterprises
总 计	**Total**	**312010**	**289046**
新城区	Xincheng	12975	12261
碑林区	Beilin	27419	26433
莲湖区	Lianhu	24655	23665
灞桥区	Baqiao	18402	17367
未央区	Weiyang	60170	59100
雁塔区	Yanta	87407	85842
阎良区	Yanliang	4935	4103
临潼区	Lintong	7010	4905
长安区	Chang'an	16951	15043
高陵区	Gaoling	6654	5408
鄠邑区	Huyi	9451	6785
蓝田县	Lantian	5996	3820
周至县	Zhouzhi	7964	4034
西咸新区	Xixian	22021	20280

注：西安市行政区不包含西咸新区单位数，西咸新区单位数按统计局代码汇总。

2-7 按统计机构分企业一套表调查单位数（2020年）

Number of Survey Units by Statistical Agencies of "One Sheet" (2020)

单位：个 (unit)

区县、开发区	Region	合计 Total	规模以上工业 Industrial Enterprises above Designed Size	限额以上批发零售住宿餐饮业 Above wholesale and Retail Accommodation and Catering Industry	资质内建筑业 Qualified Construction Enterprises	房地产开发经营企业 Real Estate Development Enterprises	规模以上服务业 Service Enterprises above Designed Size
全　市	**Total**	**9341**	**1634**	**2916**	**1361**	**1208**	**2222**
新城区	Xincheng	428	7	215	68	30	108
碑林区	Beilin	701	7	323	148	35	188
莲湖区	Lianhu	549	29	199	94	77	150
灞桥区	Baqiao	208	55	40	37	43	33
未央区	Weiyang	381	18	136	81	60	86
雁塔区	Yanta	605	37	193	146	66	163
阎良区	Yanliang	172	61	35	28	33	15
临潼区	Lintong	225	96	48	37	17	27
长安区	Chang'an	214	28	68	30	52	36
高陵区	Gaoling	253	113	54	20	36	30
鄠邑区	Huyi	213	92	55	15	35	16
蓝田县	Lantian	134	59	26	15	17	17
周至县	Zhouzhi	116	25	44	16	24	7
西咸新区	Xixian	991	230	300	105	194	162
高新区	GaoXin	1460	388	292	235	117	428
经开区	JingKai	1332	250	490	176	88	328
曲江新区	Qujiang	460		98	51	89	222
航空基地	Aviation Industry Base	99	53	12	7	15	12
航天基地	Aerospace Base	271	61	74	23	57	56
浐灞生态区	Chanba Eco-District	277	4	97	21	91	64
国际港务区	International Trade &Logistic Park	252	21	117	8	32	74

注：由于统计口径不同，一套表调查单位数与各专业有差异。

2-8 各区县企业一套表调查单位数（2020年）

Number of Survey Units of "One Sheet" by Region and Development Zone（2020）

单位：个 (unit)

区 县	Region	合计 Total	规模以上工业 Industrial Enterprises above Designed Size	限额以上批发零售住宿餐饮业 Above wholesale and Retail Accommodation and Catering Industry	资质内建筑业 Qualified Construction Enterprises	房地产开发经营企业 Real Estate Development Enterprises	规模以上服务业 Service Enterprises above Designed Size
全 市	**Total**	**9341**	**1634**	**2916**	**1361**	**1208**	**2222**
新城区	Xincheng	427	7	217	64	31	108
碑林区	Beilin	704	8	325	151	35	185
莲湖区	Lianhu	554	29	201	94	77	153
灞桥区	Baqiao	616	79	217	55	120	145
未央区	Weiyang	1904	206	737	284	219	458
雁塔区	Yanta	2245	252	550	409	250	784
阎良区	Yanliang	271	113	47	35	48	28
临潼区	Lintong	241	97	49	37	27	31
长安区	Chang'an	768	229	183	78	133	145
高陵区	Gaoling	375	202	69	21	42	41
鄠邑区	Huyi	272	141	60	18	37	16
蓝田县	Lantian	133	59	26	15	16	17
周至县	Zhouzhi	135	38	46	18	24	9
西咸新区	Xixian	696	174	189	82	149	102

2-9 按区县和国民经济行业分法人单位数（2020年）

单位：个

区　县	Region	合计 Total	农、林、牧、渔业 Agriculture Forestry Animal Husbandry and Fishery	采矿业 Mining	制造业 Manufacturing	电力、燃气及水的生产和供应业 Production and Distribution of Electricity Gas and Water
全　市	**Total**	**290366**	**5656**	**210**	**19175**	**631**
新城区	Xincheng	11825	3	2	293	6
碑林区	Beilin	25152	3	5	216	13
莲湖区	Lianhu	22912	3	2	404	15
灞桥区	Baqiao	17207	312	4	1416	41
未央区	Weiyang	57051	97	101	2625	100
雁塔区	Yanta	81996	168	39	4002	113
阎良区	Yanliang	4363	145		783	23
临潼区	Lintong	6001	731	1	783	20
长安区	Chang'an	15808	590	6	1572	43
高陵区	Gaoling	5823	580	12	989	23
鄠邑区	Huyi	8777	1029	11	1723	37
蓝田县	Lantian	5260	591	3	579	76
周至县	Zhouzhi	7437	1032	9	434	33
西咸新区	Xixian	20754	372	15	3356	88

注：西安市行政区不包含西咸新区单位数，西咸新区单位数按统计局代码汇总。

Impersonal Entities by Region and Development Zone and Industry of the National Economy（2020）

(unit)

建筑业 Construction	批发和零售业 Wholesale and Retail Trades	交通运输、仓储和邮政业 Traffic Transport Storage and Post	住宿和餐饮业 Hotels and Catering Services	信息传输、软件和信息技术服务业 Information Transmission, Software and Information Technology	金融业 Financial Intermediation
41776	**86556**	**5515**	**5853**	**19305**	**1434**
1167	4936	247	410	442	59
3230	9007	193	733	1590	103
2468	8814	541	659	1255	75
2729	5780	612	236	678	191
9614	23170	1108	846	2532	230
11979	18654	677	1694	10236	573
675	835	183	77	134	21
877	1012	129	114	136	11
2913	2810	253	377	981	69
767	1238	213	99	147	6
1051	1411	144	104	184	38
644	1350	72	97	74	5
668	2571	369	86	71	8
2994	4968	774	321	845	45

2-9 续表

单位：个

区 县	Region	房地产业 Real Estate	租赁和商务服务业 Leasing and Business Services	科学研究和技术服务业 Scientific Research Technical Services	水利、环境和公共设施管理业 Management of Water Conservancy, Environment and Public Facilities
全 市	**Total**	**13459**	**38280**	**19929**	**2254**
新城区	Xincheng	608	1589	550	63
碑林区	Beilin	1376	4331	1629	87
莲湖区	Lianhu	1158	3420	1805	143
灞桥区	Baqiao	675	1923	843	146
未央区	Weiyang	2772	6727	3321	319
雁塔区	Yanta	4148	13554	8440	633
阎良区	Yanliang	207	403	145	53
临潼区	Lintong	162	506	178	64
长安区	Chang'an	664	1924	1060	161
高陵区	Gaoling	316	446	190	54
鄠邑区	Huyi	269	595	446	119
蓝田县	Lantian	111	332	115	96
周至县	Zhouzhi	115	299	108	147
西咸新区	Xixian	878	2231	1099	169

continude

(unit)

居民服务、修理和其他服务业 Services to Households Repairs and Other Services	教育 Education	卫生和社会工作 Health and Social Work	文化、体育和娱乐业 Culture Sports and Entertainment	公共管理、社会保障和社会组织 Public Administration Social Security and Social Organizations	国际组织 International Orgnizations
6964	**6129**	**2869**	**7504**	**6867**	
344	320	158	271	357	
709	527	227	756	417	
563	459	207	512	409	
455	317	119	381	349	
1225	561	238	920	545	
1900	1180	448	3041	517	
96	140	106	71	266	
135	289	223	154	476	
413	578	210	497	687	
160	177	46	107	253	
105	338	471	136	566	
63	262	76	89	625	
62	432	175	127	691	
734	549	165	442	709	

2-10 按区县和机构类型分法人单位数（2020年）

Impersonal Entities by Agencies Types of Legal Entities Corporate Units and Region and Development Zone（2020）

单位：个 (unit)

区 县	Region	法人单位数 Number of Enterprises	企业法人 Business Entity	事业法人 Institution Entity	机关法人 Government Entity	社会团体 Social Organization	其他 Other
全 市	**Total**	**290366**	**269338**	**4173**	**1086**	**1373**	**14396**
新城区	Xincheng	11825	11113	238	89	111	274
碑林区	Beilin	25152	24185	288	70	177	432
莲湖区	Lianhu	22912	21945	281	74	128	484
灞桥区	Baqiao	17207	16282	177	62	36	650
未央区	Weiyang	57051	56048	331	124	92	456
雁塔区	Yanta	81996	80513	346	101	159	877
阎良区	Yanliang	4363	3679	138	50	65	431
临潼区	Lintong	6001	4273	300	71	42	1315
长安区	Chang'an	15808	13985	516	91	52	1164
高陵区	Gaoling	5823	4833	139	51	36	764
鄠邑区	Huyi	8777	6270	337	65	103	2002
蓝田县	Lantian	5260	3479	262	87	95	1337
周至县	Zhouzhi	7437	3632	415	67	202	3121
西咸新区	Xixian	20754	19101	405	84	75	1089

注：西安市行政区不包含西咸新区单位数，西咸新区单位数按统计局代码汇总。

2-11 按区县和登记注册类型分企业法人单位数（2020年）

The Corporate Units by Types of Corporate Registration and Region and Development Zone（2020）

单位：个 (unit)

区 县	Region	企业单位数 Number of Enterprises	内资企业 Domestic Investment Enterprises	国有企业 State-owned Enterprises	集体企业 Collective-owned Enterprises	股份合作企业 Share-holding Corperative Enterprises	联营企业 Joint Ownership Enterprises
全 市	**Total**	**269338**	**268095**	**914**	**1017**	**162**	**34**
新城区	Xincheng	11113	11094	109	133	6	6
碑林区	Beilin	24185	24081	141	123	27	1
莲湖区	Lianhu	21945	21899	145	151	17	4
灞桥区	Baqiao	16282	16195	44	67	13	2
未央区	Weiyang	56048	55876	54	58	11	1
雁塔区	Yanta	80513	80024	148	85	39	3
阎良区	Yanliang	3679	3655	26	33	7	
临潼区	Lintong	4273	4259	41	66	4	2
长安区	Chang'an	13985	13869	55	72	15	3
高陵区	Gaoling	4833	4810	30	22	2	3
鄠邑区	Huyi	6270	6236	25	66	9	
蓝田县	Lantian	3479	3472	24	41	3	2
周至县	Zhouzhi	3632	3625	36	37	1	2
西咸新区	Xixian	19101	19000	36	63	8	5

注：西安市行政区不包含西咸新区单位数，西咸新区单位数按统计局代码汇总。

2-11 续表 continued

单位：个 (unit)

区 县 Region	有限责任公司 Limited Liability Corporations	股份有限公司 Share-holding Corperation Ltd.	私营企业 Private Enterprises	港、澳、台商投资企业 Enterprises with Funds from Hong Kong, Macao and Taiwan	外商投资企业 Enterprises with Foreign Investment
全 市 Total	**13772**	**644**	**249891**	**465**	**778**
新城区 Xincheng	825	44	9924	10	9
碑林区 Beilin	899	34	22851	46	58
莲湖区 Lianhu	807	38	20735	22	24
灞桥区 Baqiao	1461	34	14573	46	41
未央区 Weiyang	1880	75	53788	70	102
雁塔区 Yanta	4156	221	73931	151	338
阎良区 Yanliang	183	12	3392	9	15
临潼区 Lintong	146	5	3987	8	6
长安区 Chang'an	1379	88	12201	30	86
高陵区 Gaoling	273	23	4457	7	16
鄠邑区 Huyi	283	8	5844	15	19
蓝田县 Lantian	148	13	3227	3	4
周至县 Zhouzhi	87	10	3399	6	1
西咸新区 Xixian	1245	39	17582	42	59

主 要 统 计 指 标 解 释

企业（单位）登记注册类型 企业或企业产业活动单位的登记注册类型，依据在市场监管部门登记注册的类型划分。机关、事业单位和社会团体及其他组织的登记注册类型，依据主要经费来源和管理方式，根据实际情况进行划分。

国有企业 指企业全部资产归国家所有，并按《中华人民共和国企业法人登记管理条例》规定登记注册的非公司制的经济组织。不包括有限责任公司中的国有独资公司。

集体企业 指企业资产归集体所有，并按《中华人民共和国企业法人登记管理条例》规定登记注册的经济组织。

股份合作企业 指以合作制为基础，由企业职工共同出资入股，吸收一定比例的社会资产投资组建，实行自主经营，自负盈亏，共同劳动，民主管理，按劳分配与按股分红相结合的一种集体经济组织。

联营企业 指两个及两个以上相同或不同所有制性质的企业法人或事业单位法人，按自愿、平等、互利的原则，共同投资组成的经济组织。联营企业包括国有联营企业、集体联营企业、国有与集体联营企业和其他联营企业。

有限责任公司 指根据《中华人民共和国公司登记管理条例》规定登记注册，由两个以上，五十个以下的股东共同出资，每个股东以其所认缴的出资额对公司承担有限责任，公司以其全部资产对其债务承担责任的经济组织。有限责任公司包括国有独资公司以及其他有限责任公司。

股份有限公司 指根据《中华人民共和国公司登记管理条例》规定登记注册，其全部注册资本由等额股份构成并通过发行股票筹集资本，股东以其认购的股份对公司承担有限责任，公司以其全部资产对其债务承担责任的经济组织。

私营企业 指由自然人投资设立或由自然人控股，以雇佣劳动为基础的营利性经济组织。包括按照《公司法》《合伙企业法》以及《个人独资企业法》规定登记注册的私营独资企业、私营合作企业、私营有限责任公司、私营股份有限公司和个人独资企业。

与港澳台商合资经营企业 指港澳台地区投资者与内地企业依照《中华人民共和国中外合资经营企业法》及有关法律的规定，按合同规定的比例投资设立，分享利润和分担风险的企业。

与港澳台商合作经营企业 指港澳台地区投资者与内地企业依照《中华人民共和国中外合作经营企业法》及有关法律的规定，依照合作合同的约定进行投资或提供条件设立，分配利润、分担风险和亏损的企业。

港澳台商独资经营企业 指依照《中华人民共和国外资企业法》及有关法律的规定，在内地由港澳台地区投资者全额投资设立的企业。

港澳台商投资股份有限公司 指根据国家有关规定，经商务部（原外经贸部）批准设立，其中港、澳、台商的股本占公司注册资本的比例达25%以上的股份有限公司。凡其中港、澳、台商的股本占公司注册资本的比例小于25%的，属于内资企业中的股份有限公司。

中外合资经营企业 指外国企业或外国人与中国内地企业依照《中华人民共和国中外合资经营企业法》及有关法律的规定，按合同规定的比例投资设立，分享利润和分担风险的企业。

中外合作经营企业 指外国企业或外国人与中国内地企业依照《中华人民共和国中外合作经营企业法》及有关法律的规定，依照合作合同的约定进行投资或提供条件设立，分配利润、分担风险和亏损的企业。

外资企业 指依照《中华人民共和国外资企业法》及有关法律的规定，在中国内地由外国投资者全额投资设立的企业。

外商投资股份有限公司 指根据国家有关规定，经商务部（原外经贸部）批准设立，其中外资的股本占公司注册资本的比例达25%以上的股份有限公司。凡其中外资股本占公司注册资本的比例小于25%的，属于内资企业中的股份有限公司。

机关、事业单位和社会团体

机关：包括国家权力机关、国家行政机关、国家监察机关、司法机关、政党机关、政协组织和其他机关法人；机关法人单位的本部，以及国家权力机关分支机构、国家行政机关分支或派出机构、监察机关分支机构、人民法院分支机构、人民检察院分支机构等。

①国家权力机关：指全国人民代表大会及其常务委员会、地方各级人民代表大会及其常务委员会和办事机构。

②国家行政机关：指国务院和地方各级人民政府及其工作部门，以及地区行政行署。

③国家监察机关：指行使监察职能的机关。

④国家司法机关：指国家审判机关和检察机关。

⑤政党机关：指中国共产党各级机关和所属办事机构、各民主党派各级机关和办事机构。

⑥政协组织：指中国人民政治协商会议全国委员会和地方各级委员会及其办事机构。

事业单位 包括①经机构编制部门批准成立和登记或备案，领取《事业单位法人证书》，取得法人资格的单位；②事业法人单位的本部及分支机构或派出机构。

社会团体 指中国公民自愿组成，为实现会员共同意愿，按照其章程开展活动的非营利性社会组织。包括①经各级民政部门核准登记，领取《社会团体法人登记证书》的各类社会团体；②由各级机构编制管理部门直接管理其机构编制的群众团体；③经国务院批准可以免于登记的社会团体。

Explanatory Notes on Main Statistical Indicators

The types of registration of enterprises (units) The types of registration of enterprises or industrial activity units of enterprises shall be divided into the types of registration of government organs, public institutions, social organizations and other organizations according to the types of registration registered in the market supervision departments, and shall be divided according to the main sources of funds and ways of management according to the actual situation.

State-owned Enterprises refer to non-corporation economic units where the entire assets are owned by the State and which have been registered in accordance with the Regulation of the People's Republic of China on the Management of Registration of Corporate Enterprises. Not included from this category are solely State-funded corporations in the limited liability corporations.

Collective-owned Enterprises refer to economic units where the assets are owned collectively and which have been registered in accordance with the Regulation of the People's Republic of China on the Management of Registration of Corporate Enterprises.

Cooperative Enterprises refer to a form of collective economic units (enterprises)where capitals come mainly from employees as their shares, with certain proportion of capital from the outside, where production is organized on the basis of independent operation, independent accounting for profits and losses, joint work, democratic management, and a distribution system that integrates remuneration according to work with dividend according to capital share.

Joint Ownership Enterprises refer to economic units established by two or more corporate enterprises or corporate institutions of the same or different ownership, through joint investment on the basis of voluntary participation, equality, and mutual benefits. They include State joint ownership enterprises; collective joint ownership enterprises; joint State-collective enterprises; and other joint ownership enterprises.

Limited Liability Corporations refer to economic units established with investment from 2 to 50 investors and registered in accordance with the Regulation of the People's Republic of China on the Management of Registration of Corporations, each investor bearing limited liability to the corporation depending on its share of investment, and the corporation bearing liability to its debt to the maximum of its total assets. Limited liability corporations include solely State-funded limited liability corporations and other limited liability corporations.

Share-holding Corporations Ltd. refer to economic units registered in accordance with the Regulation of the People's Republic of China on the Management of Registration of Corporations, with total registered capital divided into equal shares and raised through issuing stocks. Each investor bears limited liability to the corporation depending on the holding of shares, and the corporation bears liability to its debt to the maximum of its total assets.

Private Enterprises refer to profit-making economic units invested and established by natural persons, or controlled by natural persons using employed labour~ it Includs in this category are private limited liability corporations, private share-holding corporations Ltd., private partnership enterprises and Law on Individual Proprietorship provision for the registration of prirate propretorship enterprises, private partnerships, private limited liability companies and individual proprietorship enterprises.

Other Domestic-funded Enterprises refer to domestic-funded economic units other than those mentioned above.

Joint Venture Enterprises with Funds from Hong Kong, Macau and Taiwan are enterprises established by investors from Hong Kong, Macau and Taiwan with enterprises in the mainland of China in accordance with the Law of the People's Republic of China on Sino-foreign Equity Joint Ventures and other relevant laws, where the establishment of the investment and the sharing of profits and risks are stipulated under joint venture contracts.

Cooperative Enterprises with Funds from Hong Kong, Macan and Taiwan established by investors from Hong Kong, Macau and Taiwan with enterprises in the mainland of China in accordance with the Law of the People's Republic of China on Sino-foreign Contractual Joint Venture and other relevant laws, where the investment or provision of facilities and the sharing of profits and risks and are stipulated under cooperative contracts.

Enterprises with Sole (exclusive)Investment from Hong Kong, Macau and Taiwan refer to enterprises established in the mainland of China with exclusive investment from investors from Hong Kong, Macau and Taiwan in accordance with the Law of the People's Republic of China on Wholly Foreign-owned Enterprises and other relevant laws.

Share-holding Corporations Ltd. with Investment from Hong Kong, Macau and Taiwan refer to share- holding corporations Ltd. established with the approval from the former Ministry of Foreign Trade and Economic Relations in line with relevant State regulations, where the share of investment from Hong Kong, Macau or Taiwan businessmen exceeds 25% of the total registered capital of the corporation. In case the share of investmentfrom Hong Kong, Macau or Taiwan is less than 25% of thetotal registered capital, the enterprise is to be classified as domestic-funded share-holding corporation Ltd.

Joint Venture Enterprises with Foreign Investment refer to enterprises jointly established byforeign enterprises or foreigners with enterprises in themainland of China in accordance with the Law of thePeople's Republic of China on Sino-foreign Equity JointVentures and other relevant laws, where the sharing ofinvestment, profits and risks is stipulated under contract.

Cooperative Enterprises with Foreign Investment refer to enterprises jointly established by foreign enterprises or foreigners with enterprises in the mainland of China in accordance with the Law of the People's Republic of China on Sino-foreign Contractual Joint Venture and other relevant laws, According to the enterprise that invests or provides conditions for establishment in accordance with the terms of the cooperation contract, distributes profits and shares risks and losses.

Enterprises with Sole (exclusive)Foreign Investment refer to enterprises established in the mainland of China with exclusive investment from foreign investors in accordance with the Law of the People's Republic of China on Wholly Foreign-owned Enterprises and other relevant laws.

Share-holding Corporations Ltd. with Foreign Investment refer to share-holding corporations Ltd. established with the approval from the former Ministry of Foreign Trade and Economic Relations in line with relevant State regulations, where the share of investment from foreign investors exceeds 25% of the total registered capital of the corporation. In case the share of foreign investment is less than 25% ofthe total registered capital, the enterprise is to be classified as domestic-funded share-holding corporation Ltd.

Administrative Organization, Institutions and Social organizations

Administrative organization including organs of state power, organs of state administration, organs of state supervision, judicial organs, organs of political parties, organizations of the CPPCC and other organs as legal persons; The headquarters of a legal entity of a state organ, a branch of a state organ of power, a branch of a state administrative organ or its dispatched organ, a branch of a supervisory organ, a branch of a people's court, a branch of a people's procuratorate, etc.

(1)The organs of state power: The National People's Congress and its Standing Committee, the local people's congresses at various levels and their standing committees and administrative bodies.

(2)State administrative organs: refer to the State Council and local people's governments at various levels and their working departments, as well as regional administrative agencies.

(3)State supervisory organs refer to organs that exercise supervisory functions.

(4) National judicial organs: refers to the national judicial organs and procurator organs.

Political party organs: refer to the organs and subordinate offices of the Communist Party of China at all levels, and the organs and offices of the democratic parties at all levels.

The CPPCC refers to the National Committee of the Chinese People's Political Consultative Conference (CPPCC) and local committees at all levels and their administrative bodies.

Public institutions include approved by the establishment of institutions and registration or record, get the "institution legal person certificate", obtain the legal person status of the unit; (2) The headquarters and branches or dispatched offices of the institution as legal person.

Social organizations refer to non-profit social organizations formed by Chinese citizens voluntarily to carry out activities in accordance with their articles of association in order to realize the common wishes of members. Including (1) approved by the civil affairs departments at all levels to register, get the "social organization legal person registration certificate" of all kinds of social organizations; (2) The establishment management departments at all levels shall directly manage the mass organizations with their establishment; Social organizations which may be exempted from registration with the approval of the State Council.

3 国民经济核算

NATIONAL ECONOMIC ACCOUNTS

资料整理：张　冲 张　洁　段　斐 刘晓敏
Data management：Zhang Chong Zhang Jie Duan Fei Liu Xiaomin
数据审核：连　鹏
Data audit：Lian Peng

第三部分　国民经济核算

一、简要说明

1.本章资料反映西安市国民经济核算情况。

2.本章资料包括西安市生产总值、构成和指数，非公有制经济增加值及占比等。地区生产总值是根据不同产业部门、不同行业的特点和资料来源情况而采用不同方法计算的。非公有制经济增加值测算执行的是《陕西省统计局关于非公有制经济增加值测算的暂行办法（修订版）》。

3.本年鉴公布的地区生产总值以及有关的指标数据，如果遇到普查或者重大核算方法改革，在能够获得更详细的基础资料的情况下，地区生产总值的历史数据还会发生变动。

2016年，国家改革研发支出的核算方法，将能够为所有者带来经济利益的研发支出不再作为中间消耗，而是作为固定资本形成处理。根据新的核算方法，在四经普修订时对以前年份进行了调整性修订。

2003-2017年数据为第四次经济普查修订结果，2018年数据为第四次经济普查数据，2019年数据为最终核算数，2020年数据为初步核算数，2011-2019年人均GDP数据依据第七次全国人口普查修订的常住人口数据进行了修订。

4.2012年，根据国家质检总局和国家标准委颁布的《国民经济行业分类》（GB／T 4754—2011），国家统计局对《三次产业划分规定》进行了修订，将“农、林、牧、渔业”中的“农、林、牧、渔服务业”，“采矿业”中的“开采辅助活动”，“制造业”中的“金属制品、机械和设备修理业”等三个大类一并调入第三产业。2013年（含）之后三次产业分类执行国家统计局2012年制定的新《三次产业划分规定》。

5.2004年（含）之前人均GDP按户籍人口计算，2005年（含）之后按常住人口计算。

6.国民经济核算数据绝对数按当年价格计算，指数按可比价格计算。

二、主要指标

地区生产总值（亿元）	10020.39	比上年增长	5.2%
第一产业	312.75	比上年增长	3.0%
第二产业	3328.27	比上年增长	7.4%
第三产业	6379.37	比上年增长	4.2%
人均地区生产总值（元/人）	79181	比上年增长	0.8%

3 NATIONAL ECONOMIC ACCOUNTS

I.Brief introduction

1.Data in this chapter reflects the National Economic accounting situation of Xi'an.

2.Data in this chapter includes Xi'an GDP, composition, index, the added value and the proportion of the non-public sectors of the economy, etc.Data of GDP are based on different approaches in accordance with different features of various sectors, industry and data sources. The estimation of the non-public sectors of the economy is based on Interim Measures of Shaanxi Provincial Bureau on the Estimation of Value Added of the Non-Public Sectors of the Economy (Revised Edition).

3.For data of GDP and related indicators published in the Yearbook, if there are census or reformation of significant accounting method, historical data of GDP may also undergo change under the circumstance that more specific data can be obtained.

In 2016, National Bureau of Statistics reforms the Methodology of Research and Development Expenditure. It regulates that R&D expenditure which will bring economic benefit for the owners should be treated as Fixed Assets instead of Intermediate Consumption. According to new accounting method,the previous years were revised in the fourth national economic census.

The Fourth Economic Census was revised from 2003 to 2017,the data of 2018 is the results of The Fourth Economic Census, data of 2019 is final accounting data, and data of 2020 is preliminary accounting data.,the per capita GDP data from 2011 to 2019 was revised according to the resident population data revised by the Seventh National Census.

4.Classification Rules of Three Strata of Industry was adjusted by National Bureau of Statistics of China in accordance with Industrial Classification for National Economic Activities (GB/T 4754–2011) in 2012, which was promulgated by AQSIQ and SAC. Services in support of agriculture, forestry, animal husbandry and fishery, support activities for mining, repair service of metal products, machinery and equipment are categorized into the Tertiary Industry. Industrial classification is based on adjusted Classification Rules of Three Strata of Industry (2012) since 2013.

5.Per capita GDP was calculated by register population before 2005, but since 2005 it is based on permanent resident population.

6.Data on national accounts are calculated at current prices, and the indices are calculated at constant prices.

Ⅱ.Major Indicators

		Increase over Preceding Year
Gross Domestic Product(100 mil. yuan)	10020.39	5.2%
Primary Industry	312.75	3.0%
Secondary Industry	3328.27	7.4%
Tertiary Industry	6379.37	4.2%
Per Capita Gross Domestic Product (yuan/person)	79181	0.8%

3-1 主要年份地区生产总值

Gross Domestic Product in Representative Years

(本表按当年价格计算)　　(Data in the table are calculated at current prices)
单位：亿元　　(100 million yuan)

年份 Year	地区生产总值 Gross Domestic Product	第一产业 Primary Industry	第二产业 Secondary Industry	第三产业 Tertiary Industry	人均地区生产总值（元/人） Per Capita GDP (yuan/person)
1952	3.37	1.59	0.88	0.90	135
1965	12.76	2.62	7.22	2.92	323
1970	17.76	3.13	10.96	3.67	412
1975	21.33	4.14	12.63	4.56	448
1978	25.35	4.83	14.59	5.93	513
1980	31.66	4.73	18.69	8.24	623
1983	35.89	5.22	20.14	10.53	674
1984	44.14	7.45	24.17	12.52	817
1985	57.58	8.76	30.83	17.99	1049
1986	65.78	9.59	33.86	22.33	1178
1987	80.16	10.73	37.69	31.74	1409
1988	99.22	11.47	46.58	41.17	1711
1989	109.38	12.78	48.91	47.69	1861
1990	116.51	13.94	50.15	52.42	1932
1991	136.14	17.17	57.06	61.91	2224
1992	164.85	18.78	69.22	76.85	2662
1993	229.56	22.58	110.88	96.10	3661
1994	289.82	31.68	128.27	129.87	4563
1995	330.35	41.40	135.33	153.62	5131
1996	406.95	46.94	161.63	198.38	6246
1997	488.82	51.33	197.97	239.52	7424
1998	525.85	51.91	216.32	257.62	7906
1999	577.29	45.53	243.35	288.41	8599
2000	646.13	44.65	277.13	324.35	9484
2001	734.86	45.87	312.90	376.09	10628
2002	826.68	47.77	353.58	425.33	11831
2003	926.12	50.72	402.22	473.18	13052
2004	1092.35	60.21	464.95	567.19	15155
2005	1294.05	66.01	511.19	716.86	16158
2006	1512.56	70.44	612.69	829.42	18567
2007	1857.75	82.42	763.07	1012.26	22476
2008	2313.26	102.46	940.42	1270.38	27736
2009	2689.06	106.09	1105.01	1477.96	31994
2010	3195.05	133.22	1290.93	1770.89	37792
2011	3791.71	165.43	1516.30	2109.98	43723
2012	4370.16	181.12	1726.70	2462.35	48530
2013	4960.23	182.60	1946.58	2831.05	53624
2014	5576.98	191.58	2152.43	3232.97	58829
2015	5932.86	191.91	2070.47	3670.48	60912
2016	6396.36	196.66	2139.49	4060.21	63393
2017	7418.04	245.26	2452.92	4719.86	66649
2018	8499.41	258.98	2861.86	5378.56	73113
2019	9399.98	279.13	3130.80	5990.06	77494
2020	10020.39	312.75	3328.27	6379.37	79181

注：1.2004年（含）之前人均GDP按户籍人口计算，2005年（含）之后按常住人口计算。
2.2013年（含）之后三次产业分类依据国家统计局2012年制定的新《三次产业划分规定》。
3.2017年开始西咸新区由西安代管，统计范围发生变化，之前年份则不含（下同）。
4.2003-2017年数据为第四次经济普查修订结果（下同）。2018年数据为第四次经济普查数据。2019年数据为最终核算数（下同）。
5.2020年数据为初步核算数（下同）。
6.2011-2019年人均GDP数据依据第七次全国人口普查修订的常住人口数据进行了修订。

3-2 主要年份地区生产总值指数（上年=100）

Indices of Gross Domestic Product in Representative Years(preceding year = 100)

(本表按可比价格计算) (Data in the table are calculated at constant prices)

年 份	Year	地区生产总值 Gross Domestic Product	第一产业 Primary Industry	第二产业 Secondary Industry	第三产业 Tertiary Industry	人均地区生产总值 Per Capita GDP
1952		103.6	92.2	137.5	123.7	
1965		126.1	134.1	133.0	106.7	
1970		122.0	109.4	140.0	100.1	
1975		103.8	92.6	107.1	107.5	
1978		101.7	101.6	99.4	108.2	
1980		111.5	83.3	119.7	116.5	
1985		112.6	107.5	111.8	116.9	
1986		111.4	107.7	108.4	118.8	
1987		113.6	100.8	109.1	126.6	
1988		111.4	81.2	115.5	114.7	
1989		106.7	103.0	104.5	110.8	
1990		105.2	103.0	102.5	109.6	
1991		109.8	118.6	108.6	108.6	108.2
1992		115.6	109.4	118.1	115.0	114.3
1993		123.9	112.5	142.7	108.4	122.3
1994		110.3	98.4	110.6	113.2	108.8
1995		110.0	104.5	112.1	108.6	108.5
1996		114.9	106.8	118.8	111.7	113.5
1997		114.4	109.1	116.7	112.4	113.2
1998		113.3	106.5	117.5	108.8	112.1
1999		112.2	97.4	115.7	110.1	111.2
2000		113.0	103.5	115.1	111.5	111.4
2001		113.1	102.5	115.3	112.6	111.4
2002		113.3	103.1	115.0	113.0	112.1
2003		113.1	101.8	117.5	110.5	111.4
2004		113.1	106.2	115.5	111.7	111.4
2005		112.3	107.5	109.8	115.1	110.5
2006		112.9	106.8	110.5	115.2	111.0
2007		115.1	104.5	113.0	117.4	113.4
2008		114.8	107.6	113.2	116.4	113.8
2009		113.0	104.9	110.7	115.1	112.2
2010		113.6	105.7	115.0	113.2	112.9
2011		112.6	105.4	111.7	113.9	109.8
2012		111.9	106.0	110.4	113.4	107.7
2013		111.2	104.4	112.6	110.7	108.3
2014		109.7	105.0	109.4	110.2	107.0
2015		108.9	104.4	104.6	112.1	106.0
2016		108.8	103.3	107.2	110.0	105.1
2017		107.7	105.0	105.1	109.4	103.6
2018		108.2	103.3	107.1	109.1	103.6
2019		107.0	104.3	106.2	107.6	102.5
2020		105.2	103.0	107.4	104.2	100.8
平均每年增长	**Yearly Average Growth Rates**					
“一五”时期	**The First Five-Year Plan Period**	**15.8**	**5.9**	**37.7**	**16.9**	
“二五”时期	**The Second Five-Year Plan Period**	**2.0**	**-3.7**	**2.5**	**8.4**	
1963--1965年	**Readjust Period**	**14.2**	**16.1**	**23.4**	**0.3**	
“三五”时期	**The Third Five-Year Plan Period**	**7.1**	**0.1**	**11.7**	**5.4**	
“四五”时期	**The Fourth Five-Year Plan Period**	**5.0**	**4.0**	**5.3**	**5.0**	
“五五”时期	**The Fifth Five-Year Plan Period**	**6.0**	**-0.7**	**6.5**	**10.1**	
“六五”时期	**The Sixth Five-Year Plan Period**	**10.7**	**7.9**	**10.4**	**12.9**	
“七五”时期	**The Seventh Five-Year Plan Period**	**9.6**	**-1.3**	**7.9**	**15.9**	
“八五”时期	**The Eighth Five-Year Plan Period**	**13.8**	**8.5**	**17.8**	**10.7**	**12.3**
“九五”时期	**The Ninth Five-Year Plan Period**	**13.6**	**4.6**	**16.8**	**10.9**	**12.3**
“十五”时期	**The Tenth Five-Year Plan Period**	**13.0**	**4.2**	**14.6**	**12.6**	**11.4**
“十一五”时期	**The Eleventh Five-Year Plan Period**	**13.9**	**5.9**	**12.5**	**15.5**	**12.7**
“十二五”时期	**The twelfth Five-Year Plan Period**	**10.9**	**5.0**	**9.7**	**12.1**	**7.8**
“十三五”时期	**The thirteenth Five-Year Plan Period**	**7.4**	**3.8**	**6.6**	**8.0**	**3.1**

注：2011-2019年、“十二五”时期人均GDP指数依据第七次全国人口普查修订的常住人口数据进行了修订。

3-3 主要年份地区生产总值指数（1952年=100）

Indices of Gross Domestic Product in Representative Years(1952= 100)

(本表按可比价格计算) (Data in the table are calculated at constant prices)

年份 Year	地区生产总值 Gross Domestic Product	第一产业 Primary Industry	第二产业 Secondary Industry	第三产业 Tertiary Industry
1952	100.0	100.0	100.0	100.0
1965	341.6	173.3	1048.3	329.2
1970	481.6	174.3	1821.0	428.6
1975	614.2	211.9	2362.5	547.9
1978	678.7	231.3	2560.8	643.8
1980	821.4	204.2	3237.2	885.2
1983	988.4	222.5	3846.2	1154.4
1984	1213.6	278.2	4748.8	1388.7
1985	1366.8	299.1	5310.6	1632.4
1986	1523.1	322.3	5756.7	1928.9
1987	1730.0	324.9	6280.6	2441.6
1988	1926.3	263.7	7256.6	2801.2
1989	2054.8	271.6	7583.1	3104.6
1990	2162.5	279.7	7772.7	3403.6
1991	2374.4	331.7	8441.2	3696.3
1992	2744.8	362.9	9969.1	4250.7
1993	3400.8	408.2	14225.9	4607.8
1994	3751.1	401.8	15733.8	5216.0
1995	4126.2	419.9	17637.6	5664.6
1996	4741.0	448.5	20953.5	6327.4
1997	5423.7	489.3	24452.7	7112.0
1998	6145.1	521.1	28731.9	7737.9
1999	6894.8	507.6	33242.8	8519.4
2000	7791.1	525.4	38262.5	9499.1
2001	8811.7	538.5	44116.7	10696.0
2002	9983.7	555.2	50734.2	12086.5
2003	11294.6	565.2	59612.7	13355.6
2004	12778.7	600.2	68852.7	14918.2
2005	14345.3	645.3	75600.2	17170.8
2006	16198.7	689.1	83538.2	19780.8
2007	18644.8	720.1	94398.2	23222.7
2008	21407.9	774.9	106858.8	27031.2
2009	24195.2	812.8	118292.7	31112.9
2010	27478.5	859.2	136036.6	35219.8
2011	30951.8	905.6	151952.8	40115.3
2012	34625.8	959.9	167755.9	45490.8
2013	38514.2	1002.1	188893.2	50358.3
2014	42250.1	1052.2	206649.1	55494.8
2015	46001.9	1098.5	216155.0	62209.7
2016	50063.9	1134.8	231718.1	68430.7
2017	53913.8	1191.8	243508.6	74863.2
2018	58318.6	1231.1	260797.7	81675.8
2019	62400.9	1284.0	276967.2	87883.2
2020	65645.7	1322.6	297462.7	91574.3

3-4 主要年份地区生产总值构成

Composition of Gross Domestic Product in Representative Years

(本表按当年价格计算) (Data in the table are calculated at current prices)

单位：% (%)

年 份	Year	地区生产总值 Gross Domestic Product	第一产业 Primary Industry	第二产业 Secondary Industry	第三产业 Tertiary Industry
1952		100	47.18	26.11	26.71
1965		100	20.53	56.58	22.89
1970		100	17.62	61.71	20.67
1975		100	19.41	59.21	21.38
1978		100	19.05	57.55	23.40
1980		100	14.94	59.03	26.03
1985		100	15.21	53.54	31.25
1986		100	14.58	51.47	33.95
1987		100	13.39	47.02	39.59
1988		100	11.56	46.95	41.49
1989		100	11.68	44.72	43.60
1990		100	11.96	43.04	45.00
1991		100	12.61	41.91	45.48
1992		100	11.39	41.99	46.62
1993		100	9.84	48.30	41.86
1994		100	10.93	44.26	44.81
1995		100	12.53	40.97	46.50
1996		100	11.53	39.72	48.75
1997		100	10.50	40.50	49.00
1998		100	9.87	41.14	48.99
1999		100	7.89	42.15	49.96
2000		100	6.91	42.89	50.20
2001		100	6.24	42.58	51.18
2002		100	5.78	42.77	51.45
2003		100	5.48	43.43	51.09
2004		100	5.51	42.56	51.93
2005		100	5.10	39.50	55.40
2006		100	4.66	40.51	54.83
2007		100	4.44	41.07	54.49
2008		100	4.43	40.65	54.92
2009		100	3.95	41.09	54.96
2010		100	4.17	40.40	55.43
2011		100	4.36	39.99	55.65
2012		100	4.14	39.51	56.35
2013		100	3.68	39.24	57.08
2014		100	3.44	38.59	57.97
2015		100	3.23	34.90	61.87
2016		100	3.07	33.45	63.48
2017		100	3.31	33.07	63.62
2018		100	3.05	33.67	63.28
2019		100	2.97	33.31	63.72
2020		100	3.12	33.22	63.66
"一五"时期	**The First Five-Year Plan Period**	**100**	**32.88**	**43.92**	**23.20**
"二五"时期	**The Second Five-Year Plan Period**	**100**	**18.08**	**58.63**	**23.29**
1963--1965年	**Readjust Period**	**100**	**19.36**	**55.38**	**25.26**
"三五"时期	**The Third Five-Year Plan Period**	**100**	**18.60**	**57.33**	**24.07**
"四五"时期	**The Fourth Five-Year Plan Period**	**100**	**20.46**	**59.59**	**19.95**
"五五"时期	**The Fiifth Five-Year Plan Period**	**100**	**18.41**	**57.69**	**23.90**
"六五"时期	**The Sixth Five-Year Plan Period**	**100**	**16.03**	**55.01**	**28.96**
"七五"时期	**The Seventh Five-Year Plan Period**	**100**	**12.42**	**46.11**	**41.47**
"八五"时期	**The Eighth Five-Year Plan Period**	**100**	**11.44**	**43.52**	**45.04**
"九五"时期	**The Ninth Five-Year Plan Period**	**100**	**9.09**	**41.45**	**49.46**
"十五"时期	**The Tenth Five-Year Plan Period**	**100**	**5.55**	**41.95**	**52.50**
"十一五"时期	**The Eleventh Five-Year Plan Period**	**100**	**4.28**	**40.74**	**54.98**
"十二五"时期	**The Twelve Five-Year Plan Period**	**100**	**3.71**	**38.21**	**58.08**
"十三五"时期	**The thirteenth Five-Year Plan Period**	**100**	**3.10**	**33.34**	**63.56**

3-5 主要年份分行业增加值

The Value added by Industry in Representative Years

单位：亿元　　　　　　　　　　　　　　　　　　　　　　　　　　　　　(100 million yuan)

年　份 Year	地区生产总值 Gross Domestic Product	农、林、牧、渔业 Farming Forestry Animal Husbandry Fishery	工业 Industry	建筑业 Construction	批发和零售业 Wholesale and Retail Trades
1992	164.85	18.78	61.33	7.89	18.16
1993	229.56	22.58	98.88	12.00	22.63
1994	289.82	31.68	110.52	17.75	27.83
1995	330.35	41.40	112.50	22.83	33.20
1996	406.95	46.94	132.52	29.11	44.51
1997	488.82	51.33	161.97	36.00	59.31
1998	525.85	51.91	175.00	41.32	64.93
1999	577.29	45.53	194.00	49.35	70.27
2000	646.13	44.65	218.44	58.69	65.87
2001	734.86	45.87	246.90	66.00	78.38
2002	826.68	47.77	280.20	73.38	91.57
2003	926.12	50.72	319.26	82.96	94.95
2004	1092.35	60.21	372.18	92.77	123.27
2005	1294.05	66.01	393.51	117.68	139.57
2006	1512.56	70.44	465.70	146.99	164.33
2007	1857.75	82.42	569.08	193.99	184.91
2008	2313.26	102.46	672.60	267.82	225.20
2009	2689.06	106.09	763.81	341.20	278.87
2010	3195.05	133.22	875.97	414.96	329.48
2011	3791.71	165.43	1009.29	507.01	406.26
2012	4370.16	181.12	1140.83	585.87	460.05
2013	4960.23	197.76	1268.22	698.54	512.26
2014	5576.98	207.89	1387.03	791.64	552.31
2015	5932.86	209.58	1242.18	857.40	589.33
2016	6396.36	216.34	1252.91	920.05	599.08
2017	7418.04	270.83	1436.72	1047.34	653.49
2018	8499.41	286.33	1707.90	1210.79	709.16
2019	9399.98	309.68	1816.23	1370.63	788.19
2020	10020.39	346.17	1828.59	1547.44	795.83

注：1999年（含）之前，批发和零售业与住宿和餐饮业无法分类，故1999年（含）之前批发和零售业数据为批发和零售业与住宿和餐饮业合计数。

3-5 续表 continued

单位：亿元 (100 million yuan)

年 份 Year	交通运输、仓储和邮政业 Transport，Storage and Post	住宿和餐饮业 Accommodation and Catering Trade	金融业 Financial Intermediation	房地产业 Real Estate	其他服务业 Others Services
1992	15.21		16.28	1.58	25.62
1993	18.01		20.59	1.97	32.90
1994	22.02		31.19	3.76	45.07
1995	24.60		35.20	4.90	55.72
1996	32.73		40.15	7.42	73.57
1997	43.02		37.50	8.74	90.95
1998	48.64		32.95	11.95	99.15
1999	55.35		30.37	14.42	118.00
2000	43.01	18.46	33.00	16.96	147.05
2001	45.50	21.97	36.21	21.38	172.65
2002	48.25	25.27	43.48	26.90	189.86
2003	46.99	25.34	47.96	32.39	225.55
2004	49.06	35.03	58.05	37.68	264.11
2005	59.12	47.59	79.33	45.90	345.36
2006	69.07	53.60	95.95	55.31	391.17
2007	78.02	67.89	141.69	70.93	468.83
2008	98.93	81.61	170.78	92.18	601.69
2009	110.55	79.27	198.58	124.92	685.79
2010	134.29	95.93	237.40	188.10	785.70
2011	160.29	114.66	278.09	245.14	905.54
2012	184.19	124.39	350.92	280.17	1062.63
2013	194.73	121.00	446.54	303.30	1217.89
2014	211.83	125.86	597.14	343.69	1359.59
2015	239.63	141.88	683.26	427.42	1542.19
2016	268.89	143.34	743.09	474.39	1778.27
2017	297.54	153.45	834.19	562.78	2161.71
2018	316.63	164.19	916.94	658.64	2528.84
2019	348.03	187.69	976.23	797.58	2805.73
2020	353.59	159.97	1069.98	849.84	3069.00

3-6 主要年份分行业增加值指数（上年=100）

Indices of the Value added by Industry in Representative Years（preceding year = 100）

(本表按可比价格计算)　　(Data in the table are calculated at constant prices)

年份 Year	地区生产总值 Gross Domestic Product	农、林、牧、渔业 Farming Forestry Animal Husbandry Fishery	工业 Industry	建筑业 Construction	批发和零售业 Wholesale and Retail Trades
1992	115.6	109.4	118.1	118.2	130.7
1993	123.9	112.5	143.7	135.6	108.0
1994	110.3	98.4	106.8	141.3	103.1
1995	110.0	104.5	108.1	136.6	109.6
1996	114.9	106.8	117.1	126.8	116.0
1997	114.4	109.1	116.4	117.8	124.0
1998	113.3	106.5	116.1	123.4	110.7
1999	112.2	97.4	114.0	122.8	106.4
2000	113.0	103.5	113.8	120.1	111.4
2001	113.1	102.5	116.3	111.8	110.5
2002	113.3	103.1	116.4	109.3	115.3
2003	113.1	101.8	115.7	124.9	112.0
2004	113.1	106.2	114.5	119.3	109.0
2005	112.3	107.5	106.7	121.1	110.5
2006	112.9	106.8	108.5	117.2	112.9
2007	115.1	104.5	111.7	117.3	113.3
2008	114.8	107.6	111.8	117.5	114.0
2009	113.0	104.9	106.7	121.9	121.7
2010	113.6	105.7	114.0	117.3	110.9
2011	112.6	105.4	111.9	111.2	117.7
2012	111.9	106.0	110.8	109.4	111.2
2013	111.2	104.8	112.4	113.9	108.4
2014	109.7	105.2	108.3	112.3	107.6
2015	108.9	105.1	103.7	107.3	105.0
2016	108.8	104.1	108.2	106.3	103.9
2017	107.7	104.8	105.0	104.8	104.6
2018	108.2	103.5	108.3	107.1	106.1
2019	107.0	104.4	103.9	109.2	108.8
2020	105.2	103.1	105.8	109.3	101.8

注：1999年（含）之前，批发和零售业与住宿和餐饮业无法分类，故1999年（含）之前批发和零售业数据为批发和零售业与住宿和餐饮业合计数。

3-6 续表 continued

(本表按可比价格计算) (Data in the table are calculated at constant prices)

年 份 Year	交通运输、仓储和邮政业 Transport，Storage and Post	住宿和餐饮业 Accommodation and Catering Trade	金融业 Financial Intermediation	房地产业 Real Estate	其他服务业 Others Services
1992	111.3		107.6	119.5	112.2
1993	102.7		109.7	107.4	111.4
1994	102.5		126.9	160.7	114.8
1995	102.6		103.7	119.7	113.6
1996	115.1		98.7	130.8	114.2
1997	122.4		87.0	109.6	115.1
1998	114.4		88.8	138.3	110.3
1999	111.9		90.6	118.6	117.0
2000	111.7	111.7	107.7	116.6	111.7
2001	111.6	114.2	103.6	123.5	114.2
2002	106.1	116.5	104.6	106.0	116.5
2003	110.5	112.3	111.1	105.7	110.2
2004	112.3	116.9	108.4	107.7	112.5
2005	112.4	123.4	110.7	108.8	117.8
2006	112.6	116.5	109.5	118.7	117.3
2007	110.9	116.1	123.2	123.1	118.3
2008	109.2	107.5	112.3	108.7	121.6
2009	110.6	103.2	121.2	130.8	111.5
2010	116.3	112.0	114.3	133.4	110.6
2011	112.7	109.4	114.7	117.9	111.8
2012	110.4	105.4	125.4	110.8	112.7
2013	104.6	100.3	124.0	113.2	108.2
2014	105.8	100.2	120.4	107.0	109.5
2015	109.3	110.5	116.4	113.5	113.1
2016	109.0	101.2	111.9	110.9	111.9
2017	106.8	103.9	106.5	109.1	113.6
2018	106.1	104.7	105.3	105.8	112.3
2019	107.5	105.2	106.9	108.2	107.9
2020	100.8	83.4	106.9	100.8	106.8

3-7 主要年份三次产业贡献率

Three Industries Contribution Rate in Representative Years

(本表按可比价格计算)　　(Data in the table are calculated at constant prices)

单位：%　　(%)

年 份 Year	地区生产总值 Gross Domestic Product	第一产业 Primary Industry	第二产业 Secondary Industry	第三产业 Tertiary Industry
2000	100	1.8	66.9	31.3
2001	100	1.3	50.4	48.3
2002	100	1.5	49.4	49.1
2003	100	0.8	59.2	40.0
2004	100	2.4	54.3	43.3
2005	100	2.9	37.6	59.5
2006	100	2.7	32.2	65.1
2007	100	1.4	33.3	65.3
2008	100	2.2	33.9	63.9
2009	100	1.6	30.8	67.6
2010	100	1.6	40.4	58.0
2011	100	1.8	37.4	60.8
2012	100	2.0	35.0	63.0
2013	100	1.3	43.9	54.8
2014	100	1.7	38.4	59.9
2015	100	1.5	20.6	77.9
2016	100	1.2	28.6	70.2
2017	100	2.2	23.4	74.4
2018	100	1.4	29.8	68.8
2019	100	2.0	29.9	68.1
2020	100	1.8	47.9	50.3

3-8 主要年份三次产业对地区生产总值增长的拉动

Contribution of the Three Strata of Industry to GDP Growth in Representative Years

(本表按可比价格计算)　　(Data in the table are calculated at constant prices)

单位：百分点　　(percentage points)

年 份 Year	地区生产总值 Gross Domestic Product	第一产业 Primary Industry	第二产业 Secondary Industry	第三产业 Tertiary Industry
2000	13.0	0.2	8.7	4.1
2001	13.1	0.2	6.6	6.3
2002	13.3	0.2	6.6	6.5
2003	13.1	0.1	7.8	5.2
2004	13.1	0.3	7.1	5.7
2005	12.3	0.4	4.6	7.3
2006	12.9	0.3	4.2	8.4
2007	15.1	0.2	5.0	9.9
2008	14.8	0.3	5.0	9.5
2009	13.0	0.2	4.0	8.8
2010	13.6	0.2	5.5	7.9
2011	12.6	0.2	4.7	7.7
2012	11.9	0.2	4.2	7.5
2013	11.2	0.1	4.9	6.2
2014	9.7	0.2	3.7	5.8
2015	8.9	0.1	1.8	7.0
2016	8.8	0.1	2.5	6.2
2017	7.7	0.2	1.8	5.7
2018	8.2	0.1	2.4	5.7
2019	7.0	0.1	2.1	4.8
2020	5.2	0.1	2.5	2.6

3-9 分行业增加值

Value added by Industry

单位：亿元　　(100 million yuan)

指　标	Item	增加值 Value Added		指数（上年=100） Index(preceding year=100)	
		2019	2020	2019	2020
地区生产总值	**Gross Domestic Product**	**9399.98**	**10020.39**	**107.0**	**105.2**
农、林、牧、渔业	Farming Forestry Animal Husbandry Fishery	309.68	346.17	104.4	103.1
工业	Industry	1816.23	1828.59	103.9	105.8
建筑业	Construction	1370.63	1547.44	109.2	109.3
批发和零售业	Wholesale and Retail Trades	788.19	795.83	108.8	101.8
交通运输、仓储及邮政业	Transport,Storage and Post	348.03	353.59	107.5	100.8
住宿和餐饮业	Accommodation and Catering Trade	187.69	159.97	105.2	83.4
金融业	Financial Intermediation	976.23	1069.98	106.9	106.9
房地产业	Real Estate	797.58	849.84	108.2	100.8
其他服务业	Others Services	2805.73	3069.00	107.9	106.8
第一产业	Primary Industry	279.13	312.75	104.3	103.0
第二产业	Secondary Industry	3130.80	3328.27	106.2	107.4
第三产业	Tertiary Industry	5990.06	6379.37	107.6	104.2

3-10 各区县生产总值（2020年）

Gross Domestic Product by Region（2020）

单位：亿元　　　　（100 million yuan）

区 县	Region	地区生产总值 Gross Domestic Product	第一产业 Primary Industry	第二产业 Secondary Industry	第三产业 Tertiary Industry	人均地区生产总值（元） Per Capita GDP（yuan）
全 市	**Total**	**10020.39**	**312.75**	**3328.27**	**6379.37**	**79181**
新城区	Xincheng	579.05		164.41	414.64	93925
碑林区	Beilin	1060.47		256.13	804.34	142632
莲湖区	Lianhu	814.95		276.99	537.96	82194
灞桥区	Baqiao	542.06	18.94	157.90	365.22	55200
未央区	Weiyang	1319.43	1.61	580.10	737.72	87933
雁塔区	Yanta	2510.72		575.78	1934.94	126772
阎良区	Yanliang	249.10	32.42	85.67	131.01	82757
临潼区	Lintong	252.53	41.37	63.55	147.61	37440
长安区	Chang'an	1136.25	32.76	604.96	498.53	73830
高陵区	Gaoling	374.49	30.84	203.49	140.16	86388
鄠邑区	Huyi	233.61	31.10	96.94	105.57	40770
蓝田县	Lantian	142.96	32.38	22.11	88.47	28969
周至县	Zhouzhi	139.44	40.39	12.35	86.70	25034
西咸新区	Xixian	612.50	50.93	204.70	356.87	48236

注：本表数据为初步核算数。

3-11 各区县生产总值指数(2020年)(上年=100)

Indices of Gross Domestic Product by Region (2020) (preceding year = 100)

(本表按可比价格计算) (Data in the table are calculated at constant prices)

区 县	Region	地区生产总值 Gross Domestic Product	第一产业 Primary Industry	第二产业 Secondary Industry	第三产业 Tertiary Industry	人均地区生产总值 Per Capita GDP
全 市	**Total**	**105.2**	**103.0**	**107.4**	**104.2**	**100.8**
新城区	Xincheng	100.4		93.4	103.8	99.9
碑林区	Beilin	102.0		110.7	99.6	99.6
莲湖区	Lianhu	102.8		110.7	99.2	98.4
灞桥区	Baqiao	108.5	93.7	113.4	106.8	100.8
未央区	Weiyang	103.0	534.1	101.7	103.8	96.4
雁塔区	Yanta	107.3		107.2	107.3	100.8
阎良区	Yanliang	100.7	104.1	94.5	104.8	99.5
临潼区	Lintong	102.3	104.0	107.2	99.1	101.8
长安区	Chang'an	115.3	103.2	126.4	105.2	108.7
高陵区	Gaoling	102.1	103.6	99.9	106.2	99.5
鄠邑区	Huyi	102.3	102.2	103.1	101.6	101.2
蓝田县	Lantian	94.1	103.7	73.9	100.1	94.6
周至县	Zhouzhi	98.6	103.6	80.7	100.4	98.7
西咸新区	Xixian	107.2	101.7	107.7	107.7	101.3

注：本表数据为初步核算数。

3-12 主要年份非公有制经济增加值

The Added Value of Non-public-owned Economic in Representative Years

年 份 Year	非公有制经济增加值 （亿元） the Added Value of Non-public-owned Economic (100 million yuan)	非公有制经济增加值 占GDP比重（%） the Added Value of Non-public-owned Economic Percentage to GDP（%）
2005	560.32	43.3
2006	673.09	44.5
2007	854.57	46.0
2008	1101.11	47.6
2009	1309.57	48.7
2010	1587.94	49.7
2011	1916.95	50.6
2012	2246.26	51.4
2013	2589.24	52.2
2014	2939.07	52.7
2015	3132.55	52.8
2016	3377.28	52.8
2017	3931.72	53.0
2018	4539.52	53.4
2019	5109.00	54.4
2020	5317.42	53.1

注：1. 2005-2018年数据根据第四次经济普查GDP修订结果相应进行了调整。2019年数据为最终核实数。
  2. 2020年数据为初步核算数。

主要统计指标解释

生产总值（GDP） 是按市场价格计算的一个地区（或国家）所有常住单位在一定时期内生产活动的最终成果。生产总值有三种表现形态，即价值形态、收入形态和产品形态。从价值形态看，它是所有常住单位在一定时期内生产的全部货物和服务价值超过同期中间投入的全部非固定资产货物和服务价值的差额，即所有常住单位的增加值之和；从收入形态看，它是所有常住单位在一定时期内创造并分配给常住单位和非常住单位的初次收入分配之和；从产品形态看，它是所有常住单位在一定时期内最终使用的货物和服务价值与货物和服务净出口价值之和。在实际核算中，生产总值有三种计算方法，即生产法、收入法和支出法。三种方法分别从不同的方面反映生产总值及其构成。

人均生产总值 即"人均GDP"，常作为发展经济学中衡量经济发展状况的指标，是最重要的宏观经济指标之一，它是人们了解和把握一个国家或地区的宏观经济运行状况的有效工具。将一个国家核算期内（通常是一年）实现的国内生产总值与这个国家的常住人口（或户籍人口）相比进行计算，得到人均生产总值。

三次产业 指根据社会生产活动历史发展的顺序对产业结构的划分。目前我国的三次产业划分是：

第一产业是指农、林、牧、渔业（不含农、林、牧、渔服务业）。

第二产业是指采矿业（不含开采辅助活动），制造业（不含金属制品、机械和设备修理业），电力、热力、燃气及水生产和供应业，建筑业。

第三产业即服务业，是指除第一产业、第二产业以外的其他行业。

劳动者报酬 指劳动者因从事生产活动所获得的全部报酬。包括劳动者获得的各种形式的工资、奖金和津贴，既包括货币形式的，也包括实物形式的，还包括劳动者所享受的公费医疗和医药卫生费、上下班交通补贴、单位支付的社会保险费、住房公积金等。

生产税净额 指生产税减生产补贴后的余额。生产税指政府对生产单位从事生产、销售和经营活动以及因从事生产活动使用某些生产要素（如固定资产、土地、劳动力）所征收的各种税、附加费和规费。生产补贴与生产税相反，指政府对生产单位的单方面转移支出，因此视为负生产税，包括政策亏损补贴、价格补贴等。

固定资产折旧 指一定时期内为弥补固定资产损耗按照规定的固定资产折旧率提取的固定资产折旧，或按国民经济核算统一规定的折旧率虚拟计算的固定资产折旧。它反映了固定资产年当期生产中的转移价值。各类企业和企业化管理的事业单位的固定资产折旧是指实际计提的折旧费；不计提折旧的政府机关、非企业化管理的事业单位和居民住房的固定资产折旧是按照统一规定的折旧率和固定资产原值计算的虚拟折旧。原则上，固定资产折旧应按固定资产当期的重置价值计算，但是目前我国尚不具备对全社会固定资产进行重估价的基础，所以暂时只能采用上述办法。

营业盈余 指常住单位创造的增加值扣除劳动者报酬、生产税净额和固定资产折旧后的余额。它相当于企业的营业利润加上生产补贴，但要扣除从利润中开支的工资和福利等。

三次产业贡献率 各产业不变价增加值增量与不变价GDP增量之比。

三次产业拉动率 GDP增长速度与各产业贡献率之乘积。

非公有制经济 非公有制经济是指国民经济中除国有经济和集体经济以外的部分，对其中的混合制经济要依据实收资本之间的比例，按经济成分对各主要经济总量进行划分。

Explanatory Notes on Main Statistical Indicators

Gross Domestic Product (GDP) refers to the final products at market prices produced by all resident units in a country (or a region) during a certain period of time. Gross domestic product is expressed in three different perspectives, namely value, income, and products respectively. GDP in its value perspective refers to the total value of all goods and services produced by all resident units during a certain period of time, minus the total value of input of goods and services of the nature of non-fixed assets; in other words, it is the sum of the value-added of all resident units. GDP from the perspective of income includes the primary income created by all resident units and distributed to resident and non-resident units. GDP from the perspective of products refers to the value of all goods and services for final demand by all resident units plus the net exports of goods and services during a given period of time. In the practice of national accounting, gross domestic product is calculated from three approaches, namely production approach, income approach and expenditure approach, which reflect gross domestic product and its composition from different angles.For a region, it is called as Gross Regional Product (GRP) or regional GDP.

Per capita gross domestic product: "per capita GDP", often used as a measure of economic development in development economics, it is one of the most important macroeconomic indicators, and people's understanding and grasp of a country or a region effective tool of macroeconomic performance. The gross domestic product (GDP) of a country's accounting period (usually one year) is divided by the country's resident population (or household population), resulting in per capita GDP.

Three Strata of Industry Classification of economic activities into three strata of industry is a common practice in the world, although the grouping varies to some extent from country to country. In China economic activities are categorized into the following three strata of industry:

Primary industry refers to agriculture, forestry, animal husbandry and fishery and services in support of these industries.

Secondary industry refers to mining and quarrying, manufacturing, production and supply of electricity, water and gas, and construction.

Tertiary industry refers to all other economic activities not included in the primary or secondary industries.

Compensation of Employees refers to the total payment of various forms to employees for the productive activities they are engaged in. It includes wages, bonuses and allowances, which the employees earn in cash or in kind. It also includes the free medical services provided to the employees and the medicine expenses, transport subsidies and social insurance, and housing fund paid by the employers.

Net Taxes on Production refers to taxes on production less subsidies on production. The taxes on production refers to the various taxes, extra charges and fees levied on the production units on their production, sale and business activities as well as on the use of some factors of production, such as fixed assets, land and labour in the production activities they are engaged in. In contrast to taxes on production, subsidies on production refer to the unilateral government transfer to the production units and are therefore regarded as negative taxes on production. They include subsidies on the loss due to implementation of government policies, price subsidies, etc.

Depreciation of Fixed Assets refers to the depreciation of fixed assets in a given period, drawn in accordance with the stipulated depreciation rate for the purpose of compensating the wear-and-tear loss of the fixed assets or the depreciation of fixed assets imputed in accordance with the stipulated unified depreciation rate in the national economic accounting system. It reflects the value of transfer of the fixed assets in the production of the current period. The depreciation of fixed assets in various enterprises and institutions managed as enterprises refers to the depreciation expenses actually drawn. In government agencies and institutions not managed as enterprises which do not draw the depreciation expenses, as well as for the houses of residents, the depreciation of fixed assets is the imputed depreciation, which is calculated in accordance with the stipulated unified depreciation rate. In principle, the depreciation of fixed assets should be calculated on the basis of the re-purchased value of the fixed assets. However, currently the conditions in China do not facilitate the revaluation of all the fixed assets. Therefore, only the above-mentioned methods can be adopted at present.

Operating Surplus refers to the balance of the value added created by the resident units after deducting the labourers remuneration, net taxes on production and the depreciation of fixed assets. It is equivalent to the business profit of the enterprises plus subsidies to production, but the wages and welfare expenses paid from the profits should be deducted.

Three Industry Contribution Rate The ratio of all industries incremental value added to GDP increment at constant prices.

Three Industries Pulling Rate The product of GDP growth rate and the contribution rate of each industry.

Non-public Economy It refers to the part of in addition to state-owned economy and collective economy in the national economy,On which the mixed-economy should be divided according to the major economic components of total economic output based on the proportion in paid-in capital.

4 人口、从业人员与职工工资

POPULATION,EMPLOYMENT AND WAGES

资料整理：杨晓柳　张　磊
Data management：Yang Xiaoliu Zhang Lei
数据审核：冯军魁
Data audit：Feng Junkui

第四部分　人口、从业人员与职工工资

一、简要说明

（一）人口部分反映西安市人口发展变化基本情况。

1.年末常住人口、性别比例、年龄比例、城镇人口比例以及人口出生率、人口死亡率和人口自然增长率等数据，根据人口普查、1%人口抽样调查或年度人口变动情况抽样调查推算所得，2006–2009年年末常住人口根据2010年第六次全国人口普查数据进行了调整。2011–2019年常住人口及城镇化率根据2020年第七次全国人口普查数据进行了修订。

2. 户籍人口资料数据来源于西安市公安局人口统计年报，为西安原口径数据。

3.人口统计调查方法。目前人口统计调查有：在逢“0”的年份进行全国人口普查；在逢“5”的年份进行全国1%人口抽样调查；其余年份进行人口变动情况抽样调查。

（二）就业部分

1.反映西安市劳动就业与工资的基本情况。主要内容包括全社会从业人员数、城镇非私营单位从业人员数、城镇非私营单位从业人员工资、城镇登记失业率等。（城镇登记失业人数及失业率资料由市人力资源局提供并整理）

2.统计范围和调查方法

（1）城镇非私营单位是指城镇地区全部非私营法人单位，具体包括国有单位、集体单位、联营经济、股份制经济、外商投资经济、港澳台投资经济等单位。工资统计是统计单位的从业人员，而个体从业人员、自由职业者等非单位从业人员不在工资统计范围内。

根据国家统计局制定的《企业一套表统计调查制度》和《劳动工资统计调查制度》，对城镇非私营法人单位采用全面调查和抽样调查相结合的方法。

（2）城镇私营单位主要是指在内资法人单位中由自然人投资设立或由自然人控股，以雇佣劳动为基础的营利性经济组织，包括按照《公司法》《合伙企业法》《私营企业暂行条例》规定登记注册的私营有限责任公司、私营股份有限公司、私营合伙企业和私营独资企业。

根据国家统计局制定的《企业一套表统计调查制度》和《劳动工资统计调查制度》，对私营单位工资统计采用全面调查和抽样调查相结合的方法。

3.统计数据发布

由于劳动工资统计调查方法改变，按照有关规定，自2020年开始劳动工资统计年鉴取消按照登记注册类型及机构类型分组相关指标数据。

二、主要指标

年末户籍人口（万人）	977.97	比上年增长	2.2%
人口自然增长率（‰）	–	–	–个千分点
常住人口（万人）	1296	比上年增长	4.9%
男女性别比（以女性为100）	104.39	比上年减少	0.13个百分点
户籍人口密度（人／平方公里）	969	比上年增加	21人/平方公里
城镇非私营单位在岗职工年平均工资（元）	104363	比上年增长	7.7%

4 POPULATION,EMPLOYMENT AND WAGES

I.Brief Introduction

I. Population part reflects the basic conditions of development and changes of population in Xi'an.

1. Permanent population at the year–end, proportion of population by sex, proportion of population by age, proportion of urban population, birth rate, death rate and natural growth rate of population. The data are estimated by Xi'an Bureau of Statistics on the basis of population censuses, the one percent sample survey on population, or annual sample surveys on population changes. Permanent Population at the Year–end from 2006 to 2009 have been adjusted in accordance with the flash sums of the 6th National Population Census in 2010. The resident population and urbanization rate from 2011 to 2019 were revised according to the data of the seventh national census in 2020.

2. The total population with residence registration are obtained from the annual reports of population of Xi'an Public Security Bureau. It is the original caliber data of Xi'an.

3. Investigation methods. The statistical surveys on population are as follows:

The national populationcensus is conducted in the year ending with 0; the national 1 percent population sample survey is conducted in the year ending with 5; sample survey on population changes are conducted in the rest of the years.

II. Employment part

1. This part reflects the basic conditions of labour employment and wages of Xi'an, mainly including the number of all employed persons, number of urban non–private units, wages of urban non–private units employed persons, registered urban unemployment rate and etc. (the number of registered urban unemployment and registered urban unemployment rate are obtained from the Xi'an municipal human resources bureau).

2. The statistical coverage and investigation methods.

a) The urban non–private units: are non–private legal units in urban area, including state–owned units, urban collective–owned units, joint ownership units, cooperative units, foreign funded units and units with funds from Hong Kong, Macao & Taiwan etc. Wage of employed persons in urban non–private units are the persons employed in those units, except self–employed and freelancers.

In accordance withA Set of Statistical Survey System for Enterprises and The Survey System on Labour Wageby National Bureau of Statistics of China, the investigation method of non–private legal units in urban area is comprehensive survey and sample survey.

b) The urban private units: are established by natural person or controlled by natural person in legal units invested by domestic, are for–profit units based on wage–labor, including private limited liability corporations, private share holding corporations Ltd., partnership corporations and private sole proprietorship corporations registered in accordance with the Company Law,Partnership Enterprise Law and Provisional Regulations.

In accordance with A Set of Statistical Survey System for Enterprises and The Survey System on Labour Wageby National Bureau of Statistics of China, the investigation method of wage of employed persons in private legal units is combined with comprehensive survey and sampling survey.

3. Publish statistics

Due to the change of labor wage statistical survey method, according to relevant regulations, the labor wage statistical yearbook will cancel the grouping of relevant index data according to registration type and institution type from 2020.

II.Major Indicators

		Increase over Preceding Year
Total registered Population of Year–end(10 000 persons)	977.97	2.2%
Natural Growth Rate(‰)	–	– per thousand
Permanent Population(10 000 persons)	1296	4.9%
Sex Ratio (Female=100)	104.39	–0.13percentage points
Density of Population (person/sq.km)	969	21person/sq.km
Annual Average Wage of Staff and Workers in Urban Non–privite Enterprises(yuan)	104363	7.7%

4-1 主要年份人口数、人口密度和人口发展情况

Population, Population Density and Population Development in Representative Years

单位：万人 (10 000 persons)

年份 Year	总人口 Total Population	市区 Urban Area	女性人口 Number of Female	城填人口 Urban Population	人口密度 (人 / 平方公里) Density of Population (person/sq.km)	总人口指数（上年为100）Total Population Index (100 for preceding year) 全市 Whole City	市区 Urban Area
1952	252.92	92.42	118.81	57.61	254	102.6	103.1
1965	400.05	179.88	190.72	136.39	401	102.5	103.4
1970	435.12	188.12	210.47	139.12	436	101.9	101.4
1978	498.10	210.15	241.82	159.98	499	101.7	102.7
1980	511.91	221.19	249.26	172.85	513	101.4	102.6
1985	553.11	245.76	268.40	201.90	554	101.6	102.2
1986	563.97	251.80	273.30	205.92	565	102.0	102.5
1987	574.46	257.69	278.12	210.25	575	101.9	102.3
1988	585.85	264.94	283.68	216.99	587	102.0	102.8
1989	597.36	270.80	289.44	222.54	598	102.0	102.2
1990	608.89	275.69	295.29	226.98	610	101.9	101.8
1991	615.48	419.29	298.13	230.85	617	101.1	152.1
1992	623.20	429.54	301.92	236.45	624	101.3	102.4
1993	630.91	435.41	305.30	240.85	632	101.2	101.4
1994	639.45	442.30	309.17	248.35	641	101.4	101.6
1995	648.21	448.65	313.46	255.71	645	101.4	101.4
1996	654.87	454.68	316.60	261.28	653	101.0	101.3
1997	662.06	461.17	320.18	267.52	663	101.1	101.4
1998	668.22	466.31	323.20	271.75	669	100.9	101.1
1999	674.50	463.56	326.12	276.14	676	100.9	99.4
2000	688.01	483.10	332.83	285.79	689	102.0	104.2
2001	694.84	489.88	336.04	292.62	696	101.0	101.4
2002	702.59	497.38	339.51	300.05	704	101.1	101.5
2003	716.58	510.26	346.26	312.88	718	102.0	102.6
2004	725.01	516.30	350.85	318.50	717	101.2	101.2
2005	741.73	533.21	359.71	333.14	734	102.3	103.3
2006	753.11	540.97	365.74	343.78	745	101.5	101.5
2007	764.25	549.19	371.84	353.85	756	101.5	101.5
2008	772.30	554.73	376.76	363.87	764	101.1	101.0
2009	781.67	561.58	382.39	370.66	773	101.2	101.2
2010	782.73	562.65	383.93	374.64	774	100.1	100.2
2011	791.83	568.77	389.31	391.31	783	101.2	101.1
2012	795.98	572.76	392.04	398.40	788	100.5	100.7
2013	806.93	580.60	398.15	409.82	799	101.4	101.4
2014	815.29	587.16	402.83	418.16	807	101.0	101.1
2015	815.66	588.43	403.43	545.95	808	100.0	100.2
2016	824.93	629.24	408.39	552.21	817	101.1	106.9
2017	845.09	649.08	420.11	567.26	837	102.4	103.2
2018	922.82	725.58	461.31	639.62	914	109.2	111.8
2019	956.74	821.31	479.61	668.57	948	103.7	113.2
2020	977.97	842.39	491.47		969	102.2	102.6

注：本表为公安年报数据，系户籍人口。2016年起公安年报调整至11月30日，市区数1991年增加临潼、长安，2016年增加高陵，行政区划面积自2012年发生变更，调整了2012年和2013年户籍人口密度。2015年公安局户籍改革，按统计上城乡划分标准统计城镇与乡村人口。户籍人口为西安原口径数据。2019年和2020年计算的人口密度所使用的土地面积为2018年数据。由于部门制度变化，自2020年开始，城镇人口数据暂不提供。

4-2 主要年份人口自然变动情况

Natural Population Movements in Representative Years

单位：万人 (10 000 persons)

年份 Year	出生 Birth 人数 Population	出生率（‰） Birth Rate (‰)	死亡 Death 人数 Population	死亡率（‰） Death Rate (‰)	自然增长率（‰） Natural Growth Rate (‰)	迁入人口 Immigrant Population	迁出人口 Emigrant Population
1985	8.95	16.30	3.01	5.48	10.82	11.60	8.74
1986	10.14	18.15	2.78	4.97	13.18	11.79	8.39
1987	9.76	17.14	2.83	4.97	12.17	12.58	9.26
1988	9.42	16.24	2.89	4.98	11.26	13.54	8.97
1989	11.78	19.92	3.04	5.13	14.79	12.73	10.15
1990	12.40	20.55	3.45	5.72	14.83	11.82	9.86
1991	8.73	14.25	3.26	5.33	8.92	8.98	6.09
1992	8.98	14.49	3.39	5.48	9.01	13.94	9.54
1993	9.25	14.75	3.37	5.38	9.37	11.50	8.33
1994	8.08	12.71	3.16	4.97	7.74	13.40	8.59
1995	7.69	11.95	3.21	4.98	6.97	14.41	8.85
1996	7.26	11.15	3.41	5.24	5.91	11.94	8.88
1997	6.84	10.38	3.12	4.75	5.63	12.58	8.62
1998	6.40	9.62	3.10	4.66	4.96	10.89	8.36
1999	6.19	9.22	3.88	5.78	3.44	12.58	9.23
2000	8.90	13.07	4.06	5.96	7.11	17.12	9.23
2001	5.11	7.39	2.89	4.19	3.20	15.16	10.83
2002	5.34	7.64	3.08	4.41	3.23	13.90	9.41
2003	6.02	8.48	3.32	4.68	3.80	20.60	9.15
2004	6.63	9.19	4.23	5.87	3.32	15.56	10.19
2005	7.67	9.58	4.13	5.16	4.42	22.61	9.46
2006	8.13	9.98	4.45	5.46	4.52	17.23	11.75
2007	8.27	10.00	4.53	5.48	4.52	19.90	14.01
2008	8.47	10.15	4.65	5.57	4.58	18.49	15.04
2009	8.47	10.08	4.73	5.63	4.45	16.84	13.14
2010	8.23	9.73	4.51	5.34	4.39	14.09	13.50
2011	8.25	9.71	4.57	5.38	4.33	14.21	11.74
2012	8.64	10.13	4.75	5.57	4.56	12.55	13.10
2013	8.20	9.57	4.60	5.37	4.20	10.83	8.60
2014	8.70	10.11	4.71	5.47	4.64	9.10	7.61
2015	8.80	10.15	4.78	5.51	4.64	8.08	11.61
2016	10.12	11.54	4.74	5.40	6.14	6.21	4.68
2017	12.03	12.62	5.17	5.42	7.20	25.22	4.94
2018	12.23	12.47	5.38	5.48	6.99	76.53	8.02
2019	12.45	12.32	5.59	5.53	6.79	30.81	6.21
2020						22.45	7.28

注：2004年以前为公安年报数据。迁入人口和迁出人口为公安年报数据。公安数据为西安原口径数据。2010年出生、死亡、自然增长率根据人口普查数据推算得出。2005−2009年、2011−2019年出生、死亡、自然增长率为人口变动抽样调查推算数据。第七次人口普查暂未公布出生、死亡、自然增长率，暂无相关数据。

4-3 人口年龄构成和抚养比

Population Age Composition and Dependency Ratio

单位：% (%)

年 份 Year	各年龄段人口比重 Proportion of Population of All Ages 0-14岁 0-14 year old	 15-64岁 15-64 year old	 65岁及以上 65 year old and above	总抚养比 Total Dependency Ratio	少年儿童 Children	老年人口 Elderly Population
1990	25.71	69.08	5.21	44.76	37.21	7.55
2000	22.27	71.26	6.47	40.33	31.25	9.08
2010	12.89	78.65	8.46	27.15	16.39	10.76
2011	12.57	78.33	9.10	27.66	16.04	11.62
2012	12.54	78.02	9.44	28.17	16.07	12.10
2013	12.46	77.88	9.66	28.40	16.00	12.40
2014	12.52	77.46	10.02	29.10	16.16	12.94
2015	12.56	76.94	10.50	29.98	16.33	13.65
2016	12.76	76.35	10.89	30.97	16.71	14.26
2017	13.63	75.20	11.17	32.97	18.12	14.85
2018	13.75	74.96	11.29	33.40	18.34	15.06
2019	13.90	74.41	11.69	34.39	18.68	15.71
2020	15.65	73.45	10.90	36.14	21.30	14.84

注：1990年、2000年、2010年、2020年数据根据人口普查数据加工整理，2011-2019年数据根据人口变动抽样调查数据推算，自2017年起为纳入西咸新区咸阳片区后的结构。抚养比指0-14岁、65岁及以上人口占15-64岁人口的比重。

4-4 全市及各区县人口数和户数（2020年）

Population and Households by Region（2020）

单位：万人 (10 000 persons)

区 县	Region	总户数（万户） Number of Households (10 000 households)	总人口 Total Population	按性别划分Grouped by Sex 男 Male	 女 Female	迁入人口（人） Immigrant Population (person)	迁出人口（人） Emigrant Population (person)
全 市	**Total**	**310.59**	**977.97**	**486.50**	**491.47**	**224462**	**72755**
新城区	Xincheng	18.44	53.52	26.38	27.14	12475	4265
碑林区	Beilin	23.26	73.21	36.11	37.10	21526	9097
莲湖区	Lianhu	27.56	77.05	37.65	39.40	20739	6056
灞桥区	Baqiao	22.31	67.61	32.86	34.75	16188	3418
未央区	Weiyang	33.92	104.12	50.37	53.75	50101	11347
雁塔区	Yanta	42.85	135.37	66.07	69.30	58331	15392
阎良区	Yanliang	8.89	27.57	13.81	13.76	2752	1752
临潼区	Lintong	23.46	73.15	36.98	36.17	4198	2341
长安区	Chang'an	40.54	129.32	64.15	65.17	22357	6646
高陵区	Gaoling	11.67	37.30	18.39	18.91	5896	1518
鄠邑区	Huyi	19.18	64.16	32.80	31.37	3803	2136
蓝田县	Lantian	19.65	65.64	34.09	31.55	2965	4210
周至县	Zhouzhi	18.85	69.94	36.83	33.11	3131	4577

注：本表均为公安年报数据，为西安原口径数据。总户数未机械配平。由于部门制度变化，自2020年开始，取消城镇人口指标。

4–5 全市及各区县常住人口数和性别比

单位：万人

区 县	Region	常住人口 Permanent Population 2011	2012	2013	2014	2015	2016
全 市	**Total**	**887**	**914**	**936**	**960**	**988**	**1030**
新城区	Xincheng	59.0	59.1	59.2	59.4	59.4	60.0
碑林区	Beilin	62.6	64.0	64.8	65.4	66.3	67.2
莲湖区	Lianhu	74.8	76.4	79.0	80.8	82.9	85.6
灞桥区	Baqiao	64.7	67.5	69.5	72.3	75.6	82.3
未央区	Weiyang	92.1	102.7	111.2	120.4	129.8	141.0
雁塔区	Yanta	126.6	132.4	136.8	140.4	145.4	155.8
阎良区	Yanliang	28.0	28.1	28.2	28.3	28.6	28.7
临潼区	Lintong	65.8	65.9	65.9	66.0	66.1	66.4
长安区	Chang'an	113.9	117.9	120.3	125.2	130.6	138.2
高陵区	Gaoling	35.2	36.0	36.9	37.8	39.1	40.3
鄠邑区	Huyi	56.1	56.4	56.9	57.4	57.9	58.5
蓝田县	Lantian	51.5	51.2	51.0	50.6	50.2	50.1
周至县	Zhouzhi	56.5	56.4	56.3	56.1	56.0	55.9
西咸新区	Xixian						

注：2011–2019年全市及各区县常住人口为依据第七次人口普查修正后数据，数据未机械配平。2020年常住人口、城镇人口及按性别划分的人口数，根据第七次人口普查数据推算得出。自2017年起常住口径数据含西咸新区。第七次人口普查未公布出生率、死亡率和自然增长率，暂无相关数据。

Permanent Population and Sex Ratio by Region

(10 000 persons)

2017	2018	2019	2020	城镇 Urban	2020年常住人口按性别划分 Permanent Population by Gender(2020) 男 Male	女 Female	性别比（女=100） Sex Ratio (Female=100)
1134	**1191**	**1235**	**1296**	**1026.43**	**661.92**	**634.08**	**104.39**
60.7	61.3	61.5	61.8	61.80	31.59	30.21	104.57
68.5	72.4	72.9	75.8	75.80	37.76	38.04	99.26
89.9	93.4	96.4	101.9	101.90	50.64	51.26	98.79
84.1	88.3	94.3	102.1	100.13	53.51	48.59	110.13
123.9	136.4	144.5	155.6	155.60	80.11	75.49	106.12
166.4	181.1	191.2	204.9	204.90	103.53	101.37	102.13
29.0	29.6	29.9	30.3	17.67	15.77	14.53	108.53
66.9	67.0	67.3	67.6	24.68	34.45	33.15	103.92
132.7	141.1	149.1	158.7	100.99	80.84	77.86	103.83
40.9	42.0	42.5	44.2	29.01	22.62	21.58	104.82
55.9	56.4	56.9	57.7	25.70	30.13	27.57	109.29
49.9	49.7	49.5	49.2	16.80	25.51	23.69	107.68
55.8	55.8	55.7	55.7	16.22	28.72	26.98	106.45
109.6	116.4	123.5	130.5	95.33	66.74	63.76	104.67

4-6 主要年份常住人口数

Permanent Population in Representative Years

单位：万人　　　　(10 000 persons)

年 份 Year	年末常住人口 Permanent Population （year-end）	城镇 Urban	乡村 Rural
2000	741.14	450.36	290.78
2005	806.81	510.55	296.26
2006	822.52	530.94	291.58
2007	830.54	548.99	281.55
2008	837.52	565.16	272.36
2009	843.46	581.40	262.06
2010	847.41	584.71	262.70
2011	887	620.00	267.00
2012	914	659.26	254.74
2013	936	689.01	246.99
2014	960	714.94	245.06
2015	988	747.71	240.29
2016	1030	789.50	240.50
2017	1134	874.55	259.45
2018	1191	927.23	263.77
2019	1235	972.89	262.11
2020	1296	1026.43	269.57

注：2000年常住人口为普查数据。2005-2009年常住人口为人口变动抽样调查推算数据。2010年、2020年常住人口为年末常住人口数，根据人口普查数据推算得出。2011-2019年常住人口依据第七次人口普查数据进行修订。自2017年起常住口径数据为大西安范围，含西咸新区。

4-7 主要年份社会从业人数

Number of Social Laborers in Representative Years

单位：万人 (10 000 persons)

年 份 Year	合计 Total	一、按城乡分 Grouped by Urban Area and Rural Area					二、按三次产业分 Grouped by Industry		
		1.城镇 Urban	国有经济 State-owned Enterprises	集体经济 Collective Enterprises	其他经济 Others	2.乡村 Village	第一产业 Primary Industry	第二产业 Secondary Industry	第三产业 Tertiary Industry
1985	**296.80**	129.07	96.80	29.07	3.20	167.73	135.89	98.61	62.30
1986	**299.45**	132.82	101.28	28.43	3.11	166.63	127.46	100.61	71.38
1987	**312.16**	138.56	104.58	30.72	3.26	173.60	130.36	107.75	74.05
1988	**327.76**	142.24	106.46	30.73	5.05	185.52	138.87	108.12	80.77
1989	**332.65**	145.65	108.80	30.44	6.41	187.00	142.21	106.40	84.04
1990	**343.06**	147.93	110.95	29.78	7.20	195.13	149.64	106.74	86.68
1991	**347.65**	149.48	111.87	29.80	7.81	198.17	152.24	108.19	87.22
1992	**357.51**	151.67	113.19	29.97	8.51	205.84	154.75	110.22	92.54
1993	**363.70**	155.72	112.98	29.77	12.97	207.98	154.02	114.02	95.66
1994	**364.56**	154.88	113.39	27.97	13.52	209.68	153.51	108.53	102.52
1995	**372.60**	158.80	113.79	25.58	19.43	213.80	153.39	109.67	109.54
1996	**379.29**	164.54	113.29	24.82	26.43	214.75	153.43	109.17	116.69
1997	**385.14**	169.52	112.44	23.52	33.56	215.62	153.23	109.46	122.45
1998	**393.95**	177.20	106.06	21.50	49.64	216.75	153.00	110.45	130.50
1999	**400.43**	180.27	105.08	20.50	54.69	220.16	154.64	110.58	135.21
2000	**389.10**	176.45	103.46	18.40	54.59	212.65	147.03	107.26	134.81
2001	**389.30**	177.94	100.47	17.10	60.37	211.36	145.09	108.96	135.25
2002	**397.16**	181.85	100.54	16.90	64.41	215.31	143.04	111.62	142.50
2003	**404.92**	183.23	94.51	16.78	71.94	221.69	146.67	109.09	149.16
2004	**409.57**	187.53	93.43	15.41	78.69	222.04	141.81	111.70	156.06
2005	**415.83**	192.53	93.27	14.47	84.79	223.30	136.31	114.20	165.32
2006	**422.15**	196.16	84.46	14.41	97.29	225.99	135.10	116.09	170.96
2007	**436.36**	214.27	90.58	11.88	111.81	222.09	133.33	125.06	177.97
2008	**448.05**	224.20	90.17	10.60	123.43	223.85	127.87	130.23	189.95
2009	**462.52**	239.39	90.83	7.63	140.93	223.13	122.13	131.57	208.82
2010	**477.58**	252.54	94.01	5.48	153.05	225.04	117.27	145.40	214.91
2011	**495.99**	265.43	91.62	5.33	168.48	230.56	121.05	151.33	223.61
2012	**514.57**	287.65	95.33	5.10	187.22	226.92	114.92	162.35	237.30
2013	**530.71**	308.04	86.06	7.29	214.69	222.67	110.45	151.50	268.76
2014	**532.92**	316.59	84.83	6.67	225.09	216.33	105.02	151.85	276.05
2015	**528.06**	327.68	84.52	5.29	237.87	200.38	107.68	129.51	290.87
2016	**539.18**	335.07	87.15	4.85	243.07	204.11	105.12	127.88	306.18
2017	**596.21**	370.33	86.06	4.46	279.81	225.88	113.17	135.52	347.52
2018	**621.22**	398.23	80.83	3.53	313.87	222.99	101.25	154.02	365.95
2019	**645.86**	421.75	75.84	3.28	342.63	224.11	101.37	164.54	379.95
2020	**664.45**	443.29				221.16	99.97	155.84	408.64

注：1.第一产业从业人员中包括城镇农林牧渔及服务业企业人员。
2.因劳动工资统计调查制度改变，自2020年起，取消分登记注册类型、机构类型分组数据，下同。

4-8 按国民经济行业分从业人数（2020年）

单位：万人

行 业	Sector	合计 Total
总计	**Total**	**664.45**
（一）农、林、牧、渔业	Agriculture ,Forestry,Animal Husbandry and Fishery	99.97
（二）采矿业	Mining	4.87
（三）制造业	Manufacturing	77.75
（四）电力、热力、燃气及水生产和供应业	Production and Supply of Electricity,Gas,Heat and Water	7.15
（五）建筑业	Construction	66.08
（六）批发和零售业	Wholesale and Retail Trades	101.13
（七）交通运输、仓储和邮政业	Traffic,Transport,Storage and Post	43.49
（八）住宿和餐饮业	Hotels and Catering Services	54.34
（九）信息传输、软件和信息技术服务业	Information Transmission,Software and Information Technology Services	18.50
（十）金融业	Financial Intermediation	15.07
（十一）房地产业	Real Estate	19.90
（十二）租赁和商务服务业	Leasing and Business Services	31.44
（十三）科学研究和技术服务业	Scientific Research and Technical Services	18.88
（十四）水利、环境和公共设施管理业	Management of Water Conservancy, Environment and Public Facilities	3.58
（十五）居民服务、修理和其他服务业	Services to Households, Repairs and Other Services	28.32
（十六）教育	Education	33.46
（十七）卫生和社会工作	Health and Social Work	22.85
（十八）文化、体育和娱乐业	Culture, Sports and Entertainment	4.76
（十九）公共管理、社会保障和社会组织	Public Administration, Social Security and Social Organizations	12.91
（二十）国际组织	International Organizations	

Number of Employed Persons Grouped by Industry of the National Economy (2020)

(10 000 persons)

城镇非私营 Urban Non-Private Units	城镇私营及个体劳动者 Urban Private Enterprises and Individual Labors	乡村从业人员 Rural Employed Persons
213.57	**229.72**	**221.16**
0.23	1.91	97.83
4.72	0.15	
39.92	21.95	15.88
6.40	0.75	
23.36	25.06	17.66
11.33	68.30	21.50
20.23	11.46	11.80
4.90	36.89	12.55
11.41	6.13	0.96
13.53	0.73	0.81
8.93	10.97	
7.14	14.78	9.52
12.33	5.78	0.77
2.61	0.97	
0.59	14.36	13.37
22.12	3.78	7.56
10.18	3.15	9.52
2.28	2.48	
11.36	0.12	1.43

4-9 城镇非私营单位从业人员情况（2020年）

单位：人

分组	Classify	单位从业人员 Employed Persons	女性 Female
总计	**Total**	**2135688**	**857960**
（一）农、林、牧、渔业	Agriculture ,Forestry,Animal Husbandry and Fishery	2263	708
（二）采矿业	Mining	47199	23605
（三）制造业	Manufacturing	399161	121621
（四）电力、热力、燃气及水生产和供应业	Production and Supply of Electricity,Gas,Heat and Water	64049	19057
（五）建筑业	Construction	233575	39316
（六）批发和零售业	Wholesale and Retail Trades	113302	59983
（七）交通运输、仓储和邮政业	Traffic,Transport,Storage and Post	202329	53496
（八）住宿和餐饮业	Hotels and Catering Services	49000	29194
（九）信息传输、软件和信息技术服务业	Information Transmission,Software and Information Technology Services	114061	42953
（十）金融业	Financial Intermediation	135308	83279
（十一）房地产业	Real Estate	89296	37213
（十二）租赁和商务服务业	Leasing and Business Services	71437	29074
（十三）科学研究和技术服务业	Scientific Research and Technical Services	123265	37764
（十四）水利、环境和公共设施管理业	Management of Water Conservancy, Environment and Public Facilities	26102	10086
（十五）居民服务、修理和其他服务业	Services to Households, Repairs and Other Services	5913	2839
（十六）教育	Education	221289	138744
（十七）卫生和社会工作	Health and Social Work	101761	76295
（十八）文化、体育和娱乐业	Culture, Sports and Entertainment	22762	11127
（十九）公共管理、社会保障和社会组织	Public Administration, Social Security and Social Organizations	113617	41606
（二十）国际组织	International Organizations		

注：自2018年开始，表名中“全部单位”改为“城镇非私营单位”。下同。

Basic Facts on Employees in Urban Non-Private Units（2020）

(person)

在岗职工合计 Total Fully Employed Staff and Workers	其他从业人员 Other Employed Persons	单位从业人员 平均人数 Average Employment	在岗职工合计 Staff and Workers	其他从业人员 Other Employed Persons
1971092	**164596**	**2190594**	**1994047**	**196547**
2192	71	2281	2204	77
47051	148	44725	44039	686
393126	6035	416503	410606	5897
62854	1195	82202	77813	4389
211168	22407	223477	200914	22563
109709	3593	115306	110936	4370
199569	2760	239989	233796	6193
44296	4704	48915	43538	5377
113574	487	111848	111471	377
61418	73890	135086	60786	74300
86454	2842	88598	85630	2968
52250	19187	70634	51628	19006
120021	3244	121718	117644	4074
24177	1925	26016	24109	1907
5758	155	5840	5682	158
211510	9779	216757	207675	9082
96575	5186	100377	95251	5126
21675	1087	22815	21563	1252
107715	5902	113603	107455	6148

4-10 主要年份城镇非私营单位分行业从业人员年平均工资

单位：元

分 组	Classify	2010	2011
总计	**Grouped by Economic Sector**	**37870**	**41679**
（一）农、林、牧、渔业	Agriculture ,Forestry,Animal Husbandry and Fishery	21436	23567
（二）采矿业	Mining	32154	38551
（三）制造业	Manufacturing	26663	34698
（四）电力、热力、燃气及水生产和供应业	Production and Distribution of Electricity,Gas and Water	39508	47705
（五）建筑业	Construction	26875	29773
（六）批发和零售业	Wholesale and Retail Trades	25103	27996
（七）交通运输、仓储和邮政业	Traffic,Transport,Storage and Post	41737	48231
（八）住宿和餐饮业	Hotels and Catering Services	19647	22925
（九）信息传输、软件和信息技术服务业	Information Transmission,Software and Information Technology Services	45904	51135
（十）金融业	Financial Intermediation	63952	72195
（十一）房地产业	Real Estate	45273	34626
（十二）租赁和商务服务业	Leasing and Business Services	30267	31549
（十三）科学研究和技术服务业	Scientific Research and Technical Services	55456	64448
（十四）水利、环境和公共设施管理业	Management of Water Conservancy, Environment and Public Facilities	25322	26009
（十五）居民服务、修理和其他服务业	Services to Households, Repairs and Other Services	26443	23993
（十六）教育	Education	53084	54442
（十七）卫生和社会工作	Health and Social Work	44035	48836
（十八）文化、体育和娱乐业	Culture, Sports and Entertainment	31925	34717
（十九）公共管理、社会保障和社会组织	Public Administration, Social Security and Social Organizations	39964	42163
（二十）国际组织	International Organizations		

Average Wages of Urban Non-private Employees by Industry in Representative Years

(yuan)

2012	2013	2014	2015	2016	2017	2018	2019	2020
44533	**49350**	**54573**	**60557**	**67205**	**75262**	**83821**	**92359**	**99315**
31846	36658	42881	43426	48626	52020	72890	81373	90218
33489	40605	42116	46645	108827	118026	99400	106393	143464
38957	44321	49482	56686	61434	66067	73733	80703	90921
55409	59955	61252	65887	69092	77674	70021	75545	103286
35828	39507	48275	52783	60475	68025	73963	81621	93794
34382	37362	40915	46203	48210	55793	62362	68787	71766
48760	54147	59189	62816	63583	69469	88547	97746	86829
26637	29497	30914	33746	37507	41147	42970	46523	44332
63328	67495	100550	109448	137210	142407	150081	167240	174214
75652	97140	104433	106807	108569	114884	108643	114753	108142
37567	44832	48120	52423	56979	57970	65726	72780	79854
34291	42109	46828	52637	54395	53474	54940	62628	65332
68274	69951	69958	72731	79539	86199	103604	118277	129654
29938	38429	43033	45356	44062	48277	54127	59967	67155
25103	32066	32478	37019	35721	35979	56707	62097	52864
54581	59143	58451	63761	71635	86672	98158	103991	112030
56764	61602	59892	61623	74797	86521	99523	108493	114177
40833	50201	57239	61561	65974	70202	74588	81117	84900
47691	49893	47000	51681	59437	77660	84567	90877	97134

4-11 主要年份城镇非私营单位从业人数及工资总额

Number of Urban Non-Private Employees and Remuneration in Representative Years

年 份 year	单位从业人员（万人） Number of Employed Persons (10 000 persons)	从业人员工资总额（亿元） Remuneration of Employed Persons (100mil. yuan)	城镇非私营单位从业人员年平均工资（元） Annual Average Wage of Employees in Urban Non-private Units(yuan)	城镇国有单位从业人员年平均工资（元） Annual Average Wage of Employees in State-owned Units(yuan)	城镇集体单位从业人员年平均工资（元） Annual Average Wage of Employees in Urban Collective Units(yuan)	城镇非私营其它经济类型单位从业人员年平均工资（元） Average Wages of Urban Non-private Basic Facts on Employees in other Units(yuan)
1978	93.56	6.28	688	705	609	
1980	103.09	8.17	818	849	699	
1985	127.04	14.17	1148	1215	923	1409
1986	132.78	16.87	1311	1388	1048	1659
1987	135.48	19.13	1446	1544	1107	1583
1988	137.56	22.81	1702	1842	1216	2065
1989	139.86	25.64	1873	2010	1385	2188
1990	141.55	29.48	2133	2290	1545	2044
1991	142.86	26.88	2276	2435	1657	2966
1992	144.51	30.80	2545	2758	1709	3504
1993	146.03	43.25	2999	3274	1910	3551
1994	142.37	58.87	4172	4588	2337	5243
1995	141.17	67.23	4763	5168	2837	5863
1996	140.60	75.64	5407	5858	3216	6225
1997	138.89	80.83	5785	6204	3437	7487
1998	138.78	82.85	6900	7445	3964	6942
1999	115.88	90.13	7764	8238	4374	8217
2000	112.45	103.80	9179	9742	5178	9451
2001	113.93	123.12	10786	11570	5431	10781
2002	115.77	138.88	12138	12877	6230	12543
2003	116.68	155.95	13504	14217	6892	14215
2004	118.15	184.63	15473	15994	7428	17030
2005	123.66	215.67	17728	18420	7612	19066
2006	125.10	250.87	20475	21392	8494	21859
2007	129.40	319.23	25012	25696	9768	27400
2008	130.85	379.29	29749	30246	10834	33344
2009	135.64	450.48	34032	34611	11940	37307
2010	140.38	520.88	37870	38122	12505	40721
2011	154.33	658.73	41679	45217	23241	37643
2012	165.59	770.86	44533	47493	29988	41218
2013	198.42	1031.46	49350	52782	34591	47462
2014	199.41	1151.53	54573	54138	41006	55766
2015	198.46	1255.75	60557	60301	43291	61590
2016	199.19	1358.95	67205	66295	48098	68847
2017	202.29	1542.35	75262	76682	54755	74999
2018	196.23	1677.57	83821	87096	53048	82239
2019	211.31	1992.54	92359	101187	49998	88142
2020	213.57	2175.60	99315			

注：因1989年以前，西安市行政区划有几次调整，本表按1989年西安行政区划对1989年前的历史数据进行了修订。

4-12 城镇非私营单位从业人员工资总额（2020年）

Total Wages of Urban Non-Private Units Employees（2020）

单位：万元 （10 000yuan）

分组	Classify	单位从业人员工资总额 Total Wages of Employment	在岗职工工资总额 Total Wages of Employed Staff and Workers
总计	**Total**	**21755972**	**20810541**
（一）农、林、牧、渔业	Agriculture ,Forestry,Animal Husbandry and Fishery	20582	20390
（二）采矿业	Mining	641639	636728
（三）制造业	Manufacturing	3786890	3749073
（四）电力、热力、燃气及水生产和供应业	Production and Supply of Electricity, Gas,Heat and Water	849032	770103
（五）建筑业	Construction	2096072	1908256
（六）批发和零售业	Wholesale and Retail Trades	827508	805478
（七）交通运输、仓储和邮政业	Traffic,Transport,Storage and Post	2083803	2050195
（八）住宿和餐饮业	Hotels and Catering Services	216850	204860
（九）信息传输、软件和信息技术服务业	Information Transmission,Software and Information Technology Services	1948542	1941899
（十）金融业	Financial Intermediation	1460849	1197270
（十一）房地产业	Real Estate	707484	695499
（十二）租赁和商务服务业	Leasing and Business Services	461466	376569
（十三）科学研究和技术服务业	Scientific Research and Technical Services	1578122	1550336
（十四）水利、环境和公共设施管理业	Management of Water Conservancy, Environment and Public Facilities	174710	168252
（十五）居民服务、修理和其他服务业	Services to Households, Repairs and Other Services	30872	30448
（十六）教育	Education	2428318	2383374
（十七）卫生和社会工作	Health and Social Work	1146070	1109050
（十八）文化、体育和娱乐业	Culture, Sports and Entertainment	193698	187614
（十九）公共管理、社会保障和社会组织	Public Administration, Social Security and Social Organizations	1103465	1083583
（二十）国际组织	International Organizations		

4-12 续表 continued

单位：万元 (10 000 yuan)

分组	Classify	其他从业人员工资总额 Remuneration of Other Employed Persons	从业人员年平均工资（元） Average Wages of Employees (yuan)
总计	**Total**	**945431**	**99315**
（一）农、林、牧、渔业	Agriculture ,Forestry,Animal Husbandry and Fishery	192	90218
（二）采矿业	Mining	4911	143464
（三）制造业	Manufacturing	37817	90921
（四）电力、热力、燃气及水生产和供应业	Production and Supply of Electricity, Gas,Heat and Water	78929	103286
（五）建筑业	Construction	187816	93794
（六）批发和零售业	Wholesale and Retail Trades	22030	71766
（七）交通运输、仓储和邮政业	Traffic,Transport,Storage and Post	33608	86829
（八）住宿和餐饮业	Hotels and Catering Services	11990	44332
（九）信息传输、软件和信息技术服务业	Information Transmission,Software and Information Technology Services	6643	174214
（十）金融业	Financial Intermediation	263579	108142
（十一）房地产业	Real Estate	11985	79854
（十二）租赁和商务服务业	Leasing and Business Services	84897	65332
（十三）科学研究和技术服务业	Scientific Research and Technical Services	27786	129654
（十四）水利、环境和公共设施管理业	Management of Water Conservancy, Environment and Public Facilities	6458	67155
（十五）居民服务、修理和其他服务业	Services to Households, Repairs and Other Services	424	52864
（十六）教育	Education	44944	112030
（十七）卫生和社会工作	Health and Social Work	37020	114177
（十八）文化、体育和娱乐业	Culture, Sports and Entertainment	6084	84900
（十九）公共管理、社会保障和社会组织	Public Administration, Social Security and Social Organizations	19882	97134
（二十）国际组织	International Organizations		

4-13 主要年份城镇登记失业人数及失业率

Registered Unemployed Persons and Unemployment Rate in Urban Area in Representative Years

年份 year	城镇登记失业人员数（万人） Real Number of Registered Unemployed Persons (10 000 persons)	城镇登记失业率（%） Registered Unemployment in Urban Area (%)
2002		3.7
2003		4.5
2004	8.29	4.3
2005	8.45	4.3
2006	8.74	4.3
2007	8.77	4.3
2008	9.40	4.2
2009	10.02	4.3
2010	10.46	4.2
2011	10.37	3.9
2012	9.60	3.5
2013	10.13	3.4
2014	10.84	3.4
2015	10.74	3.4
2016	11.29	3.3
2017	11.51	3.3
2018	12.48	3.3
2019	12.52	3.3
2020	13.58	3.6

注：本表数据由西安市人力资源与社会保障局提供。

4-14 全市及各区县城镇化率

单位：%

区 县	Region	2011	2012	2013
全 市	**Total**	**69.90**	**72.13**	**73.61**
新城区	Xincheng	100.00	100.00	100.00
碑林区	Beilin	100.00	100.00	100.00
莲湖区	Lianhu	100.00	100.00	100.00
灞桥区	Baqiao	88.44	92.56	94.01
未央区	Weiyang	86.13	92.89	94.89
雁塔区	Yanta	100.00	100.00	100.00
阎良区	Yanliang	52.79	54.98	55.96
临潼区	Lintong	29.79	31.91	32.03
长安区	Chang'an	52.52	54.30	56.97
高陵区	Gaoling	58.33	59.47	62.33
鄠邑区	Huyi	36.03	37.30	38.57
蓝田县	Lantian	23.94	25.30	27.44
周至县	Zhouzhi	23.18	23.98	24.77
西咸新区	Xixian			

注：2011-2019年城镇化率为依据第七次人口普查修正后数据。2020年城镇化率根据第七次人口普查数据推算得出。

The Urbanization Rate by Region

(%)

2014	2015	2016	2017	2018	2019	2020
74.47	**75.68**	**76.65**	**77.12**	**77.85**	**78.78**	**79.20**
100.00	100.00	100.00	100.00	100.00	100.00	100.00
100.00	100.00	100.00	100.00	100.00	100.00	100.00
100.00	100.00	100.00	100.00	100.00	100.00	100.00
94.50	94.62	95.87	96.98	97.22	98.01	98.07
95.78	98.66	99.12	100.00	100.00	100.00	100.00
100.00	100.00	100.00	100.00	100.00	100.00	100.00
56.71	56.83	57.15	57.63	57.97	58.19	58.31
33.87	34.51	34.74	34.99	35.06	36.32	36.51
57.07	58.57	59.01	62.62	62.83	63.47	63.63
62.66	63.98	64.22	64.51	64.62	65.48	65.62
40.06	41.19	41.89	43.17	43.35	44.37	44.55
28.87	30.24	31.26	33.53	33.68	34.09	34.15
25.33	26.07	26.88	27.42	28.16	29.01	29.12
			70.84	71.62	72.98	73.07

主要统计指标解释

人口数 指一定时点、一定地区范围内的有生命的个人的总和。年度统计的年末人口数，指每年12月31日24时的人口数。

常住人口 指实际经常居住在某地区一定时间（半年以上，含半年）的人口。常住人口包括户口在本辖区人也在本辖区居住的人，户口在本辖区之外但在户口登记地半年以上的人，户口待定（无户口和口袋户口）的人，户口在本辖区但离开本辖区半年以下的人。

城镇人口和乡村人口 城镇人口是指居住在城镇范围内的全部常住人口；乡村人口是除上述人口以外的全部人口。

出生率（又称粗出生率） 指在一定时期内（通常为一年）平均每千人所出生的人数的比率，一般用千分率表示。其计算公式为：

出生率＝年出生人数／年平均人数×1000‰

式中：出生人数指活产婴儿，即胎儿脱离母体时（不管怀孕月数），有过呼吸或其他生命现象。年平均人数指年初、年底人口数的平均数，也可用年中人口数代替。

死亡率（又称粗死亡率） 指在一定时期内（通常为一年）一定地区的死亡人数与同期内平均人数（或期中人数）之比，一般用千分率表示。本资料中的死亡率指年死亡率，其计算公式为：

死亡率＝年死亡人数／年平均人数×1000‰

人口自然增长率 指在一定时期内（通常为一年）人口自然增加数（出生人数减死亡人数）与该时期内平均人数（或期中人数）之比，一般用千分率表示。计算公式为：

人口自然增长率＝（本年出生人数—本年死亡人数）／年平均人数×1000‰。

从业人员 指在16周岁及以上，从事一定社会劳动并取得劳动报酬或经营收入的人员。这一指标反映了一定时期内全部劳动力资源的实际利用情况，是研究我国基本国情国力的重要指标。

单位从业人员 指在各级国家机关、政党机关、社会团体及企业、事业单位中工作，取得工资或其他形式的劳动报酬的全部人员。包括在岗职工、再就业的离退休人员、民办教师以及在各单位中工作的外方人员和港澳台方人员、兼职人员、借用的外单位人员和第二职业者。不包括离开本单位仍保留劳动关系的职工。各单位的就业人员反映了各单位实际参加生产或工作的全部劳动力。

城镇私营和个体就业人员 城镇私营就业人员指在工商管理部门注册登记，其经营地址设在县城关镇（含城关镇）以上的私营企业就业人员；包括私营企业投资者和雇工。城镇个体就业人员指在工商管理部门注册登记，并持有城镇户口或在城镇长期居住，经批准从事个体工商经营的就业人员；包括个体经营者和在个体工商户劳动的家庭帮工和雇工。

国有单位 指资产归国家所有的经济组织。包括按《中华人民共和国企业法人登记管理条例》规定登记注册的非公司制的经济组织，以及中央、地方各级国家机关、事业单位和社会团体。

集体单位 指生产资料归集体所有，并按《中华人民共和国企业法人登记管理条例》规定登记注册的经济组织。

其他单位 包括股份合作单位、联营单位、有限责任公司、股份有限公司、港澳台商投资单位以及外商投资单位等其他登记注册类型单位。

在岗职工 指在本单位工作并由单位支付工资的人员，以及有工作岗位，但由于学习、病伤产假等原因暂未工作，仍由单位支付工资的人员。

职工工资总额 指各单位在一定时期内直接支付给本单位全部职工的劳动报酬总额。工资总额的计算原则应以直接支付给职工的全部劳动报酬为根据。各单位支付给职工的劳动报酬以及其他根据有关规定支付的工资，不论是计入成本的还是不计入成本的，不论是按国家规定列入计征奖金税项目的，还是未列入计征奖金税项目的，不论是以货币形式支付的还是以实物形式支付的，均包括在工资总额内。

职工平均工资 指企业、事业、机关单位的职工在一定时期内平均每人所得的货币工资额。它表明一定时期职工工资收入的高低程度，是反映职工工资水平的主要指标。计算公式为：

职工平均工资＝报告期实际支付的全部职工工资总额/报告期全部职工平均人数

城镇登记失业人员 指有非农业户口，在一定的劳动年龄内，有劳动能力，无业而要求就业，并在当地就业服务机构进行求职登记的人员。

城镇登记失业率 指城镇登记失业人数同城镇从业人数与城镇从业人数与城镇登记失业人数之和的比。计算公式为：

$$\text{城镇登记失业率}=\frac{\text{城镇登记失业人数}}{\text{（城镇单位就业人员-使用的农村劳动力-聘用的离退休人员-聘用的港澳台及外方人员）+不在岗职工+城镇私营业主+城镇个体户主+城镇私营企业及个体就业人员+城镇登记失业人数}}\times 100\%$$

Explanatory Notes on Main Statistical Indicators

The annual statistics on total population is taken at midnight, the 31st of December, not including residents in Taiwan province, Hong Kong SAR and Macao SAR and Chinese national residing abroad.

Permanent population refers to the population of actual habitual residence in a certain area six months or over six months. Permanent popul ation include the accounts in this area which are also living in this area, accounts outside this area but with more than half a year of household registration, accounts to be determined including people without accounts or pockets of accounts, and accounts in the area but leaving this area less than six months.

Urban Population and Rural Population Urban population refers to all people residing in cities and towns, while rural population refers to population other than urban population.

Birth Rate (or Crude Birth Rate) refers to the ratio of the number of births to the average population (or mid-period population) during a certain period of time (usually one year), expressed in ‰. Birth rate in the chapter refers to annual birth rate. The following formula is used:

$$\text{Birth Rate}=\frac{\text{Number of Births}}{\text{Annual Average Population}}\times 1000‰$$

Number of births in the formula refers to live births, i.e. when a baby has breathed or showed any vital phenomena regardless of the length of pregnancy.

Annual average population is the average of the number of population at the beginning of the year and that at the end of the year. Sometimes it is substituted by the mid-year population.

Death Rate (or Crude Death Rate) refers to the ratio of the number of deaths to the average population (or mid-period population) during a certain period of time (usually one year), expressed in ‰. Death rate in the chapter refers to annual death rate. The following formula is used:

$$\text{DeathRate}=\frac{\text{Number of Deaths}}{\text{Annual Average Population}}\times 1000‰$$

Natural Growth Rate of Population refers to the ratio of natural increase in population (number of births minus number of deaths) in a certain period of time (usually one year) to the average population (or mid-period population) of the same period, expressed in ‰. The following formula is applied:

Natural Growth Rate of Population =(Number of Births-Number of Deaths)/Annual Average Population× 1000‰

Employed Persons refer to the ones aged 16 and over who are engaged in gainful employment and thus receive remuneration payment or earn business income. This indicator reflects the actual utilization of total labour force during a certain period of time and is often used for the research on China's economic situation and national power.

Persons Employed in Various Units refer to all the persons working in government agencies of various levels, political and party organizations, social organizations, enterprises and institutions, and receiving wages or other forms of payment. They include fully-employed staff and workers, re-employed retirees, teachers in the schools run by the local people, foreigners and Chinese compatriots from Hong Kong, Macao, and Taiwan working in various units, part-time employees, employees of other units working temporarily at current posts, and employees holding the second job, but do not include persons who have left their working units while keeping their labour contract (employment relation) unchanged. This indicator reflects the total number of laborers actually engaged in production or other operations in various units.

Persons Employed in Private Enterprises and Self- Employed Individuals in Urban Areas Persons employed in private enterprises refer to the persons employed in the private enterprises which have been registered at the departments of industrial and commercial administration for which the business operation are situated at a county town (i.e. a town where the county government is located), or at urban areas with administrative hierarchy higher than a county town. The self-employed individuals in urban areas refer to persons who hold the certificates of residence in urban areas or have resided in the urban areas for a long time and have been registered at the departments of industrial and commercial administration and approved to be engaged in individual industrial or commercial business, including self-employed persons as well as helpers and hired labourers who work in individual households.

State-owned Units refer to economic units whose assets are owned by the state, including non-corporation units registered according to Regulation of the People's Republic of China on the Registration of Enterprises and

Corporations, state organs, institutions and social organizations at the central-level and local levels.

Collective–owned Units refer to economic units registered according to Regulation of the People's Republic of China on the Registration of Enterprises and Corporations where the means of production are collectively owned.

Units of Other Types of Ownership refer to units registered with other types of ownership, including cooperative units, joint ownership units, limited liability corporations, share holding corporations, units funded by entrepreneurs from Hong Kong, Macao, and Taiwan, and foreign- funded units.

Employed Staff and Workers refer to persons who work in, and receive wages from their working units, including persons who have their work posts but are temporarily absent from work for reasons of study or on sick, injury or maternal leave and still receive wages from their working units.

Total Wage Bill refers to the total remuneration payment to employed persons in various units during a certain period of time. The calculation of total wage bill is based on the total remuneration payment to employed persons . Therefore, all the wages and salaries and other payments to employed persons are included in the total wage bill regardless of sources, reckoning the cost of production or not, category, listing as items of premium taxation or not, and forms, paying in cash or in kind.

Average Wage refers to the average wage in money terms per person during a certain period of time for employed persons in enterprises, institutions, and government agencies, which reflects the general level of wage income during a certain period of time and is calculated as follows:

$$\text{Average Wage} = \frac{\text{Total Wage Bill of Employed Persons at Reference Time}}{\text{Average Number of Persons Employed at Reference Time}}$$

Registered Unemployed Persons in Urban Areas refer to the persons with non-agricultural household registration at certain working ages (16 years old to retirement age), who are capable of working, unemployed and willing to work, and have been registered at the local employment service agencies to apply for a job.

Registered Unemployment Rate in Urban Areas refers to the ratio of the number of the registered unemployed persons to the sum of the number of persons employed in various units (minus the employed rural labour force, re-employed retirees, and Hong Kong, Macao, Taiwan or foreign employees), laid-off staff and workers in urban units, owners of private enterprises in urban areas, owners of self-employed individuals in urban areas, employees of private enterprises in urban areas, employee of self-employed individuals in urban areas, and the registered unemployed persons in urban areas. The formula is as follows:

$$\text{Registered Unemployment rate in urban areas} = \frac{\text{number of registered urban unemployed persons}}{\begin{array}{c}\text{number of persons employed in urban units} - \text{employed rural labour force} - \\ \text{re-employed retirees} - \text{Hong Kong, Macao, Taiwan or foreign employees} \\ + \text{laid-off staff and workers} + \text{owners of urban private Enterprises} + \\ \text{owners of urban self-employed Individuals} + \text{employees of urban private Enterprises} \\ + \text{employees of urban self-employed Individuals} + \text{registered unemployed persons in urban areas}\end{array}} \times 100\%$$

5 固定资产投资

INVESTMENT IN FIXED ASSETS

资料整理：王　峰　张　驰
Data management：Wang Feng Zhang Chi
数据审核：席锋旭
Data audit：Xi Fengxu

第五部分　固定资产投资

一、简要说明

1.本章资料反映西安固定资产投资的基本情况、固定资产投资的结构和比例关系、固定资产投资的资金来源及固定资产投资的效果等。主要包括全社会固定资产投资、项目投资、房地产开发投资和农户投资以及分区县、开发区投资情况等。

2.固定资产投资统计的范围包括：城乡建设项目投资、房地产开发投资及农户投资。

3.固定资产投资统计的资料来源主要为国家统计局的全面统计报表。除农户固定资产投资统计采用抽样调查方法外，其他均为全面统计报表。

4.统计口径的变化。

自1997年起，除房地产开发投资、非农户投资、农户投资及城镇和工矿区私人建房投资外，固定资产投资的统计起点由5万元提高到50万元。

自2006年起，非农户固定资产投资统计改为按项目统计，调查方法由抽样调查改为全面统计报表，起点提高到50万元。城镇和工矿区私人建房投资改为按项目统计，起点为50万元。

自2011年起，除房地产开发投资、农户投资外，固定资产投资项目统计起点，由计划总投资50万元提高到500万元；统计范围从城镇扩大到农村企事业组织，并将这一统计范围定义为"固定资产投资（不含农户）"。

5.由于国家统计局对《2020年固定资产投资统计报表制度》进行了修订，取消了"房屋施工面积""房屋竣工面积""房屋竣工价值"等相关指标，本年鉴所公布的2020年度"房屋施工面积""房屋竣工面积""房屋竣工价值"等相关指标数据，均为房地产开发口径。以前年度的《全市按国民经济行业分房屋建筑面积增长速度》（5-14表）也随之取消。

二、主要指标

指标		
全社会固定资产投资	比上年增长	12.3%
#国有经济单位	比上年增长	14.5%
集体经济单位	比上年下降	51.1%
#固定资产投资	比上年增长	12.8%
#房地产开发投资	比上年增长	6.5%
商品房销售面积	比上年下降	3.0%
全市新增固定资产	比上年增长	25.0%
全市竣工住宅面积	比上年下降	18.1%

5 INVESTMENT IN FIXED ASSETS

Ⅰ.Brief Introduction

1.This chapter reflects the scale and speed of investment in fixed assets in Xi'an, the structure and proportional relationship of investment in fixed assets, the source of funds for investment in fixed assets and the effects of them during a certain period of time by describing the quantity of fixed asset activities built and purchased in the whole society during a certain period of time, mainly including total investment in fixed assets in the whole province, project investment, real estate development, farmer investment by Region and Development Zone.

2.Statistics on the investment in fixed assets cover investments in capital construction projects in urban and rural areas, investments in real estate development and rural household investment.

3.The data sources for the statistics of investment in fixed assets mainly come from complete statistical report forms, Investment in fixed assets by farm households are calculated with sample survey, and the others come from complete statistical report forms.

4.Changes in Statistical Scope

Since 1997, the cut-off point of projects covered by statistics of investment in fixed assets are raised from an investment of 50,000 yuan to 500,000 yuan, except investment in real estate development, non-farm household investment, farm household investment and private investment in housing construction in urban areas and industrial and mining areas.

Since 2006, statistics on investments in fixed assets of rural non-farm households are changed to project-based. Survey method is changed from sample survey to the system of reporting form with complete enumeration. The cut-off point has been raised to 500,00 yuan. Statistics on private investment in housing construction in urban areas and industrial and mining areas have become project-based. The cut-off point has been raised to 500,000 yuan.

Since 2011, except investment in real estate development and rural household investment, the cut-off point of statistics on investments in fixed assets are raised, amount of intended investment are raised from 500,000 yuan to 5000,000. The scope of investment statistics expends from urban to rural enterprises, and this scope of statistics is defined "investments in fixed assets(non-farm)".

5. As the National Bureau of Statistics revised the Statistical Report System of Fixed Assets Investment in 2020, and cancelled the relevant indicators such as "housing construction area", "housing completion area" and "housing completion value", the relevant indicators such as "housing construction area", "housing completion area" and "housing completion value" published in this yearbook in 2020 are all real estate development standards. In the previous year, "the growth rate of housing construction area in the whole city by national economic industry" (Table 5-14) was also cancelled.

Ⅱ.Major Indicators

	Increase over Preceding Year
Total Investment In Fixed Assets	12.3%
State-owned Enterprises	14.5%
Collective-owned Enterprises	-51.1%
Project Investment	12.8%
Real Estate Development	6.5%
Floor Space of Commercialized Buildings Sold	-3.0%
Investment Newly Increased Fixed Assets	25.0%
Total Floor Space of Building Completed	-18.1%

5-1 主要年份按类别分全社会固定资产投资增长速度

The Growth Rate of Total Investment in Fixed Assets in the Whole Country by Classifications in Representative Years

单位：% (%)

年 份 Year	全社会固定资产投资 Total Investment in Fixed Assets in the Whole Country	固定资产投资 Investment in Fixed Assets	房地产开发投资 Real Estate Investment	农户投资 Farmer Investment
1980	50.0	48.8		53.3
1981	-8.7	1.8		-37.2
1982	69.8	75.9		42.7
1983	10.2	14.3		-12.2
1984	23.2	16.6		70.5
1985	43.1	35.1		81.8
1986	20.1	28.4		-9.8
1987	22.1	24.9		8.0
1988	7.7	5.5		20.8
1989	-2.9	-2.4		-5.5
1990	-6.7	-3.1		-26.1
1991	16.6	10.6	120.9	58.4
1992	25.1	28.6	65.2	8.1
1993	95.1	102.9	122.6	49.4
1994	14.0	10.2	62.7	43.9
1995	20.9	20.5	80.1	23.3
1996	10.6	9.6	13.9	16.6
1997	2.2	-1.9	0.1	24.9
1998	32.4	45.7	54.8	-25.8
1999	27.5	24.5	15.9	53.0
2000	17.8	17.6	17.0	19.0
2001	23.8	26.6	30.0	4.8
2002	17.5	19.6	17.7	0.5
2003	41.4	45.1	57.3	4.7
2004	35.3	37.3	35.9	7.1
2005	29.1	26.8	32.7	69.6
2006	27.7	25.2	26.9	61.3
2007	34.6	37.9	35.5	
2008	32.8	33.3	39.5	26.4
2009	31.1	32.5	28.9	10.7
2010	30.0	31.1	21.0	9.9
2011	30.0	30.0	18.3	-5.0
2012	26.8	29.9	28.6	-1.7
2013	21.0	21.3	24.5	12.1
2014	15.0	15.2	10.4	45.5
2015	-12.5	-12.7	4.0	-64.3
2016	2.0	3.4	6.8	-0.5
2017	12.9	13.0	15.0	0.0
2018	8.4	8.5	7.9	2.1
2019	1.1	1.1	-2.1	-2.0
2020	12.3	12.8	6.5	-25.0

注：2015年国家取消了城乡投资分组，表中“农户投资”2014年以前为原先的农村投资。
2016年全社会固定资产投资不含跨省项目，固定资产投资不含跨省和跨市项目。

5-2 主要年份按经济类型分全社会固定资产投资增长速度

The Growth Rate of Total Investment in Fixed Assets in the Whole Country by Economic Type in Representative Years

单位：% (%)

年 份 Year	合计 Total	国有经济 State-owned	集体经济 Collective-owned	个体经济 Self-employed Individual	其他经济 Others
1985	43.1	34.8	72.0	79.0	
1986	20.1	29.3	-28.7	0.3	
1987	22.1	22.9	54.6	7.7	
1988	7.7	6.9	24.0	5.6	
1989	-2.9	-2.1	-21.5	1.7	
1990	-6.7	-4.3	-1.4	-24.3	
1991	16.6	10.0	56.9	48.9	
1992	25.1	31.2	-35.8	22.3	
1993	95.1	86.2	109.0	31.3	
1994	14.0	8.5	36.6	54.0	13.9
1995	20.9	6.8	136.2	10.3	102.6
1996	10.6	16.8	-10.7	12.3	-7.0
1997	2.2	-4.0	17.0	20.9	13.1
1998	32.4	46.0	-22.7	-29.9	64.7
1999	27.5	20.7	72.6	53.2	33.2
2000	17.8	16.9	7.6	50.4	8.9
2001	23.8	10.0	0.1	58.1	74.7
2002	17.5	13.9	-6.6	15.8	35.3
2003	41.4	32.4	63.0	64.3	47.4
2004	35.3	24.3	79.4	-33.3	94.5
2005	29.1	13.5	47.9	61.5	41.4
2006	27.7	7.3	86.9	35.8	38.5
2007	34.6	18.9	87.1	70.6	27.0
2008	32.8	45.7	19.2	-72.5	60.8
2009	31.1	34.3	17.4	94.1	29.0
2010	30.0	44.6	12.6	-44.1	28.9
2011	30.0	24.8	10.4	36.4	18.9
2012	26.8	37.9	-24.6	10.8	27.4
2013	21.0	6.6	12.9	2.1	32.7
2014	15.0	8.2	-7.5	-1.4	21.0
2015	-12.5	-4.7	-22.2	-3.4	-16.2
2016	2.0	15.9	-17.5	1.5	-15.3
2017	12.9	19.4	-9.9	15.0	21.2
2018	8.4	-2.9	-54.5		8.6
2019	1.1	5.1	44.2		-3.3
2020	12.3	14.5	-51.1		11.1

注：集体经济：包括城镇集体和农村集体。
个体经济：包括私营个体投资及城镇工矿区私人建房和农村私人建房。
2017年后数据为含西咸数据

5-3 主要年份按产业分全市固定资产投资增长速度

The Growth Rate of Total Investment in Fixed Assets in the Whole City by Three Strata of Industry in Representative Years

单位：% (%)

年 份 Year	全市固定资产投资 Total Investment in Fixed Assets in The Whole City	第一产业 Primary Industry	第二产业 Secondary Industry	工业 Industry	第三产业 Tertisry Industry
1980	48.8	3.2	68.5	65.0	36.1
1981	1.8	83.3	0.5	-8.0	0.9
1982	75.9	-63.6	93.8	98.4	66.4
1983	14.3	175.0	22.1	21.5	4.6
1984	16.6	72.7	-8.2	-9.5	45.2
1985	35.1	-5.3	58.3	61.7	18.5
1986	28.4	-11.1	24.4	29.8	33.5
1987	24.9	18.8	31.5	34.5	18.6
1988	5.5	-21.1	1.2	-0.5	10.6
1989	-2.4	-13.3	-0.1	2.7	-4.5
1990	-3.1	92.3	-7.6	-7.9	0.3
1991	10.6	8.0	13.1	12.8	8.3
1992	28.6	-63.0	25.0	23.3	34.0
1993	102.9	-30.0	57.1	52.3	145.4
1994	10.2	-57.1	10.4	15.2	10.3
1995	20.5	366.7	6.5	7.2	28.4
1996	9.6	-7.1	-9.9	-12.5	19.0
1997	-1.9	84.6	-8.9	-10.6	0.6
1998	45.7	100.0	49.4	37.9	44.3
1999	24.5	95.8	12.9	21.9	28.1
2000	17.6	-19.1	43.5	49.4	10.0
2001	26.6	13.2	10.7	12.7	32.9
2002	19.6	398.8	17.4	11.7	18.6
2003	45.1	-22.1	12.0	14.6	57.1
2004	37.3	1.2	17.3	22.0	42.3
2005	26.8	55.6	47.7	46.8	22.7
2006	25.2	90.9	48.0	47.0	19.4
2007	37.9	1.6	39.4	38.8	38.0
2008	33.3	132.8	24.3	24.3	34.9
2009	32.5	3.0	24.0	24.3	35.3
2010	31.1	62.8	21.3	12.6	33.1
2011	30.0	22.2	21.3	18.5	31.8
2012	29.9	130.5	41.5	48.1	26.2
2013	21.3	-26.4	46.3	50.2	17.8
2014	15.2	2.7	28.3	38.8	12.2
2015	-12.7	32.8	-8.2	-5.8	-14.7
2016	3.4	-10.1	-12.3	-12.0	8.3
2017	13.0	2.3	-10.2	-10.6	18.6
2018	8.5	20.8	28.6	28.7	5.4
2019	1.1	-21.0	1.5	2.0	1.3
2020	12.8	-43.6	15.5	15.2	12.8

5-4 全市按资金来源及建设性质分全市固定资产投资增长速度（2020年）

The Growth Rate of Total Investment in Fixed Assets in the Whole City by Sources of Funds and Type of Construction（2020）

单位：%　　　　　　　　　　　　　　　　　　　　　　（%）

指　标	Item	增长速度 Growth
一、投资总额	**Total Investment**	**12.8**
（一）按资金来源分	Grouped by Funds Source	
1. 国家预算内投资	State Budgetary Funds	54.2
2. 国内贷款	Domestic Loans	19.4
3. 债券	Bonds	1295.3
4. 利用外资	Utilization of Foreign Funds	32.9
5. 自筹资金	Self-raising Funds	9.9
6. 其他资金	Others	7.5
（二）按构成分	Grouped by Composition of Funds	
1. 建筑安装工程	Construction and Installation Projects	7.4
2. 设备、工器具购置	Purchasing of Equipment and Instruments	15.9
3. 其它费用	Others	34.7
（三）按建设性质分	Grouped by Type of Construction	
#新建	New Construction	12.6
扩建	Expansion	187.8
改建和技术改造	Reconstruction and Technical Transformation	42.6
二、房屋施工面积	**Floor Space Under Construction**	**-3.2**

注：从2020年起，涉及到"房屋施工面积""房屋竣工面积""房屋竣工价值"等相关指标为房地产开发统计口径。

5-5 主要年份全市新增固定资产投资及房屋竣工面积增长速度

The Growth Rate of Newly Added Fixed Assets and Floor Spaces Completed of Municipal Units in Representative Years

单位：% (%)

年 份 Year	新增固定资产 Newly Increased Fixed Assets	房屋竣工面积 Floor Space of Buildings Completed	住宅 Residential Buildings
1980	44.2	38.3	41.7
1985	1.1	-4.6	-5.9
1986	55.5	22.7	20.8
1987	24.8	-11.5	-23.5
1988	0.6	-12.3	-14.1
1989	-1.4	-15.8	-14.3
1990	22.4	18.7	26.5
1991	-12.0	-12.5	-13.7
1992	25.0	10.5	17.6
1993	86.7	26.0	28.6
1994	32.8	9.7	27.3
1995	13.0	26.4	37.0
1996	-4.1	-7.1	-1.3
1997	4.7	12.7	14.8
1998	27.6	2.2	-3.8
1999	48.2	77.9	99.8
2000	26.3	5.0	-1.1
2001	11.7	-3.1	-7.8
2002	18.6	11.7	-3.2
2003	40.4	18.7	18.9
2005	-6.3	-15.4	-13.8
2004	56.4	45.7	20.1
2006	10.6	6.0	-2.6
2007	47.5	39.4	59.4
2008	8.6	-33.4	-25.4
2009	39.8	37.3	18.6
2010	17.7	-49.3	-36.7
2011	86.7	58.9	65.3
2012	36.1	32.0	38.0
2013	6.2	-31.2	-29.4
2014	32.1	66.0	74.1
2015	-17.2	-40.3	-43.5
2016	-4.7	69.9	61.2
2017	24.6	5.5	0.6
2018	-12.2	-44.5	-53.0
2019	26.2	5.6	22.4
2020	25.0	-21.1	-18.1

5-6 全市固定资产投资增长速度（2020年）

The Growth Rate of Total Investment in Fixed Assets in the Whole City（2020）

单位：%

指 标	Item	固定资产投资 Investment in Fixed Assets	房地产开发投资 Real Estate Investment
一、本年完成投资	**Investment Completed This Year**	**12.8**	**6.5**
#住宅	Residential Buildings	7.5	-1.3
（一）按登记注册类型分	**Grouped by Registion Status**		
内资	Domestic Funded Enterprises	11.7	4.7
国有	State-owned Enterprises	-16.0	-71.3
集体	Collective-owned Enterprises	-28.9	
股份合作	Cooperative Enterprises	138.0	
联营	Joint Ownership Enterprises		
国有联营	State Joint Ownership Enterprises		
集体联营	Collective Joint Ownership Enterprises		
国有与集体联营	Joint State-collective Ownership Enterprises		
其他联营	Other Joint Ownership Enterprises		
有限责任公司	Limited Liability Corporations	15.6	4.0
国有独资公司	State-funded Corporations	51.4	13.6
其他有限责任公司	Other Limited Liability Corporations	5.3	3.2
股份有限公司	Stock Limited Corporation	-28.0	-63.2
私营	Private Enterprises	44.9	25.5
私营独资	Private -funded Enterprises	-63.9	280.6
私营合伙	Private Limited Liability Corporations	-89.1	
私营有限责任公司	Private Limited Liability Corporations	52.3	25.6
私营股份有限公司	Private Share Holding Corporations	9.3	-40.9
其他	Others	-18.7	
港澳台商投资	Enterprises Funded by Hong Kong, Macao and Taiwan	-24.5	5.3
与港澳台合资经营	Joint-venture Enterprises	-51.5	11.7
与港澳台合作经营	Cooperative Enterprises	-47.9	-47.9
港澳台独资	Wholly Funded from Hong Kong,Macao and Taiwan	42.7	27.2

5-6 续表 continued

(%)

指 标	Item	固定资产投资 Investment in Fixed Assets	房地产开发投资 Real Estate Investment
港澳台投资股份有限公司	Share-holding Corporations Ltd.	-75.1	-64.5
其他港澳台投资	Investment From Hongkong,Macao,Taiwan		
外商投资	Foreign Owned Enterprises	45.9	1078.3
中外合资经营	Joint-venture Enterprises	92.0	370.4
中外合作经营	Cooperation Enterprises		
外资企业	Foreign Funded Enterprises	43.1	2275.9
外商投资股份有限公司	Share-holding Corporations Ltd. With Foreign Funds	-61.8	-50.6
其他外商投资	Foreign Investment		
（二）按建设性质分	**Grouped by Type of Construction**		
#新建	New Construction	12.6	
扩建	Expansion	187.8	
改建和技术改造	Reconstruction	42.6	
（三）按构成分	**Grouped by Composition**		
1. 建筑安装工程	Construction and Installation Projects	7.4	0.5
2. 设备、工器具购置	Purchasing of Equipment and Instruments	15.9	-22.7
3. 其他费用	Others	34.7	23.3
二、本年新增固定资产	**Newly Increase in Fixed Assets This Year**	**25.0**	**-21.7**
三、房屋面积	**Floor Space**		
房屋施工面积	Floor Space of Buildings Under Construction	-3.2	-3.2
#住宅	Residential Buildings	-5.2	-5.2
房屋竣工面积	Floor Space of Buildings Completed	-21.1	-21.1
#住宅	Residential Buildings	-18.1	-18.1
四、本年房屋竣工价值	**Value of the Building Completed This Year**	**-15.1**	**-15.1**
#住宅	Residential Buildings	6.2	6.2

5-7 按国民经济行业分全市固定资产投资增长速度（2020年）

The Growth Rate of Investment in Fixed Assets in the Whole Country by Industry（2020）

单位：%　　(%)

行　业	Sector	固定资产投资 Investment in Fixed Assets	工业企业技术改造 Technological Transformation of Industrial Enterprises
本年完成固定资产投资	**Grouped by Sector**	**12.8**	**69.0**
（一）农、林、牧、渔业	Agriculture,Forestry,Animal Husbandry and Fishery	-40.7	
（二）采矿业	Mining	-10.8	-20.2
（三）制造业	Manufacturing	13.5	76.1
农副食品加工业	Processing of Food from Agricultural Products	82.8	2145.1
食品制造业	Manufacture of Foods	-32.1	-40.7
酒、饮料和精制茶制造业	Wine, Soft Drinks and Refined Tea Industry	-55.5	49.6
烟草制品业	Tobacco Processing		
纺织业	Textile Industry	2295.4	132.1
纺织服装、服饰业	Textile, Apparel Industry		
皮革、毛皮、羽毛及其制品和制鞋业	Leather, Fur, Feather (eiderdown) and Their Products Industry	584.5	-69.4
木材加工和木、竹、藤、棕、草制品业	Timber Processing,Bamboo,Cane, Palm Fiber and Straw Products	-97.9	
家具制造业	Furniture Manufacturing	-58.9	
造纸及纸制品业	Papermaking and Paper products	-32.7	-26.6
印刷和记录媒介复制业	Printing,Record Medium Reproduction	18.8	-56.5
文教、工美、体育和娱乐用品制造业	Culture, Education, Craft Art, Sports and Entertainment Goods Manufacturing Industry	-93.2	
石油、煤炭及其他燃料加工业	Oil, Coal and Other Fuel Processing Industries	-91.0	
化学原料和化学制品制造业	Raw Chemical Materials and Chemical Products	-40.7	-66.4
医药制造业	Medical and Pharmaceutical Products	21.0	-1.1
化学纤维制造业	Chemical Fiber	6.2	
橡胶和塑料制品业	Rubber and Plastic Products Industry	-62.3	-59.3
非金属矿物制品业	Nonmetal Mineral Products	4.3	46.7
黑色金属冶炼和压延加工业	Smelting and Pressing of Ferrous Metals	-72.3	-46.8
有色金属冶炼和压延加工业	Smelting and Pressing of Nonferrou Metals	17.4	44.5
金属制品业	Metal Products	64.3	61.2

5-7 续表 continued

单位：%　　　　　　　　　　　　　　　　　　　　　　　　　　　　　　　　　　（%）

行　业	Sector	固定资产投资 Investment in Fixed Assets	工业企业技术改造 Technological Transformation of Industrial Enterprises
通用设备制造业	General Equipment Manufacturing Industry	43.1	33.3
专用设备制造业	Special Purpose Equipment	12.2	122.1
汽车制造业	Automotive Manufacturing	-7.5	-48.2
铁路、船舶、航空航天和其他运输设备制造业	Railroad, Marine, Aerospace and other Transportation Equipment Manufacturing	8.0	13.2
电气机械和器材制造业	Electric Equipment and Machinery	14.1	-33.8
计算机、通信和其他电子设备制造业	Communication Equipment, Computer and Other Electronic Equipment Manufacturing Industry	24.4	357.9
仪器仪表制造业	Instrument Manufacturing Industry	-16.0	-67.5
其他制造业	Other Manufacturing	656.3	81.5
废弃资源综合利用业	Comprehensive Utilization of waste Resources	0.2	-69.8
金属制品、机械和设备修理业	Metal Products, Machinery and Equipment Repair Industry	-69.9	
（四）电力、热力、燃气及水生产和供应业	Production & Supply of Electricity，Heat，Gas & Water	27.3	60.8
（五）建筑业	Construction	-56.3	
（六）批发和零售业	Wholesale and Retail Trades	-60.5	
（七）交通运输、仓储和邮政业	Transport, Storage and Post	9.9	
（八）住宿和餐饮业	Hotels and Catering Services	22.8	
（九）信息传输、软件和信息技术服务业	Information Transmission,Computer Service and Software	29.6	
（十）金融业	Financial Intermediation	145.1	
（十一）房地产业	Real Estate	12.5	
（十二） 租赁和商务服务业	Leasing and Business Services	19.7	
（十三）科学研究和技术服务业	Scientific Research,Technical Service and Geologic Prospecting	31.7	
（十四）水利、环境和公共设施管理业	Management of Water Conservancy, Environment and Public Facilities	0.7	
（十五）居民服务、修理和其他服务业	Services to Households, Repairs and Other Services	-85.6	
（十六）教育	Education	135.2	
（十七）卫生和社会工作	Health and Social Work	30.2	
（十八）文化、体育和娱乐业	Culture, Sports and Entertainment	39.4	
（十九）公共管理、社会保障和社会组织	Public Administration, Social Security and Social Organizations	-34.4	
（二十）国际组织	International Organizations		

5-8 按国民经济行业分民间投资增长速度（2020年）

The Growth Rate of Private Investment of Municipal Units by Industry（2020）

单位：%　　　　　　　　　　　　　　　　　　　　　　　　（%）

行　业	Sector	民间投资 Private Investment	占民间投资比重 Rate
民间投资总计	**Total**	**7.7**	**100.0**
（一）农、林、牧、渔业	Agriculture, Forestry, Animal Husbandry and Fishery	-48.5	0.7
（二）采矿业	Mining	-0.7	
（三）制造业	Manufacturing	-2.5	11.5
（四）电力、热力、燃气及水生产和供应业	Production & Supply of Electricity,Heat, Gas & Water	65.3	1.4
（五）建筑业	Construction		
（六）批发和零售业	Wholesale and Retail Trades	-60.0	0.4
（七）交通运输、仓储和邮政业	Transportation, Storage and Post	-51.4	0.8
（八）住宿和餐饮业	Hotels and Catering Services	-25.6	1.0
（九）信息传输、软件和信息技术服务业	Information Transmission, Computer Service and Software	20.6	0.7
（十）金融业	Financial Intermediation		
（十一）房地产业	Real Estate	9.4	68.0
（十二）租赁和商务服务业	Leasing and Business Services	-11.7	2.4
（十三）科学研究和技术服务业	Scientific Research and Technical Service	25.6	0.7
（十四）水利、环境和公共设施管理业	Management of Water Conservancy, Environment and Public Facilities	89.8	7.9
（十五）居民服务、修理和其他服务业	Services to Households, Repairs and Other Services	-99.0	
（十六）教育	Education	27.8	1.3
（十七）卫生和社会工作	Health and Social Work	7.9	1.7
（十八）文化、体育和娱乐业	Culture, Sports and Entertainment	-24.2	1.3
（十九）公共管理、社会保障和社会组织	Public Administration, Social Security and Social Organizations	1183.5	0.1
（二十）国际组织	International Organizations		

5-9 按国民经济行业分基础设施投资增长速度（2020年）

The Growth Rate of Investment for Basic Infrastructure of Municipal Units by Industry（2020）

单位：%　　　　(%)

指　标	Item	比去年同期增长± Increase Over the Same Period Last Year	比重 Rate
基础设施投资总计	**Total Investment of Infrastructure**	**5.5**	**100.0**
一、电力、热力、燃气及水生产和供应业	**Production and Supply of Electricity, Heat, Gas and Water**	**27.3**	**8.6**
电力、热力的生产和供应业	The Production and Supply of Electricity and Heat	65.1	5.3
燃气的生产和供应业	The Production and Supply of Gas	-55.8	0.3
水的生产和供应业	The Production and Supply of Water	4.1	3.0
二、交通运输和邮政业	**Traffic, Transport and Post**	**12.3**	**18.0**
铁路运输业	Railway Transport Industry	-80.2	0.4
道路运输业	The Road Transport Industry	15.7	14.6
水上运输业	Water Transportation		
航空运输业	The Air Transport Industry	131.4	2.7
管道运输业	Pipeline Transportation	-93.0	
多式联运和运输代理服务业	Multimodal Transport and Transport Agency Services	-33.1	0.2
装卸搬运	Handling Service	557.8	
邮政业	The Postal Service	64.6	0.1
三、信息传输业	**Information Transmission**	**37.4**	**3.3**
电信、广播电视和卫星传输服务	Telecommunications, Radio and Television and Satellite Transmission Services	42.9	2.9
互联网和相关服务	Internet and Related Services	8.6	0.4
四、水利、环境和公共设施管理业	**Management of Water Conservancy, Environment and Public Facilities**	**0.7**	**70.1**
水利管理业	Water Resources Management Industry	179.2	2.9
生态保护和环境治理业	Ecological Protection and Environmental Control Industries	366.6	2.1
公共设施管理业	Public Facilities Management Industry	-4.5	65.1

5-10 全市固定资产投资资金来源增长速度（2020年）

The Growth Rate of Source of Funds for Total Fixed Assets Investment of Whole City（2020）

单位：%　　　　(%)

指　标	Item	固定资产投资 Investment in Fixed Assets	房地产开发 Real Estate
一、本年资金来源合计	**Total of Sources of Funds This Year**	**2.4**	**1.3**
1. 上年末结余资金	Balance of Last Year	-1.2	3.2
2. 本年实际到位资金	Fully Funded Capital this Year	2.9	0.8
(1) 国家预算资金	State Budgetary Funds	40.7	
(2) 国内贷款	Domestic Loans	9.0	-17.7
(3) 债券	Bonds	1173.1	
(4) 利用外资	Utilization of Foreign Funds	21.3	
(5) 自筹资金	Self-raising Funds	0.3	8.4
(6) 其他资金来源	Others	-1.9	-2.8
二、各项应付款合计	**Total Sums of Money to be Paid This Year**	**54.8**	**34.0**

5-11 全市按行业分施工项目（2020年）

Construction Project Grouped by Industry in the Whole City（2020）

行　业	Sector	本年新增固定资产增长速度（%）The Growth Rate of Newly Increased Fixed Assets This Year（%）	施工项目个数（个）Number of Constructing Projects(unit)
总计	**Total**	**25.0**	**3571**
（一）农、林、牧、渔业	Agriculture, Forestry, Animal Husbandry and Fishery	-90.0	77
（二）采矿业	Mining	-18.4	5
（三）制造业	Manufacturing	255.6	904
（四）电力、热力、燃气及水生产和供应业	Production & Supply of Electricity，Heat，Gas & Water	12.0	226
（五）建筑业	Construction		2
（六）批发和零售业	Wholesale and Retail Trades	12.1	37
（七）交通运输、仓储和邮政业	Transportation, Storage and Post	-19.3	139
（八）住宿和餐饮业	Hotels and Catering Services	97.7	47
（九）信息传输、软件和信息技术服务业	Information Transmission, Computer Service and Software	28.5	83
（十）金融业	Financial Intermediation		3
（十一）房地产业	Real Estate	-1.9	156
（十二）租赁和商务服务业	Leasing and Business Services	-36.7	86
（十三）科学研究和技术服务业	Scientific Research and Technical Service	13.1	85
（十四）水利、环境和公共设施管理业	Management of Water Conservancy, Environment and Public Facilities	-16.4	1303
（十五）居民服务、修理和其他服务业	Services to Households, Repairs and Other Services	-81.2	10
（十六）教育	Education	399.0	271
（十七）卫生和社会工作	Health and Social Work	-48.5	61
（十八）文化、体育和娱乐业	Culture, Sports and Entertainment	17.9	50
（十九）公共管理、社会保障和社会组织	Public Administration, Social Security and Social Organizations	-0.7	26
（二十）国际组织	International Organizations		

5-11 续表 continued

行 业	Sector	本年新开工 Newly Started This Year	本年投产项目个数（个） Projects put into Use (unit)
总计	**Total**	**1816**	**1501**
（一）农、林、牧、渔业	Agriculture, Forestry, Animal Husbandry and Fishery	63	33
（二）采矿业	Mining	2	5
（三）制造业	Manufacturing	489	335
（四）电力、热力、燃气及水生产和供应业	Production & Supply of Electricity，Heat，Gas & Water	101	87
（五）建筑业	Construction	2	
（六）批发和零售业	Wholesale and Retail Trades	12	15
（七）交通运输、仓储和邮政业	Transportation, Storage and Post	54	56
（八）住宿和餐饮业	Hotels and Catering Services	16	16
（九）信息传输、软件和信息技术服务业	Information Transmission, Computer Service and Software	45	26
（十）金融业	Financial Intermediation	2	1
（十一）房地产业	Real Estate	60	49
（十二） 租赁和商务服务业	Leasing and Business Services	33	21
（十三）科学研究和技术服务业	Scientific Research and Technical Service	42	32
（十四）水利、环境和公共设施管理业	Management of Water Conservancy, Environment and Public Facilities	748	641
（十五）居民服务、修理和其他服务业	Services to Households, Repairs and Other Services	5	6
（十六）教育	Education	98	118
（十七）卫生和社会工作	Health and Social Work	24	33
（十八）文化、体育和娱乐业	Culture, Sports and Entertainment	15	16
（十九）公共管理、社会保障和社会组织	Public Administration, Social Security and Social Organizations	5	11
（二十）国际组织	International Organizations		

5-12 全市固定资产投资效果（2020年）

Achievements of Total Assets Investment of Whole City（2020）

指 标	Item	固定资产投资 Investment in Fixed Assets	房地产开发投资 Real Estate Investment
一、建设项目投产率（%）	**Rate of Projects Put Into Use（%）**	**42.0**	
施工项目个数（个）	Number of Constructing Projects (unit)	3571	
本年投产项目个数（个）	Number of Projects Put into Use (unit)	1501	
二、固定资产交付使用率（%）	**Rate of Fixed Assets Put into Use（%）**	**37.2**	**14.9**
本年新增固定资产增长速度（%）	The Growth Rate of Newly Increased Fixed Assets This Year（%）	25.0	-21.7
本年完成投资增长速度（%）	The Growth Rate of Investment Completed This Year（%）	12.8	6.5
三、建设周期（年）	**Construction Period (year)**	**5.1**	**7.3**
计划总投资增长速度（%）	The Growth Rate of Total Planned Investment（%）	9.3	3.5
本年完成投资额增长速度（%）	The Growth Rate of Investment Completed This Year（%）	12.8	6.5
四、房屋建筑面积竣工率（%）	**Completion Rate of Buildings（%）**	**4.9**	**4.9**
本年房屋施工面积增长速度（%）	The Growth Rate of Floor Space of the Constructing Buildings This Year（%）	-3.2	-3.2
本年房屋竣工面积增长速度（%）	The Growth Rate of Floor Space of the Buildings Completed This Year（%）	-21.1	-21.1

5-13 固定资产投资新增生产能力或效益（2020年）

Newly Increased Production Capacity or Project Efficiency through Investment（2020）

能源名称	Name	累计新增生产能力或效益 Cumulative Newly Increased Production Capacity or Project Efficiency
石油加工：蒸馏设备能力（处理万吨/年）	Oil Processing : Distillation Equipment Capacity (10 000 tons/year)	
石油加工：裂变设备能力（处理万吨/年）	Oil Processing : Fission Equipment Capacity (10 000 tons/year)	
太阳能发电（万千瓦）	Solar Energy (10 000 kw)	
其他发电（万千瓦）	Others (10 000 kw)	
输电线路长度（11万伏及以上）（公里）	Length of Transmission Lines (above 110 000 VA) (km)	
载货汽车制造（辆/年）	Truck Manufacturing (car/year)	
客车制造（辆/年）	Bus Manufacturing (car/year)	
轿车制造（辆/年）	Car Manufacturing (car/year)	2958
其他汽车制造（辆/年）	Other cars Manufacturing (car/year)	4600
啤酒（万吨/年）	Beer (10 000 tons/year)	
白酒（万吨/年）	White Spirit (10 000 tons/year)	
其他酒（万吨/年）	Other Alcohols (10 000 tons/year)	
新建公路（公里）	Newly Highways (km)	
#高速公路（公里）	Expressway (km)	
一级公路（公里）	First Class (km)	
二级公路（公里）	Second Class (km)	
改建公路（公里）	Reconstructed Highways (km)	
新（扩）建客、货运站（个）	New (expanded) Passenger and Freight Stations (unit)	
新（扩）建公路客、货运站（平方米）	New (expanded) Road Passenger and Freight Station (square meter)	
飞机购置（驾）	Airplane Purchasing (set)	58
城市自来水供水能力（万吨/日）	Tap Water Supply Capacity in City(10 000 tons/day)	10.1
城市污水处理能力（万吨/日）	Waste Water Treated Capacity in City(10 000 tons/day)	28

5-14 分区县、开发区全社会固定资产投资增长速度（2020年）

The Growth Rate of Total Investment in Fixed Assets by Region and Development Zone（2020）

单位：%　　（%）

区县、开发区	Region	全社会固定资产投资 Fixed Assets Investment	固定资产投资 Investment in Fixed Assets	房地产开发投资 Real Estate Investment	农户投资 Farmer Investment
全市	**Total**	**12.3**	**12.8**	**6.5**	**-25.0**
新城区	Xincheng	13.0	13.0	-28.6	
碑林区	Beilin	4.7	4.7	-24.1	
莲湖区	Lianhu	2.9	2.9	-45.2	
灞桥区	Baqiao	10.0	10.3	-2.8	-22.6
未央区	Weiyang	21.1	21.2	27.8	-38.7
雁塔区	Yanta	9.2	9.2	22.5	
阎良区	Yanliang	9.8	10.7	-20.6	-24.8
临潼区	Lintong	-5.2	-3.4	-34.1	-26.0
长安区	Chang'an	31.1	31.7	-2.2	-23.7
高陵区	Gaoling	-6.1	-5.8	-17.0	-26.7
鄠邑区	Huyi	28.6	34.0	-30.0	-26.2
蓝田县	Lantian	-36.4	-37.1	-46.2	-26.8
周至县	Zhouzhi	31.8	50.1	13.7	-26.1
西咸新区	Xixian	11.2	11.5	11.3	-22.1
#开发区	**Development Zones**				
高新区	GaoXin	23.2	23.2	39.5	
经开区	JingKai	10.2	10.2	-14.3	
曲江新区	Qujiang	12.5	12.5	8.5	
航空基地	Aviation Industry Base	12.4	12.4	-16.8	
航天基地	Aerospace Base	30.9	30.9	0.4	
浐灞生态区	Chanba Eco-District	12.7	12.7	24.0	
国际港务区	International Trade&Logistic Park	30.6	30.6	34.4	

5-15 分区县工业投资增长速度（2020年）

The Growth Rate of Industrial Investment by Region (2020)

单位：%　　　　　　　　　　　　　　　　　　　　　　　　　　　　　　　　　　(%)

区县	Region	工业投资 Industrial Investment	工业企业技术改造 Technological Transformation of Industrial Enterprises
全　市	**Total**	**15.2**	**69.0**
新城区	Xincheng	163.1	-6.3
碑林区	Beilin	-25.3	492.9
莲湖区	Lianhu	161.3	77.7
灞桥区	Baqiao	52.6	-46.3
未央区	Weiyang	42.6	71.9
雁塔区	Yanta	-36.8	-18.5
阎良区	Yanliang	21.1	18.1
临潼区	Lintong	23.6	70.6
长安区	Chang'an	22.7	161.6
高陵区	Gaoling	-25.7	36.4
鄠邑区	Huyi	12.9	-55.3
蓝田县	Lantian	-46.2	-40.1
周至县	Zhouzhi	215.8	26.9
西咸新区	Xixian	28.5	19.7

5-16 分区县、开发区新增固定资产及房屋施工、竣工面积增长速度（2020年）

单位：%

区县、开发区	Region	本年新增固定资产 Increased Fixed Assets this Year	房屋施工面积 Floor Space of Buildings Under Construction	住宅 Residential Buildings
区县	**Region**	**23.5**	**-3.2**	**-5.2**
新城区	Xincheng	-67.8	-11.4	-13.9
碑林区	Beilin	-79.4	-62.5	-59.8
莲湖区	Lianhu	-19.7	-22.8	-23.0
灞桥区	Baqiao	433.6	5.4	5.4
未央区	Weiyang	29.1	-12.3	-16.1
雁塔区	Yanta	-22.1	-7.6	-11.8
阎良区	Yanliang	11.2	-17.7	-5.9
临潼区	Lintong	-13.7	25.7	26.3
长安区	Chang'an	509.5	-3.3	-0.8
高陵区	Gaoling	18.0	5.3	6.4
鄠邑区	Huyi	14.8	-11.7	-10.4
蓝田县	Lantian	-52.9	22.6	17.4
周至县	Zhouzhi	425.6	13.7	12.7
西咸新区	Xixian	-9.9	30.9	20.7
开发区	**Development Zones**	**149.4**	**-6.2**	**-6.4**
高新区	GaoXin	261.7	-10.2	-3.9
经开区	JingKai	6.9	-17.8	-19.6
曲江新区	Qujiang	50.9	-4.4	-13.0
航空基地	Aviation Industry Base	129.0	-15.2	-18.3
航天基地	Aerospace Base	25.7	2.3	53.9
浐灞生态区	Chanba Eco-District	-46.7	1.1	5.3
国际港务区	International Trade&Logistic Park	1853.6	74.1	79.9

The Growth Rate of Newly Added Fixed Assets and Floor Space of Constructing and Completed Buildings by Region and Development Zone（2020）

（%）

本年房屋竣工面积 Floor Space of Buildings this Year Completed	住宅 Residential Buildings	本年房屋竣工价值 Value of Buildings Completed this Year	住宅 Residential Buildings	本年商品房销售面积 Floor Space of Houses Sales this year	本年商品房销售额 Sales Income of Commercial Houses this year
-21.1	**-18.1**	**-15.1**	**6.2**	**-3.0**	**10.2**
-89.0	-93.1	-91.6	-91.4	-67.7	-68.1
-78.7	-78.5	-78.0	-79.6	-45.3	-49.1
-48.8	-40.9	-20.2	-1.9	-39.6	-27.7
1931.4	4789.3	1633.0	5942.2	23.6	28.7
-51.5	-38.6	-67.6	-28.3	-19.4	-12.2
-53.3	-82.7	-48.6	-73.0	-17.2	4.7
43.3	84.9	44.9	76.7	21.4	41.2
				5.3	7.2
144.4	312.9	172.4	509.9	-21.0	5.2
				-7.0	3.1
-14.1	-23.1	-1.3	-25.0	2.5	8.6
				-49.8	-37.9
				29.2	59.5
279.9	409.1	213.4	387.0	38.9	53.9
6.6	**108.5**	**-13.2**	**135.3**	**-7.2**	**6.3**
-18.5		-38.3		-7.6	34.8
-68.9		-75.5		-28.4	-30.7
151.4	-1.0	79.9	-9.6	-24.6	-21.4
384.5	2341.2	271.0	2297.0	-9.4	1.0
				69.2	99.4
-61.0	-74.5	-70.1	-77.0	-14.4	36.6
				79.5	73.9

5-17 主要年份房地产开发投资主要指标

单位：万平方米

指标	Item	2000	2001	2002	2003	2004	2005
本年完成投资额（亿元）	Investment Completed This Year(100 million yuan)	51.85	67.42	79.37	124.82	169.67	225.23
本年房屋施工面积	Floor Space of Buildings Under Construction This Year	763.18	743.78	1172.58	1343.12	1633.68	2174.29
#住宅	Residential Buildings	619.85	580.43	964.68	943.61	1204.01	1783.36
本年房屋竣工面积	Floor Space of Buildings Completed This Year	321.10	316.24	329.71	339.67	380.84	361.62
#住宅	Residential Buildings	295.55	269.61	290.30	289.56	308.06	316.52
本年房屋竣工价值（亿元）	Value of Floor Space of Buildings Completed this Year(100million yuan)	26.94	37.20	36.93	54.73	73.75	80.58
#住宅	Residential Buildings	22.97	28.62	30.46	44.01	55.58	68.11
本年商品房销售面积	Floor Space of Commercialized Buildings Sold	212.92	225.35	252.90	252.74	305.47	497.34
#住宅	Residential Buildings	200.77	192.20	237.04	230.28	279.90	476.39
本年商品房销售额（亿元）	Total Sales of Commercialized Buildings(100 million yuan)	32.52	47.22	51.35	54.29	81.35	171.29
#住宅	Residential Buildings	29.46	35.53	45.46	44.25	71.27	158.03
本年批准预售面积	Approved Pre-sale Area of This Year	253.03	67.44	61.02	52.35	176.40	300.07
#住宅	Residential Buildings	253.03	65.20	55.73	49.12	159.10	287.13
待售面积	Area for Sale	36.41	50.82	57.14	63.85	108.52	123.59
#住宅	Residential Buildings	24.02	34.18	44.70	52.34	72.76	99.17
房屋出租面积	Rental Housing Area	1.17	9.19	15.75	10.56	11.18	17.32
#住宅	Residential Buildings	0.02	0.10	1.13	5.43	5.78	4.09
本年新增固定资产（亿元）	Newly Increased Fixed Assets This Year(100 million yuan)	38.38	50.77	48.43	62.13	83.36	92.78

Main Indicators of Investment in Real Estate Development in Representative Years

(10 000sq.m)

2006	2007	2008	2009	2010	2011	2012	2013	2014	2015	2016	2017	2018	2019	2020
285.76	387.33	540.26	696.34	842.34	996.81	1281.90	1595.64	1761.88	1831.67	1955.82	2333.34	2518.01	2464.78	2624.48
2383.56	2915.95	3632.87	5708.63	6697.39	8247.69	9947.89	10454.27	12422.10	13392.94	14727.10	15843.92	16044.57	17475.02	16916.07
1890.27	2376.82	3079.13	4901.59	5777.71	7108.27	8294.92	8461.71	9727.60	9777.23	10468.80	11134.28	11208.59	12450.59	11800.32
399.64	483.30	443.96	542.81	463.65	631.03	1063.70	795.35	1533.70	976.64	1560.18	1634.63	977.28	1057.69	834.55
342.15	422.47	412.46	453.49	412.44	564.59	903.82	663.20	1307.64	766.58	1259.24	1281.71	623.40	761.59	623.39
82.02	101.13	106.50	168.08	145.62	213.29	310.57	279.63	442.74	301.86	456.48	571.96	330.61	372.11	316.10
65.80	77.13	96.02	137.42	128.69	185.31	260.04	222.64	368.25	236.66	351.46	448.02	208.68	231.24	245.62
621.50	833.92	760.72	1256.02	1587.81	1778.02	1538.91	1662.75	1707.71	1763.68	2047.67	2509.78	2713.46	2638.69	2559.79
584.06	782.91	715.76	1202.12	1523.24	1674.85	1383.84	1522.50	1525.95	1584.08	1877.78	2147.67	2221.27	2155.46	2086.77
206.15	281.79	296.44	488.55	707.00	1091.31	1017.74	1112.87	1100.71	1146.79	1347.08	2123.34	2753.13	2989.64	3294.01
179.47	251.74	268.92	450.71	661.27	973.71	858.53	976.19	928.74	985.35	1194.41	1743.43	2214.18	2462.79	2734.58
428.20	491.07	569.22	1125.44	1510.20	3105.76	2627.73	1787.89	842.98	751.15	717.54	634.50	1047.65		
408.11	457.54	541.20	1095.17	1452.20	2826.79	2340.69	1597.82	727.31	583.55	508.17	515.34	865.40		
112.49	45.42	55.40	40.68	34.32	59.76	102.58	74.59	187.13	296.50	378.24	379.66	240.04	202.71	149.51
85.89	38.62	35.40	28.73	26.23	45.41	83.78	61.24	143.21	185.96	215.40	176.90	59.98	55.57	29.45
8.53	10.84	34.94	38.23	28.60	8.01	15.16	15.57	7.15	19.64	48.67	57.12	51.95	26.97	25.48
3.74	5.36	4.53	6.55	0.70	3.25	4.03	0.73	0.07	1.47	1.47		2.37		
100.22	143.17	124.02	195.71	168.20	25.53	358.03	334.41	531.44	335.91	574.54	807.26	409.04	498.31	389.93

5-18　分区县、开发区房地产开发主要指标（2020年）

单位：万元

区县、开发区	Region	企业（单位）个数（个）Number of Enterprises (unit)	本年完成投资 Investment Completed This Year	本年新增固定资产 Increased Fixed Assets This Year
全　市	**Total**	**1208**	**26244750**	**3899279**
新城区	Xincheng	32	291820	72860
碑林区	Beilin	35	206012	264157
莲湖区	Lianhu	77	500567	669077
灞桥区	Baqiao	124	2560739	964692
未央区	Weiyang	191	3583254	361025
雁塔区	Yanta	242	6455957	332532
阎良区	Yanliang	48	291786	24250
临潼区	Lintong	28	458998	
长安区	Chang'an	119	2655055	414801
高陵区	Gaoling	39	433949	14362
鄠邑区	Huyi	37	120013	63736
蓝田县	Lantian	18	71457	40500
周至县	Zhouzhi	24	75996	9760
西咸新区	Xixian	194	8539147	667527
#开发区	**Development Zones**	**488**	**11313335**	**775922**
高新区	GaoXin	116	3121236	161953
经开区	JingKai	88	865028	74294
曲江新区	Qujiang	89	2562738	68249
航空基地	Aviation Industry Base	91	2511314	238272
航天基地	Aerospace Base	15	191030	
浐灞生态区	Chanba Eco-District	57	1122122	60497
国际港务区	International Trade&Logistic Park	32	939867	172657

Main Indicators of Real Estate Development by Region and Development Zone（2020）

(10 000 yuan)

房屋施工面积（平方米）Floor Space of Buildings Under Constmction(sq.m)	住宅 Residential Buildings	本年房屋竣工面积（平方米）Floor Space of Buildings Completed this Year(sq.m)	住宅 Residential Buildings	本年房屋竣工价值 Value of Buildings Completed this Year	住宅 Residential Buildings
169160711	**118003237**	**8345501**	**6233877**	**3161039**	**2456188**
4560811	3293370	110801	52169	30000	16000
2250263	1655181	602102	475961	193097	142511
11037290	9181705	1239130	1110625	636079	569359
20345200	15229331	2045234	1602385	731985	597757
30965745	19660850	897318	733114	243844	212856
32253373	19085733	615146	170355	255176	94381
2018152	1644395	87882	59461	23320	15755
3264694	2735976				
18805115	13998446	883445	638418	386552	282393
5798883	4924993	50279	46214	14362	13549
1715993	1241836	198140	109977	63406	30046
1495539	1121728	57402	57402	16073	16073
1015156	789174	42137	23569	9760	4830
33634497	23440519	1516485	1154227	557385	460678
69922274	**46147856**	**1479867**	**831438**	**585695**	**366458**
12224154	6860918	324440		118167	
11840734	6593456	168693	168693	74294	74294
12888906	8697354	144367	45168	55779	23487
16286581	11844779	361813	322232	132573	119849
987008	788758				
9177929	6623283	115772	39471	32248	10657
6516962	4739308	364782	255874	172634	138171

5-19 房地产开发投资主要指标（2020年）

Main Indicators of Investment in Real Estate Development（2020）

单位：万元 （10 000 yuan）

指标	Item	全市合计 Total	国有 State-owned	市区 Urban	市属 Municipal
一、企业（单位）个数（个）	**Number of Enterprises(unit)**	**1208**	**65**	**1017**	**1169**
二、本年完成投资	**Investment Completed This Year**	**26244750**	**1711543**	**20491167**	**24700164**
按工程用途分	Grouped by Function				
住宅	Residential Buildings	17821238	1312520	13306427	16556197
#别墅、高档公寓	Villas and Top-Grade Apartments				
办公楼	Office Buildings	2255950	90698	1953117	2206863
商业营业用房	Houses for Business Use	2398544	54094	1895671	2281840
其他	Others	3769018	254231	3335952	3655264
三、本年新增固定资产	**Increased Fixed Assets This Year**	**3899279**	**508891**	**3187044**	**3899279**
四、房屋施工面积（平方米）	**Floor Space of Buildings Under Construction (sq.m)**	**169160711**	**10364697**	**142986372**	**161629720**
#住宅	Residential Buildings	118003237	7443841	99009807	112316638
五、本年房屋竣工面积（平方米）	**Floor Space of Buildings this Year Completed (sq.m)**	**8345501**	**904404**	**6731460**	**8345501**
#住宅	Residential Buildings	6233877	666578	4998679	6233877
六、本年房屋竣工价值	**Value of Buildings Completed this Year**	**3161039**	**375065**	**2578415**	**3161039**
#住宅	Residential Buildings	2456188	263444	1974607	2456188
七、本年商品房屋销售面积（平方米）	**Floor Space of Commercialized Buildings Sold this Year(sq.m)**	**25597910**	**953951**	**20646055**	**23566782**
本年商品房销售额	Sales Income of Commercialized Buildings	32940073	1328975	27681074	30223617

5-20 商品房销售情况（2020年）

Sales of Commercial Houses（2020）

指 标	Item	全市合计 Total	国有 State-owned	市区 Urban	市属 Municipal
本年商品房销售面积（平方米）	**Floor Space of Commercialized Buildings Sold(sq.m)**	**25597910**	**953951**	**20646055**	**23566782**
现房销售面积（平方米）	**Floor Space of Completed Apartment Sales(sq.m)**	**2069874**	**49662**	**1667546**	**2042739**
期房销售面积（平方米）	**Floor Space of Forward Delivery Housing Sales(sq.m)**	**23528036**	**904289**	**18978509**	**21524043**
住宅	Residential Buildings	20867693	580361	16191032	19136766
#别墅、高档公寓	Villas and High-grade Apartments				
办公楼	Office Buildings	1906307	225509	1801467	1789686
商业营业用房	Houses for Business Use	1131652	84792	1020462	1032867
其他	Others	1692258	63289	1633094	1607463
本年商品房销售额（万元）	**Real estate sales this year(10 000Yuan)**	**32940073**	**1328975**	**27681074**	**30223617**
现房销售额（万元）	**Floor Space of Completed Apartment Sales(10 000Yuan)**	**2388100**	**32242**	**2032390**	**2371606**
期房销售额（万元）	**Floor Space of Forward Delivery Housing Sales(10 000Yuan)**	**30551973**	**1296733**	**25648684**	**27852011**
住宅	Residential Buildings	27345798	948914	22359941	24980573
#别墅高档公寓	Villas and High-grade Apartments				
办公楼	Office Buildings	2872862	232813	2773639	2725591
商业营业用房	Houses for Business Use	1684838	105806	1536623	1530105
其他	Others	1036575	41442	1010871	987348
待售面积（平方米）	**Area for Sale(sq.m)**	**1495132**	**28046**	**1324916**	**1492109**
#待售一年以上（一到三年）	Being Idle for One Year	460362	1684	447454	460362
待售三年以上（含三年）	Being Idle for Three Years	371884	15349	288702	368861
住宅	Residence	294483	8480	214807	291460
#别墅高档公寓	Villas and High-grade Apartments				
办公楼	Office Buildings	192295		192295	192295
商业营业用房	Houses for Business Use	643911	19566	561705	643911
其他	Others	364443		356109	364443
房屋出租面积（平方米）	**Rental area(sq.m)**	**254810**	**35747**	**101460**	**254810**
住宅	Residential Buildings				
办公楼	Office Buildings	22403		22403	22403
商业营业用房	Houses for Business Use	232407	35747	79057	232407
其他	Others				

5-21 房地产开发投资资金来源（2020年）

Source of Funds for Investment in Real Estate Development（2020）

单位：万元 (10 000 yuan)

指 标	Item	全市合计 Total	国有 State-owned	市区 Urban	市属 Municipal
一、本年资金来源合计	**Total**	**43871757**	**2970467**	**37126906**	**40807986**
1. 上年末结余资金	Balance of Last Year	10303491	1140871	9643687	9611155
2. 本年实际到位资金	Fully Funded Capital this Year	33568266	1829596	27483219	31196831
(1)国内贷款	Domestic Loans	2280275	243433	1913281	2085348
#银行贷款	Bank Loan	2008480	243433	1660716	1813553
非银行金融机构贷款	Loans from financial Institutions except Bank	271795		252565	271795
(2)自筹资金	Self-raising Funds	15635739	790908	11539514	14818342
(3)定金及预收款	Earnest Money and Advance payment	10559345	278901	9836835	9333345
(4)个人按揭贷款	Personal Mortgage Loan	2912487	102545	2567705	2828466
(5)其他资金	Others	2180420	413809	1625884	2131330
二、本年各项应付款合计	**Total Sums of Money to be Paid This Year**	**8954890**	**932803**	**7990416**	**8153027**
#工程款	Project Fund	5232688	337544	4672713	4809424

5-22 房地产开发经营情况（2020年）

Running of Real Estate Development（2020）

单位：万元 (10 000 yuan)

指 标	Item	全市合计 Total	国有 State-owned	市区 Urban	市属 Municipal
一、资产负债情况	**Assets and Liabilities**				
1. 资产总计	Total Assets	178271426	20421354	156181709	165165095
2. 负债合计	Total Liabilities	156367357	15808180	136982328	144586098
3. 所有者权益合计	Total Creditor's Equity	21904069	4613174	19199381	20578997
#实收资本	Held Capital	16188287	2440893	14544175	14906688
二、损益及分配情况	**Profit or Loss and the Distribution**				
1. 主营业务收入	Revenue from Principal Business	17401881	1660312	16195513	16516131
土地转让收入	Revenue of Land Transferred	33		21	33
商品房屋销售收入	Revenue of Commercial Houses Sold	16031693	1251420	15066504	15155431
自持物业收入	Self-owned Property Income	118379	16365	110157	117760
#房屋出租收入	Revenue of Houses Leased	99029	6004	90810	98410
其他收入	Other Revenue	1251775	392526	1018831	1242907
2. 主营业务成本	Cost of Principal Business	12758290	1306025	11798163	12152676
3. 主营业务税金及附加	Taxes and Other Charges on Principal Business	997833	57303	941416	937323
4. 其他业务利润	Other Business Profit	29168	3007	28309	26459
5. 销售费用	Sales Expenditures	859610	28288	710891	824329
6. 管理费用	Management Cost	727169	45592	658800	703290
7. 财务费用	Fiscal Expenditure	298401	43131	275161	297728
#利息支出	Interest Exchange	317841	96670	305189	305443
8. 营业利润	Operating Profit	2475528	247407	2291262	2259117
投资收益	Investment Revenue	298582	41353	297234	245441
营业外收入	Non-business Revenue	227777	4481	224836	227238
营业外支出	Non-business Expenditures	179805	2389	165200	178714
9. 利润总额	Total Profit	2526292	249541	2348188	2310433
10. 应付职工薪酬	Salary Payable	630876	68515	559872	591898
11. 应交增值税	Value-added Tax Payable	846118	53765	705883	834724
三、全部从业人员年平均人数（人）	**Average Number of Employed Persons（Person）**	**88598**			
四、本年应付工资总额	**Total Wages This Year**	**707484**			

注：因劳动工资统计制度改革，自2020年开始，取消登记注册类型分组数据和分区县数据，故相关分组数据暂缺。

主要统计指标解释

全社会固定资产投资 是以货币形式表现的在一定时期内全社会建造和购置固定资产的工作量以及与此有关的费用的总称。该指标是反映固定资产投资规模、结构和发展速度的综合性指标，又是观察工程进度和考核投资效果的重要依据。全社会固定资产投资按登记注册类型可分为国有、集体、联营、股份制、私营和个体、港澳台商、外商、其他等。

固定资产投资(不含农户) 指城镇和农村各种登记注册类型的企业、事业、行政单位及城镇个体户进行的计划总投资500万元及500万元以上的建设项目投资和房地产开发投资，包含原口径城镇固定资产投资加上农村企事业组织项目投资，该口径自2011年起开始使用。

房地产开发投资 指各种登记注册类型的房地产开发公司、商品房建设公司及其他房地产开发法人单位和附属于其他法人单位实际从事房地产开发或经营活动的单位统一开发的包括统代建、拆迁还建的住宅、厂房、仓库、饭店、宾馆、度假村、写字楼、办公楼等房屋建筑物和配套的服务设施，土地开发工程（如道路、给水、排水、供电、供热、通讯、平整场地等基础设施工程)的投资；不包括单纯的土地交易活动。

农户投资 是指以农户为单位进行的房屋建设(主要指住宅建设)投资、农村对农、林、牧、渔及服务行业进行的投资(如农户近年广泛进行的设施农业投资)以及农户购买生产性固定资产的投资。

固定资产投资的资金来源 根据固定资产投资的资金来源不同，分为国家预算资金、国内贷款、利用外资、自筹资金和其他资金。

（1）国家预算资金：包括一般预算、政府性基金预算、国有资本经营预算和社保基金预算等资金。

（2）国内贷款：指报告期固定资产投资单位向银行及非银行金融机构借入的用于固定资产投资的各种国内借款，包括银行利用自有资金及吸收的存款发放的贷款、上级主管部门拨入的国内贷款、国家专项贷款、地方财政专项资金安排的贷款、国内储备贷款、周转贷款等。

（3）利用外资：指报告期收到的用于固定资产建造和购置的境外资金（包括设备、材料、技术在内）。包括对外借款（外国政府、国际金融组织贷款、出口信贷、外国银行商业贷款、对外发行债券和股票）、外商直接投资及外商其他投资。不包括我国自有外汇资金（国家外汇、地方外汇、留成外汇、调剂外汇和中国银行自有资金发行的外汇贷款等）。计算利用外资时，需要折算成人民币，折算中所使用的外汇汇率按现汇计算，即按使用外汇时的汇率计算。

（4）自筹资金：指固定资产投资单位报告期收到的，由各地区、各部门及企、事业单位筹集用于固定资产投资的预算外资金，包括中央各部门、各级地方和企、事业单位的自筹资金。

（5）其他资金：指在报告期收到的除以上各种资金之外其他用于固定资产投资的资金，包括企业或金融机构通过发行各种债券筹集到的资金、社会集资、个人资金、无偿捐赠的资金及其他单位拨人的资金等。

固定资产投资按国民经济行业分 根据现有企业、事业、行政单位和建设项目建成投产后的主要产品种类或主要用途及社会经济活动性质来确定国民经济行业。一般情况下，一个建设项目或一个企业、事业单位只能属于一种国民经济行业。

固定资产投资按隶属关系分 是按建设单位或企业、事业、行政单位的主管上级机关确定的。

（1）中央：是指中共中央、人大常委会和国务院各部、委、局、总公司以及直属机构直接领导的建设项目和企业、事业、行政单位。这些单位的固定资产投资计划由国务院各部门直接编制和下达，建设中所需物资、主要设备以及建设中的问题都由中央有关部门安排和解决。

（2）地方：是由省（自治区、直辖市）、地区（州、盟、省辖市）、县（旗、县级市）三级政府及业务主管部门直接领导和管理的建设项目、企业、事业、行政单位。地方项目还包括不隶属以上各级政府及主管部门的建设项目和企业、事业单位，如外商投资企业和无主管部门的企业等。

固定资产投资按建设性质分 根据整个建设项目情况来确定。建设项目的性质一般分为新建、扩建、改建和技术改造、单纯建造生活设施、迁建、恢复、单纯购置。房地产开发单位、农户投资不划分建设性质。

（1）新建：一般指从无到有开始建设的企业、事业和行政单位或建设项目。有的单位原有基础很小，经过建设后新增的固定资产价值超过该企、事业、行政单位原有固定资产价值（原值）三倍以上的也应作为新建。

（2）扩建：指在厂内或其他地点，为扩大原有产品的生产能力（或效益）或增加新的产品生产能力，而增建主要的生产车间（或主要工程）、分厂、独立的生产线。行政、事业单位在原单位增建业务用房（如学校增建教学用房、医院增建门诊部、病房等）也作为扩建。

现有企、事业单位为扩大原有主要产品生产能力或增加新的产品生产能力，增建一个或几个主要生产车间（或主要工程）、分厂，同时进行一些更新改造工程的，也应作为扩建。

（3）改建和技术改造：指现有企业、事业单位，对原有设施进行技术改造或更新（包括相应配套的辅助性生产、生活福利设施）的建设项目。现有企业、事业单位为适应市场变化的需要，而改变企业的主要产品种类（如军工企业转产民用品等）的建设项目，应作为改建。原有产品生产作业线由于各工序（车间）之间能力不平衡，为填平补齐充分发挥原有生产能力而增建不增加本企业主要产品设计能力的车间，也应作为改建。技术改造是指企业、事业单位在现有基础上，用先进的技术代替落后的技术，用先进的工艺和装备代替落后的工艺和装备，以改变企业落后的技术经济面貌，实现以内涵为主的扩大再生产，达到提高产品质量、促进产品更新换代、节约能源、降低消耗、扩大生产规模、全面提高社会经济效益的目的。技术改造具体包括以下内容：机器设备和工具的更新改造；生产工艺改革、节约能源和原材料的改造；厂房建筑和公共设施的改造；劳动条件和生产环境的改造等。

固定资产投资按构成分 固定资产投资活动按其工作内容和实现方式分为建筑安装工程，设备工具器具购置和其他费用三个部分。

（1）建筑安装工程（建筑安装工作量）：指各种房屋、建筑物的建造工程和各种设备、装置的安装工程。包括各种房屋建造工程；各种用途设备基础和各种工业窑炉的砌筑工程及金属结构工程；为施工而进行的各种准备工作和临时工程以及完工后的清理工作等；铁路、道路的铺设，矿井的开凿及石油管道的架设等；水利工程；防空地下建筑等特殊工程；列入房屋工程预算内的暖气、卫生、通风、照明、煤气等设备的价值及装设油饰工程；列入建筑工程预算内的各种管道（蒸汽、压缩空气、石油、给排水等管道）、电力、电讯电缆导线等的敷设工程；以及各种机械设备的安装下程；为测定安装工程质量，对设备进行的试运工作；房地产开发单位进行的商品房屋开发建设工程、土地开发工程。

在建筑安装工程中，不包括被安装设备本身的价值。

（2）设备工具器具购置：指建设单位或企、事业单位购置或自制的，达到固定资产标准的设备、工具、器具的价值。新建单位及扩建单位的新建车间，按照设计或计划要求购置或自制的全部设备、工具、器具，不论是否达到固定资产标准均计入“设备工具器具购置”中。

（3）其他费用：指在固定资产建造和购置过程中发生的，除上述几项内容以外的各种应分摊计入固定资产的费用。

施工项目 指报告期内所有施工的建设项目个数，包括本年新开工的项目和以前年度开工在本年继续施工的建设项目。凡是报告期内施过工的建设项目，不论施工时间长短，均作为施工项目统计。施工项目个数可以反映一定时期固定资产投资的实际规模，与同期全部建成投产项目个数相比，可以从建设速度的角度反映固定资产投资的效果。

全部建成投产项目 指报告期内按设计文件规定的全部生产能力（或效益）建成投产，经验收合格交付使用的建设项目。

新增生产能力（或工程效益） 指通过固定资产投资活动而增加的设计能力（或工程效益）。主要指标包括建设规模、本年施工规模、自开始建设累计新增生产能力（或工程效益）、本年新增生产能力（或工程效益）等。

建设规模 指建设项目或工程设计文件中规定的全部设计能力（或工程效益）。包括已经建成投产和尚未建成投产的工程的生产能力（或工程效益）。

本年施工规模 指报告期内施工的单项工程的设计能力（或工程效益），即全部建设规模中在本年正式施工的部分。

自开始建设累计新增生产能力（或工程效益） 指自开始建设至本年底止建成投产的全部单项工程累计的新增生产能力（或工程效益）。

本年新增生产能力（或工程效益） 指在本年度内按照新增生产能力（或工程效益）的计算条件和标准，实际建成投入生产或交付使用的生产能力（或工程效益）。

房屋施工面积 指报告期内施工的全部房屋（包括地下室、半地下室以及配套房屋）建筑面积。包括本期新开工的面积和上期开工跨入本期继续施工的房屋面积，以及上期已停建在本期恢复施工的房屋面积。本期竣工和本期施工后又停缓建的房屋，其建筑面积仍计入本期房屋施工面积中。

房屋竣工面积 指在报告期内房屋建筑按照设计要求已经全部完工，达到住人和使用条件，经验收鉴定合格（或达到竣工验收标准），可正式移交使用的各栋房屋建筑面积的总和。

新增固定资产 指报告期内交付使用的固定资产价值。包括本年内建成投入生产或交付使用的工程投资和达到固定资产标准的设备、工具、器具的投资及有关应摊入的费用。该指标是表示固定资产投资成果的价值指标，也是反映建设进度，计算固定资产投资效果的重要指标。

项目建成投产率 指一定时期内全部建成投产项目个数与同期施工项目个数的比率。该指标是从建设单位建设速度的角度反映投资效果的指标。

固定资产交付使用率 指一定时期新增固定资产与同期完成投资额的比率。该指标是反映固定资产动用速度，衡量建设过程中宏观投资效果的综合指标。由于新增固定资产是较长时期内形成的结果，而投资额则是当年完成的，因此，该指标一般适宜于反映较长时期内固定资产的动用情况。

商品房销售面积 指报告期内出售商品房屋的合同总面积（即双方签署的正式买卖合同中所确定的建筑面积）。由现房销售建筑面积和期房销售建筑面积两部分组成。

商品房销售额 指报告期内出售商品房屋的合同总价款（即双方签署的正式买卖合同中所确定的合同总价）。该指标与商品房销售面积同口径，由现房销售额和期房销售额两部分组成。

Explanatory Notes on Main Statistical Indicators

Total Investment in Fixed Assets in the Whole Country refers to the volume of activities in construction and purchases of fixed assets of the whole country and related fees, expressed in monetary terms during the reference period. It is a comprehensive indicator which shows the size, structure and growth of the investment in fixed assets, providing a basis for observing the progress of construction projects and evaluating results of investment. Total investment in fixed assets in the whole country includes, by type of ownership, the investment by State-owned units, collective-owned units, joint ownership units, share-holding units, private units individuals as well as investments by entrepreneurs from Hong Kong, Macao and Taiwan, foreign investors and others.

Investment in Fixed Assets (Excluding Rural Households) refers to the investment in construction projects with a total planned investment of 5 million yuan and above by enterprises of various ownerships, public institutions, administrative units and urban self-employed individuals, and the investment in real estate development in both urban and rural areas. Since 2011, it covers the urban investment in fixed assets of original statistical ranges and project investments by rural enterprises and public institutions.

Investment in Real Estate Development refers to investment by real estate development companies, commercialized buildings construction companies and other real estate development units of various types of ownership in the construction of buildings, such as residential buildings, factory buildings, warehouses, hotels, guesthouses, holiday villages, office buildings, and the complementary service facilities and land development projects, such as roads, water supply, water drainage,power supply,heating sup ply, telecommunications, land leveling and other infrastructural projects. It does not include activities in pure land transactions.

Investmentof Rural Households refers to the Housing construction investment (mainly residential construction) taken by the Rural Households as one unit, rural investment in agriculture, forestry, animal husbandry, fishery and service industries (such as the extensive facility agriculture investment of farmers in recent years) and investment in productive fixed assets purchased by farmers.

Sources of Funds for Investment in Fixed Assets are categorized as funds from the State budget, domestic loans, foreign investment, self-raised funds, and others, depending on the sources of investment.

(1) Fund from the State budget consists of budgetary appropriation and loans from the State budget. More specifically, it includes, from the budget of the central government, capital construction fund (operation fund and non-operational fund), special expenses, loans from repayment, discount fund, expenses on innovation and trial production of new products, expenses on urban construction, expenses on temporary construction from business departments, development fund for less developed areas, as well as local budgetary fund transferred from the central budget.

(2) Domestic loans refer to loans of various forms borrowed by investing units from banks and non-bank financial institutions during the reference period for the purpose of investment in fixed assets, including loans issued by banks from their self-owned funds and deposit, loans appropriated by higher authorities, special loans by government, loans arranged by local government from special funds, domestic reserve loan, and working loan.

(3) Foreign investment refers to overseas funds received during the reference period for the construction and purchase of investment in fixed assets (covering equipment, materials and technology), including foreign borrowings (loans from foreign governments and international financial institutions, export credit, commercial loans from foreign banks, issue of bonds and stocks overseas), foreign direct investment and other foreign investments. Excluded from this category is capital in foreign exchanges owned by China (foreign exchanges owned by the central and local governments, foreign exchanges retained by enterprises, foreign exchanges by enterprises through the regulating mechanism, loans in foreign exchanges issued by the Bank of China with its own fund, etc). In calculating the utilization of foreign capital, foreign currencies are converted into Chinese Renminbi applying the current exchange rate when the foreign capitals are actually used.

(4) Self-raised funds refer to extra-budgetary funds for investment in fixed assets received during the reference period by investing units from central government ministries, local governments, enterprises and institutions, including their self-raised funds.

(5) Others refer to funds for investment in fixed assets received from sources other than those listed above, including capital raised through issuing bonds by

enterprises or financial institutions, funds raised from individuals and through donations, and funds transferred from other units.

Investment in Fixed Assets by Sector The classification of construction projects by sector is determined by enterprises, institutions, administrative units and the major products or the purpose of the projects of existing enterprises, institutional and administrative units when they are put into production or use, and by the nature of their social economic activities. In general, one project or one enterprise or institution can only be classified into one sector.

Investment in Fixed Assets by Jurisdiction of Management refers to the classification of investment by the competent authorities under which investment is made by construction units, enterprises, institutions or administrative units.

(1) Central investment refers to the investment in projects or by enterprises, institutions or administrative units which are under the direct leadership and management of the State Council and of the national commissions, ministries, agencies and State-owned large corporations. Various ministries and departments of the State Council prepare and implement plans for investment in fixed assets by those departments, and arrange and ensure the supply of materials and key equipment required for the projects.

(2) Local investment refers to the investment in projects or by enterprises, institutions or administrative units which are under the direct leadership and management of departments under the provincial, prefecture and county governments. Also included are projects by foreign-invested enterprises and enterprises without competent managing authorities.

Investment in Fixed Assets by Type of Construction Construction projects in general can be classified, by the type of construction, into new construction, expansion, reconstruction and technical transformation, purely construction of living facilities, moving, restoration and purely purchasing. However, investment by type of construction is not applied to investment by real-estate development units and investment by rural households.

(1) New construction in general refers to construction projects, which start from scratch, of enterprises, institutions, administrative agencies. In case the size of the existing unit is quite small, and the value of newly added fixed assets is more than three times of the original value, the expansion will be considered as new construction.

(2) Expansion refers to construction of new major production workshop, branch factory or independent production line within a factory or in other locations, for the purpose of increasing the production capacity (or improving efficiency) or adding new production capacity. Newly constructed accommodation for the operation of institutions and administrative organizations (such as newly constructed buildings for teaching in schools, buildings for clinics or wards in hospitals, etc.) are also classified as expansion.

Also included in expansion are investments by existing enterprises or institutions in building major production line(s) or branch factory(ies) along with some work on innovation, for the purpose of expanding the production capacity of original products or producing new products.

(3) Reconstruction and technical transformation refers to construction projects by existing enterprises or institutions in innovation or technical transformation of the old facilities (including auxiliary production equipment and welfare facilities). Also considered as reconstruction is the construction of new workshops by the existing enterprises or institutions to change the variety of products to meet the market demand (such as the production of civil products by defence industries), or to bring the designed production capacity into full play through a more balanced production process on production lines. Technical transformation refers to replacement of old technology or equipment by new technology or equipment, in order to expand the reproduction through improvement of technology contents in production, to improve product quality, to promote new products to save energy,to reduce consumption, to expand the production scale and to improve overall social-economic efficiency. Contents of technical transformation include: updating of machinery, equipment and tools; reforming production process by using energy or materials saving technology; construction of factory workshops and transformation of public facilities; improvement of working conditions and environment, etc.

Investment in Fixed Assets by Structure By their

contents and the mode of implementation, investment activities are classified into 3 categories, i.e. construction and installation, purchase of equipment and instrument, and other expenses.

(1) Construction and installation (work volume of construction and installation) refers to the construction of houses and buildings and the installation of various kinds of equipment and instruments. They include construction of houses; equipment foundations, industrial kilns and stoves, and metal structure work; preparation works and temporary works for project construction, and clearing up works post project construction; pavement of railways and roads, drilling of mines and putting up of oil pipes; construction of water conservancy; construction of underground air-raid shelters and construction of other special projects; value of equipment for heating, sanitation, ventilation, lighting, gas, painting, etc. that are covered by the budget of housing projects; laying out of various pipelines (for steam, compressed air, petroleum, tap water and sewage) and wiring and cabling for electric power and for communications; installation of various machinery and equipment; testing operation for pre- testing the quality of installation projects, and land and other development work conducted by real estate developers for commercialized housing.

The value of equipment installed is itself not included in the value of construction and installation projects.

(2) Purchase of equipment and instruments refers to the total value of equipment, tools, and instruments purchased or self-produced which come up to the cut-off point for fixed assets by the construction units or investing enterprises or institutions. Equipment, tools and instruments purchased or self-produced for new workshops by newly established or expanded units are categorized as "purchase of equipment and instruments" no matter whether they come up to the cut-off point for fixed assets.

(3) Other expenses refer to expenses arising during the construction or purchase of fixed assets other than those mentioned above.

Projects under Construction refer to number of all projects with construction activities newly started in current year or left-over from the previous year in the reference period. All projects that have construction activities undertaken during the reference period are reported as projects under construction irrespective of the length of construction work. The number of projects under construction can reflect the actual size of investment in fixed assets during a given period, and when compared with the number of projects completed and put into use during the same period, it demonstrates the results of investment in fixed assets from the angle of the speed of the construction.

Projects Completed and Put into Use refer to projects have been completed in accordance with the design documents, resulting in forming production capacity (efficiency) and have been checked and accepted after relevant tests, and have been formally delivered for use.

Newly Increased Production Capacity (or Project Efficiency) refers to the increase in design capacity (or project efficiency) through investment in fixed assets. The main indicators include: construction scale, scale of projects under construction in current year, the accumulated newly increased production capacity (project efficiency) since the start of the projects and the newly increased production capacity (project efficiency) of current year.

Construction Scale refers to the total designed production capacity (project efficiency) of the construction projects in accordance with the design document, including those have been put into operation and those that have not been completed.

Scale of Projects under Construction in Current Year refers to the designed production capacity (project efficiency) of a single project under construction in the reference period, i.e. the part of the total scale of project which is officially under construction in current year.

The Accumulated Newly Increased Production Capacity (project efficiency) since the Start of the Projects refers to the accumulated newly increased production capacity of all the single projects which have been put into use from the beginning of the projects till the end of current year.

The Newly Increased Production Capacity (project efficiency) of Current Year refers to the production capacity (project efficiency) that has been completed and put into operation in current year according to the calculation conditions and standards on newly increased production capacity (project efficiency).

Floor Space of Buildings under Construction refers to the total floor space of all the buildings (including basement, semi-basement and auxiliary buildings), including the effective area and the area occupied by the structure. This indicator is one of the important indicators in physical terms to reflect the scale and accomplishment of the construction industry and also an important basis for monitoring the progress, Calculating the cost, analyzing the efficiency and studying the supply of building materials in relation to the construction projects.

Floor Space Completed refers to the floor space of all buildings completed in the reference period, which have been appraised and accepted (or come up to the designed standards) and have been transferred to owner units.

Newly Increased Fixed Assets refer to the value of fixed that has been put into use, including investment in projects that have been completed and put into operation in current year and the investment in equipment, tools and appliance that meet the standard of fixed assets and fees that should be apportioned. This is an indicator that demonstrates the results of investment in fixed assets in monetary terms, and an important indicator to reflect the speed of construction and to calculate the efficiency of investment.

Rate of Construction Projects Completed and Put into Use refers to the ratio of the number of construction projects completed and put into use in a certain period of time to the number of projects under construction in the same period. This reflects the investment efficiency from the perspective of the speed of projects construction.

6 财　政

GOVERNMENT FINANCE

资料整理：孟　刚
Data management: Meng Gang
数据审核：边可为
Data audit: Bian Kewei

第六部分　财政

一、简要说明

本章资料主要包括地方财政收入、支出总额构成及分区县情况，由西安市统计局综合处根据西安市财政局提供资料整理。

二、主要指标

财政总收入（亿元）	1541.50	比上年增长	0.5%
一般公共预算收入（亿元）	724.14	比上年增长	3.1%
一般公共预算支出（亿元）	1347.58	比上年增长	8.1%

6　GOVERNMENT FINANCE

Ⅰ.Brief Introduction

This chapter consists of primarily data on regional revenue, expenditure of the municipal government, regional revenue and expenditure of the districts and the counties. The data are provided by the Xi'an Bureau of Finance and are compiled by Integration division of the Xi'an Bureau of Statistics.

Ⅱ.Major Indicators

		Increase over Preceding Year
Total Government Revenue(100 mil. yuan)	1541.50	0.5%
General Pubilc Budgetary Revenue(100 mil. yuan)	724.14	3.1%
General Pubilc Budgetary Expenditures(100 mil. yuan)	1347.58	8.1%

6-1 主要年份地方财政一般预算收入及支出

General Public Budgetary Revenue and Expenditure of Local Finance in Representative Years

单位：亿元 （100 million yuan）

年 份 Year	财政总收入 Fiscal Revenue	一般公共预算收入 General Public Budgetary Revenue	一般公共预算支出 General Public Budgetary Expenditure	收支差额 Balance of Payments	财政总收入比上年增长（%） Fiscal Revenue Increased over the Previous Year（%）	一般公共预算收入比上年增长（%） General Public Budget Revenue Growth over the Previous Year（%）	一般公共预算支出比上年增长（%） General Public Budget Expenditures Growth over the Previous Year（%）
2000	61.57	41.39	46.50	-5.11		14.4	
2001	75.79	51.45	54.21	-2.76	23.1	9.9	10.2
2002	99.84	54.49	63.80	-9.32	31.7	16.9	11.3
2003	120.64	64.80	72.37	-7.57	20.8	21.6	22.6
2004	133.52	75.31	84.20	-8.88	10.7	20.0	16.3
2005	163.87	73.05	97.82	-24.76	22.7	18.2	16.2
2006	195.96	85.89	119.22	-33.33	19.6	18.6	21.9
2007	260.70	112.92	161.25	-48.33	33.0	31.5	35.3
2008	324.49	145.61	226.99	-81.38	24.5	28.9	40.8
2009	399.53	181.40	276.85	-95.45	23.4	24.6	22.0
2010	510.69	241.86	371.62	-129.76	27.6	33.3	34.2
2011	649.88	318.55	494.58	-176.03	27.3	31.7	33.1
2012	753.08	396.96	597.49	-200.53	15.9	24.6	20.8
2013	902.76	501.98	729.81	-227.84	19.9	26.5	22.1
2014	1019.69	583.79	819.54	-235.75	13.0	16.3	12.3
2015	1114.98	650.99	917.24	-266.25	9.3	16.3	12.9
2016	1135.68	641.07	942.52	-301.46	8.5	11.1	2.8
2017	1364.71	654.50	1045.09	-390.59	12.6	9.8	7.1
2018	1460.39	684.70	1151.87	-467.17	13.6	10.8	10.2
2019	1533.89	702.56	1247.02	-544.45	5.0	2.6	8.3
2020	1541.50	724.14	1347.58	-623.44	0.5	3.1	8.1

注：本表数据来源于市财政局，对部分历史年份数据进行了修订。

6-2 财政收入（2020年）

Government Revenue（2020）

单位：万元 （10 000 yuan）

指　　标	Item	2020
财政总收入	**Total Government Revenue**	**15414953**
#一般公共预算收入	**General Public Budgetary Revenue**	**7241390**
一、税收收入	**Total Tax Revenue**	**5716002**
1. 国内增值税	Value-added Tax	748603
2. 改征增值税	Levying VAT	1414224
3. 企业所得税	Corporate Income Tax	668055
4. 个人所得税	Individual Income Tax	257142
5. 城市建设维护税	City Maintenance and Construction Tax	495024
6. 房产税	House Property Tax	275482
7. 城镇土地使用税	Urban Land Use Tax	105445
8. 印花税	Stamp Tax	189793
9. 车船税	Tax on the Use of Vehicles and Ships	124694
10. 土地增值税	Land Appreciation Tax	498305
11. 资源税	Resource Tax	20753
12. 环境保护税	Environmental Protection Tax	473
13. 耕地占用税	Farm Land Occupatian Tax	101409
14. 契税	Deed Tax	814795
15. 其他税收收入	Other Tax Revenue	1805
二、非税收入	**Total Non-tax Revenue**	**1525388**
1. 行政事业性收费收入	Charge of Adminnistrative and Institutional Units	228826
2. 罚没收入	Penalty Receipts	165709
3. 专项收入	Special Program Receipts	509074
4. 国有资本经营收入	State-owned Assets Profit	
5. 国有资源（资产）有偿使用收入	Revenue for the Use of State-owned Assets (Resources)	389832
6. 捐赠收入	Donation Income	887
7. 政府住房基金收入	Governmental Housing Fund Income	230787
8. 其他收入	Other Revenue	273
政府性基金预算收入	**Governmental Fund Budgetary Revenue**	**12073226**

注：本表数据来源于市财政局。

6-3 财政支出（2020年）

Government Expenditures (2020)

单位：万元 （10 000 yuan）

指 标	Item	2020
一般公共预算支出	**General Public Budgetary Expenditure**	**13475816**
1. 一般公共服务支出	Expenditure for General Public Services	1328927
2. 国防支出	Expenditure for National Defense	10498
3. 公共安全支出	Expenditure for Public Security	812113
4. 教育支出	Expenditure for Education	2333672
5. 科学技术支出	Expenditure for Science and Technology	232684
6. 文化旅游体育与传媒支出	Expenditure for Cultural, Travel,Sports and Media	338026
7. 社会保障和就业支出	Expenditure for Social Safety Net and Employment Effort	1808936
8. 卫生健康支出	Expenditure for Medical 、 Health Care and Brith Control Planning	1168057
9. 节能环保支出	Expenditure for Energy Saving	579502
10. 城乡社区支出	Expenditure for Urban and Rural Community Affairs	2003838
11. 农林水支出	Expenditure for Agriculture, Forestry and Water Conservancy	659104
12. 交通运输支出	Expenditure for Transportation	269394
13. 资源勘探工业信息等支出	Expenditure for Industry Exploration of the Power of Information	372851
14. 商业服务业等支出	Expenditure for Business Services	300341
15. 金融支出	Expenditure for Finance	169907
16. 自然资源海洋气象等支出	Natural Resources and Marine Meteorology	105066
17. 住房保障支出	Expenditure for Housing Security	449578
18. 粮油物资储备支出	Expenditure for Grain and Oil Stockpiles	39217
19. 灾害防治及应急管理支出	Expenditures for Disaster Prevention and Emergency Management	83964
20. 其他支出	Other Expenditure	97576
21. 债务付息支出	Debt Service Expenditure	311323
22. 债务发行费用支出	Debt Issuance Expenditure	1242
政府性基金预算支出	**Governmental Fund Budgetary Expenditure**	**11717073**

注：本表数据来源于市财政局。

6-4　各区县、开发区财政收入（2020年）

单位：万元

区县、开发区	Region	一般公共预算收入 General Public Budgetary Revenue	税收收入 Tax Revenue	国内增值税 Domestic value Added TaxTax
合计	**Total**	**7241390**	**5716002**	**748603**
市本级	City Level	1465472	746753	9407
新城区	Xincheng	184949	167934	27438
碑林区	Beilin	332924	302353	51941
莲湖区	Lianhu	347614	308818	54457
灞桥区	Baqiao	186308	174344	20957
未央区	Weiyang	302293	265774	37647
雁塔区	Yanta	378509	346147	43352
阎良区	Yanliang	71021	51103	8986
临潼区	Lintong	132693	69889	20741
长安区	Chang'an	202109	166794	17205
高陵区	Gaoling	125061	99656	25971
鄠邑区	Huyi	78825	58863	18716
蓝田县	Lantian	29102	23007	5562
周至县	Zhouzhi	23206	15231	3268
西咸新区	Xixian	839989	658716	60185
高新区	Gao Xin	1148150	1080604	191281
经开区	JingKai	414309	357449	86157
曲江新区	Qujiang	407434	338757	7886
航空基地	Aviation Industry Base	17043	15406	4179
航天基地	Aerospace Base	100384	90266	15950
浐灞生态区	Chanba Eco-District	242850	190969	10255
国际港务区	International Trade&Logistic ParkPark	211145	187169	27062

注：本表数据来源于市财政局。

Government Revenue by Region and Development Zone（2020）

（10 000 yuan）

一般公共预算收入 General Public Budgetary Revenue					
税收收入 Tax Revenue					
改征增值税 Levying VAT	企业所得税 Corporate Income Tax	个人所得税 Individual Income Tax	城市维护建设税 City Maintenance and Construction Tax	房产税 House Property Tax	城镇土地使用税 Urban Land Use Tax
1414224	**668055**	**257142**	**495024**	**275482**	**105445**
398851	60926	12576	106853	11775	2104
20773	41957	11904	13207	14235	3221
89886	43910	31466	27548	21869	2648
90015	33651	27019	27204	16368	5564
37187	17091	3049	13050	5186	4953
76824	30539	7600	24757	13596	7188
101519	43481	20467	30525	21227	4429
11219	5612	3134	3396	4301	1965
10232	5992	2386	6070	2942	1910
43465	25173	4738	13360	5475	2949
12658	7778	3264	9468	5186	5684
8566	3002	1693	5648	3253	1972
5040	1186	539	1701	1070	796
3963	441	1023	875	442	339
125783	55626	10601	47220	23954	18553
195589	139759	77719	83615	75877	17552
63642	50407	14443	33559	22897	9537
66439	53751	8711	17542	14014	5034
1667	1643	1033	2105	1386	1118
12288	11167	8220	5887	2558	969
11810	15946	3989	8190	3335	3340
26808	19017	1568	13244	4536	3620

6-4 续表1

单位：万元

区县、开发区	Region	一般公共预算收入 General Public Budgetary Revenue		
		税收收入 Tax Revenue		
		印花税 Stamp Tax	车船税 Tax on the Use of Vehicles and Ships	土地增值税 Land Appreciation Tax
合计	**Total**	**189793**	**124694**	**498305**
市本级	City Level	19677	104797	
新城区	Xincheng	4596		13725
碑林区	Beilin	10929		4055
莲湖区	Lianhu	10648		8133
灞桥区	Baqiao	4592		25670
未央区	Weiyang	8077		22910
雁塔区	Yanta	8789		21893
阎良区	Yanliang	1314	2408	1447
临潼区	Lintong	3030	2650	1934
长安区	Chang'an	5541	3965	14103
高陵区	Gaoling	5366	2154	8441
鄠邑区	Huyi	1269	1886	3209
蓝田县	Lantian	572	1250	1380
周至县	Zhouzhi	283	1519	1148
西咸新区	Xixian	19081	4065	96483
高新区	Gao Xin	41316		84530
经开区	JingKai	21560		21905
曲江新区	Qujiang	6665		58490
航空基地	Aviation Industry Base	315		497
航天基地	Aerospace Base	3204		14899
浐灞生态区	Chanba Eco-District	3576		65948
国际港务区	International Trade&Logistic ParkPark	9393		27505

continued 1

(10 000 yuan)

一般公共预算收入 General Public Budgetary Revenue					非税收入 Non-tax Revenue
税收收入 Tax Revenue					
资源税 Resource Tax	环境保护税 Environmental Protection Tax	耕地占用税 Farm Land Occupation Tax	契税 Deed Tax	其他各项税收收入 Other Tax Revenue	
20753	**473**	**101409**	**814795**	**1805**	**1525388**
19539	345			-97	718719
			16886	-8	17015
3			18117	-19	30571
6			35752	1	38796
1		6518	35999	91	11964
1		750	35908	-23	36519
13			50067	385	32362
		1753	5567	1	19918
74		4669	7259		62804
45		821	29954		35315
		1509	12183	-6	25405
15		1036	8598		19962
167		1539	2205		6095
67		26	1837		7975
802	128	80856	115373	6	181273
10		1932	171274	150	67546
2			33418	-78	56860
6			100254	-35	68677
			1435	28	1637
			15124		10118
			63171	1409	51881
2			54414		23976

6-4 续表2

单位：万元

区县、开发区	Region	一般公共预算收入 General Public Budgetary Revenue		
		非税收入 Non-tax Revenue		
		行政事业性收费收入 Charge of Adiministrative and Institutional Units	罚没收入 Penalty Receipts	专项收入 Special Program Receipts
合计	**Total**	**228826**	**165709**	**509074**
市本级	City Level	146681	86243	174094
新城区	Xincheng	2547	5600	7477
碑林区	Beilin	2301	2561	15347
莲湖区	Lianhu	3733	3757	16090
灞桥区	Baqiao	962	1386	6905
未央区	Weiyang	738	2458	17481
雁塔区	Yanta	4574	2866	16598
阎良区	Yanliang	3703	1415	11004
临潼区	Lintong	3241	8305	3445
长安区	Chang'an	6619	12626	6810
高陵区	Gaoling	11003	2576	5080
鄠邑区	Huyi	4181	5960	3248
蓝田县	Lantian	923	1515	3496
周至县	Zhouzhi	3469	2847	713
西咸新区	Xixian	24366	15820	100417
高新区	Gao Xin	602	2947	47589
经开区	JingKai	4334	751	20003
曲江新区	Qujiang	731	2392	10457
航空基地	Aviation Industry Base	102	194	1194
航天基地	Aerospace Base	688	1530	7336
浐灞生态区	Chanba Eco-District	856	1960	24567
国际港务区	International Trade&Logistic ParkPark	2472		9723

continued 2

(10 000 yuan)

一般公共预算收入 General Public Budgetary Revenue					政府性基金预算收入 Governmental Funds Budgetary Revenue
非税收入 Non-tax Revenue					
国有资本经营收入 State-owned Assets Profit	国有资源（资产）有偿使用收入 The Revenues of the Compensation for the Use of State-owned Resoures(Assants)	捐赠收入 Donation Income	政府住房基金收入 Governmental Housing Fund Income	其他收入 Other income	
	389832	**887**	**230787**	**273**	**12073226**
	101367		210334		1107767
	1391				53
	10362				1098
	14649	567			115837
	2662	49			508812
	15842				29771
	8319	5			
	3796				40387
	47668		145		98655
	9053		207		193683
	6709		37		126395
	5971	118	484		179392
	151		10		26351
	862		84		40788
	35716	120	4834		3296111
	6446		9689	273	2497594
	28728		3044		314880
	54097		1000		517438
	124		23		89066
	564				313541
	23602		896		587669
	11753	28			1987938

6-5 各区县、开发区财政支出（2020年）

单位：万元

区县、开发区	Region	一般公共预算支出 General Public Budgetary Expenditures	一般公共服务支出 General Public Services Expenditure	国防支出 Expenditure for National Defense	公共安全支出 Expenditure for Public Safety
合计	**Total**	**13475816**	**1328927**	**10498**	**812113**
市本级	City Level	4358775	283139	4611	444352
新城区	Xincheng	353718	27576	108	30216
碑林区	Beilin	311093	34715		27609
莲湖区	Lianhu	414568	53442	238	26342
灞桥区	Baqiao	371532	45547	488	22558
未央区	Weiyang	371215	35242	247	23495
雁塔区	Yanta	350047	55493	375	35589
阎良区	Yanliang	209821	26088		12320
临潼区	Lintong	465366	31746		17063
长安区	Chang'an	493565	47356	118	20732
高陵区	Gaoling	280141	35112	313	11244
鄠邑区	Huyi	386977	32725	1827	14543
蓝田县	Lantian	444261	43753	237	12128
周至县	Zhouzhi	428194	26074	84	13373
西咸新区	Xixian	1339388	280634	1222	56754
高新区	Gao Xin	1071645	99619	30	20248
经开区	JingKai	382694	41722		8351
曲江新区	Qujiang	499761	40858		1695
航空基地	Aviation Industry Base	38229	5968		
航天基地	Aerospace Base	115376	8998	600	3264
浐灞生态区	Chanba Eco-District	286784	33171		7941
国际港务区	International Trade&Logistic Park	502666	39949		2296

注：本表数据来源于市财政局。

Government Expenditure by Region and Development Zone（2020）

（10 000 yuan）

教育支出 Expenditure for Education	科学技术支出 Expenditure for Science and Technology	文化旅游体育与传媒支出 Expenditure for Cultural, Travel, Sports and Media	社会保障和就业支出 Expenditure for Social Safety Net and Employment Effort	卫生健康支出 Expenditure for Medical and Health Care	节能环保支出 Expenditure for Energy Saving and Environment Protection
2333672	**232684**	**338026**	**1808936**	**1168057**	**579502**
177762	72674	63871	749171	579085	138907
93471	887	2108	82205	32738	2159
100960	2122	3581	76770	23684	2307
113299	2212	3539	81070	35868	4874
114182	277	3017	50037	27996	3002
109144	450	1922	41248	23792	6678
105070	882	3276	43355	26781	6036
52559	81	2480	31812	19196	6066
117794	264	10182	106952	35894	21270
135816	308	7496	74218	52552	10572
76513	364	3483	36256	29000	6882
89398	445	4713	92101	30319	10160
95171	483	7338	97959	34636	17424
111871	275	6338	70050	31882	18693
257315	5811	30388	106833	122537	35655
172078	109489	7961	54427	35532	258591
96211	10585	9885	1602	9644	14820
93178		144548	1521	6124	2691
4881	2500	63		510	761
49767	22525	117	200	2856	2133
64885		1338	81	1637	2966
102347	50	20382	11068	5794	6855

6-5 续表1

单位：万元

区县、开发区	Region	一般公共预算支出 General Public Budgetary Expenditures			
		城乡社区支出 Expenditure for Urban and Rural Community Affairs	农林水支出 Expenditure for Agriculture, Foresty and Water Conservancy	交通运输支出 Expenditure for Transportation	资源勘探工业信息等支出 Expenditure for Industry Exploration of Information
合计	**Total**	**2003838**	**659104**	**269394**	**372851**
市本级	City Level	816635	162451	186342	40581
新城区	Xincheng	35962	1185	1222	1541
碑林区	Beilin	27228	157	490	1047
莲湖区	Lianhu	47730	2958	491	3311
灞桥区	Baqiao	45985	26786	4592	3216
未央区	Weiyang	101610	6209	1812	1064
雁塔区	Yanta	18603	7768	1426	5073
阎良区	Yanliang	28020	7835	1527	13413
临潼区	Lintong	40448	52406	4411	3720
长安区	Chang'an	43699	52748	7433	753
高陵区	Gaoling	29562	22364	6382	2128
鄠邑区	Huyi	22825	40517	13613	6067
蓝田县	Lantian	37052	76346	6859	526
周至县	Zhouzhi	28982	91202	11187	338
西咸新区	Xixian	88464	62564	16834	53081
高新区	Gao Xin	133845	11833	1915	70499
经开区	JingKai	24637	147	2458	152329
曲江新区	Qujiang	159561	5193		2673
航空基地	Aviation Industry Base	15303	294		5213
航天基地	Aerospace Base	10188	100		5743
浐灞生态区	Chanba Eco-District	156677	1677		446
国际港务区	International Trade&Logistic Park	90822	26364	400	89

continued 1

(10 000 yuan)

商业服务业等支出 Expenditure for Business Services	金融支出 Expenditure for Finance	自然资源海洋气象等支出 Natural Resources and Marine Meteorology	住房保障支出 Expenditure for Housing Support	粮油物资储备支出 Expenditure for Grain and Oil Stockpiles	灾害防治及应急管理支出 Disaster Prevention and emergency management expenditure
300341	**169907**	**105066**	**449578**	**39217**	**83964**
52325	160994	45163	156447	18637	35712
2892	1300	1072	33082	1459	1056
2411		870	4082	630	1324
1819	291	1035	28969	1360	572
473		1725	7672	576	1018
291	70	2578	4404	825	858
1128	18	2670	33970	1253	631
461	177	1817	400	1500	643
459	155	4148	11539	1148	1493
1301	158	6249	27487	1259	1428
2519		2566	8016	1575	1686
1005	85	4645	15205	1559	1044
1829	127	3661	4082	949	865
477	130	1926	8560	1450	1370
41912	724	9002	32097	3037	21643
3206	416	2352	39404	800	1345
2260		96	4093		2672
5001	5262		19974		1657
644					1
653		754	4608		1961
5602		1180	4246		855
171673		11557	1241	1200	4130

6–5 续表2 continued 2

单位：万元 （10 000 yuan）

区县、开发区	Region	一般公共预算支出 General Public Budgetary Expenditures			政府性基金预算支出 Governmental Fund Budgetary Expenditure
		其他支出 Other Expenditure	债务付息支出 Debt Service Expenditure	债务发行费用支出 Debt Issuance Expenditure	
合计	**Total**	**97576**	**311323**	**1242**	**11717073**
市本级	City Level	1822	166945	1149	2268120
新城区	Xincheng		1479		55648
碑林区	Beilin	2	1104		61817
莲湖区	Lianhu	90	5058		83552
灞桥区	Baqiao	6368	6017		223577
未央区	Weiyang	31	9245		42891
雁塔区	Yanta		650		19907
阎良区	Yanliang	100	3326		39700
临潼区	Lintong	2	4272		138420
长安区	Chang'an	190	1692		160334
高陵区	Gaoling	579	3597		147291
鄠邑区	Huyi	1180	3001		120083
蓝田县	Lantian	235	2601		29409
周至县	Zhouzhi	1570	2362		50498
西咸新区	Xixian	70975	41813	93	3515671
高新区	Gao Xin	10132	37923		1626203
经开区	JingKai		1182		350445
曲江新区	Qujiang		9825		479592
航空基地	Aviation Industry Base		2091		86197
航天基地	Aerospace Base		909		197386
浐灞生态区	Chanba Eco-District		4082		650466
国际港务区	International Trade&Logistic Park	4300	2149		1369866

主要统计指标解释

财政收入 指国家财政参与社会产品分配所取得的收入，是实现国家职能的财力保证。主要包括：

（1）税收收入：包括增值税、消费税、企业所得税、企业所得税退税、个人所得税、资源税、城市维护建设税、房产税、印花税、城镇土地使用税、土地增值税、车船税、船舶吨税、车辆购置税、关税、耕地占用税、契税、烟叶税、环境保护税和其他税收收入。

（2）非税收入：包括专项收入、行政事业性收费收入、罚没收入、国有资本经营收入、国有资源（资产）有偿使用收入、捐赠收入、政府住房基金收入和其他收入。

财政支出 指国家财政将筹集起来的资金进行分配使用，以满足经济建设和各项事业的需要。主要包括：

（1）一般公共服务支出：指政府提供基本公共管理与服务的支出，包括人大事务、政协事务、政府办公厅（室）及相关机构事务、发展与改革事务、统计信息事务、财政事务、税收事务、审计事务、海关事务、人力资源事务、纪检监察事务、商贸事务、知识产权事务、民族事务、港澳台侨事务、档案事务、民主党派及工商联事务、群众团体事务、党委办公厅（室）及相关机构事务、组织事务、宣传事务、统战事务、对外联络事务、其他共产党事务支出、网信服务、市场监督管理实务和其他一般公共服务支出。

（2）外交支出：指政府外交事务支出，包括外交管理事务、驻外机构、对外援助、国际组织、对外合作与交流、对外宣传、边界勘界联检、国际发展合作等方面的支出。

（3）国防支出：指政府用于国防方面的支出，包括用于现役部队、国防科研事业、专项工程、国防动员等方面的支出。

（4）公共安全支出：指政府维护社会公共安全方面的支出，包括武装警察部队、公安、国家安全、检察、法院、司法、监狱、强制隔离戒毒、国家保密、缉私警察、海警等。

（5）教育支出：指政府教育事务支出，包括教育管理事务、普通教育、职业教育、成人教育、广播电视教育、留学教育、特殊教育、进修及培训、教育费附加安排的支出等。

（6）科学技术支出：指用于科学技术方面的支出，包括科学技术管理事务、基础研究、应用研究、技术研究与开发、科技条件与服务、社会科学、科学技术普及、科技交流与合作、科技重大项目等。

（7）文化旅游体育与传媒支出：指政府在文化和旅游、文物、体育、新闻出版电影、广播电视等方面的支出。

（8）社会保障和就业支出：指政府在社会保障与就业方面的支出，包括人力资源和社会保障管理事务、民政管理事务、补充全国社会保障基金、行政事业单位离退休、企业改革补助、就业补助、抚恤、退役安置、社会福利、残疾人事业、红十字事业、最低生活保障、临时救助、特困人员救助供养、补充道路交通事故社会救助基金、其他生活救助、财政对基本养老保险基金的补助、财政对其他社会保险基金的补助、退役军人管理实务等。

（9）卫生健康支出：指政府卫生健康方面的支出，包括卫生健康管理事务、公立医院、基层医疗卫生机构、公共卫生、中医药、计划生育事务、行政事业单位医疗、财政对基本医疗保险基金的补助、医疗救助、优抚对象医疗、医疗保障管理事务、老龄卫生健康事务等。

（10）节能环保支出：指政府节能环保支出，包括环境保护管理事务、环境监测与监察、污染防治、自然生态保护、天然林保护、退耕还林、风沙荒漠治理、退牧还草、已垦草原退耕还草、能源节约利用、污染减排、可再生能源、循环经济、能源管理事务等支出。

（11）城乡社区支出：指政府城乡社区事务支出，包括城乡社区管理事务、城乡社区规划与管理、城乡社区公共设施、城乡社区环境卫生、建设市场管理与监督等。

（12）农林水支出：指政府用于农林水事务支出，包括农业、林业和草原、水利、南水北调、扶贫、农业综合开发、农村综合改革、普惠金融发展支出、目标价格补贴等。

（13）交通运输支出：指政府交通运输和邮政业方面的支出，包括公路水路运输、铁路运输、民用航空运输、成品油价格改革对交通运输的补贴、邮政业支出、车辆购置税支出等。

（14）资源勘探信息等支出：指政府用于资源勘探、制造业、建筑业、工业信息等方面的支出，包括资源勘探开发、制造业、建筑业、工业和信息产业监管、国有资产监管、支持中小企业发展和管理等。

（15）商业服务业支出：指政府用于商业服务业方面的支出，包括商业流通事务、涉外发展服务等。

（16）金融支出：指政府用于金融方面的支出，包括金融部门行政支出、金融部门监管支出、金融发展、金融调控等。

（17）援助其他地区支出：指用于援助方政府安排并管理的对其他地区各类援助、捐赠等资金支出。包括一般公共服务、教育、文化体育与传媒、医疗卫生、节能环保、农业、交通运输、住房保障等支出

（18）自然资源海洋气象等支出：指政府用于自然资源、海洋管理、测绘、气象等公益服务事业方面的支出。

（19）住房保障支出：指政府用于住房方面的支出，包括保障性安居工程支出、住房改革支出、城乡社区住宅等。

（20）粮油物资储备支出：指政府用于粮油物资储备方面的支出，包括粮油事务、物资事务、能源储备、粮油储备、重要商品储备等。

（21）灾害防治及应急管理支出：指政府用于灾害防治及应急管理方面的支出，包括应急管理事务、消防事务、森林消防事务、煤矿安全、地震事务、自然灾害防治、自然灾害救灾及恢复重建支出等。

（22）债务付息支出：指政府用于归还债务利息等所发生的支出。

（23）债务发行费用支出：指政府用于债务发行兑付费用的支出。

（24）其他支出：指不能划分到上述功能科目的其他政府支出。

中央财政收入和地方财政收入 指按现行分税制财政体制划分的中央本级收入和地方本级收入。属于中央财政的收入包括关税，进口货物增值税和消费税，出口货物退增值税和消费税，消费税，铁道部门、各银行总行、各保险公司总公司等集中缴纳的城市维护建设税，增值税50%部分，纳入共享范围的企业所得税60%部分，未纳入共享范围的中央企业所得税、中央企业上交的利润，个人所得税60%部分，车辆购置税，船舶吨税，证券交易印花税，海洋石油资源税，中央非税收入等。属于地方财政的收入包括地方企业上交利润，城市维护建设税（不含铁道部门、各银行总行、各保险公司总公司集中缴纳的部分），房产税，城镇土地使用税，土地增值税，车船税，耕地占用税，契税，烟叶税，印花税（不含证券交易印花税），增值税50%部分，纳入共享范围的企业所得税40%部分，个人所得税40%部分，海洋石油资源税以外的其他资源税，地方非税收入等。

中央财政支出和地方财政支出 指根据政府在经济和社会活动中的不同职责，划分中央和地方政府的责权，按照政府的责权划分确定的支出。中央财政支出包括一般公共服务，外交支出，国防支出，公共安全支出，以及中央政府调整国民经济结构、协调地区发展、实施宏观调控的支出等。地方财政支出包括一般公共服务，公共安全支出，地方统筹的各项社会事业支出等。

Explanatory Notes on Main Statistical Indicators

Government Revenue refers to income for the government finance through participating in the distribution of social products. It is the financial guarantee to ensure government functioning. The contents of government revenue include the following main items:

(1) Tax revenue, including value added tax(VAT), consumption tax, business tax, corporate income tax, corporate income tax refund ,individual income tax, resource tax, city maintenance and construct tax, house property tax, stamp tax, urban land use tax, land appreciation tax, tax on vehicles and boat operation, ship tonnage tax, vehicle purchase tax, tariffs, farm land occupation tax, deed tax, and tobacco leaf tax, etc.

(2) Non-tax revenue, including special program receipts, charge of administrative and institutional units, penalty receipts, state-owned capital operating income, state-owned resources (assets) compensation for the use of income, donation income, government housing fund income and others non-tax receipts.

Government Expenditure refers to the distribution and use of the funds which the government finance has raised, so as to meet the needs of economic construction and various causes. It includes the following main items:

(1) Expenditure for general public services: It refers to the spending on the basic public management and services which provided by governments, including the expense on affairs of People's Congress, affairs of People's Political Consultative Conference, affairs of government general office and relative institutions, affairs of development and reform, affairs of statistics, affairs of finance, affairs of taxation, affairs of audit, affairs of customs, affairs of human resources and social security, affairs of discipline inspection and supervision, affairs of population and family planning, affairs of commerce and trade, affairs of intellectual property, affairs of administration for industry and commerce, affairs of land and resources, affairs of oceanic administration, affairs of surveying and mapping, affairs of earthquake, ethnic affairs, religious affairs, affairs of Hong Kong, Macao, Taiwan, and Overseas Chinese, affairs of archives administration, affairs of democratic parties and federation of industry and commerce, affairs of mass organization, and affairs of lottery, affairs of the general office of the Party Committee and related institutions, affairs of propaganda, affairs of united front, affairs of external liaison, affairs of expenditure on other Communist Party, other affairs of Chinese Communist Party, etc.

(2) Expenditure for foreign affairs: It refers to the spending of government on foreign affairs, including the expense on administration of foreign affairs, missions overseas, external assistance, international organizations, foreign cooperation and communication, surveying and joint inspection on borderline, etc.

(3) Expenditure for national defense: It refers to the spending of government on national defense, including the expense on active force, scientific research on national defense, special projects, mobilization of national defense, etc.

(4) Expenditure for public security: It refers to the spending of government on maintaining social and public security, including the expense on armed police force, public security, state security, prosecution, courts, justice, prison, compulsory isolation and drug treatment, state secrecy, anti-smuggling police, maritime police, etc.

(5) Expenditure for education: It refers to the spending of government on education, including the expense on the administration of education, general education, regular vocational school education, adult education, radio and television education, student abroad education, special education, education and training, education surtax arrangements spending, etc.

(6) Expenditure for science and technology: It refers to the spending of government on science and technology (S&T), including the expense on the administration of S&T, basic research, applied research, research and development, conditions and services of S&T, social science, popularization of science and technology, exchanges and cooperation of S&T, major project of S&T, etc.

(7) Expenditure for culture, sport and media: It refers to the spending of government on culture, sports, radio, film, television, press and publication, etc.

(8) Expenditure for social safety net and employment effort: It refers to the spending of government on social safety net and employment, including the expense on administration of social safety net and employment, civil affairs, subsidy on National Social Security Fund, retirees of administrative units and institutions, subsidy on enterprise reform, subsidy on employment effort, pension, placement of ex-serviceman, social welfare, the handicapped undertakings, living relief of natural disasters, affairs of Red Cross Society, minimum subsistence security, temporary assistance, relief and assistance for the residents living in extreme poverty, supplementary social assistance fund for road traffic accidents, other life assistance, financial subsidy for basic old-age insurance fund, financial subsidy for other social insurance funds, etc.

(9) Expenditure for medical health care and birth control planning: It refers to government spending on health care, including health management services, public hospitals, primary health care institutions, public health, the pharmaceutical, family planning affairs, food and drug supervision and administration affairs, medical treatment of administrative institutions, financial subsidies to basic medical insurance funds, medical assistance, preferential care for the target medical treatment, etc.

(10) Expenditure for energy saving: It refers to the government energy-saving and environmental protection expenditures, including environmental management services, environmental monitoring and surveillance, pollution control, ecological protection, natural forest protection project, forest, desert sand control, pasture, grassland of cultivated farmland, energy conservation and utilization expenditure pollution reduction, renewable energy and comprehensive utilization of resources, etc.

(11) Expenditure for urban and rural community affairs: It refers to the spending of government on urban and rural community affairs, including the expense on administration of urban and rural community, planning and management of urban and rural community, public facilities of urban and rural community, housing of urban and rural community, sanitation of urban and rural community, management and supervision on the construction market, etc.

(12) Expenditure for agriculture, forestry and water conservancy: It refers to the spending of government on agriculture, forestry and water conservancy, including the expense on agriculture, forestry, water conservancy, South-to-North Water Diversion Project, poverty alleviation, agricultural comprehensive development, comprehensive agricultural reform, inclusive financial development expenditure and target price subsidies, etc.

(13) Expenditure for transportation: It refers to the spending of government on transportation and postal services, including the expense on road transport, sea transport, rail transport, civil aviation transportation, oil price reform subsidies for transportation, postal services, vehicle purchase tax, etc.

(14) Expenditure for exploration of the power of information: It refers to the spending on exploration, manufacturing, construction, industry information and other aspects of information, including resource exploration and development, manufacturing, construction, industry and information industry regulation, safety supervision, the state-owned assets supervision and support of small and medium enterprise development and management, etc.

(15) Expenditure for business services: It refers to government spending on commercial aspects of services, including commercial distribution business, tourism management and services, foreign development services, etc.

(16) Expenditure for financial: It refers to government spending on financial aspects, including administrative of financial sector, financial sector supervision, financial development, financial control, etc.

(17) Expenditure for assistance to other parts: It refers to the various types of assistance to other regions, financial donations, donors, government expenditure and management arrangements, etc.

(18) Expenditure for Land and Marine Meteorology: It refers to government spending on land resources, marine, mapping, seismic, weather and other aspects of

public service undertakings, etc.

(19) Expenditure for housing security: It refers to government spending on housing, including affordable housing projects, housing reform, urban and rural communities housing, etc.

(20) Expenditure for Grain and Oil stockpiles: It refers to government spending on supplies of grain and oil reserves, including grain and oil services, supplies services, energy reserves, grain and oil reserves, reserves of other important commodities, etc.

(21) Expenditure on disaster prevention and emergency management: refers to the government expenditure on disaster prevention and emergency management, including expenditure on emergency management, fire control, forest fire control, coal mine safety, earthquake, natural disaster prevention and control, natural disaster relief and recovery and reconstruction, etc.

(22) Expenditure for debt interest payment: It refers to the government expenditure for repayment of interest on debts, etc.

(23) Expenditure for debt issuance: It refers to the Government expenditure on debt issuance and payment fees.

(24) Other expenditure: It refers to other government spending cannot be divided into the above functions subjects.

Revenue of the Central Government and Revenue of the Local Governments refers to the revenue collected by the Central Government and that by the local governments as defined by the decentralized taxation system. In accordance with this system, the revenue of the Central Government includes tariff, VAT and consumption tax from imports, VAT and consumption tax rebate for exports, consumption tax, city maintenance and construct tax from the Ministry of Railways, head offices of banks, head offices of insurance company, which are handed over to the government in a centralized way, 50% of the value added tax, 60% the share part of the corporate income tax, unshared part of corporate income tax of the central enterprises, profit handed in by the central enterprises, 60% of individual income tax, vehicle purchase tax, ship tonnage tax, stamp tax on securities transactions, resource tax on the offshore petroleum resources, Central Government non-tax revenue, etc. The revenue of the local governments includes profit handed in by the local enterprises, city maintenance and construct tax (excluding the part of the Ministry of Railways, head offices of banks, head offices of insurance company, which are handed over to the government in a centralized way), house property tax, urban land use tax, land appreciation tax, tax on vehicles and boat operation, farm land occupation tax, deed tax, and tobacco leaf tax, stamp tax, 50% of the value added tax, 40% the share part of the corporate income tax, 40% of individual income tax, resource tax other than the tax on offshore petroleum resources, local non-tax revenue, etc.

Expenditure of the Central Government and Expenditure of the Local Governments according to the different functions of the Central Government and local governments in economic and social activities, the rights of affairs administration are demarcated between those of the Central Government and those of local governments; and the classification of the expenditure between the Central Government and local governments are made on the basis of the classification of the rights of affairs administration between them. The expenditure of the Central Government includes the expenditure for general public services, expenditure for foreign affairs, expenditure for defense, expenditure for public security, and the expenditure of the Central Government for adjusting the national economic structure; coordinating the development among different regions; and exercising macroeconomic regulation. The expenditure of the local governments includes mainly the expenditure for general public services, expenditure for public security, and expenditures for social development which are planned by local governments, etc.

7 物价指数

PRICE INDICES

资料整理：张元园　乔兴录
Data management: Zhang Yuanyuan Qiao Xinglu
数据审核：景春玲　高小琴　贾海宇
Data audit: Jing Chunling Gao Xiaoqin Jia Haiyu

第七部分　物价指数

一、简要说明

1.本章资料主要反映生产、流通、消费、投资与房地产等环节价格变动趋势和变动幅度。主要包括居民消费价格指数、商品零售价格指数、工业生产者出厂价格指数、工业生产者购进价格指数、固定资产投资价格指数和住宅销售价格指数。

2.本章资料由国家统计局西安调查队提供。

3.居民消费价格指数、商品零售价格指数资料的获取，是通过抽样调查和重点调查相结合的方式。在西安市区域内选定经营规模大、商品种类多的大型商场、超市、农贸市场和服务网点作为调查点，选择具有代表性的商品和服务项目作为样本，对其市场价格进行定期调查，以样本推断总体。

4.工业生产者出厂价格指数、工业生产者购进价格指数、固定资产投资价格指数，采取抽样调查和重点调查的方法。工业生产者出厂、工业生产者购进价格指数通过西安工业企业网上直报获取。住宅销售价格指数通过西安市月度住宅销售网签数据获取。

二、主要指标

居民消费价格总指数（上年=100）	102.1	比上年下降	0.6个百分点
商品零售价格总指数（上年=100）	101.5	比上年下降	0.6个百分点

7 PRICE INDICES

Ⅰ.Brief Introduction

1.The data on price indices in this chapter show the changing trends and change rates in the price of production, circulation, consumption, investment and real estate, including mainly consumer price indices, retail price indices, producer price indices for industrial producers, purchasing price indices for industrial producers, price indices for investment in fixed assets, and selling price indices of residential buildings.

2.The data are provided by NBS Survey Office in Xi'an.

3.The data for the calculation of consumer price indices and retail prices and retail price indices in the province are collected through stratified random sampling. Large-scale shops, supermarkets, fairs and service outlets with wide variety of commodities in Xi'an are selected as survey points. Representative commodities and services are selected as sample commodities and services. Regular surveys are conducted to collect data on market prices. The data on the population are estimated on the basis of the sample.

4.The producer price indices for industrial producers, purchasing price indices for industrial producers and price indices for investment in fixed assetsare collected through stratified random sampling. The producer price indices for industrial producers and purchasing price indices for industrial producers are collected by online direct report of Xi'an industrial enterprises. Selling price indices of residential buildings are collected by monthly data of online residential sales record.

Ⅱ.Major Indicators

		Increase over Preceding Year
Consumer Price Index(the price of preceding year=100)	102.1	-0.6 percentage points
Retail Price Index(the price of preceding year=100)	101.5	-0.6 percentage points

7-1 主要年份各种价格指数

Price Indices in Representative Years

(以上年价格为100) (the price of preceding year=100)

年 份 Year	居民消费价格指数 Consumer Price Index	商品零售价格指数 Retail Price Index	工业生产者出厂价格指数 Producer Price Indices (PPI) for Industrial Producers	工业生产者购进价格指数 Industrial Purchasing Indices （IPI） for Industrial Producers	固定资产投资价格指数 Price Index for Investment in Fixed Assets
1980	108.7	109.3			
1983	102.6	102.0			
1984	104.7	104.8			
1985	109.7	109.3			
1986	108.5	107.4			
1987	110.6	111.4			
1988	122.8	123.2			
1989	118.3	117.8			
1990	102.5	100.9			
1991	109.4	108.3			
1992	112.2	112.4			
1993	117.2	112.8	102.5	104.3	
1994	128.5	126.2	132.2	115.0	
1995	117.0	114.6	110.8	113.1	
1996	110.9	107.9	100.7	103.8	
1997	106.0	101.5	98.6	102.5	
1998	97.9	95.5	94.4	97.5	
1999	96.8	97.4	97.5	96.9	100.8
2000	100.2	98.7	99.4	102.4	102.1
2001	99.9	98.9	99.3	101.0	101.3
2002	98.6	98.5	98.2	98.4	101.2
2003	100.5	100.0	101.5	105.3	102.4
2004	102.3	101.9	102.7	110.4	103.3
2005	100.3	99.7	103.9	109.6	102.4
2006	101.6	101.5	103.2	106.1	102.0
2007	104.7	103.7	101.9	106.2	103.5
2008	106.0	105.4	103.7	108.5	110.5
2009	99.7	99.5	99.9	100.7	97.9
2010	103.5	102.7	102.3	106.3	103.8
2011	105.6	104.4	102.5	108.8	105.4
2012	102.8	102.3	100.5	97.2	101.9
2013	102.7	101.7	99.5	97.2	100.8
2014	101.4	100.7	99.5	99.5	100.8
2015	100.7	99.7	98.5	94.5	97.9
2016	100.9	100.1	97.8	97.6	100.0
2017	102.0	101.7	100.3	104.7	105.4
2018	101.9	102.2	101.1	102.7	104.7
2019	102.7	102.1	101.6	100.0	
2020	102.1	101.5	100.2	100.4	

注：本表数据来源国家统计局西安调查队。

本表2017年数据为西安原口径数据。下同。

本表2018年起PPI、IPI含西咸新区；2019年起住宅销售价格指数数据口径有变化，不含西咸地区；其他指标为西安原口径数据。下同。

2018年固定资产投资价格指数包含西咸地区，2019年固定资产投资价格调查方案变动，2019年不出价格指数。2020年固投调查暂停。

7-2 居民消费价格指数（2020年）

Residents Consumer Price Indices（2020）

(以上年价格为100) (the price of preceding year=100)

指 标	Item	2020
居民消费价格指数	**Consumer Price Index**	**102.1**
非食品烟酒价格指数	Non-Food，Tobaccol and Liquor Price Index	100.4
服务价格指数	Price Index of Service	100.8
工业品价格指数	Industrial Price Index	100.0
鲜活食品价格指数	Price Index of Fresh Food	110.3
消费品价格指数	Price Index of Consumer Goods	102.8
能源价格指数	Energy Price Index	97.8
非食品价格指数	Non-foodstuff Price Index	100.9
扣除食品和能源价格指数	Price Index with Food And Energy Excluded	101.1
扣除鲜菜鲜果价格指数	Price Index with Fresh Vegetables Fruits Excluded	102.1
扣除自有住房价格指数	Price Index with Self-owned Housing Excluded	102.4
居住（扣自有住房）价格指数	Housing (Self-owned Housing Excluded) Price Index	99.8
一、食品和烟酒	**Food，To bacco and Liquor**	**106.1**
1. 食品	Food	107.5
（1）粮食	Grain	100.9
（2）薯类	Potato	109.6
（3）豆类	Beans	112.6
（4）食用油	Cooking Oil	102.7
（5）菜	Vegetables	113.0
（6）畜肉类	Livestock Meat	133.1
（7）禽肉类	Poultry Meat	102.1
（8）水产品	Aquatic Products	104.8
（9）蛋类	Eggs	82.2
（10）奶类	Milk	103.9
（11）干鲜瓜果类	Dried Fresh Melons and Fruits	89.7
（12）糖果糕点类	Sweets and Cakes	99.3
（13）调味品	Flavouring	101.0
（14）其他食品类	Other Food	103.8
2. 茶及饮料	Tea and Drinks	100.9
3. 烟酒	Tobacco and Liquor	100.9
（1）烟草	Tobacco	100.2
（2）酒类	Liquor	102.0
4. 在外餐饮	Dining Out	104.9
二、衣着	**Clothing**	**100.4**
1. 服装	Garments	100.8
2. 鞋类	Footwear	99.3
三、居住	**Residence**	**99.6**
1. 租赁房房租	Rental Housing	99.0
2. 住房保养维修及管理	Housing Maintenance And Management	99.5
3. 水电燃料	Water,Electricity, Fuels	100.3
4. 自有住房	Private Housing	99.3

注：本表数据来源国家统计局西安调查队。

7-2 续表 continued

(以上年价格为100) (the price of preceding year=100)

指 标	Item	2020
四、生活用品及服务	**Daily Necessities and Services**	**100.6**
1.家具及室内装饰品	Furniture and Interior Decorations	100.0
2.家用器具	Household Appliances	99.4
3.家用纺织品	Home Textiles	100.9
4.家庭日用杂品	Daily Use Household Articles	101.4
5.个人护理用品	Personal Care Articles	101.5
6.家庭服务	Home Services	100.5
五、交通和通信	**Transportation And Communication**	**98.3**
1.交通	Transportation	97.8
（1）交通工具	Transportation Facility	99.8
（2）交通工具用燃料	Fuels For Vehicles	86.1
（3）交通工具使用和维修	Vehicles Use And Maintenance	98.4
（4）交通费	Traffic Fare	98.9
2.通信	Communications	99.3
（1）通信工具	Telecommunication facility	97.8
（2）通信服务	Telecommunication Service	100.0
（3）邮递服务	Postal Service	100.0
六、教育文化和娱乐	**Education, Culture And Recreation**	**102.5**
1.教育	Education	105.5
（1）教育用品	Educational Articles	101.3
（2）教育服务	Education Service	106.0
2.文化娱乐	Culture And Recreation	99.5
（1）文娱耐用消费品	Durable Consumer Goods for Cultural and Recreational Use and Service	96.6
（2）其他文娱用品	Other Recreational Articles	101.1
（3）文化娱乐服务	Cultural And Recreational Services	93.6
（4）旅游	Touring	102.6
七、医疗保健	**Health Care**	**99.8**
1.药品及医疗器具	Medical Instrument Articles	98.8
（1）中药	Traditional Chinese Medicine	101.9
（2）西药	Western Medicine	94.9
（3）滋补保健品	Health Care Articles	105.5
（4）医疗卫生器具	Medical Apparatus	98.4
（5）保健器具	Health Care Appliances	100.0
2.医疗服务	Medical Service	100.5
八、其他用品和服务	**Other Supplies And Services**	**105.7**
1.其他用品	Other Supplies	108.4
（1）首饰手表	Jewelry and Watches	115.5
（2）其他杂项用品	Other Miscellaneous Articles	98.1
2.其他服务类	Other Service	102.3

7-3 商品零售价格指数（2020年）

Retail Price Indices（2020）

(以上年价格为100)　　　　(the price of preceding year=100)

指　标	Item	2020
商品零售价格指数	**Retail Price Indices**	**101.5**
一、食品	**Food**	**107.2**
1. 粮食	Grain	100.9
2. 薯类	Potato	109.6
3. 豆类	Beans	112.6
4. 食用油	Cooking Oil	102.9
5. 菜	Vegetables	113.0
6. 畜肉类	Livestock Meat	136.7
7. 禽肉类	Poultry Meat	102.1
8. 水产品	Aquatic Products	104.8
9. 蛋类	Eggs	82.2
10. 奶类	Milk	103.9
11. 干鲜瓜果类	Dried Fresh Melons and Fruits	89.7
12. 糖果糕点类	Sweets and Cakes	99.3
13. 调味品	Flavouring	101.0
14. 其他食品类	Other Food	103.8
15. 在外餐饮	Dining Out	104.9
二、饮料、烟酒	**Drinks, Tobacco and Liquor**	**101.1**
1. 茶及饮料	Tea and Drinks	100.9
2. 烟草	Cigarette	100.2
3. 酒类	Liquor	102.0
三、服装、鞋帽	**Garments, Shoes And Hats**	**100.4**
1. 服装	Garments	100.8
2. 鞋帽袜	Footwear and Hats	99.3
3. 其他衣着配件	Other Clothing Accessories	99.1
四、纺织品	**Textiles**	**101.4**
1. 服装材料	Cotton Cloth	100.0
2. 床上用品	Blend Cloth	101.5
五、家用电器及音像器材	**Household Appliances，Music and Video Equipment**	**97.7**
1. 家庭设备	Household Facility	99.6
2. 文娱用耐用消费品	Durable Consumer Goods for Cultural and Recreational Use	93.9
3. 专业音响器材	Music and Video Equipment	102.1

注：本表数据来源国家统计局西安调查队。

7-3 续表 continued

(以上年价格为100) (the price of preceding year=100)

指 标	Item	2020
六、文化办公用品	**Cultural and Office Appliances**	**101.0**
七、日用品	**Articles for Daily Use**	**101.1**
1. 日用百货	General Merchandise for Daily Use	101.3
2. 厨具餐具茶具	Kitchenware, Tableware, Tea Set	102.5
3. 清洗用品	Daily Use Articles For Washing	100.9
4. 其他日用品	Other Daily Articles	99.6
八、体育娱乐用品	**Sports And Recreation Articles**	**101.3**
1. 体育户外用品	Sports Outdoor Articles	101.6
2. 娱乐用品	Recreation Articles	101.1
九、交通、通信用品	**Transportation And Communication Goods**	**99.4**
1. 交通运输机械	Transportation Machinery	99.6
2. 通信器材	Communication Equipment	98.1
十、家具	**Furniture**	**101.3**
十一、化妆品	**Cosmetics**	**101.7**
十二、金银饰品	**Gold , Silver and Jewelry**	**117.5**
十三、中西药品及医疗保健用品	**Traditional Chinese And Western Medicines And Health Care Articles**	**98.3**
1. 医疗卫生器具	Medical Apparatus	98.4
2. 中药	Traditional Chinese Medicine	101.9
3. 西药	Western Medicine	94.9
4. 保健器具及用品	Health Care Apparatus and Article	103.3
十四、书报杂志及电子出版物	**Books, Newspapers,Magazines And Electronic Publications**	**100.7**
1. 教材及参考书	Teaching Materials and Reference Books	101.3
2. 书报杂志	Books, Newspapers,Magazines	100.0
3. 计算机办公软件	Computer Office Software	100.0
十五、燃料	**Fuel**	**94.1**
1. 煤炭及制品	Coal and Its Products	101.7
2. 石油及制品	Oil and Its Products	91.9
十六、建筑材料及五金电料	**Building Materials And Hardware**	**98.4**
1. 建筑装潢材料	Building Decoration Materials	98.6
2. 五金水暖	Hardware Plumbing	97.4

7-4 主要年份工业生产者出厂价格指数

(上年价格=100)

类别	Classify	1999	2000	2001	2002	2003	2004
工业生产者出厂价格指数	**Producer Price Index**	**97.5**	**99.4**	**99.3**	**98.2**	**101.5**	**102.7**
按轻重工业分	Grouped by Light Industry and Heavy Industry						
轻工业	Light Industry	95.9	97.8	99.6	98.4	101.3	103.4
以农产品为原料	Using Farm Products as Raw Materials	95.2	99.2	99.0	98.4	104.5	108.7
以非农产品为原料	Using Non-farm Products as Raw Materials	97.0	95.5	100.6	98.6	99.9	100.8
重工业	Heavy Industry	98.9	100.8	99.2	98.2	101.6	101.9
采掘	Mining & Quarrying	101.5	97.5	94.8	101.3	103.4	140.5
原料	Raw Materials	102.3	107.7	101.1	101.3	111.2	109.0
加工	Processing	98.0	98.4	98.5	97.7	100.1	100.6
按生产生活资料分	by means of production and livelihood						
生产资料	Means of Production	98.3	100.5	99.1	98.0	101.8	102.7
采掘	Mining & Quarrying	101.5	97.5	94.8	101.3	103.4	140.5
原料	Raw Materials	100.2	106.4	101.1	101.0	108.1	106.6
加工	Processing	97.6	98.7	98.5	97.4	100.9	102.0
生活资料	Consumer Goods	96.5	97.3	99.9	99.1	100.5	102.5
（1）食品	Food	95.8	94.4	99.6	101.2	101.0	103.6
（2）衣着	Clothing	95.2	101.6	99.4	100.8	99.4	102.7
（3）一般日用品	Articles for Daily Use	97.6	96.9	101.9	97.9	101.2	101.2
（4）耐用消费品	Durable Consumer Goods	98.0	95.9	97.0	98.1	97.2	98.3
按工业部门分	Grouped by Industrial Sector						
1. 冶金工业	Metallurgical Industry	91.2	98.2	97.2	98.7	103.8	107.1
2. 电力工业	Power Industry	109.3	109.6	102.4	100.0	103.2	104.1
3. 煤炭及炼焦工业	Coal and Coking Industry	96.3	100.5	110.3	106.7	136.8	131.4
4. 石油工业	Petroleum Industry	107.1	134.2	96.6	100.7	118.6	110.5
5. 化学工业	Chemical Industry	96.6	96.7	100.5	99.2	100.2	100.8
6. 机械工业	Machine Manufacturing Industry	98.1	98.0	98.3	97.6	99.8	100.6
7. 建筑材料工业	Building Materials Industry	96.7	98.5	100.6	99.6	99.7	100.0
8. 森林工业	Timber Industry	97.9	98.9	98.1	98.9	100.1	100.2
9. 食品工业	Food Industry	95.5	94.3	99.8	101.1	102.8	107.5
10. 纺织工业	Textiles Industry	93.7	103.4	97.5	94.9	117.3	119.1
11. 缝纫工业	Tailoring Industry	99.1	103.5	100.0	101.1	100.2	103.6
12. 皮革工业	Leather Industry	98.0	99.2	101.0	101.8	98.7	99.6
13. 造纸工业	Paper Industry	95.3	96.7	102.3	95.0	96.9	100.2
14. 文教艺术用品工业	Cultural,Educational & Handicrafts Articles	96.7	96.4	101.1	103.4	97.5	96.5
15. 其它工业	Other Industry	98.9	104.8	107.1	99.4	103.3	105.0

注：本表数据来源国家统计局西安调查队。

Producer Price Indices (PPI) for Industrial Producers in Representative Years

(the price of preceding year = 100)

2005	2006	2007	2008	2009	2010	2011	2012	2013	2014	2015	2016	2017	2018	2019	2020
103.9	**103.2**	**101.9**	**103.7**	**99.9**	**102.3**	**102.5**	**100.5**	**99.5**	**99.5**	**98.5**	**97.8**	**100.3**	**101.1**	**101.6**	**100.2**
99.9	100.2	101.8	103.7	100.6	102.5	107.0	100.4	100.7	100.9	100.3	98.5	100.5	102.5	101.3	100.8
97.3	100.1	103.3	106.0	98.9	104.0	109.3	100.3	101.0	100.8	99.1	97.8	100.9	103.0	101.2	100.4
101.2	100.2	100.8	102.1	101.8	101.4	100.9	100.5	99.9	101.3	103.3	100.1	99.7	101.3	101.5	101.8
107.9	105.5	101.9	103.8	99.3	102.2	101.6	100.5	99.2	99.2	98.2	97.6	100.3	100.7	101.8	100.1
107.9	100.6	111.6	122.3	90.0	150.2	102.6	101.8	100.6	100.6	99.8	99.8	106.0	107.1	110.3	100.1
114.2	111.8	104.9	110.8	99.5	108.9	111.2	108.6	95.1	97.6	90.4	91.4	103.4	106.1	103.6	100.4
106.7	104.2	101.2	101.9	99.4	100.8	100.1	99.2	99.9	99.5	99.3	98.3	99.8	100.0	101.5	100.0
105.3	104.2	101.3	103.4	99.3	102.2	101.9	100.3	99.2	99.5	98.3	97.4	100.7	101.7	101.7	100.1
107.9	100.6	111.6	122.3	90.0	105.2	102.6	101.8	100.6	100.6	99.8	99.8	106.0	107.1	110.3	100.1
111.3	111.6	104.8	110.2	99.7	109.0	111.3	108.7	95.2	97.7	90.5	91.2	102.7	106.0	103.6	100.4
104.3	103.0	100.6	102.0	99.3	101.0	100.3	98.9	99.9	99.7	99.6	98.3	100.3	101.0	101.4	100.1
100.4	100.4	103.5	104.7	101.4	102.5	104.5	100.8	100.4	99.7	99.4	98.6	99.7	100.1	101.5	100.5
100.3	100.4	105.3	106.6	100.3	103.3	109.5	101.6	100.9	101.2	100.1	97.7	100.3	102.5	101.9	100.3
102.0	103.3	104.6	105.1	102.7	101.2	111.9	99.4	100.4	99.1	96.0	100.2	101.3	100.4	100.2	100.6
101.3	100.8	100.1	102.7	102.6	101.2	101.5	101.5	99.1	101.3	102.1	98.9	99.6	96.8	99.9	100.8
99.1	99.4	100.7	100.7	103.9	101.9	99.5	99.0	100.9	95.9	95.6	99.5	98.5	101.3	103.3	100.4
103.9	106.5	103.2	104.8	92.0	105.8	116.3	100.7	97.5	97.5	96.5	95.2	104.9	107.3	104.3	99.3
110.6	107.9	105.5	110.0	109.0	101.2	104.7	111.2	100.6	99.4	98.9	92.3	99.4	102.3	95.5	95.2
97.1	95.4	106.8	104.8	101.7	110.6	109.3	101.5	100.0	100.0	100.0					
121.7	117.6	104.8	115.6	96.7	114.2	108.4	108.2	89.7	97.2	81.0	95.4	102.5	107.3	107.1	101.2
103.2	100.8	101.1	104.1	102.6	100.8	104.2	100.3	99.6	100.9	100.6	96.8	100.6	97.9	99.6	99.6
104.9	103.4	101.0	101.7	99.9	100.9	99.5	99.0	100.0	99.4	99.5	98.6	99.5	100.1	101.4	100.5
98.6	98.9	98.9	101.8	101.9	99.9	100.6	99.6	99.3	99.1	99.5	98.0	106.1	118.8	114.5	95.5
101.6	101.6	101.1	101.1	101.1	101.7	105.2	103.2	103.4	101.6	91.7	99.9	100.0	102.0	102.0	100.6
98.3	99.0	106.1	109.3	98.3	104.3	110.1	101.7	101.0	101.3	99.8	97.0	99.9	102.6	101.8	100.6
89.9	102.4	98.4	99.7	97.5	108.9	107.2	88.7	103.9	99.3	96.0	93.7	103.5	102.8	100.4	96.0
100.8	103.5	104.6	105.1	102.6	101.3	113.4	99.4	100.4	99.0	93.4	100.5	102.7	100.7	100.4	101.1
101.2	100.0	99.0	99.6	99.7	99.6	98.0	99.9	99.9	100.0	118.9	99.8	99.6	100.0	100.0	100.0
101.2	100.0	100.1	104.5	98.4	100.4	103.4	99.2	98.4	98.1	98.1	100.9	109.7	106.3	97.8	99.8
98.1	100.1	99.1	99.2	102.2	99.9	100.7	106.0	97.5	100.0	102.6	98.0	99.0	100.9	99.9	100.3
103.4	105.7	111.4	104.3	99.7	100.5	104.3	101.2	99.6	100.0	100.0	99.7	96.2	93.6	101.9	105.2

7-5 主要年份工业生产者购进价格指数

Industrial Purchasing Indices (IPI) for Industrial Producers in Representative Years

(上年价格=100) (the price of preceding year=100)

指 标	Item	2000	2003	2004	2005	2006	2007	2008	2009	2010
工业生产者购进价格指数	**Industrial Producer Price Index**	**102.4**	**105.3**	**110.4**	**109.6**	**106.1**	**106.2**	**108.5**	**100.7**	**106.3**
（一）燃料、动力类	Fuel and Power	105.0	105.7	109.4	123.5	112.6	107.0	109.8	105.1	108.6
（二）黑色金属材料类	Ferrous Metals	102.7	107.4	117.4	107.6	99.2	104.8	111.3	99.2	103.1
#钢材	Steel	103.4	106.0	114.8	107.5	98.5	104.9	111.7	98.7	103.5
（三）有色金属材料和电线类	Non-Ferrous Metals and Electric Wires	105.2	105.8	114.1	107.8	116.5	110.7	99.1	93.9	113.6
（四）化工原料类	Chemical Materials	104.6	102.4	106.3	106.1	101.6	105.6	111.4	95.0	103.9
（五）木材及纸浆类	Timber and Paper Pulp	101.2	101.2	100.3	108.2	111.7	105.9	106.5	102.6	101.1
（六）建筑材料及非金属矿类	Building Materials and Non-metal ores	100.3	99.6	110.4	99.3	100.7	104.0	104.8	106.8	102.1
（七）其它工业原材料及半成品类	Other Industrial Raw Materials and Semi-Products	98.8	102.5	111.2	106.1	104.3	108.8	110.6	101.4	108.1
（八）农副产品类	Agricultural and Sideline Products	100.4	113.7	112.7	100.9	107.2	107.2	108.9	99.6	106.5
（九）纺织原料类	Textile Raw Materials	98.0	103.4	103.9	97.6	101.5	100.5	99.8	97.6	104.6

注：本表数据来源国家统计局西安调查队。

7-5 续表 continued

(上年价格=100) (the price of preceding year=100)

指 标	Item	2011	2012	2013	2014	2015	2016	2017	2018	2019	2020
工业生产者购进价格指数	**Industrial Producer Price Index**	**108.8**	**97.2**	**97.2**	**99.5**	**94.5**	**97.6**	**104.7**	**102.7**	**100.0**	**100.4**
（一）燃料、动力类	Fuel and Power	113.5	102.3	96.8	98.2	95.3	98.3	101.6	99.8	101.7	100.1
（二）黑色金属材料类	Ferrous Metals	102.9	93.4	98.0	97.9	91.6	96.0	109.0	104.1	99.4	100.0
#钢材	Steel	102.9	93.3	98.0	97.9	91.5	96.0	109.0	104.0	99.4	100.0
（三）有色金属材料和电线类	Non-Ferrous Metals and Electric Wires	118.9	93.0	94.5	96.6	96.3	99.3	117.7	115.1	104.0	103.3
（四）化工原料类	Chemical Materials	108.1	87.7	90.8	104.6	91.3	94.1	104.2	99.2	97.0	99.7
（五）木材及纸浆类	Timber and Paper Pulp	105.4	100.9	99.2	100.7	101.0	98.7	107.3	103.9	95.6	100.1
（六）建筑材料及非金属矿类	Building Materials and Non-metal ores	102.9	97.4	102.2	101.1	98.1	97.1	101.0	111.1	111.0	99.5
（七）其它工业原材料及半成品类	Other Industrial Raw Materials and Semi-Products	109.4	100.3	98.9	100.9	99.1	98.9	100.8	100.4	99.7	100.2
（八）农副产品类	Agricultural and Sideline Products	107.4	103.4	100.5	98.8	92.8	100.4	101.0	102.3	101.2	101.4
（九）纺织原料类	Textile Raw Materials	107.0	89.1	97.6	99.3	89.7	94.1	102.7	99.4	99.3	98.5

7-6 住宅销售价格指数（2020年）

Selling Price Indices of Residential Buildings（2020）

(上年价格=100) (the price of preceding year=100)

指 标	Item	2020
新建商品住宅	**New commodity residentiai house**	**108.9**
90平方米及以下	90 square meters and less	112.0
90-144平方米	90-144 square meters	108.4
144平方米以上	144 square meters and more	106.9
二手住宅	**used/second hand residential buildings**	**99.7**
90平方米及以下	90 square meters and the following	100.0
90-144平方米	90-144 square meters	98.8
144平方米以上	144 square meters and more	101.2

注：本表数据来源国家统计局西安调查队。

主要统计指标解释

居民消费价格指数 是反映一定时期内城乡居民所购买的生活消费品和服务项目价格变动趋势和程度的相对数，是对城市居民消费价格指数和农村居民消费价格指数进行综合汇总计算的结果。通过该指数可以观察和分析消费品的零售价格和服务项目价格变动对城乡居民实际生活费支出的影响程度。

商品零售价格指数 是反映一定时期内城乡商品零售价格变动趋势和程度的相对数。商品零售价格的变动与国家的财政收入、市场供需的平衡、消费与积累的比例关系有关。因此，该指数可以从一个侧面对上述经济活动进行观察和分析。

工业生产者价格指数 是反映工业产品价格变化趋势和变动幅度的统计指标，是工业企业的产品价格在不同的时间和空间条件下平均变动的相对数。工业生产者价格包括工业品第一次出售时的出厂价格和企业作为中间投入的原材料、燃料、动力购进价格，简称工业生产者出厂价格和工业生产者购进价格。工业生产者价格指数是进行国民经济核算和经济管理的主要依据。

住宅销售价格指数 是综合反映商品住宅价格水平总体变化趋势和变化辐度的相对数。

固定资产投资价格指数 是反映一定时期内固定资产投资品和取费项目价格的变动趋势和变动幅度的相对数。固定资产投资额是由建筑安装工程投资完成额、设备工器具购置投资完成额和其他费用投资完成额三部分组成的。编制固定资产投资价格指数应首先分别编制上述三部分投资的价格指数，然后采用加权算术平均法求出固定资产投资价格总指数。

该指数可以准确地反映固定资产投资中涉及的各类投资品和取费项目价格变动趋势和变动幅度，消除按现价计算的固定资产投资指标中的价格变动因素，真实地反映固定资产投资的规模、速度、结构和效益，为国家科学地制定、检查固定资产投资计划和进行国民经济核算提供科学的、可靠的依据。

Explanatory Notes on Main Statistical Indicators

Consumer Price Indices reflect the trend and degree of changes in prices of consumer goods and services purchased by urban and rural households during a given period. They are obtained by combining Consumer Price Indices of Urban Household and Consumer Price Indices of Rural Household. The Indices enable the observation and analysis of the degree of impact of the changes in the prices of retailed goods and services on the actual living expenses of urban and rural residents.

Retail Price Indices reflect the trend and degree of change in retail prices of commodities during a given period. The change in retail prices of commodities is related to government revenue, the equilibrium of market supply and demand, and the ratio of consumption to accumulation. Therefore, the retail price indices are useful from an oblique perspective for observing and analyzing the changes of the above economic activities.

Industrial Producer Price Index refelct the trend and degree of changes of industrial product price, which is the relative number of average change prices of industrial enterprises products under different condition of time and space. Including the first time of sale prices of industrial products and the price of raw materials, fuel and power as intermediate inputs, be called for short of PPI and IPI.

Industrial producer price Index is an important basis for national accounts and economic manegement.

Price Indices for Investment in Fixed Assets reflect the trend and degree of changes in prices of investment goods and projects in fixed assets during a given period. The investment in fixed assets consists of three components, namely the investment in construction and installation, the investment in purchases of equipment and instrument, and the investment in other items. Price indices for investment in fixed assets are calculated as the weighted arithmetic mean of the price indices for the three components of investment in fixed assets.

Removing the factor of price change in the aggregates of investment at current prices, this indicator shows the changes in the prices of commodities and fees involved in the investment of fixed assets, and can be used to observe the actual size, growth, structure, and efficiency of investment in fixed assets and provides reliable and scientific data for government planning and further improving the current national accounting .

8 人民生活

PEOPLE´S LIVELIHOOD

资料整理：李晓宁 张 磊
Data management：Li Xiaoning Zhang Lei
数据审核：罗朝晖
Data audit：Luo Zhaohui

第八部分　人民生活

一、简要说明

1.本章资料反映我市城乡居民生活现状和变化情况，主要包括居民家庭基本情况及生活状况、收入及支出、住房等。

2.本章资料来源于国家统计局西安调查队城乡一体化住户收支与生活状况抽样调查。

3.统计资料范围及口径变化：①2014年西安开始实施城乡住户一体化改革，新老口径存在差距。②因2018年是分市、分省数据衔接年的基数年，衔接后西安各区县新口径与老口径数据相比，绝对额有所下降。③自2018年起本章调查资料包含13区、县及西咸新区城乡住户调查数据。

4.统计调查方法：住户收支与生活状况以各市（区）为总体，采用分层、多阶段、与人口规模大小成比例的概率抽样方法，随机抽选调查住宅，确定调查户。在全市抽选出调查小区，对抽中小区中的住户进行全面摸底调查，在此基础上随机等距选出调查户参与记账调查。定期对调查小区和调查住宅进行轮换。

二、主要指标

全体居民人均可支配收入（元）	35783	比上年增长	5.0%
城镇常住居民人均可支配收入（元）	43713	比上年增长	4.5%
城镇常住居民人均消费支出（元）	25813.1	比上年下降	8.3%
农村常住居民人均可支配收入（元）	15749	比上年增长	8.0%
农村常住居民人均消费支出（元）	12958.3	比上年增长	3.2%

8 PEOPLE'S LIVELIHOOD

Ⅰ.Brief Introduction

1.The data in this chapter reflects the people's living conditions and their changes in Xi'an, consisting of the basic conditions of all households, income, expenditure, the inhabit situation and etc.

2.The data are provided by NBS Survey Office in Xi'an, collected though sample survey.

3.The field of investigation and statistics range have been changed. ①In 2014, reformed household survey programme was used in Xi'an in order to produce aggregates with the same concepts and definitions for the urban and rural population. ② Since 2018 is the base year for the data convergence of cities and provinces, the absolute amount of new caliber data of Xi'an districts and counties has declined compared with the old caliber data. ③Since 2018, the data in this chapter consists of 13 Districts (Counties) and Xi'an new area.

4. Methodology on household survey. The household survey is conducted by selecting sampled houses randomly, deciding surveyed households, with all households in the city (district) as the population, with stratified sampling, multi-stage sampling, probability sampling in proportion scale. The households in selected communities are surveyed comprehensively, and then on the basis, randomly select some households for keeping diaries. Communities and households surveyed rotate regularly.

Ⅱ.Major Indicators

		Increase over Preceding Year
Per capita disposable income of all residents(yuan)	35783	5.0%
Per capita annual disposable income of Urban residents (yuan)	43713	4.5%
Per capita consumption expenditure of Urban residents (yuan)	25813.1	-8.3%
Per capita annual disposable income of Rural residents (yuan)	15749	8.0%
Per capita consumption expenditure of Rural residents(yuan)	12958.3	3.2%

8-1 主要年份城乡居民人均收入及恩格尔系数

Per Capita Annual Income and Engel's Coefficient of Urban and Rural Households in Representative Years

年 份 Year	城镇居民人均可支配收入 Per Capita Annual Disposable Income of Urban		农村居民人均纯收入（可支配收入） Per Capita Annual Net Income of Rural（Disposable Income）		城镇居民家庭恩格尔系数（%） Engel's Coefficient of Urban Households（%）	农村居民家庭恩格尔系数（%） Engel's Coefficient of Rural Households（%）
	绝对数(元) Absolute number (yuan)	指数 1980年=100 Index year of 1980=100	绝对数(元) Absolute number (yuan)	指数 1978年=100 Index year of 1978=100		
1978			140	100.0		
1979						
1980	414	100.0	190	135.7	53.3	53.3
1985	719	173.5	351	250.7	49.5	48.5
1990	1518	366.5	610	435.7	53.1	49.5
1991	1619	390.9	707	505.0	51.6	46.7
1992	1992	481.0	783	559.3	52.5	50.9
1993	2661	642.5	870	621.4	46.4	46.0
1994	3517	849.1	1078	770.0	45.2	50.1
1995	4153	1002.5	1353	966.4	44.7	50.3
1996	5023	1212.6	1586	1132.9	42.6	49.9
1997	5344	1290.1	1846	1318.6	40.7	49.2
1998	5670	1368.7	2052	1465.7	39.8	42.4
1999	5999	1448.3	2203	1573.6	36.3	39.1
2000	6364	1536.5	2344	1674.3	36.5	36.6
2001	6705	1618.8	2490	1778.6	34.8	33.9
2002	7184	1734.3	2641	1886.4	34.4	31.1
2003	7748	1870.7	2838	2027.1	34.8	37.6
2004	8544	2062.8	3143	2245.0	36.1	35.7
2005	9628	2324.5	3460	2471.4	37.0	36.3
2006	10905	2632.9	3808	2720.0	34.4	36.8
2007	12662	3057.0	4399	3142.1	36.6	38.2
2008	15207	3671.4	5212	3722.9	36.4	37.0
2009	18963	4578.2	6275	4482.3	32.4	35.8
2010	22244	5370.4	7750	5535.7	31.3	32.5
2011	25981	6272.6	9788	6991.4	31.3	31.9
2012	29982	7238.5	11442	8172.9	32.5	33.8
2013	33100	7991.3	12930	9235.7	32.5	33.0
2014	30715	8718.5	12898	10334.7	32.3	34.2
2015	33188	9422.0	14072	11270.0	32.7	32.2
2016	35630	10119.2	15191	12171.6	29.3	26.9
2017	35837	10948.9	12190	13242.7	29.4	27.3
2018	38729	11835.8	13286	14434.5	27.1	24.4
2019	41850	12794.5	14588	15849.1	26.8	25.4
2020	43713	13370.3	15749	17117.1	28.1	28.0

注：2014年实施城乡住户一体化调查后，统计口径发生变化，新老口径存在差异。本表2014年开始为新口径数据，“农村居民人均纯收入”改为“农村居民人均可支配收入”。2014-2015年恩格尔系数按新口径进行了修订。

本表2018年起数据包含西咸新区数据。下同。

8-1表中2017年城镇、农村居民人均可支配收入已依据2018年口径进行衔接，其他年份不可比。

8-2 主要年份城乡居民人民币储蓄存款

Savings Deposit of Urban and Rural Households in Representative Years

单位：亿元 (100 million yuan)

年 份 Year	年末余额 Balance at Year-end	指数（上年=100） Index(preceding year=100)
1978	2.57	
1979	3.30	128.4
1980	4.22	127.8
1981	4.90	116.0
1982	5.97	121.9
1983	7.35	123.1
1984	10.73	146.0
1985	14.26	132.9
1986	19.45	136.4
1987	33.95	174.6
1988	40.77	120.1
1989	56.65	138.9
1990	77.09	136.1
1991	97.42	126.4
1992	120.27	123.5
1993	158.28	131.6
1994	218.74	138.2
1995	291.46	133.2
1996	394.02	135.2
1997	433.56	110.0
1998	499.68	115.3
1999	586.40	117.4
2000	675.83	115.3
2001	800.86	118.5
2002	988.04	123.4
2003	1210.56	122.5
2004	1432.86	118.4
2005	1716.76	119.8
2006	1950.53	113.6
2007	2002.38	102.7
2008	2513.70	125.5
2009	3084.20	122.7
2010	3641.09	118.1
2011	4155.65	114.1
2012	4787.03	115.2
2013	5357.05	111.9
2014	5698.15	106.4
2015	6571.18	115.3
2016	7035.81	107.1
2017	7497.30	106.6
2018	8360.33	111.5
2019	9553.29	114.3
2020	10913.05	114.2

注：1.本表数据来源于人民银行西安分行营管部,对部分历史年份数据进行了修订，为西安原口径数据。

2.2015年以后“储蓄存款”为“住户存款”。

8-3 各区县城乡居民人均可支配收入

Per Capita Income of Urban and Rural Households by Region

区 县	Region	城镇居民人均可支配收入 Per Capita Disposable Income of Urban Households			农村居民人均可支配收入 Per Capita Disposable Income of Rural Households		
		绝对数（元） Absolute number(yuan)		2020年比2019年增长% Growth of 2020 than 2019 (%)	绝对数（元） Absolute number(yuan)		2020年比2019年增长% Growth of 2020 than 2019 (%)
		2019	2020		2019	2020	
全 市	**Total**	**41850**	**43713**	**4.5**	**14588**	**15749**	**8.0**
新城区	Xincheng	48208	50233	4.2			
碑林区	Beilin	47977	50040	4.3			
莲湖区	Lianhu	47995	50155	4.5			
灞桥区	Baqiao	40328	42183	4.6	17969	19353	7.7
未央区	Weiyang	44628	46859	5.0			
雁塔区	Yanta	48685	51217	5.2			
阎良区	Yanliang	40631	42703	5.1	15808	17104	8.2
临潼区	Lintong	30810	32320	4.9	14659	15802	7.8
长安区	Chang'an	42051	44027	4.7	15928	17186	7.9
高陵区	Gaoling	38794	40579	4.6	16370	17696	8.1
鄠邑区	Huyi	24788	25854	4.3	13632	14723	8.0
蓝田县	Lantian	23893	24920	4.3	14731	15851	7.6
周至县	Zhouzhi	22407	23438	4.6	13137	14162	7.8
西咸新区	Xixian	25270	26331	4.2	14027	15177	8.2

8-4 全市居民家庭基本情况

Basic Conditions of All Households

指标名称	Item	2019	2020
调查户数（户）	**Number of Households Surveyed (household)**	**2410**	**2410**
调查户人口（人）	**Residents Surveyed(person)**		
平均每户常住人口	Average Household Size	3.0	3.0
平均每户劳动力人数	Average Number of Employed Persons	2.2	2.2
平均每劳动力负担人口	Average Number of Persons Supported by a Laborer	1.4	1.4
人均可支配收入（元）	**Annual Per Capita Disposable Income(yuan)**	**34064**	**35783**
工资性收入	Wages Income	20991.0	21346.9
经营净收入	Household Business Income	2629.9	2710.9
财产净收入	Property Income	3070.1	3426.6
转移净收入	Transfer Income	7373.0	8298.6
人均消费支出（元）	**Annual Per Capita Consumption Expenditure (yuan)**	**23691.2**	**22167.6**
食品烟酒	Food,Tobacco and Alcohol	6300.5	6221.1
衣着	Clothing	1761.8	1452.7
居住	Residence	5050.9	5367.4
生活用品及服务	Living Articles and Services	1719.7	1538.3
交通通信	Transport and Communication Services	2807.6	2535.0
教育文化娱乐	Recreation, Education and Culture Services	3223.6	2379.7
医疗保健	Medical and Health Care Services	2210.9	2193.7
其他用品和服务	Other Commodities and Services	616.2	479.7

8-5 全市居民人均可支配收入

Per Capita Annual Disposable Income of All Households

单位：元 (yuan)

指标名称	Item	2019	2020
人均可支配收入	**Annud Per Capital Disposable income**	**34064**	**35783**
一、工资性收入	**Wage income**	**20991.0**	**21346.9**
（一）工资	Wage	19837.4	19935.8
（二）实物福利	Benefits in kind	64.8	77.4
（三）其他	Others	1088.8	1333.7
二、经营净收入	**Net Income from Business**	**2629.9**	**2710.9**
（一）第一产业经营净收入	Net Income from Primary Industry Business	424.3	385.2
（二）第二产业经营净收入	Net Income from Secondary Industry Business	188.5	195.5
（三）第三产业经营净收入	Net Income from Tertiary Industry Business	2017.1	2130.2
三、财产净收入	**Net Income from Properties**	**3070.1**	**3426.6**
#利息净收入	Net interest	124.4	168.2
红利收入	Bonus	364.0	408.8
转让承包土地经营权租金净收入	Net Rental from Transfer of Contracted Land Management Rights	43.7	56.1
出租房屋财产性收入	The Property Income by Renting House	1066.0	1131.0
出租机械、专利、版权等资产的收入	The Income by Renting Assets like Mechanical, Patents, Copyright ect.	56.9	77.6
四、转移净收入	**Net Income from Transfer**	**7373.0**	**8298.6**
（一）转移性收入	Net Income from Transfer	8874.3	10059.7
（二）转移性支出	Transfer Expenditure	1501.3	1761.1

8-6 全市居民年人均消费支出

Per Capita Living Expenditure of All Households

单位：元 (yuan)

指标名称	Item	2019	2020
消费支出	**Total Living Expenditure**	**23691.2**	**22167.6**
一、食品烟酒	**Food,Tobacco and Alcohol**	**6300.5**	**6221.1**
1.食品	food	3568.8	3958.0
2.烟酒	Alcohol and tobacco	542.7	530.0
3.饮料	Drink	168.8	158.3
4.饮食服务	Catering Services	2020.2	1574.8
二、衣着	**Clothing**	**1761.8**	**1452.7**
衣类	Garments	1408.6	1158.0
鞋类	Footwear	353.2	294.7
三、居住	**Residence**	**5050.9**	**5367.4**
#租赁房房租	Rental Housing Rent	353.2	337.3
住房维修及管理	Housing Repair and Management	691.1	694.3
水电燃料及其他	Water,Electric Power Fuel and Others	1058.8	1089.7
四、生活用品及服务	**Living Articles and Services**	**1719.7**	**1538.3**
家具及室内装饰品	Furniture and Interior Decorations	235.3	268.2
家用器具	Household Appliances	495.6	314.3
家用纺织品	Household textile	124.9	108.3
家庭日用杂品	Household Articles of Daily Use	345.2	383.4
个人用品	Personal Items	430.5	375.5
家庭服务	Household Services	88.2	88.6
五、交通通信	**Transportation and Communications**	**2807.6**	**2535.0**
交通	Transportation	2016.7	1710.0
通信	Communications	790.9	825.0
六、教育文化娱乐	**Recreation, Education and Culture Services**	**3223.6**	**2379.7**
教育	Education	2041.6	1687.9
文化娱乐	Recreation	1182.0	691.8
七、医疗保健	**Medicine and Medical Services**	**2210.9**	**2193.7**
医疗器具及药品	Medical Instruments and Medicines	706.3	749.1
医疗服务	Medical Services	1504.6	1444.6
八、其他用品和服务	**Others**	**616.2**	**479.7**

8-7 全市居民家庭人均购买主要商品数量

Per Capita Annual Purchases of Major Commodities of All Households

单位：千克 (kg)

指标名称	Item	2019	2020
面粉	Flour	19.5	25.5
大米	Rice	14.3	16.0
薯类	Potato	16.7	19.2
豆类	Beans	11.4	12.4
食用植物油	Edible vegetable oil	9.5	10.3
鲜菜	Fresh vegetables	97.8	102.2
猪肉	Pork	9.7	9.5
牛肉	Beef	2.1	2.3
羊肉	Lamb	0.7	0.7
鸡	Chicken	2.8	3.3
鱼类	Fish	3.4	3.1
虾类	Shrimp	0.9	0.8
鲜蛋	Eggs	11.3	13.2
鲜奶	Milk	12.9	13.3
酸奶	Yogurt	7.4	6.6
奶粉	Milk	0.9	0.8
鲜瓜果	Fresh fruit	66.2	64.3
糕点	Cake	5.8	5.1
茶叶	Tea	0.4	0.4
卷烟（盒）	Cigarettes (box)	30.2	30.1
啤酒	Beer	3.1	3.4
白酒	Liquor	1.3	1.1
果酒	Wine	0.2	0.3
鞋（双）	Footwear (pair)	2.8	2.5
水（吨）	Water (tons)	29.5	34.4
电（度）	Electricity （kwh）	784.5	803.6
煤炭	Coal	13.9	10.1
管道天燃气（立方米）	Gas pipeline (cu.m)	74.8	87.7
罐装液化石油气	Bottled liquefied petroleum gas	2.7	3.0

8-8 全市居民家庭每百户年末耐用品拥有情况

Ownership of Major Durable Consumer Goods Every 100 Households

指标名称	Item	2019	2020
家用汽车（辆）	Automobile (unit)	36.3	39.4
摩托车（辆）	Motorcycles (unit)	10.2	10.0
助力车（台）	Strength-aid Cycle (unit)	46.0	48.4
洗衣机（台）	washing machine (unit)	98.5	101.0
电冰箱（柜）	Refrigerator (unit)	95.8	98.3
微波炉（台）	Microwave Oven (unit)	43.9	45.8
彩色电视机（台）	Color TV Set (unit)	107.0	109.0
空调（台）	Air conditioning(unit)	160.0	165.3
热水器（台）	Water heaters(unit)	87.1	91.2
洗碗机（台）	Dishwasher (unit)	1.4	1.5
排油烟机（台）	Exhauster (unit)	73.1	74.9
固定电话（部）	Ordinary Telephone (unit)	11.4	10.7
移动电话（部）	Mobile phones (unit)	255.6	254.1
#接入互联网（部）	Access to the Internet(unit)	194.4	231.9
计算机（台）	Computer（unit）	57.6	59.9
#接入互联网（台）	Access to the Internet(unit)	43.4	46.9
照相机（台）	Camera (unit)	18.9	19.7
中高档乐器（架）	High-end Instruments (unit)	7.3	8.4
健身器材（台）	Setting-up Apparatus (unit)	7.4	8.2
空气净化器（台）	Air-cleaner（unit）	12.4	13.1
吸尘器（台）	Vacuum Cleaner（unit）	11.3	12.5

8-9 城镇常住居民家庭基本情况

Basic Conditions of Urban Households

指标名称	Item	2019	2020
调查户数（户）	**Number of Households Surveyed (household)**	**1770**	**1770**
调查户人口（人）	**Residents Surveyed(person)**		
平均每户常住人口	Average Household Size	2.8	2.8
平均每户劳动力人数	Average Number of Employed Persons	2.1	2.2
平均每劳动力负担人口	Average Number of Persons Supported by a Laborer	1.3	1.3
人均可支配收入（元）	**Annual Per Capita Disposable Income(yuan)**	**41850**	**43713**
工资性收入	Wages Income	25883.5	26145.0
经营净收入	Household Business Income	2715.5	2733.9
财产净收入	Property Income	4167.3	4632.9
转移净收入	Transfer Income	9083.7	10201.2
人均消费支出（元）	**Annual Per Capita Consumption Expenditure (yuan)**	**28140.4**	**25813.1**
食品烟酒	Food,Tobacco and Alcohol	7541.3	7248.4
衣着	Clothing	2152.4	1715.5
居住	Residence	5910.1	6248.3
生活用品及服务	Living Articles and Services	2044.4	1849.3
交通通信	Transport and Communication Services	3334.8	2892.5
教育文化娱乐	Recreation, Education and Culture Services	3851.7	2736.4
医疗保健	Medical and Health Care Services	2519.2	2530.2
其他用品和服务	Other Commodities and Services	786.5	592.5

8-10 城镇常住居民人均消费支出

Per Capita Living Expenditure of Urban Households

单位：元 (yuan)

指标名称	Item	2019	2020
消费支出	**Total Living Expenditure**	**28140.4**	**25813.1**
一、食品烟酒	**Food,Tobacco and Alcohol**	**7541.3**	**7248.4**
1.食品	food	4166.3	4534.1
2.烟酒	Alcohol and tobacco	586.9	563.3
3.饮料	Drink	205.1	188.0
4.饮食服务	Catering Services	2583.0	1963.0
二、衣着	**Clothing**	**2152.4**	**1715.5**
衣类	Garments	1725.8	1370.9
鞋类	Footwear	426.6	344.6
三、居住	**Residence**	**5910.1**	**6248.3**
#租赁房房租	Rental Housing Rent	438.9	383.4
住房维修及管理	Housing Repair and Management	741.4	771.4
水电燃料及其他	Water,Electric Power Fuel and Others	1276.1	1303.4
四、生活用品及服务	**Living Articles and Services**	**2044.4**	**1849.3**
家具及室内装饰品	Furniture and Interior Decorations	281.2	332.0
家用器具	Household Appliances	576.0	377.2
家用纺织品	Household textile	147.7	129.0
家庭日用杂品	Household Articles of Daily Use	388.1	440.0
个人用品	Personal Items	547.6	458.4
家庭服务	Household Services	103.8	112.7
五、交通通信	**Transportation and Communications**	**3334.8**	**2892.5**
交通	Transportation	2402.3	1951.8
通信	Communications	932.5	940.7
六、教育文化娱乐	**Recreation, Education and Culture Services**	**3851.7**	**2736.4**
教育	Education	2310.1	1861.4
文化娱乐	Recreation	1541.6	875.0
七、医疗保健	**Medicine and Medical Services**	**2519.2**	**2530.2**
医疗器具及药品	Medical Instruments and Medicines	853.3	909.1
医疗服务	Medical Services	1665.9	1621.1
八、其他用品和服务	**Others**	**786.5**	**592.5**

8-11 城镇常住居民家庭人均购买主要商品数量

Per Capita Annual Purchases of Major Commodities of Urban Households

单位：千克 (kg)

指标名称	Item	2019	2020
面粉	Flour	17.0	22.6
大米	Rice	15.1	16.7
薯类	Potato	17.0	19.5
豆类	Beans	11.6	12.4
食用植物油	Edible vegetable oil	8.5	9.3
鲜菜	Fresh vegetables	106.1	110.5
猪肉	Pork	10.6	10.4
牛肉	Beef	2.7	3.0
羊肉	Lamb	0.9	0.8
鸡	Chicken	3.4	3.9
鱼类	Fish	4.4	3.9
虾类	Shrimp	1.2	1.1
鲜蛋	Eggs	12.2	14.3
鲜奶	Milk	15.2	15.1
酸奶	Yogurt	9.5	8.2
奶粉	Milk	1.0	0.8
鲜瓜果	Fresh fruit	75.0	72.2
糕点	Cake	6.7	6.0
茶叶	Tea	0.5	0.5
卷烟（盒）	Cigarettes (box)	27.5	27.3
啤酒	Beer	3.1	3.5
白酒	Liquor	1.5	1.3
果酒	Wine	0.2	0.2
鞋（双）	Footwear (pair)	2.8	2.5
水（吨）	Water (tons)	33.2	40.6
电（度）	Electricity （kwh）	834.6	833.1
煤炭	Coal	6.3	4.0
管道天燃气（立方米）	Gas pipeline (cu.m)	102.1	119.1
罐装液化石油气	Bottled liquefied petroleum gas	1.8	1.6

8-12 城镇常住居民家庭每百户耐用品拥有情况

Ownership of Major Durable Consumer Goods Every 100 Urban Households

指标名称	Item	2019	2020
家用汽车（辆）	Automobile (unit)	37.5	40.6
摩托车（辆）	Motorcycles(unit)	2.9	3.0
助力车（台）	Strength-aid Cycle (unit)	33.4	36.7
洗衣机（台）	washing machine (unit)	97.9	101.4
电冰箱（柜）	Refrigerator (unit)	95.7	99.0
微波炉（台）	Microwave Oven (unit)	52.8	56.0
彩色电视机（台）	Color TV Set (unit)	102.7	106.1
空调（台）	Air conditioning(unit)	173.4	180.9
热水器（台）	Water heaters(unit)	90.5	95.3
洗碗机（台）	Dishwasher (unit)	1.6	1.8
排油烟机（台）	Exhauster (unit)	85.2	88.1
固定电话（部）	Ordinary Telephone(unit)	13.6	12.6
移动电话（部）	Mobile phones (unit)	237.1	238.6
#接入互联网（部）	Access to the Internet(unit)	183.3	222.1
计算机（台）	Computer (unit)	65.3	69.2
#接入互联网（台）	Access to the Internet(unit)	51.0	55.7
照相机（台）	Camera (unit)	23.7	24.9
中高档乐器（架）	High-end Instruments (unit)	9.2	10.5
健身器材（台）	Setting-up Apparatus (unit)	9.1	10.0
空气净化器（台）	Air-cleaner(unit)	15.9	16.9
吸尘器（台）	Vacuum Cleaner(unit)	14.4	16.0

8-13 城镇常住居民家庭居住情况

Housing Conditions of Urban Households

指标名称	Item	2019	2020
调查户数（户）	**Number of Households Surveyed (household)**	**1770**	**1770**
平均每户居住人口（人）	**Average Number of Resident Population (person)**	**2.8**	**2.8**
人均现住房建筑面积（平方米/人）	**The Average Floor Area Per Person (sq.m / person)**	**34.8**	**34.9**
一、按居住空间样式分（%）	**by Living space style（%）**	**100.0**	**100.0**
单栋楼房	Single building Room	8.4	8.1
单栋平房	Single-storey House	4.8	4.6
单元房	Apartment	79.7	83.2
筒子楼或连片平房	Tube-shaped Apartment or Lace Single-storey Houses	7.1	4.1
其他	Other		
二、按主要建筑材料分（%）	**by main construction materials（%）**	**100.0**	**100.0**
钢筋混凝土	Reinforced concrete soil	63.8	65.6
砖混材料	Brick and concrete material	35.6	33.8
砖瓦砖土	Tile and brick earth	0.5	0.5
其他	Others	0.1	0.1
三、按房屋来源分（%）	**by Source of Housing（%）**	**100.0**	**100.0**
租赁住房	Rental housing	14.8	11.9
自建住房	Self-establish Housing	15.2	14.2
购买商品房	Commercial Residential Housing	35.2	36.2
购买房改住房	Private Housing through Housing Reform	17.5	19.4
购买保障性住房	Indemnificatory Housing	3.2	3.7
拆迁安置房	Resettlement Housing	8.9	9.7
继承或获赠住房	Inheriting and Donation Housing	1.3	1.3
其他	Others	3.9	3.6
四、按住户主要饮水来源情况分（%）	**By Source of main Drinking Water （%）**	**100.0**	**100.0**
经过净化处理的自来水	Purified Tap Water	89.2	92.0
受保护的井水和泉水	Protected Wells and Springs	8.5	5.6
不受保护的井水和泉水	Unprotected Wells and Springs	0.9	0.9
江河湖泊水	Rivers and Lakes Water	0.6	0.6
其他饮用水来源	Others	0.8	0.9
五、按住宅内厕所类型分（%）	**By Household Lavatory Type (%)**	**100.0**	**100.0**
水冲式卫生厕所	Sanitary Water Closet	97.3	97.6
水冲式非卫生厕所	Insanitary Water Closet	1.0	1.0
卫生旱厕	Sanitary Latrine	1.6	1.3
普通旱厕	Latrine	0.1	0.1
无厕所	No Lavatory		
六、按主要炊用能源状况分（%）	**By Cooking Fuel Condition （%）**	**100.0**	**100.0**
天然气、煤气、液化石油气	Pipeline Natural Gas，Pipeline Gas，Pipeline Liquified Petroleum Gas	81.1	87.3
煤炭	Coal		
电	Electricity	17.9	11.8
沼气	Methane		
其他	Others	1.0	0.9

8-14 农村常住居民家庭基本情况

Basic Conditions of Rural Households

指标名称	Item	2019	2020
调查户数（户）	**Number of Households Surveyed (household)**	**640**	**640**
调查户人口（人）	**Residents Surveyed(person)**		
平均每户常住人口	Average Household Size	3.7	3.5
平均每户劳动力人数	Average Number of Employed Persons	2.3	2.4
平均每劳动力负担人口	Average Number of Persons Supported by a Laborer	1.6	1.5
人均可支配收入（元）	**Annual Per Capita Disposable Income(yuan)**	**14588**	**15749**
工资性收入	Wages Income	8752.0	9225.8
经营净收入	Household Business Income	2415.9	2652.5
财产净收入	Property Income	326.4	378.8
转移净收入	Transfer Income	3093.7	3491.9
人均消费支出（元）	**Annual Per Capita Consumption Expenditure (yuan)**	**12561.4**	**12958.3**
食品烟酒	Food,Tobacco and Alcohol	3196.7	3625.8
衣着	Clothing	784.8	788.8
居住	Residence	2901.7	3141.9
生活用品及服务	Living Articles and Services	907.4	752.7
交通通信	Transport and Communication Services	1488.7	1632.0
教育文化娱乐	Recreation, Education and Culture Services	1652.2	1478.4
医疗保健	Medical and Health Care Services	1439.6	1343.6
其他用品和服务	Other Commodities and Services	190.3	195.1

8-15 农村常住居民人均消费支出

Per Capita Living Expenditure of Rural Households

单位：元 (yuan)

指标名称	Item	2019	2020
消费支出	**Total Living Expenditure**	**12561.4**	**12958.3**
一、食品烟酒	**Food,Tobacco and Alcohol**	**3196.7**	**3625.8**
1.食品	food	2074.3	2502.7
2.烟酒	Alcohol and tobacco	432.1	445.7
3.饮料	Drink	78.0	83.1
4.饮食服务	Catering Services	612.3	594.3
二、衣着	**Clothing**	**784.8**	**788.8**
衣类	Garments	615.0	620.2
鞋类	Footwear	169.8	168.6
三、居住	**Residence**	**2901.7**	**3141.9**
#租赁房房租	Rental Housing Rent	138.7	220.8
住房维修及管理	Housing Repair and Management	565.3	499.3
水电燃料及其他	Water,Electric Power Fuel and Others	515.1	549.7
四、生活用品及服务	**Living Articles and Services**	**907.4**	**752.7**
家具及室内装饰品	Furniture and External Decorations	120.7	106.8
家用器具	Household Appliances	294.4	155.6
家用纺织品	Household textile	67.9	56.1
家庭日用杂品	Household Articles of Daily Use	237.6	240.4
个人用品	Personal Items	137.7	166.2
家庭服务	Household Services	49.1	27.6
五、交通通信	**Transportation and Communications**	**1488.7**	**1632.0**
交通	Transportation	1051.9	1099.1
通信	Communications	436.8	532.9
六、教育文化娱乐	**Recreation, Education and Culture Services**	**1652.2**	**1478.4**
教育	Education	1369.6	1249.6
文化娱乐	Recreation	282.6	228.8
七、医疗保健	**Medicine and Medical Services**	**1439.6**	**1343.6**
医疗器具及药品	Medical Instruments and Medicines	338.5	344.9
医疗服务	Medical Services	1101.1	998.7
八、其他用品和服务	**Others**	**190.3**	**195.1**

8-16 农村常住居民家庭人均购买主要商品数量

Per Capita Annual Purchases of Major Commodities of Rural Households

单位：千克 (kg)

指标名称	Item	2019	2020
面粉	Flour	25.6	32.9
大米	Rice	12.4	14.4
薯类	Potato	15.9	18.7
豆类	Beans	10.8	12.4
食用植物油	Edible vegetable oil	12.1	13.0
鲜菜	Fresh vegetables	77.2	81.3
猪肉	Pork	7.7	7.3
牛肉	Beef	0.6	0.6
羊肉	Lamb	0.3	0.3
鸡	Chicken	1.4	1.7
鱼类	Fish	1.1	0.9
虾类	Shrimp	0.1	0.1
鲜蛋	Eggs	9.1	10.2
鲜奶	Milk	7.1	8.9
酸奶	Yogurt	2.2	2.6
奶粉	Milk	0.7	0.9
鲜瓜果	Fresh fruit	44.0	44.5
糕点	Cake	3.6	2.9
茶叶	Tea	0.3	0.3
卷烟（盒）	Cigarettes (box)	36.9	37.1
啤酒	Beer	3.1	2.9
白酒	Liquor	0.9	0.7
果酒	Wine	0.2	0.3
鞋（双）	Footwear（pair）	2.7	2.6
水（吨）	Water (tons)	20.2	18.6
电（度）	Electricity （kwh）	659.3	729.2
煤炭	Coal	33.0	25.4
管道天燃气（立方米）	Gas pipeline (cu.m)	6.6	8.5
罐装液化石油气	Bottled liquefied petroleum gas	4.8	6.6

8-17 农村常住居民家庭平均每百户耐用品拥有情况

Ownership of Major Durable Consumer Goods Every 100 Rural Households

指标名称	Item	2019	2020
家用汽车（辆）	Automobile (unit)	32.3	35.9
摩托车（辆）	Motorcycles (unit)	34.1	32.0
助力车（台）	Strength-aid Cycle (unit)	87.6	85.1
洗衣机（台）	washing machine (unit)	100.2	99.8
电冰箱（柜）	Refrigerator (unit)	96.3	96.2
微波炉（台）	Microwave Oven (unit)	14.8	13.8
彩色电视机（台）	Color TV Set (unit)	121.0	118.0
空调（台）	Air conditioning(unit)	115.6	116.0
热水器（台）	Water heaters(unit)	75.6	78.5
洗碗机（台）	Dishwasher (unit)	0.5	0.3
排油烟机（台）	Exhauster (unit)	33.0	33.4
固定电话（部）	Ordinary Telephone (unit)	4.4	4.7
移动电话（部）	Mobile phones (unit)	316.7	302.6
#接入互联网（部）	Access to the Internet(unit)	231.2	262.6
计算机（台）	Computer（unit）	32.2	30.7
#接入互联网（台）	Access to the Internet(unit)	18.4	19.1
照相机（台）	Camera (unit)	3.0	3.2
中高档乐器（架）	High-end Instruments (unit)	1.0	1.8
健身器材（台）	Setting-up Apparatus (unit)	2.1	2.6
空气净化器（台）	Air-cleaner（unit）	0.8	1.0
吸尘器（台）	Vacuum Cleaner（unit）	1.0	1.1

8-18 农村常住居民家庭居住情况

Housing Conditions of Rural Households

指标名称	Item	2019	2020
调查户数（户）	**Number of Households Surveyed (household)**	**640**	**640**
平均每户居住人口（人）	**Average Number of Resident Population (person)**	**3.7**	**3.5**
人均现住房建筑面积（平方米/人）	**The Average Floor Area Per Person (sq.m / person)**	**49.1**	**50.2**
一、按居住空间样式分（%）	**by Living space style（%）**	**100.0**	**100.0**
单栋楼房	Single building Room	51.4	53.7
单栋平房	Single-storey House	45.1	43.7
单元房	Apartment	2.6	2.0
筒子楼或连片平房	Tube-shaped Apartment or Lace Single-storey Houses		
其他	Other	0.9	0.6
二、按主要建筑材料分（%）	**by main construction materials（%）**	**100.0**	**100.0**
钢筋混凝土	Reinforced concrete soil	16.1	19.6
砖混材料	Brick and concrete material	78.5	75.1
砖瓦砖土	Tile and brick earth	4.5	5.2
竹草土坯	Bamboo grass mud		
其他	Others	0.9	0.1
三、按房屋来源分（%）	**by Source of Housing（%）**	**100.0**	**100.0**
租赁住房	Rental housing	3.0	3.1
自建住房	Self-establish Housing	95.2	95.0
购买商品房	Commercial Residential Housing	0.5	0.4
购买房改住房	Private Housing through Housing Reform		
购买保障性住房	Indemnificatory Housing		
拆迁安置房	Resettlement Housing	1.2	0.8
继承或获赠住房	Inheriting and Donation Housing		
其他	Others	0.1	0.7
四、按住户主要饮水来源情况分（%）	**By Source of main Drinking Water （%）**	**100.0**	**100.0**
经过净化处理的自来水	Purified Tap Water	51.7	55.4
受保护的井水和泉水	Protected Wells and Springs	41.1	38.8
不受保护的井水和泉水	Unprotected Wells and Springs	6.7	4.5
江河湖泊水	Rivers and Lakes Water	0.2	0.7
其他饮用水来源	Others	0.3	0.6
五、按住宅内厕所类型分（%）	**By Household Lavatory Type (%)**	**100.0**	**100.0**
水冲式卫生厕所	Sanitary Water Closet	65.4	70.0
水冲式非卫生厕所	Insanitary Water Closet	20.0	18.1
卫生旱厕	Sanitary Latrine	14.2	9.9
普通旱厕	Latrine	0.4	2.0
无厕所	No Lavatory		
六、按主要炊用能源状况分（%）	**By Cooking Fuel Condition （%）**	**100.0**	**100.0**
天然气、煤气、液化石油气	Pipeline Natural Gas，Pipeline Gas，Pipeline Liquified Petroleum Gas	8.8	23.0
煤炭	Coal	0.7	0.1
电	Electricity	76.6	66.8
沼气	Methane		
其他	Others	13.9	10.1

主要统计指标解释

住户 指居住在一个住宅内，共同分享生活开支或收入的一群人。居住在同一房间内、不共同分享生活开支的人群，每个人都视为一个住户。住家保姆、住家家庭帮工视为单独的住户。

常住成员指住户成员中，经常在家居住、或者调查期内居住时间超过一半的人员，以及本住户供养的学生。

可支配收入 指调查户在调查期内获得的、可用于最终消费支出和储蓄的总和，即调查户可以用来自由支配的收入。可支配收入既包括现金，也包括实物收入。按照收入的来源，可支配收入包含四项，分别为：工资性收入、经营净收入、财产净收入和转移净收入。计算公式为：

可支配收入＝工资性收入＋经营净收入＋财产净收入＋转移净收入

工资性收入 指就业人员通过各种途径得到的全部劳动报酬和各种福利，包括受雇于单位或个人、从事各种自由职业、兼职和零星劳动得到的全部劳动报酬和福利。

经营净收入 指住户或住户成员从事生产经营活动所获得的净收入，是全部经营收入中扣除经营费用、生产性固定资产折旧和生产税之后得到的净收入。计算公式具体为：

经营净收入＝经营收入－经营费用－生产性固定资产折旧－生产税

财产净收入 指住户或住户成员将其所拥有的金融资产、住房等非金融资产和自然资源交由其他机构单位、住户或个人支配而获得的回报并扣除相关的费用之后得到的净收入。

财产性净收入=财产性收入－财产性支出

转移性收入 指国家、单位、社会团体对住户的各种经常性转移支付和住户之间的经常性收入转移。包括养老金或退休金、社会救济和补助、政策性生产补贴、政策性生活补贴、经常性捐赠和赔偿、报销医疗费、住户之间的赡养收入，以及本住户非常住成员寄回带回的收入等。计算公式为：

转移净收入＝转移性收入－转移性支出

消费支出 指住户用于满足家庭日常生活消费需要的全部支出，包括用于消费品的支出和用于服务性消费的支出。根据用途不同，消费支出可划分为食品烟酒、衣着、居住、生活用品及服务、交通通信、教育文化娱乐、医疗保健、其他用品及服务八大类。

农村居民人均纯收入（老口径） 指农村住户当年从各个来源得到的家庭总收入扣除相关费用性支出后，最终归农村居民所有的收入总和，按照农村住户人口平均的纯收入水平。计算公式为：

纯收入=总收入－家庭经营费用支出－税费支出－生产性固定资产折旧－赠送农村内部亲友

Explanatory Notes on Main Statistical Indicators

Households refer to persons living and sharing economically together in one house. When people don`t share living expenses, every single person are deemed to be one household. Live-in Nanny and family helpers are deemed to be one household.

Usual Resident Population refers to persons staying at home regularly or for over half of time in survey period and students provided by the by the household.

Disposable Income of Households refers to the actual income of households for purpose of final expenditure and savings in survey period, households can use that at their disposable. It includes income both in cash and in kind. By sources of income, disposable income includes four categories: income from wages and salaries, net business income, net income from properties and net income from transfer. The formula is:

Disposable Income of Households = Income from Wages and Salaries + Net Business Income + Net Income from Properties + Net Income from Transfer

Income from Wages and Salaries refers to remuneration of labour and salaries from all kinds of sources, including those employed by other units or individuals, freelance work, part-time jobs, and sporadic labour.

Net Business Income refers to net income earned by households and their members engaged in production and business activities. It refers to the operating revenue minus operating costs, depreciation of productive fixed assets, and production tax. The formula is:

Net Business Income = Operating Revenue - Operating Costs - Depreciation of Productive Fixed Assets - Production Tax

Net Income from Properties refers to net income received as returns by households or members of financial assets, non-financial assets such as housing, to other institutions, households and individuals, and minus relevant costs. The formula is:

Net Income from Properties = Property Income – Property Expenditure

Income from Transfer refersto the regular transfer from country, institutions, social communities to households and between households. It includes old-age and retirement pension, regular donation and compensation, applying for medical fees, supporting income between households, income from non-usual-residing members of households, etc.

Net Income from Transfer The formula is:

Net Income from Transfer = Income from Transfer – Expenditure from Transfer

Consumption Expenditure of Households refers to all expenditure of households for living expenditure to satisfy family daily living. It includesexpenditure on eight categories: food tobacco and liquor; clothing; residence; household facilities, articles and services; transport and communications; education, cultural and recreational activities; health care and medical services, and miscellaneous goods and services.

The Average Per Capita Net Income of Rural Residents (the old range) refers to the total income of rural households from all sources minus all corresponding expenses. The formula is:

Net Income = Total Income –Household Operation Expenses – Taxes and Fees Paid – Taxes and Fees Depreciation of Fixed Assets for Production – Gifts to Non-rural Relatives

9 城市公用事业

URBAN PUBLIC UTILITIES

资料整理：陈超毅
Data management：Chen Chaoyi
数据审核：刘栋婷
Data audit：Liu Dongting

第九部分　城市公用事业

一、简要说明

本章资料主要包括城市供水、供燃气、供热、公共交通、市政设施、市政设施水平、城市规模及用地状况、园林绿地、环境卫生等情况，由西安市统计局服务业与社会科技处根据西安市住房和城乡建设局、市交通局、市轨道交通集团有限公司及市水务局等提供的数据整理。

二、主要指标

人均公园绿地面积（平方米）	11.79	比上年增加	1.82
人均城市道路面积（平方米）	18.13	比上年减少	0.21
供水普及率（%）	98.67	比上年提高	0.4个百分点
燃气普及率（%）	99.87	比上年降低	0.09个百分点

9　URBAN PUBLIC UTILITIES

Ⅰ.Brief Introduction

Data in this chapter reflects basic condition of urban public utilities of Xi'an City. Data on public utilities primarily consists of urban water supply, gas sales, urban heating, public transportation, municipal facilities, level of municipal construction, scale of the city, condition of land utilization, parks, greenbelt and environmental sanitation. Data in this chapter is compiled by Tertiary Industry and Social Science & Technology Division of Xi'an Bureau of Statistics according to the data provided by Housing and Urban Planning Construction of Xi'an , Xi'an Rail Transit Group Company Limited and Xi'an Metro Office.

Ⅱ.Major Indicators

		Increase over Preceding Year
Per Capita Public Green Areas (sq.m)	11.79	1.82
Per Captia Area of Roads (sq.m)	18.13	-0.21
Water-Consuming Popularization (%)	98.67	0.4 percenage points
Gas-Consuming Popularization (%)	99.87	-0.09 percenage points

9-1 城市（县城）供水

Urban (County) Water Supply

指 标	Item	2010	2015	2016	2017	2018	2019	2020
年末水厂个数（个）	Number of Water Factory at Year-end (unit)	9	22	22	24	22	28	28
供水综合生产能力（万立方米/日）	Total Volume of Water Supply (10 000 cu.m/day)	197.40	211.50	219.38	206.47	215.10	287.22	300.41
#地下水	Groundwater	55.80	62.86	64.61	65.11	89.86	86.64	113.37
年末供水管道总长度（公里）	Length of Water Supply Pipelines at Year-end (km)	2416.00	4371.05	4522.46	4899.56	4959.94	4977.08	5991.32
全年供水总量（万立方米）	Total Annual Volume of Water Supply (10 000 cu.m)	41089.00	56055.25	59953.03	89215.62	90394.45	75392.33	76943.51
#生产运营用水	For Productive Use	6267.00	16146.29	16567.21	43095.31	39453.60	22675.54	21173.30
居民家庭用水	For Residential Use	20944.00	30742.79	32182.87	34896.60	39078.56	39962.46	41774.05
用水人口（万人）	Population with Access to Tap Water (10 000 persons)	410.90	463.05	475.00	506.26	589.90	642.91	672.05

注：本表数据来源于市住房和城乡建设局、市水务局。
本表2017年及以后年份数据含西咸新区。

9-2 城市（县城）供燃气

Gas Supply in Urban Area（County）

指 标	Item	2010	2015	2016	2017	2018	2019	2020
一、天然气	**Natural Gas**							
供气管道长度（公里）	Total Length of Gas Pipelines (km)	4488	7465.73	8199.80	9174.87	10659.68	11928.62	12636.49
供气总量（万立方米）	Total Gas Supply(10 000 cu.m)	109052	196826.38	206068.05	231168.38	285215.47	320847.29	329150.02
#销售气量	Volume of Gas Sales	104055	189066.21	201078.36	224419.93	279030.23	311544.57	320566.43
#家庭用量	Residential Households	20989	65952.81	67024.75	105249.81	100959.64	103357.70	121623.10
用气人口（万人）	Population with Access to Gas (10 000 persons)	333	437.96	452.11	477.01	588.40	646.89	671.05
二、液化石油气	**Liquefied Petroleum Gas**							
供气总量（吨）	Total Gas Supply (ton)	11469	5030.30	4955.50	7607.20	31023.54	9965.79	12449.70
#销售气量	Volume of Gas Sales	11441	4950.00	4875.20	7478.90	30397.32	9865.50	12286.60
#家庭用量	Residential Households	7376	4064.00	4056.00	6081.47	8881.82	7241.36	6936.00
用气人口（万人）	Population with Access to Gas (10 000 persons)	31.20	19.50	17.60	13.02	13.65	7.11	9.16

注：本表数据来源于市住房和城乡建设局。
本表2017年及以后年份数据含西咸新区。

9-3 城市（县城）集中供热

Heating in Urban Area（County）

指 标	Item	2010	2015	2016	2017	2018	2019	2020
供热能力	Heating Capacity							
蒸汽（吨/小时）	Steam (tons/hour)	2235	3013	3013	6200	4325	4425	3690
热水（兆瓦）	Hot Water (megawatts)	3531	17191.90	17765.90	14477.00	14465.47	15414.44	17226.21
供热总量(万吉焦)	Volume Supplied (10 000 gigajoules)							
蒸汽	Steam	1674	1671.14	1789.13	2813.00	1972.08	2042.18	1709.25
热水	Hot Water	2570	4241.30	5032.84	6338.00	6532.89	7538.46	8596.49
集中供热管道长度（公里）	Length of Centralized Heating Pipelines(km)	541	1054.41	1141.24	1842.00	1516.83	1739.61	1826.96
集中供热面积（万平方米）	Heated Area (10 000sq.m)	6094	16690.65	19566.81	29118.90	24922.93	27615.69	29153.07
#住宅	Residential Buildings	5009	14730.49	17282.39	17541.10	20751.73	22778.29	24473.31

注：本表数据来源于市住房和城乡建设局。
本表2017年及以后年份数据含西咸新区。

9-4 城市公共交通

Urban Public Traffic

指 标	Item	2010	2015	2016	2017	2018	2019	2020
运营车辆（辆）	Operating Vehicles (unit)	7107	7781	7829	7780	8743	10566	9363
标准运营车辆（标台）	Standard Vehicles (unit)	8139	9061	9140	9243	10712	13092	11710
公交客运总量（万人次）	Total of Bus Passenger(10 000 person-times)	162400	161032	147089	133465	135919	145280	73927
公交客运收入（万元）	Bus Passenger Transport Income (10 000 yuan)	129397	137492	129132	165072	126590	159040	85016
出租汽车数（辆）	Number of Taxis (unit)	12786	14459	14459	14509	14609	16832	16923
地铁运营线路长度（公里）	Length of Subway Lines in Operation(km)		50.94	88.97	88.97	126.70	132.41	244.27
地铁客运量（万人次）	Total of Subway Passenger(10 000 person-times)		34209.35	40815.75	60534.01	74624.64	94383.62	72528.87

注：本表数据来源于市交通局和市轨道交通集团有限公司。
本表数据为西安原口径。

9-5 市政设施

Municipal Facilities

指　标	Item	2010	2015	2016	2017	2018	2019	2020
一、道路长度（公里）	Length of Roads (km)	2662	3570.58	3683.14	4398.83	4712.47	5141.85	5283.95
二、道路面积（万平方米）	Area of Roads (10 000 sq.m)	5965	8457.14	8618.93	10063.55	10834.70	11998.06	12345.21
三、人行道面积（万平方米）	Area of Sidewalks (10 000 sq.m)	1834	2381.20	2423.70	2814.31	2886.16	3105.42	
四、桥梁数（座）	Number of Bridges (unit)	347	448	449	491	502	439	454
#立交桥	Overpasses	71	106	107	127	126	99	103
五、路灯盏数（盏）	Number of Street Lights (unit)	291754	343465	349808	382979	383174	461408	464069
六、排水管道长度（公里）	Length of Drainage Pipelines (km)	3765	4984.94	5161.83	5802.36	6126.11	6445.80	6959.60
七、污水年排放量（万立方米）	Annual Discharge Volume of Sewage (10 000 cu.m)	34706	62092	56578	58303	70374	74617	78629
八、污水处理厂处理能力（万立方米/日）	Daily Disposal Capacity of Sewage (10 000 cu.m/day)	106.5	200.6	212.1	147.6	225.1	229.7	242.4
九、污水年处理量（万立方米）	Yearly Disposal Capacity of Sewage Disposal Plant (10 000 cu.m)	25088	57034	52011	54279	66048	71917	75881

注：本表数据来源于市住房和城乡建设局。
本表2017年及以后年份数据含西咸新区。
2020年立交桥数、路灯盏数来源于市城市管理和综合执法局。
2020年人行道面积数据暂缺。

9-6 城市（县城）设施水平

Urban（County）Municipal Facilities

指　标	Item	2010	2015	2016	2017	2018	2019	2020
一、人均日生活用水量（升）	Per Capita Daily Consumption of Tap Water For Residential Use (liters)	186.20	187.79	191.35	199.09	189.56	176.07	176.38
二、供水普及率（%）	Water-Consuming Popularization(%)	98.8	100	100	99.25	97.85	98.27	98.67
三、燃气普及率（%）	Gas-Consuming Popularization(%)	97.0	98.79	98.89	96.07	99.90	99.96	99.87
四、人均城市道路面积（平方米）	Per Captia Area of Roads (sq.m)	15.4	18.26	18.15	19.73	17.97	18.34	18.13
五、建成区排水管道密度（公里/平方公里）	Density of Drainage Pipelines in Developed Areas (km/sq.km)	9.5	9.09	9.12	1.46	7.88	7.96	8.58
六、污水处理率（%）	Rate of Sewerage Disposal(%)	84.0	91.85	91.93	93.10	93.85	96.38	96.51
七、园林绿化	Afforestation and Parks and Gardens							
人均公园绿地面积（平方米）	Per Capita Public Green Areas (sq.m)	9.1	11.47	11.61	12.04	9.97	9.97	11.79
建城区绿地率（%）	Rate of Green Areas in Developed Areas(%)	29.2	34.03	34.95	36.78	35.23	36.02	38.11
八、生活垃圾无害化处理率（%）	Rate of No Harm Disposal of Garbage(%)	93.9	98.09	96.70	98.11	98.97	98.87	98.75

注：本表数据来源于市住房和城乡建设局。
本表2017年及以后年份数据含西咸新区。
本表供水普及率指标2016年及以前数据为用水普及率。

9-7 城市（县城）园林绿化

Urban（County） Parks,Gardens and Green Areas in Cities

指 标	Item	2010	2015	2016	2017	2018	2019	2020
一、公园个数（个）	**Number of Parks (unit)**	**68**	**91**	**95**	**103**	**104**	**117**	**149**
二、公园面积（公顷）	**Area of Parks (hectares)**	**1335**	**2599.83**	**2647.40**	**3259.70**	**3272.70**	**3490.53**	**4803.83**
三、绿地面积（公顷）	**Total Area of Parks,Gardens and Green Areas (hectares)**	**12140**	**20582.44**	**22502.87**	**30703.66**	**31680.89**	**32586.46**	**36034.00**
#公园绿地面积	Public Green Areas	3526	5310.58	5517.08	6142.98	6010.08	6522.65	8027.79
四、年末绿化覆盖面积（公顷）	**Coverage Space of Green Areas at year-end (hectares)**	**15646**	**25639.88**	**27617.83**	**35936.49**	**35939.67**	**36885.61**	**40560.79**
五、建成区绿化覆盖率（%）	**Coverage of Green Areas in Developed Areas (%)**	**37.50**	**42.04**	**42.57**	**40.79**	**38.53**	**39.32**	**41.54**

注：本表数据来源于市住房和城乡建设局。
本表2017年及以后年份数据含西咸新区。

9-8 城市（县城）环境卫生

Urban（County） Environment Sanitation

指 标	Item	2010	2015	2016	2017	2018	2019	2020
清扫面积（万平方米）	Area Under Cleaning Program (10 000 sq.m)	6290	9842	9137	12241	7790	10527	12552
生活垃圾清运量（万吨）	Volume of Residential Garbage Disposal (10 000 tons)	237	359.16	371.51	422.25	430.68	396.78	301.45
公共厕所（座）	Number of Public Lavatories (unit)	1257	2239	2314	3274	4030	3551	3612
市容环卫专用车辆设备总数（辆）	Special Vehicles of Environmental Sanitation (unit)	1042	2050	2000	2571	3305	2491	3133

注：本表数据来源于市住房和城乡建设局。
本表2017年及以后年份数据含西咸新区。
按照住房和城乡建设部门意见，个别指标数据进行了修订。

9-9 市区及县供水（2020年）

Urban and County Water Supply（2020）

指　标	Item	西安 Xi'an	市区 City	蓝田 Lantian	周至 ZhouZhi
年末水厂个数（个）	Number of Water Factory at Year-end (unit)	28	26	1	1
供水综合生产能力	Total Volume of Water Supply	300.41	292.66	3.74	4.01
（万立方米/日）	(10 000 cu.m/day)				
#地下水	Groundwater	113.37	106.95	3.74	2.68
年末供水管道总长度	Length of Water Supply Pipelines	5991.32	5743.12	126.36	121.84
（公里）	at Year-end (km)				
全年供水总量	Total Annual Volume of Water Supply	76943.51	75758.08	645.22	540.21
（万立方米）	(10 000 cu.m)				
#生产运营用水	For Productive Use	21173.30	20815.14	283.06	75.10
居民家庭用水	For Residential Use	41774.05	41228.15	273.15	272.75
用水人口（万人）	Population with Access to Tap Water	672.05	655.45	8.60	8.00
	(10 000 persons)				

注：本表数据来源于市住房和城乡建设局、市水务局。
本表数据含西咸新区。

9-10 市区及县供燃气（2020年）

Urban and County Gas Supply（2020）

指 标	Item	西安 Xi'an	市区 Urban	蓝田 Lantian	周至 ZhouZhi
一、天然气	**Natural Gas**				
管道长度（公里）	Total Length of Gas Pipelines (km)	12636.49	12343.76	124.73	168.00
供气总量（万立方米）	Total Gas Supply(10 000 cu.m)	329150.02	322730.46	2788.11	3631.45
#销售气量	Volume of Gas Sales	320566.43	314269.82	2667.16	3629.45
#家庭用量	Residential Households	121623.10	119488.24	1214.86	920.00
用气人口（万人）	Population with Access to Gas (10 000 persons)	671.05	657.15	7.70	6.20
二、液化石油气	**Liquefied Petroleum Gas**				
供气总量（吨）	Total Gas Supply (ton)	12449.70	9552.00	1087.50	1810.20
#销售气量	Volume of Gas Sales	12286.60	9421.60	1055.00	1810.00
#家庭用量	Residential Households	6936.00	4161.00	975.00	1800.00
用气人口（万人）	Population with Access to Gas (10 000 persons)	9.16	6.97	0.98	1.21

注：本表数据来源于市住房和城乡建设局。
本表数据含西咸新区。

9-11 市区及县集中供热（2020年）

Urban and County Heating（2020）

指 标	Item	西安 Xi'an	市区 Urban	蓝田 Lantian	周至 ZhouZhi
供热能力	Heating Capacity				
蒸汽（吨/小时）	Steam (tons/hour)	3690.00	3690.00		
热水（兆瓦）	Hot Water (megawatts)	17226.21	17219.79		6.42
供热总量(万吉焦)	Volume Supplied(10 000 gigajoules)				
蒸汽	Steam	1709.25	1709.25		
热水	Hot Water	8596.49	8589.82		6.67
集中供热管道长度（公里）	Length of Centralized Heating Pipelines(km)	1826.96	1823.66		3.30
供热面积（万平方米）	Heated Area (10 000sq.m)	29153.07	29139.08		13.99
#住宅	Residential Buildings	24473.31	24462.17		11.14

注：本表数据来源于市住房和城乡建设局。
本表数据含西咸新区。

9-12 市区及县市政设施（2020年）

Urban and County Municipal Facilities（2020）

指 标	Item	西安 Xi'an	市区 Urban	蓝田 Lantian	周至 ZhouZhi
一、道路长度（公里）	**Length of Roads (km)**	**5283.95**	**5159.13**	**76.46**	**48.36**
二、道路面积（万平方米）	**Area of Roads (10 000 sq.m)**	**12345.21**	**12107.34**	**138.79**	**99.08**
三、人行道面积（万平方米）	**Area of Sidewalks (10 000 sq.m)**				
四、桥梁数（座）	**Number of Bridges (unit)**	**454**	**440**	**8**	**6**
#立交桥	Crossroads	103	103		
五、路灯盏数（盏）	**Number of Street Lights (unit)**	**464069**	**454274**	**4017**	**5778**
六、排水管道长度（公里）	**Length of Drainage Pipelines (km)**	**6959.60**	**6798.03**	**97.47**	**64.10**
七、污水年排放量（万立方米）	**Annual Discharge Volume of Sewage (10 000 cu.m)**	**78629**	**77560**	**544**	**525**
八、污水处理厂处理能力（万立方米/日）	**Daily Disposal Capacity of Sewage (10 000 cu.m/day)**	**242.4**	**236.8**	**3.0**	**2.6**
九、污水年处理量（万立方米）	**Yearly Disposal Capacity of Sewage Disposal Plant (10 000 cu.m)**	**75881**	**74971**	**447**	**463**

注：本表数据来源于市住房和城乡建设局。
本表数据含西咸新区。
2020年立交桥数、路灯盏数来源于市城市管理和综合执法局。
人行道面积数据暂缺。

9-13 市区及县市政设施水平（2020年）

Urban and County Municipal Facilities Level（2020）

指 标	Item	西安 Xi'an	市区 Urban	蓝田 Lantian	周至 ZhouZhi
一、人均日生活用水量（升）	**Per Capita Daily Consumption of Tap Water For Residential Use (liter)**	**176.38**	**177.70**	**104.62**	**144.96**
二、供水普及率（%）	**Water-Consuming Popularization (%)**	**98.67**	**98.68**	**97.95**	**98.52**
三、燃气普及率（%）	**Gas-Consuming Popularization (%)**	**99.87**	**99.99**	**98.86**	**91.26**
四、人均城市道路面积（平方米）	**Per Captia Area of Roads (sq.m)**	**18.13**	**18.23**	**15.81**	**12.20**
五、建成区排水管道密度（公里/平方公里）	**Density of Drainage Pipelines (km/sq.km)**	**8.58**	**8.72**	**4.12**	**3.99**
六、污水处理率（%）	**Rate of Sewerage Disposal (%)**	**96.51**	**96.66**	**82.26**	**88.19**
七、园林绿化	**Afforestation and Parks and Gardens**				
人均公园绿地面积（平方米）	Per Capita Public Green Areas (sq.m)	11.79	11.85	8.80	10.10
建城区绿地率（%）	Rate of Green Areas in Developed Areas(%)	38.11	38.51	32.07	17.00
八、生活垃圾无害化处理率（%）	**Rate of No Harm Disposal of Garbage (%)**	**98.75**	**99.96**		**100.00**

注：本表数据来源于市住房和城乡建设局。
本表数据含西咸新区。

主要统计指标解释

建成区面积 城市行政区内实际已成片开发建设、市政公用设施和公共设施基本具备的区域。对核心城市，它包括集中连片的部分以及分散的若干个已经成片建设起来，市政公用设施和公共设施基本具备的地区；对一城多镇来说，它包括由几个连片开发建设起来的，市政公用设施和公共设施基本具备的地区组成。因此建成区范围，一般是指建成区外轮廓线所能包括的地区，也就是这个城市实际建设用地所达到的范围。

供水综合生产能力 指按供水设施取水、净化、送水、出厂输水干管等环节设计能力计算的综合生产能力。包括在原设计能力的基础上，经挖、革、改增加的生产能力。计算时，以四个环节中最薄弱的环节为主确定能力。

供水管道长度 指从送水泵至用户水表之间所有管道的长度。不包括新安装尚未使用、水厂内以及用户建筑物内的管道。在同一条街道埋设两条或两条以上管道时，应按每条管道的长度计算。

供水总量 指报告期供水企业（单位）供出的全部水量。包括有效供水量和漏损水量。

用水普及率 指报告期末城区内用水人口与总人口的比率。计算公式:

$$用水普及率=\frac{用水人口（含暂住人口）}{人口+暂住人口}\times 100\%$$

供气管道长度 指报告期末从气源厂压缩机的出口或门站出口至各类用户引入管之间的全部已经通气投入使用的管道长度。不包括煤气生产厂、输配站、液化气储存站、灌瓶站、储配站、气化站、混气站、供应站等厂（站）内的管道。

供气总量 指报告期燃气企业（单位）向用户供应的燃气数量。包括销售量和损失量。

燃气普及率 指报告期末城区内使用燃气的人口与总人口的比率。计算公式：

$$燃气普及率=\frac{用气人口（含暂住人口）}{人口+暂住人口}\times 100\%$$

供热能力 指供热企业（单位）向城市热用户输送热能的设计能力。不是热电厂的生产能力。

供热总量 指在报告期供热企业（单位）向城市热用户输送全部蒸汽和热水的总热量。

供热管道长度 指从各类热源到热用户建筑物接入口之间的全部蒸汽和热水的管道长度。不包括各类热源厂内部的管道长度。

供热面积 指供热企业（单位）向城市各类房屋建筑物、构筑物及其附属设施供热的全部建筑面积。

道路长度 指道路长度和与道路相通的桥梁、隧道的长度，按车行道中心线计算。

道路面积 指道路实际铺装面积和与道路相通的广场、桥梁、隧道的铺装面积（统计时，将人行道面积单独统计）。

人行道面积按道路两侧面积相加计算，包括步行街和广场，不含人车混行的道路。

排水管道长度 指所有排水总管、干管、支管、检查井及连接井进出口等长度之和。计算时按单管计算，即在同一条街道上如有两条或两条以上并排的排水管道时，应按每条排水管道的长度相加计算。

绿化覆盖面积 指城市中的乔木、灌木、草坪等所有植被的垂直投影面积。包括公园绿地、防护绿地、生产绿地、附属绿地、其他绿地的绿化种植覆盖面积、屋顶绿化覆盖面积以及零散树木的覆盖面积，不含各类绿地中的水域面积以及没有被植被覆盖的面积（硬化道路、无屋顶绿化的建筑物等）。乔木树冠下重迭的灌木和草本植物不重复计算。

人均城市道路面积 指报告期末城区内平均每人拥有的城市道路面积。计算公式：

$$人均城市道路面积=\frac{城区道路面积}{城区人口+城区暂住人口}$$

建成区排水管道密度 指报告期末建成区排水管道分布的疏密程度，计算公式：

$$排水管道密度=\frac{排水管道长度}{建成区面积}$$

污水处理率 指报告期内污水处理总量与污水排放总量的比率。计算公式：

$$污水处理率=\frac{污水处理总量}{污水排放总量}\times 100\%$$

人均公园绿地面积 指报告期末城区内平均每人拥有的公园绿地面积。计算公式：

$$人均公园绿地面积=\frac{城区公园绿地面积}{城区人口+城区暂住人口}$$

建成区绿地率 指报告期末建成区内绿地面积与建成区面积的比率。计算公式：

$$建成区绿地率=\frac{建成区绿地面积}{建成区面积}\times 100\%$$

Explanatory Notes on Main Statistical Indicators

Area of the Constructed Regions refers to developed and built city administrative area where basic municipal utilities and public facilities complete constructed. To core city, it includes part of contiguous centralized and a number of decentralized part where basic municipal utilities and public facilities complete constructed. To a multi-city town, it consists of several contiguous developed and build area where municipal utilities and public facilities with basic composition. Therefore, the range of built-up area, generally refers to the built-up areas in the contour line, which is the actual construction site of the city achieved range.

Production Capacity of Water Supply refers to the designed overall production capacity of water facilities, covering the four segments of water collection, purification, conveyance, and out flow through trunk pipelines. Increased capacity through transformation and innovation projects is included as well. The capacity is determined mainly on the weakest of the above-mentioned four segments.

Length of Water Supply Pipelines at Year-end refers to the total length of all the pipelines between the water pumps and the user water meters, excluding pipelines newly installed but not used yet, pipeline in the water factory, and pipeline in the user's buildings.

Volume of Water Supply refers to the total volume of water supplied by water-works(units) during the reference period, including both the effective water supply and loss during the water supply.

Coverage Rate of Urban Population with Access to Tap Water refers to the ratio of the urban population with access to tap water to the total urban population . The formula is :

$$\text{Coverage of urban population with access to tap water} = \frac{\text{population with access to tap water}}{\text{population}} \times 100\%$$

Length of Gas Pipeline refers to the total length of pipelines in use between the outlet of the compressor of gas-work of outlet gas stations and the leading pipe of users , excluding pipelines within gasworks , delivery stations ,LPG storage stations ,refilling stations, gas-mixing stations and supply stations.

Volume of Gas Supply refers to the total volume of gas provided to users by gas-producing enterprises (units) in a year , including the volume sold and the volume lost .

Coverage Rate of Urban Population with Access to Gas refers to the ratio of the urban population with access to gas to the total urban population at the end of the reference period. The formula is :

$$\text{Coverage rate of urban population with access to gas} = \frac{\text{population with access to gas}}{\text{population}} \times 100\%$$

City Heating capacity in Urban Areas refers to the designed capacity of heating enterprises (units) in supplying heating energy to urban users during the reference period .

City Quantity of Heat Supplied in Urban Areas refers to the total quantity of heat from steam and hot water urban users by heating enterprises (units) during the reference period .

City Length of Urban Heating Pipelines refers to the total length of steam or hot water pipelines for sources of heat to the leading pipelines of the building of the users, excluding internal pipelines in heat generating enterprises.

Heated Area refers to the total structure area of heat supplied to urban constructions, structures and ancillary facilities by heating enterprises (units) during the reference period .

Length of Paved Roads refers to the length of roads with paved surface including bridges and tunnels connected with roads. Length of the roads is measured by the central lines .

Area of Paved Roads refers to the actual pavement area of roads and the actual pavement area of squares, bridges and tunnels connecting to the roads (the area of sidewalk pavements is calculated separately).

The area of sidewalk pavements is the sum of area of roads on sides of road, including pedestrian streets and squares, excluding roads for both pedestrians and vehicles .

Length of exhaust pipelines refers to the total length of all main drain piles, trunk pipes ,branch pipes, access manholes, and connector well entrances and exits, and so on. The whole length is calculated as of single pipes. Namely, if there are two or more drain pipes parallel on a street, the length of every pipe shall be summed.

Total area of green land refers to vertical projection area of all vegetation including trees, shrubs, lawns. Including parks, protective green space, production green space, green subsidiaries, green plants covering area, covering an area other green spaces, green roofs and covering area of scattered trees, excluding kinds of water area in kinds of green area and the area not covered by vegetation(hardened road, building of no green roof). shrubs and herbaceous plants overlap under the canopy of trees do not double counting.

Per Capita Area of Paved Roads refers to the area of urban roads per capita at the end of the reporting period. The formula is :

$$\text{Per capita area of paved roads} = \frac{\text{Area of urban roads}}{\text{Urban population+temporary resident population}}$$

Density of Drainage Pipelines refers to density of drainage pipelines in developed areas at the end of the reporting period. The formula is :

$$\text{Density of drainage pipelines} = \frac{\text{Length of drainage pipelines}}{\text{Ares of developed areas}}$$

Rate of Sewerage Disposal refers to the ratio of waste water disposed with the total discharge of waste water in the reporting period. The formula is:

$$\text{Rate of Sewerage Disposal} = \frac{\text{Waste Water Disposed}}{\text{Total Discharge of Waste Water}} \times 100\%$$

Per Capita Area of Public Green refers to the area of public green areas per capita at end of the reporting period. The formula is :

$$\text{Per capita area of public green} = \frac{\text{Area of public green areas}}{\text{Urban population+temporary resident population}}$$

Coverage of Green Areas in Developed Areas refers to the ratio of green areas in built-up areas with the area of developed areas at the end of reporting period. The formula is:

$$\text{Coverage of green land in developed areas} = \frac{\text{Area of green land in developed aresa}}{\text{Area of developed areas}} \times 100\%$$

10 环境保护

ENVIRONMENT PROTECTION

资料整理：张　育
Data management: Zhang Yu
数据审核：马建华
Data audit: Ma Jianhua

第十部分　环境保护

一、简要说明

本章资料反映环境保护、工业污染排放及处理利用情况、危险废物集中处置情况、生活及其他污染情况和工业污染治理项目建设情况，由西安市统计局能源与环境统计处根据西安市环保局提供的数据资料整理。本章数据不包含西咸新区。

二、主要指标

全年环境空气质量达标天数（天）	250	比上年增加	25

10　ENVIRONMENT PROTECTION

Ⅰ.Brief Introduction

This chapter contains information that reflect environment protection, discharge and treatment of industrial pollutant, centralized treatment of dangerous wastes, domestic pollution and other pollution, construction of projects of industrial pollution treatment. Data in this chapter is compiled by General Division of the Xi'an Bureau of Statistics according to the reported data from Xi'an Environment Protection Bureau. Data from Xixian is not contained in this chapter from 2017.

Ⅱ.Major Indicators

		Increase over Preceding Year
Days of Air Quality up to the Standards（days）	250	25

10-1 城市环境保护（2020年）

Urban Environmental Protection (2020)

指 标	Item	2020
一、饮用水环境	**Potable Water Environment**	
全市饮用水水质达标率(%)	Compliance Rate of the City's Potable Water Quality (%)	100
二、大气环境	**Atmospheric Environment**	
颗粒物（PM10）年平均浓度（微克/立方米）	Particulate matter (PM10) Annual average concentration (μg / m^3)	88
颗粒物（PM2.5）年平均浓度（微克/立方米）	Particulate matter (PM2.5) Annual average concentration (μg / m^3)	51
二氧化硫浓度年平均值（微克/立方米）	Annual Average Concentration of Sulphur Dioxide (μg / m^3)	8
二氧化氮浓度年平均值（微克/立方米）	Annual Average Concentration of Nitrogen Dioxide (μg / m^3)	41
一氧化碳第95百分位数（微克/立方米）	The 95th percentile of carbon monoxide (μg / m^3)	1.5
臭氧八小时第90百分位数（微克/立方米）	Ozone eight hours 90th percentile (μg / m^3)	159
全年环境空气质量达标天数(天)	Days of Air Quality up to the Standards(days)	250
全年环境空气质量达标率(%)	Annual compliance rate of Ambient Air Quality(%)	68.3
三、声环境	**Voice**	
1、功能区噪声平均值(昼/夜)	Average Noise Value of Functional Districts（day/night)	
0类区(dB(A)/dB(A))	Class 0(dB(A)/dB(A))	48/43
1类区(dB(A)/dB(A))	Class 1(dB(A)/dB(A))	51/62
2类区(dB(A)/dB(A))	Class 2(dB(A)/dB(A))	54/49
3类区(dB(A)/dB(A))	Class 3(dB(A)/dB(A))	59/54
4类区(dB(A)/dB(A))	Class 4(dB(A)/dB(A))	68/64
2、道路交通噪声平均值(dB(A))	Average Noise Value of Road Traffic(dB(A))	69.4
3、区域噪声平均值(dB(A))	Average Noise Value of Region(dB(A))	55.8
四、环境污染治理	**Environmental pollution treatment**	
当年完成环保验收项目环境保护投资（亿元）	Year Completed Investment in Environmental Protection Projects of Environmental acceptance(100 million yuan)	9.03

注：本表数据来源于市生态环境局。表中当年完成环保验收项目环境保护投资额包含市本级及区县、开发区。
本表不含西咸新区。下同。

10–2 主要年份工业“三废”排放及处理利用情况

指　标	Item	2000	2010
一、工业废水排放量（万吨）	**Volume of Waste Water Discharge (10 000 tons)**	**9145**	**13840**
工业废水处理量（万吨）	Volume of Industrial Wastewater Disposal (10 000 tons)		10673.52
废水治理设施数（套）	Number of Facilities for Treatment of Waste Water (sets)		267
二、工业废气排放量（亿立方米）	**Total Volume of Industrial Waste Gas Emission (100 million cu.m)**	**275.97**	**791.56**
废气治理设施数（套）	Number of Facilities for Treatment of Waste Gas(sets)		816
三、工业固体废物产生量（万吨）	**Volume of Industrial Solid Wastes Produced (10 000 tons)**	**107**	**267.29**
工业固体废物处置量（万吨）	Volume of Industrial Solid Wastes Treated (10 000 tons)	20	3.56
工业固体废物综合利用量（万吨）	Volume of Industrial Solid Waste Utilized (10 000 tons) in a Comprehensive Way	63	262
工业固体废物综合利用率（%）	Percentage of Volume of Industrial Solid Waste Utilized in a Comprehensive Way(%)	58.88	98.05
四、工业锅炉（台/蒸吨）	**Industrial Boilers (units/tons)**		

注：1.本表数据来源于市生态环境局。
2.2010年全国统一进行了污染源普查动态更新调查工作，“十二五”的环境统计体系与污染源普查体系相衔接，与“十一五”环境统计口径不同。
3.工业固体废物综合利用率依据环境统计口径计算。

Discharge and Treatment of Waste Gas, Water & Solid Wastes in Repersentative Years

2011	2012	2013	2014	2015	2016	2017	2018	2019	2020
13148	**10223.73**	**8972.97**	**6339.85**	**5203.56**	**4029.83**	**4247.57**	**4163.40**	**3913.70**	**2998.24**
12632.38	9089.04	6798.71	5818.27	4783.6	4264.99	4448.08	4091.10	3955.70	3384.43
314	312	295	305	315	266	275	299	311	311
1018.46	**1043.31**	**844.11**	**901.23**	**1108.48**	**1034.46**	**1444.60**	**1040.40**	**1067.30**	**1194.32**
745	649	661	740	801	834	1048	1225	1641	1271
279	**259.14**	**255.78**	**252.66**	**238.53**	**195.99**	**190.30**	**198.70**	**206.66**	**183.07**
6	9.24	9.68	17.54	20.95	28.66	28.00	78.10	22.70	27.09
271	248.58	244.08	233.52	216.64	167.20	159.80	118.30	182.98	156.00
97.30	95.92	95.43	92.43	90.82	85.31	83.97	59.50	87.50	85.21
	503/8785	**576/13466**	**520/14177**	**501/18278**	**480/12791.8**	**457/14682.3**	**466/17078.2**	**478/16955.3**	**455/17065.5**

10-3 工业污染排放及处理利用情况（2020年）

Discharge and Treatment of Industrial Pollution （2020）

指　标	Item	2020
一、被调查企业基本情况	**Basic condition of Enterprises investigated**	
1. 企业数（个）	Number of Enterprises (units)	561
2. 工业总产值（亿元）	Gross Industry Output Value (100 millian yuan)	4032.09
3. 工业锅炉数（台/蒸吨）	Industrial Boilers (units/tons)	455/17065.5
4. 工业炉窑数（座）	Number of Industrial Grates (items)	328
二、工业废水	**Industrial Waste Water**	
1. 工业取水量（万吨）	Industrial water intake (10000 tons)	6782.25
2. 工业废水排放量（万吨）	Volume of Industrial Waste Water Discharged (10 000 tons)	2998.24
3. 工业废水处理量（万吨）	Volume of Industrial Wastewater Disposal (10 000 tons)	3384.43
4. 废水治理设施数（套）	Number of Facilities for Treatment of Waste Water (sets)	311
5. 废水治理设施处理能力（万吨/日）	Disposal Capacity of Facilities for Treatment of Waste Water (10 000 tons/day)	22.23
6. 废水治理设施运行费用（万元）	Operating Expense of Facilities for Treatment of Waste Water (10 000 yuan)	35473.82
三、工业废气	**Industrial Waste Gas**	
1. 煤炭消费量（万吨）	Total Coal Consumption (10 000 tons)	480.56
2. 燃料油消费量（不含车船用）（万吨）	Fuel Oil Consumption (10 000 tons)	0.18
3. 天然气消费量（亿立方米）	Natural Gas Consumption (100 millian cu.m)	9.18
4. 工业废气排放总量（亿立方米）	Total Volume of Industrial Waste Gas Emission (100 millian cu.m)	1194.32
5. 废气治理设施数（套）	Number of Facilities for Treatment of Waste Gas (sets)	1271
6. 废气治理设施处理能力（万立方米/时）	Disposal Capacity of Facilities for Treatment of Waste Gas (10 000 cu.m./h)	9877.49
7. 废气治理设施设备运行费用（万元）	Operating Expense of Facilities for Treatment of Waste gas(10 000 yuan)	32329.06
8. 二氧化硫产生量（吨）	Sulfur dioxide production (tons)	88509.01
9. 二氧化硫排放量（吨）	Volume of Sulphur Dioxide Emission (tons)	1506.45
10. 氮氧化物产生量（吨）	Production of nitrogen oxides(tons)	14547.05
11. 氮氧化物排放量（吨）	Nitrogen oxide emissions(tons)	2917.46
12. 烟（粉）尘产生量（吨）	Tobacco (powder) dust production(tons)	246531.09
13. 烟（粉）尘排放量（吨）	The smoke (powder) dust emissions(tons)	1797.40
四、工业固体废物	**Industrial Solid Waste**	
1. 工业固体废物产生量（万吨）	Volume of Industrial Solid Waste Produced (10 000tons)	183.07
2. 工业固体废物综合利用量（万吨）	Volume of Industrial Solid Waste Utilized (10 000tons)	156.00
3. 工业固体废物综合利用率（%）	Percentage of Industrial Solid Waste Utilized（%）	85.21
4. 工业固体废物贮存量（万吨）	Volume of Industrial Solid Waste Accumulated (10 000tons)	0.06
5. 工业固体废物处置量（万吨）	Volume of Industrial Solid Waste Treated (10 000tons)	27.09
6. 工业固体废物倾倒丢弃量（吨）	Volume of Industrial Solid Waste Discharged (tons)	17.57

注：本表数据来源于市生态环境局。

10-4 城市污水处理情况（2020年）

Urban Sewage Treatment（2020）

指　标	Item	2020
一、污水处理厂数（座）	**Number of Sewage Treatment Works(units)**	**42**
污水处理厂处理能力（万吨/日）	Daily Disposal Capacity of Sewage(10 000 tons/day)	287.55
二、污水处理	**Sewgae Disposal**	
污水实际处理量（万吨）	Volume of Sewgae Disposal(10 000 tons)	95288.01
生活污水处理量	Volume of Domestic Sewgae Disposal	92113.55
工业污水处理量	Volume of Industrial Sewage Disposal	3154.46
三、再生水（万吨）	**Utilization(10 000 tons)**	
生产量	Production	6333.66
利用量	Utilization	5473.37
四、化学需氧量去除量（吨）	**Volume of COD Removed (tons)**	**316523.95**
五、氨氮去除量（吨）	**Volume of Ammonia and Nitrogen Removed(tons)**	**28794.55**
六、总磷去除量（吨）	**Volume of Total Phosphorus Removed(tons)**	**4189.13**
七、污泥生产量（万吨）	**Volume of Sludge Produced(10 000 tons)**	**55.52**
八、污泥处置量（万吨）	**Volume of Sludge Disposal(10 000 tons)**	**55.51**
九、污泥倾倒丢弃量（吨）	**Dumping sludge discards (tons)**	**80.00**
十、本年运行费用（万元）	**Operating Expense(10 000 yuan)**	**89735.41**

注：本表数据来源于市生态环境局。

10-5 危险废物（医疗废物）集中处理情况（2020年）

Condition of Concentrated Disposal of Dangerous Wastes（Medical Wastes）（2020）

指　标	Item	2020
一、危险废物集中处理（置）厂数（个）	**Number of Colleted Dangerous Wastes Treated Plants(items)**	**1**
二、医疗废物集中处理（置）厂数（个）	**The number of Manufacturing Plants of Medical waste treatment (units)**	**1**
三、危险废物设计处置能力（吨/日）	**Design hazardous waste disposal capacity (tons / day)**	**74**
四、实际处置危险废物量（吨）	**The actual amount of hazardous waste disposal (tons)**	**15121.2**
五、危险废物综合利用量（吨）	**Volume of Dangerous Wastes Utilized in a Comprehensive Way (tons)**	**76.8**
六、焚烧残渣流向（千克）	**Flow Direction of Residuum after Burning (kg)**	
1. 焚烧残渣量	Volume of Residuum after Burning	3679.2
2. 焚烧残渣安全填埋处置量	Secure landfill disposal incineration residues	3679.2
3. 焚烧飞灰产生量	Fly ash production	252.8
4. 焚烧飞灰安全填埋处置量	Fly ash landfill disposal safety	252.8
七、当年运行费用（万元）	**Operating Expenses in Current year(10 000 yuan)**	**5550**

注：本表数据来源于市生态环境局。

10-6 生活及其他污染情况（2020年）

Domestic Pollution and Other Conditions（2020）

指　标	Item	2020
一、基本情况	**Basic Condition**	
1. 生活天然气消费量（万立方米）	Volume of Living natural gas consumption (10 000 cu.m)	271500
2. 生活用水总量（万吨）	Volume of Living water (10 000 tons)	70300
二、污染排放情况	**Discharge of Pollutant**	
1. 城镇生活污水排放量（万吨）	Volume of Urban Domestic Sewage Discharged(10 000 tons)	53583
2. 生活污水处理量（万吨）	Volume of Domestic Sewgae Disposal(10 000 tons)	92114
3. 生活CDD产生量（吨）	Volume of Life CDD production (tons)	305047
4. 生活CDD排放量（吨）	Volume of Life CDD emissions (tons)	271639
5. 生活氨氮产生量（吨）	Volume of Ammonia and Nitrogen in Urban Domestic Sewage Produced (tons)	32359
6. 生活氨氮排放量（吨）	Volume of Ammonia and Nitrogen in Urban Domestic Sewage Discharged (tons)	3912
7. 二氧化硫排放量（吨）	Volume of Domestic and Other Sulphur Dioxide Emission (tons)	6516
8. 氮氧化物排放量（吨）	Volume of Ammonia and Nitrogen in Urban Domestic Sewage Discharged (tons)	5305
9. 烟尘排放量（吨）	Volume of Soot Emission (tons)	18912

注：本表数据来源于市生态环境局。

10-7 工业污染治理项目建设情况（2020年）

Condition of Anti-Industrial-Pollution Projects（2020）

指 标	Item	2020
一、工业企业数（个）	**Number of Industrial Enterprises (units)**	**7**
二、老工业污染源项目治理本年施工总数（个）	**The total number of construction projects of Old industrial pollution sources control this year(units)**	**4**
#工业废水治理项目	Treatment of Waste Water	
工业废气治理项目	Treatment of Waste Gas	2
工业固体废物治理项目	Treatmen of Solid Wastes	
三、老工业污染源项目治理本年竣工总数（个）	**The Total Number of Old Industrial Pollution Control Projects Completed this year(units)**	**2**
#工业废水治理项目	Treatment of Waste Water	
工业废气治理项目	Treatment of Waste Gas	2
工业固体废物治理项目	Treatmen of Solid Wastes	
四、老工业污染源治理项目本年完成投资（万元）	**Investment completed in Old industrial pollution control projects this Year(10 000 yuan)**	**1979**
#废水治理项目	Treatment of Waste Water	
废气治理项目	Treatment of Waste Gas	579
固体废物治理项目	Treatmen of Solid Wastes	
五、老工业污染源治理项目本年投资来源（万元）	**Source of Investment in Old industrial pollution control projects this Year(10 000 yuan)**	**1979**
#政府其他补助	Other Government Subsidies	
企业自筹	Self-raising Funds	**1979**
银行贷款	Lonans	
六、“三同时”项目竣工验收数（个）	**Number of "Three simultaneous"project completion and acceptance (a)**	
七、“三同时”竣工验收项目实际环保投资（万元）	**"Three simultaneous" actual environmental investment completed and accepted (10 000 yuan)**	
八、“三同时”项目废水治理新增处理能力（万吨/日）	**"Three simultaneous"Add processing capacity of wastewater treatment (10 000 tons / day)**	
九、“三同时”项目废气治理新增处理能力（万立方米/时）	**"Three simultaneous"Add processing capacity of Exhaust treatment (10 000 cu.m/h)**	

注：本表数据来源于市生态环境局。
“三同时”指建设项目中防治污染的措施，必须与主体工程同时设计，同时施工，同时投产使用。
2020年环统系统中已无“三同时”项目相关描述。

10-8 各区县、开发区环境保护基本情况（2020年）

区县、开发区	Region	本年完成环保验收项目环保投资额（万元）Investment Completed in accepted Environmental projects this year (10 000 yuan)	工业二氧化硫排放量（吨）Volume of Industrial Sulphur Dioxide Discharged (tons)
全　市	**Total**	**90317.8**	**1506.4**
新城区	Xincheng	5248.7	0.2
碑林区	Beilin	33.2	187.6
莲湖区	Lianhu	1818.0	30.5
灞桥区	Baqiao		221.2
未央区	Weiyang	5059.9	65.7
雁塔区	Yanta	970.7	118.0
阎良区	Yanliang	547.5	1.4
临潼区	Lintong	3254.7	2.4
长安区	Chang'an	326.1	295.2
高陵区	Gaoling	1860.1	13.9
鄠邑区	Huyi		322.9
蓝田县	Lantian	3840.0	123.5
周至县	Zhouzhi	1608.8	0.1
高新区	GaoXin	21309.2	1.0
经开区	JingKai	10154.2	70.9
航天基地	Aerospace Base	7416.9	52.1

注：本表数据来源于市生态环境局。
环境统计中污水处理厂个数包含部分大学园区及部分大型小区的污水处理厂。
区县、开发区环保验收项目环保投资额未包括市本级完成数。

Condition of Environment Protection by Regions（2020）

工业化学需氧量排放量（吨） Volume of COD Removed (tons)	垃圾处理站数（座） Number of Rubbish Disposal Works (units)	污水处理厂数（个） Number of Sewage Treatment Works (units)
1431.0	**2**	**42**
14.8		
102.1		2
124.7		3
35.0		6
21.9		3
101.9		2
55.7		2
71.2		6
82.1		1
421.6	1	3
4.1	1	4
5.9		2
129.5		6
69.4		2
33.3		

主 要 统 计 指 标 解 释

工业用水 指工矿企业在生产过程中用于制造、加工、冷却、空调、净化、洗涤等方面的用水，按新水取用量计，不包括企业内部的重复利用水量。

工业废水排放量 指经过企业厂区所有排放口排到企业外部的工业废水量。包括生产废水、外排的直接冷却水、超标排放的矿井地下水和与工业废水混排的厂区生活污水，不包括外排的间接冷却水（清污不分流的间接冷却水应计算在内）。

直接排入海的 指经企业位于海边的排放口，直接排入海的废水量。直接排放指废水经过工厂的排污口直接排入海，而未经过城市下水道或其他中间体，也不受其他水体的影响。

工业废水排放达标量 指报告期内废水中各项污染物指标都达到国家或地方排放标准的外排工业废水量，包括未经处理外排达标的，经废水处理设施处理后达标排放的，以及经污水处理厂处理后达标排放的。

生活污水排放量 指城镇居民每年排放的生活污水。用人均系数法测算。测算公式为：

$$\text{生活污水排放量}=\text{城镇生活污水排放系数}\times\text{市镇非农业人口}\times 365$$

生活污水中化学需氧量（COD）排放量 指城镇居民每年排放的生活污水中的COD的量。用人均系数法测算。测算公式为：

$$\text{城镇生活污水中COD产生系数}=\text{城镇牛活污水中COD排放量}\times\text{市镇非农业人口}\times 365$$

化学需氧量（COD） 指用化学氧化剂氧化水中有机污染物时所需的氧量。COD值越高，表示水中有机污染物污染越重。

工业废气排放量 指报告期内企业厂区内燃料燃烧和生产工艺过程中产生的各种排入大气的含有污染物的气体的总量，以标准状态（273K，101325Pa）计算。测算公式为：

$$\text{工业废气排放量}=\text{燃料燃烧过程中废气排放量}+\text{生产工艺过程中废气排放量}$$

生活及其他SO_2排放量 以生活及其他煤炭消费量和其含硫量为基础，根据以下公式计算：

$$\text{生活及其他}SO_2\text{排放量}=\text{生活及其他煤炭消费量}\times\text{含硫量}\times 0.8\times 2$$

工业SO_2排放量 指报告期内企业在燃料燃烧和生产工艺过程中排入大气的SO_2总量，计算公式为：

$$\text{工业}SO_2\text{排放量}=\text{燃料燃烧过程中}SO_2\text{排放量}+\text{生产工艺过程中}SO_2\text{排放量}$$

工业烟尘排放量 指企业厂区内燃料燃烧过程中产生的烟气中夹带的颗粒物排放量。

生活及其他烟尘排放量 指除工业生产活动以外的所有社会、经济活动及公共设施的经营活动中燃烧所排放的烟尘纯重量。以生活及其他煤炭消费量为基础进行测算。

工业粉尘排放量 指企业在生产工艺过程中排放的能在空气中悬浮一定时间的固体颗粒物排放量。如钢铁企业的耐火材料粉尘、焦化企业的筛焦系统粉尘、烧结机的粉尘、石灰窑的粉尘、建材企业的水泥粉尘等。不包括电厂排入大气的烟尘。

工业固体废物产生量 指报告期内企业在生产过程中产生的固体状、半固体状和高浓度液体状废弃物的总量，包括危险废物、冶炼废渣、粉煤灰、炉渣、煤矸石、尾矿、放射性废物和其他废物等；不包括矿山开采的剥离废石和掘进废石（煤矸石和呈酸性或碱性的废石除外）。酸性或碱性废石指采掘的废石其流经水、雨淋水的pH值小于4或pH值大于10.5者。

危险废物 指列入国家危险废物名录或根据国家规定的危险废物鉴别标准和鉴别方法认定的，具有爆炸性、易燃性、易氧化性、毒性、腐蚀性、易传染疾病等危险特性之一的废物。

工业固体废物综合利用量 指报告期内企业通过回收、加工、循环、交换等方式，从固体废物中提取或者使其转化为可以利用的资源、能源和其他原材料的固体废物量（包括当年利用往年的工业固体废物贮存量），如用作农业肥料、生产建筑材料、筑路等。综合利用量由原产生固体废物的单位统计。

工业固体废物综合利用率 指工业固体废物综合利用量占丁业固体废物产生量（包括综合利用往年贮存量）的百分率。计算公式为：

$$\text{工业固体废物综合利用率}=\frac{\text{工业固体废物综合利用量}}{\text{工业固体废物产生量}+\text{综合利用往年贮存量}}\times 100\%$$

工业固体废物贮存量 指报告期内企业以综合利用或处置为目的，将固体废物暂时贮存或堆存在专设的贮存设施或专设的集中堆存场所内的数量。专设的固体废物贮存场所或贮存设施必须有防扩散、防流失、防渗漏、防止污染大气、水体的措施。

工业固体废物处置量 指报告期内企业将固体废物焚烧或者最终置于符合环境保护规定要求的场所，并不再回取的工业固体废物量（包括当年处置往年的工业固体废物贮存量）。处置方式有填埋（其中危险废物应安全填埋）、焚烧、专业贮存场（库）封场处理、深层灌注、回填矿井及海洋处置（经海洋管理部门同意投海处置）等。

工业固体废物排放量 指报告期内企业将所产生的固体废物排到固体废物污染防治设施、场所以外的数量，不包括矿山开采的剥离废石和掘进废石（煤矸石和呈酸性或碱性的废石除外）。

"三废"综合利用产品产值 指报告期内利用"三废"作为主要原料生产的产品价值（现行价）；已经销售或准备销售的应计算产品价值，留作生产自用的不应计算产品价值。

生活垃圾清运量 指报告期内收集和运送到各生活垃圾处理厂（场）和生活垃圾最终消纳点的生活垃圾数量。生活垃圾指城市日常生活或为城市日常生活提供服务的活动中产生的固体废物以及法律行政规定的视为城市生活垃圾的固体废物。包括：居民生活垃圾、商业垃圾、集市贸易市场垃圾、街道清扫垃圾、公共场所垃圾和机关、学校、厂矿等单位的生活垃圾。

生活垃圾无害化处理率 指报告期生活垃圾无害化处理量与生活垃圾产生量的比率。在统计上，由于生活垃圾产生量不易取得，可用清运量代替。计算公式为：

$$\text{生活垃圾无害化处理率}=\frac{\text{生活垃圾无害化处理量}}{\text{生活垃圾产生量}}\times 100\%$$

Explanatory Notes on Main Statistical Indicators

Water Used by Industry refers to new withdrawals of water, excluding reuse of water within enterprises.

Waste Water Discharged by Industry refers to the volume of waste water discharged by industrial enterprises through all their outlets, including waste water from production process, directly cooled water, groundwater from mining wells which does not meet discharge standards and sewage from households mixed with waste water produced by industrial activities, but excluding indirectly cooled water discharged (It should be included if the discharge is not separated from waste water).

Waste Water Directly Discharged into Sea refers to the volume of waste water directly discharged into sea through outlets of enterprises situated by sea without going through municipal sewerage networks or any other intermediates or being affected by any other water bodies.

Industrial Waste Water Meeting Discharge Standards refers to volume of industrial waste water discharge which, with or without treatment, reaches national or local standards with regard to all pollutants.

Urban Non-industrial Waste Water Discharge refers to annual discharge of non-industrial waste water by urban households. It is estimated by per capita coefficient using the formula:

$$\text{Urban non-industrial waste water discharge} = \text{urban non-industrial waste water discharge coefficient} \times \text{urban non-alagricultur population} \times 365$$

Volume of Chemical Oxygen Demand (COD) Generated by Urban Non-industrial Waster Water refers to chemical oxygen demand generated through the annual discharge of non-industrial waste water by urban households. It is estimated as:

$$\text{Volume of chemical oxygen demand (cod) generated by urban non-industrial waster water} = \text{Coefficient of COD generated through urban non-industrial waste water} \times \text{urban non-agricultural population} \times 365$$

Chemical Oxygen Demand (COD) refers to the amount of oxygen required when chemical oxidants are used to oxidize organic pollutants in water. A higher value of COD corresponds to more serious pollution by organic pollutants.

Industrial Waste Air Emission refers to the discharge into atmosphere of waste air containing pollutants generated from fuel burning and production processes in enterprises within a given period of time. It is calculated at standard status (273K, 101325Pa) as:

$$\text{Industrial waste air emission} = \text{tnoissimehrough fuel burning} + \text{tnoissimehrough production process}$$

SO_2 Emission through Non-industrial and Other Activities is calculated on the basis of consumption of coal by households and other activities and the sulphur content of coal with the following formula:

$$SO_2 \text{ emission through non-industrial and other activities} = \text{of coalby households andother activities} \times \text{sulphur content} \times 0.8 \times 2$$

SO_2 Emission through Industrial Activities refers to volume of sulphur dioxide emission from fuel burning and production process by enterprises during a given period of time. It is calculated as:

$$SO_2 \text{ emission through industrial activities} = SO_2 \text{emission from fuel burning} + SO_2 \text{ emission from production process}$$

Industrial Soot Emission refers to the volume of soot in smoke emitted in the process of fuel burning in the premises of enterprises.

Soot Emission by Consumption and Others refers to the net volume of soot emitted by fuel burning from all social and economic activities and operations of public facilities other than industrial activities. It is calculated on the basis of coal consumption by households and others.

Industrial Dust Emission refers to volume of dust emitted by production process of enterprises and suspended in the air for a given period of time, including dust from refractory material of iron and steel works, dust from coke-screening systems and sintering machines of coke plants, dust from lime kilns and dust from cement production in building material enterprises, but excluding soot and dust emitted from power plants.

Industrial Solid Wastes Produced refers to total volume of solid, semi-solid and high concentration liquid residues produced by industrial enterprises from production process in a given period of time, including hazardous wastes, slag, coal ash, gangue, tailings, radioactive residues and other wastes, but excluding stones stripped or dug out in mining - gangue and acid or alkaline stones not included (a stone is acid or alkaline according to the pH value of the water being below 4 or above 10.5 when the stone is in, or soaked by water).

Hazardous Wastes refers to those included in the national hazardous wastes catalogue or specified as any one of the following properties in the national hazardous wastes identification standards: explosive, ignitable, oxidizable, toxic, corrosive or liable to cause infectious diseases or lead to other dangers.

Industrial Solid Wastes Utilized refers to volume of solid wastes from which useful materials can be extracted or which can be converted into usable resources, energy or other materials by means of reclamation, processing, recycling and exchange (including utilizing in the year the stocks of industrial solid wastes of the previous year). Examples of such utilizations include fertilizers, building materials and road materials. The information shall be collected by the producing units of the wastes.

Rate of Utilization of Industrial Solid Wastes refers to the percentage of industrial solid wastes utilized over industrial solid wastes produced (including stocks of the previous years). It is calculated as:

$$\text{Rate of utilization of industrial solid wastes} = \frac{\text{volume of industrial solid wastes utilized}}{\text{industrial solid wastesproduced+ stock of previous years}} \times 100\%$$

Stock of Industrial Solid Wastes refers to the volume of solid wastes placed in special facilities or special sites for purposes of utilization or disposal. The sites or facilities should take measures against dispersion, loss, seepage, and air and water contamination.

Industrial Solid Wastes Disposed refers to the quantity of industrial solid wastes which are burnt or placed ultimately in the sites meeting the requirements for environmental protection and not salvaged or recycled (including disposition in the year of those wastes of previous years). The disposition includes landfill (Safe landfills should be conducted for hazardous wastes), incineration, containment spaces, deep underground disposal, backfill in mining pits and disposal at sea.

Industrial Solid Wastes Discharged refers to the volume of industrial solid wastes discharged by producing enterprises to disposal facilities or to other sites. The wastes exclude stones stripped or dug from mining (gangue and acid or alkaline waste stones not included).

Output Value of Products Made from Waste Gas, Waste Water and Solid Wastes refers to the current value of products with waste gas, waste water and solid wastes as main materials of production. Products sold and ready to sell shall be included while those produced for own use shall not be included.

Consumption Wastes Transported refers to volume of consumption wastes collected and transported to disposal factories or sites. Consumption wastes are solid wastes produced from urban households or from service activities for urban households, and solid wastes regarded by laws and regulations as urban consumption wastes, including those from households, commercial activities, markets, cleaning of streets, public sites, offices, schools, factories, mining units and other sources.

Ratio of Consumption Wastes Treated refers to consumption wastes treated over that produced. In practical statistics, as it is difficult to estimate, the volume of consumption wastes produced is replaced with that transported. It is calculated as:

$$\text{Ratio of consumption wastes treated} = \frac{\text{consumption wastes treated}}{\text{consumption wastes produced}} \times 100\%$$

11 农　业

AGRICULTURE

资料整理：薛　丰　张喜兰　马秋娟　吴光卫　罗文毅　赵明正

Data management：Xue Feng　Zhang Xilan　Ma Qiujuan　Wu Guangwei　Luo Wenyi　Zhao Mingzheng

数据审核：马　琰　柳红卫

Data audit：Ma yan　Liu Hongwei

第十一部分　农业

一、简要说明

1.本章资料反映西安农业生产和农村经济的基本情况。内容主要包括农林牧渔业产值、主要农产品产量、造林、水利水保、农业机械拥有量、农村经济效益主要指标、区县农业生产情况等方面统计资料。粮食、畜牧业相关指标数据表由国家统计局西安调查队负责完成。

2.农业统计范围包括主要涉农区县的农业生产经营活动。

3.涉及主要年份数据资料，按照《陕西省根据第三次全国农业普查结果核定和修订常规年报相关数据方案》要求，对2007–2017年数据进行了修订。其中，畜牧业中猪牛羊禽修订了2013–2017年数据。11–1、11–3、11–5、11–7表不做修订。

二、主要指标

指标	数值		增长
农林牧渔业总产值（亿元）	564.41	比上年增长	3.2%
农作物播种面积（万亩）	538.40	比上年增长	0.1%
粮食产量（万吨）	144.58	比上年增长	3.4%

11 AGRICULTURE

Ⅰ.Brief Introduction

1. Data in this chapter reflects basic condition of agriculture production of Xi'an city. The mainly including output of agriculture, forestry, animal husbandry and fishery, output of major products, forestation, water conservancy and protection, quantity of agricultural machinery and agricultural base county. The data table of grain and animal husbandry indicators is completed by XI'AN Investigation Team of National Bureau of Statistics.

2. Rural social and economic statistics cover social and economic activities in all townships except county towns.

3. Data related to major years, revised the data from 2007 to 2017 by Shaanxi Province in accordance with the results of the third national agricultural census approved and revised the regular annual report data programmed. Among them, animal husbandry such as hog, cattle, sheep are revised the data from 2013 to 2017.

Ⅱ.Major Indicators

		Increase over Preceding Year
Gross Output Value of Farming, Forestry, Animal Husbandry and Fishery (100 mil. Yuan)	564.41	3.2%
Sown Area of Crops(10 000 mu)	538.40	0.1%
Grain Output(10 000 tons)	144.58	3.4%

11-1 主要年份乡村从业人员及基础设施情况

Rural Employees and Basic Facilities in Representative Years

指 标	Item	2000	2005	2010	2011	2012	2013	2014
一、乡村从业人员数（万人）	**Number of Rural Workers (10000 persons)**	**212.65**	**223.30**	**225.04**	**230.56**	**226.92**	**222.67**	**216.33**
#女性	Female	99.07	103.22	103.25	109.61	107.63	106.70	104.03
#农林牧渔业	Forestry Animal Husbandry and Fishery	146.07	137.69	116.58	116.15	113.29	108.48	110.30
二、自来水受益村数（个）	**The Number of Tap Water Villages (unit)**	**1527**	**1756**	**2184**	**2400**	**2545**	**2650**	**2765**
三、通有线电视村数（个）	**The Number of Villages connected with cable TV (unit)**							
四、通宽带村数（个）	**The Number of Villages connected to broadband (unit)**							

11-1 续表 continued

指　标	Item	2015	2016	2017	2018	2019	2020
一、乡村从业人员数（万人）	**Number of Rural Workers (10000 persons)**	**200.38**	**204.11**	**225.88**	**222.99**	**224.11**	**221.16**
#女性	Female	96.46	98.10	107.16	105.88	105.89	103.57
#农林牧渔业	Forestry Animal Husbandry and Fishery	105.10	102.32	110.38	97.65	97.83	98.42
二、自来水受益村数（个）	**The Number of Tap Water Villages (unit)**	**2718**	**2507**	**2706**	**2027**	**1966**	**1944**
三、通有线电视村数（个）	**The Number of Villages connected with cable TV (unit)**		**2338**	**2328**	**1750**	**1637**	**1645**
四、通宽带村数（个）	**The Number of Villages connected to broadband (unit)**		**2720**	**2694**	**2070**	**1964**	**1950**

11-2 各区县乡村从业人员数（2020年）

Number of Rural Employees by Region（2020）

单位：万人 (10 000 persons)

区 县	Region	乡村从业人员数合计 Total number of employees in rural areas	女性 Female employees	农林牧渔业 Forestry Animal Husbandry and Fishery
全 市	**Total**	**221.16**	**103.57**	**98.42**
新城区	Xincheng			
碑林区	Beilin			
莲湖区	Lianhu			
灞桥区	Baqiao	14.22	5.83	4.07
未央区	Weiyang	0.08	0.01	0.02
雁塔区	Yanta			
阎良区	Yanliang	10.34	4.66	6.44
临潼区	Lintong	31.66	14.29	21.04
长安区	Chang'an	37.13	16.94	9.78
高陵区	Gaoling	8.20	3.63	2.50
鄠邑区	Huyi	26.77	12.49	12.04
蓝田县	Lantian	29.00	18.32	12.18
周至县	Zhouzhi	33.27	14.01	18.16
西咸新区	Xixian	30.49	13.39	12.19

11-3 主要年份农业机械年末拥有量

指 标	Item	2005	2009	2010
农业机械总动力（千瓦）	Total Power of Agricultural Machinery(kw)	2239001	2616053	2677334
大中型拖拉机（台）	Large and Medium Tractors(unit)	8415	11479	14675
小型拖拉机（台）	Mini-tractors(unit)	26326	18406	14194
拖拉机配套农具（台）	Number of Tactor Towing Farm Machinery(unit)	67217	55614	53608
农用水泵（台）	Agricultural Water Pump(unit)	77567	80174	77367
节水灌溉类机械（套）	Equipment in Water-saving Irrigation(set)	1290	1799	1710
联合收割机（台）	Combine Harvesters(unit)	4802	6155	6718
机动脱粒机（台）	Motorized Huller (unit)	13870	11960	13231

注：1.本表数据来源于市农业农村局，2017年西咸新区由西安代管，2017年、2018年数据不含西咸新区，2019年及以后数据含西咸新区。
2.2017年以前大中型拖拉机动力标准为14.7千瓦及以上，小型拖拉机动力标准为2.2-14.7千瓦（含2.2千瓦）。2018年及以后大中型拖拉机动力标准为22.1千瓦以上，小型拖拉机动力标准为22.1千瓦及以下。
3.表中“农用水泵”“节水灌溉类机械”和“机动脱粒机”三项指标由于部门报表制度发生变化，2020年暂无数据。

Possession of Agricultural Machinery year end in Representative Years

2011	2012	2013	2014	2015	2016	2017	2018	2019	2020
2890247	2983979	3108354	3203302	3253733	2615435	2543023	2429137	2456028	2478420
12585	12987	12927	9946	9652	10177	9275	8580	8938	9357
13008	11471	8971	7538	8447	9175	8501	8226	6009	6264
65833	60035	58515	53257	54120	59805	50559	47582	45635	47677
75426	80982	80575	79849	79695	79681	76916	70533	62397	
1733	2106	2218	2562	2517	2476	2366	2135	1869	
7854	8502	9114	7815	8144	8458	7656	7390	7685	7947
13407	14493	14700	14749	14504	14272	14169	14074	12813	

11-4 各区县农业机械年末拥有量（2020年）

指 标	Item	西安市 Xi' an	新城区 Xincheng	碑林区 Beilin	莲湖区 Lianhu	灞桥区 Baqiao
农业机械总动力（千瓦）	Total Power of Agricultural Machinery(kw)	2478420				118900
大中型拖拉机（台）	Large and Medium Tractors(unit)	9357				
小型拖拉机（台）	Mini-tractors(unit)	6264				20
拖拉机配套农具（台）	Number of Tactor Towing Farm Machinery(unit)	47677				200
农用水泵（台）	Agricultural Water Pump(unit)					
节水灌溉类机械（套）	Equipment in Water-saving Irrigation(set)					
联合收割机（台）	Combine Harvesters(unit)	7947				20
机动脱粒机（台）	Motorized Huller (unit)					

注：本表数据来源于市农业农村局。

Possession of Agricultural Machinery year end in Representative Years (2020)

未央区 Weiyang	雁塔区 Yanta	阎良区 Yanliang	临潼区 Lintong	长安区 Chang'an	高陵区 Gaoling	鄠邑区 Huyi	蓝田县 Lantian	周至县 Zhouzhi	西咸新区 Xixian
		140045	423218	360200	250011	511900	247200	341683	37063
		483	1228	1342	1634	1971	915	1243	298
		265		916	142	1327	931	2425	20
		2282	9834	4800	6500	9834	6238	6637	914
		470	1787	1121	902	2544	394	328	265

11-5 主要年份农业机械化、化肥、水利情况

指　标	Item	2000	2005	2008
一、农业机械化水平（万亩）	**Statistics on Agricultural Machinery (10 000 mu)**			
当年机械耕地面积（实际）	Area Ploughed by Tractors	366.81	360.68	404.42
当年机械播种面积（作业）	Seeded Area by Tractors	482.74	485.62	539.81
当年机械收获面积（作业）	Harvest Area by Tractors	272.83	271.77	313.11
二、农用化肥施用量（吨）	**Use of Agricultural Fertilizers and Insecticides(ton)**			
按折纯法计算合计	Standard Consumption	196343	211790	225949
氮肥	Nitrogenous Fertilizer	102982	107645	112000
磷肥	Phosphate Fertilizer	18658	19368	18855
钾肥	Potash Fertilizer	15921	17055	17077
复合肥	Compound Fertilizer	39313	57009	66247
三、农用塑料薄膜使用量（公斤）	**Plastic Sheet for Agricultural Use(kg)**	**1622198**	**1855383**	**2122310**
四、农用柴油使用量（吨）	**Diesel Oil for Agricultural Use (ton)**	**52706**	**50832**	**51097**
五、农药使用量（公斤）	**Pesticide (kg)**	**1559333**	**1427879**	**1465819**
六、农村水利化情况（万亩）	**Irrigation and Water Conservancy (10 000 mu)**			
有效灌溉面积	Effective Irrigation Area	335.97	280.10	274.48
旱涝保收面积	Stable-Harvesting Arable Land	294.06	255.37	249.31

注：1.本表第一部分数据来源于市农业农村局，第六部分数据来源于市水务局。
2.2017年西咸新区由西安代管，2017年、2018年第一部分和第六部分数据不含西咸新区，2019年及以后第六部分不含西咸新区。

Agricultural Machinery,Chemical Fertilizers,Water Conservancy, in Representative Years

2009	2010	2011	2012	2013	2014	2015	2016	2017	2018	2019	2020
413.70	367.32	427.03	425.40	425.21	549.07	533.21	518.07	498.57	465.25	417.01	409.26
544.86	548.28	507.55	529.99	523.15	509.58	492.90	499.36	532.61	501.27	469.46	451.77
342.82	403.50	413.93	428.28	443.57	466.21	474.10	488.85	470.66	456.27	393.97	406.26
230299	235532	239497	243281	239701	251217	246284	242871	255267	252662	243916	251814
112275	108868	110412	113662	109497	116055	108833	111150	115631	113745	103059	103218
18457	18315	18026	18061	18023	18505	18584	18033	19072	18456	16797	16551
16534	17997	18095	21267	18973	20110	21986	21779	21486	21228	20969	20753
71042	78811	81764	90291	93208	96547	96881	91909	99078	99233	103091	111292
2141969	**2450496**	**2533372**	**2683201**	**2678745**	**2657870**	**2770750**	**2880480**	**3157710**	**3380130**	**3350070**	**3241783**
51346	**61917**	**61637**	**57451**	**62563**	**74935**	**59360**	**55982**	**67510**	**67091**	**61141**	**57954**
1325459	**1243105**	**1242773**	**1252490**	**1210060**	**1220638**	**1174883**	**1126305**	**1703736**	**1506859**	**1367993**	**1346652**
273.17	281.28	262.32	267.84	240.22	248.34	244.72	259.78	256.13	282.83	245.72	228.01
247.60	234.15	214.62	211.31	196.96	189.69	188.50	201.70	184.91	184.78	193.44	195.00

11-6 各区县农业机械化、化肥、水利情况（2020年）

指　标	Item	西安市 Xi'an	新城区 Xincheng	碑林区 Beilin	莲湖区 Lianhu
一、农业机械化水平（万亩）	**Statistics on Agricultural Machinery (10 000 mu)**				
当年机械耕地面积（实际）	Area Ploughed by Tractors	409.26			
当年机械播种面积（作业）	Seeded Area by Tractors	451.77			
当年机械收获面积（作业）	Harvest Area by Tractors	406.26			
二、农用化肥施用量（吨）	**Use of Agricultural Fertilizers and Insecticides(ton)**				
按折纯法计算合计	Standard Consumption	251814			
氮肥	Nitrogenous Fertilizer	103218			
磷肥	Phosphate Fertilizer	16551			
钾肥	Potash Fertilizer	20753			
复合肥	Compound Fertilizer	111292			
三、农用塑料薄膜使用量（公斤）	**Plastic Sheet for Agricultural Use(kg)**	**3241783**			
四、农用柴油使用量（吨）	**Diesel Oil for Agricultural Use (ton)**	**57954**			
五、农药使用量（公斤）	**Pesticide (kg)**	**1346652**			
六、农村水利化情况（万亩）	**Irrigation and Water Conservancy (10 000 mu)**				
有效灌溉面积	Effective Irrigation Area	228.01			
旱涝保收面积	Stable-Harvesting Arable Land	195.00			

注：本表第一部分数据来源于市农业农村局，第六部分数据来源于市水务局。

Agricultural Machinery,Chemical Fertilizers, Water Conservancy by Region（2020）

灞桥区 Baqiao	未央区 Weiyang	雁塔区 Yanta	阎良区 Yanliang	临潼区 Lintong	长安区 Chang'an	高陵区 Gaoling	鄠邑区 Huyi	蓝田县 Lantian	周至县 Zhouzhi	西咸新区 Xixian
9.11			45.95	93.10	37.66	35.26	45.71	50.40	30.92	61.15
8.75			38.70	102.58	50.73	31.73	57.90	60.27	41.41	59.70
7.58			31.75	100.45	45.94	28.20	50.46	55.10	36.25	50.53
2729	178		31599	46683	15296	12701	30690	45668	52412	13858
926	68		14406	16635	6245	4020	14207	28213	15068	3430
158	14		1663	4898	973	1805	1685	2617	1897	841
711	39		2912	1910	2779	1500	2443	3628	4448	383
934	57		12618	23240	5299	5376	12355	11210	30999	9204
7537	**15012**		**1559137**	**223544**	**161320**	**34000**	**504331**	**373550**	**101536**	**261816**
206	**258**		**3421**	**8179**	**7254**	**1890**	**11228**	**9026**	**3300**	**13192**
6773	**320**		**187487**	**208797**	**62871**	**155750**	**59797**	**68563**	**164911**	**431383**
4.46	1.11		21.59	47.25	31.53	20.30	39.63	10.65	51.49	
	1.11		22.56	47.25	22.13	20.30	42.91		38.74	

11-7 主要年份农林牧渔业总产值及指数

Gross Output Value of Farming,Forestry,Animal Husbandry,Fishery and Related Indices in Representative Years

单位：万元 (10 000 yuan)

年份 Year	农林牧渔业总产值（现价） Gross Output Value (At current prices)	农业 Farming	林业 Forestry	牧业 Animal Husbandry	渔业 Fishery	农林牧渔专业及辅助性活动 Farming, Forestry, Animal Husbandry, Fishery and Auxiliary Activities	指数（上年=100）（可比价） Indices(preceding year=100) (At cinstant prices)
1970	40617	35965	713	3896	43		111.2
1975	55322	47378	1509	6403	32		93.9
1978	65423	56519	1444	7427	33		104.7
1980	65322	54004	1177	10106	35		85.0
1985	134933	105888	2559	26186	300		106.4
1990	262073	191088	3134	65840	2011		102.5
1991	295620	208324	3362	81070	2864		108.6
1992	321155	219160	4225	94045	3725		108.6
1993	387068	261959	5031	115810	4268		112.8
1994	565056	359609	7819	192140	5488		102.4
1995	754597	513348	7185	228598	5466		106.8
1996	786003	552726	7573	219214	6490		102.1
1997	836201	585973	9226	233623	7379		110.3
1998	853279	625465	8146	212045	7623		107.5
1999	739905	530029	8883	194552	6441		100.7
2000	743712	514845	8482	212612	7773		104.3
2001	767511	527160	8427	223861	8063		102.8
2002	797444	539978	11378	238761	7327		103.0
2003	837857	551398	10550	269610	6299		101.5
2004	967946	580798	12773	314517	6728	53130	108.4
2005	1065437	657262	13086	329856	7340	57893	107.7
2006	1141484	686748	15188	346626	7017	85905	107.2
2007	1317442	790316	15845	395003	9147	107131	105.3
2008	1629892	943261	23365	521950	11348	129968	107.8
2009	1695468	1034208	22663	486142	11830	140625	106.5
2010	2124191	1389118	26787	538396	12830	157060	107.4
2011	2501236	1651250	34453	616943	14856	183734	106.6
2012	2785682	1827705	62291	643347	19877	232462	106.0
2013	3057732	2038346	80199	648800	22773	267614	104.9
2014	3232984	2196966	86889	633519	24030	291580	105.1
2015	3308141	2251512	97776	613417	19519	325917	105.1
2016	3467506	2357901	102222	621737	19640	366006	104.2
2017	4373298	3009278	135570	729219	22700	476531	104.8
2018	4612088	3230380	169157	679813	26268	506470	103.5
2019	4993219	3493828	184739	727047	21867	565738	104.3
2020	5644139	3924251	236065	849948	18895	614980	103.2

注：本表2007-2017年数根据第三次全国农业普查结果进行了修订。

11-8 主要年份农林牧渔业总产值指数

Related Indices of Gross Output Value of Farming,Forestry,Animal Husbandry and Fishery in Representative Years

年 份 Year	农林牧渔业总产值指数（上年=100）（可比价） Gross Output Value Index of Farming, Forestry, Animal Husbandry and Fishery (preceding year = 100) (At constant prices)	农业 Farming	林业 Forestry	牧业 Animal Husbandry	渔业 Fishery	农林牧渔专业及辅助性活动 Farming, Forestry, Animal Husbandry, Fishery and Auxiliary Activities
2005	107.7	108.0	98.7	107.3	112.6	108.0
2006	107.2	106.0	102.5	109.3	104.5	109.0
2007	105.3	106.4	101.3	102.4	106.3	109.0
2008	107.8	107.9	112.2	106.0	100.5	114.0
2009	106.5	105.4	121.3	106.8	107.4	110.2
2010	107.4	108.7	115.2	104.3	92.7	108.9
2011	106.6	108.2	105.7	102.9	102.1	107.8
2012	106.0	105.6	143.0	104.8	113.4	108.5
2013	104.9	104.3	131.3	104.0	110.1	105.9
2014	105.1	105.8	105.7	103.2	106.0	105.9
2015	105.1	106.7	113.8	100.2	71.2	106.2
2016	104.2	104.8	114.7	100.6	100.1	106.6
2017	104.8	105.0	111.0	103.0	104.3	106.2
2018	103.5	102.8	131.0	100.1	111.4	105.1
2019	104.3	104.7	120.1	98.0	86.4	105.5
2020	103.2	101.6	144.5	100.1	90.7	103.4

11-9 主要年份农林牧渔业总产值构成

Gross Output Value and Its Composition of Farming, Forestry, Animal Husbandry and Fishery at Current Price in Representative Years

单位：% (%)

年 份 Year	农林牧渔业总产值（现价） Gross Output Value (At current prices)	农业 Farming	林业 Forestry	牧业 Animal Husbandry	渔业 Fishery	农林牧渔专业及辅助性活动 Farming, Forestry, Animal Husbandry, Fishery and Auxiliary Activities
2005	100.0	61.7	1.2	31.0	0.7	5.4
2006	100.0	60.9	1.3	31.5	0.6	5.7
2007	100.0	60.0	1.2	30.0	0.7	8.1
2008	100.0	57.9	1.4	32.0	0.7	8.0
2009	100.0	61.0	1.3	28.7	0.7	8.3
2010	100.0	65.4	1.3	25.3	0.6	7.4
2011	100.0	66.0	1.4	24.7	0.6	7.3
2012	100.0	65.6	2.2	23.1	0.7	8.4
2013	100.0	66.7	2.6	21.2	0.7	8.8
2014	100.0	68.0	2.7	19.6	0.7	9.0
2015	100.0	68.1	3.0	18.5	0.6	9.8
2016	100.0	68.0	2.9	17.9	0.6	10.6
2017	100.0	68.8	3.1	16.7	0.5	10.9
2018	100.0	70.0	3.7	14.7	0.6	11.0
2019	100.0	70.0	3.7	14.6	0.4	11.3
2020	100.0	69.5	4.2	15.1	0.3	10.9

11-10 各区县农林牧渔业总产值(2020年)

Gross Output Value of Farming, Forestry, Animal Husbandry and Fishery by Region (2020)

单位：万元 (10 000 yuan)

区 县	Region	农林牧渔业总产值（现价）Gross Output Value (At current prices)	农业 Farming	林业 Forestry	牧业 Animal Husbandry	渔业 Fishery	农林牧渔专业及辅助性活动 Farming, Forestry, Animal Husbandry, Fishery and Auxiliary Activities
全 市	**Total**	**5644139**	**3924251**	**236065**	**849948**	**18895**	**614980**
新城区	Xincheng						
碑林区	Beilin						
莲湖区	Lianhu						
灞桥区	Baqiao	342532	256522	8486	27862	120	49542
未央区	Weiyang	28476	14906	10494	306	352	2418
雁塔区	Yanta						
阎良区	Yanliang	557053	425779	5620	71030	183	54441
临潼区	Lintong	770480	484907	14078	183789	4760	82946
长安区	Chang'an	561784	390229	9213	89261	4029	69052
高陵区	Gaoling	601632	391501	15153	97975	3087	93916
鄠邑区	Huyi	547410	363818	28079	99918	1578	54017
蓝田县	Lantian	588042	362135	44263	122429	3317	55898
周至县	Zhouzhi	719245	489286	65307	90637	522	73493
西咸新区	Xixian	927485	745168	35372	66741	947	79257

11-11 各区县农林牧渔业总产值指数和构成（2020年）

Gross Output Value and Its Composition of Farming, Forestry, Animal Husbandry and Fishery at Current Price by Region（2020）

单位：%　　　　(%)

区县	Region	农林牧渔业总产值 Gross Output Value	农业 Farming	林业 Forestry	牧业 Animal Husbandry	渔业 Fishery	农林牧渔专业及辅助性活动 Farming, Forestry, Animal Husbandry, Fishery and Auxiliary Activities
全市指数	**Total**	**103.2**	**101.6**	**144.5**	**100.1**	**90.7**	**103.4**
新城区	Xincheng						
碑林区	Beilin						
莲湖区	Lianhu						
灞桥区	Baqiao	95.7	92.1	147.1	106.2	31.3	103.9
未央区	Weiyang	438.9	627.7	727.8	35.6	0.0	112.5
雁塔区	Yanta						
阎良区	Yanliang	104.1	102.0	854.3	107.7	63.4	104.5
临潼区	Lintong	104.1	101.3	385.8	105.2	92.3	103.7
长安区	Chang'an	103.2	102.8	283.9	97.9	85.0	103.2
高陵区	Gaoling	103.6	102.0	303.0	93.3	218.9	104.8
鄠邑区	Huyi	102.4	104.5	108.9	93.5	70.1	102.3
蓝田县	Lantian	103.6	104.3	134.3	94.0	70.3	102.7
周至县	Zhouzhi	103.6	103.2	107.3	102.7	111.8	103.0
西咸新区	Xixian	101.7	99.3	143.2	111.1	69.1	102.0
全市构成	**Total**	**100.0**	**69.5**	**4.2**	**15.1**	**0.3**	**10.9**
新城区	Xincheng						
碑林区	Beilin						
莲湖区	Lianhu						
灞桥区	Baqiao	100.0	74.9	2.5	8.1		14.5
未央区	Weiyang	100.0	52.3	36.9	1.1	1.2	8.5
雁塔区	Yanta						
阎良区	Yanliang	100.0	76.4	1.0	12.8		9.8
临潼区	Lintong	100.0	62.9	1.8	23.9	0.6	10.8
长安区	Chang'an	100.0	69.5	1.6	15.9	0.7	12.3
高陵区	Gaoling	100.0	65.1	2.5	16.3	0.5	15.6
鄠邑区	Huyi	100.0	66.5	5.1	18.3	0.3	9.8
蓝田县	Lantian	100.0	61.6	7.5	20.8	0.6	9.5
周至县	Zhouzhi	100.0	68.0	9.1	12.6	0.1	10.2
西咸新区	Xixian	100.0	80.3	3.8	7.2	0.1	8.6

注：1.总产值指数按可比价计算，上年=100。
　　2.总产值构成按现价计算。

11-12 主要年份农林牧渔业增加值

Value-Added of Farming, Forestry, Animal Husbandry and Fishery in Representative Years

单位：万元 (10 000 yuan)

年 份 Year	农林牧渔业增加值（现价） Value-Added of Farming,Forestry,Animal Husbandry and Fishery (At current prices)	农业 Farming	林业 Forestry	牧业 Animal Husbandry	渔业 Fishery	农林牧渔专业及辅助性活动 Farming, Forestry, Animal Husbandry, Fishery and Auxiliary Activities
2017	2708351	1953733	78658	406750	11740	257470
2018	2861844	2097265	98148	379191	13586	273654
2019	3096776	2267013	107115	405837	11310	305501
2020	3461645	2511807	141282	463791	10587	334178

注：本表2017年数根据第三次全国农业普查结果进行了修订。

11-13 主要年份农林牧渔业增加值指数

Indices of Value-Added of Farming, Forestry, Animal Husbandry and Fishery in Representative Years

年 份 Year	农林牧渔业增加值指数（上年=100）（可比价） Value-Added Index of Farming, Forestry, Animal Husbandry and Fishery (preceding year = 100) (At constant prices)	农业 Farming	林业 Forestry	牧业 Animal Husbandry	渔业 Fishery	农林牧渔专业及辅助性活动 Farming, Forestry, Animal Husbandry, Fishery and Auxiliary Activities
2008	107.6	107.6	112.0	105.8	100.0	114.0
2009	106.3	103.6	114.6	111.2	106.3	108.8
2010	106.9	107.9	108.7	104.3	94.0	108.9
2011	106.7	108.1	106.1	102.8	102.7	108.1
2012	106.0	105.6	142.8	104.8	113.4	108.5
2013	104.8	104.3	131.3	104.0	110.1	105.9
2014	105.2	105.8	104.1	103.2	106.0	105.9
2015	105.1	106.5	114.0	100.5	71.3	106.2
2016	104.1	104.5	112.6	100.5	100.3	106.9
2017	104.8	105.1	111.0	102.3	104.3	106.2
2018	103.5	102.8	131.0	100.1	111.4	105.1
2019	104.4	104.8	120.1	98.1	86.4	105.5
2020	103.1	101.6	144.7	100.1	90.8	103.4

11-14 各区县农林牧渔业增加值（2020年）

Value-Added of Farming, Forestry, Animal Husbandry, and Fishery by Region（2020）

单位：万元 (10 000 yuan)

区 县	Region	农林牧渔业增加值（现价） Value-Added of Farming,Forestry,Animal Husbandry and Fishery (At current prices)	农业 Farming	林业 Forestry	牧业 Animal Husbandry	渔业 Fishery	农林牧渔专业及辅助性活动 Farming, Forestry, Animal Husbandry, Fishery and Auxiliary Activities
全 市	**Total**	**3461645**	**2511807**	**141282**	**463791**	**10587**	**334178**
新城区	Xincheng						
碑林区	Beilin						
莲湖区	Lianhu						
灞桥区	Baqiao	216793	167974	5728	15679	57	27355
未央区	Weiyang	17622	10060	5772	145	164	1481
雁塔区	Yanta						
阎良区	Yanliang	353983	280826	3285	39967	103	29802
临潼区	Lintong	460783	308114	8852	94424	2250	47143
长安区	Chang'an	364172	279662	5805	39204	2909	36592
高陵区	Gaoling	367695	240570	10039	56346	1473	59267
鄠邑区	Huyi	335815	233742	16355	59942	1015	24761
蓝田县	Lantian	352767	223633	27308	71083	1764	28979
周至县	Zhouzhi	440487	314956	36167	52505	242	36617
西咸新区	Xixian	551528	452270	21971	34496	610	42181

11-15 各区县农林牧渔业增加值指数(2020年)

Indices of Value-Added of Farming, Forestry, Animal Husbandry and Fishery by Region (2020)

区 县	Region	农林牧渔业增加值指数(上年=100)(可比价) Value-Added Index of Farming, Forestry, Animal Husbandry and Fishery (preceding year = 100) (At constant prices)	农业 Farming	林业 Forestry	牧业 Animal Husbandry	渔业 Fishery	农林牧渔专业及辅助性活动 Farming, Forestry, Animal Husbandry, Fishery and Auxiliary Activities
全 市	**Total**	**103.1**	**101.6**	**144.7**	**100.1**	**90.8**	**103.4**
新城区	Xincheng						
碑林区	Beilin						
莲湖区	Lianhu						
灞桥区	Baqiao	94.9	91.5	140.6	107.5	33.3	104.7
未央区	Weiyang	448.3	623.8	713.9	35.5		124.0
雁塔区	Yanta						
阎良区	Yanliang	104.1	102.2	885.2	108.3	65.6	104.4
临潼区	Lintong	104.0	101.1	386.6	105.9	93.3	103.6
长安区	Chang'an	103.2	102.7	268.3	97.6	87.0	102.9
高陵区	Gaoling	103.8	101.9	324.2	93.5	229.3	105.1
鄠邑区	Huyi	102.2	104.6	109.0	92.1	70.7	102.3
蓝田县	Lantian	103.6	104.2	130.5	94.3	73.3	102.6
周至县	Zhouzhi	103.5	103.2	107.3	103.3	92.2	102.5
西咸新区	Xixian	101.7	99.5	140.7	111.5	72.2	101.1

11-16 主要年份粮食生产情况

Statistics on Food Production in Representative Years

单位：万亩、万吨 （10 000 mu,10 000 ton）

年 份 Year	粮食播种面积 Grain Sowing Area	小麦 Wheat	玉米 Corn	粮食产量 Grain Crops	夏粮 Summer Grain	小麦 Wheat	秋粮 Autumn Grain	稻谷 Rice	玉米 Corn
1980	706.35	324.17	273.14	114.40	56.60	52.20	57.80	4.70	47.70
1985	704.36	378.20	271.14	150.10	76.10	74.80	74.00	5.10	65.10
1990	731.42	387.20	282.14	172.40	91.70	89.70	80.70	5.50	70.40
1991	731.37	389.19	283.14	178.80	91.10	89.20	87.70	5.00	77.50
1992	715.50	384.60	273.60	183.40	101.70	99.60	81.70	4.70	72.30
1993	713.49	380.40	273.69	190.00	101.10	99.00	88.90	4.90	78.60
1994	719.00	375.90	272.40	157.40	86.90	84.90	70.50	4.50	61.40
1995	690.63	370.41	259.55	175.30	99.80	97.40	75.50	3.40	67.80
1996	709.00	366.30	286.80	187.50	80.10	78.40	107.40	3.40	95.60
1997	670.83	367.71	248.79	190.50	114.30	112.30	76.20	3.50	69.40
1998	705.03	370.17	285.45	212.70	104.40	104.00	108.30	3.20	99.10
1999	709.95	371.94	294.00	204.40	95.50	94.40	108.90	2.90	99.70
2000	697.55	369.89	283.70	201.90	92.60	91.60	109.30	3.10	100.50
2001	678.05	359.19	278.57	197.10	98.10	97.20	98.90	2.70	91.30
2002	655.59	350.64	271.95	192.40	94.50	93.50	97.90	2.10	91.60
2003	632.55	336.05	261.89	176.30	98.20	96.70	78.10	1.60	72.30
2004	630.63	311.52	286.50	195.80	97.80	96.00	98.00	1.70	91.60
2005	642.75	325.10	287.87	205.50	100.00	99.10	105.50	1.60	99.30
2006	648.00	313.23	307.89	193.50	86.00	85.40	107.40	1.40	101.20
2007	646.06	296.48	327.93	192.52	73.97	71.97	118.55	1.51	113.83
2008	605.57	294.42	292.34	185.48	87.95	87.36	97.53	0.80	94.02
2009	578.01	285.73	273.35	177.91	81.90	81.03	96.01	0.78	92.49
2010	559.09	277.34	264.07	174.51	81.29	80.71	93.22	0.56	89.47
2011	525.12	259.98	240.74	167.05	78.35	76.66	88.70	0.54	84.37
2012	508.16	256.22	233.84	167.67	79.69	79.02	87.98	0.44	84.18
2013	465.64	236.98	211.66	151.68	67.73	67.05	83.95	0.29	80.04
2014	437.10	224.27	200.39	140.77	68.72	68.15	72.05	0.16	69.99
2015	413.31	215.61	189.60	141.42	72.34	71.95	69.08	0.00	67.71
2016	401.95	209.78	180.80	135.39	68.86	68.45	66.53	0.07	64.09
2017	424.14	228.89	180.39	139.89	75.26	74.90	64.63	0.05	60.96
2018	419.56	227.84	177.58	142.14	74.28	73.86	67.86	0.06	64.36
2019	409.71	221.62	174.43	139.89	70.62	70.22	69.27	0.06	65.85
2020	408.15	218.75	176.22	144.58	72.58	72.21	72.00	0.06	68.64

注：1.本表2007-2017年数根据第三次全国农业普查结果进行了修订。
2.本表数据自2020年起来源于国家统计局西安调查队。

11-17 各区县粮食生产情况(2020年)

Statistics on Food Production by Region (2020)

单位：万亩、万吨 (10 000 mu,10 000 ton)

区县	Region	粮食播种面积 Grain Sowing Area	小麦 Wheat	玉米 Corn	粮食产量 Grain Crops	夏粮 Summer Grain	小麦 Wheat	秋粮 Autumn Grain	稻谷 Rice	玉米 Corn
全　市	**Total**	**408.15**	**218.75**	**176.22**	**144.58**	**72.58**	**72.21**	**72.00**	**0.06**	**68.64**
新城区	Xincheng									
碑林区	Beilin									
莲湖区	Lianhu									
灞桥区	Baqiao	6.79	4.15	2.53	2.40	1.48	1.48	0.93		0.91
未央区	Weiyang	0.02	0.02		0.01	0.01	0.01			
雁塔区	Yanta									
阎良区	Yanliang	27.00	13.75	13.23	11.93	5.96	5.96	5.97		5.96
临潼区	Lintong	100.21	52.95	42.65	34.65	16.84	16.84	17.81		16.21
长安区	Chang'an	48.23	29.85	17.80	16.66	9.53	9.53	7.13	0.05	7.00
高陵区	Gaoling	26.33	13.06	12.11	12.48	5.74	5.74	6.73		6.21
鄠邑区	Huyi	54.74	27.81	26.14	20.04	9.79	9.61	10.25		10.21
蓝田县	Lantian	60.20	35.18	20.89	17.89	9.81	9.68	8.07	0.01	7.44
周至县	Zhouzhi	37.99	18.77	17.85	12.48	5.91	5.86	6.58		6.32
西咸新区	Xixian	46.64	23.23	23.01	16.05	7.52	7.52	8.53		8.36

注：本表数据来源于国家统计局西安调查队。

11-18 主要年份粮食单位面积产量

Grain Output Per Unit Area in Representative Years

单位：公斤/亩 （kg/mu）

年份 Year	粮食作物 Grain Crops	夏粮 Summer Grain	小麦 Wheat	秋粮 Autumn Grain	玉米 Corn
1990	236	232	232	241	249
1991	245	229	229	264	274
1992	256	259	259	253	264
1993	266	260	260	274	287
1994	219	226	226	211	225
1995	254	263	263	243	261
1996	265	214	214	321	333
1997	284	305	306	257	279
1998	302	278	279	328	347
1999	288	253	254	327	339
2000	289	247	248	338	354
2001	291	270	271	314	328
2002	293	266	267	326	337
2003	279	287	288	269	276
2004	310	308	308	313	320
2005	320	304	305	336	345
2006	299	273	273	323	329
2007	298	247	246	342	347
2008	306	297	297	315	322
2009	308	284	284	331	338
2010	312	292	291	333	339
2011	318	297	295	340	350
2012	330	309	308	352	360
2013	326	284	283	370	378
2014	322	304	304	342	349
2015	342	333	334	352	357
2016	337	326	326	349	354
2017	330	325	327	333	338
2018	339	324	324	357	362
2019	341	317	317	371	378
2020	354	330	330	383	389

注：1.本表2007-2017年数根据第三次全国农业普查结果进行了修订。
2.本表数据自2020年起来源于国家统计局西安调查队。

11-19 各区县粮食单位面积产量（2020年）

Grain Output Per Unit Area by Region (2020)

单位：公斤/亩 （kg/mu）

区 县	Region	粮食作物 Grain Crops	夏粮 Summer Grain	小麦 Wheat	秋粮 Autumn Grain	玉米 Corn
全 市	**Total**	**354**	**330**	**330**	**383**	**389**
新城区	Xincheng					
碑林区	Beilin					
莲湖区	Lianhu					
灞桥区	Baqiao	354	356	356	351	358
未央区	Weiyang	346	347	347	341	341
雁塔区	Yanta					
阎良区	Yanliang	442	433	433	451	451
临潼区	Lintong	346	318	318	377	380
长安区	Chang'an	345	319	319	388	394
高陵区	Gaoling	474	440	440	508	513
鄠邑区	Huyi	366	343	346	391	391
蓝田县	Lantian	297	276	275	328	356
周至县	Zhouzhi	329	311	312	346	354
西咸新区	Xixian	344	324	324	364	363

注：本表数据来源于国家统计局西安调查队。

11-20 主要年份主要经济作物生产情况

Production of Main Cash Crop in Representative Years

单位：万亩、万吨 (10 000 mu,10 000 ton)

年份 Year	经济作物播种面积 Sown Area of Cash Crops	油料 Oil-bearing	蔬菜 Vegetables	经济作物产量 Economic Crop Yield 油料 Oil-bearing	油菜籽 Rapeseeds	蔬菜 Vegetables
1980	129.08	10.01	24.02	0.54	0.50	40.13
1985	91.05	8.01	45.03	0.75	0.39	86.44
1990	84.99	12.00	51.03	1.35	0.94	119.32
1991	89.04	13.01	47.03	1.20	0.74	117.41
1992	105.15	16.20	54.60	1.49	0.87	128.12
1993	108.14	14.84	63.90	1.40	1.00	145.80
1994	102.10	13.80	59.90	1.08	0.78	135.26
1995	94.11	18.57	57.59	2.17	1.90	133.60
1996	88.40	18.80	55.50	1.83	1.55	138.01
1997	84.95	15.53	59.36	1.86	1.65	142.11
1998	84.96	14.69	60.95	1.67	1.36	148.87
1999	83.13	12.74	60.68	1.30	1.00	153.24
2000	87.39	13.46	64.35	1.34	0.95	162.14
2001	85.11	11.87	61.77	1.23	0.90	152.80
2002	95.51	11.40	67.71	1.22	0.84	169.74
2003	104.51	11.04	69.44	1.13	0.70	169.67
2004	123.20	9.74	77.55	1.14	0.84	180.96
2005	115.16	9.51	83.33	1.16	0.89	195.70
2006	121.49	8.58	87.03	1.08	0.87	189.30
2007	107.48	7.18	75.31	0.93	0.74	168.98
2008	104.91	8.04	75.86	1.08	0.86	180.60
2009	106.55	7.75	77.23	1.04	0.84	195.07
2010	106.80	7.77	78.06	1.01	0.84	207.11
2011	106.33	7.40	78.98	1.00	0.84	214.13
2012	104.74	6.25	79.54	0.83	0.74	227.96
2013	104.31	5.93	80.82	0.77	0.71	243.92
2014	106.09	5.21	81.72	0.71	0.59	257.86
2015	107.47	4.86	82.50	0.68	0.57	267.91
2016	100.68	4.13	81.43	0.58	0.50	268.87
2017	124.36	4.28	104.64	0.62	0.55	354.74
2018	127.90	4.61	107.74	0.67	0.57	373.69
2019	128.19	4.66	107.72	0.67	0.59	378.58
2020	130.25	5.20	109.45	0.74	0.71	381.31

注：本表2007-2017年数根据第三次全国农业普查结果进行了修订。

11-21 各区县主要经济作物生产情况(2020年)

Production of Main Cash Crop by Region (2020)

单位：万亩、万吨 (10 000 mu,10 000 ton)

区 县	Region	经济作物播种面积 Sown Area of Cash Crops	油料 Oil-bearing	蔬菜 Vegetables	瓜果 Fruits Class
全 市	**Total**	**130.25**	**5.20**	**109.45**	**14.36**
新城区	Xincheng				
碑林区	Beilin				
莲湖区	Lianhu				
灞桥区	Baqiao	3.44	0.19	3.11	0.13
未央区	Weiyang	0.64		0.61	0.03
雁塔区	Yanta				
阎良区	Yanliang	22.54	0.07	15.52	6.94
临潼区	Lintong	19.78	0.68	17.02	1.57
长安区	Chang'an	11.97	0.67	9.47	1.81
高陵区	Gaoling	14.47		14.31	0.16
鄠邑区	Huyi	10.74	0.22	8.87	1.63
蓝田县	Lantian	9.94	2.50	6.13	1.16
周至县	Zhouzhi	9.55	0.34	8.67	0.06
西咸新区	Xixian	27.18	0.53	25.73	0.88

11-21 续表 continued

单位：万亩、万吨 (10 000 mu,10 000 ton)

区 县	Region	经济作物产量 Economic Crop Yield			
		油料 Oil-bearing	油菜籽 Rapeseeds	蔬菜 Vegetables	瓜果 Fruits Class
全 市	**Total**	**0.74**	**0.71**	**381.31**	**49.10**
新城区	Xincheng				
碑林区	Beilin				
莲湖区	Lianhu				
灞桥区	Baqiao	0.03	0.02	9.98	0.24
未央区	Weiyang			0.83	0.03
雁塔区	Yanta				
阎良区	Yanliang	0.01	0.01	75.98	27.14
临潼区	Lintong	0.09	0.09	53.97	6.34
长安区	Chang'an	0.10	0.10	20.08	3.83
高陵区	Gaoling			63.09	0.74
鄠邑区	Huyi	0.04	0.02	30.17	5.03
蓝田县	Lantian	0.34	0.34	11.80	2.78
周至县	Zhouzhi	0.05	0.05	22.92	0.14
西咸新区	Xixian	0.08	0.08	92.50	2.83

11-22 主要年份主要经济作物单位面积产量

Main Cash Crop of Per Unit Area in Representative Years

单位：公斤/亩 (kg/mu)

年份 Year	油料 Oil-bearing	油菜籽 Rapeseeds	蔬菜 Vegetables
1990	103	101	2349
1991	94	89	2332
1992	92	101	2344
1993	94	107	2282
1994	79	84	2260
1995	117	128	2320
1996	86	100	2489
1997	76	129	2395
1998	114	121	2443
1999	102	106	2526
2000	102	112	2520
2001	104	113	2474
2002	107	115	2507
2003	102	110	2444
2004	117	129	2333
2005	121	132	2349
2006	125	135	2175
2007	130	131	2244
2008	134	137	2381
2009	134	130	2526
2010	130	130	2653
2011	135	133	2711
2012	133	129	2866
2013	129	122	3018
2014	136	129	3155
2015	139	132	3247
2016	141	132	3302
2017	144	138	3390
2018	146	137	3468
2019	144	135	3514
2020	142	139	3484

注：本表2007-2017年数根据第三次全国农业普查结果进行了修订。

11-23 各区县主要经济作物单位面积产量（2020年）

Main Cash Crop of Per Unit Area by Region（2020）

单位：公斤/亩 （kg/mu）

区县	Region	油料 Oil-bearing	油菜籽 Rapeseeds	蔬菜 Vegetables	瓜果 Fruits Class
全市	**Total**	**142**	**139**	**3484**	**3419**
新城区	Xincheng				
碑林区	Beilin				
莲湖区	Lianhu				
灞桥区	Baqiao	136	136	3207	1895
未央区	Weiyang			1367	933
雁塔区	Yanta				
阎良区	Yanliang	144	144	4896	3910
临潼区	Lintong	150	143	3171	4050
长安区	Chang'an	144	144	2119	2116
高陵区	Gaoling			4408	4745
鄠邑区	Huyi	171	136	3401	3082
蓝田县	Lantian	134	134	1923	2394
周至县	Zhouzhi	154	144	2643	2380
西咸新区	Xixian	149	149	3595	3230

11-24 设施农业生产情况（2020年）

Agricultural Production Facilities (2020)

指　标	Item	面积（亩）Seeded Area (mu)	产量（吨）output (ton)
一、蔬菜	**Vegetables**	**267508**	**1136569**
芹菜	Celery	68792	334966
油菜	Rape	8369	21990
菠菜	Spinach	20695	57790
黄瓜	Cucumber	23568	109161
西红柿	Tomato	24686	97889
生姜	Ginger	90	325
辣椒	Chilli	14992	60797
其他蔬菜	Other Vegetables	106316	453651
二、瓜果类	**Fruits class**	**102554**	**378479**
其中：草莓	Strawberry	17095	34558
三、花卉苗木	**Flower seedling wood**	**14382**	
四、食用菌	**Edible Fungi**		**4978**
干品	Dry Product		740
鲜品	Fresh Product		4238
其中：蘑菇	Mushroom		3859
五、其他作物	**Others**	**6783**	
补充资料：设施数量（个）	Number of Facilities (unit)		137241
设施占地面积（亩）	Area of Facilities(mu)	247946	
设施实际使用面积（亩）	Actual use area of the facility(mu)	231764	

注：2020年起，其他作物面积含设施园林水果面积。

11-25 主要年份林业生产情况

Statistics on Forestry in Representative Years

指　标	Item	2000	2005	2010	2015	2016	2017	2018	2019	2020
一、营林情况	**Afforestation**									
当年造林面积合计（万亩）	Build Forestry Areas(10 000 mu)	27.47	16.56	16.10	8.28	4.51	4.07	3.56	3.83	3.40
封山育林面积（万亩）	Hill-closeure for Afforestation Areas(10 000 mu)	18.78	18.65	55.10	44.00	43.80	28.80	28.80		
零星（四旁）植树（万株）	Planting(10 000 plants)	731	1064	509	516	462	687	656		
育苗面积（万亩）	Raise Seedlings Areas(10 000 mu)	2.05	5.99	11.95	19.84	22.78	48.24	61.02	68.63	76.66
二、主要林产品产量（吨）	**Main Forestry Product(ton)**									
核桃	Walnuts	997	3351	7875	24344	24097	36639	36970	38732	34580
板栗	Chinese Chestnut	744	2076	7736	8225	8223	8970	9282	9042	9137
花椒	Pepper	140	525	1420	204	402	293	1044	937	826
三、村及村以下采伐木材（万立方米）	**Timber Harvested at or below Village Level (10 000 cu.m)**	1.62	1.87	3.30	0.07	0.28		0.37		

注：本表数据第一、三部分来源于市自然资源和规划局。

11–26 各区县林业生产情况（2020年）

Statistics On Forestry by Region (2020)

区 县 Region	当年造林面积（亩）Build Forestry Areasin in The Year(mu)	零星植树（万株）Planting (10 000 plants)	育苗面积（亩）Raise Seedlings Areas(mu)	核桃产量（吨）Output of Walnuts (ton)	板栗产量（吨）Output of Chinese Chestnut (ton)
全 市 Total	**34027**		**766620**	**34580**	**9137**
新城区 Xincheng					
碑林区 Beilin					
莲湖区 Lianhu					
灞桥区 Baqiao	857		705	2312	115
未央区 Weiyang					
雁塔区 Yanta					
阎良区 Yanliang	830		4545	128	
临潼区 Lintong	6115		82455	6392	350
长安区 Chang'an	2512		71070	3788	943
高陵区 Gaoling	1200		54000	6	
鄠邑区 Huyi	1775		84000	631	21
蓝田县 Lantian	10427		173265	15758	5962
周至县 Zhouzhi	6533		193035	4522	1746
西咸新区 Xixian	3778		103545	1043	

注：本表前三项指标数据来源于市自然资源和规划局。

11–27 主要年份果业生产情况

Statistics on Fruits in Representative Years

指标	Item	2000	2005	2010	2015	2016	2017	2018	2019	2020
果园面积合计（万亩）	**Areas of Orchards (10 000 mu)**	**47.86**	**55.55**	**63.26**	**61.00**	**62.73**	**72.72**	**74.28**	**74.53**	**75.93**
苹果园	Apple Orchards	12.15	5.96	3.07	1.04	0.99	6.03	6.08	6.07	5.95
梨园	Pears Orchards	5.79	3.01	1.64	0.74	1.06	0.95	0.97	1.10	1.11
葡萄园	Grapes Orchards	1.89	3.02	6.42	10.94	11.65	12.55	12.61	11.98	12.04
桃园	Peach Orchards	3.47	8.66	7.68	5.33	5.82	5.99	6.19	5.96	6.43
猕猴桃园	Chinese Goosebeery Orchards	16.83	4.33	20.36	27.69	27.97	28.19	29.32	30.09	30.90
杏园	Apricot Orchards	0.62	2.50	2.21	1.31	1.25	1.63	1.74	1.95	1.87
柿子园	Presimmons Orchards	1.96	2.69	2.08	0.21	0.22	0.19	0.27	0.36	0.46
石榴园	Pomegranate Orchards			3.31	2.93	2.93	3.33	3.24	3.24	3.56
水果产量（万吨）	**Output of Fruits (10 000ton)**	**34.36**	**51.29**	**66.11**	**73.33**	**75.53**	**89.80**	**89.15**	**97.18**	**100.93**
苹果	Apple	8.94	5.34	2.96	1.71	1.70	6.93	6.91	7.07	6.97
梨	Pears	6.55	5.71	3.61	2.11	2.20	2.28	2.27	2.03	2.20
葡萄	Grapes	1.66	3.10	6.20	11.48	13.07	16.45	16.62	16.86	18.31
桃	Peach	2.70	8.98	9.85	7.76	8.61	9.92	10.51	11.02	10.75
猕猴桃	Chinese Goosebeery	9.66	13.79	24.87	35.30	35.47	36.84	35.83	42.45	45.10
杏	Apricot			3.71	2.57	2.53	2.57	2.45	2.61	2.63
柿子	Persimmon			3.01	0.81	0.26	0.33	0.40	0.41	0.43
石榴	Pomegranate			2.93	2.54	2.44	3.20	3.32	3.51	4.01

注：本表2007–2017年数根据第三次全国农业普查结果进行了修订。

11-28 各区县果业生产情况（2020年）

Area and Output of Fruits by Region (2020)

区 县	Region	果园面积（亩） Orchard (mu)	水果产量（吨） Output of Fruits(ton)
全 市	**Total**	**759261**	**1009332**
新城区	Xincheng		
碑林区	Beilin		
莲湖区	Lianhu		
灞桥区	Baqiao	63187	77899
未央区	Weiyang	199	288
雁塔区	Yanta		
阎良区	Yanliang	17589	30613
临潼区	Lintong	77336	85843
长安区	Chang'an	36629	54280
高陵区	Gaoling	18550	28403
鄠邑区	Huyi	80750	109953
蓝田县	Lantian	63973	67680
周至县	Zhouzhi	309400	435094
西咸新区	Xixian	91648	119279

11-29 果品加工、销售及生产服务情况（2020年）

指标	Item	西安市 Xi' an	灞桥区 Baqiao
一、果品加工企业数（个）	**Number of Fruit Processing Enterprises(unit)**	**35**	
其中：苹果加工企业数量	Number of Apple Processing Enterprises		
猕猴桃加工企业数	Number of Kiwi Processing Enterprises	26	
二、果品加工企业果汁加工能力（吨）	**Processing Ability of Fruit Juice in Fruit Processing Enterprises(ton)**	**3850**	
其中：苹果汁加工能力	Processing Ability of Apple Juice		
三、当年果品加工企业鲜果消耗量（吨）	**Fresh Fruit Consumption of Fruit Processing Enterprise in the Year(ton)**	**75350**	
其中：加工消耗苹果数量	Number of Fresh Apple Consumption		
加工消耗猕猴桃数量	Number of Fresh Kiwi Consumption	60000	
四、仓储能力（吨）	**Storage Capacity(ton)**	**392290**	**200**
其中：气调库	Gas Reservoir	62305	200
机械库	Machine Shop	329985	
五、果业合作（个）	**Fruit Industry Cooperation(unit)**	**1328**	**80**
六、果苗木繁育中心（个）	**Fruit Seedling Breeding Center(unit)**	**20**	
七、果业服务投入（万元）	**Service Investment in Fruit Industry(10000 yuan)**	**677**	**25**
1. 技术培训投入	Technical Training Investment	175	20
2. 科研投入	Scientific Research Investment	132	
3. 生产技术指导投入	Production Technology Guidance Investment	370	5
八、果品销售方式（吨）	**Fruit Sales Mode(ton)**	**1156600**	**78600**
1. 产地批发市场	Product Wholesale Market	578140	50838
2. 采供商	Supplier	240114	
3. 专卖、直销店	Franchised and Direct Outlets	16770	
4. 超级市场	Supermarket	36320	1382
5. 电子商务	Electronic Commerce	129418	2800
6. 农产品加工厂	Agricultural Product Processing Plant	66993	
7. 其它	Others	88845	23580
九、按销售区域分（吨）	**By the Sales Area(ton)**	**1156600**	**78600**
1. 国内市场	Domestic market	1116600	78600
2. 国际市场	International Market	40000	
附记：累计建成绿色果园面积（亩）	Cumulative Green Orchard Area(mu)	5950	
建成有机果园面积(亩)	Construction of Organic Orchard Area(mu)	6246	

The Situation of Fruit Processing, Sales and Production Service (2020)

未央区 Weiyang	阎良区 Yanliang	临潼区 Lintong	长安区 Chang'an	高陵区 Gaoling	鄠邑区 Huyi	蓝田县 Lantian	周至县 Zhouzhi	西咸新区 Xixian
		4			**2**	**3**	**26**	
							26	
		2600			**1000**	**250**		
		2600			**12400**	**350**	**60000**	
							60000	
	17650	**4885**	**1040**	**2005**	**9700**		**355310**	**1500**
	17650	2650	1000	2005	2450		36350	
		2235	40		7250		318960	1500
	13	**77**	**18**	**9**	**62**	**25**	**1023**	**21**
	13				**3**		**2**	**2**
3		**445**	**7**	**13**	**130**	**3**	**10**	**41**
		82	5	9	20		10	29
3		74			50			5
		289	2	4	60	3		7
	30613	**61550**	**50800**	**28403**	**108600**	**68900**	**587400**	**141734**
		12000	34200	9000	71900	58500	300700	41002
		11000	12300	14400	20350	4200	104800	73064
		300	500	3200	2150		6500	4120
			840		3500		27600	2998
		12000	2960	1400	7300	3260	87800	11898
		2000			3400	350	60000	1243
	30613	24250		403		2590		7409
	30613	**61550**	**50800**	**28403**	**108600**	**68900**	**587400**	**141734**
	30613	61550	50800	28403	108600	68900	547400	141734
							40000	
					2600	650	1380	1320
			4500			650	856	240

11-30 主要年份畜牧业生产情况

Statistics on Livestock Husbandry in Representative Years

指标	Item	2013	2014	2015	2016	2017	2018	2019	2020
一、活牲畜年末存栏（头）	**Live Animals in Stock at Year-end (head)**	**55619**	**58737**	**56100**	**61179**	**51075**	**50705**	**51704**	**52595**
1. 牛	Cattle	54900	58100	55900	61000	50900	50556	51567	52505
#肉牛	Farm Cattle	15673	17317	18465	23736	21509	21325	23258	27594
奶牛	Dairy Cattle	31479	33887	30705	31061	28819	28681	27895	24884
2. 马（匹）	Horses	220	219	200	176	175	149	137	90
3. 驴	Donkeys	52	59						
4. 骡	Mules	447	359		3				
二、猪年末存栏（头）	**Pigs in Stock at Year-end(head)**	**377300**	**377100**	**366800**	**363000**	**335700**	**312882**	**296612**	**301322**
#能繁殖的母猪	Female Hogs of Reprductive Ability	60900	58700	56300	55600	51800	44304	41317	42202
三、羊年末存栏（只）	**Sheep and Goats in Stock at Year-end(head)**	**84100**	**101700**	**107600**	**109800**	**75200**	**74200**	**71900**	**72625**
1. 山羊	Goats	82145	98974	104033	107260	73769	72942	71198	67978
#奶山羊	Milch Goats	68370	69093	65180	66388	62120	60619	69052	
2. 绵羊	Sheeps	1955	2726	3567	2540	1431	1258	702	4647
四、家禽年末存栏（万只）	**Poultry in Stock at Year-end (10 000 heads)**	**663.37**	**663.05**	**702.69**	**702.42**	**642.73**	**625.83**	**643.67**	**641.63**
五、年末养蜂箱数（箱）	**Honey (box)**	**23346**	**22485**	**19536**	**21420**	**20377**	**19129**	**23033**	

注：1.本表2013-2017年数据根据第三次全国农业普查结果进行了修订。
2.本表数据自2020年起来源于国家统计局西安调查队。
3.2020年“奶山羊”和“养蜂箱数”数据国家统计局陕西调查总队未反馈。

11-31 各区县畜牧业生产情况（2020年）

Statistics On Livestock, Animal Husbandry by Region (2020)

区 县	Region	活牲畜年末存栏（头） Live Animals In Stock at Year-end (head)	牛 Cattle	肉牛 Beef cattle	奶牛 Dairy Cattle	马（匹） Horses (head)	驴 Donkeys	骡 Mutes
全 市	**Total**	**52595**	**52505**	**27594**	**24884**	**90**		
新城区	Xincheng							
碑林区	Beilin							
莲湖区	Lianhu							
灞桥区	Baqiao	1114	1039	163	875	75		
未央区	Weiyang							
雁塔区	Yanta							
阎良区	Yanliang	6094	6094	2478	3616			
临潼区	Lintong	17883	17883	4644	13239			
长安区	Chang'an	2089	2089	947	1142			
高陵区	Gaoling	4593	4593	2888	1705			
鄠邑区	Huyi	3799	3799	2677	1122			
蓝田县	Lantian	10412	10412	9252	1160			
周至县	Zhouzhi	5592	5577	4461	1090	15		
西咸新区	Xixian	1019	1019	84	935			

注：本表数据来源于国家统计局西安调查队。

11-31 续表 continued

区 县	Region	猪年末存栏（头） Swine (head)	能繁殖的母猪 breeding sows	羊年末存栏（只） Sheep and Goats (head)	山羊 Goats	奶山羊 Milch Goats	家禽年末存栏（万只） Poultry (10 000 head)	年末养蜂箱数（箱） Honey (box)
全 市	**Total**	**301322**	**42202**	**72625**	**67978**		**641.63**	
新城区	Xincheng							
碑林区	Beilin							
莲湖区	Lianhu							
灞桥区	Baqiao	6947	1244	1783	1783		5.10	
未央区	Weiyang							
雁塔区	Yanta							
阎良区	Yanliang	15033	2255	9645	8490		54.70	
临潼区	Lintong	61384	6891	21768	18806		163.73	
长安区	Chang'an	20150	2856	3740	3740		69.20	
高陵区	Gaoling	21527	3229	5181	4797		69.00	
鄠邑区	Huyi	56603	7982	5828	5828		74.40	
蓝田县	Lantian	35842	5321	20771	20771		105.00	
周至县	Zhouzhi	63204	9340	1964	1902		67.20	
西咸新区	Xixian	20632	3084	1945	1861		33.30	

11-32 主要年份畜禽产品产量

Production of animal products in Representative Years

单位：吨 (ton)

年 份 Year	肉类总产量 Output of Meat	猪 肉 Pork	牛 肉 Beef	羊 肉 Mutton	禽 肉 Poultry	奶类产量 Output of Milk	牛 奶 Cow Milk	禽 蛋 Poultry Eggs	蜂蜜（公斤） Honey(kg)
2013	66100	43900	4000	3300	13100	73834	41700	48700	380000
2014	70900	47400	4400	3700	13400	80961	42200	47900	376800
2015	72100	47100	4400	4100	14500	76779	40800	51000	351582
2016	68700	44200	3700	4400	14600	79281	43100	62900	371409
2017	58708	36900	4600	3300	12300	116491	83300	52785	404337
2018	54496	35932	3439	989	12473	115200	80446	52610	308015
2019	51437	33531	3329	927	12257	123711	80060	53874	322965
2020	45596	28482	3354	1001	12292	140291	85255	52242	391867

注：1.本表2013—2017年数据根据第三次全国农业普查结果进行了修订。
2.本表数据自2020年起来源于国家统计局西安调查队。

11-33 各区县主要畜禽产品产量（2020年）

Production of animal products by Region (2020)

单位：吨 (ton)

区县 Region	肉类总产量 Output of Meat	猪肉 Pork	牛肉 Beef	羊肉 Mutton	禽肉 Poultry	奶类产量 Output of Milk	牛奶 Cow Milk	禽蛋 Poultry Eggs	蜂蜜（公斤） Honey(kg)
全市 Total	**45596**	**28482**	**3354**	**1001**	**12292**	**140291**	**85255**	**52242**	**391867**
新城区 Xincheng									
碑林区 Beilin									
莲湖区 Lianhu									
灞桥区 Baqiao	906	603	107	29	165	3951	2396	374	7618
未央区 Weiyang									
雁塔区 Yanta									
阎良区 Yanliang	2605	1083	448	155	919	23363	13210	4214	2790
临潼区 Lintong	11714	7821	667	281	2762	68654	44699	13132	20164
长安区 Chang'an	4164	2398	207	88	1423	5574	4080	9105	52540
高陵区 Gaoling	3484	1965	174	97	1140	11205	7540	3951	
鄠邑区 Huyi	6095	3887	381	86	1647	6706	3267	6894	60139
蓝田县 Lantian	7022	3820	840	199	2163	12812	4241	7279	166442
周至县 Zhouzhi	6778	4992	408	31	1343	4112	3596	5175	81162
西咸新区 Xixian	2827	1912	123	37	730	3914	2226	2121	1012

注：本表数据来源于国家统计局西安调查队。

11-34 主要年份水产品养殖面积和产量

Output of Aquatic Products and Aquaculture Area in Representative Years

单位：万亩、吨 （10 000 mu,ton）

年 份 Year	水产品养殖面积 Aquaculture Area of Aquatic Products	水产品产量 Output of Aquatic Products
1990	2.55	4258
1991	2.63	4949
1992	2.80	6015
1993	2.97	7132
1994	3.10	7900
1995	3.21	8517
1996	3.51	8910
1997	3.46	10054
1998	3.40	10480
1999	3.38	11061
2000	3.35	11384
2001	3.17	12480
2002	3.31	12017
2003	2.48	9967
2004	2.46	9721
2005	2.38	9370
2006	1.60	11937
2007	1.38	12402
2008	1.40	12487
2009	1.52	13044
2010	2.24	11850
2011	2.20	11800
2012	2.95	14010
2013	2.19	14200
2014	2.31	14218
2015	2.26	14190
2016	1.96	13449
2017	2.24	13832
2018	2.23	13528
2019	1.82	13614
2020	1.54	11302

注：本表数据2010年起来源于市水务局，2019年起来源于市农业农村局。

11-35 各区县水产品养殖面积和产量（2020年）

Output of Aquatic Products and Aquaculture Area by Region (2020)

单位：亩、吨 (mu,ton)

区 县	Region	水产品养殖面积 Aquaculture Area of Aquatic Products	水产品产量 Output of Aquatic Products
全 市	**Total**	**15435**	**11302**
新城区	Xincheng		
碑林区	Beilin		
莲湖区	Lianhu		
灞桥区	Baqiao	1080	106
未央区	Weiyang	240	300
雁塔区	Yanta		
阎良区	Yanliang	180	225
临潼区	Lintong	4965	3300
长安区	Chang'an	3352	4267
高陵区	Gaoling	180	225
鄠邑区	Huyi	362	1212
蓝田县	Lantian	3165	950
周至县	Zhouzhi	1281	415
西咸新区	Xixian	630	302

注：本表数据来源于市农业农村局。

11-36 农业科技、教育情况（2020年）

Agricultural Science and Technology Education（2020）

指标	Item	2020
农业研究开发机构（个）	Agricultural research and development institutions (unit)	212
农业科技人员（人）	Agricultural scientific and technical personnel(persons)	2190
农业科研成果（个）	Agricultural scientific research achievements (unit)	23
农民技能培训人数（万人）	The number of peasants skills training(10000 persons)	11.72
良种推广面积（万亩）	Thoroughbred promotion area (10000 mu)	518.25
农业信息站（个）	Information station of Agricultural (unit)	2670

注：本表数据来源于市农业农村局。

11-37 主要年份农产品人均占有量

Per Capita Output of Major Farm Products in Representative Years

单位：公斤/人 (kg/ person)

年份 Year	粮食 Grain	油料 Oil-bearing Crops	猪牛羊肉 Pork Beef and Mutton	禽蛋 Poultry Eggs	奶类 Milk	水果 Fruits	蔬菜 Vegetables
1978	266.7	0.2	5.4	0.9	3.3	6.8	91.7
1979	288.6	0.6	6.7	1.0	4.0	5.1	97.3
1980	223.5	1.1	5.9	1.2	4.1	6.9	78.4
1985	271.4	1.4	6.8	5.7	10.2	7.6	156.3
1990	298.7	2.1	9.4	9.2	14.2	11.5	196.0
1995	270.4	3.4	15.7	21.8	20.5	37.5	206.1
2000	293.5	1.9	17.9	20.1	35.7	49.9	235.7
2005	277.1	1.6	21.1	15.9	56.9	69.1	263.8
2010	206.4	1.2	13.8	14.6	74.8	78.2	245.0
2011	192.7	1.2	13.9	14.5	74.7	74.5	247.0
2012	186.2	0.9	14.0	14.4	74.0	74.8	253.1
2013	164.0	0.8	5.5	5.3	8.0	77.8	263.7
2014	148.5	0.7	5.9	5.1	8.5	77.1	272.0
2015	145.2	0.7	5.7	5.2	7.9	75.3	275.1
2016	134.2	0.6	5.2	6.2	7.9	74.9	266.5
2017	129.3	0.6	4.1	4.9	10.8	83.0	327.9
2018	122.3	0.6	3.5	4.5	9.9	76.7	321.5
2019	115.3	0.6	3.1	4.4	10.2	80.1	312.1
2020	114.2	0.6	2.6	4.1	11.1	79.8	301.3

注：1.本表2013—2017年数据根据第三次全国农业普查结果进行了修订。
2.本表2011—2020年数据根据第七次全国人口普查结果进行了修订。

11-38 主要年份农村经济效益指标

Main Indicators of Rural Economic Benefit in Representative Years

年份 Year	每一劳动力创造的 Average Labor Force Production 农林牧渔业总产值（元） Gross Output Value of Farming,Forestry, Animal Husbandry, Fishery (yuan)	粮食（公斤） Grain Crops(kg)	油料（公斤） Oil-bearing Crops(kg)	每百元物耗生产的总产值（元） Output per 100-Yuan of Material Consumed(yuan)
1978	504.7	1024.6	0.7	
1979	549.0	1096.5	2.3	
1980	483.1	846.1	4.0	
1981	502.8	840.5	5.5	
1982	631.5	1058.9	3.6	
1983	606.5	1053.2	2.6	
1984	850.7	1154.2	3.4	
1985	1020.1	1134.6	5.6	
1986	1132.2	1236.4	9.5	
1987	1280.3	1277.2	11.7	
1988	1558.4	1148.0	6.5	
1989	1605.3	1231.9	9.5	
1990	1766.3	1279.1	10.0	233.3
1991	1958.8	1326.6	8.9	238.4
1992	2093.7	1360.7	11.1	241.8
1993	2528.9	1409.7	10.4	240.1
1994	3705.0	1167.8	8.0	227.6
1995	4953.0	1300.6	16.1	225.9
1996	5154.8	1391.2	13.6	234.5
1997	5493.0	1413.4	13.8	239.2
1998	5615.9	1578.1	12.4	247.0
1999	4826.5	1516.6	9.7	251.7
2000	5091.5	1498.0	9.9	250.2
2001	5328.5	1462.4	9.1	248.6
2002	5617.4	1427.5	9.1	265.9
2003	5761.2	1308.1	8.4	254.3
2004	6885.4	1452.7	8.5	261.7
2005	7737.9	1524.7	8.6	262.9
2006	8415.5	1435.7	8.0	263.1
2007	9983.6	1458.9	7.0	259.6
2008	12888.6	1466.7	8.5	257.7
2009	13922.4	1460.9	8.5	259.7
2010	18220.9	1496.9	8.7	258.7
2011	21534.5	1438.2	8.6	271.0
2012	24588.9	1480.0	7.3	269.8
2013	28187.1	1398.2	7.1	269.9
2014	29310.8	1276.2	6.4	270.3
2015	31476.1	1345.6	6.5	268.3
2016	33888.8	1323.2	5.7	265.9
2017	39620.4	1267.3	5.6	262.7
2018	47231.8	1455.6	6.9	263.5
2019	51037.4	1429.9	6.8	263.3
2020	57346.4	1469.0	7.5	258.6

主要统计指标解释

农林牧渔业总产值 指以货币表现的农、林、牧、渔业全部产品和对农林牧渔业生产活动进行的各种支持性服务活动的价值总量，它反映一定时期内农林牧渔业生产总规模和总成果。1957年以前的农林牧渔业总产值中包括了厩肥和农民自给性手工业（如农民自制衣服、鞋、袜，自己从事粮食初步加工等）。1958年及以后，林业中增加了村及村以下竹木采伐产值；牧业中取消了厩肥产值；副业中取消了农民自给性手工业产值，增加了村及村以下办的工业产值；渔业中增加了海洋捕捞水产品产值。1980年及以后，在副业中增加了农民家庭兼营工业商品部分的产值。从1984年起村及村以下工业产值划归工业。从1993年起取消副业，将野生动物的捕猎划入牧业，野生植物采集和农民家庭兼营商品性工业划归农业。从2003年起，执行新的国民经济行业分类标准，农林牧渔业总产值中包括了农林牧渔服务业产值。林业中增加了森林采运业产值。农业中取消了家庭兼营商品性工业产值，将野生林产品的采集划归林业。第三次农业普查以后，由于主要农产品年报数据与普查数据之间存在一定的差距，根据农业普查结果对主要农产品年报数据进行了修正，并对产值进行了相应修正。

农林牧渔业总产值的计算方法通常是按农、林、牧、渔业产品及其副产品的产量分别乘以各自单位产品价格求得；少数生产周期较长，当年没有产品或产品产量不易统计的，则采用间接方法匡算其产值；然后将四业产品产值及农林牧渔服务业产值相加即为农林牧渔业总产值。

粮食产量 指全社会的产量。包括国有经济经营的、集体统一经营的和农民家庭经营的粮食产量，还包括工矿企业办的农场和其他生产单位的产量。粮食除包括稻谷、小麦、玉米、高粱、谷子及其他杂粮外，还包括薯类和豆类。其产量计算方法，豆类按去豆荚后的干豆计算；薯类（包括甘薯和马铃薯，不包括芋头和木薯）1963年以前按每4公斤鲜薯折1公斤粮食计算，从 1964年开始改为按5公斤鲜薯折1公斤粮食计算。城市郊区作为蔬菜的薯类（如马铃薯等）按鲜品计算，并且不作粮食统计。其他粮食一律按脱粒后的原粮计算。1989年以前全国粮食产量数据主要靠全面报表取得，1989年开始使用抽样调查数据。

棉花产量 指全社会的产量。包括春播棉和夏播棉。产量按皮棉计算。不包括木棉。

油料产量 指全部油料作物的生产量。包括花生、油菜籽、芝麻、向日葵籽、胡麻籽（亚麻籽）和其他油料。不包括大豆、木本油料和野生油料。花生以带壳干花生计算。

水产品产量 指人工养殖的水产品和天然生长的水产品的捕捞量。包括海水的鱼类、虾蟹类、贝类和藻类以及内陆水域的鱼类、虾蟹类和贝类，不包括淡水生植物。水产品产量是通过各级水产和统计部门逐级上报取得数据。1995年及以前，贝类中牡蛎按鲜肉计算；蚶、蛤、蛙按5斤鲜品折1斤计算。1996年以后则统一按鲜品计算。

猪、牛、羊肉产量 指当年出栏并已屠宰、除去头蹄下水后带骨肉（即胴体重）的重量。包括全社会范围内的产量。1996年前为各级逐级上报数据。1996年第一次农业普查以后，由于畜牧业产品年报数据与普查数据之间存在一定的差距，根据普查结果对畜牧业年报数据进行了修正。1999年以后，国家统计局在部分地区开展了猪、牛、羊、禽等主要畜禽品种的抽样调查，并用抽样数据作为国家定案数据使用。未开展抽样调查的地区和品种，仍使用各级统计部门逐级上报数据。2008年，根据第二次农业普查结果，对2006年、2007年畜牧业年报数据进行了修正。2019年，根据第三次农业普查结果，对2013—2017年畜牧业年报数据进行了修正。

畜禽存栏头（只）数 指报告期末农村各种合作经济组织和国营农场、农民个人、机关、团体、学校、工矿企业、部队等单位以及城镇居民饲养的大牲畜、猪、羊、家禽等畜禽的存栏数。

常用耕地 是指耕地总资源中专门种植农作物并经常进行耕种、能够正常收获的土地。包括当年实际耕种的熟地；弃耕、休闲不满三年，随时可以复耕的地；开荒利用三年以上的地。不包括临时种植农作物的坡度在25度以上的陡坡地；在河套、湖畔、库区临时开发的成片或零星土地；也不包括已列为国家和省（区、市）退耕计划但临时耕种的土地。

农作物播种面积 指实际播种或移植有农作物的面积。凡是实际种植有农作物的面积，不论种植在耕地上还是种植在非耕地上，均包括在农作物播种面积中。在播种季节基本结束后，因遭灾而重新改种和补种的农作物面积，也包括在内。它是反映我国耕地面积利用情况的一个重要指标。目前，农作物播种面积主要包括粮食、棉花、油料、糖料、麻类、烟叶、蔬菜和瓜类、药材和其他农作物九大类。

有效灌溉面积 指具有一定的水源，地块比较平整，灌溉工程或设备已经配套，在一般年景下，当年能够进行正常灌溉的耕地面积。在一般情况下，有效灌溉面积应等于灌溉工程或设备已经配备，能够进行正常灌溉的水田和水浇地面积之和。它是反映我国耕地抗旱能力的一个重要指标。

农用化肥施用量 指本年内实际用于农业生产的化肥数量，包括氮肥、磷肥、钾肥和复合肥。化肥施用量要求按折纯量计算数量。折纯量是指把氮肥、磷肥、钾肥分别按含氮、含五氧化二磷、含氧化钾的百分之百成份进行折算后的数量。复合肥按其所含主要成分折算。公式为：

折纯量=实物量×某种化肥有效成份含量的百分比

农业机械总动力 指主要用于农、林、牧、渔业的各种动力机械的动力总和。包括耕作机械、排灌机械、收获机械、农用运输机械、植物保护机械、牧业机械、林业机械、渔业机械和其他农业机械【内燃机按引擎马力折成瓦（特）计算、电动机按功率折成瓦（特）计算】。不包括专门用于乡、镇、村、组办工业、基本建设、非农业运输、科学试验和教学等非农业生产方面用的动力机械与作业机械。这个指标的统计数据主要来源于农机部门。

Explanatory Notes on Main Statistical Indicators

Gross Output Value of Agriculture, Forestry, Animal Husbandry and Fishery refers to the total value of products of agriculture, forestry, animal husbandry and fishery, and total value of services in support of agriculture, forestry, animal husbandry and fishery activities. It reflects the total scale and results of agricultural production during a given period. Prior to 1957, China's gross agricultural output value included barnyard manure and handicraft products for self- consumption (clothes, shoes, stockings, and initial grain processing undertaken by peasants). Since 1958, cutting and felling of bamboo and trees by villages and other cooperative organizations under villages have been included in forestry; value of barnyard manure has been excluded from animal husbandry; self consumed handicrafts have not been included from sideline occupations, while the output value of industries run by villages and cooperative organizations under village has been included in sideline occupations; and the output value of fish catches by motor fishing boats has been added to fishery. Since 1980, the value of handicraft products made for sale by individuals in households has been added to sideline occupations. Since 1984, industries run by villages and under villages have been included in the sector of industry. Since 1993, the subdivision of sideline occupations has been cancelled, and the hunting of wild animals has been classified into animal husbandry, and the gathering of wild plants and commodity industry run by rural household have been included in farming. A new industrial classification of economic activities was introduced in 2003. Under the new classification, value of services to agriculture, forestry, animal husbandry and fishery is included in the gross output value of agriculture, value of wood felling and transport is included in forestry, value of industrial output by rural households is not included in agriculture, and the collection of wild forest products is taken from agriculture and included in forestry. The third Agriculture Census of China revealed some discrepancy between the main agricultural products from the annual reports and that from the census. According to the result of the First Agriculture census, efforts were made to adjust the output value of main agricultural to make the figures from the annual reports consistent with the census data.

Gross output value of agrieulture is obtained by multiplying the output of each product or by-product by its price, resulting in the output value of each single item. For a small number of products, annual output of which is not available or difficult to get due to the long production (growing) process involved, the output value is estimated through an indirect approach. The sum of output values of all products of agriculture, forestry, animal husbandry and fishery and services in support to those industries is then equal to the gross output value of agriculture.

Grain Output refers to the total output in the whole country including grains produced by State farms, collective units, rural households, as well as by farms affiliated to industrial and mining enterprises and other production units. Grain includes rice, wheat, corn, sorghum, millet and other miscellaneous grains as well as tubers and beans. Output of beans refers to dry beans without pods. The output of tubers (sweet potatoes and potatoes, not including taros and cassava) are converted into that of grain at the ratio 4:1, i.e. 4 kilograms of fresh tubers were equivalent to 1 kilogram of grain up to 1963. Since 1964 the ratio for conversion has been 5:1. Tubers supplied as vegetables (such as potatoes) in cities and suburbs are calculated as fresh vegetables and their output is not included in the output of grain. Output of all other grains refers to husked grain. Data on grain production before 1989 were obtained through the Comprehensive Statistical Reporting System. Since 1989, data from sample surveys are used.

Cotton Output refers to cotton production in the whole country including cotton planted in spring and in autumn. Output is measured as the weight of ginned cotton. Ceiba is not included.

Output of Oil–bearing Crops refers to the total production of oil-bearing crops of various kinds, including peanuts (dry, in shell), rapeseeds, sesame, sunflower seeds, flax seeds, and other oil-bearing crops. Soybeans, oil-bearing woody plants, and wild oil-bearing crops are not included.

Output of Aquatic Products refers to catches of both artificially cultured and naturally grown aquatic products, including fish, shrimps, crabs and shellfish in sea and inland water as well as seaweed. Freshwater plants are not included. Data on output of aquatic products are reported by aquatic product and statistical agencies level by level. Before 1995, among the shellfish, oyster was counted as fresh meat; 5 kilograms of ark shell, clams and frogs are equivalent to 1 kilogram of fresh aquatic products; they have all been counted as flesh aquatic products since 1996.

Output of Pork, Beef, and Mutton refers to the meat of slaughtered hogs, cattle, sheep and goats with head, feet, and offal taken away. Data refers to the production of the whole country. The First Agricultural Census of China in 1996 revealed some discrepancy between the production of animal products from the annual reports and that from the census. Efforts were made to adjust the output value of animal husbandry to make the figures from the annual reports consistent with the census data. Since 1999, the NBS conducted sample surveys for the major animal husbandry products, such as hogs, cattle, sheep and goats and fowls, and the data from sample surveys are used as national finalized data. Those products, which are not covered by the sample survey, are still reported by statistical agencies level by level. In 2007. the data on animal husbandry from 2000 to 2006 were revised according to the results of the Second Agriculture Census of China. In 2008, A Monitoring and Survey Program was set up on main livestock, the data on the main livestock such as hog, cattle, sheep and poultry became the official data based on the sampling survey. In 2019, data from the annual husbandry report 2013 to 2017 were revised based on the results of the third agricatural census.

Number of Livestock or Poultry in Stock at Beginning (or End) of Period refers to the total number of large animals, pigs, sheep, fowls, etc. raised by rural cooperative organizations, State farms, rural individuals, government agencies, schools, industrial and mining enterprises, army, and urban residents at the beginning (or end) of the reference period.

Regularly Cultivated Land refers to farmland among the total land resources which is exclusively used for farming and is under regular cultivation with harvest in normal years. Included are currently cultivated land, land that has been abandoned or put in idle for less than 3 years and could be re-used for cultivation at any time, and new-claimed land that has been put into cultivation for more than 3 years. Excluded under this category are steep slope land over 25 degrees under temporary cultivation, land (large or small plots) that is claimed along river bends, lake sides or banks of reservoirs, as well as land that has been designated under the "Green for Grain" programmes of the state and provincial governments but is still temporarily under cultivation.

Sown Area of Crops refers to area of transplanted with crops regardless of being land sown or in cultivated area or non-cultivated area. Area of land re-sown due to lso included. This is an important indicator that can reflect the utilization condition of the cultivated land in China. At present, the sown area of crops mainly include the following 9 categories of crops: grain, cotton, oil-bearing crops, sugar crops, flax crops, tobacco, vegetables and melons, medicinal materials and other farm crops.natural disasters is also included. This is an important indicator that can reflect the utilization condition of the cultivated land in China. At present, the sown area of crops mainly include the following 9 categories of crops: grain, cotton, oil-bearing crops, sugar crops, flax crops, tobacco, vegetables and melons, medicinal materials and other farm crops.

Irrigated Area refers to area of land that are effectively irrigated, i.e. relatively level land, where there are water sources or complete sets of irrigation facilities to lift and move adequate water for irrigation purpose under normal conditions. Under normal situations, irrigated area is the sum of watered fields and irrigated fields where irrigation systems or equipment have been installed for regular irrigation purpose. This important indicator reflects drought resistance capacity of the cultivated land in China.

Consumption of Chemical Fertilizers in Agriculture refers to the quantity of chemical fertilizers applied in agriculture in the year, including nitrogenous fertilizer, phosphate fertilizer, potash fertilizer, and compound fertilizer. The consumption of chemical fertilizers is calculated in terms of volume of effective components by means of converting the gross weight of the respective fertilizers into weight containing effective component (e.g. nitrogen content in nitrogenous fertilizer, phosphorous pentoxide contents in phosphate fertilizer, and potassium oxide contents in potash fertilizer). Compound fertilizer is converted in regard to its major components. The formula is:

Volume of effective component= physical quantity × effective component of certain chemical fertilizer (%)

Total Power of Agricultural Machinery refers to total mechanical power of machinery used in agriculture, forestry, animal husbandry and fishery, including machinery for ploughing, irrigation and drainage, harvesting, transport, plant protection, animal husbandry, forestry and fishery and other agricultural machineries. (For the power of internal combustion engines, it is converted from its horsepower into watts while for electric motors the output power is converted into watts.) Machinery employed for non-agricultural purposes, such as the machines used in township-run and village-run industry, construction, non-agricultural transport, scientific experiments and teaching, are not included. Data are mainly from agricultural machinery agencies.

12 工　业

INDUSTRY

资料整理：罗延庆　左　宇　陈小兵　李　玫　沈佳慧　张思敏　王　玥
Data management：Luo Yanqing　Zuo Yu　Chen Xiaobing　Li Mei　Shen Jiahui　Zhang Simin　Wang Yue
数据审核：刘　婷
Data audit：Liu Ting

第十二部分　工业

一、简要说明

1.本章资料反映西安市工业经济方面的基本情况。

2.本章资料包括规模以上工业企业按企业登记类型、轻重工业、企业规模、工业行业大类分组的主要经济指标和经济效益指标，主要工业产品产量，主要产品生产能力。

3.规模以上工业企业统计范围。

1998年至2006年为全部国有及年主营业务收入在500万元及以上非国有工业企业。

2007年至2010年为年主营业务收入在500万元及以上工业企业。

2011年起提高到年主营业务收入在2000万元及以上工业企业。

4.数据来源。

根据国家统计局制定的《企业一套表统计调查制度》和《工业统计报表制度》，对规模以上工业法人单位采用全面调查的方法，从国家一套表平台采集。

二、主要指标

规模以上工业企业单位数（个）	1667	比上年增长	2.2%
规模以上工业增加值（快报数）	–	比上年增长	7.0%
规模以上工业出口交货值（亿元）（快报数）	788.98	比上年增长	13.6%

12 INDUSTRY

Ⅰ.Brief Introduction

1. This chapter reflects the basic conditions of the industrial sector.

2. This chapter mainly including economic indicators of industrial enterprises above designated size; as well as their economic indicators, efficiency indicators, output and production capacity of key industrial products classified by type of registration by light and heavy industries, by size of enterprise, by branch of industry.

3. The Scopes of Industrial Statistics

The scopes of industrial statistics are all State-owned industrial enterprises and non-State-owned industrial enterprises with revenue from principal business over 5 million yuan from 1998 to 2006.

The scopes of industrial statistics are all industrial enterprises with revenue from principal business over 5 million yuan from 2007 to 2010.

The scopes of industrial statistics are raised to all industrial enterprises with revenue from principal business over 20 million yuan from 2011.

4.Sources of Data

According to the A set of table survey system for enterprises and System of industrial statistical report forms by the National Bureau of Statistics, the method of comprehensive investigation shall be adopted for industrial legal entities above the designated size, collected from a set of table platforms by the National Bureau of Statistics.

Ⅱ.Major Indicators

		Increase over Preceding Year
Number of industrial Enterprises Gross Output Above Designated Size(item)	1667	2.2%
Industrial added value above designated size	–	7.0%
Export delivery value above designated size (100million yuan)	788.98	13.6%

12-1 主要年份规模以上工业企业主要经济指标

Major Economic Indicators of Industrial Enterprises above Designated Size in Representative Years

单位：亿元 (100 million yuan)

年份 Year	企业单位数（个） Number of Enterprises (unit)	平均用工人数（万人） Average Number of Employed Persons (10 000person)	资产总计 Total Assets	负债合计 Total Liabilites	所有者权益合计 Owners' Equities	主营业务收入 Revenue from Principal Business	利润总额 Total Profits	利税总额 Total Pre-tax Profits
1998	793	51.71	810.56	548.68	261.88	346.84	-1.26	14.82
1999	770	45.64	853.90	577.94	275.96	346.26	8.26	27.30
2000	816	43.25	958.05	622.46	323.72	420.42	16.11	36.29
2001	785	40.12	1054.36	657.88	384.65	451.62	17.97	40.84
2002	771	38.48	1065.76	643.78	412.27	541.64	25.43	51.31
2003	735	36.55	1195.69	733.04	460.97	645.53	33.82	64.99
2004	1066	38.08	1333.91	869.30	464.60	812.46	38.57	74.23
2005	902	37.92	1503.85	977.42	508.82	980.97	28.72	67.25
2006	904	37.94	1651.67	1062.11	578.33	1183.51	61.46	110.23
2007	937	38.55	1940.52	1254.01	686.51	1561.25	106.22	168.54
2008	1032	40.17	2426.13	1518.86	907.27	1928.05	84.89	168.63
2009	1131	43.42	2913.56	1779.38	1130.76	2384.52	177.20	280.68
2010	1126	47.11	3592.13	2069.29	1515.65	3011.19	245.37	373.56
2011	891	50.42	3975.38	2295.49	1678.19	3381.27	172.94	312.78
2012	970	49.23	4775.92	2835.55	1926.72	3758.56	167.77	320.57
2013	1056	48.36	5127.69	3049.36	2071.72	4171.21	211.26	392.14
2014	1146	49.65	6048.34	3607.62	2436.06	4566.20	226.17	401.20
2015	1150	50.59	6740.26	3860.55	2926.55	4374.11	206.88	341.40
2016	1220	49.54	7473.07	4158.75	3302.36	5028.28	290.96	438.59
2017	1403	51.11	7862.59	4162.97	3595.73	5710.70	367.77	532.35
2018	1474	51.87	8409.16	4603.87	3805.29	6055.58	399.52	573.30
2019	1631	49.75	9449.95	5096.70	4349.39	6483.80	325.60	465.42
2020	1667	50.16	10638.17	5871.38	4736.91	6650.76	466.63	610.93

注：2013年数据为第三次全国经济普查数据。2018年数据为全国第四次经济普查数据。下同。

12-2 各区县规模以上工业企业主要经济指标（2020年）

单位：亿元

区　县	Region	企业单位数（个）Number of Enterprises (unit)	平均用工人数（万人）Average Number of Employed Persons (10 000 persons)	资产合计 Total Assets
新城区	Xincheng	11	2.86	543.08
碑林区	Beilin	7	0.26	77.87
莲湖区	Lianhu	33	4.24	910.62
灞桥区	Baqiao	82	1.88	256.55
未央区	Weiyang	182	6.72	1266.05
雁塔区	Yanta	264	7.92	1485.96
阎良区	Yanliang	116	3.22	657.28
临潼区	Lintong	96	1.76	460.51
长安区	Chang'an	213	8.13	2674.38
高陵区	Gaoling	202	4.70	1021.41
鄠邑区	Huyi	133	3.77	439.40
蓝田县	Lantian	60	0.54	82.24
周至县	Zhouzhi	38	0.28	33.50
西咸新区	Xixian	230	3.89	729.33

Major Economic Indicators of Industrial Enterprises above Designated Size by Region (2020)

(100 million yuan)

负债合计 Total Liabilites	所有者权益合计 Total Owners' Equities	营业收入 Revenue	利润总额 Total Profits	利税总额 Total Pre-tax Profits
345.35	197.72	376.78	11.62	19.88
48.12	29.76	28.49	1.70	2.24
434.14	476.47	429.54	25.32	38.78
164.90	91.47	166.06	6.77	10.51
709.24	549.07	913.78	47.01	56.58
771.91	706.48	700.82	65.64	84.96
347.19	309.81	302.59	10.47	13.98
292.35	164.19	311.05	17.21	24.05
1188.87	1484.53	1724.90	199.81	232.41
693.51	323.45	1072.96	48.67	65.43
283.65	155.75	424.38	17.27	33.79
61.26	20.99	50.77	2.98	3.78
14.35	18.99	21.60	0.46	0.88
516.54	208.24	374.48	11.69	23.65

12-3 规模以上工业企业主要工业产品产量（2020年）

Major Output of Industrial Enterprises above Designated Size（2020）

产品名称	Name of Products	2020	比上年增长（%） Increase over Preceding Year (%)
自来水生产量(亿立方米)	Tap Water Production (100 million cu.m)	7.41	4.9
大米(万吨)	Rice (10 000 ton)	1.06	-40.2
小麦粉(万吨)	Wheat Flour (10 000 ton)	64.49	47.6
精制食用植物油(万吨)	Edible Vegetable Oil (10 000 ton)	18.50	-8.8
鲜、冷藏肉（万吨）	Fresh/Frozen Meat(10 000 ton)	4.29	-45.2
饲料（万吨）	Mixed Feed(10 000 ton)	93.97	26.5
#配合饲料	Compound feed	22.29	40.1
混合饲料	Mixed feed	69.54	21.1
方便面(万吨)	Instant Noodle(10 000 ton)	16.83	10.7
乳制品(万吨)	Dairy Products (10 000 ton)	60.42	-16.8
液体乳	Milk	57.43	-0.3
固体及半固体乳制品	Solid and semi-solid dairy products	2.99	-80.1
饮料酒(万千升)	Beverage Wine (10 000 kiloliter)	34.39	-4.1
#白酒（折65度，商品量）	Liquor (as 65 degree, amount of goods)	…	-75.7
啤酒	Beer	31.52	-11.1
葡萄酒	Wine	0.23	-35.2
饮料(万吨)	Beverage (10 000 ton)	162.56	-21.5
#碳酸饮料类（汽水）	Carbonated Beverage	41.09	-4.6
果汁和蔬菜汁饮料	Juice and Fruit Beverage	9.15	-48.2
包装饮用水类	Canned Drinking Water	68.09	-32.8
纱(万吨)	Yarn (10 000 ton)	2.09	-24.5
棉纱	Cotton Yarn	1.04	-5.0
棉混纺纱	Blend Fabric	0.44	-25.5
化学纤维纱	Pure Chemical-Fibre Yarn	0.61	-43.6
布(亿米)	Cloth (100 million m)	0.99	-17.9

12-3 续表1 continued1

产品名称	Name of Products	2020	比上年增长（%）Increase over Preceding Year (%)
棉布	Cotton Cloth	0.48	-4.4
棉混纺布	Blend Fabric	0.25	-17.0
化学纤维短纤布	Chemical Fiber short fiber Cloth	0.26	-35.2
人造板（万立方米）	Artificial Board (10 000 cu.m)	13.85	24.3
纤维板	Fibre Board	13.85	24.3
家具（万件）	Furniture (10 000unit)	36.31	-52.4
#木质家具	Wooden Furniture	20.07	-41.4
软体家具	Soft Furniture (inc.: Sofa ,Mattress etc.)	3.97	-28.2
机制纸及纸板（外购原纸加工除外）（万吨）	Machine Made Paper(not including processing of procured base paper)(10 000 ton)	4.22	-63.0
纸制品（万吨）	Paper-Made Products (10 000 ton)	10.51	-13.8
#瓦楞纸箱	Corrugated Paper	8.78	-9.0
单色印刷品（万令）	Monochrom Printed products(10 000 ream)	61.71	-48.3
多色印刷品（万对开色令）	Colored Printed products(10 000 ream)	588.65	-46.8
化学农药原药(折有效成分100%)(万吨)	Chemical Pesticide(100% effective content)(10 000 ton)	0.10	24.9
涂料（万吨）	Construction Paint(10 000 ton)	0.91	-35.0
合成洗涤剂（万吨）	Synthetic Detergents (10 000 ton)	4.13	-15.7
#合成洗衣粉	Washing Power	1.21	12.8
液体洗涤剂	Liquid detergent	2.06	-35.3
化学原料药（万吨）	Chemical Medicine (10 000 ton)	0.10	4.9
中成药（万吨）	Traditional Chinese Medicine (10 000 ton)	1.19	-4.7
化学纤维（万吨）	Chemicai Fiber(10 000 ton)	3.71	-13.6
#人造纤维（纤维素纤维）	Man-made Fiber	3.71	-6.8
塑料制品（万吨）	Plastic Product (10 000 ton)	20.22	-31.7
水泥（万吨）	Cement (10 000 ton)	221.69	5.1

12-3 续表2 continued2

产品名称	Name of Products	2020	比上年增长（%）Increase over Preceding Year（%）
硅酸盐水泥熟料（万吨）	Portland Cement Clinker (10 000 ton)	78.08	1.9
水泥混凝土电杆（万根）	Cement Pole(10 000 unit)	2.45	-31.3
商品混凝土(万立方米)	Ready-mixed Concrete (10 000 cu.m)	4527.16	5.6
沥青和改性沥青防水卷材（万平方米）	Asphalt and Modified Bitumen Membrane(10 000 sq.m)	2675.87	1.6
钢化玻璃(万平方米)	Toughened Glass(10 000 sq.m)	60.03	-87.0
日用玻璃制品（万吨）	Glassware(10 000 ton)		
钢材（万吨）	Rolled-steel Final Products (10 000 ton)	39.99	19.3
#线材（盘条）	Wire Rod	20.30	36.7
其他钢材	Other steel	12.12	0.5
铝材(万吨)	Aluminum Material (10 000 ton)	2.31	-0.6
单晶硅（万千克）	Monocrystalline Silicon (10 000kg)	163.86	-7.1
多晶硅（万千克）	Polycrystalline Silicon(10 000kg)	148.09	-85.6
工业锅炉（蒸发量吨）	Industrial Boiler steam(ton)	1036.70	-28.4
发动机（万千瓦）	Engine (10 000 kw)	595.44	52.9
#汽车发动机（万千瓦）	Motor Engine(10 000 kw)	595.44	52.9
金属切削机床(万台)	Metal-cutting Machines (10 000 unit)	0.45	41.1
泵(万台)	Pump (Liquid pump)(10 000 unit)	0.51	42.5
风机（万台）	Fan(10 000 unit)	467.56	679.4
气体压缩机（万台）	Gas Compressor(10 000 unit)	82.64	6.9
阀门（万吨）	Valves (10 000 ton)	0.49	-17.0
铸铁件（万吨）	Iron Castings (10 000 ton)	1.55	-10.1
铸钢件（万吨）	Steel Castings (10 000 ton)		
锻件（万吨）	Forgings (10 000 ton)	0.97	-1.4
矿山专用设备（万吨）	Mining Equipment (10 000 ton)	1.73	10.5
炼油、化工生产专用设备（万吨）	Oil Refining and Chemical industry Machine(10 000 ton)	0.32	-26.2

12-3 续表3 continued 3

产品名称	Name of Products	2020	比上年增长（%） Increase over Preceding Year （%）
金属冶炼设备（万吨）	Metal Smelting Equipments(10 000 ton)	0.57	38.5
金属轧制设备（万吨）	Metal-rolling Machine(10 000 ton)	0.55	-83.0
印刷专用设备（吨）	Printing Equipment(ton)	33.00	-82.0
环境污染防治专用设备(万台/套)	Special Equipment for Environment Protection(10 000 unit)	1.17	0.8
#大气污染防治设备	Equipment for Preventing Atmospheric Pollution	1.01	9.9
汽车（万辆）	Motor Vehicle(10 000unit)	49.83	16.9
其中：基本型乘用车（轿车）	Basic Type Passenger Vehicles(car)	10.11	-28.5
#轿车（排量≤1升）	Car0L-1.0L Gas Displacement(1.0L included)	4.10	-39.6
轿车（1升＜排量≤1.6升）	Car1.0L-1.6L Gas Displacement(1.6L included)	6.00	-18.2
运动型多用途乘用车（SUV）	Sports Utility Vehicle (SUV)	15.33	65.6
载货汽车	Trucks	24.39	26.8
其中：新能源汽车	New Energy Vehicles	5.95	-36.3
改装汽车（万辆）	Refit Trucks (10 000 unit)	1.48	5.9
铁路货车（万辆）	Freight(10 000 unit)	0.27	-39.6
电动机（万千瓦）	Electric motor (10 000 kw)	259.58	-12.1
#直流电动机	DC motors	18.36	-46.0
交流电动机	Alternating Current Motor	241.22	-7.7
变压器（亿千伏安）	Transformer(100 million KVA)	1.83	5.3
高压开关板（万面）	High-voltage Switch Panel(10 000 unit)	0.82	-5.0
低压开关板（万面）	Low-voltage Switch Panel(10 000 unit)	0.95	34.4
电力电缆(万千米)	Electric Power Cables(10 000 km)	19.15	3.4
通信及电子网络用电缆(万对千米)	Communication Cables(10 000 pair km)	4.01	11.4
光缆（万芯千米）	Optical Cable (10 000 Core.km)	912.52	34.8
绝缘制品(万吨)	Insulating Products (10 000 ton)	1.95	-54.1
电子元件（亿只）	Electronic Components(100 million unit)	45.19	-3.0
工业自动化调节仪表与控制系统（万台/套）	Automatization Meter and System (10 000 unit)	4.07	-44.8

12-3 续表4 continued 4

产品名称	Name of Products	2020	比上年增长（%） Increase over Preceding Year （%）
分析仪器及装置（万台/套）	Analysis Instruments and Apparatus(10 000 set)	0.12	27.4
化学试剂（万吨）	Chemicals Reagents(10 000 ton)	14.14	-10.7
起重机（吨）	Crane (ton)	1270.00	-13.7
减速机（万台）	Reducer (10 000 unit)	3.74	104.2
模具（万套）	Molds (10 000 set)	0.14	-67.9
电动自行车（万辆）	Electric Bicycle (10 000 car)	1.28	-97.6
电力电容器（万千乏）	Power Capacitors (10 000 kvar)	6165.01	-7.8
高压开关设备（11万伏以上）（万台）	High Voltage Switchgear (above 110,000 volt) (10 000a)	2.10	1.5
灯具及照明装置（万套/台/个）	Lamps and lighting Equipment (10 000set /a)	6.54	-39.6
半导体分立器件（亿只）	Discrete Semiconductor Devices (100million unit)	81.25	57.1
工业仪表（万台/个）	Industrial Instrumentation (10 000a)	67.24	-0.8
环境监测专用仪器仪表（万台）	Special Equipment for Prevention and Control of Environmental Pollution(10 000 unit)	1.00	-3.8
集成电路圆片（万片）	Integrated Circuit Wafer (10 000 pieces)	205.90	43.7
锂离子电池（万只）	Lithium Ion Battery (10 000 unit)	2068.00	17.4
太阳能电池（万千瓦）	Solar Cell (10 000 kw)	379.64	1691.6
智能手机（万台）	Smart Phones (10 000 sets)	1699.74	48.9
光纤（万千米）	Optical Fiber(10 000 km)	732.05	29.7
3D打印设备（台）	3D Printing Equipment(unit)	206	19.1
移动通信基站设备（万块射频模块）	Mobile Communication Base Station Equipment (10 000 RF modules)	391.93	11.0
民用无人机（架）	Civilian Drone(unit)	70	-6.7
发电量（亿千瓦小时）	Electricity(100 million kwh)	154.27	3.6
火力发电量	Thermal Power	153.07	3.7
水力发电量	Hydropower	0.77	-16.2
太阳能发电量	Solar Power	0.43	9.5

12-4 主要年份规模以上工业企业经济效益指标

Indicators of Economic Performance of Industrial Enterprises above Designated Size in Representative Years

年 份 Year	总资产贡献率 (%) Ratio of Total Assets to Industrial Output Value (%)	资产负债率 (%) Assets-Liability Ratio (%)	流动资产周转次数 (次/年) Rate of Annual Turnover Working Capitals (times/year)	成本费用利润率 (%) Ratio of Profits to Cost (%)	全员劳动生产率 (元/人·年) Overall Labor Productivity (yuan/person·year)	产品销售率 (%) Proportion of Industrial Products Sold (%)
1998		67.7	0.9	-266.1	19185	95.3
1999		67.7	0.9	2.5	22878	95.9
2000		65.0	1.0	4.2	29496	97.1
2001	5.8	62.4	0.9	4.1	38267	96.7
2002	6.2	60.4	1.1	5.1	46940	96.7
2003	7.0	61.3	1.1	5.7	58801	96.3
2004	6.9	65.2	1.2	5.0	66752	97.9
2005	8.4	65.0	1.3	3.1	82815	97.5
2006	7.8	64.3	1.4	5.5	97561	98.2
2007	10.2	64.6	1.6	7.3	129706	96.8
2008	8.6	62.6	1.5	4.6	150641	96.1
2009	11.3	61.1	1.7	8.1	161289	97.6
2010	12.2	57.6	1.7	8.8	188483	97.1
2011	8.6	57.7	1.5	5.2	194105	97.4
2012	7.7	59.4	1.5	4.5	230032	96.7
2013	8.5	59.5	1.5	5.2	264324	95.7
2014	7.4	59.7	1.4	5.2	266789	94.9
2015	5.7	57.3	1.3	4.8	268182	94.5
2016	6.4	55.7	1.3	6.0	277240	96.0
2017	7.2	53.0	1.4	6.6	294393	97.3
2018	7.3	54.8	1.3	6.7		96.2
2019	5.4	53.9	1.2	5.1		94.0
2020	6.1	55.2	1.1	7.1		93.0

注：产品销售率2019年和2020年数据为快报数。

12-5 规模以上工业企业主要经济指标（2020年）

单位：万元

分组	Classify	企业单位数（个）Number of Enterprises (unit)	亏损企业 Loss Making Enterprises
总计	**Total**	**1667**	**334**
#亏损企业	Deficit Enterprises	334	334
按隶属关系分	**Grouped by Jurisdiction of Management**		
#中央企业	Central Enterprises	112	14
地方企业	Provincial Enterprises	180	46
按登记注册类型分组	**Grouped by Registion Status**		
内资企业	Domestic Investment Enterprises	1543	302
国有	State-owned Enterprises	35	2
集体	Collective-owned Enterprises	3	1
股份合作	Share-holding Corperative	5	2
联营	Joint Ownership Enterprises		
有限责任公司	Limited Liability Corporations	473	98
股份有限公司	Share-holding Corperation Ltd.	100	20
私营	Private Enterprises	926	178
其他	Other Domestic Funded Enterprises	1	1
港澳台商投资	Enterprises with Funds from Hong Kong,Macao and Taiwan	22	6
外商投资	Foreign Funded Enterprises	102	26
按轻重工业分	**Grouped by Light Industry and Heavy Industry**		
轻工业	Light Industry	360	90
重工业	Heavy Industry	1307	244
按企业规模分	**Grouped by Size of Enterprises**		
大型企业	Large-size	66	8
中型企业	Medium-size	178	30
小型企业	Small-size	1298	257
微型企业	Microenterprise	125	39
按控股情况分	**Grouped by Cast strand**		
国有控股	State owned shares	326	58

Major Economic Indicators of Industrial Enterprises above Designated Size（2020）

(10 000yuan)

平均用工人数（人）Average Number of Employed Persons (person)	资产总计 Total Assets	流动资产合计 Total Working Capitals	固定资产原价 Origing Value of Fixed Assets	累计折旧 Accumulative Total Depreciation
501597	**106381653**	**61511762**	**49029576**	**22600128**
71694	17017697	8934281	7291540	1850827
144327	26300585	15638422	13257035	6833156
89609	28817774	16828560	9561049	3649103
432606	87793053	54543795	31081501	13269872
48985	10049965	5140251	6466063	3064592
360	9021	6530	2243	631
875	116678	97004	13654	6525
215753	40279657	24991570	16199469	7002135
56479	19532004	11960883	3833603	1753800
109995	17731110	12305636	4551170	1434050
159	74619	41920	15300	8140
26042	3397721	1929384	1294930	569466
42949	15190879	5038584	16653144	8760789
80159	11604386	7166584	4400372	1890836
421438	94777268	54345178	44629204	20709292
264449	63957670	35270499	34832106	17524711
102596	18114848	11609273	5659254	2404125
129001	22097077	13924543	6861120	2619331
5551	2212059	707447	1677096	51961
254543	55824047	33940418	24057047	10969419

12-5 续表1

单位：万元

分　组	Classify	负债合计 Total Liabilites	流动负债合计 Total Working Liabilities
总计	**Total**	**58713812**	**48075928**
#亏损企业	Deficit Enterprises	11619434	8712871
按隶属关系分	**Grouped by Jurisdiction of Management**		
#中央企业	Central Enterprises	13834019	11290801
地方企业	Provincial Enterprises	17980110	14493433
按登记注册类型分组	**Grouped by Registion Status**		
内资企业	Domestic Investment Enterprises	50848155	41463315
国有	State-owned Enterprises	6777123	4922527
集体	Collective-owned Enterprises	4491	3673
股份合作	Share-holding Corperative	93359	79122
联营	Joint Ownership Enterprises		
有限责任公司	Limited Liability Corporations	23503639	18819673
股份有限公司	Share-holding Corperation Ltd.	9574443	7900325
私营	Private Enterprises	10813444	9656341
其他	Other Domestic Funded Enterprises	81656	81656
港澳台商投资	Enterprises with Funds from Hong Kong,Macao and Taiwan	2332653	2064648
外商投资	Foreign Funded Enterprises	5533004	4547965
按轻重工业分	**Grouped by Light Industry and Heavy Industry**		
轻工业	Light Industry	6750337	5331510
重工业	Heavy Industry	51963475	42744418
按企业规模分	**Grouped by Size of Enterprises**		
大型企业	Large-size	34978764	29685917
中型企业	Medium-size	9378432	7581261
小型企业	Small-size	12564251	10552042
微型企业	Microenterprise	1792365	256708
按控股情况分	**Grouped by Cast strand**		
国有控股	State owned shares	32866582	26238234

continued1

(10 000yuan)

所有者权益合计 Total Owners' Equities	实收资本 Total Capital Hold	营业收入 Total Revenue	主营业务收入 Revenue from Principal Business	营业成本 Total Cost	税金及附加 Taxs and Other Changes
47369061	**18916462**	**68982258**	**66507599**	**58922934**	**400038**
5231603	3075689	7493579	7200864	6729242	39136
12432702	4937902	14454228	14179408	12959830	69480
10687103	3709668	20140775	18759288	17694821	80560
36646262	13934734	57254674	55191413	49346196	274113
3272842	1364063	5730367	5663212	5067005	24718
2952	1582	10519	10519	8736	64
23319	8229	48470	48466	41023	117
16588823	7209461	27540502	25898020	23898331	150237
9942623	2344493	8912516	8734409	7623870	34662
6822741	3002908	14992259	14816759	12688271	64157
-7037	4000	20042	20029	18961	159
1065068	288287	3047963	2753237	2730905	66406
9657730	4693441	8679620	8562948	6845834	59519
4815097	1908637	8954052	8768300	6478293	59850
42553963	17007825	60028206	57739298	52444642	340188
28978905	10136137	43514049	41706335	38642760	255096
8736414	3516516	10856870	10595057	8554634	63458
9533285	5105540	14065977	13873477	11251244	77881
120457	158269	545363	332730	474297	3602
22791045	9121254	33582636	31898502	29941456	166749

12-5 续表2

单位：万元

分　组	Classify	销售费用 Expenses for Sales	管理费用 Expenses for Management	研发费用 R&D Expenses
总计	**Total**	**2138785**	**2608143**	**1585147**
#亏损企业	Deficit Enterprises	318726	376020	157800
按隶属关系分	**Grouped by Jurisdiction of Management**			
#中央企业	Central Enterprises	178823	663776	386895
地方企业	Provincial Enterprises	601609	616193	281598
按登记注册类型分组	**Grouped by Registion Status**			
内资企业	Domestic Investment Enterprises	1609686	2139093	1305002
国有	State-owned Enterprises	42065	251198	130189
集体	Collective-owned Enterprises	845	465	
股份合作	Share-holding Corperative	3215	1106	309
联营	Joint Ownership Enterprises			
有限责任公司	Limited Liability Corporations	813124	1039597	638689
股份有限公司	Share-holding Corperation Ltd.	210408	277950	160354
私营	Private Enterprises	539842	567717	374592
其他	Other Domestic Funded Enterprises	186	1060	870
港澳台商投资	Enterprises with Funds from Hong Kong,Macao and Taiwan	65034	114796	27669
外商投资	Foreign Funded Enterprises	464065	354254	252476
按轻重工业分	**Grouped by Light Industry and Heavy Industry**			
轻工业	Light Industry	1050474	477545	118284
重工业	Heavy Industry	1088311	2130598	1466863
按企业规模分	**Grouped by Size of Enterprises**			
大型企业	Large-size	846489	1333317	921885
中型企业	Medium-size	677042	473960	259604
小型企业	Small-size	592979	749441	392620
微型企业	Microenterprise	22275	51425	11037
按控股情况分	**Grouped by Cast strand**			
国有控股	State owned shares	579579	1249148	751846

continued2

(10 000yuan)

财务费用 Financial cost	营业利润 Operating Profit	利润总额 Total Profits	亏损企业亏损总额 Total Loss of Deficit Enterprises	利税总额 Total Pre-tax Profits	应付职工薪酬 Salary Payable	本年应交增值税 Value Added Tax Payable
498651	**4509013**	**4666317**	**419142**	**6109346**	**6407976**	**1042992**
214493	-433832	-419142	419142	-372881	808696	7125
74344	567359	581185	88000	871185	2310676	220519
98497	1223344	1274421	113579	1590261	1372011	235281
392340	3284599	3441121	369589	4609375	5470261	894141
49357	234253	242125	7202	366215	766286	99373
57	352	369	35	893	965	460
1733	559	85	330	732	5659	530
132778	1480872	1547357	190198	2165837	2847210	468243
89589	967001	1003371	72702	1154894	820463	116862
118707	602857	649107	97831	921582	1028217	208318
120	-1296	-1292	1292	-777	1462	356
26902	57878	57730	4452	166001	257979	41866
79408	1166536	1167467	45102	1333970	679736	106985
115563	854585	877033	62886	1154205	771947	217322
383088	3654428	3789284	356257	4955142	5636030	825670
173640	2716516	2725583	46157	3470072	4218188	489394
120204	787684	839792	125813	1133645	1097839	230395
177438	1012829	1098856	199360	1490902	1074256	314165
27369	-8015	2086	47812	14727	17693	9039
188278	1384852	1456961	231823	2115213	3829947	491503

12-5 续表3

单位：万元

分　组	Classify	企业单位数（个） Number of Enterprises (unit)	亏损企业 Loss Making Enterprises
集体控股	Collective shares	11	5
私人控股	Private holdings	1192	235
港澳台控股	Hong Kong and Macao Holdings	16	3
外商投资	Foreign Investment	65	14
其他	Others	57	19
按工业行业大类分	**Grouped by Sector**		
煤炭开采和洗选业	Mining and Washing of Coal		
石油和天然气开采业	Extraction of Petroleum and Natural Gas		
黑色金属矿采选业	Mining and Processing of Ferrous Metal Ores		
有色金属矿采选业	Mining and Processing of Non-ferrous Metal Ores		
非金属矿采选业	Mining and Processing of Nonmetal Ores		
开采专业及辅助性活动	Mining Professional and Auxiliary Activity	10	1
其他采矿业	Mining of other Ores		
农副食品加工业	Processing of Food from Agricultural Porducts	41	5
食品制造业	Manufacture of Foods	49	13
酒、饮料和精制茶制造业	Manufacture of Alcohol,Beverages and Tea	16	7
烟草制品业	Manufacture of Tobacco	2	
纺织业	Manufacture of Textile	18	6
纺织服装、服饰业	Textile, apparel industry	3	
皮革、毛皮、羽毛及其制品和制鞋业	Manufacture of Leather, Fur, Feather and Related Products, and Shoes	2	2
木材加工和木、竹、藤、棕、草制品业	Processing of Timber, Manufacture of Wood,Plam and Straw Products	3	2
家具制造业	Manufacture of Furniture	12	3
造纸和纸制品业	Manufacture of Paper and Paper Products	22	3
印刷和记录媒介复制业	Printing,Reproduction of Recording Media	29	9

continued3

(10 000yuan)

平均用工人数（人） Average Number of Employed Persons (person)	资产总计 Total Assets	流动资产合计 Total Working Capitals	固定资产原价 Origing Value of Fixed Assets	累计折旧 Accumulative Total Depreciation
1551	187556	110508	61537	29966
193391	34400223	22157818	7923479	2759309
4550	518376	278340	233703	152622
33664	13381884	3939408	15812314	8382557
13898	2069567	1085271	941496	306254
12713	1288038	890242	794157	539817
5066	1019914	723162	317960	161804
14918	973075	516190	503923	237289
6609	1057677	487493	514628	299650
648	66207	36684	52240	24112
6265	325186	153751	217650	87652
1024	95427	80878	15663	6037
779	75040	52599	9572	6200
417	107817	52977	31463	11323
1261	78098	38269	40921	9794
2194	170102	93175	60964	21379
6246	667436	388691	492933	334401

12-5 续表4

单位：万元

分 组	Classify	负债合计 Total Liabilites	流动负债合计 Total Working Liabilities
集体控股	Collective shares	99542	75539
私人控股	Private holdings	20045210	17256768
港澳台控股	Hong Kong and Macao Holdings	186044	124607
外商投资	Foreign Investment	4540499	3616240
其他	Others	975936	764539
按工业行业大类分	**Grouped by Sector**		
煤炭开采和洗选业	Mining and Washing of Coal		
石油和天然气开采业	Extraction of Petroleum and Natural Gas		
黑色金属矿采选业	Mining and Processing of Ferrous Metal Ores		
有色金属矿采选业	Mining and Processing of Non-ferrous Metal Ores		
非金属矿采选业	Mining and Processing of Nonmetal Ores		
开采专业及辅助性活动	Mining Professional and Auxiliary Activity	467953	463593
其他采矿业	Mining of other Ores		
农副食品加工业	Processing of Food from Agricultural Porducts	584878	489711
食品制造业	Manufacture of Foods	464603	434814
酒、饮料和精制茶制造业	Manufacture of Alcohol,Beverages and Tea	577584	483070
烟草制品业	Manufacture of Tobacco	12044	7544
纺织业	Manufacture of Textile	185267	79351
纺织服装、服饰业	Textile, apparel industry	54559	54119
皮革、毛皮、羽毛及其制品和制鞋业	Manufacture of Leather, Fur, Feather and Related Products, and Shoes	26526	21816
木材加工和木、竹、藤、棕、草制品业	Processing of Timber, Manufacture of Wood,Plam and Straw Products	49883	8388
家具制造业	Manufacture of Furniture	42004	37751
造纸和纸制品业	Manufacture of Paper and Paper Products	104430	85725
印刷和记录媒介复制业	Printing,Reproduction of Recording Media	249996	222663

continued4

(10 000yuan)

所有者权益合计 Total Owners' Equities	实收资本 Total Capital Hold	营业收入 Total Revenue	主营业务收入 Revenue from Principal Business	营业成本 Total Cost	税金及附加 Taxs and Other Changes
86436	47022	105297	100318	78557	596
14225563	4819313	26317611	25606671	21905425	169607
332332	175715	425244	415843	305565	2672
8841240	4203277	7403671	7357096	5765423	53305
1092445	549882	1147798	1129169	926508	7110
820084	486940	857812	841567	767886	5352
435035	113625	1274718	1257471	1144946	2199
508470	207301	1128028	1102525	870970	6743
480093	162330	709695	696803	499674	12017
54163	35471	25641	25279	15253	666
135599	55740	141563	128405	123593	1298
40868	27500	40863	40682	32484	236
48514	41000	38136	37670	32473	352
57934	13668	7381	6180	5784	169
36093	15461	58863	58295	48790	378
65672	32513	159074	150521	142225	534
417439	230081	599476	594118	492894	3629

12-5 续表5

单位：万元

分 组	Classify	销售费用 Expenses for Sales	管理费用 Expenses for Management	研发费用 R&D Expenses
集体控股	Collective shares	5781	11390	1167
私人控股	Private holdings	1060447	968653	550180
港澳台控股	Hong Kong and Macao Holdings	41722	25799	13037
外商投资	Foreign Investment	422285	299235	230549
其他	Others	28972	53919	38369
按工业行业大类分	**Grouped by Sector**			
煤炭开采和洗选业	Mining and Washing of Coal			
石油和天然气开采业	Extraction of Petroleum and Natural Gas			
黑色金属矿采选业	Mining and Processing of Ferrous Metal Ores			
有色金属矿采选业	Mining and Processing of Non-ferrous Metal Ores			
非金属矿采选业	Mining and Processing of Nonmetal Ores			
开采专业及辅助性活动	Mining Professional and Auxiliary Activity	3555	19334	37903
其他采矿业	Mining of other Ores			
农副食品加工业	Processing of Food from Agricultural Porducts	29766	34821	3812
食品制造业	Manufacture of Foods	130173	52164	5354
酒、饮料和精制茶制造业	Manufacture of Alcohol,Beverages and Tea	117412	28901	1976
烟草制品业	Manufacture of Tobacco	1315	5979	
纺织业	Manufacture of Textile	3405	8989	4414
纺织服装、服饰业	Textile, apparel industry	2380	3580	1012
皮革、毛皮、羽毛及其制品和制鞋业	Manufacture of Leather, Fur, Feather and Related Products, and Shoes	1495	1752	531
木材加工和木、竹、藤、棕、草制品业	Processing of Timber, Manufacture of Wood,Plam and Straw Products	327	2662	
家具制造业	Manufacture of Furniture	3581	4595	
造纸和纸制品业	Manufacture of Paper and Paper Products	4158	5220	132
印刷和记录媒介复制业	Printing,Reproduction of Recording Media	15374	42341	11664

continued5

(10 000yuan)

财务费用 Financial cost	营业利润 Operating Profit	利润总额 Total Profits	亏损企业亏损总额 Total Loss of Deficit Enterprises	利税总额 Total Pre-tax Profits	应付职工薪酬 Salary Payable	本年应交增值税 Value Added Tax Payable
467	7193	8516	2609	11563	12215	2451
224294	1907403	1981438	142438	2593175	1798658	442129
6140	29641	31488	1836	32064	47306	-2096
70438	1062205	1061502	23775	1200309	569424	85502
9034	117719	126412	16662	157023	150426	23501
-4309	33267	32502	396	41946	266796	4093
8502	55123	60610	968	70659	39716	7850
4014	94868	96611	7721	132850	107256	29496
3609	46731	48225	12637	83506	65163	23264
-212	2687	2576		4948	8613	1707
429	2484	2962	2993	6258	31592	1997
698	802	1249		2988	5673	1503
234	-786	-738	738	43	4726	429
1235	-1245	-601	868	-313	754	120
951	569	849	1100	2564	6327	1337
1820	6962	7938	148	10771	10397	2299
4433	33079	35024	5353	53830	93304	15177

12-5 续表6

单位：万元

分 组	Classify	企业单位数（个） Number of Enterprises (unit)	亏损企业 Loss Making Enterprises
文教、工美、体育和娱乐用品制造业	Manufacture of Articles For Cultural,Educational and Sports Activities	8	3
石油、煤炭及其他燃料加工业	Petroleum, coal and other fuel processing industries	7	3
化学原料和化学制品制造业	Manufacture of Raw Chemical Materials and Chemical Products	82	18
医药制造业	Manufacture of Medicines	70	20
化学纤维制造业	Manufacture of Chemical Fibers	3	
橡胶和塑料制品业	Manufacture of Rubber and Plastics	44	7
非金属矿物制品业	Manufacture of Non-metallic Mineral Products	194	45
黑色金属冶炼和压延加工业	Smelting and Pressing of Ferrous Metals	14	1
有色金属冶炼和压延加工业	Smelting and Pressing of Non-ferrous Metals	47	9
金属制品业	Manufacture of Metal Products	108	19
通用设备制造业	Manufacture of General Purpose Machinery	97	17
专用设备制造业	Manufacture of Special Equipment	140	26
汽车制造业	Manufacture of Motor Vehicle	73	9
铁路、船舶、航空航天和其他运输设备制造业	Railways,Shipbuilding,Aerospace and Other Transportation Equipment Manufacturing Industry	103	14
电气机械和器材制造业	Manufacture of Electric Equipment and Machinery	171	29
计算机、通讯和其他电子设备制造业	Manufacture of Communication Equipment, Computers and other Electronic Equipment	138	25
仪器仪表制造业	Manufacture of Measuring Instruments and Machinery	71	11
其他制造业	Manufacture of Other Manufacturing	7	1
废弃资源综合利用业	Recycling and Disposal of Waste	4	1
金属制品、机械和设备修理业	Metal Products,Machinery and Equipment Repair Industry	13	4
电力、热力生产和供应业	Production and Supply of Electric Power and Heat Power	31	9
燃气生产和供应业	Gas Mining and Supplying Industry	20	4
水的生产和供应业	Production and Supply of Water	15	8

continued6

(10 000yuan)

平均用工人数（人） Average Number of Employed Persons (person)	资产总计 Total Assets	流动资产合计 Total Working Capitals	固定资产原价 Origing Value of Fixed Assets	累计折旧 Accumulative Total Depreciation
555	38009	25632	10091	1970
2642	152463	106674	27968	14668
18150	3029689	1836049	1435715	373003
18277	2799305	1761274	796719	259935
722	169788	98293	161675	89201
9941	2499098	1602624	756415	195771
20372	3805570	2833082	1197884	479879
1596	204597	144417	96230	40985
8414	2951779	1920322	689776	242348
20935	2361545	1374379	1048093	449107
20262	4924124	3832413	975047	472750
27150	5729604	3943551	1063991	448988
55120	10678186	8071752	2723347	1335128
65691	12634515	8285521	3323106	1704319
51915	12848194	8906622	3767978	1336700
71766	22321026	8530772	16720153	8266409
15796	2825045	2081090	699561	307256
908	79692	53854	34202	14622
240	51597	29984	15635	3079
1814	189878	98660	56767	19421
19010	6262810	1451484	7597367	3932059
7898	2721041	713690	1892915	598855
4283	1180082	295513	886871	274216

12-5 续表7

单位：万元

分组	Classify	负债合计 Total Liabilites	流动负债合计 Total Working Liabilities
文教、工美、体育和娱乐用品制造业	Manufacture of Articles For Cultural,Educational and Sports Activities	14269	7501
石油、煤炭及其他燃料加工业	Petroleum, coal and other fuel processing industries	116202	116172
化学原料和化学制品制造业	Manufacture of Raw Chemical Materials and Chemical Products	1840084	1074486
医药制造业	Manufacture of Medicines	1276393	1090549
化学纤维制造业	Manufacture of Chemical Fibers	62468	62408
橡胶和塑料制品业	Manufacture of Rubber and Plastics	1858595	1230667
非金属矿物制品业	Manufacture of Non-metallic Mineral Products	2760742	2450746
黑色金属冶炼和压延加工业	Smelting and Pressing of Ferrous Metals	120735	108832
有色金属冶炼和压延加工业	Smelting and Pressing of Non-ferrous Metals	1144638	817753
金属制品业	Manufacture of Metal Products	1756046	1299396
通用设备制造业	Manufacture of General Purpose Machinery	3050943	2858968
专用设备制造业	Manufacture of Special Equipment	2817706	2403539
汽车制造业	Manufacture of Motor Vehicle	7356559	6869233
铁路、船舶、航空航天和其他运输设备制造业	Railways,Shipbuilding,Aerospace and Other Transportation Equipment Manufacturing Industry	6047144	5233483
电气机械和器材制造业	Manufacture of Electric Equipment and Machinery	7310020	6859278
计算机、通讯和其他电子设备制造业	Manufacture of Communication Equipment, Computers and other Electronic Equipment	9683763	6996495
仪器仪表制造业	Manufacture of Measuring Instruments and Machinery	1441290	1338595
其他制造业	Manufacture of Other Manufacturing	40999	36277
废弃资源综合利用业	Recycling and Disposal of Waste	35343	32089
金属制品、机械和设备修理业	Metal Products,Machinery and Equipment Repair Industry	54189	42368
电力、热力生产和供应业	Production and Supply of Electric Power and Heat Power	4664898	2900740
燃气生产和供应业	Gas Mining and Supplying Industry	1524508	1235329
水的生产和供应业	Production and Supply of Water	916551	622481

continued7

(10 000yuan)

所有者权益合计 Total Owners' Equities	实收资本 Total Capital Hold	营业收入 Total Revenue	主营业务收入 Revenue from Principal Business	营业成本 Total Cost	税金及附加 Taxs and Other Changes
20650	14117	15449	14738	11737	158
36262	54732	122042	109500	110192	265
1114333	492978	1684201	1572825	1289836	8583
1499034	359640	2163980	2161458	1093198	20226
107320	95052	222858	222856	184222	1372
637936	465370	1051020	1023798	905919	5819
989484	590676	3130677	3094079	2728389	18102
83862	65638	504516	501365	482895	1485
1807141	600378	968895	924876	773404	6528
602332	522993	1613531	1571230	1395414	6545
1878572	471831	2465184	2448284	2058737	15040
2909497	1027322	2528638	2493165	1853355	17037
3319919	1201383	12947754	11541851	11780168	99609
6586652	2223150	5426292	5371803	4566814	21998
5514695	2087658	9092733	8874012	8201025	38562
12615110	4871270	12569611	12432842	10731529	67215
1383755	347196	1702780	1691957	1325048	6415
38693	21367	34959	33759	25282	311
16254	13000	70852	70845	67156	754
135689	142601	92791	91585	71825	708
1582976	1235324	3525768	3444639	3287422	19001
1135736	419306	1793344	1679166	1622252	7045
253198	171848	213136	197452	180147	3690

12-5 续表8

单位：万元

分 组	Classify	销售费用 Expenses for Sales	管理费用 Expenses for Management	研发费用 R&D Expenses
文教、工美、体育和娱乐用品制造业	Manufacture of Articles For Cultural,Educational and Sports Activities	648	1994	3
石油、煤炭及其他燃料加工业	Petroleum, coal and other fuel processing industries	3813	6210	286
化学原料和化学制品制造业	Manufacture of Raw Chemical Materials and Chemical Products	51190	90474	55987
医药制造业	Manufacture of Medicines	600057	214565	44511
化学纤维制造业	Manufacture of Chemical Fibers	1118	5213	2179
橡胶和塑料制品业	Manufacture of Rubber and Plastics	34512	30237	22859
非金属矿物制品业	Manufacture of Non-metallic Mineral Products	95187	110047	38702
黑色金属冶炼和压延加工业	Smelting and Pressing of Ferrous Metals	5128	7539	1219
有色金属冶炼和压延加工业	Smelting and Pressing of Non-ferrous Metals	12567	51300	52436
金属制品业	Manufacture of Metal Products	20596	90335	46406
通用设备制造业	Manufacture of General Purpose Machinery	66968	159948	72623
专用设备制造业	Manufacture of Special Equipment	128744	148270	115181
汽车制造业	Manufacture of Motor Vehicle	241984	248671	168447
铁路、船舶、航空航天和其他运输设备制造业	Railways,Shipbuilding,Aerospace and Other Transportation Equipment Manufacturing Industry	87029	268096	140714
电气机械和器材制造业	Manufacture of Electric Equipment and Machinery	294090	338411	182850
计算机、通讯和其他电子设备制造业	Manufacture of Communication Equipment, Computers and other Electronic Equipment	69681	339999	478777
仪器仪表制造业	Manufacture of Measuring Instruments and Machinery	49280	109359	76685
其他制造业	Manufacture of Other Manufacturing	1652	3396	3253
废弃资源综合利用业	Recycling and Disposal of Waste	968	1745	223
金属制品、机械和设备修理业	Metal Products,Machinery and Equipment Repair Industry	638	13288	2257
电力、热力生产和供应业	Production and Supply of Electric Power and Heat Power	7300	90750	8256
燃气生产和供应业	Gas Mining and Supplying Industry	45887	47395	3620
水的生产和供应业	Production and Supply of Water	6810	20565	876

continued8

(10 000yuan)

财务费用 Financial cost	营业利润 Operating Profit	利润总额 Total Profits	亏损企业亏损总额 Total Loss of Deficit Enterprises	利税总额 Total Pre-tax Profits	应付职工薪酬 Salary Payable	本年应交增值税 Value Added Tax Payable
384	526	694	115	1233	2624	381
2675	-1705	-1500	1959	563	5237	1798
46753	272394	277345	26653	312482	116425	26553
26283	169485	177206	13661	303257	237241	105826
718	22059	22141		28541	12124	5028
33158	47772	47864	5071	72555	82391	18873
29190	111652	118862	26466	233029	166428	96066
1925	4815	5210	316	10975	12962	4280
15143	61052	63412	20722	91350	98422	21411
14718	62752	70989	21088	100547	239688	23013
3728	125780	135073	15964	209346	247161	59234
28793	285127	319106	57923	399436	315774	63293
-1707	507602	514020	4063	791078	814044	177449
24818	343627	352556	11589	436784	949528	62230
54902	330126	340791	55723	414487	826346	35134
95860	1589505	1596387	71471	1799151	839182	135549
3318	157926	163540	4805	192640	238128	22685
831	544	928	114	2486	6609	1247
2152	882	1036	129	7187	1672	5397
112	4636	5840	6632	10427	25770	3880
61575	66473	89492	22683	171587	375997	63093
15787	82585	88207	2744	113599	101279	18347
16131	-11138	-10087	16329	-3443	52625	2955

12-6 规模以上国有及国有控股工业企业主要经济指标（2020年）

单位：万元

分 组	Classify	企业单位数（个） Number of Enterprises (unit)	亏损企业 Loss Making Enterprises
总计	**Total**	**326**	**58**
#亏损企业	Deficit Enterprises	58	58
按隶属关系分	**Grouped by Jurisdiction of Management**		
#中央企业	Central Enterprises	110	14
地方企业	Provincial Enterprises	216	44
按轻重工业分	**Grouped by Light Industry and Heavy Industry**		
轻工业	Light Industry	32	7
重工业	Heavy Industry	294	51
按企业规模分	**Grouped by Size of Enterprises**		
大型企业	Large-size	43	5
中型企业	Medium-size	80	12
小型企业	Small-size	169	35
微型企业	Microenterprise	34	6
按工业行业大类分	**Grouped by Sector**		
煤炭开采和洗选业	Mining and Washing of Coal		
石油和天然气开采业	Extraction of Petroleum and Natural Gas		
黑色金属矿采选业	Mining and Processing of Ferrous Metal Ores		
有色金属矿采选业	Mining and Processing of Non-ferrous Metal Ores		
非金属矿采选业	Mining and Processing of Nonmetal Ores		
开采专业及辅助性活动	Mining Professional and Auxiliary Activity	2	
其他采矿业	Mining of Other Ores		
农副食品加工业	Processing of Food from Agricultural Porducts	1	1
食品制造业	Manufacture of Foods	8	1
酒、饮料和精制茶制造业	Manufacture of Alcohol,Beverages and Tea	1	
烟草制品业	Manufacture of Tobacco	1	
纺织业	Manufacture of Textile	5	1
纺织服装、服饰业	Textile, apparel industry		
皮革、毛皮、羽毛及其制品和制鞋业	Manufacture of Leather, Fur, Feather and Related Products, and Shoes	1	1
木材加工和木、竹、藤、棕、草制品业	Processing of Timber, Manufacture of Wood,Plato and Straw Products		

Major Economic Indicators of State-owned and State-holding Share Industrial Enterprises above Designated Size (2020)

(10 000yuan)

平均用工人数（人）Average Number of Employed Persons (person)	资产总计 Total Assets	流动资产合计 Total Working Capitals	固定资产原价 Origing Value of Fixed Assets	累计折旧 Accumulative Total Depreciation
254543	**55824047**	**33940418**	**24057047**	**10969419**
24082	6994304	2926755	4140029	971498
143440	26239752	15594269	13222656	6812743
111103	29584296	18346149	10834391	4156676
20830	3299522	2167213	1337984	667736
233713	52524525	31773205	22719063	10301684
177850	38618879	24272099	17193007	8874554
51111	10103552	6091872	3393113	1360815
23095	5626244	3279651	2091923	710634
2487	1475372	296796	1379003	23417
11808	1168597	793291	749921	510737
110	122526	81090	27073	20860
2903	124029	82130	73998	41178
1286	249470	128009	53472	36841
496	39371	24769	32402	18138
4983	252807	99647	200230	79470
616	65913	43810	8877	5779

12-6 续表1

单位：万元

分　组	Classify	负债合计 Total Liabilites	流动负债合计 Total Working Liabilities
总计	**Total**	**32866582**	**26238234**
#亏损企业	Deficit Enterprises	4810460	3025613
按隶属关系分	**Grouped by Jurisdiction of Management**		
#中央企业	Central Enterprises	13802207	11260253
地方企业	Provincial Enterprises	19064375	14977981
按轻重工业分	**Grouped by Light Industry and Heavy Industry**		
轻工业	Light Industry	2088930	1349971
重工业	Heavy Industry	30777652	24888263
按企业规模分	**Grouped by Size of Enterprises**		
大型企业	Large-size	22659695	19260659
中型企业	Medium-size	5215905	3941309
小型企业	Small-size	3575510	2926649
微型企业	Microenterprise	1415472	109617
按工业行业大类分	**Grouped by Sector**		
煤炭开采和洗选业	Mining and Washing of Coal		
石油和天然气开采业	Extraction of Petroleum and Natural Gas		
黑色金属矿采选业	Mining and Processing of Ferrous Metal Ores		
有色金属矿采选业	Mining and Processing of Non-ferrous Metal Ores		
非金属矿采选业	Mining and Processing of Nonmetal Ores		
开采专业及辅助性活动	Mining Professional and Auxiliary Activity	421580	417556
其他采矿业	Mining of Other Ores		
农副食品加工业	Processing of Food from Agricultural Porducts	32245	22244
食品制造业	Manufacture of Foods	59291	57641
酒、饮料和精制茶制造业	Manufacture of Alcohol,Beverages and Tea	155482	94076
烟草制品业	Manufacture of Tobacco	3074	3074
纺织业	Manufacture of Textile	145494	49514
纺织服装、服饰业	Textile, apparel industry		
皮革、毛皮、羽毛及其制品和制鞋业	Manufacture of Leather, Fur, Feather and Related Products, and Shoes	23424	18713
木材加工和木、竹、藤、棕、草制品业	Processing of Timber, Manufacture of Wood,Plato and Straw Products		

continued1

(10 000yuan)

所有者权益合计 Total Owners' Equities	实收资本 Total Capital Hold	营业收入 Total Revenue	主营业务收入 Revenue from Principal Business	营业成本 Total Cost	税金及附加 Taxs and Other Changes
22791045	**9121254**	**33582636**	**31898502**	**29941456**	**166749**
2105861	1400702	1796956	1652545	1674648	14974
12403681	4927508	14328253	14055733	12848814	68612
10387364	4193746	19254384	17842769	17092643	98137
1210592	562143	2043679	1988738	1696707	19333
21580453	8559111	31538957	29909764	28244750	147415
15959183	5441141	25114943	23719903	22569821	121221
4887648	2327455	4978002	4854304	4343603	27773
2050733	1299856	3311940	3260455	2872566	16637
-106519	52802	177752	63839	155466	1118
747017	470000	791374	776163	712117	4806
90281	10000	1649	1265	1321	15
64738	30100	260737	246808	224743	1025
93988	28790	269516	269516	196407	8638
36297	27400	11840	11731	5619	394
107313	32421	91641	78880	81375	1082
42490	34500	34434	33968	29466	339

12-6 续表2

单位：万元

分 组	Classify	销售费用 Expenses for Sales	管理费用 Expenses for Management	研发费用 R&D Expenses
总计	**Total**	**579579**	**1249148**	**751846**
#亏损企业	Deficit Enterprises	43602	133916	50807
按隶属关系分	**Grouped by Jurisdiction of Management**			
#中央企业	Central Enterprises	176921	662543	386725
地方企业	Provincial Enterprises	402659	586605	365121
按轻重工业分	**Grouped by Light Industry and Heavy Industry**			
轻工业	Light Industry	79061	83380	29460
重工业	Heavy Industry	500518	1165768	722386
按企业规模分	**Grouped by Size of Enterprises**			
大型企业	Large-size	412425	883147	524812
中型企业	Medium-size	93521	207718	132260
小型企业	Small-size	62695	128916	92852
微型企业	Microenterprise	10938	29367	1922
按工业行业大类分	**Grouped by Sector**			
煤炭开采和洗选业	Mining and Washing of Coal			
石油和天然气开采业	Extraction of Petroleum and Natural Gas			
黑色金属矿采选业	Mining and Processing of Ferrous Metal Ores			
有色金属矿采选业	Mining and Processing of Non-ferrous Metal Ores			
非金属矿采选业	Mining and Processing of Nonmetal Ores			
开采专业及辅助性活动	Mining Professional and Auxiliary Activity	2764	14698	37738
其他采矿业	Mining of Other Ores			
农副食品加工业	Processing of Food from Agricultural Porducts		1236	
食品制造业	Manufacture of Foods	10723	12529	95
酒、饮料和精制茶制造业	Manufacture of Alcohol,Beverages and Tea	29626	4643	
烟草制品业	Manufacture of Tobacco	957	3000	
纺织业	Manufacture of Textile	1113	5944	2572
纺织服装、服饰业	Textile, apparel industry			
皮革、毛皮、羽毛及其制品和制鞋业	Manufacture of Leather, Fur, Feather and Related Products, and Shoes	1232	1492	319
木材加工和木、竹、藤、棕、草制品业	Processing of Timber, Manufacture of Wood,Plato and Straw Products			

continued2

(10 000yuan)

财务费用 Financial cost	营业利润 Operating Profit	利润总额 Total Profits	亏损企业亏损总额 Total Loss of Deficit Enterprises	利税总额 Total Pre-tax Profits	应付职工薪酬 Salary Payable	本年应交增值税 Value Added Tax Payable
188278	**1384852**	**1456961**	**231823**	**2115213**	**3829947**	**491503**
85789	-239664	-231823	231823	-195500	224654	21349
73827	557134	570949	88000	857630	2299999	218070
114451	827718	886012	143823	1257583	1529948	273434
21287	146504	145762	8872	211591	229984	46495
166992	1238348	1311199	222951	1903622	3599963	445008
79572	1072494	1092019	24857	1578295	2971230	365055
36560	200515	236005	83671	343001	593948	79223
48399	121730	132022	81981	192269	259158	43610
23747	-9887	-3085	41314	1649	5611	3616
-4475	29452	28327		35014	260793	1881
426	-1349	-202	202	-182	542	5
112	12271	12127	2260	17119	26412	3967
-2550	34409	34425		52187	19333	9124
-282	2150	1957		3475	5734	1125
128	2529	2294	1750	4540	26559	1164
146	-645	-598	598	85	4170	344

12-6 续表3

单位：万元

分组	Classify	企业单位数（个） Number of Enterprises (unit)	亏损企业 Loss Making Enterprises
家具制造业	Manufacture of Furniture		
造纸和纸制品业	Manufacture of Paper and Paper Products		
印刷和记录媒介复制业	Printing,Reproduction of Recording Media	6	2
文教、工美、体育和娱乐用品制造业	Manufacture of Articles For Cultural,Educational and Sports Activities	1	
石油、煤炭和其他燃料加工业	Petroleum, coal and other fuel processing industries		
化学原料及化学制品制造业	Manufacture of Raw Chemical Materials and Chemical Products	19	4
医药制造业	Manufacture of Medicines	2	1
化学纤维制造业	Manufacture of Chemical Fibers	2	
橡胶和塑料制品业	Manufacture of Rubber and Plastics	5	1
非金属矿物制品业	Manufacture of Non-metallic Mineral Products	16	4
黑色金属冶炼和压延加工业	Smelting and Pressing of Ferrous Metals	2	
有色金属冶炼和压延加工业	Smelting and Pressing of Non-ferrous Metals	16	5
金属制品业	Manufacture of Metal Products	16	2
通用设备制造业	Manufacture of General Purpose Machinery	24	5
专用设备制造业	Manufacture of Special Equipment	31	3
汽车制造业	Manufacture of Motor Vehicle	18	1
铁路、船舶、航空航天和其他运输设备制造业	Railways,Shipbuilding,Aerospace and Other Transportation Equipment Manufacturing Industry	35	1
电气机械和器材制造业	Manufacture of Electric Equipment and Machinery	32	4
计算机、通讯和其他电子设备制造业	Manufacture of Communication Equipment, Computers and other Electronic Equipment	33	4
仪器仪表制造业	Manufacture of Measuring Instruments and Machinery	9	1
其他制造业	Manufacture of Other Manufacturing		
废弃资源综合利用业	Recycling and Disposal of Waste	1	
金属制品、机械和设备修理业	Metal Products,Machinery and Equipment Repair Industry	2	
电力、热力的生产和供应业	Production and Supply of Electric Power and Heat Power	20	7
燃气生产和供应业	Gas Mining and Supplying Industry	8	3
水的生产和供应业	Production and Supply of Water	9	6

continued3

(10 000yuan)

平均用工人数（人） Average Number of Employed Persons (person)	资产总计 Total Assets	流动资产合计 Total Working Capitals	固定资产原价 Origing Value of Fixed Assets	累计折旧 Accumulative Total Depreciation
3604	476058	287382	392402	280201
100	2781	2471	385	227
12849	967657	463244	806291	120610
669	52248	37436	24202	12747
521	90925	65432	84318	54878
7142	2286398	1478553	655320	161187
3454	635611	473287	176894	56866
666	130350	95701	72426	33590
4301	2504033	1610728	559556	196131
12209	1626056	894312	769165	353970
10585	4037910	3200697	692128	326565
13041	3271295	2238179	604943	271859
25244	6700895	5652717	1293534	718977
56420	11057638	7188821	2981912	1590499
21728	5209037	3799471	1576505	853529
21927	4278255	1969513	1930899	339533
8757	2005180	1430638	572938	246320
92	16747	3133	10588	1379
874	56233	26640	6665	2978
17903	5189745	976257	7147782	3830926
6450	2237445	535447	1673594	532770
3805	968838	257616	878628	270678

12-6 续表4

单位：万元

分 组	Classify	负债合计 Total Liabilites	流动负债合计 Total Working Liabilities
家具制造业	Manufacture of Furniture		
造纸和纸制品业	Manufacture of Paper and Paper Products		
印刷和记录媒介复制业	Printing,Reproduction of Recording Media	125458	114238
文教、工美、体育和娱乐用品制造业	Manufacture of Articles For Cultural,Educational and Sports Activities	631	631
石油、煤炭和其他燃料加工业	Petroleum, coal and other fuel processing industries		
化学原料及化学制品制造业	Manufacture of Raw Chemical Materials and Chemical Products	766804	335757
医药制造业	Manufacture of Medicines	15672	15416
化学纤维制造业	Manufacture of Chemical Fibers	9161	9121
橡胶和塑料制品业	Manufacture of Rubber and Plastics	1719636	1114303
非金属矿物制品业	Manufacture of Non-metallic Mineral Products	453311	416648
黑色金属冶炼和压延加工业	Smelting and Pressing of Ferrous Metals	83009	78194
有色金属冶炼和压延加工业	Smelting and Pressing of Non-ferrous Metals	894947	609877
金属制品业	Manufacture of Metal Products	1238375	843718
通用设备制造业	Manufacture of General Purpose Machinery	2628269	2489552
专用设备制造业	Manufacture of Special Equipment	1592419	1338372
汽车制造业	Manufacture of Motor Vehicle	4649711	4453685
铁路、船舶、航空航天和其他运输设备制造业	Railways,Shipbuilding,Aerospace and Other Transportation Equipment Manufacturing Industry	5430723	4664475
电气机械和器材制造业	Manufacture of Electric Equipment and Machinery	2251963	2060844
计算机、通讯和其他电子设备制造业	Manufacture of Communication Equipment, Computers and other Electronic Equipment	3149871	1980833
仪器仪表制造业	Manufacture of Measuring Instruments and Machinery	1095932	1015878
其他制造业	Manufacture of Other Manufacturing		
废弃资源综合利用业	Recycling and Disposal of Waste	10639	8639
金属制品、机械和设备修理业	Metal Products,Machinery and Equipment Repair Industry	11798	9760
电力、热力的生产和供应业	Production and Supply of Electric Power and Heat Power	3815716	2435542
燃气生产和供应业	Gas Mining and Supplying Industry	1274972	1004242
水的生产和供应业	Production and Supply of Water	806977	575693

continued4

(10 000yuan)

所有者权益合计 Total Owners' Equities	实收资本 Total Capital Hold	营业收入 Total Revenue	主营业务收入 Revenue from Principal Business	营业成本 Total Cost	税金及附加 Taxs and Other Changes
350600	184919	451227	447508	365494	2879
2150	200	2019	2019	1184	14
124457	110641	607748	541916	497775	3430
36577	14490	51412	51351	36531	401
81764	74052	139927	139925	118440	720
566762	402844	859170	833300	747809	4924
182300	150314	426191	423569	386274	2492
47341	38911	356801	354456	344295	1144
1609085	484591	537398	508058	406458	4828
387681	375686	949582	926191	822386	2780
1415034	196645	1872760	1861566	1611474	10642
1678875	619703	1236358	1223161	1033881	7732
2049477	856284	9287567	8191795	8539920	30185
5626916	1896838	4626160	4584798	4021023	15648
2957074	799895	3022850	2897098	2897837	20951
1105806	525706	1394985	1383754	1087597	11245
909248	183721	1228279	1221043	1024521	3066
6108	5000	5514	5507	2753	112
44435	46247	28712	28712	21596	307
1374029	1114134	3315232	3251012	3148674	17707
901675	319028	1545808	1442931	1422583	6022
151528	88192	175746	160501	151903	3222

12-6 续表5

单位：万元

分 组	Classify	销售费用 Expenses for Sales	管理费用 Expenses for Management	研发费用 R&D Expenses
家具制造业	Manufacture of Furniture			
造纸和纸制品业	Manufacture of Paper and Paper Products			
印刷和记录媒介复制业	Printing,Reproduction of Recording Media	10001	32797	8326
文教、工美、体育和娱乐用品制造业	Manufacture of Articles For Cultural,Educational and Sports Activities		577	
石油、煤炭和其他燃料加工业	Petroleum, coal and other fuel processing industries			
化学原料及化学制品制造业	Manufacture of Raw Chemical Materials and Chemical Products	15825	41614	25422
医药制造业	Manufacture of Medicines	4602	3272	234
化学纤维制造业	Manufacture of Chemical Fibers	498	3249	1969
橡胶和塑料制品业	Manufacture of Rubber and Plastics	26913	19172	19383
非金属矿物制品业	Manufacture of Non-metallic Mineral Products	5311	10640	8935
黑色金属冶炼和压延加工业	Smelting and Pressing of Ferrous Metals	3171	3742	258
有色金属冶炼和压延加工业	Smelting and Pressing of Non-ferrous Metals	5872	34476	35106
金属制品业	Manufacture of Metal Products	3111	54964	38012
通用设备制造业	Manufacture of General Purpose Machinery	37044	110439	52632
专用设备制造业	Manufacture of Special Equipment	38120	61911	51990
汽车制造业	Manufacture of Motor Vehicle	178431	108958	131335
铁路、船舶、航空航天和其他运输设备制造业	Railways,Shipbuilding,Aerospace and Other Transportation Equipment Manufacturing Industry	52807	216137	107172
电气机械和器材制造业	Manufacture of Electric Equipment and Machinery	75178	166793	98261
计算机、通讯和其他电子设备制造业	Manufacture of Communication Equipment, Computers and other Electronic Equipment	27793	131010	73113
仪器仪表制造业	Manufacture of Measuring Instruments and Machinery	9873	71556	47656
其他制造业	Manufacture of Other Manufacturing			
废弃资源综合利用业	Recycling and Disposal of Waste	416	1158	
金属制品、机械和设备修理业	Metal Products,Machinery and Equipment Repair Industry	15	3913	399
电力、热力的生产和供应业	Production and Supply of Electric Power and Heat Power	797	78147	7301
燃气生产和供应业	Gas Mining and Supplying Industry	30877	32590	3620
水的生产和供应业	Production and Supply of Water	6511	18493	

continued5

(10 000yuan)

财务费用 Financial cost	营业利润 Operating Profit	利润总额 Total Profits	亏损企业亏损总额 Total Loss of Deficit Enterprises	利税总额 Total Pre-tax Profits	应付职工薪酬 Salary Payable	本年应交增值税 Value Added Tax Payable
2117	32977	32749	3474	47229	77723	11601
-1	245	245		369	578	110
8124	56066	59669	14781	75260	65961	12162
-186	6580	6572	588	8945	4862	1972
-140	13030	13076		17656	8919	3860
29070	41039	39956	2907	61258	68765	16378
5953	7054	7320	7416	21665	48026	11853
1040	3680	3530		7539	8097	2865
9931	41815	42771	19937	63446	65057	15847
9570	43439	50065	17264	59667	169032	6823
-2402	89316	93936	11081	145585	167371	41007
11225	68647	91032	31497	130522	178845	31758
-29277	383371	388550	560	524101	529841	105366
19750	215153	218608	6978	262483	858488	28228
14688	118347	120430	21714	209387	336355	68006
48400	4905	8469	54427	39647	217248	19933
-4347	99351	98491	578	109038	166118	7481
391	811	814		1306	992	380
34	2730	3116		5734	12631	2311
43579	31062	49744	16219	136160	362892	68710
14222	60890	63179	2610	84560	90070	15359
13031	-14471	-13689	14984	-8584	48537	1884

12-7 规模以上外商及港澳台商投资工业企业主要经济指标（2020年）

单位：万元

分　组	Classify	企业单位数（个）Number of Enterprises (unit)	亏损企业 Loss Making Enterprises
总计	**Total**	**124**	**32**
#亏损企业	Deficit Enterprises	32	32
按登记注册类型分组	**Grouped by Type of Registration**		
港澳台商投资	Enterprises with Funds from Hong Kong, Macao &Taiwan	22	6
与港澳台商合资经营	Cooperative Enterprises	13	5
与港澳台商合作经营	Joint-venture Enterprises	1	
港澳台商独资	Enterprises with Sole Investment	8	1
港澳台商投资股份有限公司	Share-holding Corporations Ltd. With their Investment		
其他港澳台投资	Other		
外商投资	Foreign Funded Enterprises	102	26
中外合资经营	Joint-venture Enterprises	55	13
中外合作经营	Cooperation Enterprises		
外资企业	Foreign Funded Enterprises	43	11
外商投资股份有限公司	Share-holding Corporations Ltd. With Foreign Funds	4	2
其他外商投资	Other		
按轻重工业分	**Grouped by Light Industry and Heavy Industry**		
轻工业	Light Industry	31	10
重工业	Heavy Industry	93	22
按企业规模分	**Grouped by Size of Enterprises**		
大型企业	Large-size	10	1
中型企业	Medium-size	31	6
小型企业	Small-size	79	24
微型企业	Microenterprise	4	1
按工业行业大类分	**Grouped by Sector**		
煤炭开采和洗选业	Mining and Washing of Coal		
石油和天然气开采业	Extraction of Petroleum and Natural Gas		
黑色金属矿采选业	Mining and Processing of Ferrous Metal Ores		
有色金属矿采选业	Mining and Processing of Non-ferrous Metal Ores		
非金属矿采选业	Mining and Processing of Nonmetal Ores		
开采专业及辅助性活动	Mining Professional and Auxiliary Activity		
其他采矿业	Mining of Other Ores		

Major Economic Indicators of Foreign,Hong Kong,Macao and Taiwan Invested Industrial Enterprises above Designated Size（2020）

(10 000 yuan)

平均用工人数（人） Average Number of Employed Persons (person)	资产总计 Total Assets	流动资产合计 Total Working Capitals	固定资产原价 Origing Value of Fixed Assets	累计折旧 Accumulative Total Depreciation
68991	**18588600**	**6967968**	**17948075**	**9330255**
7850	1311496	583186	752090	339125
26042	3397721	1929384	1294930	569466
22907	3186824	1793644	1146759	477844
54	1645	1422	985	762
3081	209252	134318	147186	90859
42949	15190879	5038584	16653144	8760789
17805	3241950	2075967	1509040	716758
21069	10931509	2431734	14760985	7941331
4075	1017420	530883	383120	102701
16210	2666499	1385842	1500441	666941
52781	15922101	5582126	16447633	8663315
40994	13880975	4054485	15635778	8183746
19047	2670658	1799413	1145828	607234
8919	2025203	1105154	1161162	536687
31	11765	8916	5307	2588

12-7 续表1

单位：万元

分 组	Classify	负债合计 Total Liabilites	流动负债合计 Total Working Liabilities
总计	**Total**	**7865657**	**6612613**
#亏损企业	Deficit Enterprises	776304	584061
按登记注册类型分组	**Grouped by Type of Registration**		
港澳台商投资	Enterprises with Funds from Hong Kong, Macao &Taiwan	2332653	2064648
与港澳台商合资经营	Cooperative Enterprises	2250648	1986605
与港澳台商合作经营	Joint-venture Enterprises	125	125
港澳台商独资	Enterprises with Sole Investment	81881	77918
港澳台商投资股份有限公司	Share-holding Corporations Ltd. With their Investment		
其他港澳台投资	Other		
外商投资	Foreign Funded Enterprises	5533004	4547965
中外合资经营	Joint-venture Enterprises	1811466	1734871
中外合作经营	Cooperation Enterprises		
外资企业	Foreign Funded Enterprises	3179345	2347449
外商投资股份有限公司	Share-holding Corporations Ltd. With Foreign Funds	542193	465645
其他外商投资	Other		
按轻重工业分	**Grouped by Light Industry and Heavy Industry**		
轻工业	Light Industry	1514165	1376715
重工业	Heavy Industry	6351492	5235898
按企业规模分	**Grouped by Size of Enterprises**		
大型企业	Large-size	5528362	4586802
中型企业	Medium-size	1441489	1386059
小型企业	Small-size	887854	633180
微型企业	Microenterprise	7952	6572
按工业行业大类分	**Grouped by Sector**		
煤炭开采和洗选业	Mining and Washing of Coal		
石油和天然气开采业	Extraction of Petroleum and Natural Gas		
黑色金属矿采选业	Mining and Processing of Ferrous Metal Ores		
有色金属矿采选业	Mining and Processing of Non-ferrous Metal Ores		
非金属矿采选业	Mining and Processing of Nonmetal Ores		
开采专业及辅助性活动	Mining Professional and Auxiliary Activity		
其他采矿业	Mining of Other Ores		

continued 1

(10 000 yuan)

所有者权益合计 Total Owners' Equities	实收资本 Total Capital Hold	营业收入 Total Revenue	主营业务收入 Revenue from Principal Business	营业成本 Total Cost	税金及附加 Taxs and Other Changes
10722798	**4981728**	**11727583**	**11316185**	**9576739**	**125925**
535047	449780	596463	583379	498607	4150
1065068	288287	3047963	2753237	2730905	66406
936176	225917	2752361	2466598	2507014	64730
1520	714	1939	1935	1694	11
127372	61656	293663	284705	222196	1665
9657730	4693441	8679620	8562948	6845834	59519
1430484	790686	2682237	2586086	2124030	10370
7752019	3843046	4964950	4944429	4056739	42540
475227	59710	1032433	1032433	665066	6609
1152335	489124	2689428	2668474	1895450	15158
9570464	4492604	9038155	8647711	7681289	110767
8352613	3627741	8084484	7728129	6762308	106196
1229168	654932	2273619	2234127	1773349	11257
1137349	693709	1350390	1336440	1023006	8435
3668	5346	19091	17490	18077	37

12-7 续表2

单位：万元

分 组	Classify	销售费用 Expenses for Sales	管理费用 Expenses for Management	研发费用 R&D Expenses
总计	**Total**	**529100**	**469050**	**280145**
#亏损企业	Deficit Enterprises	60190	42644	19381
按登记注册类型分组	**Grouped by Type of Registration**			
港澳台商投资	Enterprises with Funds from Hong Kong, Macao &Taiwan	65034	114796	27669
与港澳台商合资经营	Cooperative Enterprises	27153	102615	24316
与港澳台商合作经营	Joint-venture Enterprises	131	139	
港澳台商独资	Enterprises with Sole Investment	37751	12041	3353
港澳台商投资股份有限公司	Share-holding Corporations Ltd. With their Investment			
其他港澳台投资	Other			
外商投资	Foreign Funded Enterprises	464065	354254	252476
中外合资经营	Joint-venture Enterprises	183847	97056	37120
中外合作经营	Cooperation Enterprises			
外资企业	Foreign Funded Enterprises	107751	147963	215234
外商投资股份有限公司	Share-holding Corporations Ltd. With Foreign Funds	172468	109236	122
其他外商投资	Other			
按轻重工业分	**Grouped by Light Industry and Heavy Industry**			
轻工业	Light Industry	399548	170949	13130
重工业	Heavy Industry	129551	298102	267015
按企业规模分	**Grouped by Size of Enterprises**			
大型企业	Large-size	306560	303462	217980
中型企业	Medium-size	161813	89779	34084
小型企业	Small-size	60587	74424	28081
微型企业	Microenterprise	139	1385	0
按工业行业大类分	**Grouped by Sector**			
煤炭开采和洗选业	Mining and Washing of Coal			
石油和天然气开采业	Extraction of Petroleum and Natural Gas			
黑色金属矿采选业	Mining and Processing of Ferrous Metal Ores			
有色金属矿采选业	Mining and Processing of Non-ferrous Metal Ores			
非金属矿采选业	Mining and Processing of Nonmetal Ores			
开采专业及辅助性活动	Mining Professional and Auxiliary Activity			
其他采矿业	Mining of Other Ores			

continued 2

(10 000 yuan)

财务费用 Financial cost	营业利润 Operating Profit	利润总额 Total Profits	亏损企业亏损总额 Total Loss of Deficit Enterprises	利税总额 Total Pre-tax Profits	应付职工薪酬 Salary Payable	本年应交增值税 Value Added Tax Payable
106311	**1224414**	**1225196**	**49553**	**1499972**	**937715**	**148851**
21957	-49641	-49553	49553	-39139	78385	6264
26902	57878	57730	4452	166001	257979	41866
24163	44260	43059	4010	144644	226248	36855
-5	-31	17		98	413	71
2743	13649	14654	441	21259	31318	4940
79408	1166536	1167467	45102	1333970	679736	106985
17582	267725	271129	21488	325711	199051	44212
39019	841310	838628	15756	917340	355627	36172
22808	57501	57710	7858	90919	125057	26600
34027	206012	206933	18619	280806	251607	58715
72284	1018403	1018263	30935	1219166	686108	90136
60633	871688	863035	2679	1063440	635854	94209
25555	196180	200179	18743	245774	197574	34338
20304	157055	162001	27747	190739	103947	20304
-182	-509	-18	385	18	341	

12-7 续表3

单位：万元

分 组	Classify	企业单位数（个） Number of Enterprises (unit)	亏损企业 Loss Making Enterprises
农副食品加工业	Processing of Food from Agricultural Porducts	1	
食品制造业	Manufacture of Foods	7	3
酒、饮料和精制茶制造业	Manufacture of Alcohol,Beverages and Tea	6	2
烟草制品业	Manufacture of Tobacco		
纺织业	Manufacture of Textile		
纺织服装、服饰业	Textile, apparel industry		
皮革、毛皮、羽毛及其制品和制鞋业	Manufacture of Leather, Fur, Feather and Related Products, and Shoes		
木材加工和木、竹、藤、棕、草制品业	Processing of Timber,Manufacture of Wood,Plam and Straw Products		
家具制造业	Manufacture of Furniture		
造纸和纸制品业	Manufacture of Paper and Paper Products	2	
印刷和记录媒介复制业	Printing,Reproduction of Recording Media	1	
文教、工美、体育和娱乐用品制造业	Manufacture of Articles For Cultural,Educational and Sports Activities		
石油、煤炭和其他燃料加工业	Petroleum, coal and other fuel processing industries	1	
化学原料及化学制品制造业	Manufacture of Raw Chemical Materials and Chemical Products	8	4
医药制造业	Manufacture of Medicines	5	2
化学纤维制造业	Manufacture of Chemical Fibers	2	
橡胶和塑料制品业	Manufacture of Rubber and Plastics	1	
非金属矿物制品业	Manufacture of Non-metallic Mineral Products	7	2
黑色金属冶炼和压延加工业	Smelting and Pressing of Ferrous Metals		
有色金属冶炼和压延加工业	Smelting and Pressing of Non-ferrous Metals	4	2
金属制品业	Manufacture of Metal Products	5	1
通用设备制造业	Manufacture of General Purpose Machinery	6	3
专用设备制造业	Manufacture of Special Equipment	11	2
汽车制造业	Manufacture of Motor Vehicle	11	1
铁路、船舶、航空航天和其他运输设备制造业	Railways,Shipbuilding,Aerospace and Other Transportation Equipment Manufacturing Industry	7	2
电气机械和器材制造业	Manufacture of Electric Equipment and Machinery	11	3
计算机、通讯和其他电子设备制造业	Manufacture of Communication Equipment, Computers and other Electronic Equipment	14	1
仪器仪表制造业	Manufacture of Measuring Instruments and Machinery	3	
其他制造业	Manufacture of Other Manufacturing	1	
废弃资源综合利用业	Recycling and Disposal of Waste		
金属制品、机械和设备修理业	Metal Products,Machinery and Equipment Repair Industry	7	3
电力、热力生产和供应业	Production and Supply of Electric Power and Heat Power	1	
燃气生产和供应业	Gas Mining and Supplying Industry	2	1
水的生产和供应业	Production and Supply of Water		

continued 3

(10 000 yuan)

平均用工人数（人） Average Number of Employed Persons (person)	资产总计 Total Assets	流动资产合计 Total Working Capitals	固定资产原价 Origing Value of Fixed Assets	累计折旧 Accumulative Total Depreciation
34	1284	1117	201	53
4926	344864	188118	215501	106779
4038	627709	279838	371709	229304
337	41588	16332	19482	8757
28	2752	2351	401	111
2300	102690	72081	2077	1037
616	403695	128366	438858	183863
4727	880645	491712	370995	88472
393	119575	62563	138067	85653
48	11812	5679	5600	336
1261	314412	206615	186783	104894
389	54764	29172	28528	11506
821	80910	44777	60315	28886
1474	140421	93151	74755	44280
2140	428606	322455	105013	55926
25140	3505702	2126721	1350464	590347
1574	270504	238672	57360	42108
2963	953346	617139	446151	186893
11829	9337856	1647296	13642867	7430502
644	111144	103094	21074	13725
54	1645	1422	985	762
554	84879	44585	42314	14175
100	114149	18124	565	115
2601	653651	226591	368008	101770

12-7 续表4

单位：万元

分组	Classify	负债合计 Total Liabilites	流动负债合计 Total Working Liabilities
农副食品加工业	Processing of Food from Agricultural Porducts	520	520
食品制造业	Manufacture of Foods	170868	165674
酒、饮料和精制茶制造业	Manufacture of Alcohol,Beverages and Tea	379227	350736
烟草制品业	Manufacture of Tobacco		
纺织业	Manufacture of Textile		
纺织服装、服饰业	Textile, apparel industry		
皮革、毛皮、羽毛及其制品和制鞋业	Manufacture of Leather, Fur, Feather and Related Products, and Shoes		
木材加工和木、竹、藤、棕、草制品业	Processing of Timber,Manufacture of Wood,Plam and Straw Products		
家具制造业	Manufacture of Furniture		
造纸和纸制品业	Manufacture of Paper and Paper Products	26992	16036
印刷和记录媒介复制业	Printing,Reproduction of Recording Media	1035	1035
文教、工美、体育和娱乐用品制造业	Manufacture of Articles For Cultural,Educational and Sports Activities		
石油、煤炭和其他燃料加工业	Petroleum, coal and other fuel processing industries	82377	82346
化学原料及化学制品制造业	Manufacture of Raw Chemical Materials and Chemical Products	177465	69395
医药制造业	Manufacture of Medicines	455570	364595
化学纤维制造业	Manufacture of Chemical Fibers	59859	59839
橡胶和塑料制品业	Manufacture of Rubber and Plastics	4660	4660
非金属矿物制品业	Manufacture of Non-metallic Mineral Products	187788	156171
黑色金属冶炼和压延加工业	Smelting and Pressing of Ferrous Metals		
有色金属冶炼和压延加工业	Smelting and Pressing of Non-ferrous Metals	41039	30137
金属制品业	Manufacture of Metal Products	50344	48904
通用设备制造业	Manufacture of General Purpose Machinery	46810	34117
专用设备制造业	Manufacture of Special Equipment	158705	150187
汽车制造业	Manufacture of Motor Vehicle	2411738	2192965
铁路、船舶、航空航天和其他运输设备制造业	Railways,Shipbuilding,Aerospace and Other Transportation Equipment Manufacturing Industry	72426	68325
电气机械和器材制造业	Manufacture of Electric Equipment and Machinery	648586	643315
计算机、通讯和其他电子设备制造业	Manufacture of Communication Equipment, Computers and other Electronic Equipment	2270554	1639253
仪器仪表制造业	Manufacture of Measuring Instruments and Machinery	24713	23213
其他制造业	Manufacture of Other Manufacturing	125	125
废弃资源综合利用业	Recycling and Disposal of Waste		
金属制品、机械和设备修理业	Metal Products,Machinery and Equipment Repair Industry	29090	19414
电力、热力生产和供应业	Production and Supply of Electric Power and Heat Power	62465	6562
燃气生产和供应业	Gas Mining and Supplying Industry	502702	485088
水的生产和供应业	Production and Supply of Water		

continued 4

(10 000 yuan)

所有者权益合计 Total Owners' Equities	实收资本 Total Capital Hold	营业收入 Total Revenue	主营业务收入 Revenue from Principal Business	营业成本 Total Cost	税金及附加 Taxs and Other Changes
764	200	2995	2984	2424	13
173996	82817	404825	400055	297727	3505
248483	85521	376633	364565	265097	2104
14596	6540	54921	52243	47352	164
1716	120	2251	2251	1876	8
20313	33660	69534	69533	65753	19
226229	176695	241357	240175	200243	1040
425076	80632	1050365	1049772	657005	7507
59717	45800	139789	139788	109170	1081
7152	7300	7614	6832	6321	41
126624	54450	193933	190554	147993	1633
13725	18449	28452	27931	26271	233
30565	25203	88529	88172	76015	732
93611	84759	107737	107391	92824	688
269900	91035	299595	298212	230276	1930
1093963	287305	3238919	2932196	2878133	67438
197934	57574	136844	134413	97726	1080
304760	271779	922347	912157	737845	1757
7067302	3337437	3705861	3697529	3080399	32082
86431	10668	89765	89149	52885	588
1520	714	1939	1935	1694	11
55789	71974	44262	43059	38647	198
51685	40398	22167	22159	7018	242
150949	110700	496952	443131	456044	1831

12-7 续表5

单位：万元

分　组	Classify	销售费用 Expenses for Sales	管理费用 Expenses for Management	研发费用 R&D Expenses
农副食品加工业	Processing of Food from Agricultural Porducts	34	138	
食品制造业	Manufacture of Foods	62768	15965	1292
酒、饮料和精制茶制造业	Manufacture of Alcohol,Beverages and Tea	80710	18269	24
烟草制品业	Manufacture of Tobacco			
纺织业	Manufacture of Textile			
纺织服装、服饰业	Textile, apparel industry			
皮革、毛皮、羽毛及其制品和制鞋业	Manufacture of Leather, Fur, Feather and Related Products, and Shoes			
木材加工和木、竹、藤、棕、草制品业	Processing of Timber,Manufacture of Wood,Plam and Straw Products			
家具制造业	Manufacture of Furniture			
造纸和纸制品业	Manufacture of Paper and Paper Products	2132	1069	
印刷和记录媒介复制业	Printing,Reproduction of Recording Media	175	49	
文教、工美、体育和娱乐用品制造业	Manufacture of Articles For Cultural,Educational and Sports Activities			
石油、煤炭和其他燃料加工业	Petroleum, coal and other fuel processing industries		1291	
化学原料及化学制品制造业	Manufacture of Raw Chemical Materials and Chemical Products	8377	9370	1472
医药制造业	Manufacture of Medicines	190335	114407	1950
化学纤维制造业	Manufacture of Chemical Fibers	841	3769	391
橡胶和塑料制品业	Manufacture of Rubber and Plastics	583	652	
非金属矿物制品业	Manufacture of Non-metallic Mineral Products	931	9547	3855
黑色金属冶炼和压延加工业	Smelting and Pressing of Ferrous Metals			
有色金属冶炼和压延加工业	Smelting and Pressing of Non-ferrous Metals	1026	2039	656
金属制品业	Manufacture of Metal Products	1988	4176	1255
通用设备制造业	Manufacture of General Purpose Machinery	5870	6714	2118
专用设备制造业	Manufacture of Special Equipment	10154	18496	13000
汽车制造业	Manufacture of Motor Vehicle	50131	115183	29227
铁路、船舶、航空航天和其他运输设备制造业	Railways,Shipbuilding,Aerospace and Other Transportation Equipment Manufacturing Industry	4947	7452	8222
电气机械和器材制造业	Manufacture of Electric Equipment and Machinery	77536	26040	7127
计算机、通讯和其他电子设备制造业	Manufacture of Communication Equipment, Computers and other Electronic Equipment	4953	82780	208556
仪器仪表制造业	Manufacture of Measuring Instruments and Machinery	6055	5093	563
其他制造业	Manufacture of Other Manufacturing	131	139	
废弃资源综合利用业	Recycling and Disposal of Waste			
金属制品、机械和设备修理业	Metal Products,Machinery and Equipment Repair Industry	72	7178	437
电力、热力生产和供应业	Production and Supply of Electric Power and Heat Power		1185	
燃气生产和供应业	Gas Mining and Supplying Industry	19353	18051	
水的生产和供应业	Production and Supply of Water			

continued 5

(10 000 yuan)

财务费用 Financial cost	营业利润 Operating Profit	利润总额 Total Profits	亏损企业亏损总额 Total Loss of Deficit Enterprises	利税总额 Total Pre-tax Profits	应付职工薪酬 Salary Payable	本年应交增值税 Value Added Tax Payable
-1	387	391		493	244	89
759	58464	58518	5968	77631	41460	15608
5767	4431	4517	7890	18089	38211	11467
898	5629	5831		7282	2637	1287
11	133	138		205	138	59
2287	184	183		1304	2840	1102
6512	13094	13165	6420	15548	9958	1343
16029	65885	67008	1037	105657	134128	31142
774	17579	17605		22313	6697	3627
-26	29	30		71	345	
3163	27732	31042	4205	40733	9487	8058
448	-2059	-1714	2458	-1361	3198	120
1280	3168	3157	682	5714	8288	1825
480	-232	732	3087	1245	16378	-175
1460	25661	24841	3282	30195	28921	3424
23158	117242	116730	560	247175	248984	63008
1631	16392	16435	1301	22409	25955	4895
10046	76568	79139	5943	82538	51188	1642
30115	739690	732745	162	766761	251181	1934
-742	25365	25492		27368	8993	1288
-5	-31	17		98	413	71
-118	-2003	-1929	6424	-1316	9511	415
2447	11275	11287		4401	1271	-7129
-63	19832	19837	135	25418	37292	3750

12-8 规模以上大中型工业企业主要经济指标（2020年）

单位：万元

分　组	Classify	企业单位数（个）Number of Enterprises (unit)	亏损企业 Loss Making Enterprises
总计	**Total**	**244**	**38**
#亏损企业	Deficit Enterprises	38	38
按隶属关系分	**Grouped by Jurisdiction of Management**		
#中央企业	Central Enterprises	57	7
地方企业	Provincial Enterprises	50	9
按登记注册类型分组	**Grouped by Registion Status**		
内资企业	Domestic Investment Enterprises	203	31
国有	State-owned Enterprises	17	2
集体	Collective-owned Enterprises		
股份合作	Share-holding Corperative	1	1
联营	Joint Ownership Enterprises		
有限责任公司	Limited Liability Corporations	107	13
股份有限公司	Share-holding Corperation Ltd.	40	7
私营	Private Enterprises	38	8
其他	Other Domestic Funded Enterprises		
港澳台商投资	Enterprises with Funds from Hong Kong,Macao and Taiwan	7	1
外商投资	Foreign Funded Enterprises	34	6
按轻重工业分	**Grouped by Light Industry and Heavy Industry**		
轻工业	Light Industry	58	8
重工业	Heavy Industry	186	30
按企业规模分	**Grouped by Size of Enterprises**		
大型企业	Large-size	66	8
中型企业	Medium-size	178	30

Major Economic Indicators of Large and Medium-sized Industrial Enterprises above Designated Size (2020)

(10 000 yuan)

平均用工人数（人） Average Number of Employed Persons (person)	资产总计 Total Assets	流动资产合计 Total Working Capitals	固定资产原价 Origing Value of Fixed Assets	累计折旧 Accumulative Total Depreciation
367045	**82072517**	**46879772**	**40491360**	**19928836**
42842	10024123	5829561	3648946	1090993
138651	24835264	14747480	12468580	6676018
74383	24534627	14896732	7455017	3314048
307004	65520885	41025875	23709754	11137856
46800	9344951	4781382	6201417	3012816
652	94893	79001	7825	3386
175776	31814897	20620634	12312801	6141563
47576	16859795	10199954	3298184	1541770
36200	7406350	5344904	1889528	438322
24689	3118034	1804501	1260561	553381
35352	13433599	4049396	15521045	8237599
49843	7778803	4745348	3076099	1326256
317202	74293714	42134424	37415260	18602581
264449	63957670	35270499	34832106	17524711
102596	18114848	11609273	5659254	2404125

12-8 续表1

单位：万元

分组	Classify	负债合计 Total Liabilites	流动负债合计 Total Working Liabilities
总计	**Total**	**44357196**	**37267178**
#亏损企业	Deficit Enterprises	6665436	5720695
按隶属关系分	**Grouped by Jurisdiction of Management**		
#中央企业	Central Enterprises	12836714	10691616
地方企业	Provincial Enterprises	14929191	12867126
按登记注册类型分组	**Grouped by Registion Status**		
内资企业	Domestic Investment Enterprises	37387345	31294317
国有	State-owned Enterprises	6317238	4690636
集体	Collective-owned Enterprises		
股份合作	Share-holding Corperative	85977	73187
联营	Joint Ownership Enterprises		
有限责任公司	Limited Liability Corporations	17717971	15100437
股份有限公司	Share-holding Corperation Ltd.	8363463	6830977
私营	Private Enterprises	4902697	4599080
其他	Other Domestic Funded Enterprises		
港澳台商投资	Enterprises with Funds from Hong Kong,Macao and Taiwan	2225625	2015977
外商投资	Foreign Funded Enterprises	4744226	3956884
按轻重工业分	**Grouped by Light Industry and Heavy Industry**		
轻工业	Light Industry	4666339	3488408
重工业	Heavy Industry	39690858	33778770
按企业规模分	**Grouped by Size of Enterprises**		
大型企业	Large-size	34978764	29685917
中型企业	Medium-size	9378432	7581261

continued 1

(10 000 yuan)

所有者权益合计 Total Owners' Equities	实收资本 Total Capital Hold	营业收入 Total Revenue	主营业务收入 Revenue from Principal Business	营业成本 Total Cost	税金及附加 Taxs and Other Changes
37715319	**13652653**	**54370919**	**52301392**	**47197394**	**318554**
3358687	1662623	5185266	5068804	4673583	23668
11998549	4638947	13193459	12970169	11832893	64308
9605436	2915095	18481100	17211978	16314838	72384
28133538	9369980	44012816	42339137	38661737	201101
3027713	1233485	5530874	5465895	4903940	23716
8915	1754	36721	36721	30869	49
14096926	5563660	22700545	21248498	19821602	125459
8496332	1785420	7923245	7798789	6953263	28115
2503652	785661	7821431	7789234	6952064	23762
892409	193369	2898851	2604721	2623558	65790
8689372	4089304	7459252	7357535	5912099	51664
3112464	1077255	6349893	6228742	4525944	43318
34602855	12575399	48021026	46072650	42671450	275236
28978905	10136137	43514049	41706335	38642760	255096
8736414	3516516	10856870	10595057	8554634	63458

12-8 续表2

单位：万元

分　组	Classify	销售费用 Expenses for Sales	管理费用 Expenses for Management	研发费用 R&D Expenses
总计	**Total**	**1523531**	**1807277**	**1181490**
#亏损企业	Deficit Enterprises	177668	189710	94291
按隶属关系分	**Grouped by Jurisdiction of Management**			
#中央企业	Central Enterprises	162028	627870	357799
地方企业	Provincial Enterprises	550942	515224	235421
按登记注册类型分组	**Grouped by Registion Status**			
内资企业	Domestic Investment Enterprises	1055158	1414036	929426
国有	State-owned Enterprises	38280	239962	124159
集体	Collective-owned Enterprises			
股份合作	Share-holding Corperative	2940	554	
联营	Joint Ownership Enterprises			
有限责任公司	Limited Liability Corporations	667940	793340	508456
股份有限公司	Share-holding Corperation Ltd.	146652	217781	117012
私营	Private Enterprises	199346	162398	179799
其他	Other Domestic Funded Enterprises			
港澳台商投资	Enterprises with Funds from Hong Kong,Macao and Taiwan	60292	105221	17520
外商投资	Foreign Funded Enterprises	408081	288020	234544
按轻重工业分	**Grouped by Light Industry and Heavy Industry**			
轻工业	Light Industry	829274	323659	62762
重工业	Heavy Industry	694257	1483618	1118728
按企业规模分	**Grouped by Size of Enterprises**			
大型企业	Large-size	846489	1333317	921885
中型企业	Medium-size	677042	473960	259604

continued 2

(10 000 yuan)

财务费用 Financial cost	营业利润 Operating Profit	利润总额 Total Profits	亏损企业亏损总额 Total Loss of Deficit Enterprises	利税总额 Total Pre-tax Profits	应付职工薪酬 Salary Payable	本年应交增值税 Value Added Tax Payable
293844	**3504200**	**3565375**	**171970**	**4603717**	**5316027**	**719789**
116044	-173638	-171970	171970	-181644	608215	-33342
61444	517775	530151	47157	798976	2245904	204517
47227	1168418	1207342	52273	1500565	1243085	220839
207656	2436332	2502161	150548	3294503	4482599	591242
49248	216197	221562	7202	346583	744787	101305
1740	123	-10	10	142	4769	103
40240	1257840	1291681	78798	1806050	2471427	388910
71044	760644	786104	40527	901636	737029	87417
45383	201529	202824	24011	240093	524587	13507
24294	44386	43420	2260	157670	244713	48460
61895	1023482	1019794	19162	1151544	588715	80087
88196	557869	561768	25129	762903	575105	157817
205648	2946330	3003607	146841	3840814	4740923	561972
173640	2716516	2725583	46157	3470072	4218188	489394
120204	787684	839792	125813	1133645	1097839	230395

12-8 续表3

单位：万元

分组	Classify	企业单位数（个）Number of Enterprises (unit)	亏损企业 Loss Making Enterprises
按控股情况分	**Grouped by Cast strand**		
国有控股	State owned shares	123	17
集体控股	Collective shares	1	
私人控股	Private holdings	84	16
港澳台控股	Hong Kong and Macao Holdings	5	
外商投资	Foreign Investment	26	5
其他	Others	5	
按工业行业大类分	**Grouped by Sector**		
煤炭开采和洗选业	Mining and Washing of Coal		
石油和天然气开采业	Extraction of Petroleum and Natural Gas		
黑色金属矿采选业	Mining and Processing of Ferrous Metal Ores		
有色金属矿采选业	Mining and Processing of Non-ferrous Metal Ores		
非金属矿采选业	Mining and Processing of Nonmetal Ores		
开采专业及辅助性活动	Mining Professional and Auxiliary Activity	2	
其他采矿业	Mining of other Ores		
农副食品加工业	Processing of Food from Agricultural Porducts	5	
食品制造业	Manufacture of Foods	14	3
酒、饮料和精制茶制造业	Manufacture of Alcohol,Beverages and Tea	5	1
烟草制品业	Manufacture of Tobacco	1	
纺织业	Manufacture of Textile	3	1
纺织服装、服饰业	Textile, apparel industry	1	
皮革、毛皮、羽毛及其制品和制鞋业	Manufacture of Leather, Fur, Feather and Related Products, and Shoes	1	1
木材加工和木、竹、藤、棕、草制品业	Processing of Timber, Manufacture of Wood,Plam and Straw Products		
家具制造业	Manufacture of Furniture	2	
造纸和纸制品业	Manufacture of Paper and Paper Products		
印刷和记录媒介复制业	Printing,Reproduction of Recording Media	5	1

continued 3

(10 000 yuan)

平均用工人数（人） Average Number of Employed Persons (person)	资产总计 Total Assets	流动资产合计 Total Working Capitals	固定资产原价 Origing Value of Fixed Assets	累计折旧 Accumulative Total Depreciation
228961	48722431	30363971	20586121	10235369
508	57475	45136	16389	8435
96496	20033062	12586530	4206166	1368709
3432	234839	157828	193767	131769
29456	12280851	3406301	14953231	7999552
8192	743860	320007	535686	185003
12329	1232807	849169	772352	528230
2187	245133	177509	118143	80102
10909	581684	331443	348776	173866
5150	839142	401517	383221	249728
496	39371	24769	32402	18138
4626	198708	59891	196727	77367
739	63112	51443	12015	3846
616	65913	43810	8877	5779
485	38335	16189	21129	6903
3830	468557	282594	362529	261451

12-8 续表4

单位：万元

分组	Classify	负债合计 Total Liabilites	流动负债合计 Total Working Liabilities
按控股情况分	**Grouped by Cast strand**		
国有控股	State owned shares	27875600	23201968
集体控股	Collective shares	33126	26553
私人控股	Private holdings	11947464	10397899
港澳台控股	Hong Kong and Macao Holdings	79467	75714
外商投资	Foreign Investment	4018301	3244559
其他	Others	403238	320485
按工业行业大类分	**Grouped by Sector**		
煤炭开采和洗选业	Mining and Washing of Coal		
石油和天然气开采业	Extraction of Petroleum and Natural Gas		
黑色金属矿采选业	Mining and Processing of Ferrous Metal Ores		
有色金属矿采选业	Mining and Processing of Non-ferrous Metal Ores		
非金属矿采选业	Mining and Processing of Nonmetal Ores		
开采专业及辅助性活动	Mining Professional and Auxiliary Activity	436376	432016
其他采矿业	Mining of other Ores		
农副食品加工业	Processing of Food from Agricultural Porducts	95034	89812
食品制造业	Manufacture of Foods	324252	302955
酒、饮料和精制茶制造业	Manufacture of Alcohol,Beverages and Tea	507689	417801
烟草制品业	Manufacture of Tobacco	3074	3074
纺织业	Manufacture of Textile	119905	27484
纺织服装、服饰业	Textile, apparel industry	42066	42066
皮革、毛皮、羽毛及其制品和制鞋业	Manufacture of Leather, Fur, Feather and Related Products, and Shoes	23424	18713
木材加工和木、竹、藤、棕、草制品业	Processing of Timber, Manufacture of Wood,Plam and Straw Products		
家具制造业	Manufacture of Furniture	23865	23444
造纸和纸制品业	Manufacture of Paper and Paper Products		
印刷和记录媒介复制业	Printing,Reproduction of Recording Media	152456	129269

continued 4

(10 000 yuan)

所有者权益合计 Total Owners' Equities	实收资本 Total Capital Hold	营业收入 Total Revenue	主营业务收入 Revenue from Principal Business	营业成本 Total Cost	税金及附加 Taxs and Other Changes
20846831	7768596	30092945	28574208	26913425	148994
24349	10000	32953	32483	21470	214
8085596	1785425	16822873	16326680	14432883	116494
155372	78114	290884	281989	212631	1977
8262550	3840589	6575925	6539882	5133997	47900
340622	169931	555340	546151	482988	2975
796431	471109	817802	801700	733111	5144
150099	28500	469791	468489	409552	766
257432	120660	939215	919571	716023	5334
331454	103161	621533	610201	442139	10290
36297	27400	11840	11731	5619	394
78803	17864	72882	60121	69307	978
21047	7500	18586	18405	13959	140
42490	34500	34434	33968	29466	339
14470	6060	29117	29117	23462	190
316100	165689	455912	453330	371064	2629

12-8 续表5

单位：万元

分组	Classify	销售费用 Expenses for Sales	管理费用 Expenses for Management	研发费用 R&D Expenses
按控股情况分	**Grouped by Cast strand**			
国有控股	State owned shares	505946	1090864	657071
集体控股	Collective shares	2198	4553	
私人控股	Private holdings	587293	423976	282002
港澳台控股	Hong Kong and Macao Holdings	37934	16419	2388
外商投资	Foreign Investment	382895	256607	221539
其他	Others	7265	14857	18489
按工业行业大类分	**Grouped by Sector**			
煤炭开采和洗选业	Mining and Washing of Coal			
石油和天然气开采业	Extraction of Petroleum and Natural Gas			
黑色金属矿采选业	Mining and Processing of Ferrous Metal Ores			
有色金属矿采选业	Mining and Processing of Non-ferrous Metal Ores			
非金属矿采选业	Mining and Processing of Nonmetal Ores			
开采专业及辅助性活动	Mining Professional and Auxiliary Activity	2858	16930	37752
其他采矿业	Mining of other Ores			
农副食品加工业	Processing of Food from Agricultural Porducts	14972	9825	2742
食品制造业	Manufacture of Foods	117083	38341	2338
酒、饮料和精制茶制造业	Manufacture of Alcohol,Beverages and Tea	108955	20318	24
烟草制品业	Manufacture of Tobacco	957	3000	
纺织业	Manufacture of Textile	441	5017	
纺织服装、服饰业	Textile, apparel industry	1714	2617	345
皮革、毛皮、羽毛及其制品和制鞋业	Manufacture of Leather, Fur, Feather and Related Products, and Shoes	1232	1492	319
木材加工和木、竹、藤、棕、草制品业	Processing of Timber, Manufacture of Wood,Plam and Straw Products			
家具制造业	Manufacture of Furniture	1331	2540	
造纸和纸制品业	Manufacture of Paper and Paper Products			
印刷和记录媒介复制业	Printing,Reproduction of Recording Media	10436	31252	8648

continued 5

(10 000 yuan)

财务费用 Financial cost	营业利润 Operating Profit	利润总额 Total Profits	亏损企业亏损总额 Total Loss of Deficit Enterprises	利税总额 Total Pre-tax Profits	应付职工薪酬 Salary Payable	本年应交增值税 Value Added Tax Payable
116132	1273009	1328024	108528	1921295	3565178	444278
123	4409	4681		5845	5309	950
111044	1209379	1217542	47876	1528249	1105292	194213
3022	16343	17092		23567	34011	4497
58688	975825	971902	15566	1087799	513910	67996
4835	25234	26134		36962	92327	7853
-4513	32275	31174		39496	264832	3178
112	31845	31720		38389	15498	5904
2275	67272	67526	4949	98095	85773	25235
3052	38070	37881	7723	67912	55628	19741
-282	2150	1957		3475	5734	1125
70	-113	-579	1750	1377	24070	978
594	-453	497		1567	4456	931
146	-645	-598	598	85	4170	344
748	846	1190		2109	2686	729
3024	33885	34135	1078	48278	76487	11514

12-8 续表6

单位：万元

分组	Classify	企业单位数（个） Number of Enterprises (unit)	
			亏损企业 Loss Making Enterprises
文教、工美、体育和娱乐用品制造业	Manufacture of Articles For Cultural,Educational and Sports Activities		
石油、煤炭和其他燃料加工业	Petroleum, coal and other fuel processing industries	1	
化学原料及化学制品制造业	Manufacture of Raw Chemical Materials and Chemical Products	7	1
医药制造业	Manufacture of Medicines	13	
化学纤维制造业	Manufacture of Chemical Fibers	1	
橡胶和塑料制品业	Manufacture of Rubber and Plastics	3	1
非金属矿物制品业	Manufacture of Non-metallic Mineral Products	9	
黑色金属冶炼和压延加工业	Smelting and Pressing of Ferrous Metals	1	
有色金属冶炼和压延加工业	Smelting and Pressing of Non-ferrous Metals	7	2
金属制品业	Manufacture of Metal Products	9	2
通用设备制造业	Manufacture of General Purpose Machinery	10	4
专用设备制造业	Manufacture of Special Equipment	23	6
汽车制造业	Manufacture of Motor Vehicle	17	1
铁路、船舶、航空航天和其他运输设备制造业	Railways,Shipbuilding,Aerospace and Other Transportation Equipment Manufacturing Industry	28	2
电气机械和器材制造业	Manufacture of Electric Equipment and Machinery	18	7
计算机、通讯和其他电子设备制造业	Manufacture of Communication Equipment, Computers and other Electronic Equipment	40	3
仪器仪表制造业	Manufacture of Measuring Instruments and Machinery	6	
其他制造业	Manufacture of Other Manufacturing		
废弃资源综合利用业	Recycling and Disposal of Waste		
金属制品、机械和设备修理业	Metal Products,Machinery and Equipment Repair Industry	1	
电力、热力生产和供应业	Production and Supply of Electric Power and Heat Power	7	1
燃气生产和供应业	Gas Mining and Supplying Industry	3	1
水的生产和供应业	Production and Supply of Water	1	

continued 6

(10 000 yuan)

平均用工人数（人） Average Number of Employed Persons (person)	资产总计 Total Assets	流动资产合计 Total Working Capitals	固定资产原价 Origing Value of Fixed Assets	累计折旧 Accumulative Total Depreciation
2300	102690	72081	2077	1037
11028	1165845	772593	213020	71165
11600	2044782	1258291	573994	166186
329	50213	35730	23608	3548
7066	2271968	1470375	649572	160746
3674	767721	547047	200382	85562
390	59196	43446	47711	22339
5016	2362833	1504723	510472	182803
13006	1559825	847930	796015	350976
11671	3979428	3146613	730772	360151
16121	3606944	2564441	771872	331473
49505	10027718	7604114	2531483	1261476
57952	11249282	7403660	2949032	1556735
40863	10643353	7313807	3443009	1188567
61008	19850907	7403447	15668568	8146153
9014	1976930	1421255	572418	255169
758	16975	15761	1091	231
16636	4042557	564368	6522554	3653077
5265	1953805	444848	1550148	520137
2476	566783	206912	477391	205897

12-8 续表7

单位：万元

分组	Classify	负债合计 Total Liabilites	流动负债合计 Total Working Liabilities
文教、工美、体育和娱乐用品制造业	Manufacture of Articles For Cultural,Educational and Sports Activities		
石油、煤炭和其他燃料加工业	Petroleum, coal and other fuel processing industries	82377	82346
化学原料及化学制品制造业	Manufacture of Raw Chemical Materials and Chemical Products	637858	421212
医药制造业	Manufacture of Medicines	880340	733463
化学纤维制造业	Manufacture of Chemical Fibers	2610	2570
橡胶和塑料制品业	Manufacture of Rubber and Plastics	1714271	1108939
非金属矿物制品业	Manufacture of Non-metallic Mineral Products	498468	449956
黑色金属冶炼和压延加工业	Smelting and Pressing of Ferrous Metals	31463	26997
有色金属冶炼和压延加工业	Smelting and Pressing of Non-ferrous Metals	771930	493346
金属制品业	Manufacture of Metal Products	1231439	851799
通用设备制造业	Manufacture of General Purpose Machinery	2577322	2433573
专用设备制造业	Manufacture of Special Equipment	1764490	1431747
汽车制造业	Manufacture of Motor Vehicle	6951163	6523065
铁路、船舶、航空航天和其他运输设备制造业	Railways,Shipbuilding,Aerospace and Other Transportation Equipment Manufacturing Industry	5549353	4782848
电气机械和器材制造业	Manufacture of Electric Equipment and Machinery	6263872	5861673
计算机、通讯和其他电子设备制造业	Manufacture of Communication Equipment, Computers and other Electronic Equipment	8273171	6478917
仪器仪表制造业	Manufacture of Measuring Instruments and Machinery	1014053	938619
其他制造业	Manufacture of Other Manufacturing		
废弃资源综合利用业	Recycling and Disposal of Waste		
金属制品、机械和设备修理业	Metal Products,Machinery and Equipment Repair Industry	7503	5603
电力、热力生产和供应业	Production and Supply of Electric Power and Heat Power	2806896	1923570
燃气生产和供应业	Gas Mining and Supplying Industry	1138074	958292
水的生产和供应业	Production and Supply of Water	432404	272010

continued 7

(10 000 yuan)

所有者权益合计 Total Owners' Equities	实收资本 Total Capital Hold	营业收入 Total Revenue	主营业务收入 Revenue from Principal Business	营业成本 Total Cost	税金及附加 Taxs and Other Changes
20313	33660	69534	69533	65753	19
527987	83099	449288	409892	323248	2580
1164442	172396	1790204	1789705	930147	15776
47603	49252	83069	83069	75052	291
557697	394544	849674	824842	739969	4874
269253	68158	628539	608801	503652	3548
27733	28811	56764	54421	49482	508
1590903	474098	500981	464594	377007	4383
328386	319366	949715	925606	824277	2455
1402105	204634	1790022	1782629	1536652	10747
1842454	585866	1492689	1481106	1109125	11278
3076555	1074239	12284668	10890562	11238792	96646
5699930	1909688	4839008	4794014	4168806	17367
4379481	1450992	7591129	7405528	7028313	31226
11577736	4406152	11783454	11687300	10169279	63178
962878	183933	1237592	1231002	1009518	3287
9473	10000	20057	20057	15770	283
1235661	935923	3054576	3009353	2913541	16442
815730	246399	1300435	1245577	1194648	5602
134379	39000	128409	117170	110663	1861

12-8 续表8

单位：万元

分 组	Classify	销售费用 Expenses for Sales	管理费用 Expenses for Management	研发费用 R&D Expenses
文教、工美、体育和娱乐用品制造业	Manufacture of Articles For Cultural,Educational and Sports Activities			
石油、煤炭和其他燃料加工业	Petroleum, coal and other fuel processing industries		1291	
化学原料及化学制品制造业	Manufacture of Raw Chemical Materials and Chemical Products	12267	35168	18510
医药制造业	Manufacture of Medicines	476421	177164	24344
化学纤维制造业	Manufacture of Chemical Fibers	277	1444	1788
橡胶和塑料制品业	Manufacture of Rubber and Plastics	26284	18281	19380
非金属矿物制品业	Manufacture of Non-metallic Mineral Products	25148	24579	21619
黑色金属冶炼和压延加工业	Smelting and Pressing of Ferrous Metals	2418	2542	250
有色金属冶炼和压延加工业	Smelting and Pressing of Non-ferrous Metals	5889	31778	29104
金属制品业	Manufacture of Metal Products	4989	55207	36940
通用设备制造业	Manufacture of General Purpose Machinery	38928	113292	46965
专用设备制造业	Manufacture of Special Equipment	64909	69759	50888
汽车制造业	Manufacture of Motor Vehicle	215719	213630	155772
铁路、船舶、航空航天和其他运输设备制造业	Railways,Shipbuilding,Aerospace and Other Transportation Equipment Manufacturing Industry	66477	219310	110115
电气机械和器材制造业	Manufacture of Electric Equipment and Machinery	241597	270231	142292
计算机、通讯和其他电子设备制造业	Manufacture of Communication Equipment, Computers and other Electronic Equipment	41906	265959	413868
仪器仪表制造业	Manufacture of Measuring Instruments and Machinery	15801	72544	46822
其他制造业	Manufacture of Other Manufacturing			
废弃资源综合利用业	Recycling and Disposal of Waste			
金属制品、机械和设备修理业	Metal Products,Machinery and Equipment Repair Industry		2105	399
电力、热力生产和供应业	Production and Supply of Electric Power and Heat Power	174	63833	6830
燃气生产和供应业	Gas Mining and Supplying Industry	18794	26919	3437
水的生产和供应业	Production and Supply of Water	5553	10911	

continued 8

(10 000 yuan)

财务费用 Financial cost	营业利润 Operating Profit	利润总额 Total Profits	亏损企业亏损总额 Total Loss of Deficit Enterprises	利税总额 Total Pre-tax Profits	应付职工薪酬 Salary Payable	本年应交增值税 Value Added Tax Payable
2287	184	183		1304	2840	1102
31952	26439	26489	9031	35317	59837	6248
21210	149650	153215		249200	194131	80209
-56	4480	4536		6227	5427	1400
29099	40941	39856	2907	61044	68245	16314
3591	45337	46722		72275	43949	22005
213	720	556		2477	6111	1413
9352	39499	40350	15775	56443	67125	11710
6929	25343	31930	13036	43845	190416	9459
-2491	81436	86303	11348	137444	175531	40394
10607	230423	254415	15003	304063	203680	38370
-6049	462565	466825	2317	724209	772493	160738
19920	260786	263475	7244	321421	873690	40579
45368	175722	178816	47280	211975	735994	1934
74874	1550604	1546701	26286	1726887	732149	117008
-5273	116418	115778		127137	168097	8073
44	1471	1477		4051	11567	2291
34117	27166	42571	4324	132749	344062	73737
11252	59786	60203	1322	79408	82526	13602
1672	100	71		5458	38826	3527

12-9 规模以上高技术产业工业企业主要经济指标（2020年）

单位：万元

行 业	Sector	企业单位数（个） Number of Enterprises (unit)	亏损企业 Loss Making Enterprises
总计	**Total**	**385**	**75**
一、医药制造业	**Pharmaceutical Manufacturing**	**70**	**20**
（一）化学药品制造	Chemical manufacturing	28	5
化学药品原料药制造	Chemical raw materials Medicine manufacturing	10	1
化学药品制剂制造	Chemical preparations manufacturing	18	4
（二）中药饮片加工	Chinese medicine Pieces processing	2	
（三）中成药生产	Chinese medicine production	25	10
（四）兽用药品制造	Veterinary pharmaceutical manufacturing	4	1
（五）生物药品制造	Biopharmaceutical manufacturing	5	2
（六）卫生材料及医药用品制造	Sanitary materials and medical supplies manufacturing	1	
（七）药用辅料及包装材料	Pharmaceutical Excipients and Packaging Materials	5	2
二、航空、航天及设备制造业	**Aviation, Aerospace and Equipment Manufacturing Industry**	**76**	**11**
（一）飞机制造	Aircraft Manufacturing	21	3
（二）航天器及运载火箭制造	Spacecraft and Launch Vehicles Manufacturing	3	
（三）航空、航天相关设备制造	Aviation and aerospace-related equipment manufacturing	40	4
（四）其他航空航天器制造	Other aerospace manufacturing	6	
（五）航空航天器修理	Aerospace vehicle repair	6	4
三、电子及通讯设备制造业	**Electronic and communication equipment manufacturing**	**146**	**25**
（一）电子工业专用设备制造	Electronic equipment manufacturing	10	
（二）光纤、光缆及锂离子电池制造	Optical Fiber, Cable and Lithium-ion Battery Manufacturing	4	2
（三）通信设备、雷达及配套设备制造	Communications Equipment, Radar and Ancillary Equipments	32	5
（四）广播电视设备制造	Broadcasting and TV Equipment	2	1
（五）非专业视听设备制造	Non-professional audiovisual equipment manufacturing	1	
（六）电子器件制造	Electronic device manufacturing	41	5
（七）电子元件及电子专用材料制造	Electronic components and electronic materials manufacturing	40	7
（八）智能消费设备制造	Smart consumer device manufacturing	3	1
（九）其他电子设备制造	Other electronic equipment manufacturing	13	4
四、计算机及办公设备制造业	**Computer and office equipment manufacturing**	**6**	**2**
（一）计算机整机制造	Computer machine manufacturing		
（二）计算机零部件制造	Computer parts manufacturing	1	1
（三）计算机外围设备制造	Computer peripheral equipment manufacturing	1	
（四）工业控制计算机及系统制造	Industrial Control Computer and System Manufacturing	4	1
（五）信息安全设备制造	Information Security Equipment Manufacturing		
（六）其他计算机制造	Other computer manufacturing		
（七）办公设备制造	Office Equipment manufacturing		
五、医疗设备及仪器仪表制造业	**Medical equipment and instrumentation manufacturing**	**86**	**16**
（一）医疗仪器设备及器械制造	Medical equipment and device manufacturing	17	5
（二）通用仪器仪表制造	General Measuring Instruments and Machinery Manufacturing	41	8
（三）专用仪器仪表制造	Special Measuring Instruments and Machinery Manufacturing	18	1
（四）光学仪器制造	Optical Instruments Manufacturing	5	1
（五）其他仪器仪表制造业	Other instrumentation manufacturing	5	1
六、信息化学品制造业	**Information chemicals manufacturing**	**1**	**1**
信息化学品制造	Information Chemical Manufacturing	1	1

Major Economic Indicators of High Technology Industry

Industrial Enterprises above Designated Size（2020）

(10 000 yuan)

平均用工人数（人）Average Number of Employed Persons (person)	资产总计 Total Assets	流动资产合计 Total Working Capitals	固定资产原价 Origing Value of Fixed Assets	累计折旧 Accumulative Total Depreciation
168040	**40677943**	**20530715**	**21875871**	**10595697**
18277	**2799305**	**1761274**	**796719**	**259935**
9440	1551193	986739	563879	164940
1258	249287	199042	40085	15564
8182	1301906	787697	523794	149376
108	20051	12906	1681	245
6594	878308	545813	170060	65850
396	60957	53581	11313	5430
1079	234343	124119	35317	16527
59	2979	1797	1550	467
601	51474	36320	12918	6476
56108	**11186571**	**7238712**	**3015813**	**1557816**
41878	8335923	5555466	2111193	1155792
4636	1199537	555991	422484	185489
8037	1283277	892242	410457	197278
1062	267289	185964	36755	11441
495	100545	49050	34923	7817
75209	**23254717**	**8976722**	**17306278**	**8447193**
910	102660	82062	20533	6810
3126	943790	454421	582640	176948
25526	3186976	2272860	799316	426072
260	26806	24056	2771	1927
60	7204	5582	5806	531
23802	11111661	2700203	14256757	7632573
19215	7640969	3278486	1578851	178456
1015	86709	43976	44024	16996
1295	147942	115077	15581	6881
593	**112759**	**90533**	**17048**	**2975**
85	5477	4659	1037	237
240	82788	63495	14431	2051
268	24495	22379	1580	688
17694	**3249973**	**2421554**	**724713**	**319639**
2195	460744	361618	44706	19538
4948	544651	439281	65538	29449
2941	545691	455500	56122	31323
7066	1628594	1127713	538659	231187
544	70293	37442	19688	8141
159	**74619**	**41920**	**15300**	**8140**
159	74619	41920	15300	8140

12-9 续表1

单位：万元

行　业	Sector	负债合计 Total Liabilites	流动负债合计 Total Working Liabilities
总计	**Total**	**18855643**	**15004630**
一、医药制造业	**Pharmaceutical Manufacturing**	**1276393**	**1090549**
（一）化学药品制造	Chemical manufacturing	626917	519609
化学药品原料药制造	Chemical raw materials Medicine manufacturing	67786	59292
化学药品制剂制造	Chemical preparations manufacturing	559131	460318
（二）中药饮片加工	Chinese medicine Pieces processing	10492	10263
（三）中成药生产	Chinese medicine production	539917	466568
（四）兽用药品制造	Veterinary pharmaceutical manufacturing	25060	21422
（五）生物药品制造	Biopharmaceutical manufacturing	40613	39294
（六）卫生材料及医药用品制造	Sanitary materials and medical supplies manufacturing	620	620
（七）药用辅料及包装材料	Pharmaceutical Excipients and Packaging Materials	32774	32774
二、航空、航天及设备制造业	**Aviation, Aerospace and Equipment Manufacturing Industry**	**5441692**	**4656115**
（一）飞机制造	Aircraft Manufacturing	4051813	3562900
（二）航天器及运载火箭制造	Spacecraft and Launch Vehicles Manufacturing	669414	466589
（三）航空、航天相关设备制造	Aviation and aerospace-related equipment manufacturing	620849	536699
（四）其他航空航天器制造	Other aerospace manufacturing	71394	68033
（五）航空航天器修理	Aerospace vehicle repair	28222	21893
三、电子及通讯设备制造业	**Electronic and communication equipment manufacturing**	**10406272**	**7644783**
（一）电子工业专用设备制造	Electronic equipment manufacturing	56477	51451
（二）光纤、光缆及锂离子电池制造	Optical Fiber, Cable and Lithium-ion Battery Manufacturing	705606	634800
（三）通信设备、雷达及配套设备制造	Communications Equipment, Radar and Ancillary Equipments	1772859	1490274
（四）广播电视设备制造	Broadcasting and TV Equipment	15812	12271
（五）非专业视听设备制造	Non-professional audiovisual equipment manufacturing	2619	2619
（六）电子器件制造	Electronic device manufacturing	3133007	2301030
（七）电子元件及电子专用材料制造	Electronic components and electronic materials manufacturing	4635590	3073088
（八）智能消费设备制造	Smart consumer device manufacturing	14148	13461
（九）其他电子设备制造	Other electronic equipment manufacturing	70156	65790
四、计算机及办公设备制造业	**Computer and office equipment manufacturing**	**39573**	**37962**
（一）计算机整机制造	Computer machine manufacturing		
（二）计算机零部件制造	Computer parts manufacturing	4954	4121
（三）计算机外围设备制造	Computer peripheral equipment manufacturing	21203	20953
（四）工业控制计算机及系统制造	Industrial Control Computer and System Manufacturing	13416	12888
（五）信息安全设备制造	Information Security Equipment Manufacturing		
（六）其他计算机制造	Other computer manufacturing		
（七）办公设备制造	Office Equipment manufacturing		
五、医疗设备及仪器仪表制造业	**Medical equipment and instrumentation manufacturing**	**1610057**	**1493565**
（一）医疗仪器设备及器械制造	Medical equipment and device manufacturing	184744	170792
（二）通用仪器仪表制造	General Measuring Instruments and Machinery Manufacturing	294736	273481
（三）专用仪器仪表制造	Special Measuring Instruments and Machinery Manufacturing	218097	206977
（四）光学仪器制造	Optical Instruments Manufacturing	895894	826728
（五）其他仪器仪表制造业	Other instrumentation manufacturing	16586	15586
六、信息化学品制造业	**Information chemicals manufacturing**	**81656**	**81656**
信息化学品制造	Information Chemical Manufacturing	81656	81656

continued 1

(10 000 yuan)

所有者权益合计 Total Owners' Equities	实收资本 Total Capital Hold	营业收入 Total Revenue	主营业务收入 Revenue from Principal Business	营业成本 Total Cost	税金及附加 Taxs and Other Changes
21776123	**7788406**	**22277074**	**22042036**	**17980315**	**112292**
1499034	**359640**	**2163980**	**2161458**	**1093198**	**20226**
919982	191252	1566313	1564693	901532	12349
181500	57550	215051	215051	155597	1040
738481	133702	1351262	1349642	745935	11309
9559	6000	7152	7152	5882	41
318808	92733	451546	450740	140976	6245
35897	7748	9714	9644	6772	102
193730	49027	89210	89210	18371	1176
2359	500	4208	4208	1861	37
18700	12380	35836	35810	17805	276
5744733	**1918760**	**4514272**	**4474850**	**3879699**	**14430**
4283966	1419568	3296113	3269854	2967780	8522
530123	79547	504499	497239	390629	795
662427	297577	586976	582277	430146	4106
195895	36233	90806	90806	59267	749
72323	85834	35878	34674	31877	259
12826292	**5087064**	**13490140**	**13310407**	**11541304**	**67808**
46184	18776	58418	46678	43147	421
238184	228825	918736	885163	803426	571
1414117	409103	3698493	3666199	3352639	11961
10994	3808	27232	26611	20259	136
4585	290	7432	7432	7108	15
7978654	3712215	5084817	5052965	4124135	40156
2983226	656695	3557919	3490237	3088514	13692
72561	11564	35250	34941	24333	302
77787	45788	101844	100183	77743	554
73186	**31808**	**56625**	**54276**	**36798**	**399**
523	523	5718	5718	5587	2
61585	27600	33828	31488	20408	294
11078	3685	17078	17070	10803	103
1639915	**387135**	**2032016**	**2021016**	**1410354**	**9270**
276000	53439	354120	353943	104171	3044
249914	113137	394272	390735	293256	2248
327594	58503	278681	277423	177036	2366
732700	145537	973858	967940	812753	1463
53707	16519	31085	30975	23138	149
-7037	**4000**	**20042**	**20029**	**18961**	**159**
-7037	4000	20042	20029	18961	159

12-9 续表2

单位：万元

行 业	Sector	销售费用 Expenses for Sales	管理费用 Expenses for Management
总计	**Total**	**871109**	**911289**
一、医药制造业	**Pharmaceutical Manufacturing**	**600057**	**214565**
（一）化学药品制造	Chemical manufacturing	342069	150627
化学药品原料药制造	Chemical raw materials Medicine manufacturing	8548	6757
化学药品制剂制造	Chemical preparations manufacturing	333522	143870
（二）中药饮片加工	Chinese medicine Pieces processing	219	388
（三）中成药生产	Chinese medicine production	198492	51966
（四）兽用药品制造	Veterinary pharmaceutical manufacturing	1141	447
（五）生物药品制造	Biopharmaceutical manufacturing	53121	6802
（六）卫生材料及医药用品制造	Sanitary materials and medical supplies manufacturing	512	420
（七）药用辅料及包装材料	Pharmaceutical Excipients and Packaging Materials	4504	3915
二、航空、航天及设备制造业	**Aviation, Aerospace and Equipment Manufacturing Industry**	**49070**	**216096**
（一）飞机制造	Aircraft Manufacturing	34123	137465
（二）航天器及运载火箭制造	Spacecraft and Launch Vehicles Manufacturing	1074	25708
（三）航空、航天相关设备制造	Aviation and aerospace-related equipment manufacturing	10638	40778
（四）其他航空航天器制造	Other aerospace manufacturing	2909	6820
（五）航空航天器修理	Aerospace vehicle repair	325	5325
三、电子及通讯设备制造业	**Electronic and communication equipment manufacturing**	**131786**	**349844**
（一）电子工业专用设备制造	Electronic equipment manufacturing	2761	3238
（二）光纤、光缆及锂离子电池制造	Optical Fiber, Cable and Lithium-ion Battery Manufacturing	60786	11415
（三）通信设备、雷达及配套设备制造	Communications Equipment, Radar and Ancillary Equipments	10672	64634
（四）广播电视设备制造	Broadcasting and TV Equipment	1827	1684
（五）非专业视听设备制造	Non-professional audiovisual equipment manufacturing	102	79
（六）电子器件制造	Electronic device manufacturing	19442	125616
（七）电子元件及电子专用材料制造	Electronic components and electronic materials manufacturing	30008	130017
（八）智能消费设备制造	Smart consumer device manufacturing	1237	4754
（九）其他电子设备制造	Other electronic equipment manufacturing	4951	8407
四、计算机及办公设备制造业	**Computer and office equipment manufacturing**	**1442**	**4808**
（一）计算机整机制造	Computer machine manufacturing		
（二）计算机零部件制造	Computer parts manufacturing	250	488
（三）计算机外围设备制造	Computer peripheral equipment manufacturing	403	2338
（四）工业控制计算机及系统制造	Industrial Control Computer and System Manufacturing	789	1982
（五）信息安全设备制造	Information Security Equipment Manufacturing		
（六）其他计算机制造	Other computer manufacturing		
（七）办公设备制造	Office Equipment manufacturing		
五、医疗设备及仪器仪表制造业	**Medical equipment and instrumentation manufacturing**	**88569**	**124917**
（一）医疗仪器设备及器械制造	Medical equipment and device manufacturing	41388	17300
（二）通用仪器仪表制造	General Measuring Instruments and Machinery Manufacturing	25256	24907
（三）专用仪器仪表制造	Special Measuring Instruments and Machinery Manufacturing	18219	18324
（四）光学仪器制造	Optical Instruments Manufacturing	2105	62129
（五）其他仪器仪表制造业	Other instrumentation manufacturing	1601	2257
六、信息化学品制造业	**Information chemicals manufacturing**	**186**	**1060**
信息化学品制造	Information Chemical Manufacturing	186	1060

continued 2

(10 000 yuan)

研发费用 R&D Expenses	财务费用 Financial cost	营业利润 Operating Profit	利润总额 Total Profits	亏损企业亏损总额 Total Loss of Deficit Enterprises	利税总额 Total Pre-tax Profits	应付职工薪酬 Salary Payable	本年应交增值税 Value Added Tax Payable
735896	**160458**	**2400588**	**2428031**	**115606**	**2835128**	**2213101**	**294805**
44511	**26283**	**169485**	**177206**	**13661**	**303257**	**237241**	**105826**
25891	22737	114852	115599	7687	186905	169395	58957
10737	5651	26810	26991	494	30405	9573	2373
15153	17086	88043	88607	7193	156500	159822	56584
256	160	207	232		311	423	39
11408	2092	41326	47258	4050	91875	49806	38373
448	282	522	701	73	920	2073	117
4177	-47	5523	5930	412	13498	10185	6392
253	11	1137	1144		1401	334	221
2078	1047	5916	6343	1439	8346	5025	1727
110476	**24030**	**242506**	**248435**	**16385**	**292046**	**824657**	**29181**
36262	16020	109283	110632	1968	124374	599171	5220
37959	811	54562	55464		58250	106921	1992
27282	6453	67440	69909	7785	91145	99298	17129
7504	656	14146	14601		19358	13268	4008
1469	90	-2926	-2171	6632	-1080	5999	832
483075	**105421**	**1648086**	**1655497**	**74786**	**1853891**	**875408**	**130586**
4284	738	3790	3907		5851	7507	1523
3997	10208	63097	63706	4280	59194	35214	-5083
42970	9479	226286	230400	3358	304042	234596	61681
1098	123	2484	2510	8	4497	2984	1852
	7	469	469		485	690	
371880	39082	846860	846336	6300	926288	388285	39796
48125	45406	500493	502849	54267	544218	180823	27678
3403	10	1811	1835	963	3277	12409	1140
7319	368	2796	3486	5610	6039	12900	1999
3983	**1385**	**8306**	**8503**	**965**	**10305**	**6496**	**1403**
	236	-844	-733	733	-732	477	
2426	948	6794	6798		7721	3213	629
1558	201	2357	2438	232	3316	2806	774
92982	**3220**	**333501**	**339683**	**8517**	**376407**	**267837**	**27454**
17000	409	176698	177242	3712	185568	32156	5281
20270	2087	30183	33102	3622	47043	50675	11693
11636	5219	53784	57124	1146	65627	33230	6137
41681	-4920	71746	70486	1	75644	147502	3696
2394	425	1091	1730	36	2524	4275	646
870	**120**	**-1296**	**-1292**	**1292**	**-777**	**1462**	**356**
870	120	-1296	-1292	1292	-777	1462	356

12-10 规模以上工业企业主要经济效益指标（2020年）

行 业	Sector	总资产贡献率（%） Ratio of Total Assets to Industrial Output Value（%）	资产负债率（%） Assets-Liability Ratio（%）
总计	**Total**	**6.1**	**55.2**
按工业行业大类分	**Grouped by Sector**		
煤炭开采和洗选业	Mining and Washing of Coal		
石油和天然气开采业	Extraction of Petroleum and Natural Gas		
黑色金属矿采选业	Mining and Processing of Ferrous Metal Ores		
有色金属矿采选业	Mining and Processing of Non-ferrous Metal Ores		
非金属矿采选业	Mining and Processing of Nonmetal Ores		
开采专业及辅助性活动	Mining Professional and Auxiliary Activity	2.8	36.3
其他采矿业	Mining of Other Ores		
农副食品加工业	Processing of Food from Agricultural Porducts	7.6	57.4
食品制造业	Manufacture of Foods	14.4	47.8
酒、饮料和精制茶制造业	Manufacture of Alcohol,Beverages and Tea	8.5	54.6
烟草制品业	Manufacture of Tobacco	7.2	18.2
纺织业	Manufacture of Textile	2.0	57.0
纺织服装、服饰业	Textile, Garments industry	3.8	57.2
皮革、毛皮、羽毛及其制品和制鞋业	Manufacture of Leather, Fur, Feather and Related Products	0.4	35.4
木材加工和木、竹、藤、棕、草制品业	Processing of Timber, Manufacture of Wood,Plam and Straw Products	0.8	46.3
家具制造业	Manufacture of Furniture	4.4	53.8
造纸和纸制品业	Manufacture of Paper and Paper Products	7.3	61.4
印刷和记录媒介复制业	Printing,Reproduction of Recording Media	8.6	37.5
文教、工美、体育和娱乐用品制造业	Manufacture of Articles For Cultural,Educational and Sports Activities	3.5	37.5

Major Indicators of Economic Performance of Industrial Enterprises above Designated Size (2020)

流动资产周转率 (次/年) Rate of Annual Turnover Working Capitals (times/year)	成本费用利润率 (%) Ratio of Profits to Cost (%)	营业收入利润率 (%) Profit Margin of Operating Income (%)	每百元资产实现营业收入（元） Operating Income per 100 yuan of Assets (yuan)
1.1	**7.1**	**6.8**	**64.8**
1.0	3.9	3.8	66.6
1.8	5.0	4.8	125.0
2.2	9.1	8.6	115.9
1.5	7.4	6.8	67.1
0.7	11.5	10.0	38.7
0.9	2.1	2.1	43.5
0.5	3.1	3.1	42.8
0.7	-2.0	-1.9	50.8
0.1	-6.0	-8.2	6.9
1.5	1.5	1.4	75.4
1.7	5.2	5.0	93.5
1.5	6.2	5.8	89.8
0.6	4.7	4.5	40.7

12-10 续表1

行　业	Sector	总资产贡献率（%） Ratio of Total Assets to Industrial Output Value（%）	资产负债率（%） Assets-Liability Ratio（%）
石油、煤炭和其他燃料加工业	Petroleum, coal and other fuel processing industries	2.0	76.2
化学原料及化学制品制造业	Manufacture of Raw Chemical Materials and Chemical Products	11.6	60.7
医药制造业	Manufacture of Medicines	11.1	45.6
化学纤维制造业	Manufacture of Chemical Fibers	17.2	36.8
橡胶和塑料制品业	Manufacture of Rubber and Plastics	4.0	74.4
非金属矿物制品业	Manufacture of Non-metallic Mineral Products	6.7	72.5
黑色金属冶炼和压延加工业	Smelting and Pressing of Ferrous Metals	6.1	59.0
有色金属冶炼和压延加工业	Smelting and Pressing of Non-ferrous Metals	3.4	38.8
金属制品业	Manufacture of Metal Products	4.8	74.4
通用设备制造业	Manufacture of General Purpose Machinery	4.3	62.0
专用设备制造业	Manufacture of Special Equipment	7.3	49.2
汽车制造业	Manufacture of Motor Vehicle	7.4	68.9
铁路、船舶、航空航天和其他运输设备制造业	Railways, Shipbuilding,Aerospace and Other Transportation Equipment Manufacturing Industry	3.6	47.9
电气机械和器材制造业	Manufacture of Electric Equipment and Machinery	3.3	56.9
计算机、通讯和其他电子设备制造业	Manufacture of Communication Equipment, Computers and other Electronic Equipment	8.4	43.4
仪器仪表制造业	Manufacture of Measuring Instruments and Machinery	6.7	51.0
其他制造业	Manufacture of Other Manufacturing	3.5	51.5
废弃资源综合利用业	Recycling and Disposal of Waste	14.7	68.5
金属制品、机械和设备修理业	Metal Products,Machinery and Equipment Repair Industry	5.7	28.5
电力、热力生产和供应业	Production and Supply of Electric Power and Heat Power	3.6	74.5
燃气生产和供应业	Gas Mining and Supplying Industry	4.3	56.0
水的生产和供应业	Production and Supply of Water	1.2	77.7

continued 1

流动资产周转率（次/年）Rate of Annual Turnover Working Capitals (times/year)	成本费用利润率（%）Ratio of Profits to Cost (%)	营业收入利润率（%）Profit Margin of Operating Income (%)	每百元资产实现营业收入（元）Operating Income per 100 yuan of Assets (yuan)
1.1	-1.2	-1.2	80.1
0.9	18.1	16.5	55.6
1.2	9.0	8.2	77.3
2.3	11.5	9.9	131.3
0.7	4.7	4.6	42.1
1.1	4.0	3.8	82.3
3.5	1.0	1.0	246.6
0.5	7.0	6.5	32.8
1.2	4.5	4.4	68.3
0.6	5.7	5.5	50.1
0.6	14.0	12.6	44.1
1.6	4.1	4.0	121.3
0.7	6.9	6.5	43.0
1.0	3.8	3.8	70.8
1.5	13.6	12.7	56.3
0.8	10.5	9.6	60.3
0.7	2.7	2.7	43.9
2.4	1.4	1.5	137.3
0.9	6.6	6.3	48.9
2.4	2.6	2.5	56.3
2.5	5.1	4.9	65.9
0.7	-4.5	-4.7	18.1

12-11 规模以上大中型工业企业主要经济效益指标（2020年）

行 业	Sector	总资产贡献率（%） Ratio of Total Assets to Industrial Output Value (%)	资产负债率（%） Assets-Liability Ratio (%)
总计	**Total**	**5.9**	**54.1**
按国民经济行业分	**Grouped by Sector**		
煤炭开采和洗选业	Mining and Washing of Coal		
石油和天然气开采业	Extraction of Petroleum and Natural Gas		
黑色金属矿采选业	Mining and Processing of Ferrous Metal Ores		
有色金属矿采选业	Mining and Processing of Non-ferrous Metal Ores		
非金属矿采选业	Mining and Processing of Nonmetal Ores		
开采专业及辅助性活动	Mining Professional and Auxiliary Activity	2.8	35.4
其他采矿业	Mining of other Ores		
农副食品加工业	Processing of Food from Agricultural Porducts	15.8	38.8
食品制造业	Manufacture of Foods	17.9	55.7
酒、饮料和精制茶制造业	Manufacture of Alcohol,Beverages and Tea	8.8	60.5
烟草制品业	Manufacture of Tobacco	8.1	7.8
纺织业	Manufacture of Textile	0.7	60.3
纺织服装、服饰业	Textile, apparel industry	3.4	66.7
皮革、毛皮、羽毛及其制品和制鞋业	Manufacture of Leather, Fur, Feather and Related Products, and Shoes	0.4	35.5
木材加工和木、竹、藤、棕、草制品业	Processing of Timber,Manufacture of Wood,Plam and Straw Products		
家具制造业	Manufacture of Furniture	7.5	62.3
造纸和纸制品业	Manufacture of Paper and Paper Products		
印刷和记录媒介复制业	Printing,Reproduction of Recording Media	10.7	32.5
文教、工美、体育和娱乐用品制造业	Manufacture of Articles For Cultural,Educational and Sports Activities		

Major Economic Indicators of Large and Medium-sized Industrial Enterprises above Designated Size（2020）

流动资产周转率（次/年）Rate of Annual Turnover Working Capitals (times/year)	成本费用利润率（%）Ratio of Profits to Cost (%)	营业收入利润率（%）Profit Margin of Operating Income (%)	每百元资产实现营业收入（元）Operating Income per 100 yuan of Assets (yuan)
1.2	**6.9**	**6.6**	**66.3**
1.0	4.0	3.8	66.3
2.7	7.3	6.8	191.7
2.8	7.7	7.2	161.5
1.6	6.6	6.1	74.1
0.5	21.1	16.5	30.1
1.2	-0.8	-0.8	36.7
0.4	2.6	2.7	29.5
0.8	-1.8	-1.7	52.2
1.8	4.2	4.1	76.0
1.6	8.0	7.5	97.3

12-11 续表1

行　业	Sector	总资产贡献率（%） Ratio of Total Assets to Industrial Output Value (%)	资产负债率（%） Assets-Liability Ratio (%)
石油、煤炭和其他燃料加工业	Petroleum, coal and other fuel processing industries	3.5	80.2
化学原料及化学制品制造业	Manufacture of Raw Chemical Materials and Chemical Products	5.5	54.7
医药制造业	Manufacture of Medicines	12.4	43.1
化学纤维制造业	Manufacture of Chemical Fibers	12.3	5.2
橡胶和塑料制品业	Manufacture of Rubber and Plastics	3.8	75.5
非金属矿物制品业	Manufacture of Non-metallic Mineral Products	10.0	64.9
黑色金属冶炼和压延加工业	Smelting and Pressing of Ferrous Metals	4.5	53.2
有色金属冶炼和压延加工业	Smelting and Pressing of Non-ferrous Metals	2.6	32.7
金属制品业	Manufacture of Metal Products	3.3	79.0
通用设备制造业	Manufacture of General Purpose Machinery	3.4	64.8
专用设备制造业	Manufacture of Special Equipment	8.6	48.9
汽车制造业	Manufacture of Motor Vehicle	7.1	69.3
铁路、船舶、航空航天和其他运输设备制造业	Railways,Shipbuilding,Aerospace and Other Transportation Equipment Manufacturing Industry	3.0	49.3
电气机械和器材制造业	Manufacture of Electric Equipment and Machinery	2.1	58.9
计算机、通信和其他电子设备制造业	Manufacture of Communication Equipment, Computers and other Electronic Equipment	9.1	41.7
仪器仪表制造业	Manufacture of Measuring Instruments and Machinery	6.1	51.3
其他制造业	Manufacture of Other Manufacturing		
废弃资源综合利用	Recycling and Disposal of Waste		
金属制品、机械和设备修理业	Metal Products,Machinery and Equipment Repair Industry	24.1	44.2
电力、热力生产和供应业	Production and Supply of Electric Power and Heat Power	4.1	69.4
燃气生产和供应业	Gas Mining and Supplying Industry	4.2	58.3
水的生产和供应业	Production and Supply of Water	1.5	76.3

continued 1

流动资产周转率 （次/年） Rate of Annual Turnover Working Capitals (times/year)	成本费用利润率 （%） Ratio of Profits to Cost （%）	营业收入利润率 （%） Profit Margin of Operating Income （%）	每百元资产实现 营业收入（元） Operating Income per 100 yuan of Assets (yuan)
1.0	0.3	0.3	67.7
0.6	6.3	5.9	38.5
1.4	9.4	8.6	87.6
2.3	5.8	5.5	165.4
0.6	4.8	4.7	37.4
1.2	8.1	7.4	81.9
1.3	1.0	1.0	95.9
0.3	8.9	8.1	21.2
1.1	3.4	3.4	60.9
0.6	5.0	4.8	45.0
0.6	19.5	17.0	41.4
1.6	4.0	3.8	122.5
0.7	5.8	5.4	43.0
1.0	2.3	2.4	71.3
1.6	14.1	13.1	59.4
0.9	10.2	9.4	62.6
1.3	8.1	7.4	118.2
5.4	1.4	1.4	75.6
2.9	4.8	4.6	66.6
0.6	0.1	0.1	22.7

12-12 规模以上工业主要产品生产能力（2020年）

Production Capacity of Major Products of Industrial Enterprises above Designated Size (2020)

指 标	Item	2020
棉纺锭/纺纱量（锭/吨）	Cotton Spindles / Spinning Volume (ingot/ton)	201408
气流纺锭/纺纱量（头/吨）	Rotor Spinning / Spinning Volume (head/ton)	1056
棉布织机（台）	Cotton Loom (unit)	4391
原油加工能力（吨）	Crude Oil Processing Capacity (ton)	140000
烧碱(折100%)（吨）	Caustic Soda (ton)	22000
农用氮、磷、钾化学肥料总计(折纯)（吨）	Chemical Fertilizers (ton)	80000
初级形态塑料（吨）	Primary Plastic (ton)	27500
化学纤维（吨）	Chemical Fibre (ton)	40000
硅酸盐水泥熟料（吨）	Portland Cement Clinker (ton)	1500000
水泥（吨）	Cement (ton)	3616145
平板玻璃（重量箱）	Plate Glass (weight case)	6846881
粗钢（吨）	Crude Steel (ton)	5000
钢材（吨）	Rolled Steel (ton)	607948
金属切削机床（台）	Metal-cutting Machine Tools (set)	7524
挖掘机（台）	Excavator (set)	180
汽车（辆）	Motor Vehicles (unit)	540000
其中：乘用车	Passenger Vehicle (unit)	300000
其中：新能源乘用车	New Energy Passenger Car (unit)	130000
商用车	Commercial Vehicle (unit)	240000
太阳能电池（千瓦）	Solar Cell (kw)	9818599
微型计算机设备（台）	Micro Computer Equipment (set)	350
移动通信手持机（台）	Mobile Telephones (set)	20092121
彩色电视机（台）	Color TV Set (set)	600000
发电设备容量总计（万千瓦）	Total Capacity of Power Generation Equipment (10 000 kw)	363
其中：火电设备容量	Thermal Power	356

主要统计指标解释

工业 指从事自然资源的开采，对采掘品和农产品进行加工和再加工的物质生产部门。具体包括：（1）对自然资源的开采，如采矿、晒盐等（但不包括禽兽捕猎和水产捕捞）；（2）对农副产品的加工、再加工，如粮油加工、食品加工、缫丝、纺织、制革等；（3）对采掘品的加工、再加工，如炼铁、炼钢、化工生产、石油加工、机器制造、木材加工等，以及电力、自来水、煤气的生产和供应等；（4）对工业品的修理、翻新，如机器设备的修理、交通运输工具（如汽车）的修理等。

工业统计调查单位为独立核算法人工业企业。

独立核算法人工业企业指从事工业生产经营活动的单位。独立核算法人工业企业应同时具备以下条件：①依法成立，有自己的名称、组织机构和场所，能够承担民事责任；②独立拥有和使用资产，承担负债，有权与其他单位签订合同；③独立核算盈亏，并能够编制资产负债表。

国有及国有控股企业 指国有企业加上国有控股企业。国有企业（即原全民所有制工业或国营工业）指企业全部资产归国家所有，并按《中华人民共和国企业法人登记管理条例》规定登记注册的非公司制的经济组织。包括国有企业、国有独资公司和国有联营企业。1957年以前的公私合营和私营工业，后均改造为国营工业，1992年改为国有工业，这部分工业的资料不单独分列时，均包括在国有企业内。国有控股企业是对混合所有制经济的企业进行的“国有控股”分类。它是指这些企业的全部资产中国有资产（股份）相对其他所有者中的任何一个所有者占资（股）最多的企业。该分组反映了国有经济控股情况。

本篇涉及的其他企业登记注册类型的解释详见综合篇。

轻工业 指主要提供生活消费品和制作手工工具的工业。按其所使用的原料不同，可分为两大类：（1）以农产品为原料的轻工业，是指直接或间接以农产品为基本原料的轻工业。主要包括食品制造、饮料制造、烟草加工、纺织、缝纫、皮革和毛皮制作、造纸以及印刷等工业；（2）以非农产品为原料的轻工业，是指以工业品为原料的轻工业。主要包括文教体育用品、化学药品制造、合成纤维制造、日用化学制品、日用玻璃制品、日用金属制品、手工工具制造、医疗器械制造、文化和办公用机械制造等工业。

重工业 指为国民经济各部门提供物质技术基础的主要生产资料的工业。按其生产性质和产品用途，可以分为下列三类：（1）采掘（伐）工业，是指对自然资源的开采，包括石油开采、煤炭开采、金属矿开采、非金属矿开采等工业；（2）原材料工业，指向国民经济各部门提供基本材料、动力和燃料的工业。包括金属冶炼及加工、炼焦及焦炭、化学、化工：原料、水泥、人造板以及电力、石油和煤炭加工等工业；（3）加工工业，是指对工业原材料进行再加工制造的工业。包括装备国民经济各部门的机械设备制造工业、金属结构、水泥制品等工业，以及为农业提供的生产资料如化肥、农药等工业。

根据上述划分原则，修理业中以重工业产品为修理作业对象的划为重工业，反之划为轻工业。

资产总计 指企业拥有或控制的能以货币计量的经济资源，包括各种财产、债权和其他权利。资产按流动性分为流动资产、长期投资、固定资产、无形资产、递延资产和其他资产。该指标根据企业会计“资产负债表”中“资产总计”项目的期末数增列。

流动资产 指企业可以在一年内或者超过一年的一个生产周期内变现或者耗用的资产，包括现金及各种存款、短期投资，应收及预付款项、存货等。

固定资产原价 指企业在建造、购置、安装、改建、扩建、技术改造某项固定资产时所支出的全部货币总额。它一般包括买价、包装费、运杂费和安装费等。

固定资产净值 指固定资产原价减去历年已提折旧额后的净额。计算公式为：

固定资产净值=固定资产原价-累计折旧

负债合计 指企业所承担的能以货币计量，将以资产或劳务偿付的债务，偿还形式包括货币、资产或提供劳务。负债一般按偿还期长短分为流动负债和长期负债。根据会计“资产负债表”中“负债合计”的年末数填列。

所有者权益合计 指企业投资人对企业净资产的所有权。企业净资产为企业全部资产与企业全部负债的差额，包括实收资本、资本公积、盈余公积、未分配利润等。根据会计“资产负债表”中“所有者权益”项的期末数填列。

营业收入 指企业从事销售商品、提供劳务和让渡资产使用权等生产经营活动形成的经济利益流入。包括“主营业务收入”和“其他业务收入”。根据会计“利润表”中“营业收入”项目的本年累计数填报。

主营业务收入 指会计“利润表”中对应指标的本年累计数。未执行2001年《企业会计制度》的企业，用“产品销售收入”的本期累计数代替。

营业成本 指企业从事销售商品、提供劳务和让渡资产使用权等生产经营活动发生的实际成本。“营业成本”应当与“营业收入”进行配比。包括“主营业务成本”和“其他业务成本”。根据会计“利润表”中“营业成本”项目的本年累计数填报。

税金及附加 指企业因从事生产经营活动按税法规定应缴纳的消费税、城市维护建设税、资源税、环境保护税、教育附加及房产税、土地使用税、车船使用税、印花税等相关税费。根据会计“利润表”中“税金及附加”项目的本年累计数填报。

销售费用 指企业在销售商品和材料、提供劳务的过程中发生的各种费用，包括保险费、包装费、展览费和广告费、商品维修费、预计产品质量保证损失、运输费、装卸费等以及为销售本企业商品而专设的销售机构（含销售网点、售后服务网点等）的职工薪酬、业务费、折旧费等经营费用。

管理费用 指企业为组织和管理企业生产经营所发生的费用，包括企业在筹建期间内发生的开办费、董事会和行政管理部门在企业经营管理中发生的，或者应当由企业统一负担的公司经费等，不包含“研发费用”。执行企业会计准则的企业，根据会计“利润表”中“管理费用”项目的本年累计数填报。执行《小企业会计准则》的企业，应将会计“利润表”中“管理费用”项目本年累计数减“研发费用”项目本年累计数后填报。执行其他企业会计制度的企业以及未执行财政部《关于修订印发2019年度一般企业财务报表格式的通知》（财会[2019]6号）的企业，在会计“利润表”中“管理费用”项目的本年累计数的基础上，根据会计“管理费用”科目下和“研究费用”明细科目，将“研发费用”剔除后填报。

研发费用 指企业在新知识、新技术、新产品、新工艺等的研究与开发过程中发生的费用化支出，以及计入“管理费用”会计科目的企业自行开发无形资产的摊销。费用化支出主要包括研发活动的人工费用、直接投入费用、用于研发活动的仪器、设备的折旧费、用于研发活动的软件、专利权、非专利技术的摊销费用、新产品设计费、新工艺规程制定费以及其他研发活动相关费用。执行企业会计准则的企业，根据会计“利润表”中“研发费用”项目的本年累计数填报。执行《小企业会计准则》的企业，根据会计“利润表”中“研发费用”项目的本年累计数填报。执行其他企业会计制度的企业以及会计“利润表”未列示“研发费用”或“研究费用”的企业，根据会计“管理费用”科目下“研究费用”明细科目的本期发生额，以及“管理费用”科目下“无形资产摊销”明细科目的本期发生额分析填报。

财务费用 指企业为筹集生产经营所需资金等而发生的筹资费用，包括企业生产经营期间发生的利息支出（减利息收入）、汇兑损失（减汇兑收益）以及相关的手续费等。根据会计“利润表”中“财务费用”项目的本年累计数填报。

利润总额 指企业在生产经营过程中各种收入扣除各种耗费后的盈余，反映企业在报告期内实现的盈亏总额，包括营业利润、补贴收入、投资净收益和营业外收支净额。根据会计“利润表”中的对应指标的本期累计数填列。

本年应交增值税 指企业按税法规定，从事货物销售或提供加工、修理修配劳务等增加货物价值的活动本期应交纳的税金。指企业在报告期应交增值税额。计算公式为：

本年应交增值税=销项税额-（进项税额-进项税额转出）-出口抵减内销产品应纳税额-减免税款+出口退税

本年进项税额 指工业企业在报告期内购入货物或接受应税劳务而支付的、准予从销项税额中抵扣的增值税额。

本年销项税额 指工业企业在报告期内销售货物或提供应税劳务应收取的增值税额。

总资产贡献率 反映企业全部资产的获利能力，是企业经营业绩和管理水平的集中体现，是评价和考核企业盈利能力的核心指标。计算公式为：

总资产贡献率（%）=（利润总额+税金总额+利息支出）/平均资产总额×100%

公式中：税金总额为产品销售税金及附加与应交增值税之和；平均资产总额为期初期末资产之和的算术平均值。

资产负债率 该指标既反映企业经营风险的大小，也反映企业利用债权人提供的资金从事经营活动的能力。计算公式为：

资产负债率（%）=负债总额/资产总额×100%

资产与负债均为报告期期末数。

流动资产周转次数 指一定时期内流动资产完成的周转次数，反映投入工业企业流动资金的周转速度。计算公式为：

流动资产周转次数 = 产品销售收入 / 全部流动资产平均余额

公式中：全部流动资产平均余额为期初和期末的流动资产之和的算术平均值。

成本费用利润率 反映企业投入的生产成本及费用的经济效益，同时也反映企业降低成本所取得的经济效益。计算公式为：

成本费用利润率（%）=利润总额 / 成本费用总额 ×100%

公式中：成本费用总额为产品销售成本、销售费用、管理费用、财务费用之和。

产品销售率 该指标反映工业产品已实现销售的程度，是分析工业产销衔接情况，研究工业产品满足社会需求的指标。计算公式为：

产品销售率（%）=工业销售产值 / 工业总产值（现价）×100%

Explanatory Notes on Main Statistical Indicators

Industry refers to the material production sector which is engaged in the extraction of natural resources and processing and reprocessing of minerals and agricultural products, including (1) extraction of natural resources, such as mining, salt production (but not including hunting and fishing); (2) processing and reprocessing of farm and sideline produces, such as rice husking, flour milling, wine making, oil pressing, silk reeling, spinning and weaving, and leather making; (3) manufacture of industrial products, such as steel making, iron smelting, chemicals manufacturing, petroleum processing, machine building, timber processing; water and gas production and electricity generation and supply; (4)repairing of industrial products such as the repairing of machinery and means of transport (including cars).

In industrial statistics surveys, the units of enquiry are corporate industrial enterprises with independent accounting systems.

Corporate industrial enterprises with independent accounting systems refer to enterprises engaging in industrial production activities, which meet the following requirements: (1) They are established legally, having their own names, organizations, location and able to take civil liability; (2) They possess and use their assets independently, assume liabilities and are entitled to sign contracts with other units; (3) They are financially independent and compile their own balance sheets.

State-owned and State-holding Enterprises refer to state-owned enterprises plus State-holding enterprises. State-owned enterprises (originally known as State-run enterprises with ownership by the whole society) are non-corporate economic entities registered in accordance with the Regulation of the People's Republic of China on the Management of Registration of Legal Enterprises, where all assets are owned by the State. Included in this category are State-owned enterprises, State-funded corporations and State-owned joint-operation enterprises. Joint State- private industries and private industries, which existed before 1957, were transformed into state-run industries since 1957, and into State-owned industries after 1992. Statistics on those enterprises are included in the State- owned industries instead of being grouped them separately. State-holding enterprises are a sub- classification of enterprises with mixed ownership, referring to enterprises where the percentage of State assets (or shares by the State) is larger than any other single share holder of the same enterprise. This sub- classification illustrates the control of the State over a particular industry.

For explanation of enterprises of other types of registration covered in this chapter, please refer to General Survey.

Light Industry refers to the industry that produces consumer goods and hand tools. It consists of two categories, depending on the materials used:

(1) Industries using farm products as raw materials. These are the branches of light industry which directly or indirectly use farm products as basic raw materials, including the manufacture of food and beverages, tobacco processing, textile, clothing, fur and leather manufacturing, paper making, printing, etc.

(2) Industries using non-farm products as raw materials. These are the branches of light industry which use manufactured goods as raw materials, including the manufacture of cultural, educational articles and sports goods, chemicals, synthetic fibre, chemical products for daily use, glass products for daily use, metal products for daily use, hand tools, medical apparatus and instruments, and the manufacture of cultural and office machinery.

Heavy Industry refers to the industry which produces capital goods, and provides various sectors of the national economy with necessary material and technical basis for production. It consists of the following three branches according to the purpose of production or the use of products:

(1) Mining, quarrying and logging industry, which refers to the industry that extracts natural resources, including extraction of petroleum, coal, metal and non-metal ores.

(2) Raw materials industry refers to the industry that provides various sectors of the national economy with raw materials, fuels and power. It includes smelting and processing of metals, coking and coke chemistry, chemical materials and building materials such as cement, plywood, and power, petroleum refining and coal dressing

(3) Manufacturing industry which refers to the industry that processes raw materials. It includes machine-building industries which equip sectors of the national economy; industries producing metal structure and cement products; and industries producing means of agricultural production, such as chemical fertilizers and pesticides.

In accordance with the above principles of classification, the repairing trades, which are engaged primarily in repairing products of heavy industry, are classified as heavy industry while those which are engaged in repairing products of light industry are classified as light industry.

Total Assets refer to all economic resources, in monetary term, these are owned or controlled by enterprises, including properties, creditor's equity and other economic rights of all forms. Classified by the degree of liquidity, total assets include working capitals, long-term investment, fixed assets, intangible assets, deferred assets and other assets. Data on this indicator can be obtained by the year-end figures of total assets in the Assets and Liability Table of accounting records of enterprises.

Working Capital refers to capital that an enterprise can cash or use during one year or one production cycle that may exceed one year, including cash and savings deposits of various forms, short-term investment, money receivable and prepaid money, inventories, etc.

Original Value of Fixed Assets refers to the total value, in monetary terms, that an enterprise spent on fixed assets, through construction, purchase, installation, transformation, expansion or technical upgrading. Generally, it covers cost of purchase, packing, transportation and installation, etc.

Net Value of Fixed Assets refers to the original value of fixed assets minus depreciation over the years, i.e.:

Net value of fixed assets = original value of fixed assets - cumulative depreciation

Total Liabilities refer to payable liabilities of enterprises that have to be repaid in terms of money, assets or labour services. In terms of payment, it can be divided into liquid liabilities and long-term liabilities. Data on this item is obtained from the ending figures on total liabilities from the Assets and Liability Table from the enterprises.

Total Equity refers to the ownership of net assets of enterprise by its investors. Net assets equal total assets minus total liabilities of the enterprise, including the paid-in capital, accumulation of capital and operating surplus and non-distributed profits. Data are obtained from the ending figures on "total equity" from the "balance sheets" .

Operating Income It refers to the inflow of economic interests generated by an enterprise's production and operation activities such as selling goods, providing labor services and transferring the right to use assets. Operating income includes "main business income" and "other business income". The current year's cumulative counting is reported according to the item of "Operating income" in the accounting "income statement".

Revenue from Principal Business refers to the annual accumulation of the corresponding item in the "profit table" of the accountant. For enterprises that do not follow the 2001 Enterprise Accounting Standards, the year-end accumulation of revenue from the sales of products is used as a substitute.

Operating Cost It refers to the actual cost incurred by an enterprise in such production and operation activities as selling goods, providing labor services and transferring the right to use assets. "Operating cost" shall be matched with "operating revenue". Include "main business cost" and "other business cost". The current year's cumulative counting is reported according to the operating cost item in the accounting "income statement".

Taxes and Surcharges It refers to the consumption tax payable in accordance with the tax law for an enterprise engaged in production and business activities, including urban maintenance and construction tax, resource tax, environmental protection tax, education surcharge, property tax, land use tax, vehicle and vessel use tax, stamp tax and other related taxes. It is filled according to the cumulative number of taxes and additional items in the accounting income statement for this year.

Sales Cost It refers to the enterprises in the process of selling goods and materials to provide services of all kinds of costs, including insurance premium package exhibition and advertising goods maintenance product quality assurance is expected loss freight handling charge and so on and designed for sales of the enterprise products sales organizations (including sales outlets after-sales service network, etc.) of business expenses such as depreciation of employee compensation fees.

Cost management It refers to the enterprise for the cost of production in which the enterprise organization and management, including enterprise organization expenses the board of directors in the preparation period and the administrative departments in the enterprise management, or shall be borne by the enterprise unified company funds, etc., does not include the development costs, perform the enterprise accounting standard for business enterprises according to the management of project cost accounting profit statement this year accumulative fill in the implementation of accounting standards for small business enterprises, should be to reduce the management cost accounting profit statement project this year accumulative R&D projects this year accumulative after fill in Perform other enterprise accounting system of enterprises and not issued by the Ministry of Finance on revising the 2019 annual general enterprise financial report format to inform (finance and accounting) [2019] 6 enterprises, management of project cost in accounting profit this year accumulative frequency, on the basis of administrative subjects and research expenses according to the accounting detail course, will cost out the development is allowed.

R & D Expenses It refer to the expenses incurred by enterprises in the research and development process of new knowledge, new technology, new products and new processes. It mainly includes the labor cost of research and development activities, direct input cost, depreciation cost of instruments and equipment used in research and development activities, amortization cost of software, patent right and non-patent technology used in research and development activities, new product design fee, new process procedure formulation fee and other related costs of research and development activities. An enterprise implementing the accounting standards for business enterprises shall fill in the current year's cumulative count of the items of "Research and development expenses" in the accounting "income statement". The enterprises implementing the Accounting Standards for Small Enterprises shall fill in the current year's accumulations according to the items of "research expenses" in the accounting "income statement". Enterprises implementing accounting systems of other enterprises and enterprises that do not list "RESEARCH and development expenses" or "research expenses" in the accounting "income statement" shall fill in the amount incurred in the current period according to the relevant items of "Research expenses" under the accounting "administrative expenses".

Total Profits refers to the balance of various incomes minus various spendings in the course of operation, reflecting the total profits and losses of enterprises in reporting period. It includes: operating profits, income from subsidies, net investment income and net income from activities other than operation. Data are obtained from the annual accumulation of the corresponding item in the "profit table" of the accountant.

Value-added Tax Payable in the Current Year refers to the payable tax of enterprises which engaged in selling of goods or providing services that bring added value to the goods, such as processing, repairing, fitting and other activities should be paid according to Tax Law. It refers to the amount of the value-added tax which should be paid by the enterprises during the reference period. The formula is as tollows:

Value-added Tax Payable in the Current Year = tax on sales-(tax on purchase-transferred tax on purchase)- exports deduct tax payable on domestic sales-tax relief+the export tax rebate.

Tax on Purchase in Current Year refers to goods purchased by industrial enterprises or value added tax that should be paid but being granted the right to deduct from the tax on sales.

Tax on Sales in Current Year refers to value added tax on industrial enterprises from sales of goods or taxable services that should be charged value added tax.

Ratio of Profits, Taxes and Interests to Average Assets reflects the profit-making capability of all assets of the enterprise and is a key indicator manifesting the performance and management and evaluating the profit-making potential of the enterprise. It is calculated as

$$\text{Ratio of Profits, Taxes and Interests toAverageAssets(\%)} = \frac{\text{otal profits+ total taxes+ interest payment}}{\text{average assets}} \times 100\%$$

In the above formula, total taxes is the sum of tax and extra charges on the sales of products and value-added tax payable; and average assets is the arithmetic mean of the sum of beginning assets and ending assets.

Ratio of Debts to Assets reflects both the operation risk and the capability of the enterprise in making use of the capital from the creditors. It is calculated as follows:

$$\text{Ratio of Debts toAssets(\%)} = \frac{\text{total debts}}{\text{total assets}} \times 100\%$$

Both assets and debts are figures at the end of the reference period.

Turnover of Working Capital refers to the number of times of turnover of working capital in a given period of time, which reflects the speed of the turnover of working capital of industrial enterprises, and is calculated as follows:

$$\text{Turnover of Working Capital} = \frac{\text{sales revenue of products}}{\text{average balance of total working capital}}$$

In the above formula, average balance of total working capital refers to the arithmetic mean of the sum of working capital at the beginning and at the end of the reference period.

Ratio of Profits to Total Industrial Costs refers to the ratio of profits realized in a given period to the total costs in the same period, which reflects the economic efficiency of input cost and is calculated as follows:

$$\text{Ratio of Profits to Total Industrial Cost (\%)} = \frac{\text{total profits}}{\text{total costs}} \times 100\%$$

Total costs in the above formula are the sum of cost of products sold, marketing cost, management cost and financial cost.

Sales Ratio of Products is an indicator reflecting the actual sale of industrial products, analyzing the production-selling and supply-demand relations. It is calculated as:

$$\text{Sales Ratio of Products (\%)} = \frac{\text{value of industrial sales}}{\text{gross industrial output value (current prices)}} \times 100\%$$

13 能 源

ENERGY

资料整理：于元英　张　育　李　婷
Data management：Yu Yuanying　Zhang Yu　Li Ting
数据审核：马建华
Data audit：Ma Jianhua

第十三部分　能源

一、简要说明

本章资料包括规模以上工业能源购消存情况、全市单位GDP能耗、规模以上工业企业用水情况等，由西安市统计局能源与环境处提供。

二、主要指标

规模以上工业综合能源消费量（万吨标准煤）	582.36	比上年下降	10.1%
单位GDP能耗（吨标准煤/万元）	0.300	比上年下降	7.52%

13　ENERGY

Ⅰ.Brief Introduction

Data in this chapter reflects energy purchases consumption and inventory of industrial enterprises above designated size,energy consumption per unit of GDP in whole city, and statistics on water use of industrial enterprises above designated size. data in this chapter are provided and compiled by Energy and Environment Division of the Xi'an Bureau of Statistics.

Ⅱ.Major Indicators

		Increase over Preceding Year
Comprehensive Energy Consumption Above Designated Size(10 000 Tons of Standard Coal)	582.36	-10.1%
Energy Consumption of GDP per Unit (Tons of Standard Coal /10 000 yuan)	0.300	-7.52%

13-1 全市及各区县单位GDP能耗增长率

Grouth Rates of Energy Consumption per Unit of GDP by Region

单位：%（%）

区 县	Region	2010	2011	2012	2013	2014	2015	2016	2017	2018	2019	2020
西安市	**Xi'an**	**-2.06**	**-3.56**	**-3.51**	**-3.57**	**-5.89**	**-3.20**	**-3.83**	**-4.61**	**-5.99**	**-4.78**	**-7.52**
新城区	Xincheng	-1.15	-3.51	-3.50	-3.50	-5.39	-3.27	-3.58	-3.27	-4.72	-4.19	-9.92
碑林区	Beilin	-0.91	-3.89	-3.50	-3.50	-6.06	-3.20	-3.66	-3.65	-5.42	-4.37	-10.98
莲湖区	Lianhu	-3.58	-3.84	-3.60	-3.61	-7.76	-3.14	-3.58	-5.93	-6.12	-3.50	-11.01
灞桥区	Baqiao	-4.20	-3.81	-3.62	-3.64	-5.20	-3.30	-3.75	-6.95	-8.25	-3.98	-10.41
未央区	Weiyang	-1.31	-3.60	-3.60	-3.60	-7.60	-4.16	-3.86	-4.49	-4.48	-2.95	-2.80
雁塔区	Yanta	-4.18	-3.61	-3.61	-3.60	-3.89	-3.58	-3.55	-6.36	-6.54	-5.86	-9.09
阎良区	Yanliang	-0.61	-3.38	-3.50	-3.50	-7.59	-3.00	-3.46	-3.99	-4.32	-2.91	-2.74
临潼区	Lintong	-4.81	-3.52	-3.51	-3.51	-8.07	-3.00	-3.46	-6.29	-5.71	-5.18	-1.64
长安区	Chang'an	-2.08	-3.60	-3.63	-3.63	-3.40	-4.10	-3.56	-5.10	-4.56	-2.95	-4.26
高陵区	Gaoling	-3.82	-3.93	-3.52	-3.54	-7.32	-3.00	-3.52	-4.00	-5.88	-2.90	-2.05
鄠邑区	Huyi	-2.99	-3.85	-3.60	-3.62	-3.40	-3.82	-3.84	-3.89	-5.86	-4.13	-6.35
蓝田县	Lantian	-2.06	-3.39	-3.40	-3.30	-5.48	-3.17	-3.84	-3.27	-5.21	-3.35	5.47
周至县	Zhouzhi	-2.06	-3.30	-3.30	-3.30	-7.63	-2.90	-3.50	-3.64	-5.59	-2.96	-11.62
西咸新区	Xixian									-12.51	-12.31	-26.33

注：单位GDP能耗中GDP按可比价计算。

13–2 主要年份全社会用电量

单位：万千瓦时

指 标	Sector	2000	2007	2008	2009
总 计	**Total**	**732373**	**1482896**	**1605089**	**1724067**
A、全行业用电量合计	Total of Industry of Electricity	599855	1215799	1293574	1358483
1. 第一产业	Primary Industry	77579	120134	127054	99083
2. 第二产业	Secondary Industry	354245	700026	724852	766029
3. 第三产业	Tertiary Industry	168031	395639	441668	493371
B、城乡居民生活用电	Electricity Consumption of and Rural ResidentsUrban	132518	267097	311515	365585
1. 乡村	Rural	31281	38395	63072	99941
2. 城市	City	101237	228702	248443	265644
一、农、林、牧、渔业	Agriculture,Forestry,Animal Husbandry and Fishery	77579	120134	127054	99083
二、工业	Industry	345175	674990	696291	724920
三、建筑业	Construction	9070	25036	28561	41108
四、交通运输、仓储及邮政业	Traffic,Transport, Storage and Post	22904	53825	56614	62031
五、信息传输、软件和信息技术服务业	Information Transmission,Computer Services and Software		21938	26680	29328
六、批发和零售业	Wholesale and Retail Trades		107343	111676	122203
七、住宿和餐饮业	Hotels and Catering Services				
八、金融业	Financial Intermediation		67674	81674	102400
九、房地产业	Real Estate				
十、租赁和商务服务业	Leasing and Business Services				
十一、公共事业及管理组织	Public Utilities and Management Organization		144859	165024	177409

注：1.本表数据来源于国网陕西省供电公司西安供电公司和国网陕西电力公司西咸供电公司。
2.2017年及以后为包含西咸新区数据。
3.2018年采用新行业分类标准，所以2017年及之前的农、林、牧、渔业、批发和零售业、住宿和餐饮业、金融业、房地产业、租赁和商务服务业无法分类，故2017年及之前农、林、牧、渔业为农、林、牧、渔、水利业合计，批发和零售业为商业、住宿和餐饮业合计，金融业为金融、房地产、商务及居民服务业合计。

Electricity Consumption of the Whole Society in Representative Years

(10 000 kw. h)

2010	2011	2012	2013	2014	2015	2016	2017	2018	2019	2020
1993751	**2167453**	**2352571**	**2554679**	**2753213**	**2844836**	**3120582**	**3613693**	**3967465**	**4184997**	**4150188**
1499903	1590486	1706859	1854696	2002503	2049492	2216797	2586468	2821250	3031213	3043246
108720	117984	109086	110405	95997	89970	87825	102033	28998	26057	31941
883259	910360	932622	991202	1086105	1088866	1147294	1388903	1430389	1470195	1487484
507924	562142	665151	753089	820401	870656	981678	1095531	1361863	1534962	1523821
493848	576966	645713	699982	750710	795344	903785	1027226	1146216	1153784	1106942
142059	169898	197937	216148	235938	241920	263871	288571	321715	347306	333809
351789	407068	447776	483834	514773	553424	639914	738655	824501	806478	773134
108720	117984	109086	110405	95997	89970	87825	102033	100432	75902	70414
838317	859796	875018	920024	998132	997115	1062188	1287836	1326060	1345516	1361355
44942	50564	57605	71179	87973	91750	85106	101068	110600	131824	129172
58509	66684	69633	78722	88805	90914	109911	128970	149353	174658	191568
30760	33191	37444	39551	42662	46203	61950	77104	90433	105752	124898
148418	166558	199970	228117	253199	277248	301414	334387	302014	371987	387667
								94270	98522	85667
116163	131236	150832	165833	180824	185329	212666	232317	13599	13908	13891
								180942	214133	202529
								25860	30222	36738
154074	164473	207271	240866	254911	270962	295737	322753	427688	468790	439347

13-3 规模以上工业企业能源购进、消费及库存（2020年）

能源名称	Name	年初库存量 Stock (year-beginning)	购进量 Purchases	其中：购自省外 Wherein: purchased from outside the province
原煤(吨)	Raw Coal (ton)	995301	8659898	
洗精煤（用于炼焦）（吨）	Washed Coal(Coking Coal)(ton)			
其他洗煤(吨)	Other Washed Coals(ton)	86615	119889	1661
煤制品（吨）	Briquettes(ton)			
焦炭(吨)	Coke(ton)		360	360
其他焦化产品(吨)	Other Coking Products(ton)			
焦炉煤气(万立方米)	Coke Oven Gas(10000 cu.m)			
高炉煤气(万立方米)	Blast Furnace Gas(10000 cu.m)			
转炉煤气(万立方米)	Converter Gas(10000 cu.m)			
其他煤气(万立方米)	Other Gas(10000 cu.m)			
天然气（万立方米）	Natural Gas(10 000cu.m)	542	118323	
液化天然气（吨）	Liquefied Natural Gas (ton)	616	11446	
氢气（万立方米）	hydrogen(10000cu.m)		384	
原油(吨)	Crude Oil(ton)			
汽油(吨)	Gasoline(ton)	48	13551	516
煤油(吨)	Kerosene(ton)	37	90	
柴油(吨)	Diesel Oil(ton)	2607	86913	201
燃料油(吨)	Fuel Oil(ton)	364	1731	
液化石油气(吨)	LPG(ton)		20677	
炼厂干气(吨)	Refinery Gas(ton)			
石脑油(吨)	Naphtha(ton)			
润滑油（吨）	Lubricating Oil (ton)	40	4311	877
石蜡(吨)	Paraffin(ton)			
溶剂油（吨）	Solvent Oil (ton)			
石油焦(吨)	Petrol Coke(ton)			
石油沥青(吨)	Petroleum Asphalt(ton)	566	22167	
其它石油制品(吨)	Other Petroleum Products(ton)	71	1736	
热力(百万千焦)	Heat (1 million kilo-joule)		10151534	
电力(万千瓦时)	Electricity(10 000kwh)		923964	
煤矸石(用于燃料)(吨)	Coal Gangue(used for fuel)(ton)			
城市生活垃圾(用于燃料)(吨)	City Domestic Waste(used for fuel)(ton)	31779		
生物燃料（吨标准煤）	Biofuel(tons of SCE)	543	15268	5715
余热余压（百万千焦）	Residual Heat and Pressure(million of KJ)		239517	
工业废料(用于燃料)(吨)	Industrial Waste(used for fuel)(ton)			
其他燃料（吨标准煤）	Other Fuels(ton of SCE)	269	1217	
能源合计(吨标准煤)	Total Energy(ton of SCE)			

Energy Purchases, Consumption and Inventory of Industrial Enterprises above Designated Size (2020)

购进金额 (千元) Purchase amount (Thousand Dollars)	工业 生产消费 Industrial Production Consume	用于原材料 as Raw Material	运输工具消费 Means of transport Consume	期末库存量 Stock (year-end)
3627195	9088116	246619		506740
78872	161366			39857
1080	360			
2996733	117421	4041	62	300
40136	11422		865	48
20977	384			
97079	13518		9839	26
636	93			33
518149	90346	111	50863	1265
6961	1450			111
67476	20673	20447		
41377	4190	1563		158
49320	20903			949
20812	1806			1
1183555	6009626			
5368630	1063177		2282	
	1346324			15000
8447	15174			637
143710	563079			
3026	1219			
14274170	9948026	282256		

13-4 规模以上工业企业分行业主要能源品种消费量（2020年）

Major Energy Consumption above Designated Size by Industry（2020）

行　业	Sector	原煤 (吨) Raw Coal (ton)	天然气 (万立方米) Natural Gas(10 000 cu.m)
总　计	**Total**	**9088116**	**117421**
煤炭开采和洗选业	Mining and Washing of Coal		
石油和天然气开采业	Extraction of Petroleum and Natural Gas		
黑色金属矿采选业	Mining and Processing of Ferrous Metal Ores		
有色金属矿采选业	Mining and Processing of Non-ferrous Metal Ores		
非金属矿采选业	Mining and Processing of Nonmetal Ores		
开采专业及辅助性活动	Mining Professional and Auxiliary Activity		329
其他采矿业	Mining of other Ores		
农副食品加工业	Processing of Food from Agricultural Porducts	213232	1890
食品制造业	Manufacture of Foods		3045
酒、饮料和精制茶制造业	Manufacture of Alcohol,Beverages and Tea		1915
烟草制品业	Manufacture of Tobacco		
纺织业	Manufacture of Textile		255
纺织服装、服饰业	Textile, apparel industry		34
皮革、毛皮、羽毛及其制品和制鞋业	Manufacture of Leather, Fur, Feather and Related Products, and Shoes		
木材加工和木、竹、藤、棕、草制品业	Processing of Timber, Manufacture of Wood,Plam and Straw Products		
家具制造业	Manufacture of Furniture		73
造纸和纸制品业	Manufacture of Paper and Paper Products		965
印刷和记录媒介复制业	Printing,Reproduction of Recording Media		501
文教、工美、体育和娱乐用品制造业	Manufacture of Articles For Cultural,Educational and Sports Activities		
石油、煤炭及其他燃料加工业	Processing of Petroleum, Cokeing,Processing of Nuclear and Nuclear Fuel		253
化学原料和化学制品制造业	Manufacture of Raw Chemical Materials and Chemical	337899	6230
医药制造业	Manufacture of Medicines		2007
化学纤维制造业	Manufacture of Chemical Fibers		
橡胶和塑料制品业	Manufacture of Rubber and Plastics	37494	16229
非金属矿物制品业	Manufacture of Non-metallic Mineral Products	111189	2621
黑色金属冶炼和压延加工业	Smelting and Pressing of Ferrous Metals		277
有色金属冶炼和压延加工业	Smelting and Pressing of Non-ferrous Metals		869
金属制品业	Manufacture of Metal Products		486
通用设备制造业	Manufacture of General Purpose Machinery		264
专用设备制造业	Manufacture of Special Equipment		162
汽车制造业	Manufacture of Motor Vehicle		4546
铁路、船舶、航空航天和其他运输设备制造业	Railways,Shipbuilding,Aerospace and Other Transportation Equipment Manufacturing Industry		95
电气机械和器材制造业	Manufacture of Electric Equipment and Machinery		2521
计算机、通讯和其他电子设备制造业	Manufacture of Communication Equipment, Computers and other Electronic Equipment		5126
仪器仪表制造业	Manufacture of Measuring Instruments and Machinery		32
其他制造业	Manufacture of Other Manufacturing		9
废弃资源综合利用业	Recycling and Disposal of Waste		
金属制品、机械和设备修理业	Metal Products,Machinery and Equipment Repair Industry		4
电力、热力的生产和供应业	Production and Supply of Electric Power and Heat Power	8388302	64035
燃气生产和供应业	Gas Mining and Supplying Industry		2648
水的生产和供应业	Production and Supply of Water		

13-4 续表 continued

行 业	Sector	汽油（吨）Gasoline (ton)	柴油（吨）Diesel Oil (ton)	热力（百万千焦）Heat (million kilo joule)	电力（万千瓦时）Electricity (10 000 kwh)
总 计	**Total**	**13518**	**90346**	**6009626**	**1063177**
煤炭开采和洗选业	Mining and Washing of Coal				
石油和天然气开采业	Extraction of Petroleum and Natural Gas				
黑色金属矿采选业	Mining and Processing of Ferrous Metal Ores				
有色金属矿采选业	Mining and Processing of Non-ferrous Metal Ores				
非金属矿采选业	Mining and Processing of Nonmetal Ores				
开采专业及辅助性活动	Mining Professional and Auxiliary Activity	1137	11641		3269
其他采矿业	Mining of other Ores				
农副食品加工业	Processing of Food from Agricultural Porducts	348	307	2029542	16355
食品制造业	Manufacture of Foods	443	1059	483185	15650
酒、饮料和精制茶制造业	Manufacture of Alcohol,Beverages and Tea	51	62	105967	11514
烟草制品业	Manufacture of Tobacco	7	38	85629	581
纺织业	Manufacture of Textile	42		23714	15978
纺织服装、服饰业	Textile, apparel industry	41	17		207
皮革、毛皮、羽毛及其制品和制鞋业	Manufacture of Leather, Fur, Feather and Related Products, and Shoes	30		6582	150
木材加工和木、竹、藤、棕、草制品业	Processing of Timber, Manufacture of Wood,Plam and Straw Products	19			2073
家具制造业	Manufacture of Furniture	113	183		1848
造纸和纸制品业	Manufacture of Paper and Paper Products	69	53		3512
印刷和记录媒介复制业	Printing,Reproduction of Recording Media	242	257	113596	9533
文教、工美、体育和娱乐用品制造业	Manufacture of Articles For Cultural,Educational and Sports Activities	21	9		200
石油、煤炭及其他燃料加工业	Processing of Petroleum, Cokeing,Processing of Nuclear and Nuclear Fuel	426	146		908
化学原料和化学制品制造业	Manufacture of Raw Chemical Materials and Chemical	409	651	352765	75645
医药制造业	Manufacture of Medicines	527	72	286148	13794
化学纤维制造业	Manufacture of Chemical Fibers			1277605	5763
橡胶和塑料制品业	Manufacture of Rubber and Plastics	126	4371	2420	31132
非金属矿物制品业	Manufacture of Non-metallic Mineral Products	438	58282	4952	44595
黑色金属冶炼和压延加工业	Smelting and Pressing of Ferrous Metals	44	10		5982
有色金属冶炼和压延加工业	Smelting and Pressing of Non-ferrous Metals	257	132	4032	29742
金属制品业	Manufacture of Metal Products	942	268	12477	16601
通用设备制造业	Manufacture of General Purpose Machinery	490	129	273	12643
专用设备制造业	Manufacture of Special Equipment	1375	1245	40752	13302
汽车制造业	Manufacture of Motor Vehicle	2410	6821	353169	131526
铁路、船舶、航空航天和其他运输设备制造业	Railways,Shipbuilding,Aerospace and Other Transportation Equipment Manufacturing Industry	621	214	40248	14577
电气机械和器材制造业	Manufacture of Electric Equipment and Machinery	1116	538	575683	82657
计算机、通讯和其他电子设备制造业	Manufacture of Communication Equipment, Computers and other Electronic Equipment	482	44	205067	299109
仪器仪表制造业	Manufacture of Measuring Instruments and Machinery	420	25	3737	1968
其他制造业	Manufacture of Other Manufacturing	41	16		643
废弃资源综合利用业	Recycling and Disposal of Waste		168		978
金属制品、机械和设备修理业	Metal Products,Machinery and Equipment Repair Industry	50			802
电力、热力的生产和供应业	Production and Supply of Electric Power and Heat Power	144	3482	2083	171119
燃气生产和供应业	Gas Mining and Supplying Industry	400	84		6251
水的生产和供应业	Production and Supply of Water	237	22		22570

13-5 规模以上工业企业分行业综合能源消费量（2020年）

Comprehensive Energy Consumption by Sector above Designated Size（2020）

单位：吨标准煤 (ton of SCE)

行 业	Scetor	2020	比上年增长(%) Increase over Preceding Year (%)
总 计	**Total**	**5823637**	**-10.1**
煤炭开采和洗选业	Mining and Washing of Coal		
石油和天然气开采业	Extraction of Petroleum and Natural Gas		
黑色金属矿采选业	Mining and Processing of Ferrous Metal Ores		
有色金属矿采选业	Mining and Processing of Non-ferrous Metal Ores		
非金属矿采选业	Mining and Processing of Nonmetal Ores		
开采专业及辅助性活动	Mining Professional and Auxiliary Activity	27388	-17.9
其他采矿业	Mining of other Ores		
农副食品加工业	Processing of Food from Agricultural Porducts	176133	0.5
食品制造业	Manufacture of Foods	77944	-13.2
酒、饮料和精制茶制造业	Manufacture of Alcohol,Beverages and Tea	40640	-0.8
烟草制品业	Manufacture of Tobacco	3700	-4.8
纺织业	Manufacture of Textile	23722	-19.2
纺织服装、服饰业	Textile, apparel industry	797	-3.5
皮革、毛皮、羽毛及其制品和制鞋业	Manufacture of Leather, Fur, Feather and Related Products, and Shoes	453	-29.4
木材加工和木、竹、藤、棕、草制品业	Processing of Timber, Manufacture of Wood,Plam and Straw Products	5707	6.8
家具制造业	Manufacture of Furniture	3507	-30.5
造纸和纸制品业	Manufacture of Paper and Paper Products	17845	4.7
印刷和记录媒介复制业	Printing,Reproduction of Recording Media	22976	-12.0
文教、工美、体育和娱乐用品制造业	Manufacture of Articles For Cultural,Educational and Sports Activities	306	-85.0
石油、煤炭及其他燃料加工业	Processing of Petroleum, Cokeing,Processing of Nuclear and Nuclear Fuel	7377	12.9
化学原料和化学制品制造业	Manufacture of Raw Chemical Materials and Chemical Products	464694	-59.2
医药制造业	Manufacture of Medicines	54038	-12.4
化学纤维制造业	Manufacture of Chemical Fibers	50649	-8.9
橡胶和塑料制品业	Manufacture of Rubber and Plastics	96836	3.6
非金属矿物制品业	Manufacture of Non-metallic Mineral Products	340479	3.6
黑色金属冶炼和压延加工业	Smelting and Pressing of Ferrous Metals	21018	9.1
有色金属冶炼和压延加工业	Smelting and Pressing of Non-ferrous Metals	48919	-0.8
金属制品业	Manufacture of Metal Products	28980	-3.7
通用设备制造业	Manufacture of General Purpose Machinery	19986	-0.2
专用设备制造业	Manufacture of Special Equipment	23810	-12.7
汽车制造业	Manufacture of Motor Vehicle	210175	10.7
铁路、船舶、航空航天和其他运输设备制造业	Railways,Shipbuilding,Aerospace and Other Transportation Equipment Manufacturing Industry	21972	-10.3
电气机械和器材制造业	Manufacture of Electric Equipment and Machinery	156983	1.4
计算机、通信和其他电子设备制造业	Manufacture of Communication Equipment, Computers and other Electronic Equipment	445098	27.3
仪器仪表制造业	Manufacture of Measuring Instruments and Machinery	3621	-22.7
其他制造业	Manufacture of Other Manufacturing	1000	4.6
废弃资源综合利用业	Recycling and Disposal of Waste	1447	-27.8
金属制品、机械和设备修理业	Metal Products,Machinery and Equipment Repair Industry	1116	-5.9
电力、热力生产和供应业	Production and Supply of Electric Power and Heat Power	3358115	-1.6
燃气生产和供应业	Gas Mining and Supplying Industry	38088	-19.5
水的生产和供应业	Production and Supply of Water	28118	-6.2

13-6 规模以上工业企业用水情况（2020年）

Statistics on Water Use of Industrial Enterprises above Designated Size（2020）

指 标	Item	取水量（万立方米）Water Use (10 000 cu.m)	外供水量（万立方米）Outward Water Supply (10 000 cu.m)
合 计	**Total**	**89621.45**	**76619.48**
地表淡水	Surface fresh water	59631.68	1826.33
地下淡水	Underground fresh water	14256.66	949.18
自来水	Tap Water	14771.76	73843.97
陆地苦咸水	Land lake Salt water		
矿井水	Mine Water	7.26	
雨水	Rain Water	4.06	
再生水	Reclaimed Water	948.99	
其他水	Other Water	1.04	
外排水量	Efflux capacity	28947.94	
重复用水量	Repeated water consumption	152959.28	

13-7 规模以上工业企业分行业用水情况（2020年）

Volume of Water Use of Industrial Enterprises above Designated Size by Industry (2020)

行　业	Sector	取水量（万立方米） Water Use (10 000 cu.m)
总　计	**Total**	**89621.45**
煤炭开采和洗选业	Mining and Washing of Coal	
石油和天然气开采业	Extraction of Petroleum and Natural Gas	
黑色金属矿采选业	Mining and Processing of Ferrous Metal Ores	
有色金属矿采选业	Mining and Processing of Non-ferrous Metal Ores	
非金属矿采选业	Mining and Processing of Nonmetal Ores	
开采专业及辅助性活动	Mining Professional and Auxiliary Activity	127.00
其他采矿业	Mining of other Ores	
农副食品加工业	Processing of Food from Agricultural Porducts	243.74
食品制造业	Manufacture of Foods	613.36
酒、饮料和精制茶制造业	Manufacture of Alcohol,Beverages and Tea	514.23
烟草制品业	Manufacture of Tobacco	10.26
纺织业	Manufacture of Textile	68.90
纺织服装、服饰业	Textile, apparel industry	2.95
皮革、毛皮、羽毛及其制品和制鞋业	Manufacture of Leather, Fur, Feather and Related Products, and Shoes	1.22
木材加工和木、竹、藤、棕、草制品业	Processing of Timber, Manufacture of Wood,Plam and Straw Products	1.46
家具制造业	Manufacture of Furniture	11.22
造纸和纸制品业	Manufacture of Paper and Paper Products	11.65
印刷和记录媒介复制业	Printing,Reproduction of Recording Media	57.45
文教、工美、体育和娱乐用品制造业	Manufacture of Articles For Cultural,Educational and Sports Activities	1.21
石油、煤炭及其他燃料加工业	Processing of Petroleum, Cokeing,Processing of Nuclear and Nuclear Fuel	2.84
化学原料和化学制品制造业	Manufacture of Raw Chemical Materials and Chemical Products	426.25
医药制造业	Manufacture of Medicines	310.41
化学纤维制造业	Manufacture of Chemical Fibers	62.37
橡胶和塑料制品业	Manufacture of Rubber and Plastics	158.21
非金属矿物制品业	Manufacture of Non-metallic Mineral Products	520.04
黑色金属冶炼和压延加工业	Smelting and Pressing of Ferrous Metals	4.68
有色金属冶炼和压延加工业	Smelting and Pressing of Non-ferrous Metals	143.72
金属制品业	Manufacture of Metal Products	79.29
通用设备制造业	Manufacture of General Purpose Machinery	73.25
专用设备制造业	Manufacture of Special Equipment	128.97
汽车制造业	Manufacture of Motor Vehicle	795.19
铁路、船舶、航空航天和其他运输设备制造业	Railways,Shipbuilding,Aerospace and Other Transportation Equipment Manufacturing Industry	83.94
电气机械和器材制造业	Manufacture of Electric Equipment and Machinery	718.05
计算机、通讯和其他电子设备制造业	Manufacture of Communication Equipment, Computers and other Electronic Equipment	2046.80
仪器仪表制造业	Manufacture of Measuring Instruments and Machinery	29.64
其他制造业	Manufacture of Other Manufacturing	3.23
废弃资源综合利用业	Recycling and Disposal of Waste	5.63
金属制品、机械和设备修理业	Metal Products,Machinery and Equipment Repair Industry	12.03
电力、热力的生产和供应业	Production and Supply of Electric Power and Heat Power	4289.23
燃气生产和供应业	Gas Mining and Supplying Industry	27.49
水的生产和供应业	Production and Supply of Water	78035.54

13-7 续表 continude

行 业	Sector	外供水量（万立方米）Outward Water Suppiy (10 000 cu.m)
总 计	**Total**	**76619.48**
煤炭开采和洗选业	Mining and Washing of Coal	
石油和天然气开采业	Extraction of Petroleum and Natural Gas	
黑色金属矿采选业	Mining and Processing of Ferrous Metal Ores	
有色金属矿采选业	Mining and Processing of Non-ferrous Metal Ores	
非金属矿采选业	Mining and Processing of Nonmetal Ores	
开采专业及辅助性活动	Mining Professional and Auxiliary Activity	
其他采矿业	Mining of other Ores	
农副食品加工业	Processing of Food from Agricultural Porducts	
食品制造业	Manufacture of Foods	
酒、饮料和精制茶制造业	Manufacture of Alcohol,Beverages and Tea	
烟草制品业	Manufacture of Tobacco	
纺织业	Manufacture of Textile	
纺织服装、服饰业	Textile, apparel industry	
皮革、毛皮、羽毛及其制品和制鞋业	Manufacture of Leather, Fur, Feather and Related Products, and Shoes	
木材加工和木、竹、藤、棕、草制品业	Processing of Timber, Manufacture of Wood,Plam and Straw Products	
家具制造业	Manufacture of Furniture	0.03
造纸和纸制品业	Manufacture of Paper and Paper Products	
印刷和记录媒介复制业	Printing,Reproduction of Recording Media	
文教、工美、体育和娱乐用品制造业	Manufacture of Articles For Cultural,Educational and Sports Activities	
石油、煤炭及其他燃料加工业	Processing of Petroleum, Cokeing,Processing of Nuclear and Nuclear Fuel	
化学原料和化学制品制造业	Manufacture of Raw Chemical Materials and Chemical Products	
医药制造业	Manufacture of Medicines	
化学纤维制造业	Manufacture of Chemical Fibers	
橡胶和塑料制品业	Manufacture of Rubber and Plastics	
非金属矿物制品业	Manufacture of Non-metallic Mineral Products	
黑色金属冶炼和压延加工业	Smelting and Pressing of Ferrous Metals	
有色金属冶炼和压延加工业	Smelting and Pressing of Non-ferrous Metals	
金属制品业	Manufacture of Metal Products	
通用设备制造业	Manufacture of General Purpose Machinery	1.55
专用设备制造业	Manufacture of Special Equipment	2.24
汽车制造业	Manufacture of Motor Vehicle	
铁路、船舶、航空航天和其他运输设备制造业	Railways,Shipbuilding,Aerospace and Other Transportation Equipment Manufacturing Industry	
电气机械和器材制造业	Manufacture of Electric Equipment and Machinery	
计算机、通讯和其他电子设备制造业	Manufacture of Communication Equipment, Computers and other Electronic Equipment	
仪器仪表制造业	Manufacture of Measuring Instruments and Machinery	
其他制造业	Manufacture of Other Manufacturing	
废弃资源综合利用业	Recycling and Disposal of Waste	
金属制品、机械和设备修理业	Metal Products,Machinery and Equipment Repair Industry	
电力、热力的生产和供应业	Production and Supply of Electric Power and Heat Power	162.55
燃气生产和供应业	Gas Mining and Supplying Industry	
水的生产和供应业	Production and Supply of Water	76453.11

13-8 分区县规模以上工业企业综合能源消费量（2020年）

Comprehensive Energy Consumption above Designated Size by Region（2020）

单位：吨标准煤 (ton of SCE)

区 县	Region	综合能源消费量 Comprehensive Energy Consumption	增速（%） Growth Rate（%）
全 市	**Total**	**5823637**	**-10.1**
新城区	Xincheng	24373	-8.7
碑林区	Beilin	88951	-17.9
莲湖区	Lianhu	183040	-8.1
灞桥区	Baqiao	776170	-1.9
未央区	Weiyang	267207	-13.4
雁塔区	Yanta	301907	-7.8
阎良区	Yanliang	48432	-0.8
临潼区	Lintong	111195	17.4
长安区	Chang'an	684852	17.2
高陵区	Gaoling	232656	10.4
鄠邑区	Huyi	842869	5.6
蓝田县	Lantian	180754	46.3
周至县	Zhouzhi	19058	-9.0
西咸新区	Xixian	2062173	-27.3

主要统计指标解释

单位生产总值能耗 指一定时期内，一个国家或地区每生产一个单位的生产总值所消耗的能源。计算公式为：

单位生产总值能耗=能源消费总量/生产总值

工业企业能源消费量 指工业企业在工业生产活动和非工业生产活动中消费的能源，包括工业生产活动中作为燃料、动力、原料、辅助材料使用的能源，生产工艺中使用的能源，用于能源加工转换的能源；非工业生产活动中使用的能源。具体包括：

（1）用于本企业产品生产、工业性作业和其他生产性活动的能源；

（2）用于技术更新改造措施、新技术研究和新产品试制以及科学试验等方面的能源；

（3）用于经营维修、建筑及设备大修理、机电设备和交通运输工具等方面的能源；

（4）用于劳动保护的能源；

（5）生产交通运输工具的企业（如造船厂、汽车制造厂），向成品轮船、汽车中添加动力用油，应算作企业的能源消费，但不作为工业生产消费，应作为非工业生产消费和交通运输工具消费。

（6）其他非生产消费的能源。

工业生产能源消费量 指工业企业为进行工业生产活动所消费的能源。主要包括：

（1）用于本企业产品生产、工业性作业的能源，包括用作原料、材料、燃料、动力的能源；作为能源加工转换企业，还包括用作加工转换的能源（这部分能源不能理解为用作原材料，用作原材料的概念见后面的解释）；

（2）产品生产过程中作为辅助材料使用的能源；

（3）生产工艺过程使用的能源；

（4）新技术研究、新产品试制、科学试验使用的能源；

（5）为了工业生产活动而在进行的各种修理过程中使用的能源；

（6）生产区内的劳动保护用能等。

用于原材料的能源消费量 指能源产品不作能源使用，即不作燃料、动力使用，而作为生产另外一种产品（非能源产品）的原料或作为辅助材料使用，作原料使用时通常构成这种产品的实体。它与用作加工转换的区别是：用作加工转换，投入的是能源，产出的主要产品还是能源（或产出的产品属于加工转换过程中产生的不作能源使用的其他副产品和联产品）。而用作原材料时，投入的是能源，产出的主要产品是能源范畴以外的产品，包括产出的某种产品在广义上可以用作能源（比如可以燃烧以提供热量），但通常意义上不作能源使用的产品。

非工业生产能源消费量 指在工业企业能源消费中，除“工业生产能源消费”以外的能源消费，即非工业生产用能和工业企业附属的不从事工业生产活动的非独立核算单位用能。比如本企业施工单位进行技术更新改造、维修等过程用能，非生产区的劳动保护用能，科研单位、农场、车队、学校、医院、食堂、托儿所等单位用能。但是必须注意，上述单位如果是独立核算的，其用能既不能包括在“工业企业能源消费”中，亦不能包括在“非工业生产能源消费”中。

生产交通运输工具的企业（如造船厂、汽车制造厂），向成品轮船、汽车中添加动力用油，应算作企业的非工业生产消费。

综合能源消费量 指企业（单位）在报告期内工业生产实际消费的各种能源（扣除能源加工转换和能源回收利用等重复因素）的总和。计算综合能源消费量时，需要将各种能源品种的消费量换算成按照标准计量单位（如：吨标准煤）计量的消费量。

取水量 指企业从各种水源直接提取或者从市场购买的用于厂区、办公区内工业生产活动的水量，以实际获得的新水量为准。

外供水量 指企业外供给其他单位的水或水产品的量，以离厂水量为准。包括外供给其他企业或市场的原水、自来水、海水淡化水、矿泉水、纯净水等。不包括直流冷却水量、再生水（中水）、未利用直接排放的矿井水和雨水量、北方地区供暖企业供给城镇热力网内循环的热水量、进入城镇污水管网和直接排到自然环境中的水量。

Explanatory Notes on Main Statistical Indicators

Energy Consumption per Unit of GDP refers to the energy consumption per unit of Gross Domestic Product in a country or the Gross Regional Product in a region in the same reference period. The formula is:

Energy Consumption per Unit of GDP= Total Energy Consumption/Gross Domestic Product

Energy Consumption of Industrial Enterprises refers to the energy consumed by industrial enterprises in industrial production activities and non-industrial production activities, including energy used as fuel, power, raw materials and auxiliary materials in industrial production activities, energy used in production processes, energy for processing and conversion, and energy in the course of use of non-industrial production activities. Specifically, it includes:

(1)Energy used for the production, industrial operation and other productive activities of the enterprise;

(2)Energy for technological upgrading, new technology research and trial production of new products and scientific experiments.

(3) Energy for maintenance, construction and equipment repair, electrical and mechanical equipment and transportation.

(4) Energy for labor protection;

(5)Enterprises manufactured means of conveyance (such as making shipyards and automobile manufacturers), adding power oil to the finished product ships and cars, should be used as the energy consumption of the enterprises, but not as industrial production and consumption, it should be included in the consumption of non-industrial production and transportation means.

(6)Other non-productive energy sources.

Energy Consumption of Industrial Production refers to the energy consumed by industrial enterprises in industrial production activities. It mainly includes:

(1)Energy for the production and industrial operation of the products of the enterprise, including energy for raw materials, materials, fuel and power; as energy processing and conversion enterprises, including energy for processing and conversion (this part of the energy cannot be understood as raw materials, the concept of raw material is explained later)

(2)Energy used as auxiliary material during the production of products;

(3)Energy used in the production process;

(4)Energy for new technology research, trial production of new products and scientific test;

(5)Energy used in various repair processes for industrial production activities;

(6)Labor protection energy in the production area.

Energy Consumption for Raw Materials refers the energy products are not used for energy use, that is, not to be used as fuel and power, but as raw materials for the production of another product (non-energy products) or as auxiliary materials, which usually constitute the entity of this product when used as a raw material. The difference between it and the conversion of processing is that it is used as a process conversion, which is invested in energy, the main product of the output still is energy (or the produced product belongs to other by-products and associated products that are not used for energy use in the process of processing and conversion). When used as raw materials, energy is invested, and the main product is beyond the energy category, including a product that can be used as a source of energy in the broad sense (for example, to be burned to provide heat), but in general, it is not used for energy use.

Non-industry Consumption Energy refers to the energy consumed by industrial enterprises except for industrial production activities, means that energy consumed by non-industry production and it is not independent accounting units which was engaged in industrial production activities affiliated to industrial enterprises. For example, the energy consumption of technical renovation, maintenance and other processes carried out by construction units of this enterprise, labor protection for non-production areas, energy consumption of scientific research units, farms, motorcade, schools, hospitals, canteens, nursery schools and other units. However, it must be noted that if the above-mentioned units are independently accounted, their use can neither be included in the "industrial energy consumption" nor in the "non-industrial production energy consumption".

Enterprises manufactured means of conveyance(such as making shipyards and automobile manufacturers) adding power oil to finished ships and cars, should be regarded as non-industrial production and consumption of enterprises.

Comprehensive Energy Consumption refers to the sum of the various energy sources for the actual consumption of industrial production during the reporting period (the repeating factors of the conversion of energy processing and energy recovery and utilizationhave been deducted). When calculating the comprehensive energy consumption, it is necessary to convert the consumption of various types of energy into the consumption measured in accordance with the standard unit of measurement (e.g. tons of standard coal).

Water Intake refers to the amount of water directly extracted from a variety of water sources or purchased from the market for industrial production activities in the factory and office areas, which is based on the actual new amount of water.

External Water Supply refers to the quantity of water or aquatic products supplied to other units by the enterprises, taking the quantity of water away from the plant as the criterion. It includes raw water, tap water, desalination water, mineral water, purified water, etc., which are supplied to other enterprises or markets. Direct current cooling water, reclaimed water (water), unused mine water and rain water, the hot water in the urban heat network supplied by the heating enterprises in the north are not included.

14 建筑业

CONSTRUCTION

资料整理：杨雪峰
Data management: Yang Xuefeng
数据审核：席锋旭
Data audit: Xi Fengxu

第十四部分　建筑业

一、简要说明

1.本章资料反映我市建筑业概况和发展情况。包括建筑业企业基本情况和生产经营情况。主要指标有企业个数、签订合同额、本年新签合同额、建筑业总产值、从事建筑业活动的平均人数、房屋施工面积、营业利润、应交增值税、劳动生产率等。

2.本章资料统计范围，根据建筑业发展的实际情况，建筑业统计范围从2002年年报起由原具有建筑业资质等级四级及四级以上的独立核算的建筑业企业调整为具有建筑业资质的独立核算建筑业企业。

3.本章建筑业企业统计数据是根据国家统计局制定的《建筑业统计报表制度》整理汇总的。资质以内建筑业统计报表由国家统计局根据企业实际情况采取全面调查的方法布置、收集，2011年年报开始由资质内建筑业企业通过联网直报系统上报。

4.2019年年报取消劳务分包建筑业企业生产经营情况表。

二、主要指标

企业个数（个）	1361	比上年增长	5.7%
#国有及国有控股企业	193	比上年增长	7.2%
建筑业总产值（亿元）	5124.37	比上年增长	13.5%
#国有及国有控股企业	4002.19	比上年增长	15.4%
房屋建筑竣工面积（万平方米）	3486.09	比上年增长	27.9%
房屋建筑面积竣工率（%）	17.2	比上年提高	1.3个百分点

14 CONSTRUCTION

I. Brief Introduction

1.Main Contents:Data in this chapter show the general situation and the development of the construction industry in Xi'an. They cover the situation of production and management of the construction enterprises, including the number of enterprises; total contract value; newly signed contract value; gross output value of the construction industry; the average number of employed persons engage in the activities of construction enterprises; floor space of building completed in construction enterprises; profits of construction enterprises; value-added tax payable; labour productivity and etc.

2.Scope of Statistics:In view of the development of the construction industry, starting from 2002 the scope of construction statistics has been adjusted to include all the construction enterprises of various types of ownership with qualification certificates and independent accounting systems, replacing the previous criteria that required construction enterprises of various types of ownership to have qualification certificates at or above Class 4 with independent accounting systems.

3.Sources of Data and Methods of Survey:Data on construction enterprises are collected in accordance with the Statistical Reporting System of Constructionby the National Bureau of Statistics. The construction statistical reports are deployed and collected through comprehensive survey by National Bureau of Statistics in accordance with the real conditions of the enterprises. Since 2011,construction enterprises with qualification certificates reported through internet.

4.The annual report cancels the production and operation table of labor subcontracting construction enterprises in 2019.

Ⅱ.Major Indicators

		Increase over Preceding Year
Number of Enterprises(item)	1361	5.7%
#State-owned or State Holding Majority Shares	193	7.2%
Total Output Value of Construction(100 mil. yuan)	5124.37	13.5%
State-owned or State Holding Majority Shares	4002.19	15.4%
Floor Space of Buildings Completed(10 000 sq.m)	3486.09	27.9%
Rate of Floor Space of Buildings Completed(%)	17.2	1.3 percentage points

14-1 主要年份建筑业总产值

Total Output Value of Construction in Representative Years

单位：亿元　　(100 million yuan)

年份 Year	单位数（个） Number of Enterprises (unit)	建筑业总产值 Total Output Value of Construction	国有及国有控股 State-owned or State Holding Majority Shares	集体企业 Collective-owned Enterprises
2000	184	105.93	78.87	14.87
2001	205	114.81	91.82	15.47
2002	223	133.47	85.03	15.35
2003	204	177.11	119.99	13.40
2004	244	244.42	201.68	16.59
2005	235	326.65	276.68	19.61
2006	217	416.48	348.20	23.65
2007	279	604.75	432.63	32.67
2008	328	915.12	676.12	460.14
2009	326	1074.55	875.19	47.15
2010	324	1334.00	1034.04	58.39
2011	336	1619.09	1278.33	79.42
2012	396	1874.23	1364.70	96.83
2013	420	2228.41	1702.08	154.87
2014	539	2586.33	1981.24	95.02
2015	706	2650.41	2044.05	69.73
2016	893	2897.55	2288.23	63.35
2017	1055	3304.54	2588.18	70.56
2018	1209	3925.72	3083.48	52.99
2019	1288	4514.38	3467.90	47.48
2020	1361	5124.37	4002.19	24.67

注：1、1996年以后建筑业年报统计范围由往年的县及县以上（含县级建制镇）各种经济类型的建筑企业，改为具有建筑业资质等级三级及三级以上的各种经济类型的建筑施工企业；2002年改为具有建筑业资质等级的各种经济类型的建筑施工企业。
2、本表资料含劳务分包企业。
3、由于统计口径变化，对部分年份建筑业总产值相关数据进行了修订。

14-2 全市建筑施工总承包企业基本情况（2020年）

Basic Situation of Construction General Contracting Contractors in Whole City（2020）

指　标	Item	合计 Total	国有及国有控股 State-owned or State Holding Majority Shares
企业单位数（个）	Number of Enterprises (unit)	906	155
#二级以上企业	Special and First and Second Class Enterprise	686	135
计算劳动生产率的平均人数（万人）	Average Number of Employed Persons in Calculation of Labor Productivity (10 000 persons)	94.50	68.95
#二级以上企业	Special and First and Second Class Enterprise	91.58	67.92
建筑业总产值（亿元）	Total Output Value of Construction(100 million yuan)	4733.26	3833.75
#二级以上企业	Special and First and Second Class Enterprise	4587.30	3764.92
全员劳动生产率	Overall Labor Productivity	50.09	55.60
按总产值计算（万元/人）	Calculated by Total Output Value(10 000yuan/person)		

14-3 施工总承包和专业承包建筑企业生产情况（2020年）

分组	Classify	签订的合同额（万元）Contract Value (10 000 yuan)	上年结转合同额（万元）Contract Value Carried Over from last year (10 000 yuan)	本年新签合同额（万元）Contract Value Signed in this year (10 000 yuan)
总计	**Total**	**141073683**	**62437593**	**78636091**
#国有及国有控股	State-owned and State Holding Majority Shares	119098085	53897744	65200341
一、按登记注册类型分	**Grouped by Registion Status**			
内资	Domestic Investment Enterprises	140325422	62186825	78138598
国有企业	State-owned Enterprises	2475468	647984	1827483
集体企业	Collective-owned Enterprises	436847	154499	282348
股份合作企业	Share-holding Corperative Enterprises	4950		4950
联营企业	Joint Ownership Enterprises	89680	4522	85159
国有独资公司	State-owned Company	25375306	11934383	13440923
其他有限责任公司	Limited Liability Corporations	92977458	41979788	50997671
股份有限公司	Share-holding Corperation Ltd.	1551761	821329	730432
私营企业	Private Enterprises	17413953	6644320	10769633
其他企业	Others			
港澳台商投资企业	Enterprises with Funds from Hong Kong,Macao and Taiwan	92244	70913	21331
外商投资企业	Enterprises with Foreign Investment	656017	179855	476162
二、按国民经济行业分	**Grouped by Sector**			
房屋建筑业	Building Engineering Construction	50737362	20133396	30603967
土木工程建筑业	Civil Engineering Construction	84667590	40982280	43685310
建筑安装业	Installation of Construction	3757171	818388	2938784
建筑装饰和其他建筑业	Architectural Decoration and Other Construction	1911560	503530	1408030
三、按隶属关系分	**Grouped by Administrative Relationship**			
中央	Central	77108330	38324554	38783776
地方	Region	34236753	12204544	22032209
其他	Others	29728600	11908495	17820105
四、按企业资质等级分	**Grouped by Class of Enterprises**			
1. 施工总承包	Overall Contractor for Construction	134793395	60913142	73880252
#特级	Special Class	81592504	37648603	43943900
一级	First Class	40214805	17425340	22789465
二级	Second Class	10540923	4723838	5817086
2. 专业承包	Special Contractor	6280289	1524451	4755838
#一级	First Class	4419679	1047638	3372041
二级	Second Class	1137517	257426	880091

Main Indicators on General Constructing Contractors and Professional Contractors（2020）

建筑业总产值（万元）Total Output Value of Constrution (10 000 yuan)	在外省完成的产值 Output Value in Other Provinces	建筑工程产值 Output Value of Constrution	安装工程产值 Output Value of Installation	其他产值 Others	竣工产值（万元）Completed Output Value (10 000 yuan)	房屋建筑施工面积（平方米）Number of Projects under Constrution (sq.m)	新开工面积 New Construction Area
51243738	**24377440**	**45700638**	**3491009**	**2052091**	**17332920**	**202187514**	**61692070**
40021879	21913464	37142776	1635354	1243749	14437921	163878799	51025024
50912390	24361580	45454849	3405450	2052091	17152226	200732633	61618155
1134509	182540	864881	197958	71670	389018	3936608	378712
246685		199064	37150	10471	147839	1735725	1090873
4800		4800					
64330		64330			1042	31837	19413
9319119	5284679	8943980	154496	220643	5079553	28975071	7218957
30656146	16107479	27935333	1758922	961891	8811457	133594566	41683536
746977	492438	703450	43527		420216	6099756	2584619
8739825	2294444	6739012	1213397	787417	2303101	26359070	8642045
43625	14060	36952	6674		9364	940568	72915
287723	1800	208837	78886		171330	514313	1000
20234713	6116771	18267075	1318463	649175	8583738	178508560	52630926
27410022	17092333	25370489	1067729	971804	7987853	17402374	7093574
2266083	806468	988054	964251	313778	314465	3534247	817111
1332921	361867	1075020	140566	117335	446864	2742333	1150459
23665590	18393584	22944962	541131	179496	7973687	58458573	20650177
13826775	2586520	12065765	1050828	710182	5495608	83261511	23934533
13751373	3397336	10689910	1899051	1162413	3863625	60467430	17107360
47332596	23356365	42756769	2710324	1865503	15823621	197920178	59718615
24783857	14006051	23185867	1155733	442257	7298818	128884167	36329466
15521252	7667394	13873721	839575	807957	6838833	53618451	17530105
5567891	1217819	4399881	616897	551112	1184007	14284365	5541005
3911143	1021075	2943869	780685	186589	1509299	4267336	1973455
2636615	759830	1974842	556171	105602	1155854	2198701	1491137
739911	146446	539652	126961	73298	231350	1381981	307848

14-3 续表

分 组	Classify	房屋竣工面积（平方米）Floor Space of Buildings Completed (sq.m)	房屋竣工价值（万元）Housing Completion Value (10 000 yuan)
总计	**Total**	**34860928**	**8509206**
#国有及国有控股	State-owned and State Holding Majority Shares	24724107	6866285
一、按登记注册类型分	**Grouped by Registion Status**		
内资	Domestic Investment Enterprises	34720045	8331950
国有企业	State-owned Enterprises	486684	88579
集体企业	Collective-owned Enterprises	653503	109200
股份合作企业	Share-holding Corperative Enterprises		
联营企业	Joint Ownership Enterprises	12420	1042
国有独资公司	State-owned Company	3820117	1094509
其他有限责任公司	Limited Liability Corporations	20827444	5554202
股份有限公司	Share-holding Corperation Ltd.	1957697	334536
私营企业	Private Enterprises	6962180	1149882
其他企业	Others		
港澳台商投资企业	Enterprises with Funds from Hong Kong,Macao and Taiwan	60563	9077
外商投资企业	Enterprises with Foreign Investment	80320	168180
二、按国民经济行业分	**Grouped by Sector**		
房屋建筑业	Building Engineering Construction	31641785	7941893
土木工程建筑业	Civil Engineering Construction	1549215	458021
建筑安装业	Installation of Construction	702171	50142
建筑装饰和其他建筑业	Architectural Decoration and Other Construction	967757	59150
三、按隶属关系分	**Grouped by Administrative Relationship**		
中央	Central	6918786	1794670
地方	Region	15084796	4326955
其他	Others	12857346	2387582
四、按企业资质等级分	**Grouped by Class of Enterprises**		
1. 施工总承包	Overall Contractor for Construction	32070232	8352328
#特级	Special Class	18080247	5043327
一级	First Class	10933091	2467458
二级	Second Class	2660349	520280
2. 专业承包	Special Contractor	2790696	156878
#一级	First Class	1038605	84720
二级	Second Class	268560	13970

continued

从事建筑业活动的平均人数（人）Average Number of Employed Persons in Construction Enterprises Productivity(person)	建筑业企业期末从业人员数（人）The Number of Employees in Construction Enterprises at the end of Period (person)	工程技术人员 Technical Personnel	自有机械设备年末净值（万元）The Net Value of Machinery and Equipment Owned at the end of the Year (10 000 yuan)	自有机械设备年末总台数（台）The Total Number of Machinery and Equipment Owned owned (stand)	自有机械设备年末总功率（千瓦）Total Power of Machinery and Equipment Owned at the end of the Year (kw)	企业总产值（万元）Gross Output Value of Enterprises (10 000 yuan)
1029851	**867328**	**123788**	**655902**	**52504**	**3292317**	**56518630**
719925	600354	79442	502374	30651	2685366	44797438
1027528	864995	123356	655892	52494	3292217	56187163
36766	34199	4386	10826	4852	102716	1139835
11515	11608	2584	6190	2296	21758	260743
223	251	33	1231	46	4460	4800
1079	1095	282	6283	33	2004	66392
165789	111885	22822	140338	7649	654817	9562587
542455	451364	53617	358216	18973	1909704	35198094
18485	19310	2074	4763	688	17577	747780
251216	235283	37558	128046	17957	579181	9206932
1340	1450	195				43625
983	883	237	10	10	100	287842
449035	355674	47033	87375	18762	406682	20556730
499270	445010	64834	553061	28036	2815908	32269645
48524	35169	6664	6529	2795	36425	2332636
33022	31475	5257	8938	2911	33302	1359619
444975	395480	47081	456720	19997	2356507	28215710
224172	154622	26316	45653	10574	309837	13990488
360704	317226	50391	153529	21933	625973	14312433
944967	797896	110453	624435	47665	3179984	52448779
427576	307599	40070	286376	16129	1624716	29351726
353922	342037	39594	196540	16229	983177	15642499
134327	120757	25163	122492	12592	403916	5799720
84884	69432	13335	31467	4839	112333	4069851
49675	37204	7791	9518	3008	64382	2683731
18329	16379	3599	16586	1441	28014	788263

14–4 施工总承包和专业承包建筑业企业主要指标（2020年）

指 标	Item	企业数（个） Number of Enterprises (unit)	总产值（万元） Total Output Value (10 000 yuan)	从事建筑业活动的平均人数（人） Average Number of Employed Persons in Construction Enterprises (person)
总计	**Total**	**1361**	**51243738**	**1029851**
#国有及国有控股	State-owned and State Holding Majority Shares	193	40021879	719925
一、按登记注册类型分	**Grouped by Registion Status**			
内资	Domestic Investment Enterprises	1353	50912390	1027528
国有企业	State-owned Enterprises	22	1134509	36766
集体企业	Collective-owned Enterprises	36	246685	11515
股份合作企业	Share-holding Corperative Enterprises	1	4800	223
联营企业	Joint Ownership Enterprises	2	64330	1079
国有独资公司	State-owned Company	61	9319119	165789
其他有限责任公司	Limited Liability Corporations	146	30656146	542455
股份有限公司	Share-holding Corperation Ltd.	9	746977	18485
私营企业	Private Enterprises	1076	8739825	251216
其他企业	Others			
港澳台商投资企业	Enterprises with Funds from Hong Kong,Macao and Taiwan	2	43625	1340
外商投资企业	Enterprises with Foreign Investment	6	287723	983
二、按国民经济行业分	**Grouped by Sector**			
房屋建筑业	Building Engineering Construction	484	20234713	449035
土木工程建筑业	Civil Engineering Construction	474	27410022	499270
建筑安装业	Installation of Construction	188	2266083	48524
建筑装饰和其他建筑业	Architectural Decoration and Other Construction	215	1332921	33022
三、按隶属关系分	**Grouped by Administrative Relationship**			
中央	Central	63	23665590	444975
地方	Region	117	13826775	224172
其他	Others	1181	13751373	360704
四、按企业资质等级分	**Grouped by Class of Enterprises**			
1. 施工总承包	Overall Contractor for Construction	906	47332596	944967
#特级	Special Class	25	24783857	427576
一级	First Class	182	15521252	353922
二级	Second Class	479	5567891	134327
2. 专业承包	Special Contractor	455	3911143	84884
#一级	First Class	185	2636615	49675
二级	Second Class	191	739911	18329

Major Indicators of General Construction Contractors and Professional Contractors (2020)

建筑业企业期末人数（人） The Number of Employees in Construction Enterprises at the End of Period (person)	利润总额（万元） Total Profit (10000 yuan)	利税总额（万元） Total Profits and Taxes (10000 yuan)	按总产值计算劳动生产率（万元/人） Productivity by Gross Output Value (10000 yuan/person)	产值利润率(%) Profit Rate of Output Value (%)	产值利税率(%) Profit and Tax Rate of Output Value (%)	资产总计（万元） Total Assets (10000 yuan)	负债总计（万元） Total Liabilities (10000 yuan)	资产负债率(%) Asset Liability Ratio (%)
867328	**1541139**	**2498641**	**49.76**	**3.0**	**4.9**	**72004622**	**56871380**	**79.0**
600354	1268574	1856025	55.59	3.2	4.6	57150734	47060901	82.3
864995	1505504	2445993	49.55	3.0	4.8	71617982	56609467	79.0
34199	14062	35698	30.86	1.2	3.1	928234	763393	82.2
11608	6786	18990	21.42	2.8	7.7	353195	267137	75.6
251	376	1369	21.52	7.8	28.5	18406	15098	82.0
1095	1429	3957	59.62	2.2	6.2	118713	67890	57.2
111885	492929	688705	56.21	5.3	7.4	16520699	12978651	78.6
451364	807666	1229715	56.51	2.6	4.0	42188103	35086615	83.2
19310	2920	10151	40.41	0.4	1.4	249301	162702	65.3
235283	179338	457410	34.79	2.1	5.2	11241331	7267982	64.7
1450	2326	3626	32.56	5.3	8.3	110691	101220	91.4
883	33308	49022	292.70	11.6	17.0	275949	160693	58.2
355674	494209	874046	45.06	2.4	4.3	27268250	22591294	82.8
445010	927854	1401588	54.90	3.4	5.1	39560502	30579381	77.3
35169	92797	151231	46.70	4.1	6.7	3732598	2702591	72.4
31475	26278	71774	40.36	2.0	5.4	1443272	998114	69.2
395480	697121	970218	53.18	2.9	4.1	28323914	22825274	80.6
154622	489838	747046	61.68	3.5	5.4	22308988	18622670	83.5
317226	354180	781377	38.12	2.6	5.7	21371720	15423436	72.2
797896	1435232	2256874	50.09	3.0	4.8	66999914	53360976	79.6
307599	881949	1171250	57.96	3.6	4.7	37594224	31101550	82.7
342037	334632	625558	43.86	2.2	4.0	18619467	15013045	80.6
120757	115961	289701	41.45	2.1	5.2	8534782	5934424	69.5
69432	105906	241766	46.08	2.7	6.2	5004708	3510403	70.1
37204	75003	164074	53.08	2.8	6.2	3169385	2260468	71.3
16379	20510	44629	40.37	2.8	6.0	1082977	691284	63.8

14-5 施工总承包和专业承包建筑业企业财务状况（2020年）

单位：万元

指 标	Item	资产总计 Total Assets	流动资产合计 Total Current Assets
总计	**Total**	**72004622**	**59749068**
#国有及国有控股	State-Owned and State Holding Majority Shares	57150734	46368866
一、按登记注册类型分	**Grouped by Registion Status**		
内资	Domestic Investment Enterprises	71617982	59363964
国有企业	State-owned Enterprises	928234	738938
集体企业	Collective-owned Enterprises	353195	306062
股份合作企业	Share-holding Corperative Enterprises	18406	13512
联营企业	Joint Ownership Enterprises	118713	91974
国有独资公司	State-owned Company	16520699	12968270
其他有限责任公司	Limited Liability Corporations	42188103	34920385
股份有限公司	Share-holding Corperation Ltd.	249301	211427
私营企业	Private Enterprises	11241331	10113396
其他企业	Others		
港澳台商投资企业	Enterprises with Funds from Hong Kong, Macao and Taiwan	110691	110603
外商投资企业	Enterprises with Foreign Investment	275949	274501
二、按国民经济行业分	**Grouped by Sector**		
房屋建筑业	Building Engineering Construction	27268250	24874916
土木工程建筑业	Civil Engineering Construction	39560502	30267168
建筑安装业	Installation of Construction	3732598	3332732
建筑装饰和其他建筑业	Architectural decoration and other Construction	1443272	1274252
三、按隶属关系分	**Grouped by Administrative Relationship**		
中央	Central	28323914	21033864
地方	Region	22308988	19551841
其他	Others	21371720	19163363
四、按企业资质等级分	**Grouped by Class of Enterprises**		
1. 施工总承包	Overall Contractor for Construction	66999914	55365685
#特级	Special Class	37594224	30130207
一级	First Class	18619467	16463274
二级	Second Class	8534782	7244680
2. 专业承包	Special Contractor	5004708	4383383
#一级	First Class	3169385	2809521
二级	Second Class	1082977	933843

Financial Status of General Constructing Contractors and Professional Contractors（2020）

(10 000yuan)

固定资产原价 Original Value of Fixed Assets	累计折旧 Accumulated Depreciation	本年折旧 Depreciation of This Year	负债合计 Total Liabilities	流动负债合计 Total Current Liabilities	非流动负债合计 Non Current Liabilities	所有者权益合计 Total Owners' Equity	实收资本 Paid in Capital
4520781	**2461860**	**352430**	**56871380**	**53473715**	**3034878**	**15133242**	**9485942**
3392084	1933474	270975	47060901	44261015	2786944	10089833	5596754
4519006	2460880	351945	56609467	53227953	3018728	15008515	9475642
202875	43242	6261	763393	733609	29769	164842	111592
40803	15368	2404	267137	259124	2613	86058	69672
2492	1724	40	15098	14945	153	3308	4947
6226	2358	37	67890	43222	24668	50823	34200
1295935	861026	121135	12978651	12114324	857606	3542048	1690276
2008111	1088077	152272	35086615	33144031	1926633	7101488	4315768
20226	7832	1145	162702	161931	770	86599	44050
942338	441252	68651	7267982	6756766	176516	3973349	3205136
118	31	12	101220	85070	16150	9471	5500
1657	950	473	160693	160693		115256	4800
855521	369318	48685	22591294	21251122	1133292	4676956	3051853
3419016	1973941	283739	30579381	28708393	1733912	8981121	5395904
142444	73440	12232	2702591	2542411	145051	1030007	661436
103799	45162	7773	998114	971789	22622	445158	376749
2846078	1683527	232964	22825274	21473292	1345261	5498640	3096706
483092	217222	35347	18622670	17437906	1180467	3686318	1790932
1191611	561111	84119	15423436	14562518	509150	5948284	4598304
4186301	2292697	328709	53360976	50158354	2882781	13638937	8459250
1892872	1089566	140498	31101550	29137542	1964008	6492673	3141812
1478245	821686	121006	15013045	14333810	551904	3606422	2785381
647884	276537	48975	5934424	5411932	340051	2600358	1976946
334480	169163	23721	3510403	3315361	152096	1494305	1026692
203424	110314	12487	2260468	2165579	76085	908917	605083
85082	42468	7542	691284	651773	25616	391693	301955

14-5 续表

单位：万元

指 标	Item	营业收入 Total Revenue	主营业务收入 Main Business Income
总计	**Total**	**55874986**	**52005195**
#国有及国有控股	State-Owned and State Holding Majority Shares	43472767	40671222
一、按登记注册类型分	**Grouped by Registion Status**		
内资	Domestic Investment Enterprises	55443375	51611649
国有企业	State-owned Enterprises	888967	832313
集体企业	Collective-owned Enterprises	299948	273360
股份合作企业	Share-holding Corperative Enterprises	26922	25701
联营企业	Joint Ownership Enterprises	85694	54826
国有独资公司	State-owned Company	11534301	10598603
其他有限责任公司	Limited Liability Corporations	32933078	30959166
股份有限公司	Share-holding Corperation Ltd.	205653	189165
私营企业	Private Enterprises	9468812	8678516
其他企业	Others		
港澳台商投资企业	Enterprises with Funds from Hong Kong, Macao and Taiwan	73336	68937
外商投资企业	Enterprises with Foreign Investment	358275	324609
二、按国民经济行业分	**Grouped by Sector**		
房屋建筑业	Building Engineering Construction	19795538	18558972
土木工程建筑业	Civil Engineering Construction	31920061	29714699
建筑安装业	Installation of Construction	2654164	2350381
建筑装饰和其他建筑业	Architectural decoration and other Construction	1505223	1381144
三、按隶属关系分	**Grouped by Administrative Relationship**		
中央	Central	26061912	24530415
地方	Region	14327967	13210616
其他	Others	15485107	14264165
四、按企业资质等级分	**Grouped by Class of Enterprises**		
1. 施工总承包	Overall Contractor for Construction	51379338	47931691
#特级	Special Class	29221963	27567955
一级	First Class	14402324	13384616
二级	Second Class	6136883	5551500
2. 专业承包	Special Contractor	4495648	4073504
#一级	First Class	2936461	2675322
二级	Second Class	938486	828975

continued 1

(10 000yuan)

营业成本 Total Cost	主营业务成本 Main Business Costs	税金及附加 Taxs and Other Charges	主营业务税金及附加 The Main Business Tax and Surcharges	管理费用 Management Costs	营业利润 Operating Profit	利润总额 Total Profit	应付职工薪酬 Payable to Employees	应交增值税 Value Added Tax Payable
52537324	**52005195**	**160560**	**155377**	**1242179**	**1527470**	**1541139**	**5832846**	**796942**
41045752	40671222	91209	88789	727879	1249566	1268574	4489796	496242
52142367	51611649	159292	154110	1236142	1492635	1505504	5794417	781197
837304	832313	3594	3589	31619	13937	14062	103428	18042
273639	273360	1926	1878	13589	6418	6786	32824	10278
25701	25701	138	138	719	360	376	4573	855
80067	54826	471	326	2918	1407	1429	2689	2057
10738070	10598603	28845	27908	240416	490749	492929	1027358	166931
31204658	30959166	67053	65200	545792	789689	807666	3690846	354996
190089	189165	802	802	8569	1521	2920	20142	6429
8792839	8678516	56464	54270	392521	188553	179338	912559	221609
70347	68937	286	286	937	2305	2326	997	1014
324610	324609	982	982	5099	32530	33308	37431	14732
18762559	18558972	59835	57503	363438	488073	494209	2251653	320002
29995437	29714699	84782	82744	690758	923987	927854	3237706	388952
2392937	2350381	8969	8498	108144	89614	92797	218489	49465
1386392	1381144	6974	6633	79838	25796	26278	124998	38522
24719620	24530415	45680	44310	399933	687029	697121	3051504	227417
13385877	13210616	38394	37712	273291	477934	489838	1190088	218814
14431828	14264165	76486	73356	568955	362507	354180	1591255	350711
48388260	47931691	140273	135675	1037614	1424450	1435232	5402864	681369
27702027	27567955	54686	53668	410937	869894	881949	2957304	234615
13533547	13384616	53276	52357	291002	326556	334632	1643747	237650
5691500	5551500	26197	23713	281943	126200	115961	618836	147543
4149065	4073504	20287	19702	204565	103019	105906	429982	115573
2707111	2675322	14376	14177	117156	73472	75003	224241	74695
857268	828975	3659	3278	56492	19116	20510	89559	20460

14-6 各区县建筑业主要经济指标（2020年）

Major Indicators of Construction Enterprises by Region（2020）

区 县	Region	企业个数（个）Number of Enterprises (unit)	总产值（亿元）Total Output Value (100 million yuan)	从事建筑业活动的平均人数（万人）Average Number of Employed Persons in Construction Enterprises Labor Productivity(10 000person)	全员劳动生产率（万元/人）Overall Labor Productivity (10 000 yuan/person)	利税总额（亿元）Total Pre-tax Profits (100 million yuan)
全 市	**Total**	**1361**	**5124.37**	**102.99**	**49.76**	**249.86**
新城区	Xincheng	66	357.65	4.32	82.79	10.62
碑林区	Beilin	148	1012.23	19.13	52.91	42.08
莲湖区	Lianhu	94	406.23	8.63	47.07	29.85
灞桥区	Baqiao	57	353.74	6.09	58.09	13.42
未央区	Weiyang	270	1095.99	27.57	39.75	47.59
雁塔区	Yanta	412	1251.39	22.32	56.07	68.43
阎良区	Yanliang	35	26.62	0.77	34.57	1.57
临潼区	Lintong	37	10.35	0.45	23.00	0.64
长安区	Chang'an	68	256.57	6.18	41.52	17.65
高陵区	Gaoling	21	17.96	1.44	12.47	0.45
鄠邑区	Huyi	18	14.53	0.54	26.91	1.21
蓝田县	Lantian	15	5.98	0.29	20.62	1.09
周至县	Zhouzhi	17	4.86	0.23	21.13	0.25
西咸新区	Xixian	103	310.29	5.04	61.57	15.01

注：本表数据依据施工总承包和专业承包企业数据加工整理。

14-7 各区县建筑业房屋施工及竣工面积（2020年）

Floor Space of Buildings under Construction & Completed by Region（2020）

区 县	Region	房屋建筑施工面积（万平方米）Floor Space under Construction (10 000sq.m)	本年新开工面积 Newly Started This Year	房屋建筑竣工面积（万平方米）Floor Space of Buildings Completed (10 000sq.m)	竣工房屋价值（亿元）Value of Buildings Completed (100 million yuan)
全 市	**Total**	**20218.75**	**6169.21**	**3486.09**	**850.92**
新城区	Xincheng	605.38	238.59	94.24	30.45
碑林区	Beilin	6074.85	1737.22	1136.54	304.91
莲湖区	Lianhu	2863.14	620.76	471.84	126.35
灞桥区	Baqiao	489.82	303.09	11.70	1.50
未央区	Weiyang	5480.63	1892.63	762.56	189.15
雁塔区	Yanta	2993.58	736.00	529.11	124.49
阎良区	Yanliang	39.71	23.22	7.72	1.49
临潼区	Lintong	82.40	55.67	19.54	2.41
长安区	Chang'an	225.97	87.86	132.95	6.46
高陵区	Gaoling	79.58	29.94	39.14	5.64
鄠邑区	Huyi	68.50	30.84	26.83	5.67
蓝田县	Lantian	21.63	14.39	10.97	2.11
周至县	Zhouzhi	8.51	1.06	1.12	0.21
西咸新区	Xixian	1185.06	397.94	241.85	50.10

14-8 各区县建筑业企业主要经济效益指标（2020年）

Major Economic Performance Indicators on Construction Enterprises by Region（2020）

区 县	Region	人均利润总额（元/人） Per Profit (yuan/person)	人均利税（元/人） Per Pre-Tax Profits (yuan/person)	人均竣工产值（元/人） Per Output Value of Buildings Completed (yuan/person)	人均施工面积（平方米/人） Per Floor Space of Buildings Under Construcyion (sq.m/person)	人均竣工面积（平方米/人） Per Floor Space of Buildings Completed (sq.m/person)
全 市	**Total**	**14965**	**24262**	**168305**	**196**	**34**
新城区	Xincheng	15299	24604	907445	140	22
碑林区	Beilin	13591	22002	209114	318	59
莲湖区	Lianhu	23800	34604	220113	332	55
灞桥区	Baqiao	15090	22057	179207	80	2
未央区	Weiyang	10712	17259	97070	199	28
雁塔区	Yanta	18615	30654	109889	134	24
阎良区	Yanliang	11276	20451	179836	52	10
临潼区	Lintong	1272	14111	89427	181	43
长安区	Chang'an	17281	28562	43402	37	22
高陵区	Gaoling	-165	3126	47141	55	27
鄠邑区	Huyi	8019	22501	120089	128	50
蓝田县	Lantian	21579	37434	150156	74	38
周至县	Zhouzhi	3103	11288	68014	38	5
西咸新区	Xixian	15887	29789	130874	235	48

14-8 续表 continued

区 县	Region	产值利润率（%） Ratio of Profits to Output Value (%)	产值利税率（%） Ratio of Pre-tax Profits to Output Value (%)	资产利润率（%） Ratio of Profits to Assets (%)	资产利税率（%） Ratio of Pre-tax Profits to Assets (%)	资产负债率（%） Ratio of Debts to Assets (%)
全 市	**Total**	**3.0**	**4.9**	**2.1**	**3.5**	**79.0**
新城区	Xincheng	1.8	3.0	1.6	2.5	88.8
碑林区	Beilin	2.6	4.2	1.8	2.9	84.2
莲湖区	Lianhu	5.1	7.3	2.4	3.4	85.0
灞桥区	Baqiao	2.6	3.8	2.5	3.7	69.7
未央区	Weiyang	2.7	4.3	2.2	3.6	76.2
雁塔区	Yanta	3.3	5.5	2.1	3.4	76.5
阎良区	Yanliang	3.2	5.9	3.3	6.0	68.3
临潼区	Lintong	0.6	6.2	0.1	1.5	54.0
长安区	Chang'an	4.2	6.9	3.8	6.3	77.0
高陵区	Gaoling	-0.1	2.5	-0.1	1.4	65.5
鄠邑区	Huyi	3.0	8.3	2.9	8.0	65.0
蓝田县	Lantian	10.5	18.2	11.0	19.0	57.0
周至县	Zhouzhi	1.4	5.2	1.1	3.9	55.4
西咸新区	Xixian	2.6	4.8	2.2	4.2	73.7

主要统计指标解释

建筑业统计单位 指从事房屋、构筑物建造和设备安装活动的法人企业。建筑业法人企业应具有建筑业资质并能够独立核算，同时其应具备以下条件：①依法成立，有自己的名称、组织机构和场所，能够承担民事责任；②独立拥有和使用资产，承担负债，有权与其他单位签订合同；③独立核算盈亏，能够编制资产负债表。

建筑业总产值 是以货币形式表现的建筑业企业在一定时期内生产的建筑业产品和提供的服务的总和。建筑业总产值包括：

（1）建筑工程产值：指列入建筑工程预算内的各种工程价值。

（2）安装工程产值：指设备安装工程价值，不包括被安装设备本身的价值。

（3）其他产值：建筑业总产值中除建筑工程、安装工程以外的产值。包括房屋构筑物修理产值、非标准设备制造产值、总包企业向分包企业收取的管理费以及不能明确划分的施工活动所完成的产值。

a. 房屋构筑物修理产值：指房屋和构筑物修理所完成的产值，但不包括被修理房屋、构筑物本身价值和生产设备的修理价值。

b. 非标准设备制造产值：指加工制造没有定型的非标准生产设备的加工费和原材料价值（如化工厂、炼油厂用的各种罐、槽，矿井生产统一使用的各种漏斗、三角槽、阀门等）以及附属加工厂为本企业承建工程制作的非标准设备的价值。

建筑业增加值 指建筑业企业在报告期内以货币形式表现的建筑业生产经营活动的最终成果。

从2004年第一次全国经济普查开始，建筑业现价增加值按生产法和分配法（收入法）两种方法计算，以收入法的计算结果为准，即从收入的角度出发，根据生产要素在生产过程中应得的收入份额计算。具体计算方法：经济普查年度建筑业增加值按照《经济普查年度GDP核算方案》计算，非经济普查年度建筑业增加值按照《非经济普查年度GDP核算方案》计算。

房屋建筑施工面积 指在报告期内施过工的全部房屋建筑面积，包括本期新开工的房屋面积、上期施工跨入本期继续施工的房屋面积、上期停缓建在本期恢复施工的房屋面积、本期竣工的房屋面积及本期施工后又停缓建的房屋面积。

房屋建筑竣工面积 指在报告期内房屋建筑按照设计要求全部完工，达到了使用条件，经验收鉴定合格，正式移交使用单位的房屋建筑面积。

Explanatory Notes on Main Statistical Indicators

Statistical Unit in the Construction Industry refers to a corporate enterprise engaged in the construction of buildings and structures and in the installation of equipment. A corporate construction enterprise should have qualification certificates with independent accounting system, and should meet the following 3 requirements: a) being set up in line with relevant legal basis, having its full name, organization and location, and capable of taking civil liabilities; b) independently possessing and using its assets and assuming its liabilities, and entitled to sign contracts with other institutions; and c) making independent accounts of its profits and losses, and capable of compiling its own balance sheet.

Gross Output Value of Construction refers to total of construction products and services, expressed in money terms, produced or rendered by construction and installation enterprises during a given period of time. It includes:

(1)Output value of construction projects: the value of projects covered by the project budgets;

(2) Output value of installation projects: the value of the installation of equipment, (excluding the value of the equipment to be installed);

(3)Other output values: the output value of construction industry apart from that of construction projects and installation projects. It includes: output value of repair of buildings and structures; output value of non-standard equipment manufacturing; overhead expenses received by contracted enterprises from the sub-contracted enterprises and the completed output value of construction activities for which there is no clear definition.

a. Output value of repair of buildings and structures: the value created through the repairs of buildings or structures. It does not include the value of buildings or structures being repaired and the value of the repair of production equipment;

b. Output value of manufactured non-standard equipment: the value of non-standard production equipment, including raw materials and manufacturing cost, made for the construction project (i.e., chemical plant; kettles or tanks used by refineries; various fillers, triangle tanks, valves used by mines). It also includes the output value of equipment manufactured by subsidiary workshops.

Value-added of Construction refers to the final result of the activities of production and operation of enterprises of the construction industry in monetary terms during the reference period.

Starting from the 2004 economic census, value-added of construction is calculated by both production approach and income approach, with the figures from the income approach as the final figures. Under the income approach, calculation starts from the perspective of income and is based on the share of income derived from the production process by the relevant factors of production. Specifically, value-added of construction for the Census years is calculated in accordance with the Programme of Compilation of GDP and National Accounts for the Year of Economic Census, and value-added of construction for other years is calculated in accordance with the Programme of Compilation of GDP and National Accounts for the Non Economic Census Years.

Floor Space of Buildings Under Construction refers to floor space of buildings under construction during the reference period, including the floor space of buildings for which construction has newly started; buildings for which construction has started earlier and is continuing during the reference period; and buildings for which construction has been suspended earlier but has restarted during the reference period; buildings completed during the reference period; and buildings under construction but construction has subsequently been during the reference period.

Floor Space of Buildings Completed refers to the floor space of buildings that are completed in the reference period in accordance with the requirements of the design, up to the standard for being put into use, and having been checked and accepted by departments concerned as qualified ones.

15 运输邮电和信息化

TRANSPORT,POSTAL TELECOMMUNICATION SERVICE AND INFORMATIZATION

资料整理：王家峰　刘志杰
Data management：Wang Jiafeng　Liu Zhijie
数据审核：刘栋婷
Data audit：Liu Dongting

第十五部分　运输邮电和信息化

一、简要说明

本章资料包括交通运输业和邮电通信业的基本情况，主要是交通运输工具、货物和旅客运输量、邮电业务、邮政局所及服务点等基本情况，以及一套表单位信息化情况。运输邮电资料由西安市统计局服务业和社会科技统计处根据有关部门提供资料整理。信息化资料主要根据国家统计联网直报平台一套表单位的信息化统计数据整理。2017年起运输邮电数据为西安原口径数据，信息化数据为包含西咸新区数据。

二、主要指标

邮电业务总量（亿元）	1721.55	比上年增长	21.1%
全社会车辆数（万辆）	398.01	比上年增长	10.7%
#民用小轿车	220.38	比上年增长	8.0%

15　TRANSPORT,POSTAL TELECOMMUNICATION SERVICES AND INFORMATIZATION

Ⅰ.Brief Introduction

Data in this chapter consists of primarily basic condition of transportation, postal service and communication, mainly including transportation facility amount of goods and passenger transportation, basic data of postal service, post offices and service establishments of Xi'an City. Data on transportation industry in this chapter is compiled by Tertiary Industry and Social&Science and Technology Division of the Xi'an Bureau of Statistics according to the data provided by department concerned of the municipal government. Data on informationization are obtained from data in "Five Top" Units of National Statistical Networking Platrform. Since 2017, the range of data on transportation, post and communication industry is the original range in Xi'an and data on informationization includes data in XiXian.

Ⅱ.Major Indicators

		Increase over Preceding Year
Amount of Postal and Telecommunication Service(100 mil. yuan)	1721.55	21.1%
Number of Vehides in the whole Sciety(10 000 unit)	398.01	10.7%
Civil Car	220.38	8.0%

15-1 主要年份各种交通线路和桥梁

Transportation Routes and Bridges in Representative Years

年 份 Year	公路里程 （公里） Length of Highways (km)	桥 梁 （座） Bridges (seat)	桥梁长度 （米） Length of Bridge (m)
1989	2563		
1990	2586		
1991	2785		
1992	2786		
1993	2801		
1994	2830		
1995	2852		
1996	2877		
1997	3026		
1998	3047		
1999	2789		
2000	3010		
2001	3298		
2002	7862	629	29799
2003	8360	629	29799
2004	8360	629	29799
2005	8500	634	46973
2006	9530	634	46973
2007	9672	1319	91412
2008	11895	1710	151996
2009	12378	1856	154866
2010	12378	1856	154866
2011	12599	1863	149743
2012	13127	2190	214978
2013	13135	2213	224962
2014	13251	2213	224949
2015	13328	2323	250910
2016	13356	2423	256058
2017	13383	2435	286841
2018	14722	2413	292710
2019	13386	2436	300939
2020	13755	2447	321458

注：1.本表数据来自市交通局。
2.民航通航里程2013年统计口径发生较大变化，从2018年起此数据不再统计。
3.2018年桥梁数和桥梁长度重新进行了修订。
4.本表数据为西安原口径数据。

15-1 续表 continued

年 份 Year	永久式桥梁 （座） Permanent Bridges (seat)	永久式桥梁长度 （米） Length of Permanent Bridges (m)	民航通航里程 （重复航线）（公里） Length of Total Civil Aviation Routes(km)
1989			
1990			
1991			
1992			65007
1993			83215
1994			100800
1995			119753
1996			126433
1997			173010
1998			180000
1999			141284
2000			139764
2001			154614
2002	629	29799	211000
2003	629	29799	381800
2004	629	29799	386953
2005	632	46915	485749
2006	632	46915	418852
2007	1275	90716	553355
2008	1657	150980	515524
2009	1803	153850	587904
2010	1803	153850	742375
2011	1811	148810	898628
2012	2138	213985	981450
2013	2161	223970	70643568
2014	2171	224165	78626210
2015	2286	250175	93375419
2016	2386	255322	92561215
2017	2399	286164	113501600
2018	2438	292960	
2019	2414	300416	
2020	2431	321044	

15-2 各种交通线路里程和桥梁数（2020年）

Length of Transportation Routes and Number of Bridges (2020)

指　　标	Item	2020
公路里程（公里）	**Length of Highways (km)**	**13755**
等级公路	Expressways and Class I to IV Highways	13460
高速	Expressway	652
一级	First Class	434
二级	Second Class	1289
三级	Third Class	1094
四级	Forth Class	9992
等外公路	Highways below Class IV	295
桥梁	**Bridges**	
永久式桥梁	Permanent	
座（座）	Seat (seat)	2431
长度（米）	Length (m)	321044
民航航线条数（条）	**Length of Civil Aviation routes(Article)**	**383**
国际航线（条）	International routes(Article)	92

注：1.本表数据来自市交通局，为西安原口径数据。
　　2.民航通航里程从2018年起此数据不再统计。

15-3 主要年份全社会车辆数

Possession of Civil Vehicles in Representative Years

单位：辆、台 (unit)

年份 Year	合计 Total	汽车 Motor	载客汽车 Passenget Vehicles	载货汽车 Ordinary Trucks	摩托车 Motorcycles	拖拉机 Tractors
1999	**279335**	133192	63772	44348		38023
2000	**310252**	138318	89783	44974		37177
2001	**369988**	172436	110744	55453		31355
2002	**454998**	206653	134527	64623	176960	36083
2003	**516719**	242599	163872	70781	191834	34733
2004	**512802**	276012	195524	74557	156709	34755
2005	**544586**	377628	240923	82463	131440	34741
2006	**608155**	393778	296078	89772	131449	33236
2007	**840376**	522616	360081	97614	284594	32028
2008	**875005**	595735	430472	89093	247079	30176
2009	**1012937**	754803	567326	113430	224121	31347
2010	**1253461**	961283	739038	145740	259239	29151
2011	**1445811**	1174874	928669	171649	241132	25600
2012	**1633257**	1380125	1123105	186412	224279	24458
2013	**1862063**	1634885	1372371	207058	200419	21898
2014	**2139024**	1926012	1658714	224409	190625	17484
2015	**2394052**	2191023	1929195	224322	179619	18099
2016	**2588479**	2444000	2191862	226915	119771	19352
2017	**2885557**	2716361	2451906	243998	145207	17776
2018	**3256344**	3098008	2804240	272474	134264	16808
2019	**3594233**	3427557	3137323	269155	158203	
2020	**3980103**	3734527	3424924	290062	235573	

注：本表数据来自市车管所，为西安原口径数据。

15-4 全社会车辆数（2020年）

Possession of Civil Vehicles（2020）

单位：辆 (unit)

指　标	Item	2020
合计	**Total**	**3980103**
民用汽车	Motor	3734527
#私人汽车拥有量	Possession of Private Vehicles	3368136
载客汽车	Passenger Vehicles	3424924
#大　型	Large	19937
轿　车	Car	2203821
普通载货汽车	Ordinary Trucks	290062
#重、中型	Heavy and Medium	66849
#三轮汽车	Three Wheelers Cars	1930
摩托车	Motorcycle	235573
普通摩托车	Bicycle Motor	207278
挂车	Articulated Trailers	10003
其他类型车	Others	

注：本表数据来自市车管所，为西安原口径数据。

15-5 主要年份交通运输量及周转量

Passenger Traffic and Kilometers and Freight Traffic and Ton-kilometers in Representative Years

年 份 Year	客运量 （万人次） Passenger Traffic (10 000 person-times)	旅客周转量 （万人公里） Passenger-Km (10 000 person-Km)	货运量 （万吨） Freight Traffic (10 000 tons)	货物周转量 （万吨公里） Freight Ton-Km (10 000 ton-Km)
1978	1334		3723	
1979	1420		3919	
1980	1508		3655	
1981	1839		3379	
1982	2340		4067	
1983	3054		4225	
1984	2899		4966	
1985	2404		5681	
1986	2186		5409	
1987	3781		6294	
1988	5721		6968	
1989	6092		8742	
1990	5748		6980	
1991	4193		3389	
1992	4368		8233	
1993	8036		8406	
1994	8321		8754	
1995	9069		9590	
1996	9854		10577	
1997	8922		9358	
1998	9223		9429	
1999	10311	2130383	9766	3452383
2000	8068	2507896	6999	3691963
2001	9078	2658037	7728	4229430
2002	12399	2524444	9482	4544040
2003	11413	2596402	9392	5037684
2004	10832	3112374	14845	5850029
2005	10479	1607568	12051	1249525
2006	11245	1721217	11832	1354318
2007	12466	1753464	15124	1473182
2008	26501	2529007	27560	3490707
2009	28693	2582025	30606	3766806
2010	30294	2942957	34323	4301680
2011	33375	3223544	39239	5212010
2012	36154	3387448	44924	5958742
2013	38289	3634915	50119	6471497
2014	25719	3091147	42039	6234128
2015	26904	3241463	46270	6430083
2016	23671	2909172	23888	5521252
2017	24287	3267158	25497	5979131
2018	26057	3624193	26219	5188953
2019	26315	3875080	27426	5190086
2020	14338	2314604	25713	5026965

注：1.本表数据由市交通局、西安铁路局、咸阳机场、长安航空公司、东方航空公司西北分公司提供，2018年起铁路数据为西铁局西安辖区数据，与以前年度不可比。
2.2016年陕西省公路运输统计计算系数变化，因此与往年数据不可比。
3.本表数据为西安原口径数据。

15-6 交通运输量及运输周转量

Passenger Traffic and Kilometers and Freight Traffic and Ton-kilometers

指　标	Item	2019	2020
一、客运量合计（万人次）	**Passenger Traffic(10 000 person-times)**	**26315**	**14338**
铁路	Railways	6332	3745
公路	Highways	15261	7486
民航	Civil Aviation	4722	3107
二、旅客周转量合计（万人公里）	**Passenger-Km (10 000 person-Km)**	**3875080**	**2314604**
铁路	Railways	819035	480108
公路	Highways	877786	465858
民航	Civil Aviation	2178259	1368638
三、货运量合计（万吨）	**Freight Traffic(10 000 tons)**	**27426**	**25713**
铁路	Railways	487	471
公路	Highways	26901	25204
民航	Civil Aviation	38	38
四、货物周转量合计（万吨公里）	**Freight Ton-Kin (10 000 ton-Km)**	**5190086**	**5026965**
铁路	Railways	1242489	1279281
公路	Highways	3934603	3736745
民航	Civil Aviation	12994	10939

注：1.本表数据由市交通局、西安铁路局、咸阳机场、长安航空公司、东方航空公司西北分公司提供，2018年起铁路数据为西铁局西安辖区数据。
2.本表数据为西安原口径数据。

15-7 主要年份邮政电信情况

年份 Year	邮电业务总量（万元） Business Volume of Postal and Telecommunication Services(10 000 yuan)	电信业务总量 Business Volume of Telecommunication Services	邮政业务总量 Business Volume of Postal Services
1978	1420		
1979	1616		
1980	1640		
1981	1713		
1982	2154		
1983	2250		
1984	2484		
1985	2972		
1986	3244		
1987	3911		
1988	5327		
1989	5973		
1990	7843		
1991	5700		
1992	6610		
1993	36581		
1994	54034		
1995	76450		
1996	104566		
1997	124601		
1998	204927		
1999	306457		
2000	461628		
2001	367620		
2002	515259	470492	44767
2003	820943	770673	50270
2004	1027415	975045	52370
2005	1320447	1261033	59414
2006	1867560	1796533	71027
2007	2267633	2191250	76383
2008	2646662	2564524	82138
2009	2989246	2900836	88410
2010	3231059	3167750	63309
2011	2005025	1944329	60696
2012	2162035	2098273	63762
2013	2479430	2313630	165800
2014	2922011	2695332	226679
2015	3315324	2983024	332300
2016	3831119	3299859	531260
2017	4398547	3728783	669764
2018	7395253	6621776	773477
2019	14217000	13096111	1120889
2020	17215477	15810239	1405238

注：1.2002年及以后，邮政电信机构分离；2001—2010年邮电业务总量按2000年不变价格计算；2011年后邮电业务总量按2010年不变价格计算，故与以往年份不可比。
2.本表数据为西安原口径数据。
3.本表数据由市邮政管理局，中国联通、中国电信、中国移动等西安分公司提供。

Basic Statistic on Postal and Telecommunication Service in Representative Years

固定电话年末用户数（户） Number of Immobile Telephone at Year-end (subscriber)	农村电话用户数 Number of Telephone in Rural Areas at Year-end	移动电话用户年末数（户） Number of Mobile Phone at Year-end (subscriber)	互联网年末宽带用户数（户） Number of Broad Band Net User (subscriber)
12828	1062		
13487	1052		
14024	1086		
14497	1125		
15357	1129		
16922	1156		
18611	1203		
21624	1239		
26373	1235		
30200	1290		
34265	1357		
39506	1498		
45267	1668		
49516	2479		
60727	2613		
101327	2671		
197398	5067		
299485	8386		
430270	13654		
573244	21202		
736998	37863		
874586	74761		
1242637	170199		
1711500	259374	1277400	17183
2095230	358803	1964200	35230
2538393	415593	2412392	160900
2934424	480276	3500900	243448
3214806	500847	4199570	339280
3159639	467526	5510720	508775
3145819	419446	6645863	586213
3068807	383869	7377575	813987
2891009	358238	11200566	1167916
2617691	335048	14230800	1461804
2703640	320189	16141463	1841027
3110176	335864	18035397	2023059
3191112	330602	21606662	2670473
3066575	372823	20253157	2779458
2920773	306336	17669953	2899714
2843336	314457	17395026	3358343
2732174	294055	18542137	3467859
2622787	244984	18580879	3924786
2500807	206246	17113569	4386532
2389480	191674	17044663	4792399

15-8 邮政业务及服务网点

Postal Service and Branch Post Office

指标	Item	2011	2012	2013	2014	2015	2016	2017	2018	2019	2020
一、邮政业务总量（万元）	Business Volume of Postal Services(10 000 yuan)	60696	63077	165800	226679	332300	531260	669764	773477	1120889	1405238
二、邮政业务收入（万元）	Gross Income of Post Services (10 000 yuan)	65174	71778	177100	213893	307008	439867	544555	616823	794417	912500
其中：快递业务收入	Express Delivery Business Income			97100	134306	207451	331605	413699	475783	624260	757100
三、函件（万件）	Number of Letters (10 000 pcs)	3061	2769	2856	2112	1707	1367	1360	1081	1028	902
四、包件（万件）	Parcels (10 000 pcs)	91	50	89	71	69	51	48	49	31	26
五、汇票（万张）	Money Order (10 000 pcs)	112	90	148	81	48	17	15	11	16	12
六、报纸订销累计份数（万份）	Accumulated Newspaper Prescribing and Sales Volume (10 000 pcs)	12603	13052	14495	14338	14457	14395	14744	14915	14749	14462
七、杂志订销累计份数（万份）	Accumulated Magazine Prescribing and Sales Volume (10 000 pcs)	564	613	1628	1572	1285	1155	956	1059	760	656
八、特快专递类业务（万件）	Express Mail Service Volume (10 000 pcs)	1901	129	22211	22289	23724	43941	64961	86995	63110	69815
九、集邮业务量（万枚）	Stamps For Collection (10 000 pcs)	1060	2312	1431	1477	1920	1607	1687	1135	51	54
十、邮政营销网点（处）	Number of Post Office Branch Establishments (unit)	277	279	269	280	299	297	297	297	297	308
#设在农村的局所	In it: Number of Post Offices in Rural Area	50	115	110	123	140	149	149	148	148	148
十一、邮政信筒信箱（个）	Number of Mailboxes(unit)	1108	1108	1108	1170	1170	422	422	290	417	246

注：1.本表数据来自市邮政管理局，2013年邮政数据统计口径变化，对部分历史数据进行了修订。
2.本表数据为西安原口径数据。

15-9 电信业务情况

Telecommunication Service

指 标	Item	2011	2012	2013	2014	2015	2016	2017	2018	2019	2020
一、电信业务总量（万元）	**Business Volume of Telecommunication Services (10 000 yuan)**	**1944329**	**2098273**	**2313630**	**2695332**	**2983024**	**3299859**	**3728783**	**6621776**	**13096111**	**15810239**
二、电信业务总收入（万元）	**Gross Income of Telecommunication Services (10 000 yuan)**	**1029629**	**1162257**	**1316435**	**1356705**	**1338203**	**1420708**	**1451625**	**1495207**	**1465283**	**1547138**
三、固定电话年末用户数（万户）	**Number of Immobile Telephone at Year-end(10 000 subscribers)**	**270.36**	**311.02**	**319.11**	**306.66**	**292.08**	**284.33**	**273.22**	**262.28**	**250.08**	**238.95**
#农村电话年末户数（万户）	Number of Telephone in Rural Areas at Year-end(10 000 subscribers)	32.02	33.59	33.06	37.28	30.63	31.45	29.41	24.50	20.62	19.17
四、电话交换机总容量（万门）	**Capacity (number) of Telephone Switchboard (10 000 lines)**	**441.49**	**420.38**	**378.02**	**230.01**	**145.08**	**75.92**				
五、移动电话用户年末数（万户）	**Number of Mobile Phone at Year-end (10 000 subscribers)**	**1614.15**	**1803.54**	**2160.67**	**2025.32**	**1767.00**	**1739.50**	**1854.21**	**1858.09**	**1711.36**	**1704.47**
#4G电话用户数	4G Mobile Phone Subscribers						1113.03	1369.00	1499.18	1439.45	1353.40
六、互联网年末用户数（万户）	**Number of Broad Band Net User (10 000 subscribers)**	**184.10**	**202.31**	**267.05**	**277.95**	**289.97**	**335.83**	**346.79**	**392.48**	**438.65**	**479.24**

注：本表数据由中国联通、中国电信、中国移动等西安分公司提供，为西安原口径数据。

15-10　一套表单位信息化基本情况（2020年）

单位：个

指　标	Item	企业数 Number of Enterprises
总计	**Total**	**9046**
按国民经济门类分	**According To the Categories of National Economy**	
采矿业	Mining Industry	10
制造业	Manufacturing Industry	1517
电力、热力、燃气及水生产和供应业	Electricity, Heat, Gas and Water Production and Supply	62
建筑业	Construction Business	1343
批发和零售业	Wholesale and Retail Trade	2051
交通运输、仓储和邮政业	Transportation, Warehousing and Postal Services	232
住宿和餐饮业	Accommodation and Catering Industry	735
信息传输、软件和信息技术服务业	Information Transmission, Software and Information Technology	326
房地产业	Estate	1415
租赁和商务服务业	Leasing and Business Services	440
科学研究和技术服务业	Scientific Eesearch and Eechnical Services	408
水利、环境和公共设施管理业	Management of Water Wonservancy, Environment and Public Facilities	67
居民服务、修理和其他服务业	Services of Households, Repairs and Other Services	75
教育	Education	24
卫生和社会工作	Health and Social Service	74
文化、体育和娱乐业	Culture, Sports and Entertainment	267

注：一套表单位包括规模以上工业企业、限额以上批零住餐企业、资质以内建筑业企业、规模以上服务业企业、房地产开发经营企业。

Basic Statistics on Informatization of "One Sheet" Units (2020)

(unit)

使用计算机的企业 Computer-used Enterprise	有信息技术人员的企业 Enterprises with Information Technology Personnel	有局域网的企业 LAN Enterprises	使用信息化管理的企业 Enterprises Managed by Information Technology	有信息化投入的企业 Enterprises with Informatization Input
9043	**6700**	**6780**	**8728**	**7003**
10	8	6	10	8
1517	1357	1302	1484	1368
62	52	50	62	55
1343	1008	950	1295	1081
2051	1343	1461	1949	1461
232	152	168	224	170
735	532	539	713	552
325	308	282	318	301
1415	925	1019	1362	1013
438	304	314	423	294
408	337	320	401	335
67	53	45	66	50
75	58	53	72	56
24	23	21	24	22
74	67	63	74	67
267	173	187	251	170

15-11 一套表单位信息化设施及投入情况（2020年）

指 标	Item	期末使用计算机数量（台）Computers Used at the End of Period（unit）
总计	**Total**	**790858**
按国民经济门类分	**According To the Categories of National Economy**	
采矿业	Mining Industry	9020
制造业	Manufacturing Industry	184633
电力、热力、燃气及水生产和供应业	Electricity, Heat, Gas and Water Production and Supply	8000
建筑业	Construction Business	90965
批发和零售业	Wholesale and Retail Trade	75107
交通运输、仓储和邮政业	Transportation, Warehousing and Postal Services	31516
住宿和餐饮业	Accommodation and Catering Industry	17486
信息传输、软件和信息技术服务业	Information Transmission, Software and Information Technology	199263
房地产业	Estate	44643
租赁和商务服务业	Leasing and Business Services	22529
科学研究和技术服务业	Scientific Eesearch and Eechnical Services	68803
水利、环境和公共设施管理业	Management of Water Wonservancy, Environment and Public Facilities	5566
居民服务、修理和其他服务业	Services of Households, Repairs and Other Services	1516
教育	Education	5984
卫生和社会工作	Health and Social Service	14930
文化、体育和娱乐业	Culture, Sports and Entertainment	10897

注：一套表单位包括规模以上工业企业、限额以上批零住餐企业、资质以内建筑业企业、规模以上服务业企业、房地产开发经营企业。

Information Technology Facilities and Investment of "One Sheet" Units (2020)

信息技术人员 （人） Information Technology Personnel （Person）	拥有网站个数 （个） Number of Websites Owned （unit）
47791	**5606**
55	6
8504	1379
460	37
4704	777
3979	899
1236	110
1207	312
17808	348
2854	739
2273	298
3139	347
257	38
166	34
250	32
271	79
628	171

15–12　一套表单位信息化管理情况（2020年）

单位：个

指　标	Item	企业数 Number of Enterprises	使用信息化管理的企业 Number of Enterprises Managed by Information Technology
总计	**Total**	**9046**	**8728**
按国民经济门类分	**According To the Categories of National Economy**		
采矿业	Mining Industry	10	10
制造业	Manufacturing Industry	1517	1484
电力、燃气及水的生产供应业	Electricity, Heat, Gas and Water Production and Supply	62	62
建筑业	Construction Business	1343	1295
批发和零售业	Wholesale and Retail Trade	2051	1949
交通运输、仓储和邮政业	Transportation, Warehousing and Postal Services	232	224
住宿和餐饮业	Accommodation and Catering Industry	735	713
信息传输、软件和信息技术服务业	Information Transmission, Software and Information Technology	326	318
房地产业	Estate	1415	1362
租赁和商务服务业	Leasing and Business Services	440	423
科学研究和技术服务业	Scientific Eesearch and Eechnical Services	408	401
水利、环境和公共设施管理业	Management of Water Wonservancy, Environment and Public Facilities	67	66
居民服务、修理和其他服务业	Services of Households, Repairs and Other Services	75	72
教育	Education	24	24
卫生和社会工作	Health and Social Service	74	74
文化、体育和娱乐业	Culture, Sports and Entertainment	267	251

注：一套表单位包括规模以上工业企业、限额以上批零住餐企业、资质以内建筑业企业、规模以上服务业企业、房地产开发经营企业。

Information Management Situation of "One Sheet" Units (2020)

(unit)

财务管理 Financial Management	购销存管理 Purchase and Sale Management	生产制造管理 Manufacturing Management	物流配送管理 Logistics Distribution Management	客户关系管理 Customer Relationship Management	人力资源管理 Human Resource Management	其他 Others
7899	**3836**	**1287**	**887**	**2563**	**3251**	**1378**
10	6	2		4	4	1
1371	988	765	259	450	535	150
58	26	20	3	11	25	6
1206	242	133	40	260	476	236
1686	1359	97	391	646	530	227
204	58	14	69	48	85	45
613	355	38	43	217	207	136
304	122	38	17	136	191	50
1248	344	86	24	438	633	265
391	62	12	12	138	195	71
374	87	50	9	98	192	92
58	17	4		7	22	14
57	23	6	6	18	26	17
23	7	1		5	11	7
66	55	4	3	22	28	16
230	85	17	11	65	91	45

15-13 一套表单位电子商务交易情况（2020年）

指　标	Item	企业数（个） Number of Enterprises (unit)
总计	**Total**	**9046**
按国民经济门类分	**According To the Categories of National Economy**	
采矿业	Mining Industry	10
制造业	Manufacturing Industry	1517
电力、燃气及水的生产供应业	Electricity, Heat, Gas and Water Production and Supply	62
建筑业	Construction Business	1343
批发和零售业	Wholesale and Retail Trade	2051
交通运输、仓储和邮政业	Transportation, Warehousing and Postal Services	232
住宿和餐饮业	Accommodation and Catering Industry	735
信息传输、软件和信息技术服务业	Information Transmission, Software and Information Technology	326
房地产业	Estate	1415
租赁和商务服务业	Leasing and Business Services	440
科学研究和技术服务业	Scientific Eesearch and Eechnical Services	408
水利、环境和公共设施管理业	Management of Water Wonservancy, Environment and Public Facilities	67
居民服务、修理和其他服务业	Services of Households, Repairs and Other Services	75
教育	Education	24
卫生和社会工作	Health and Social Service	74
文化、体育和娱乐业	Culture, Sports and Entertainment	267

注：一套表单位包括规模以上工业企业、限额以上批零住餐企业、资质以内建筑业企业、规模以上服务业企业、房地产开发经营企业。

E-commerce Transactions of "One Sheet" Units（2020）

有电子商务交易的企业（个）Enterprises with Ecommerce Transactions（unit）	有电子商务销售的企业 Ecommerce Sales Enterprises	有电子商务采购的企业 E-Commerce Purchases Enterprises	拥有电子商务交易平台的企业（个）With Ecommerce Trading Platform Enterprises（unit）	全年电子商务销售金额（万元）Sales of Ecommerce (10 000 yuan)	全年电子商务采购金额（万元）Purchases of Ecommerce (10 000 yuan)
1177	**956**	**468**	**78**	**11221769**	**5755833**
149	90	83	6	289709	188290
2	1	1	1	6947	2
64	5	61		295	2255312
345	332	145	37	9458042	2582524
13	8	7	4	160371	4585
382	374	53	3	214510	1807
54	33	31	12	925367	691119
27	6	23	3	3976	2004
39	32	15	8	47584	23287
30	12	24	1	9414	5376
12	11	2	1	4031	21
9	6	6		699	40
3	3	3		78930	1084
8	6	5		2081	157
40	37	9	2	19813	225

主要统计指标解释

公路里程 指在一定时期内实际达到《公路工程技术标准JTJ01–88》规定的等级公路，并经公路主管部门正式验收交付使用的公路里程数。包括大中城市的郊区公路以及通过小城镇街道部分的公路里程和桥梁、隧道渡口的长度，不包括大中城市的街道、厂矿、林区生产用道和农业生产用道的里程。两条或多条公路共同经由同一路段，只计算一次，不得重复计算里程长度。它是反映公路建设发展规模的重要指标，也是计算运输网密度等指标的基础资料。

民用航空航线里程 指民航运输定期班机飞行的航线长度的总和。航线长度按机场之间的距离计算，通常有两种计算方法：一是将每条航线长度相加称为重复计算航线里程；一是将两线或两条以上航线经过同一区段里程，只计算一次航线长度称为不重复计算航线里程。一般常用的是后者，它能确切反映民航运输网的规模，是表明民航事业为国民经济服务和方便人民生活程度的主要指标。

货（客）运量 指在一定时期内，各种运输工具实际运送的货物（旅客）数量。它是反映运输业为国民经济和人民生活服务的数量指标，也是制定和检查运输生产计划、研究运输发展规模和速度的重要指标。货运按吨计算，客运按人计算。货物不论运输距离长短、货物类别，均按实际重量统计。旅客不论行程远近或票价多少，均按一人一次客运量统计；半价票、小孩票也按一人统计。

货物（旅客）周转量 指在一定时期内，由各种运输工具运送的货物（旅客）数量与其相应运输距离的乘积之总和。它是反映运输业生产总成果的重要指标，也是编制和检查运输生产计划，计算运输效率、劳动生产率以及核算运输单位成本的主要基础资料。计算货物周转量通常按发出站与到达站之间的最短距离，也就是计费距离计算。计算公式为：

货物（旅客）周转量=Σ货物（旅客）运输量×运输距离

民用汽车拥有量 指报告期末，在公安交通管理部门按照《机动车注册登记工作规范》，已注册登记领有民用车辆牌照的全部汽车数量。汽车拥有量统计的主要分类：根据汽车结构分为载客汽车、载货汽车及其他汽车；根据汽车所有者不同分为个人（私人）汽车、单位汽车；根据汽车的使用性质分为营运汽车、非营运汽车；根据汽车大小规格不同载客汽车分为大型、中型、小型和微型，载货汽车分为重型、中型、轻型和微型。

邮电业务总量 指以价值量形式表现的邮电通信企业为社会提供各类邮电通信服务的总数量。邮电业务量按专业分类包括函件、包件、汇票、报刊发行、邮政快件、特快专递、邮政储蓄、集邮、公众电报、用户电报、传真、长途电话、出租电路、无线寻呼、移动电话、分组交换数据通信、出租代维等。计算方法为各类产品乘以相应的平均单价（不变价）之和，再加上出租电路和设备、代用户维护电话交换机和线路等的服务收入。它综合反映了一定时期邮电业务发展的总成果，是研究邮电业务量构成和发展趋势的重要指标。计算公式为：

邮电业务总量=Σ（各类邮电业务量×不变单价）+出租代维及其他业务收入

移动电话用户 是指通过移动电话交换机进入移动电话网、占用移动电话号码的电话用户。用户数量以报告期末在移动电话营业部门实际办理登记手续进入移动电话网的户数进行计算，一部移动电话统计为一户。

电话用户 指接入国家公众固定电话网，并按固定电话业务进行经营管理的电话用户。1997年以前，电话用户分为市内电话用户和农村电话用户。“市内电话用户”是指接入县城及县以上城市的电话网上的电话用户；“农村电话用户”是指接入县邮电局农话台及县以下农村电话交换点，以县城为中心（除市活用户外）联通县、乡（镇）、行政村、村民小组的用户。从1997年起，电话用户数分组调整为以用户所在区域划分为“城市电话用户”和“乡村电话用户”，与过去的按市内电话和农村电话划分方法不同。而电话用户总数、电话机总部数统计范围不变。

农村电话用户 指县城关区以下的集镇和农村接入局用交换机的电话用户数。

局用交换机容量 是指安装在本地电信运营商内用于接续本地固定电话的电话交换机容量，有倍增设备按倍增后的数量计数。包括现用和备用的人工或自动交换机的全部容量。

计算机数 指报告期末企业（单位）使用的计算机数量，包括台式机、笔记本电脑和平板电脑。

信息技术人员 指专职从事信息技术系统的制定、设计、开发、安装、操作、维护、管理和评估的人员。

信息化投入 包括企业（单位）一次性投入和运

营维护投入。

一次性投入 包括企业（单位）购置各类硬件和软件的实际支出。

运营维护投入 包括企业（单位）更新维护各类信息通信硬件和软件的实际支出。

互联网 指在世界范围内的公共计算机网络。它提供一系列通信服务（包括万维网）的接入，并传送电子邮件、新闻、娱乐和数据文件等。

全年电子商务销售金额 指报告期内企业（单位）借助网络订单而销售的商品和服务总额。借助网络订单指通过网络接受订单，付款和配送可以不借助于网络。

全年电子商务采购金额 指报告期内企业（单位）借助网络订单而采购的商品和服务总额。借助网络订单指通过网络发送订单，付款和配送可以不借助于网络。

Explanatory Notes on Main Statistical Indicators

Length of Highways refers to the length of highways which are built in conformity with the grades specified by the highway engineering standard formulated by the Ministry of Communications, and have been formally checked and accepted by the departments of highways and put into use. The length of highways includes that of the suburb highways at large and medium- sized cities,highways passing through streets at small cities and towns,and also the length of bridges, tunnel and ferries. It does not include the length of streets in big and medium-sized cities and highways built for the production purpose at factories, mines, forest areas and agricultural areas. If two or more highways go the same section of the way, the length of the section is only calculated for once and no duplication is allowed. The length of highways is an important indicator to show the development of the highway construction and to provide essential information to calculate the transport network density.

Length of Civil Aviation Routes refers to the length of all routes for regular civil aviation flights. There are usually two ways to calculate the distance between airports connected by the route length: one is to put the length of all air routes together, called duplicated calculation of the length of the routes; the other is not to allow the duplication in calculation when two or more routes passing the same section of aviation routes. The latter is usually used, as it can precisely show the size of the civil aviation network and indicate the extent of civil aviation serving the national economy and the people.

Freight (Passenger) Traffic refers to the volume of freight (passenger) transported with various means. Freight transport is calculated in tons and passenger traffic is calculated in the number of persons. Despite the type of freight and travelling distance, the freight transport is calculated in the actual weight of the goods: and despite the travelling distance and ticket price, the passenger traffic is calculated by the principle that one person can be counted only once in one travel. The passenger who travel with a half price ticket or a child ticket is also calculated as one person. The freight (passenger) traffic provides a quantitative measure to show how the transport industry serves the national economy and people, and is also an important indicator for planning the transport industry and for studying the development scale and speed of the transport industry.

Freight Ton-kilometers(Passenger-kilometers) refer to the sum of the products of the volume of transported cargo (passengers) multiplying by the transport distance, usually using ton-kilometer and passenger-kilometer as units for measurement. Normally, the shortest distance between the departure station and the destination station (i.e., the payable distance) is the basis to calculate the freight ton-kilometers. This is an important indicator to show the total results of the transport industry, to prepare and examine the transport plan and to measure the efficiency, the labour productivity and the unit cost of transport.

The formula is as follows:

Freight Ton-kilometers(Passenger-kilometers)=Σ {Freight (Passenger) Traffic × Distance of Transportation }

Measuring unit: ton-kilometer (person-kilometer)

Possession of Civil Motor Vehicles refer to the total numbers of vehicles that are registered and received vehicles license tags according to the Work Standard for Motor Vehicles Registration formulated by the Transport Management Office under the department of public security at the end of the reference period. They are divided into categories. According to the structure of motor vehicles, they are divided into passenger vehicles, trucks and others; according to ownership into private vehicles and vehicles for the unit' s use; according to kind of usage into working vehicles and non-working vehicles; and according to size of vehicles into large passenger vehicles, medium-sized passenger vehicles, small passenger vehicles and mini passenger vehicles, heavytrucks, light-heavy trucks, light trucks and mini-trucks.

Business Volume of Post and Telecommunications refers to the total amount of post and telecommunications services, expressed in value terms, provided by the post and telecommunications departments for the society. Post and telecommunication services can be classified asletters, parcels, remittance, issue of newspapers and magazines, fast mail service, express mail service, savings deposits, stamps for collection, public and individual telegraph service, facsimiles, long-distance telephone service,leasing of telephone lines, urban paging service, mobile telephone service, data transfer and transmission, etc. The accounting approach is to multiply the service products of all types with their average unit price (constant price) to get sum of business value, plus income from other services such as leasing of telephone lines and equipment, maintenance of telephone switchboards and lines on behalf of customers. This indicator reflects the overall results of post and telecommunications service during a given period, and is important to study the composition of business service and the development of post and telecommunications service.

The formula is as follows:

Business Volume of Post and Telecommunications= Σ (Transaction of Post and Telecommunication Service x Constant Price) + Income from Leasing, Maintenance and other Services

Mobile Telephone Subscribers refer to the persons who own mobile telephone numbers and are connected with the mobile telephone communication network through the mobile telephone switchboards. The number of subscribers is calculated by the subscribers who have completed registration at mobile communication business centers and entered into the mobile telephone network. One mobile telephone is taken as a subscriber.

Telephone Subscribers refer to subscribers that are connected to the public line telephone network provided with telephone services. Before 1997, telephone subscribers were classified as city subscribers and village subscribers. City subscribers referred to those connected to city telephone networks in county towns and cities, while village subscribers referred to those connected to village telephone stations at and below counties. Since 1997, the classification of telephone subscribers was modified on the basis of physical location of the subscribers as Urban telephone subscribers and rural telephone subscribers , which is different from the previous classification of categorizing local telephones and rural telephones , while the definition of total subscribers and total number of telephones remain unchanged.

Rural Telephone Subscribers refer to telephone subscribers, located at towns under county town and country, that are connected to the public line telephone network.

Capacity of Office Telephone Exchanges refers to the capacity (measured in gate) of telephone exchanges installed in the offices of local telecommunication service providers for communication between fixed telephones. It includes the capacity of both manual and automatic exchanges in use and for stand-by purpose. Equipment with expansion function is to be counted by the expanded capacity.

The number of computer srefers to the number of computers used in an enterprise or a company at the end of the reporting period, including desktops, laptops, and tablet computers.

Information technology personnel refers topeople who is engaged in the formulation, design, development, installation, operation, maintenance, management and evaluation of an information technology system.

Informatization Input includes the One-time investment input and operation maintenance investment of an enterprise or a company.

One-time Investment Input includes the actual expenditure in purchasing all kinds of hardware and software of an enterprise or a company.

Operation and Maintenance Input includesthe actual expenditure inupdating and maintenance of all kinds of information communication hardware and software of anenterprise or a company.

The Internet refers to the public computer network around the world. It provides access to a range of communications services including the world wide web, and transmits e-mail, news, entertainment, and data files,etc.

The amount of E-commerce sales during the whole year the total amount of goods and services sold by means of network orders of an enterprise or a company during the reporting period.By means of network ordersmeans that the orders are received over the network, but the payment and distribution can be made without the network.

The amount of E-commerce purchases during the whole year refers to the total amount of goods and services purchased by means of network orders of an enterprise or a company during the reporting period.

By means of network orders means that the orders are sent over the network, but the payment and distribution can be made without the network.

16 国内贸易

DOMESTIC TRADE

资料整理：杨　骏　赵琳瑛　胡树建　李鹏涛　闫小溪　刘琼之

Data management: Yang Jun Zhao Linying Hu Shujian Li Pengtao Yan Xiaoxi Liu Qiongzhi

数据审核：赵　晖

Data audit: Zhao Hui

第十六部分　国内贸易

一、简要说明

1.本章资料反映西安市批发和零售业、住宿和餐饮业的发展与经营状况，主要内容包括：社会消费品零售总额，限额以上批发和零售业、住宿和餐饮业基本情况、连锁经营情况，重点交易市场情况等。

2.限额以上企业指年主营业务收入2000万元及以上的批发企业（单位）；500万元及以上的零售业企业（单位）；200万元及以上的住宿和餐饮业企业（单位）。

3.批发业、零售业、住宿业、餐饮业大中小微型企业划分按照《统计上大中小微型企业划分办法（2017）》标准执行。

二、主要指标

社会消费品零售总额（亿元）	4989.33	比上年下降	2.9%

16　DOMESTIC TRADE

I.Brief Introduction

1.This chapter reflects the management and development of wholesale and retail trades, hotels and catering services in Xi'an , mainly including: total retail sales of consumer goods, the basic conditions enterprises above designated size in wholesale and retail trades, hotels and catering services, the conditions of chain stores,focus on transaction markets, etc.

2.Enterprises above designated size cover wholesale enterprises with revenue from principal business over 20 million yuan, retail enterprises with revenue from principal business over 5 million yuan, hotel and catering services enterprises with revenue from principal business over 2 million yuan.

3.The division standard of large/medium/small/mini sized enterprises of wholesale, retail trades, hotels and catering services is based on the division standard of large/medium/small/mini sized enterprises in 2017.

Ⅱ .Maior Indicators

		Increase over Preceding Year
Total Retail Sales of Consumer Goods (100 mil. yuan)	4989.33	-2.9%

16-1 主要年份社会消费品零售额

Total Retail Sales of Consumer Goods in Representative Years

单位：亿元 (100 million yuan)

年份 Year	社会消费品零售总额 Total Retail Sales of Consumer Goods	城镇 Urban	乡村 Village	批发和零售贸易业 Wholesale Trades and Retail Trades	住宿和餐饮业 Accommodation and Catering Trade	其他行业 Others
1978	12.70	8.82	3.88	11.01	0.53	0.21
1980	15.88	11.53	4.35	13.05	0.80	0.20
1985	32.92	26.09	6.83	25.04	1.69	0.48
1986	37.50	29.25	8.25	28.88	1.97	0.64
1987	43.86	34.62	9.24	33.32	2.50	0.49
1988	59.65	47.74	11.91	44.84	2.97	0.78
1989	68.05	54.60	13.45	54.41	2.98	0.76
1990	72.77	59.42	13.35	57.46	3.79	0.90
1991	81.04	66.93	14.11	60.35	4.43	1.26
1992	100.84	89.17	11.67	71.86	6.13	2.30
1993	117.10	105.97	11.13	77.12	7.60	2.75
1994	148.95	135.48	13.47	92.46	9.39	3.53
1995	188.35	167.54	20.81	116.54	12.08	3.76
1996	225.71	200.65	25.06	146.85	16.03	4.07
1997	268.49	241.79	26.70	171.65	22.46	4.23
1998	296.71	262.04	34.67	186.74	31.53	4.35
1999	330.13	289.24	40.89	212.31	35.51	4.95
2000	368.96	324.63	44.33	238.41	42.40	5.56
2001	416.95	368.46	48.49	272.26	50.16	6.01
2002	473.12	421.77	51.35	318.35	52.91	6.64
2003	518.67	463.95	54.72	454.32	55.00	9.36
2004	601.12	541.21	59.91	529.43	59.09	12.60
2005	698.37	629.71	68.66	617.36	66.23	14.79
2006	819.32	739.33	80.00	724.42	78.04	16.86
2007	979.18	884.40	94.78	866.67	93.42	19.10
2008	1233.44	1115.35	118.09	1082.92	128.84	21.68
2009	1469.37	1404.26	65.11	1313.89	155.47	
2010	1765.42	1694.79	70.63	1575.73	189.69	
2011	2146.43	2071.87	74.55	1921.76	224.67	
2012	2530.95	2453.11	77.84	2273.52	257.43	

年份 Year	社会消费品零售总额 Total Retail Sales of Consumer Goods	按销售单位所在地分 By Location of Establishments 城镇零售额 Urban Areas	城区 Urban District	乡村零售额 Rural Areas	按消费形态分By Consumption Patterns 商品零售 Retail Sales	餐饮收入 Catering income
2013	2898.62	2808.37	2245.35	90.25	2669.52	229.10
2014	3277.33	3174.09	2749.92	103.24	3034.94	242.39
2015	3620.90	3501.23	3011.94	119.67	3345.59	275.32
2016	4012.44	3876.23	3479.35	136.20	3713.16	299.28
2017	4422.72	4264.73	3667.72	157.99	4075.53	347.18
2018	4854.70	4759.97	4067.48	94.73	4476.48	378.22
2019	5140.93	5039.17	4280.42	101.76	4733.65	407.28
2020	4989.33	4881.52	4145.45	107.81	4636.57	352.77

注：本表1993年到2017年数据根据第四次经济普查结果进行了修订，2018年为经普数。

16-2 社会消费品零售总额

Total Retail Sales of Consumer Goods

单位：亿元 (100 million yuan)

分 类	Classify	2019	2020
社会消费品零售总额	**Total Retail Sales of Consumer Goods**	**5140.93**	**4989.33**
（一）按销售单位所在地分	Grouped by Region		
（1）城镇	Urban	5039.17	4881.52
#城区	District	4280.42	4145.45
（2）乡村	Village	101.76	107.81
（二）按消费形态分	Grouped by Consumption Patterns		
（1）商品零售	Retail Sales	4733.65	4636.57
（2）餐饮收入	Catering Income	407.28	352.77

16-3 各区县社会消费品零售总额

Total Retail Sales of Consumer Goods by Region

单位：亿元 (100 million yuan)

区 县	Region	2005	2010	2011	2012	2013	2014	2015	2016	2017	2018	2019	2020
全 市	**Total**	**698.37**	**1765.42**	**2146.43**	**2530.95**	**2898.62**	**3277.33**	**3620.90**	**4012.44**	**4422.72**	**4854.70**	**5140.93**	**4989.33**
新城区	Xincheng	58.12	121.94	145.61	167.61	187.08	209.82	235.49	255.50	259.80	292.82	293.11	252.50
碑林区	Beilin	130.35	269.18	321.45	368.06	412.03	468.74	523.35	566.28	568.99	584.86	622.29	556.00
莲湖区	Lianhu	124.47	238.27	284.80	326.71	367.14	411.75	453.14	490.72	493.16	507.10	553.76	482.37
灞桥区	Baqiao	32.63	86.80	117.08	163.08	224.57	262.22	296.24	341.66	366.32	417.48	448.66	516.66
未央区	Weiyang	103.08	372.62	454.94	542.65	631.55	717.33	773.27	875.42	772.86	865.32	904.20	909.49
雁塔区	Yanta	156.02	462.69	563.77	659.18	739.97	826.95	915.51	991.33	1006.54	1107.71	1162.36	1144.40
阎良区	Yanliang	6.55	14.80	17.90	20.72	23.17	25.83	28.19	30.51	31.27	34.81	38.33	37.22
临潼区	Lintong	13.25	25.26	30.52	35.19	38.80	44.02	47.55	51.36	54.25	61.57	64.77	55.09
长安区	Chang'an	39.55	92.22	111.30	129.03	142.84	161.78	181.97	199.95	211.78	240.51	251.33	232.46
高陵区	Gaoling	11.68	32.86	40.68	51.68	57.26	65.08	73.15	102.17	110.09	127.80	142.11	177.86
鄠邑区	Huyi	8.21	17.92	21.52	24.67	27.47	31.03	34.58	37.79	38.91	44.05	46.78	41.25
蓝田县	Lantian	8.15	16.96	20.26	23.24	25.64	28.94	31.84	34.88	36.67	42.91	47.63	39.20
周至县	Zhouzhi	6.31	13.91	16.61	19.15	21.11	23.83	26.63	34.88	36.44	40.77	40.85	34.33
西咸新区	Xixian									435.65	487.00	524.74	510.51

注：本表2017年及之前年份数据根据第四次经济普查结果进行了修订。

16-4 限额以上批发和零售贸易企业财务状况（2020年）

单位：万元

分组	Classify	单位数（个）Number (unit)	资产总计 Total Assets	流动资产合计 Circulating Funds
总计	**Total**	**2120**	**40878799.0**	**33146634.6**
一、批发企业	**Wholesale Enterprises**	**1211**	**28753717.5**	**24965675.3**
1. 按登记注册类型分组	Grouped by Category of Commodities			
内资企业	Domestic Funded Enterprises	1181	23090710.0	19992544.6
国有	State-owned Enterprises	23	1461614.0	1312778.9
集体	Collective-owned Enterprises	3	1902.8	1807.4
股份合作	Corperative Enterprises			
联营	Joint Ownership Enterprises			
国有联营	State Joint Ownership Enterprises			
集体联营	Collective Joint Ownership Enterprises			
国有与集体联营	Joint State-collective Enterprises			
其他联营	Others Joint Ownership Enterprises			
有限责任公司	Limited Liability Corporations	259	13880847.2	11887071.7
国有独资公司	State Funded Corporations	29	3155705.9	2816539.5
其他有限责任公司	Other Limited Liability Corporations	230	10725141.3	9070532.2
股份有限公司	Share-holding Corporations Ltd.	19	1758654.6	1337126.2
私营	Private Enterprises	876	5986693.0	5453256.1
私营独资	Private-funded Enterprises	3	10122.8	9933.1
私营合伙	Private Partnership Enterprises			
私营有限责任公司	Private Limited Liability Corporations	863	5828333.9	5322113.2
私营股份有限公司	Private Share-holding Corporations Ltd.	10	148236.3	121209.8
其他	Other Enterprises	1	998.4	504.3
港澳台商投资	Enterprises with Funds from Hong Kong, Macao &Taiwan	7	82972.1	73126.7
外商投资	Foreign Funded Enterprises	23	5580035.4	4900004.0
2. 按国民经济行业分组	Grouped by Sector			

Financial Status of Wholesale and Retail Enterprises above Designated Size（2020）

(10 000 yuan)

固定资产原价 Original Value of Fixed Assets	累计折旧 Accumulated Depreciation	负债合计 Total Liabilities	流动负债合计 Circulating Liabilities	所有者权益合计 Total Owners' Equities	实收资本 Paid in Capital	营业收入 Total Revenue	主营业务收入 Revenue from Principal Business
3103107.7	**1160160.7**	**30393348.9**	**27700972.8**	**10493450.1**	**10135960.8**	**93531368.6**	**92715198.4**
1085049.9	**432207.8**	**21859356.5**	**20528769.9**	**6887199.9**	**4802747.0**	**72673415.7**	**72227564.2**
990287.6	413358.4	16754845.6	15684037.8	6328703.3	4525241.7	56969443.6	56530773.5
140240.7	74792.8	856912.5	813049.0	604701.5	129701.5	3687253.3	3684137.3
176.3	68.2	1957.0	1955.9	-54.2	54.0	4902.6	4902.6
375343.6	136763.1	9754906.2	9078279.6	4124337.4	3159560.4	32549569.9	32247076.5
64983.9	21397.5	2382425.1	2259085.5	773280.8	574275.8	8488341.7	8290584.5
310359.7	115365.6	7372481.1	6819194.1	3351056.6	2585284.6	24061228.2	23956492.0
150672.3	50687.4	1459386.5	1336881.3	299268.1	207392.6	5150045.8	5107081.4
322487.3	150073.6	4681466.7	4453655.3	1299668.8	1028033.2	15575725.0	15485628.7
357.8	168.2	8854.1	8354.1	1268.7	1150.0	18225.7	18166.0
309508.7	143886.5	4593226.3	4372226.3	1229550.1	971034.6	15432922.1	15343289.1
12620.8	6018.9	79386.3	72574.9	68850.0	55848.6	124577.2	124173.6
1367.4	973.3	216.7	216.7	781.7	500.0	1947.0	1947.0
6974.7	1321.4	62475.9	62476.0	20496.2	26089.8	235054.0	229808.8
87787.6	17528.0	5042035.0	4782256.1	538000.4	251415.5	15468918.1	15466981.9

16-4 续表1

单位：万元

分 组	Classify	营业成本 Total Cost	税金及附加 Taxs and Other Changes
总计	**Total**	**88706667.9**	**293683.3**
一、批发企业	**Wholesale Enterprises**	**70315349.2**	**232388.4**
1. 按登记注册类型分组	Grouped by Category of Commodities		
内资企业	Domestic Funded Enterprises	54810384.4	226522.2
国有	State-owned Enterprises	3230536.7	184159.8
集体	Collective-owned Enterprises	4707.1	22.9
股份合作	Corperative Enterprises		
联营	Joint Ownership Enterprises		
国有联营	State Joint Ownership Enterprises		
集体联营	Collective Joint Ownership Enterprises		
国有与集体联营	Joint State-collective Enterprises		
其他联营	Others Joint Ownership Enterprises		
有限责任公司	Limited Liability Corporations	31772854.5	24861.8
国有独资公司	State Funded Corporations	8362323.5	6342.6
其他有限责任公司	Other Limited Liability Corporations	23410531.0	18519.2
股份有限公司	Share-holding Corporations Ltd.	5016251.7	2441.8
私营	Private Enterprises	14784258.1	15035.9
私营独资	Private-funded Enterprises	16956.8	16.7
私营合伙	Private Partnership Enterprises		
私营有限责任公司	Private Limited Liability Corporations	14650437.1	14899.5
私营股份有限公司	Private Share-holding Corporations Ltd.	116864.2	119.7
其他	Other Enterprises	1776.3	
港澳台商投资	Enterprises with Funds from Hong Kong, Macao &Taiwan	227471.6	166.3
外商投资	Foreign Funded Enterprises	15277493.2	5699.9
2. 按国民经济行业分组	Grouped by Sector		

continued 1

(10 000 yuan)

销售费用 Sale Expenses	管理费用 Management Expenses	财务费用 Financial Expenses	营业利润 Business Profits	利润总额 Total Profits	应付职工薪酬 Salary Payable	所得税费用 Income Tax Expenses	应交增值税 Value Added Tax Payable
2646938.0	**1000624.8**	**323600.6**	**723168.1**	**782167.2**	**1168678.2**	**192095.1**	**583996.9**
990739.2	**477996.7**	**213875.7**	**511036.8**	**528380.3**	**499381.4**	**115828.7**	**268150.7**
954224.2	432593.1	133589.4	454091.2	469593.7	455858.4	100563.4	259791.1
48371.1	37571.4	11696.1	178119.6	181369.2	58643.1	46493.4	60622.1
115.6	38.4	9.7	8.7	8.7	225.4	3.5	530.2
331615.0	184352.4	77760.9	174256.6	184934.2	200701.8	26749.4	91722.6
37081.5	42628.4	8261.3	-10431.3	-8094.9	47732.5	3765.7	23311.4
294533.5	141724.0	69499.6	184687.9	193029.1	152969.3	22983.7	68411.2
100649.6	7105.0	10909.3	11975.8	10298.9	52003.3	2988.3	3987.7
473459.9	203503.9	33213.4	89594.8	92847.0	144214.0	24328.8	102928.5
94.4	883.8	29.7	79.0	79.0	200.2	15.6	55.0
468399.9	199452.7	32536.0	90132.4	93968.6	142135.4	24119.5	100352.1
4965.6	3167.4	647.7	-616.6	-1200.6	1878.4	193.7	2521.4
13.0	22.0		135.7	135.7	70.8		
2320.0	9628.1	863.6	-5365.1	-5680.3	2479.7	358.4	-473.8
34195.0	35775.5	79422.7	62310.7	64466.9	41043.3	14906.9	8833.4

16-4 续表2

单位：万元

分 组	Classify	单位数（个）Number (unit)	资产总计 Total Assets	流动资产合计 Circulating Funds
农、林、牧产品批发	Wholesale of Agricultural,Forestry and Animal Husbandry Products	12	109629.2	75707.8
食品、饮料及烟草制品批发	Wholesale of food Beverages and Tobaccos	132	2492397.6	2053338.7
纺织、服装及家庭服务器批发	Wholesale of Textiles, Garments and Daily Articles	52	629852.8	598936.8
文化、体育用品及器材批发	Wholesale of Culture, Sports Appliances and Equipments	47	497744.9	361496.7
医药及医疗器材批发	Wholesale of Medicines and Medical Appliances	175	3823417.1	3531585.9
矿产品、建材及化工产品批发	Wholesale of Mineral Products, Building Materials and Chemical Products	509	17775250.2	15136649.5
机械设备、五金产品及电子产品批发	Wholesale of Machinery, Hardware, and Electronic Equipment	247	3206586.4	3006996.6
贸易经纪与代理	Trade Broker and Agency	4	79030.9	77734.1
其他批发	Other wholesale not Classified Elsewhere	33	139808.4	123229.2
二、零售企业	**Retail Trade**	**909**	**12125081.5**	**8180959.3**
1. 按登记注册类型分组	Grouped by Category of Commodities			
内资企业	Domestic Funded Enterprises	846	8449020.9	5888334.9
国有	State-owned Enterprises	9	266268.0	172175.1
集体	Collective-owned Enterprises	11	10677.9	4944.1
股份合作	Corperative Enterprises			
联营	Joint Ownership Enterprises			
国有联营	State Joint Ownership Enterprises			
集体联营	Collective Joint Ownership Enterprises			
国有与集体联营	Joint State-collective Enterprises			
其他联营	Others Joint Ownership Enterprises			
有限责任公司	Limited Liability Corporations	228	3633952.8	2328683.6
国有独资公司	State Funded Corporations	10	488228.8	209812.9

continued 2

(10 000 yuan)

固定资产原价 Original Value of Fixed Assets	累计折旧 Accumulated Depreciation	负债合计 Total Liabilities	流动负债合计 Circulating Liabilities	所有者权益合计 Total Owners' Equities	实收资本 Paid in Capital	营业收入 Total Revenue	主营业务收入 Revenue from Principal Business
20470.6	7149.8	77779.6	73492.4	31849.6	25247.0	126519.1	126381.4
235932.3	96092.3	1346582.3	1137320.3	1142591.1	345117.7	3632658.2	3571944.8
16709.3	11077.8	502396.4	495311.9	127038.3	57209.9	1028711.5	1009379.3
32413.2	13604.3	304453.7	287938.0	193291.2	122647.8	826372.4	822038.1
180665.5	64924.4	3170740.6	3042718.4	651760.5	424833.9	4835489.4	4818648.3
459587.9	175833.3	13640313.1	12754092.1	4132981.8	3484147.6	55310102.3	55174850.0
128999.1	58547.6	2638063.3	2564581.6	567875.6	318713.7	6386488.5	6179386.1
1044.6	485.3	70567.1	70246.8	8463.8	4322.4	184146.6	182824.6
9227.4	4493.0	108460.4	103068.4	31348.0	20507.0	342927.7	342111.6
2018057.8	**727952.9**	**8533992.4**	**7172202.9**	**3606250.2**	**5333213.8**	**20857952.9**	**20487634.2**
1236463.1	419401.3	6128696.5	4989179.6	2335485.5	4731868.1	11322597.5	11064668.4
104458.8	23784.4	105121.0	102493.2	161147.0	12955.7	242102.8	237495.8
3635.5	858.2	6616.3	4893.4	4061.6	614.2	20394.8	20316.4
474780.1	182036.1	2450073.8	1995032.9	1195131.7	730416.6	4697411.6	4569738.6
121212.3	13958.2	207084.0	165448.1	281144.8	230263.5	263874.5	259093.3

16-4 续表3

单位：万元

分组	Classify	营业成本 Total Cost	税金及附加 Taxs and Other Changes
农、林、牧产品批发	Wholesale of Agricultural,Forestry and Animal Husbandry Products	123363.5	41.5
食品、饮料及烟草制品批发	Wholesale of food Beverages and Tobaccos	3042194.8	185725.2
纺织、服装及家庭服务器批发	Wholesale of Textiles, Garments and Daily Articles	946799.0	1008.3
文化、体育用品及器材批发	Wholesale of Culture, Sports Appliances and Equipments	760670.6	755.0
医药及医疗器材批发	Wholesale of Medicines and Medical Appliances	4468874.4	9247.4
矿产品、建材及化工产品批发	Wholesale of Mineral Products, Building Materials and Chemical Products	54397636.8	28276.2
机械设备、五金产品及电子产品批发	Wholesale of Machinery, Hardware, and Electronic Equipment	6073410.2	6733.9
贸易经纪与代理	Trade Broker and Agency	174804.8	69.2
其他批发	Other wholesale not Classified Elsewhere	327595.1	531.7
二、零售企业	**Retail Trade**	**18391318.7**	**61294.9**
1. 按登记注册类型分组	Grouped by Category of Commodities		
内资企业	Domestic Funded Enterprises	10074449.3	29406.1
国有	State-owned Enterprises	184028.8	1721.2
集体	Collective-owned Enterprises	17508.0	208.8
股份合作	Corperative Enterprises		
联营	Joint Ownership Enterprises		
国有联营	State Joint Ownership Enterprises		
集体联营	Collective Joint Ownership Enterprises		
国有与集体联营	Joint State-collective Enterprises		
其他联营	Others Joint Ownership Enterprises		
有限责任公司	Limited Liability Corporations	4207529.1	12647.7
国有独资公司	State Funded Corporations	228715.3	817.6

continued 3

(10 000 yuan)

销售费用 Sale Expenses	管理费用 Management Expenses	财务费用 Financial Expenses	营业利润 Business Profits	利润总额 Total Profits	应付职工薪酬 Salary Payable	所得税费用 Income Tax Expenses	应交增值税 Value Added Tax Payable
2200.0	2408.3	491.0	163.4	594.1	2290.5	33.2	1079.0
132856.3	73819.2	2634.9	215948.7	226279.5	110070.5	58240.2	69789.8
50685.3	17662.8	3307.4	6125.6	6773.4	17795.7	2277.2	5527.3
24752.0	25398.3	1222.7	10929.2	11002.1	21998.1	1425.9	2771.0
160508.3	100897.7	61474.0	66668.1	67423.2	97580.9	14885.4	58622.8
466292.3	169581.6	123751.1	132526.3	134404.6	168140.9	39227.9	78646.2
141952.7	79369.2	19698.4	75803.5	78945.3	77042.0	-1026.5	48401.1
5290.7	2218.7	625.9	1097.2	1352.3	1303.7	390.2	170.1
6201.6	6640.9	670.3	1774.8	1605.8	3159.1	375.2	3143.4
1656198.8	**522628.1**	**109724.9**	**212131.3**	**253786.9**	**669296.8**	**76266.4**	**315846.2**
812186.5	348213.4	86186.0	34281.7	68366.8	426208.7	31778.8	206332.2
12493.0	12436.5	1266.0	28712.8	29626.8	16857.4	6261.3	6612.6
962.7	1312.5	56.4	392.7	387.3	1220.6	33.0	441.3
321504.3	129854.8	23718.4	50362.5	72130.4	178288.8	12557.4	113174.8
19854.8	11996.5	1701.3	35840.5	36118.7	23607.1	938.8	4655.0

16-4 续表4

单位：万元

分 组	Classify	单位数（个） Number (unit)	资产总计 Total Assets	流动资产合计 Circulating Funds
其他有限责任公司	Other Limited Liability Corporations	218	3145724.0	2118870.7
股份有限公司	Share-holding Corporations Ltd.	8	858002.0	586880.5
私营	Private Enterprises	585	3641711.6	2765753.6
私营独资	Private-funded Enterprises	18	13377.8	9032.8
私营合伙	Private Partnership Enterprises	1	402.8	325.6
私营有限责任公司	Private Limited Liability Corporations	564	3601773.3	2732433.6
私营股份有限公司	Private Share-holding Corporations Ltd.	2	26157.7	23961.6
其他	Other Enterprises	5	38408.6	29898.0
港澳台商投资	Enterprises with Funds from Hong Kong, Macao &Taiwan	26	1616024.4	1185076.7
外商投资	Foreign Funded Enterprises	37	2060036.2	1107547.7
2. 按国民经济行业分组	Grouped by Sector			
综合零售	Integrated Retail	116	3793852.4	2273161.3
食品、饮料及烟草制品专门零售	Food, Beverages and Tobaccos Special Retail Trade	68	179538.2	153191.6
纺织、服装及日用品专门零售	Special Retail of Textiles,Garments and Daily Consumer Articles	61	961324.4	719051.3
文化、体育用品及器材专门零售	Retail of Culture,Sports Appliances and Equipments	58	329873.2	213834.7
医药及医疗器材专门零售	Retail of Medicines and Medical Appliances	45	497892.1	432489.4
汽车、摩托车、零配件和燃料及其他动力销售	Retail of Automobiles, Motorcycles, Spare Parts and Fuel and Other Power	331	4285547.1	2792439.4
家用电器及电子产品专门零售	Special Retail of Household Electric Appliances and Electronic Products	90	874742.6	693680.4
五金、家具及室内装饰材料专门零售	Special Retail of Hardware,Furniture and Decoration Materials	28	330720.3	218773.3
货摊、无店铺及其他零售业	Non-shop and Other Retail	112	871591.2	684337.9

continued 4

(10 000 yuan)

固定资产原价 Original Value of Fixed Assets	累计折旧 Accumulated Depreciation	负债合计 Total Liabilities	流动负债合计 Circulating Liabilities	所有者权益合计 Total Owners' Equities	实收资本 Paid in Capital	营业收入 Total Revenue	主营业务收入 Revenue from Principal Business
353567.8	168077.9	2242989.8	1829584.8	913986.9	500153.1	4433537.1	4310645.3
51912.2	35436.7	468542.8	353323.7	389459.2	346257.4	254142.6	245538.9
591219.2	173223.5	3078944.0	2514523.1	566676.0	3637574.2	5972853.1	5861548.7
3720.1	1106.3	11032.0	10082.2	2345.8	1969.1	42984.2	42966.6
104.1	3.8	258.9	258.9	143.9	100.0	3397.2	3397.2
585517.1	170916.5	3051670.0	2488199.0	554011.7	3626055.1	5879511.4	5768224.6
1877.9	1196.9	15983.1	15983.0	10174.6	9450.0	46960.3	46960.3
10457.3	4062.4	19398.6	18913.3	19010.0	4050.0	135692.6	130030.0
240402.8	111558.6	1011572.7	903178.8	604451.7	199511.1	2491692.2	2402374.8
541191.9	196993.0	1393723.2	1279844.5	666313.0	401834.6	7043663.2	7020591.0
951674.2	336587.6	2687597.2	1982952.8	1093560.6	1238786.7	3625308.6	3436781.8
18676.2	7663.4	162673.2	131828.7	15820.6	47159.2	267443.2	261306.8
163349.5	68376.6	516085.2	441310.1	444598.0	195417.2	1221484.3	1199908.5
118205.6	13183.1	235923.5	193140.3	93611.7	92531.3	252790.5	247651.2
22593.2	9448.8	385076.2	358110.8	112815.9	41699.4	658282.5	653397.2
642027.8	256103.5	3152267.6	2793520.8	1170531.8	3203321.6	8296426.6	8194147.4
10964.3	7617.4	478122.1	466570.4	391770.5	269712.6	1036170.6	1021270.2
52388.6	15834.8	251058.3	211244.0	79001.0	147221.4	296482.8	281198.1
38178.4	13137.7	665189.1	593525.0	204540.1	97364.4	5203563.8	5191973.0

16-4 续表5

单位：万元

分 组	Classify	营业成本 Total Cost	税金及附加 Taxs and Other Changes
其他有限责任公司	Other Limited Liability Corporations	3978813.8	11830.1
股份有限公司	Share-holding Corporations Ltd.	218152.2	521.7
私营	Private Enterprises	5316110.3	13990.8
私营独资	Private-funded Enterprises	37139.5	259.8
私营合伙	Private Partnership Enterprises	2395.9	28.9
私营有限责任公司	Private Limited Liability Corporations	5243305.4	13521.4
私营股份有限公司	Private Share-holding Corporations Ltd.	33269.5	180.7
其他	Other Enterprises	131120.9	315.9
港澳台商投资	Enterprises with Funds from Hong Kong, Macao &Taiwan	2077992.0	10394.8
外商投资	Foreign Funded Enterprises	6238877.4	21494.0
2. 按国民经济行业分组	Grouped by Sector		
综合零售	Integrated Retail	3013296.6	20780.6
食品、饮料及烟草制品专门零售	Food, Beverages and Tobaccos Special Retail Trade	220932.2	621.6
纺织、服装及日用品专门零售	Special Retail of Textiles,Garments and Daily Consumer Articles	939200.2	5684.5
文化、体育用品及器材专门零售	Retail of Culture,Sports Appliances and Equipments	201333.8	925.6
医药及医疗器材专门零售	Retail of Medicines and Medical Appliances	516010.4	2321.3
汽车、摩托车、零配件和燃料及其他动力销售	Retail of Automobiles, Motorcycles, Spare Parts and Fuel and Other Power	7607989.7	19830.1
家用电器及电子产品专门零售	Special Retail of Household Electric Appliances and Electronic Products	926711.4	1123.7
五金、家具及室内装饰材料专门零售	Special Retail of Hardware,Furniture and Decoration Materials	223892.3	1400.7
货摊、无店铺及其他零售业	Non-shop and Other Retail	4741952.1	8606.8

continued 5

(10 000 yuan)

销售费用 Sale Expenses	管理费用 Management Expenses	财务费用 Financial Expenses	营业利润 Business Profits	利润总额 Total Profits	应付职工薪酬 Salary Payable	所得税费用 Income Tax Expenses	应交增值税 Value Added Tax Payable
301649.5	117858.3	22017.1	14522.0	36011.7	154681.7	11618.6	108519.8
33455.2	24368.3	11102.3	-28018.8	-40295.0	10550.4	1223.3	1820.6
440390.2	178743.0	49759.1	-21204.0	2181.3	216160.2	7753.0	83043.4
3255.9	2260.3	55.6	154.5	142.2	1314.9	48.8	552.4
528.6	430.8	0.1	13.0	13.2	224.8	0.5	10.5
425096.9	174404.1	49709.9	-21731.5	1221.8	209701.9	7543.7	81342.8
11508.8	1647.8	-6.5	360.0	804.1	4918.6	160.0	1137.7
3381.1	1498.3	283.8	4036.5	4336.0	3131.3	3950.8	1239.5
282340.4	74303.3	10075.3	42828.5	42004.7	150807.6	8167.9	38744.3
561671.9	100111.4	13463.6	135021.1	143415.4	92280.5	36319.7	70769.7
474239.0	155535.8	40270.0	-52129.5	-54449.2	202581.9	10394.5	39034.6
31989.5	10983.2	2025.1	-891.4	521.1	16924.2	2477.5	6966.7
187774.6	69124.9	5831.5	18646.8	39705.5	98572.1	6212.8	35387.5
29467.6	20846.2	700.9	-1280.3	-388.6	25354.0	724.7	5339.7
96413.2	20683.5	5632.9	22272.7	23259.5	55939.6	3367.6	13414.5
330158.1	134363.4	43247.2	182517.4	190907.9	191443.2	48273.5	91434.9
92217.3	23921.1	2591.5	25096.4	27226.2	39264.4	223.5	48913.8
31489.0	29397.3	7309.3	5918.2	6221.8	7343.7	912.7	4191.9
382450.5	57772.7	2116.5	11981.0	20782.7	31873.7	3679.6	71162.6

16-5 限额以上住宿和餐饮企业财务状况（2020年）

单位：万元

分组	Classify	单位数（个） Number (unit)	资产总计 Total Assets	流动资产合计 Circulating Funds
总计	**Total**	**796**	**4107614.2**	**1789034.1**
一、住宿业	**Hotel Services**	**441**	**3348942.3**	**1368319.0**
1.按登记注册类型分组	Grouped by Type of Registration			
内资企业	Domestic Funded Enterprises	426	2625635.3	1042928.8
国有	State-owned Enterprises	19	136660.3	30945.0
集体	Collective-owned Enterprises	1	119.1	108.3
股份合作	Cooperative Enterprises			
联营	Joint Ownership Enterprises			
国有联营	State Joint Ownership Enterprises			
集体联营	Collective Joint Ownership Enterprises			
国有与集体联营	Joint State-collective Enterprises			
其他联营	Others Joint Ownership Enterprises			
有限责任公司	Limited Liability Corporations	98	1721964.1	614252.0
国有独资公司	State Sole Funded Corporations	7	142897.6	16939.9
其他有限责任公司	Other Limited Liability Corporations	91	1579066.5	597312.1
股份有限公司	Share-holding Corporations Ltd.			
私营	Private Enterprises	308	766891.8	397623.5
私营独资	Private-funded Enterprises	6	5219.5	4316.7
私营合伙	Private Partnership Enterprises			
私营有限责任公司	Private Limited Liability Corporations	301	758914.9	390568.9
私营股份有限公司	Private Share-holding Corporations Ltd.	1	2757.4	2737.9
其他	Other Enterprises			
港澳台商投资	Enterprises with Funds from Hong Kong, Macao &Taiwan	6	183523.7	81391.2
外商投资	Foreign Funded Enterprises	9	539783.3	243999.0
2.按国民经济行业分组	Grouped by Sector			
旅游饭店	Tourist Hotel	172	2719835.4	1054117.0
一般旅馆	Normal Hotel	250	561299.1	300716.2
民宿服务	Home and Lodging Services	4	844.6	513.2
露营地服务	Campsite Services	1	9383.9	503.4
其他住宿业	Others	14	57579.3	12469.2

注：本表统计范围为法人单位。

Finacial Status of Hotels and Catering Enterprises above Designated Size (2020)

(10 000 yuan)

固定资产原价 Original Value of Fixed Assets	累计折旧 Accumulated Depreciation	负债合计 Total Liabilities	流动负债合　计 Circulating Liabilities	所有者权益合计 Total Owners' Equities	实收资本 Paid in Capital	营业收入 Total Revenue	主营业务收入 Revenue from Principal Business
2385405.5	**977291.8**	**3627438.9**	**2942203.9**	**474938.9**	**1222580.6**	**1323158.1**	**1286774.7**
2181779.8	**866808.6**	**3071337.7**	**2473983.3**	**273500.3**	**1005360.9**	**563319.4**	**546867.2**
1695923.9	702595.7	2344191.0	1826519.8	277340.0	749676.5	495007.3	479948.0
139345.4	68953.1	115296.0	65159.5	20956.9	43175.9	38241.5	37531.2
265.2	254.4	154.4	154.4	-35.3	200.0	64.0	64.0
1226190.0	497773.0	1477591.9	1150256.3	243607.5	531235.9	218271.8	209593.3
135704.8	45781.2	75335.3	39516.6	67562.3	26638.5	14691.6	14425.4
1090485.2	451991.8	1402256.6	1110739.7	176045.2	504597.4	203580.2	195167.9
330123.3	135615.2	751148.7	610949.6	12810.9	175064.7	238430.0	232759.5
1069.6	414.0	5103.8	4019.0	115.7	330.0	1541.3	1541.3
328720.9	134887.9	742714.4	603600.1	13268.3	174634.7	235858.1	230187.6
332.8	313.3	3330.5	3330.5	-573.1	100.0	1030.6	1030.6
181271.4	99342.7	163542.7	97349.7	19981.0	91384.4	26295.8	25469.7
304584.5	64870.2	563604.0	550113.8	-23820.7	164300.0	42016.3	41449.5
1967009.4	777668.5	2552298.9	2036781.9	165836.3	805370.3	376349.3	363945.2
173404.2	79031.7	485901.6	409191.4	72993.4	187992.6	168013.6	163968.6
168.8	111.9	809.8	654.4	34.8		597.9	597.9
7256.4	540.2	5440.4	468.8	3943.5	5000.0	1303.6	1303.6
33941.0	9456.3	26887.0	26886.8	30692.3	6998.0	17055.0	17051.9

16-5 续表1

单位：万元

分 组	Classify	营业成本 Total Cost	税金及附加 Taxs and Other Changes
总计	**Total**	**679161.1**	**13470.5**
一、住宿业	**Hotel Services**	**270881.3**	**10827.8**
1.按登记注册类型分组	Grouped by Type of Registration		
内资企业	Domestic Funded Enterprises	237625.4	7286.2
国有	State-owned Enterprises	17639.6	1246.1
集体	Collective-owned Enterprises	64.3	0.2
股份合作	Cooperative Enterprises		
联营	Joint Ownership Enterprises		
国有联营	State Joint Ownership Enterprises		
集体联营	Collective Joint Ownership Enterprises		
国有与集体联营	Joint State-collective Enterprises		
其他联营	Others Joint Ownership Enterprises		
有限责任公司	Limited Liability Corporations	119626.4	4469.2
国有独资公司	State Sole Funded Corporations	3575.3	364.5
其他有限责任公司	Other Limited Liability Corporations	116051.1	4104.7
股份有限公司	Share-holding Corporations Ltd.		
私营	Private Enterprises	100295.1	1570.7
私营独资	Private-funded Enterprises	638.8	7.7
私营合伙	Private Partnership Enterprises		
私营有限责任公司	Private Limited Liability Corporations	99238.7	1561.1
私营股份有限公司	Private Share-holding Corporations Ltd.	417.6	1.9
其他	Other Enterprises		
港澳台商投资	Enterprises with Funds from Hong Kong, Macao &Taiwan	11835.0	1125.4
外商投资	Foreign Funded Enterprises	21420.9	2416.2
2.按国民经济行业分组	Grouped by Sector		
旅游饭店	Tourist Hotel	189760.7	9529.1
一般旅馆	Normal Hotel	75847.7	997.3
民宿服务	Home and Lodging Services	173.1	92.2
露营地服务	Campsite Services	359.1	0.1
其他住宿业	Others	4740.7	209.1

continued 1

(10 000 yuan)

销售费用 Sale Expenses	管理费用 Management Expenses	财务费用 Financial Expenses	营业利润 Business Profits	利润总额 Total Profits	应付职工薪酬 Salary Payable	所得税费用 Income Tax Expenses	应交增值税 Value Added Tax Payable
447450.3	**321576.5**	**58963.8**	**-174024.5**	**-156154.5**	**358963.8**	**8451.2**	**10386.9**
180151.0	**235921.6**	**52674.5**	**-176637.4**	**-164541.8**	**177845.2**	**1746.5**	**6032.1**
163126.3	209166.7	25159.1	-136912.6	-126653.8	160678.3	870.8	5490.0
15374.8	22134.3	2050.7	-20104.6	-19707.0	20344.2	78.2	690.7
	81.2	-0.3	-81.5	-81.5	115.6	0.6	0.6
66640.4	99350.8	15479.8	-77362.3	-74341.0	83390.2	871.1	2915.9
8513.2	8206.0	432.8	-6284.5	-5789.1	8022.9	1.9	727.0
58127.2	91144.8	15047.0	-71077.8	-68551.9	75367.3	869.2	2188.9
81111.1	87600.4	7628.9	-39364.2	-32524.3	56828.3	-79.1	1882.8
801.8	252.9	2.7	-161.2	-154.3	409.9	0.3	38.0
80007.7	86894.9	7620.5	-39054.2	-32303.1	56064.5	-79.4	1828.8
301.6	452.6	5.7	-148.8	-66.9	353.9		16.0
7732.7	10610.6	1631.4	-6200.5	-5757.9	10277.1	405.7	290.9
9292.0	16144.3	25884.0	-33524.3	-32130.1	6889.8	470.0	251.2
109631.0	171374.0	48130.7	-141541.5	-131943.2	133600.5	1714.9	4138.3
57269.0	57223.7	3971.3	-29066.8	-26590.6	39027.5	17.7	1744.4
413.2	27.5	4.1	-69.7	-64.2	106.2	0.5	2.7
357.0	544.1	159.1	-115.9	-110.5	381.2		
12480.8	6752.3	409.3	-5843.5	-5833.3	4729.8	13.4	146.7

16-5 续表2

单位：万元

分 组	Classify	单位数（个） Number (unit)	资产总计 Total Assets	流动资产合计 Circulating Funds
二、餐饮业	**Catering Trade**	**355**	**758671.9**	**420715.1**
1.按登记注册类型分组	Grouped by Type of Registration			
内资企业	Domestic Funded Enterprises	343	607005.2	353655.0
国有	State-owned Enterprises	2	4305.3	1685.9
集体	Collective-owned Enterprises			
股份合作	Cooperative Enterprises			
联营	Joint Ownership Enterprises			
国有联营	State Joint Ownership Enterprises			
集体联营	Collective Joint Ownership Enterprises			
国有与集体联营	Joint State-collective Enterprises			
其他联营	Others Joint Ownership Enterprises			
有限责任公司	Limited Liability Corporations	76	151597.2	93859.8
国有独资公司	State Sole Funded Corporations	3	13052.3	4762.4
其他有限责任公司	Other Limited Liability Corporations	73	138544.9	89097.4
股份有限公司	Share-holding Corporations Ltd.	4	197470.1	83365.7
私营	Private Enterprises	261	253632.6	174743.6
私营独资	Private-funded Enterprises	11	3827.9	2235.9
私营合伙	Private Partnership Enterprises			
私营有限责任公司	Private Limited Liability Corporations	249	246909.5	170871.9
私营股份有限公司	Private Share-holding Corporations Ltd.	1	2895.2	1635.8
其他	Other Enterprises			
港澳台商投资	Enterprises with Funds from Hong Kong, Macao &Taiwan	5	83055.4	40024.8
外商投资	Foreign Funded Enterprises	7	68611.3	27035.3
2.按国民经济行业分组	Grouped by Sdctor			
正餐服务	Dinner	331	582077.1	339212.3
快餐服务	Fast Food	12	101686.4	32390.6
饮料及冷饮服务	Beverages and Cold Drinks	7	65563.0	43712.3
餐饮配送及外卖送餐服务	Catering Distribution and Takeaway Servic	1	1432.3	1414.2
其他餐饮业	Other Catering Services	4	7913.1	3985.7

continued 2

(10 000 yuan)

固定资产原价 Original Value of Fixed Assets	累计折旧 Accumulated Depreciation	负债合计 Total Liabilities	流动负债合计 Circulating Liabilities	所有者权益合计 Total Owners' Equities	实收资本 Paid in Capital	营业收入 Total Revenue	主营业务收入 Revenue from Principal Business
203625.7	**110483.2**	**556101.2**	**468220.6**	**201438.6**	**217219.7**	**759838.7**	**739907.5**
152450.6	83966.8	468923.0	396763.4	136950.1	197646.9	534282.1	521490.6
4260.6	2042.4	1680.8	1680.8	2624.5	2904.1	4759.0	4759.0
55866.9	31780.4	153130.5	140670.3	-1197.4	41040.5	128144.0	126739.2
15919.7	7563.4	10036.8	9120.0	3015.5	4731.2	5787.5	5677.4
39947.2	24217.0	143093.7	131550.3	-4212.9	36309.3	122356.5	121061.8
21691.0	13269.8	88500.4	76567.6	108969.7	61507.7	65808.3	60117.7
70632.1	36874.2	225611.3	177844.7	26553.3	92194.6	335570.8	329874.7
2377.1	1124.0	2619.9	1475.7	836.9	686.7	4250.4	4088.1
67288.0	35402.5	222734.9	176112.5	23077.7	61507.9	328596.1	323066.4
967.0	347.7	256.5	256.5	2638.7	30000.0	2724.3	2720.2
22512.3	11519.6	45249.5	35573.7	37805.9	4995.3	73860.2	73860.2
28662.8	14996.8	41928.7	35883.5	26682.6	14577.5	151696.4	144556.7
144505.2	82238.3	455415.2	384420.2	125947.4	167038.1	496021.3	482852.4
43703.7	21680.7	61516.2	44055.8	40170.2	46035.6	182919.9	176179.5
10398.9	4804.3	28706.3	29615.2	36439.1	3146.0	74540.0	74519.5
38.1	30.2	123.2	135.1	1309.1		2327.8	2327.8
4979.8	1729.7	10340.3	9994.3	-2427.2	1000.0	4029.7	4028.3

16-5 续表3

单位：万元

分　组	Classify	营业成本 Total Cost	税金及附加 Taxs and Other Changes
二、餐饮业	**Catering Trade**	**408279.8**	**2642.7**
1.按登记注册类型分组	Grouped by Type of Registration		
内资企业	Domestic Funded Enterprises	294265.4	2475.3
国有	State-owned Enterprises	3976.9	69.8
集体	Collective-owned Enterprises		
股份合作	Cooperative Enterprises		
联营	Joint Ownership Enterprises		
国有联营	State Joint Ownership Enterprises		
集体联营	Collective Joint Ownership Enterprises		
国有与集体联营	Joint State-collective Enterprises		
其他联营	Others Joint Ownership Enterprises		
有限责任公司	Limited Liability Corporations	74383.6	370.6
国有独资公司	State Sole Funded Corporations	5644.8	100.5
其他有限责任公司	Other Limited Liability Corporations	68738.8	270.1
股份有限公司	Share-holding Corporations Ltd.	37207.9	544.5
私营	Private Enterprises	178697.0	1490.4
私营独资	Private-funded Enterprises	2412.3	24.8
私营合伙	Private Partnership Enterprises		
私营有限责任公司	Private Limited Liability Corporations	175154.2	1465.6
私营股份有限公司	Private Share-holding Corporations Ltd.	1130.5	
其他	Other Enterprises		
港澳台商投资	Enterprises with Funds from Hong Kong, Macao &Taiwan	23090.5	62.6
外商投资	Foreign Funded Enterprises	90923.9	104.8
2.按国民经济行业分组	Grouped by Sdctor		
正餐服务	Dinner	276491.4	2374.7
快餐服务	Fast Food	96823.7	120.5
饮料及冷饮服务	Beverages and Cold Drinks	31892.8	54.6
餐饮配送及外卖送餐服务	Catering Distribution and Takeaway Servic	757.5	1.4
其他餐饮业	Other Catering Services	2314.4	91.5

continued 3

(10 000 yuan)

销售费用 Sale Expenses	管理费用 Management Expenses	财务费用 Financial Expenses	营业利润 Business Profits	利润总额 Total Profits	应付职工薪酬 Salary Payable	所得税费用 Income Tax Expenses	应交增值税 Value Added Tax Payable
267299.3	**85654.9**	**6289.3**	**2612.9**	**8387.3**	**181118.6**	**6704.7**	**4354.8**
189342.1	66686.9	6052.1	-12693.5	-6621.9	131236.9	1911.9	3715.3
191.8	510.9	0.1	9.5	28.6	361.8	40.3	233.4
42297.2	16883.0	2033.1	-6884.5	-5557.7	30376.4	191.0	226.0
249.1	1029.8	167.1	-1181.4	-1145.0	2306.9		43.6
42048.1	15853.2	1866.0	-5703.1	-4412.7	28069.5	191.0	182.4
28765.5	8322.2	1260.1	1224.9	2304.8	25683.8	-44.6	1752.6
118087.6	40970.8	2758.8	-7043.4	-3397.6	74814.9	1725.2	1503.3
1033.0	410.8	37.8	439.9	468.2	1042.3	33.0	44.2
115396.7	40481.9	2715.0	-7335.1	-3719.3	73366.4	1692.2	1459.1
1657.9	78.1	6.0	-148.2	-146.5	406.2		
41374.5	3124.6	519.1	6114.6	5989.0	24044.9	1618.4	454.3
36582.7	15843.4	-281.9	9191.8	9020.2	25836.8	3174.4	185.2
175093.0	62366.8	5257.6	-13354.0	-7353.6	125122.8	1846.7	4113.2
58607.9	17738.1	444.1	9916.8	9142.2	39823.7	2446.3	295.8
32113.7	3942.1	-162.2	6700.5	7069.3	15180.7	2411.3	-83.0
947.3		5.1	616.4	636.9	463.3		
537.4	1607.9	744.7	-1266.8	-1107.5	528.1	0.4	28.8

16-6 限额以上批发和零售贸易业商品购进、销售、库存总额(2020年)

单位：万元

分组	Classify	单位数（个）Number (unit)	商品购进额 Total Purchases	进口 Imports
总计	**Total**	**2154**	**98911459.4**	**8078391.7**
一、批发企业	**Wholesale Enterprises**	**1214**	**82108356.4**	**7706778.6**
1.按登记注册类型分组	Grouped by Type of Registration			
内资企业	Domestic Funded Enterprises	1181	65203534.7	1434444.0
国有	State-owned Enterprises	23	3687483.0	1104.0
集体	Collective-owned Enterprises	3	5299.2	
有限责任公司	Limited Liability Corporations	259	35273772.8	1377408.4
国有独资公司	State Sole Funded Corporations	29	9079259.7	117574.9
其他有限责任公司	Other Limited Liability Corporations	230	26194513.1	1259833.5
股份有限公司	Share-holding Corporations Ltd.	19	10193245.5	904.8
私营	Private Enterprises	876	16041981.9	55026.8
私营独资	Private-funded Enterprises	3	19122.8	
私营合伙	Private Partnership Enterprises			
私营有限责任公司	Private Limited Liability Corporations	863	15888201.5	55026.8
私营股份有限公司	Private Share-holding Corporations Ltd.	10	134657.6	
其他	Other Enterprises	1	1752.3	
港澳台商投资	Enterprises with Funds from Hong Kong, Macao &Taiwan	7	214946.4	
外商投资	Foreign Funded Enterprises	23	16670592.2	6272334.6
个体经营户	Individusl Enterprises	3	19283.1	
2.按国民经济行业分组	Grouped by Economic Sector			
农、林、牧产品批发	Wholesale of Agricultural,Forestry and Animal Husbandry Products	12	136336.4	
食品、饮料及烟草制品批发	Wholesale of Food, Beverages and Tobacco Products	133	3109146.5	1804.4
纺织、服装及家庭用品批发	Wholesale of Textiles, Garments and Daily Articles	53	1030355.1	7167.5
文化、体育用品及器材批发	Wholesale of Culture, Sports Articles and Equipments	47	825601.8	
医药及医疗器材批发	Wholesale of Medicines and Medical Appliances	175	4961894.4	6285.1
矿产品、建材及化工产品批发	Wholesale of Mineral Products, Building Materials and Chemical Products	509	65006787.8	5178192.0

Total Purchases,Sales and Inventories of Wholesale and Retail Enterprises above Designated Size（2020）

(10 000 yuan)

商品销售额		批发额		零售额	期末商品库存额
	公共网络商品销售额		出口		Value of
Sales Value	Public Network Sales	Wholesale Trade	Exports	Retail Trade	Stock at Final goods
107666576.7	**13573515.9**	**84353284.0**	**6588316.7**	**23249166.4**	**4649360.9**
84646773.6	**7121412.8**	**83707768.3**	**6588256.8**	**885846.8**	**2941475.8**
67700364.6	7121130.1	66795873.2	1062915.1	851332.9	2548662.9
4154571.4	1530254.6	4152927.1		1644.3	167710.5
5213.9		5205.6			465.1
35839346.8	609505.1	35737889.7	409529.3	96197.0	1417046.2
9211537.9	3620.7	9190280.3	61619.6	21257.6	246630.5
26627808.9	605884.4	26547609.4	347909.7	74939.4	1170415.7
10519809.2	4765991.4	10037020.3	261923.6	482788.9	60601.9
17179476.3	215167.7	16861399.6	391462.2	270186.6	902831.6
20270.1		17834.2		2435.9	269.5
17019325.9	215167.7	16703685.1	391462.2	267750.7	883932.4
139880.3		139880.3			18629.7
1947.0	211.3	1430.9		516.1	7.6
262262.2		258794.1		3468.1	8271.0
16662013.0	282.7	16631737.0	5525341.7	30276.0	381150.8
22133.8		21364.0		769.8	3391.1
135419.6	100.3	135274.9	203.2	144.7	14052.8
3841979.1	1546855.0	3681439.0	12036.4	117849.2	301495.8
1148209.4	29849.3	1095458.3	242117.2	51546.2	159778.4
897416.7	1769.1	894434.3	8731.9	2982.4	55070.7
5407443.3	151394.5	5370765.3	10410.7	35830.0	547765.8
65824259.7	5260282.9	65195152.4	3959751.7	621122.6	1512248.9

16-6 续表1

单位：万元

分　组	Classify	单位数（个）Number (unit)	商品购进额 Total Purchases	进口 Imports
机械设备、五金产品及电子产品批发	Wholesale of Machinery, Hardwares, Transport Means and Electronic Products	248	6510615.0	2498334.8
贸易经纪与代理	Trade Manage and Agent	4	190036.1	14994.8
其他批发	Other Wholesales	33	337583.3	
3.按经营形式分组	Grouped by Means of Operation			
独立门店	Independent Shop	593	40656370.9	7082712.6
连锁总店	Headquarter of Chain Store	2	97570.0	
连锁门店	Chain Store			
其他	Other	619	41354415.5	624066.0
二、零售企业	**Retail Trade**	**940**	**16803103.0**	**371613.1**
1.按登记注册类型分组	Grouped by Registration Status			
内资企业	Domestic Funded Enterprises	846	11103434.5	183689.4
国有	State-owned Enterprises	9	150349.8	
集体	Collective-owned Enterprises	11	19656.1	
有限责任公司	Limited Liability Corporations	228	4349342.2	105994.2
国有独资公司	State Sole Funded Corporations	10	272134.2	8307.4
其他有限责任公司	Other Limited Liability Corporations	218	4077208.0	97686.8
股份有限公司	Share-holding Corporations Ltd.	8	168042.6	
私营	Private Enterprises	585	6270262.7	77695.2
私营独资	Private-funded Enterprises	18	43097.0	
私营合伙	Private Partnership Enterprises	1	3883.8	
私营有限责任公司	Private Limited Liability Corporations	564	6172170.0	77695.2
私营股份有限公司	Private Share-holding Corporations Ltd.	2	51111.9	
其他	Other Enterprises	5	145781.1	
港澳台商投资	Enterprises with Funds from Hong Kong, Macao &Taiwan	26	2212531.3	86145.5
外商投资	Foreign Funded Enterprises	37	3454962.2	101778.2
个体经营户	Individusl Enterprises	31	32175.0	
2.按国民经济行业分组	Grouped by Registered Kind			
综合零售	General Retail Sales Trade	136	3156522.8	26.3
食品、饮料及烟草制品专门零售	Retail of Food, Beverage and Tobaccos	69	225361.7	531.0
纺织、服装及日用品专门零售	Retail of Textiles, Garments and Daily Articles	63	803919.9	1155.5
文化、体育用品及器材专门零售	Retail of Culture, Sports Articles and Equipments	61	225683.1	8307.4

continued 1

(10 000 yuan)

商品销售额 Sales Value	公共网络商品销售额 Public Network Sales	批发额 Wholesale Trade	出口 Exports	零售额 Retail Trade	期末商品库存额 Value of Stock at Final goods
6823497.0	68436.0	6768840.4	2276071.6	54226.6	326272.4
193493.4		193493.4	78324.6		13329.6
375055.4	62725.7	372910.3	609.5	2145.1	11461.4
41814240.6	195937.3	41016570.8	6214934.2	749397.9	1276562.0
101048.4		100351.1		697.3	1732.9
42731484.6	6925475.5	42590846.4	373322.6	135751.6	1663180.9
23019803.1	**6452103.1**	**645515.7**	**59.9**	**22363319.6**	**1707885.1**
12315488.7	1448731.8	465754.5	59.9	11838766.4	1247614.1
325922.0				325922.0	15864.6
21978.3		394.4		21583.9	1854.5
4971871.2	398809.8	135172.2	59.9	4826072.8	512581.5
278518.4	994.6	36657.2	59.9	241861.2	34991.2
4693352.8	397815.2	98515.0		4584211.6	477590.3
268584.2	8518.6			268584.2	15122.4
6575323.7	1041403.4	330177.9		6244804.2	692285.8
47948.0	3336.1			47948.0	4427.0
3838.8				3838.8	45.8
6471861.1	1038067.3	330177.9		6141341.6	678569.3
51675.8				51675.8	9243.7
151809.3		10.0		151799.3	9905.3
2665803.5	232704.6	148045.9		2517757.6	314402.0
7942877.7	4764750.8	30724.5		7912153.2	129272.5
95633.2	5915.9	990.8		94642.4	16596.5
3962871.7	227877.1	13503.2		3949364.6	321845.5
303523.7	21386.9	39588.2		253318.2	36227.5
1399686.8	22058.3	138721.2		1260965.6	251890.1
265913.8	8536.7	34644.7	59.9	231269.1	80392.5

16-6 续表2

单位：万元

分组	Classify	单位数（个）Number (unit)	商品购进额 Total Purchases	进口 Imports
医药及医疗器材专门零售	Retail of Medicines and Medical Appliances	45	633946.1	
汽车、摩托车、零配件和燃料及其他动力销售	Sales of automobiles, motorcycles, spare parts and fuel and other power	335	8518328.9	356200.0
家用电器及电子产品专门零售	Retail of Household Electronic Equipments and Products	90	802250.3	
五金、家具及室内装饰材料专门零售	Retail of Hardwares, Furniture and Room Decorative Building	29	251856.6	
货摊、无店铺及其他零售业	No Fixed Stores and Other Retails	112	2185233.6	5392.9
3.按经营形式分组	Grouped by Means of Operation			
独立门店	Independent Shop	683	12324106.9	366315.9
连锁总店	Headquarter of Chain Store	40	872795.2	
连锁门店	Chain Store	34	324637.2	26.3
其他	Other	183	3281563.7	5270.9
4.按零售业态分组	Grouped by Retail Size			
有店铺	Retail of Shop	792	14476467.1	357912.8
食杂店	Grocery Store	4	9073.4	
便利店	Convenience Store	18	132557.8	
折扣店	Dime Store			
超市	Supermarket	78	234951.9	26.3
大型超市	Larget Supermarket	13	2299031.3	
仓储会员店	Warehouse Club	5	18211.2	
百货店	Department Store	60	613671.2	
专业店	Special Store	282	5079935.7	65737.1
专卖店	Monopoly Store	290	5695002.8	292149.4
家居建材商店	Home-building Material Store	14	212564.0	
购物中心	Shopping Center	9	17528.6	
厂家直销中心	Factory Outlet Center	19	163939.2	
无店铺零售	Retail of No-shop	148	2326635.9	13700.3
电视购物	TV Shopping	1	84030.8	
邮购	Mail Order	1	572.8	
网上商店	Online Stores	102	2067208.2	5392.9
自动售货亭	Vending Machine			
电话购物	Tele Shopping			
其他	Others	44	174824.1	8307.4

continued 2

(10 000 yuan)

商品销售额 Sales Value	公共网络商品销售额 Public Network Sales	批发额 Wholesale Trade	出口 Exports	零售额 Retail Trade	期末商品库存额 Value of Stock at Final goods
727021.4	10546.8	48755.9		678265.5	111339.5
9117294.6	340446.1	161188.4		8956106.2	776106.8
1164381.1	135357.2	115233.2		1048806.3	62974.5
316696.7	6787.6	21228.8		295467.9	16295.5
5762413.3	5679106.4	72652.1		5689756.2	50813.2
14147619.5	808672.0	265512.7	59.9	13881765.2	1251941.0
1083830.5	25242.3	803.2		1083027.3	147537.1
644351.2	138465.7	31433.7		612917.5	33623.9
7144001.9	5479723.1	347766.1		6785609.6	274783.1
17097873.4	767632.4	523038.6		16563872.0	1636302.4
17607.5	0.1			17607.5	1336.9
160422.9	6142.4	1916.8		147888.8	21910.0
275925.6	4378.8	7195.9		268725.8	29332.0
1621858.6	176573.8	10734.6		1611124.0	215999.9
22024.4				22024.4	4736.8
2036402.9	50882.0	2251.0		2034151.9	75115.5
6005942.5	196788.4	109568.8		5896373.7	542209.4
6312291.5	326044.0	364863.5		5947086.4	709688.6
265106.2	4095.7	10686.6		254419.6	10626.3
203306.8				203306.8	5722.8
176984.5	2727.2	15821.4		161163.1	19624.2
5921929.7	5684470.7	122477.1	59.9	5799447.6	71582.7
89171.5	89171.5			89171.5	803.2
561.1	516.8			561.1	
5630258.7	5590290.9	73156.8		5557096.9	49433.6
201938.4	4491.5	49320.3	59.9	152618.1	21345.9

16-7 限额以上住宿和餐饮业经营情况（2020年）

单位：万元

分 组	Classify	单位数（个）Number (unit)	营业额 Business Revenue
总计	**Total**	**908**	**1532150.3**
一、住宿业	**Lodging Services**	**467**	**714779.3**
1. 按国民经济行业分组	Grouped by Economic Sector		
旅游饭店	Tour Restaurant	193	515536.7
一般旅馆	Common Hotel	255	179491.7
民宿服务	Home and Lodging Services	4	600.0
露营地服务	Campsite Services	1	1303.7
其他住宿业	Others	14	17847.2
2. 按登记注册类型分组	Grouped by Registration Status		
内资企业	Domestic Funded Enterprises	449	634130.8
国有	State-owned Enterprises	24	54616.5
集体	Collective-owned Enterprises	1	64.7
股份合作	Corperative Enterprises		
联营	Joint Ownership Enterprises		
有限责任公司	Limited Liability Corporations	108	300198.8
国有独资公司	State-funded Corporations	7	15340.0
其他有限责任公司	Other Limited Liability Corporations	101	284858.8
股份有限公司	Stock Limited Corporation	3	20574.5
私营	Private Enterprises	311	249418.1
私营独资	Private-funded Enterprises	6	1584.8
私营合伙	Private Partnership Enterprises		
私营有限责任公司	Private Limited Liability Corporations	304	246786.7
私营股份有限公司	Private Share Holding Corporations	1	1046.6
其他	Others	2	9258.2
港澳台商投资	Enterprises Funded by Hong Kong, Macao and Taiwan	7	48731.7

注：此表统计范围为法人企业、大个体及产业活动单位。

Statistic on Hotel Services and Catering Services above Designed Size（2020）

(10 000 yuan)

客房收入 From Hotel Room	公共网络客房收入 Public Network Room Revenue	餐费收入 From Meals	公共网络餐费收入 Public Network Catering Revenue	商品销售额 Merchandise sales
409028.8	**72591.2**	**984538.2**	**90328.7**	**42583.7**
399034.5	**71629.0**	**240188.3**	**8017.6**	**16887.2**
251268.9	39727.2	200398.9	6918.8	15288.2
136803.0	31466.8	32057.1	1092.1	1402.6
592.4	334.5	5.1		2.5
1115.6		166.8		21.3
9254.6	100.5	7560.4	6.7	172.6
358925.6	66397.5	208326.0	7718.5	16178.3
23400.5	3021.0	20251.9	102.0	993.1
64.7	11.2			
149656.9	20882.4	117992.6	4355.2	3366.8
7705.4	593.3	5510.9		203.2
141951.5	20289.1	112481.7	4355.2	3163.6
4996.5	1578.5	5099.3	751.6	9580.9
176073.8	38794.6	60725.0	2509.7	2237.5
1135.3	58.0	258.9	0.6	18.4
174393.5	38729.8	59964.5	2509.1	2219.1
545.0	6.8	501.6		
4733.2	2109.8	4257.2		
23554.3	1255.8	19232.0	68.2	105.6

16-7 续表

单位：万元

分　组	Classify	单位数（个） Number (unit)	营业额 Business Revenue
外商投资	Foreign Funded Enterprises	10	31621.9
个体经营	Individual Enterprises	1	294.9
二、餐饮业	**Catering Trade**	**441**	**817371.0**
1. 按国民经济行业分组	Grouped by Economic Sector		
正餐服务	Dinner Services	415	539596.5
快餐服务	Fast Food Services	12	192765.3
饮料及冷饮服务	Beverages and Cold Drinks	7	78010.3
餐饮配送及外卖送餐服务	Catering Distribution and Takeaway Servic	1	2327.8
其他餐饮业	Other Catering Services	6	4671.1
2. 按登记注册类型分组	Grouped by Registration Status		
内资企业	Domestic Funded Enterprises	351	558341.9
国有	State-owned Enterprises	5	9888.9
集体	Collective-owned Enterprises		
股份合作	Corperative Enterprises		
联营	Joint Ownership Enterprises		
有限责任公司	Limited Liability Corporations	81	139820.0
国有独资公司	State-funded Corporations	3	5860.6
其他有限责任公司	Other Limited Liability Corporations	78	133959.4
股份有限公司	Stock Limited Corporation	4	66630.2
私营	Private Enterprises	261	342002.8
私营独资	Private-funded Enterprises	11	4345.4
私营合伙	Private Partnership Enterprises		
私营有限责任公司	Private Limited Liability Corporations	249	334903.4
私营股份有限公司	Private Share Holding Corporations	1	2754.0
其他	Others		
港澳台商投资	Enterprises Funded by Hong Kong, Macao and Taiwan	5	78250.0
外商投资	Foreign Funded Enterprises	7	160650.3
个体经营	Individual Enterprises	78	20128.8

continued

(10 000 yuan)

客房收入 From Hotel Room	公共网络客房收入 Public Network Room Revenue	餐费收入 From Meals	公共网络餐费收入 Public Network Catering Revenue	商品销售额 Merchandise sales
16259.7	3969.6	12630.3	230.9	603.3
294.9	6.1			
9994.3	**962.2**	**744349.9**	**82311.1**	**25696.5**
9775.1	830.6	482214.1	35873.2	18703.0
		185633.5	13576.7	60.0
		70793.3	32202.1	6488.8
		2327.8		
219.2	131.6	3381.2	659.1	444.7
9509.8	944.8	502929.3	59533.6	17875.8
1235.3		8127.7		453.2
3407.8	359.8	128718.5	23779.5	4234.7
322.7		3987.1		1150.7
3085.1	359.8	124731.4	23779.5	3084.0
593.2	50.5	47512.2	8725.4	4782.2
4273.5	534.5	318570.9	27028.7	8405.7
137.6		4094.7	82.1	113.1
4135.9	534.5	311726.3	25571.6	8292.6
		2749.9	1375.0	
124.2		71633.1	17259.8	5538.5
269.0	17.4	150469.6	4063.2	1712.8
91.3		19317.9	1454.5	569.4

16-8 限额以上批发和零售业主要商品分类销售额（2020年）

Sale Values of Wholesale and Retail Enterprises above Designated Size by Category of Main Commodities（2020）

单位：万元　　(10 000 yuan)

分　组	Classify	销售合计 Total Sales Value	批发 Wholesale Value	零售 Retail Value
总计	**Total**	**103307783.0**	**79581088.7**	**23726694.3**
其中：通过公共网络实现的商品销售	Sales Achieved through the Public Network	12856906.0	6891182.3	5965723.7
粮油、食品类	Cereals, Oils and Foodstuffs	3233737.2	1379580.3	1854156.9
#粮油类	Grain and Oil	1064743.5	435675.8	629067.7
肉禽蛋类	Meat, Poultry and Eggs	433149.0	85610.8	347538.2
水产品类	Aquatic Products	103356.7	21894.4	81462.3
蔬菜类	Vegetables	801964.5	650446.3	151518.2
干鲜果品类	Fresh and Dried Fruit Category	341778.1	76439.3	265338.8
饮料类	Beverages	526851.7	181193.5	345658.2
烟酒类	Tobacco and Liquor	2509797.6	2035735.0	474062.6
服装、鞋帽、针纺织品类	Clothing, Shoes, Hats and Textiles	3191662.1	372629.1	2819033.0
#服装类	Clothing	2354920.3	109684.3	2245236.0
鞋帽类	Shoes and Hats	577709.0	127946.8	449762.2
针纺织品类	Knitwear and Textiles	212767.1	112679.1	100088.0
化妆品类	Cosmetics	938921.6	34947.6	903974.0
金银珠宝类	Gold,Silver and Jewelry	785921.9	279440.8	506481.1
日用品类	Articles for Daily Use	1011262.4	131760.5	879501.9
#可穿戴智能设备	Wearable intelligent device	5308.3	52.7	5255.6
五金、电料类	Hardwear and Electrical Materials	236177.0	198535.5	37641.5
体育、娱乐用品类	Sports and Recreation Articles	296096.2	15003.0	281093.2
#照相器材类	Photography Equipment	84030.9		84030.9
书报杂志类	Newspapers and Magazines	434023.4	242314.9	191708.5
电子出版物及音像制品类	E-journal and Video Products	14362.9	9.0	14353.9
家用电器和音像器材类	Household Appliances and Video Products	2216707.6	530158.3	1686549.3
中西药品类	Traditional Chinese and Western Medicine	5111240.9	4395325.2	715915.7
#西药	Western Medicine	4071994.8	3540932.4	531062.4
中草药及中成药	Chinese Herbal Medicine and Traditional Chinese Medicine	232407.3	142213.3	90194.0
文化办公用品类	Cultural and Official Goods	1254014.4	384568.1	869446.3
#计算机及其配套产品	Computers and Ancillary Products	971689.8	173302.0	798387.8
家具类	Furniture	285867.5	7426.1	278441.4
通讯器材类	Communication Appliances	1322831.2	202237.1	1120594.1
煤炭及制品类	Coal and Related Products	8661240.1	8661240.1	
木材及制品类	Wood and Wooden Products	44901.7	44901.7	
石油及制品类	Petroleum and Related Products	13557515.5	11044548.1	2512967.4
化工材料及制品类	Raw Chemical Materials	4130254.3	4130254.3	
#化肥类	Chemical Fertilizers	138763.2	138763.2	
金属材料类	Metal Materials	36737844.0	36737844.0	
建筑及装潢材料类	Buildings and Decoration Materials	870295.9	677692.5	192603.4
机电产品及设备类	Mechanical and Electrical Products	4232741.1	4208235.2	24505.9
#农机类	Agricultural Machinery	35272.7	35272.7	
汽车类	Automobile	8589048.8	980673.6	7608375.2
种子饲料类	Seeds and Feedstuff	31384.4	31384.4	
棉麻类	Cotton,Hemp	9080.8	9080.8	
其他类	Others	3074000.8	2664370.0	409630.8

注：本表为定期季度报表数据。

16-9 亿元以上商品交易市场成交情况（2020年）

Basic Statistics on Commodity Exchange Markets of Transaction Value over 100 Million Yuan（2020）

分 组	Classify	年末出租摊位数（个）Number of Rental Booths at Year-end (unit)	成交额（万元）Turnover (10 000 yuan)
1. 粮油、食品类	Cereals, Oils and Foodstuffs	8990	4527666
#粮油类	Grain and Oil	535	329433
肉禽蛋类	Meat, Poultry and Eggs	834	379060
水产品类	Aquatic Products	829	380841
蔬菜类	Vegetables	2694	1236400
干鲜果品类	Fresh and Dried Fruit Category	4084	2201847
2. 饮料类	Beverages	318	17790
3. 烟酒类	Tobacco and Liquor	143	14090
4. 服装、鞋帽、针纺织品类	Clothing, Shoes, Hats and Textiles	5821	344637
#服装类	Clothing	3615	141265
鞋帽类	Shoes and Hats	1232	142822
针纺织品类	Knitwear and Textiles	974	60550
5. 化妆品类	Cosmetics	105	3305
6. 金银珠宝类	Gold,Silver and Jewelry	5	985
7. 日用品类	Articles for Daily Use	618	37382
#可穿戴智能设备	Wearable intelligent device	43	1290
8. 五金、电料类	Hardwear and Electrical Materials	47	2101
9. 体育、娱乐用品类	Sports and Recreation Articles	202	13493
10. 书报杂志类	Newspapers and Magazines		
11. 电子出版物及音像制品类	E-journal and Video Products	3	26
12. 家用电器和音像器材类	Household Appliances and Video Products	84	9341
13. 中西药品类	Traditional Chinese and Western Medicine		
#西药	Western Medicine		
中草药及中成药	Chinese Herbal Medicine and Traditional Chinese Medicine		
14. 文化办公用品类	Cultural and Official Goods	1601	168674
#计算机及其配套产品	Computer and Related Products	1404	148932
15. 家具类	Furniture	1583	396767
16. 通讯器材类	Communication Appliances	431	29658
17. 煤炭及制品类	Coal and Related Products		
18. 木材及制品类	Wood and Wooden Products		
19. 石油及制品类	Petroleum and Related Products		
20. 化工材料及制品类	Raw Chemical Materials	156	142795
#化肥类	Chemical Fertilizers		
21. 金属材料类	Metal Materials	62	182700
22. 建筑及装潢材料类	Buildings and Decoration Materials	6813	3005445
23. 机电产品及设备类	Mechanical and Electrical Products	724	135873
#农机类	Agricultural Machinery		
24. 汽车类	Automobile	1505	176265
25. 种子饲料类	Seeds and Feedstuff		
26. 棉麻类	Cotton,Hemp	15	83
27. 其他类	Others	1016	17782

16-10 批发和零售业连锁经营情况（2020年）

Basic Statistics on Chain Business of Wholesale and Retail Trades (2020)

指 标	Item	本年合计 Total	上年合计 Total Last Year	本年直营店 Regular Chain
一、门店总数（个）	**Number of Stores(unit)**	**3108**	**3179**	**2704**
二、年末从业人员数（人）	**Employees at Year-end(person)**	**24546**	**27403**	**22172**
三、年末零售营业面积（平方米）	**Operating Area of Retail at Year-end(sq.m)**	**1042995**	**1015402**	**1004785**
四、连锁门店商品购进额（万元）	**Purchases Value of Chain Stores(10 000 yuan)**	**3042656**	**3362811**	**2998102**
其中：统一配送商品购进额	Centralized Purchases and Delivery	2675501	2932944	2634611
其中：自有配送中心配送商品购进额	Self Centralized Purchases and Delivery	2350890	2540878	2317735
非自有配送中心配送商品购进额	Non-self Centralized Purchases and Delivery	204846	275090	204786
五、连锁门店商品销售额（万元）	**Sales Value of Chain Store(10 000 yuan)**	**3932759**	**4274140**	**3883864**
其中：零售额	Retail Value	1943600	2205003	1895855

注：上年同期数为本年在库企业加报数据。

16-10 续表 continued

指 标	Item	上年直营店 Regular Chain Last Year	本年加盟店 Franchise	上年加盟店 Franchise Last Year
一、门店总数（个）	**Number of Stores(unit)**	**2882**	**404**	**297**
二、年末从业人员数（人）	**Employees at Year-end(person)**	**26231**	**2374**	**1172**
三、年末零售营业面积（平方米）	**Operating Area of Retail at Year-end(sq.m)**	**995419**	**38210**	**19983**
四、连锁门店商品购进额（万元）	**Purchases Value of Chain Stores(10 000 yuan)**	**3327964**	**44555**	**34847**
其中：统一配送商品购进额	Centralized Purchases and Delivery	2900612	40889	32332
其中：自有配送中心配送商品购进额	Self Centralized Purchases and Delivery	2516367	33155	24511
非自有配送中心配送商品购进额	Non-self Centralized Purchases and Delivery	275090	60	
五、连锁门店商品销售额（万元）	**Sales Value of Chain Store(10 000 yuan)**	**4233450**	**48895**	**40690**
其中：零售额	Retail Value	2164350	47745	40653

16-11　住宿和餐饮业连锁经营情况（2020年）

Basic Statistics on Chain Business of Hotels and Catering Services（2020）

指　标	Item	本年合计 Total	上年合计 Total Last Year
一、门店总数（个）	**Number of Stores(unit)**	**717**	**674**
二、年末从业人员数（人）	**Employees at Year-end(person)**	**16318**	**17919**
三、年末餐饮营业面积（平方米）	**Operating Area of Retail at Year-end(sq.m)**	**210433**	**203033**
四、客房数（间）	**Guest Rooms(room)**	**532**	**532**
五、床位数（张）	**Guest Beds(bed)**	**886**	**886**
六、餐位数（位）	**Dining Seats(set)**	**85052**	**97330**
七、连锁门店商品购进（采购）额（万元）	**Purchases Value of Chain Stores(10 000 yuan)**	**135554**	**140339**
其中：统一配送商品购进（采购）额	Centralized Purchases and Delivery	120338	125324
其中：自有配送中心配送商品购进（采购）额	Self Centralized Purchases and Delivery	73707	75594
非自有配送中心配送商品购进（采购）额	Non-self Centralized Purchases and Delivery	35884	40390
八、连锁门店商品营业额（万元）	**Sales Value of Chain Store(10 000 yuan)**	**329238**	**363685**
其中：餐费收入	Catering Revenues	316936	352901
商品销售额	Sales Value	9312	9677

注：上年同期数为本年在库企业加报数据。

16-11　续表　continued

指　标	Item	本年直营店 Regular Chain	上年直营店 Regular Chain Last Year
一、门店总数（个）	**Number of Stores(unit)**	**717**	**674**
二、年末从业人员数（人）	**Employees at Year-end(person)**	**16318**	**17919**
三、年末餐饮营业面积（平方米）	**Operating Area of Retail at Year-end(sq.m)**	**210433**	**203033**
四、客房数（间）	**Guest Rooms(room)**	**532**	**532**
五、床位数（张）	**Guest Beds(bed)**	**886**	**886**
六、餐位数（位）	**Dining Seats(set)**	**85052**	**97330**
七、连锁门店商品购进（采购）额（万元）	**Purchases Value of Chain Stores(10 000 yuan)**	**135554**	**140339**
其中：统一配送商品购进（采购）额	Centralized Purchases and Delivery	120338	125324
其中：自有配送中心配送商品购进（采购）额	Self Centralized Purchases and Delivery	73707	75594
非自有配送中心配送商品购进（采购）额	Non-self Centralized Purchases and Delivery	35884	40390
八、连锁门店商品营业额（万元）	**Sales Value of Chain Store(10 000 yuan)**	**329238**	**363685**
其中：餐费收入	Catering Revenues	316936	352901
商品销售额	Sales Value	9312	9677

16-12 近年限额以上住宿和餐饮业经营情况

单位：个、亿元

分 组	Classify	2017	
		单位数 Number of Enterprises	营业额 Business Revenue
总计	**Total**	**716**	**142.38**
一、住宿业	**Lodging Services**	**319**	**68.04**
1. 按登记注册类型分组	Grouped by Registration Status		
内资企业	Domestic Funded Enterprises	301	57.61
国有	State-owned Enterprises	25	5.77
集体	Collective-owned Enterprises	1	0.04
股份合作	Cooperative Enterprises		
联营	Joint Ownership Enterprises		
国有联营	State Joint Ownership Enterprises		
集体联营	Collective Joint Ownership Enterprises		
国有与集体联营	Joint State-collective Ownership Enterprises		
其他联营	Other Joint Ownership Enterprises		
有限责任公司	Limited Liability Corporations	138	35.02
国有独资公司	State-funded Corporations	8	3.87
其他有限责任公司	Other Limited Liability Corporations	130	31.15
股份有限公司	Stock Limited Corporation	4	1.92
私营	Private Enterprises	133	14.86
私营独资	Private-funded Enterprises	2	0.10
私营合伙	Private Partnership Enterprises		
私营有限责任公司	Private Limited Liability Corporations	129	14.68
私营股份有限公司	Private Share Holding Corporations	2	0.08
其他	Others		
港澳台商投资	Enterprises Funded by Hong Kong, Macao and Taiwan	7	5.21
外商投资	Foreign Funded Enterprises	9	5.14
个体经营	Individual Enterprises	2	0.08
2. 按国民经济行业分组	Grouped by Economic Sector		
旅游饭店	Tour Restaurant	193	54.26
一般旅馆	Common Hotel	116	11.61
民宿服务	Home and Lodging Services		
露营地服务	Campsite Services		
其他住宿业	Others	10	2.17

注：本表统计范围为法人、个体及产业活动单位。

Statistic on Hotel Services and Catering Services above Designed Size

(unit，100 million yuan)

2018		2019		2020	
单位数 Number of Enterprises	营业额 Business Revenue	单位数 Number of Enterprises	营业额 Business Revenue	单位数 Number of Enterprises	营业额 Business Revenue
742	**166.64**	**873**	**192.26**	**908**	**153.22**
353	**81.53**	**436**	**92.15**	**467**	**71.48**
337	70.84	420	81.07	449	63.41
21	5.07	21	5.04	24	5.46
1	0.03	2	0.06	1	0.01
134	40.03	150	45.26	108	30.02
6	3.01	9	3.49	7	1.53
128	37.02	141	41.77	101	28.49
5	2.24	4	2.31	3	2.06
175	23.30	242	28.27	311	24.94
4	0.13	5	0.23	6	0.16
168	22.53	234	27.69	304	24.68
3	0.64	3	0.36	1	0.10
1	0.17	1	0.14	2	0.93
7	5.62	8	6.83	7	4.87
8	5.05	7	4.20	10	3.16
1	0.02	1	0.05	1	0.03
184	61.97	189	67.94	193	51.55
154	16.78	227	21.26	255	17.95
2	0.10	5	0.13	4	0.06
		1	0.12	1	0.13
13	2.68	14	2.69	14	1.78

16-12 续表

单位：个、亿元

分　组	Classify	2017	
		单位数 Number of Enterprises	营业额 Business Revenue
二、餐饮业	**Catering Trade**	**397**	**74.34**
1. 按登记注册类型分组	Grouped by Registration Status		
内资企业	Domestic Funded Enterprises	364	56.40
国有	State-owned Enterprises	4	1.03
集体	Collective-owned Enterprises		
股份合作	Cooperative Enterprises		
联营	Joint Ownership Enterprises		
国有联营	State Joint Ownership Enterprises		
集体联营	Collective Joint Ownership Enterprises		
国有与集体联营	Joint State-collective Ownership Enterprises		
其他联营	Other Joint Ownership Enterprises		
有限责任公司	Limited Liability Corporations	144	22.36
国有独资公司	State-funded Corporations	2	0.67
其他有限责任公司	Other Limited Liability Corporations	142	21.69
股份有限公司	Stock Limited Corporation	5	8.58
私营	Private Enterprises	208	23.31
私营独资	Private-funded Enterprises	13	0.65
私营合伙	Private Partnership Enterprises		
私营有限责任公司	Private Limited Liability Corporations	192	22.49
私营股份有限公司	Private Share Holding Corporations	3	0.17
其他	Others	3	1.12
港澳台商投资	Enterprises Funded by Hong Kong, Macao and Taiwan	7	3.97
外商投资	Foreign Funded Enterprises	5	11.66
个体经营	Individual Enterprises	21	2.31
2. 按国民经济行业分组	Grouped by Economic Sector		
正餐服务	Dinner Services	384	58.74
快餐服务	Fast Food Services	10	15.25
饮料及冷饮服务	Beverage and Cold Beverage Services		
餐饮配送及外卖送餐服务	Catering Distribution and Takeaway Servic		
其他餐饮业	Other Catering Services	3	0.35

continued

(unit，100 million yuan)

2018		2019		2020	
单位数 Number of Enterprises	营业额 Business Revenue	单位数 Number of Enterprises	营业额 Business Revenue	单位数 Number of Enterprises	营业额 Business Revenue
389	**85.11**	**437**	**100.11**	**441**	**81.74**
360	61.16	375	72.91	351	55.83
6	1.31	6	1.50	5	0.99
136	22.48	121	22.32	81	13.98
4	1.32	3	1.40	3	0.59
132	21.16	118	20.92	78	13.40
4	9.48	3	10.07	4	6.66
213	26.67	244	37.81	261	34.20
11	0.64	11	0.58	11	0.43
201	25.97	231	37.15	249	33.49
1	0.06	2	0.08	1	0.28
1	1.22	1	1.21		
6	7.65	6	8.79	5	7.83
6	13.93	6	15.52	7	16.07
17	2.37	50	2.89	78	2.01
369	63.17	412	71.43	415	53.96
11	17.43	11	19.68	12	19.28
4	3.83	9	8.14	7	7.80
1	0.26	1	0.24	1	0.23
4	0.42	4	0.63	6	0.47

主要统计指标解释

批发业 指向其他批发或零售单位（含个体经营者）及其他企事业单位、机关团体等批量销售生活用品、生产资料的活动，以及从事进出口贸易和贸易经纪与代理的活动，包括拥有货物所有权，并以本单位(公司)的名义进行交易活动,也包括不拥有货物的所有权，收取佣金的商品代理、商品代售活动；还包括各类商品批发市场中固定摊位的批发活动，以及以销售为目的的收购活动。

零售业 指百货商店、超级市场、专门零售商店、品牌专卖店、售货摊等主要面向最终消费者（如居民等）的销售活动，以互联网、邮政、电话、售货机等方式的销售活动，还包括在同一地点，后面加工生产，前面销售的店铺（如面包房）；谷物、种子、饲料、牲畜、矿产品、生产用原料、化工原料、农用化工产品、机械设备（乘用车、计算机及通信设备除外）等生产资料的销售不作为零售活动；多数零售商对其销售的货物拥有所有权，但有些则是充当委托人的代理人，进行委托销售或以收取佣金的方式进行销售。

住宿业 指为旅行者提供短期留宿场所的活动，有些单位只提供住宿，也有些单位提供住宿、饮食、商务、娱乐一体的服务，不包括主要按月或按年长期出租房屋住所的活动。

餐饮业 指通过即时制作加工、商业销售和服务性劳动等，向消费者提供食品和消费场所及设施的服务。

社会消费品零售总额 企业（单位、个体户）通过交易直接售给个人、社会集团非生产、非经营用的实物商品金额，以及提供餐饮服务所取得的收入金额。个人包括城乡居民和入境人员，社会集团包括机关、社会团体、部队、学校、企事业单位、居委会或村委会等。

批发和零售业商品购进、销售、库存总额 指各种登记注册类型的批发和零售业企业（单位）以本企业（单位）为总体的，从国内、国外市场购进的商品总量，销售和出口的商品总量、库存的商品总量等情况。该指标可以反映商品流转过程中商品的购进、销售、库存之间的比例关系和存在的问题。

商品购进总额 从本企业以外的单位和个人购进（包括从国外直接进口）作为转卖或加工后转卖的商品金额（含增值税）。商品购进包括：（1）从工农业生产者、批发和零售业、住宿和餐饮业、出版社或报社的出版发行部门和其他服务业等企事业单位和个体经营户购进的商品；（2）从机关、社会团体购进的商品；（3）从海关、市场管理部门购进的缉私和没收的商品；（4）从居民收购的废旧商品等。不包括：（1）企业为本单位自身经营用，不是作为转卖而购进的商品，如材料物资、包装物、低值易耗品、办公用品等；（2）未通过买卖行为而收入的商品，如接受其他部门移交的商品、借入的商品、收入代其他单位保管的商品、其他单位赠送的样品、加工回收的成品等；（3）经本单位介绍，由买卖双方直接结算，本单位只收取手续费的业务；（4）销售退回和买方拒付货款的商品；（5）商品溢余；（6）期货交易商品。

进口 直接从国外进口或委托外贸企业代理进口的商品金额，不包括从国内有关单位购进的进口商品。对外贸易企业只统计自主经营进口的商品，不统计受托代理进口的商品。

商品销售总额 指对本单位以外的单位和个人出售的商品金额（包括售给本单位消费用的商品，含增值税）。商品销售包括：（1）售给个人和社会集团消费用的商品；（2）售给农业、工业、建筑业、服务业等国民经济各行业用于生产、经营用的商品，包括售予批发和零售业作为转卖或加工后转卖的商品；（3）对国（境）外直接出口的商品。不包括：（1）未通过买卖行为付出的商品，如因机构变动移交给其他企业单位的商品、借出的商品、归还受其他单位委托代保管的商品、付出的加工原料和赠送给其他单位的样品等；（2）促销返券所销售的、不计入营业收入的商品；（3）经本单位介绍，由买卖双方直接结算，本单位只收取手续费的业务；（4）未发生所有权转移的商品预付卡销售，如加油卡；（5）汽车维修、电话卡销售等服务性经济活动；（6）购货退回的商品；（7）商品损耗和损失；（8）出售本单位自用的废旧物资；（9）期货交易商品；（10）自来水供应企业、电力企业、天然气供应企业提供的水、电、气。

出口 直接向国（境）外出口商品和委托外贸企业代理出口的商品金额，商品出口不包括售给外贸企业出口或加工后出口的商品，以及在国内市场以外币销售的商品。外贸企业只统计自主经营出口的商品，不包括受托代理出口的商品。

库存总额 指报告期末各种登记注册类型的批发和零售业企业（单位）已取得所有权的商品。它反映批发和零售业企业（单位）的商品库存情况和对市场商品供应的保证程度。商品库存包括：（1）存放在批发和零售业经营单位（如门市部、批发站、经营处）仓库、货场、货柜和货架中的商品；（2）挑选、整理、包装中的商品；（3）已记入购进而尚未运到本单位的商品，即发货单或银行承兑凭证已到而货未到的商品；（4）寄放他处的商品，如因购货方拒绝承付而暂时存放在购货方的商品和已办完加工成品收回手续而未提回的商品；（5）委托其他单位代销(未作销售或调出)尚未售出的商品；（6）代其他单位购进尚未交付的商品。不包括所有权不属于本单位的商品、委托外单位加工生产尚未收回成品的商品、外贸企业代理其他单位从国外进口尚未付给订货单位的商品、代国家物资储备部门保管的商品等。

住宿和餐饮业营业额 指住宿和餐饮业单位在经营活动中，因提供服务或销售商品等取得的全部收入（含增值税），收入主要来源于提供客房、餐费服务、商品销售和其他服务，如商务服务。不包括多产业法人企业附营的其他行业产业活动单位的餐费收入、商品销售收入等各项收入。其中，客房收入指住宿和餐饮业单位在经营活动中因提供住宿服务取得的收入（含增值税）。不包括多产业法人企业附营的其他行业产业活动单位的客房收入。餐费收入指本单位为顾客提供就餐服务取得的收入（含增值税）。包括：经烹饪、调制加工后出售的各种食品，如主食、炒菜、凉拌菜等的收入。不包括多产业法人企业附营的其他行业产业活动单位的餐费收入。

连锁总店（总部） 指负责连锁企业资源（商号、商誉、经营模式、服务标准、管理模式等）的开发、配置、控制或使用等功能的企业核心管理机构。连锁经营是指经营同类商品或服务，使用统一商号的若干店铺，在同一总店（总部）的管理下，采取统一采购或特许经营等方式，实现规模效益的组织形式，包括直营连锁、特许连锁和自愿连锁三种形式。其中，直营连锁是指连锁店铺由连锁公司全资或控股开设，在总部的直接控制下，开展统一经营的连锁经营形式；特许连锁是指拥有注册商标、企业标志、专利、专有技术等经营资源的企业（特许人），以合同形式将其拥有的经营资源许可其他经营者（被特许人）使用，被特许人按合同约定在统一的经营模式下开展经营，并向特许人支付特许经营费用的连锁经营形式；自愿连锁是指若干个店铺或企业自愿组合起来，在不改变各自资产所有权关系的情况下，以同一个品牌形象面对消费者，以共同进货为纽带开展的连锁经营形式。

Explanatory Notes on Main Statistical Indicators

Wholesale Trade refers to the activities of selling wholesale commodities for daily use and capital goods to enterprises of wholesale and retail trades (including self-employed individuals) and other enterprises, institutions and government organs and organizations, and the activities of engaging in import and export and acting as a trade agent. The wholesaler may have the ownership of the commodities for wholesale and trade in the name of its own (a company), and the wholesaler can act as commission agent or commodity broker without the ownership of commodities. Also included are the wholesale activities at the fixed stalls in wholesale market and the acquisition for sales purpose.

Retail Trade refers to the activities of department store, supermarket, franchised store, brand store, retail stall and on-the-spot-making-selling store selling commodities to the final consumers (residents) by any means including internet, post, telephone, sales machine. It also includes shops with sales and production located in the same places (such as bakeries). Retail trade excludes the activities of sales of capital goods such as grain, seed, feed, livestock, mineral products, raw material for production, industrial chemicals, chemical products for agricultural use, machine and equipment (excluding vehicles, computers and communication equipment). Most retailers have the ownership of commodities to sell, but some are acting as agents or brokers to make transactions for a commission.

Hotel Services refer to the accommodation services provided to visitors. Some units may provide only accommodation while others provide a combination of accommodation, meals, business services and/or recreational facilities. It excludes activities related to the provision of long-term primary residences in facilities such as apartments typically leased on a monthly or annual basis.

Catering Services refer to the activities of providing foods, serving locations and facilities to customers through instant processing, commercial sales and service-type labor.

Total Retail Sales of Consumer Goods refer to the amount obtained by enterprises (units, self-employed individuals) through direct sales of non-production and non-business physical commodity to individuals, social institutions, and revenue from providing catering services. Individuals include rural and urban households, population from abroad, social institutions include government agencies, social organizations, military units, schools, institutions, neighbourhood (village) committees.

Purchase, Sales and Stock of Commodities by Wholesale and Retail Trades refer to the total volume of commodities purchased, total volume of sales and exports, and the stock of commodities by wholesale and retail enterprises (establishments) of different status of registration from domestic and overseas markets. This indicator reflects the relationship among purchase, sales and stock of commodities in the circulation of goods and reveals the existing problems.

Total Purchases of Commodities refer to the total value of purchases of commodities by enterprises (establishments) from other establishments or individuals (including direct import from abroad) for the purpose of re-selling, either with or without further processing of the commodities purchased. The commodities include: (1) commodities purchased from agricultural and industrial producer, wholesaler, retailer, publishing house and other enterprises, institutions and individual operators of service business; (2) commodities purchased from institutions and government departments; (3) confiscated goods purchased from the customs authorities or market management agencies; (4) second-hand goods and wastes purchased from residents; The commodities exclude (1) commodities purchased by enterprises (establishments) for use in their own business operation, commodities obtained without buying or selling procedures such as materials, consumable goods of low value, office appliance, etc. (2) received goods without trading, such as goods handed over from others, borrowed goods, preserved goods for others, donated goods from others, processed and retrieved goods, etc. (3) goods of direct settlement between buyer and seller with handling fees introduced by others, (4) goods returned or refused to pay by the buyer, (5) excessive goods, (6) futures trading commodities.

Import refers to the amount of goods imported directly from abroad or imported entrusted to foreign trade enterprises as agents, excluding imports purchased from relevant domestic units. Foreign trade enterprises only count imported goods independently, not imported goods entrusted by agents.

Total Sales of Commodities refer to value of commodities sold by the establishments to other establishments and individuals (including goods sold for self consumption, including the value-added tax). The commodities include: (1) commodities sold to individuals and social groups for their consumption; (2) commodities sold to establishments in all industries for their production and operation, including agriculture, industry, construction, and catering services including commodities sold to wholesale and retail establishments for re-selling, with or without further processing; and (3) commodities for direct export to abroad. Excluded are (1) extended commodities without trading, such as goods handed over to other enterprises and institutions because of the change of organizations, lent goods, returned goods preserved for others, extended processing materials and samples donated to others, (2) goods sold by coupon rebates that are not included in business income, (3) goods of direct settlement between buyer and seller with handling fees introduced by others, (4) prepaid cards for goods without transfer of ownership, such as gas cards, (5) Service-oriented economic activities such as automobile maintenance and telephone card sales, (6) goods returned after purchase, (7) damaged and spoiled goods, (8) waste and used goods of self use, (9) futures trading commodities, (10) water, electricity and gas supplied by water supply enterprises, electric power enterprises and natural gas supply enterprises.

Export refers to the amount of goods exported directly to foreign countries (borders) or exported entrusted to foreign trade enterprises as agents. Commodity export does not include goods sold to foreign trade enterprises for export or exported after processing, as well as goods sold in foreign currencies in the domestic market. Foreign trade enterprises only count the goods they export independently, excluding those exported by trusted agents.

Total Stock of Commodities refers to total commodities possessed by wholesaler and retailer of various types of registration status at the end of the reference period, reflecting the commodity stock level of various wholesaler and retailer and the potential for market supply. It includes: (1) Commodities located in storage, garages, counters, and shelves of operating places (such as sale stores, wholesale centres, and operating offices); (2) Commodities in the process of being selected, sorted, and packed; (3) Commodities not arrived but recorded as purchase in the account, i.e. commodities not arrived but payment receipts for the commodities from the sellers or the banks arrived; (4)Commodities deposited in other places rather than places mentioned above, for instance: commodities in the hold of purchasers temporarily due to the refusal of payment and commodities not taken back after going through the formalities; (5) Commodities entrusted to other units to sell but not sold yet; (6) Commodities purchased for other units but not delivered yet. Commodities not included as stock are those not owned by the enterprises (units), commodities on commission for processing but not yet delivered, imported commodities of agency of foreign trade enterprise but not yet delivered to ordering units and finally those put in stock on behalf of the state material reserves units.

Business Revenue of Hotels and Catering Services refers to total revenue (including VAT) of hotels and catering services received from providing services or selling commodities through business activities, income comes mainly from providing hotels, catering services, selling of commodities and other services, such as commodity services. It does not include revenue such as meal fees, selling of commodities of other industrial units affiliated with multi industrial legal entities. Income from hotels refers to income (including VAT) of hotels and catering services by providing lodging services through business activities. Income from catering services refers to income (including VAT) from providing catering services, including selling of cooked or prepared foods, such as staple food, cooked dishes, or cold dishes. It does not include meal fees of other industrial units affiliated with multi industrial legal entities.

Chain Head Stores (headquarter) refer to the core leading stores responsible for development, allocation, administration and utilization of resources (name of stores, brand of stores, operation model, service standard, management way, etc.) of chain stores. Chain stores refers to the stores engaged in providing homogeneous commodities or services, with the central leadership of head store (headquarters) and guided by common policies, conduct centralized purchase and distributed selling of commodities, in order to gain better efficiency through standardized operation. The chain stores include regular chain stores, franchise chain stores and voluntary chain stores.

Regular Chain store refers to chain stores that are invested or controlled by the headquarters. They operate under direct and unified management from the headquarters.

Franchise chain store refers to the chain stores (franchisees) which are franchised with operation resources such as trade marks, names, patent and operation know-how by the franchisors in form of contract and pay the operation fees to the franchisors.

Voluntary chain store refers to the stores operate jointly on the voluntary bases while maintaining their status of independent legal entities with full ownership of their assets. They sell goods of same brand from same channel of resource to the consumers.

17 对外经济贸易和旅游

FOREIGN TRADE AND ECONOMIC COOPERATION TOURISM

资料整理：李鹏涛
Data management: Li Pengtao
数据审核：赵　晖
Data audit: Zhao Hui

第十七部分　对外经济贸易和旅游

一、简要说明

本章资料包括对外经济贸易、利用外资和旅游等方面资料，由西安市统计局贸易外经处根据西安市商务局、投资合作局、文旅局和西安海关提供资料整理。

二、主要指标

进出口总值（亿元）	3473.84	比上年增长	7.1%
#出　口	1775.98	比上年增长	2.6%
实际利用外资（亿美元）	76.77	比上年增长	8.8%

17　FOREIGN TRADE AND ECONOMIC COOPERATION,TOURISM

Ⅰ.Brief Introduction

Data in this chapter consists of data on foreign trade, using of foreign capital and fund and tourism. Data on foreign economy and trade and tourism are compiled and provided by Foreign Economy Division of the Xi'an Bureau of Statistics according to the data from Xi'an Municipal Bureau of Commerce, Xi'an Municipal Bureau of Investment Cooperation. Xi'an Customs District and Xi'an Municipal Administration of Culture and Tourism Committee.

Ⅱ.Major Indicators

		Increase over Preceding Year
Total Imports and Exports (100 mil.yuan)	3473.84	7.1%
#Exports	1775.98	2.6%
Actual Utilized Foreign Investments (USD 100 mil.)	76.77	8.8%

17-1 主要年份外资、外贸基本情况

Main Indicators on Foreign Investments and International Trading in Representative Years

指　标	Item	2000	2005	2010	2014*	2015*
一、新设立外商投资企业（个）	**Number of New Foreign-Invested Enterprises (unit)**	**135**	**157**	**82**	**103**	**73**
合同外资（万美元）	Contracted Foreign Investments (USD 10 000)	54123	121499	119689	255321	193684
实际利用外资（万美元）	Actual Utilized Foreign Investments (USD 10 000)	15633	57113	156653	370310	400833
二、进出口总值（万美元）	**Total Imports and Exports (USD 10 000)**	**173696**	**390146**	**1039273**	**15321514**	**17616896**
进口总值	Total Imports	67634	126705	507544	7974693	9418142
出口总值	Total Exports	106062	263441	531729	7346822	8198754
进出口差额(出口-进口)	Balance of Imports and Exports	38428	136736	24185	-627871	-1219388
三、国际旅游人数总计（万人次）	**Total Number of International Tourists (10 000 person-times)**	**65.03**	**77.56**	**84.18**		
#外国人	Foreigners	54.65	65.86	73.21		
港、澳、台同胞	Chinese Compatriot From Hong Kong, Macao and Taiwan	10.38	11.70	10.97		
四、国际旅游者人天数总计（万人天）	**Total Number of Days of International Tourists (10 000 person days)**	**162.69**	**224.93**	**241.67**		
#外国人	Foreigners	131.44	190.99	211.48		
港、澳、台同胞	Chinese Compatriot From Hong Kong, Macao and Taiwan	31.15	33.94	30.19		
五、国际旅游收入（亿元）	**Earning of International Tourism (100 millon yuan)**	**22.41**	**33.54**	**42.40**		
#商品收入	Income from Mercantile	7.71	11.25	11.87		
劳务收入	Income from Labour Service	14.70	22.29	30.53		
六、国际旅游者在西安人均停留天数（天）	**Number of Days of Average Tourists Staying in Xi'an (day)**	**2.5**	**2.9**	**2.9**		

注：1.2014年起市文化和旅游局未发布国际旅游统计数据。
2.本表“新设立外商投资企业”2018年前名称为“利用外资签定协议项目”，“合同外资”2016年前名称为“利用外资签订协议金额”，“实际利用外资”2016年前名称为“外商实际直接投资额”。
3.本表来源于市商务局、西安海关、市文化和旅游局、市投资合作局。2018年及以后利用外资包含西咸新区，进出口总值为西安原口径数据。
4.*号表示2014年起进出口数据计量单位由“万美元”更改为“万元”。

17-1 续表 continued

指 标	Item	2016*	2017*	2018*	2019*	2020*
一、新设立外商投资企业（个）	**Number of New Foreign-Invested Enterprises (unit)**	**72**	**143**	**219**	**237**	**212**
合同外资（万美元）	Contracted Foreign Investments (USD 10 000)	102103	464954	475508	196410	735596
实际利用外资（万美元）	Actual Utilized Foreign Investments (USD 10 000)	450466	530680	635370	705738	767702
二、进出口总值（万美元）	**Total Imports and Exports (USD 10 000)**	**18299476**	**25450843**	**33032389**	**32425181**	**34738438**
进口总值	Total Imports	8826392	9928641	13460734	15122342	16978644
出口总值	Total Exports	9473084	15522202	19571655	17302839	17759794
进出口差额(出口-进口)	Balance of Imports and Exports	646692	5593561	6110921	2180497	781150
三、国际旅游人数总计（万人次）	**Total Number of International Tourists (10 000 person-times)**					
#外国人	Foreigners					
港、澳、台同胞	Chinese Compatriot From Hong Kong, Macao and Taiwan					
四、国际旅游者人天数总计（万人天）	**Total Number of Days of International Tourists (10 000 person days)**					
#外国人	Foreigners					
港、澳、台同胞	Chinese Compatriot From Hong Kong, Macao and Taiwan					
五、国际旅游收入（亿元）	**Earning of International Tourism (100 millon yuan)**					
#商品收入	Income from Mercantile					
劳务收入	Income from Labour Service					
六、国际旅游者在西安人均停留天数（天）	**Number of Days of Average Tourists Staying in Xi'an (day)**					

17–2 主要年份利用外资情况

Utilization of Foreign Capital in Representative Years

单位：万美元 (USD 10 000)

年　份 Year	合同外资 Contracted Foreign Investments	实际利用外资 Actual Utilized Foreign Investments
1983	3500	800
1985	8361	1106
1986	19919	4010
1987	3218	5552
1988	2423	6758
1989	1645	11632
1990	415	1154
1991	591	1094
1992	24165	5200
1993	57289	8996
1994	20321	15240
1995	28956	18653
1996	35978	20510
1997	27214	22057
1998	40034	22286
1999	40390	13801
2000	54123	15633
2001	60736	17687
2002	70692	20281
2003	96380	25557
2004	78312	27595
2005	121499	57113
2006	182525	82463
2007	143978	111567
2008	118230	114738
2009	60027	121872
2010	119689	156653
2011	120083	200522
2012	360264	247800
2013	251874	312994
2014	255321	370310
2015	193684	400833
2016	102103	450466
2017	464954	530680
2018	475508	635370
2019	196410	705738
2020	735596	767702

注：本表数据来源于市投资合作局。2018年及以后数据包含西咸新区。

17-3 外国和港澳台地区在西安投资情况（2020年）

Foreign, Hong Kong, Macao and Taiwan Investment Situation in Xi'an (2020)

单位：万美元 (USD 10 000)

指　标	Item	新设立外商投资企业（个）Number of New Foreign-Invested Enterprises(unit)	合同外资 Contracted Foreign Investments	实际利用外资 Actual Utilized Foreign Investments
合计数	**Total**	**212**	**735596**	**767702**
一、按国民经济行业分组	**By Sector**			
（一）农、林、牧、渔业	Agriculture, Forestry, Animal Husbandry and Fishery	2	23780	
（二）采矿业	Mining			
（三）制造业	Manufacturing	9	289412	406286
（四）电力、燃气及水的生产供应业	Generation and Supply of Electricity, Production and Supply of Gas and Water	1	151	564
（五）建筑业	Construction	5	253	18722
（六）批发和零售业	Wholesale and Retail Trades	65	2582	115491
（七）交通运输、仓储和邮政业	Transportation, Storage and Post	3	6809	20434
（八）住宿和餐饮业	Hotels and Catering Services	13	178	1848
（九）信息传输、软件和信息技术服务业	Information Transmission, Computer Service and Software	23	26696	1306
（十）金融业	Financial Intermediation			16120
（十一）房地产业	Real Estate	8	41685	57696
（十二）租赁和商务服务业	Leasing and Business Services	40	325723	92609
（十三）科学研究和技术服务业	Scientific Research and Technical Service	19	16168	14864
（十四）水利、环境和公共设施管理业	Management of Water Conservancy, Environment and Public Facilities	4	1600	19942
（十五）居民服务、修理和其他服务业	Services to Households, repairs and other services	7	284	454
（十六）教育	Education	2	9	1159
（十七）卫生和社会工作	Health and social work	2	22	

注：本表数据来源于市投资合作局。本表数据包含西咸新区。

17-3 续表 continued

单位：万美元 (USD 10 000)

指 标	Item	新设立外商投资企业（个） Number of New Foreign-Invested Enterprises(unit)	合同外资 Contracted Foreign Investments	实际利用外资 Actual Utilized Foreign Investments
（十八）文化、体育和娱乐业	Culture, Sports and Entertainment	9	244	207
（十九）公共管理、社会保障和社会组织	Public administration, social security and social organizations			
（二十）国际组织	International Organizations			
二、按投资国别、地区分组	**By Country(Region)**			
中国香港	Hong Kong,China	51	419465	278520
中国澳门	Macao,China	1	14	2329
中国台湾	Taiwan,China	21	1397	2496
日本	Japan	3	198	34357
马来西亚	Malaysia			
新加坡	Singapore	7	3502	326614
韩国	Korea Rep.	15	267265	70259
德国	Germany	2	3492	1923
意大利	Italy	2	25	
法国	France	2	12	3258
英国	United Kingdom	5	235	9838
瑞士	Switzerland		121	574
丹麦	Denmark			
加拿大	Canada			127
美国	United States	6	623	26022
澳大利亚	Australia	3	2870	404
维尔京群岛	Virgin Is.(E)		5349	945
其它	Others	94	31028	10036

17-4 各区县、开发区实际利用外资

Actual Utilized Investment by Foreign Entrepreneurs by Region and Development Zone

单位：万美元 (USD 10 000)

区县及开发区	Region and Economic Development Zone	2011	2012	2013	2014	2015	2016	2017	2018	2019	2020
区县合计	**Sum of Region**	**49726**	**58119**	**45164**	**51423**	**59765**	**67874**	**72527**	**119635**	**129183**	**124666**
新城区	Xincheng	6765	7800	5012	6500	7775	8768	10340	11947	11609	12097
碑林区	Beilin	6273	7800	5103	5871	6873	9360	9941	10570	11450	12127
莲湖区	Lianhu	7405	7800	5100	5843	6873	7532	8656	9392	9820	10398
灞桥区	Baqiao	6001	7397	6124	6933	8148	9056	9601	10570	11450	9200
未央区	Weiyang	6202	7800	6000	6834	7870	8614	9433	10380	11260	9420
雁塔区	Yanta	6912	8190	6179	6847	8074	8907	9843	10772	11450	9077
阎良区	Yanliang	2070	2200	2200	2346	2555	2801	3000	3200	3360	3460
临潼区	Lintong	2000	2400	2400	2504	2765	3031	1102	4094	3680	3855
长安区	Chang'an	2300	2768	3003	3360	3961	4440	4762	5200	5620	4476
高陵区	Gaoling	1089	1100	1100	1182	1478	1621	1740	1860	1960	2020
鄠邑区	Huyi	1060	1115	1173	1288	1339	1479	1700	1666	1600	1180
蓝田县	Lantian	600	650	660	707	1283	1401	1490	1862	3185	1530
周至县	Zhouzhi	1050	1100	1110	1210	773	864	920	920		
西咸新区	Xixian								37202	42739	45826
开发区合计	**Sum of Economic Development Zones**	**150797**	**189681**	**267830**	**318887**	**311265**	**381023**	**458153**	**515513**	**576495**	**643037**
高新区	GaoXin	64935	81776	132632	149387	167112	203870	260293	287000	321383	356615
经开区	JingKai	54201	68202	81423	103009	114538	129186	145000	167000	186900	206800
曲江新区	Qujiang	21002	26433	33870	41436		20588	24212	26500	29600	32488
航空基地	Aviation Industry Base	1701	2072	2640	3082	3636	4186	2045	5250	6000	8931
航天基地	Aerospace Base	2030	2403	3000	3501	3980	4567	5117	6100	6599	9853
浐灞生态区	Chanba Eco-District	3856	4837	7266	8453	9800	10833	12402	13600	15000	16460
国际港务区	International Trade&Logistic Park	1571	2082	3469	5050	6429	7793	9083	10063	11013	11890
其它	**Others**					**29803**	**1569**		**222**	**60**	

注：本表数据来源于市投资合作局。2018年及以后数据包含西咸新区。2011-2015年开发区合计含沣东新城。

17-5 主要年份进出口总值

Total Imports and Exports in Representative Years

单位：万美元 (USD 10 000)

年 份 Year	进出口总值 Total Imports and Exports	出口总值 Total Exports	进口总值 Total Imports
1987	13596	7540	6056
1990	38229	28290	9939
1992	70467	53060	17407
1993	93330	62393	30937
1994	104752	76897	27855
1995	137510	110163	27347
1996	143187	91745	51442
1997	150668	107753	42915
1998	180589	100492	80097
1999	172919	94495	78424
2000	173696	106062	67634
2001	169914	87948	81966
2002	186966	112479	74487
2003	230932	140327	90605
2004	309295	203539	105756
2005	390146	263441	126705
2006	415403	272862	142541
2007	536162	347133	189029
2008	704029	447113	256916
2009	724618	333114	391504
2010	1039273	531729	507544
2011	1260179	582662	677517
2012	1301446	729878	571568
2013	1798534	847819	950715
2014*	15321514	7346822	7974693
2015*	17616896	8198754	9418142
2016*	18299476	9473084	8826392
2017*	25450843	15522202	9928641
2018*	33032389	19571655	13460734
2019*	32425181	17302839	15122342
2020*	34738438	17759794	16978644

注：本表数据来源于西安海关。2014年起数据计量单位由“万美元”更改为“万元”。本表数据为西安原口径数据。

17-6 外贸商品进出口总值分国别和地区（2020年）

Total Value of Imports and Exports by Country and Region（2020）

单位：万元 (10 000 yuan)

国别和地区	Country and Region	进出口总值 Total Imports and Exports	出口 Exports
亚洲	**Asia**	**25519768**	**12681901**
#中国香港	Hong Kong,China	2543349	2543349
中国台湾	Taiwan,China	7202058	1770578
日本	Japan	2077696	375065
菲律宾	Phiilippines	112370	77648
马来西亚	Malaysia	1247681	930288
韩国	Korea	8934885	4541306
非洲	**Africa**	**457584**	**308519**
#埃及	Egypt	121831	121549
突尼斯	Tunisia	3811	3318
埃塞俄比亚	Ethiopia	3393	3393
博茨瓦纳	Botswana	195	195
南非	South Africa	141900	34230
欧洲	**Europe**	**4373165**	**2671777**
#德意志联邦国	Germany	1013364	522836
法国	France	436821	347305
意大利	Italy	154940	60479
荷兰	Netherland	777996	575418
英国	England	242983	177706
瑞士	Switzerland	76276	9762
西班牙	Spain	179285	148343
俄罗斯联邦	Russia	249879	138580
拉丁美洲	**Latin America**	**1088363**	**616276**
#哥伦比亚	Colombia	13205	13204
巴西	Brazil	276141	111284
阿根廷	Argentina	7454	5934
北美洲	**North America**	**2645907**	**1330846**
#加拿大	Canada	175754	47541
美国	America	2470153	1283305
大洋洲及太平洋岛屿	**Oceanic and Pacific Islands**	**645224**	**149461**
#澳大利亚	Australia	629810	141383
新西兰	New Zealand	12360	6624

注：本表数据来源于西安海关，为西安原口径数据。

17-7 主要商品分大类出口金额

Export Value of Major Merchandise by Type

单位：万美元 (USD 10 000)

商品分类	HS Section and Division	2000	2005
食用蔬菜、根及块茎	Edible Vegetables, Certain,Roots and Tubers	1095	1190
蔬菜、水果、坚果或植物其他部分的制品	Vegetables, Fruits, Nuts, or Products Made of Other Parts of Plants	2076	10531
矿砂、矿渣及矿灰	Ores,Slags and Ash	4083	63247
无机化学品；贵金属、稀土金属、放射性元素及其同位素的有机及无机化合物	Inorganic Chemicals,Organic or Inorganic Compounds of Precious Metals,of Rare Earth Metals,of Radioactive Elements or of Isotopes	3714	10997
有机化学品	Organic Chemicals	2367	8569
羊毛、动物细毛或粗毛、马毛纱线及其机织物	Wool ,Fine or Coarse Animal Hair; Horsehair Yarn and Woven Fabric	810	903
棉花	Cotton	3197	3240
化学纤维短纤	Short Staple Chemical Fibers	5061	1471
针织或钩编的服装及衣着附件	Articles of Apparel and Clothing Accessories, Knitted or Crocheted	6753	5736
非针织或非钩编的服装及衣着附件	Articles of Apparel and Clothing Accessories, not Knitted or Crocheted	7269	5068
其它纺织制成品；成套物品；旧衣着及旧纺织品	Other Made Up Textile Articles;Sets;Worn Clothing and Worn Textile Articles;Rags Articles	1649	3000
鞋靴、护膝和类似品及其零件	Footwear,Gaiters and The Like;Parts of Such Articles Headgear and Parts Thereof	1347	1368
玻璃及其制品	Glass and Glassware	3376	8576
钢铁	Iron and Steel	3534	5314
钢铁制品	Articles of Iron or Steel	5535	13959
铅及制品	Lead Articles Thereof	1371	12
锌及制品	Zinc Articles Thereof	4031	135
其他贱金属、金属陶瓷及其制品	Other Base Metals,Germets;Articles Thereof		
贱金属工具、器具、利口器、餐匙、餐叉及其零件	Tools,Implements,Cutlery,Spoons and Forks, of Base Metal;Parts Thereof of Base Metal		
核反应堆、锅炉、机器、机械器具及其零件	Nuclear Reactors ,Boilers, Machinery and Mechanical Appliances; and Parts Thereof	10915	30832
电机、电气设备及其零件；录音机及放声机、电视图象、声音的录制和重放设备及其零件、附件	Electrical Machinery and Equipment and Parts Thereof;Sound Recorders and Repreducers, Television Image and Sound Recordes and Repreducers, and Parts and Accessories of Such Articles	8339	23605
光学、照相、电影、计量、检验、医疗或外科仪器及设备、精密仪器及设备；上述物品的零配件、附件	Optical,Photographic,Cinematographic,Measuring, Checking,Precision Medical or Surgical Instruments and Apparatus;Parts and Accessories Thereof	2020	2341
家具、寝具、褥垫、弹簧床垫、软床垫及类似的填充制品；未列名灯具及照明装置；发光标志、发光铭牌及类似品；活动房屋	Mattresses,Mattress Supports,Cushions and Similar Stuffed Furnishings;Lamps and Lighting Fittings, not Elsewhere Specified or Included;Illuminated Signs,Illuminated	2587	4773

注：1.本表数据来源于西安海关。2014年起数据计量单位由“万美元”更改为“万元”。本表数据为西安原口径数据。
2.个别年份数据根据海关最新提供数据进行了修正。

17-7 续表

单位：万美元

商品分类	HS Section and Division	2007	2008
食用蔬菜、根及块茎	Edible Vegetables, Certain,Roots and Tubers	1232	1374
蔬菜、水果、坚果或植物其他部分的制品	Vegetables, Fruits, Nuts, or Products Made of Other Parts of Plants	37426	29270
矿砂、矿渣及矿灰	Ores,Slags and Ash	47378	40502
无机化学品；贵金属、稀土金属、放射性元素及其同位素的有机及无机化合物	Inorganic Chemicals,Organic or Inorganic Compounds of Precious Metals,of Rare Earth Metals,of Radioactive Elements or of Isotopes	16508	15882
有机化学品	Organic Chemicals	11182	13954
羊毛、动物细毛或粗毛、马毛纱线及其机织物	Wool ,Fine or Coarse Animal Hair; Horsehair Yarn and Woven Fabric	1065	720
棉花	Cotton	3255	3213
化学纤维短纤	Short Staple Chemical Fibers	1767	1181
针织或钩编的服装及衣着附件	Articles of Apparel and Clothing Accessories, Knitted or Crocheted	5345	4371
非针织或非钩编的服装及衣着附件	Articles of Apparel and Clothing Accessories, not Knitted or Crocheted	3875	3623
其它纺织制成品；成套物品；旧衣着及旧纺织品	Other Made Up Textile Articles;Sets;Worn Clothing and Worn Textile Articles;Rags Articles	3090	3187
鞋靴、护膝和类似品及其零件	Footwear,Gaiters and The Like;Parts of Such Articles Headgear and Parts Thereof	348	380
玻璃及其制品	Glass and Glassware	6246	6538
钢铁	Iron and Steel	11366	11966
钢铁制品	Articles of Iron or Steel	17329	26568
铅及制品	Lead Articles Thereof	1650	2
锌及制品	Zinc Articles Thereof	2470	46
其他贱金属、金属陶瓷及其制品	Other Base Metals,Germets;Articles Thereof	23414	27576
贱金属工具、器具、利口器、餐匙、餐叉及其零件	Tools,Implements,Cutlery,Spoons and Forks, of Base Metal;Parts Thereof of Base Metal		
核反应堆、锅炉、机器、机械器具及其零件	Nuclear Reactors ,Boilers, Machinery and Mechanical Appliances; and Parts Thereof	47381	75911
电机、电气设备及其零件；录音机及放声机、电视图象、声音的录制和重放设备及其零件、附件	Electrical Machinery and Equipment and Parts Thereof;Sound Recorders and Repreducers, Television Image and Sound Recordes and Repreducers, and Parts and Accessories of Such Articles	33393	56758
光学、照相、电影、计量、检验、医疗或外科仪器及设备、精密仪器及设备；上述物品的零配件、附件	Optical,Photographic,Cinematographic,Measuring, Checking,Precision Medical or Surgical Instruments and Apparatus;Parts and Accessories Thereof	4230	6348
家具、寝具、褥垫、弹簧床垫、软床垫及类似的填充制品；未列名灯具及照明装置；发光标志、发光铭牌及类似品；活动房屋	Mattresses,Mattress Supports,Cushions and Similar Stuffed Furnishings;Lamps and Lighting Fittings, not Elsewhere Specified or Included;Illuminated Signs,Illuminated	8301	8296

continued

(USD 10 000)

2009	2010	2011	2012	2013	2014*	2015*	2016*	2017*	2018*	2019*	2020*
803	2633	2016	1961	2699	2686	2039	2555	1129	659	1337	1000
21920	22189	36763	2576	49361	132663	112701	102768	149311	131711	79123	62463
6141	5247	4709	1679	1686	14977	96	178	346	25	2	4
9774	13645	11735	8911	12588	67764	44508	49950	52192	52289	61278	49903
16294	18881	20067	17890	28694	109986	109654	117162	148719	176287	185794	195107
460	923	796	562	2433	15782	3005	5648	3153	5680	5731	1130
2346	3277	2628	2185	5827	9252	14309	6429	5301	5531	9583	3281
2217	1951	2586	2375	8245	13685	11581	11178	14502	12923	14903	14132
3617	3830	3366	12316	6491	29551	37030	31646	36441	30570	15335	12534
2919	3134	3262	7050	4861	33872	23610	19393	40633	52971	22579	54999
2813	3170	2838	4412	4471	18906	15677	15187	26219	19425	37534	137812
367	544	1003	5252	6293	20186	5032	2292	18614	18514	19469	5553
5574	6691	8073	10995	13856	54453	45991	46764	46059	49904	44400	52181
4254	9622	16681	8407	6730	31854	20390	27589	28467	34424	26844	19000
11943	12149	25319	24259	33546	102720	88740	100956	164963	151403	132817	126743
1	2	2	4913	16	3		26	19	1	12	
78	10	10	11	59	109	93	20	334	48	83	95
11276	20723	28092	21397	24030	106691	95442	83309	103608	115801	122230	93007
2777	3374	3641	5176	5992	30653	25321	24868	33582	41004	38312	42354
52372	102893	99631	127795	211009	1929864	2744726	3431041	6147739	8252801	4882165	4356460
53355	118140	137105	183536	327931	3113155	3625079	4264312	7044093	8971300	10051890	10977973
5255	9489	11066	14908	17879	112646	119117	107892	108613	149348	170976	247596
4769	4992	3860	25644	23595	52352	42140	40142	77439	83975	26295	28047

17-8 主要商品分大类进口金额

Import Value of Major Merchandise by Type

单位：万美元 (USD 10 000)

商品分类	HS Section and Division	2000	2005	2010	2014*	2015*
无机化学品；贵金属、稀土金属、放射性元素及其同位素的有机及无机化合物	Inorganic Chemicals,Organic or Inorganic Compounds of Precious Metals,of Rare Earth Metals,of Radioactive Elements or of Isotopes	1467	317	7513	166549	185175
有机化学品	Organic Chemicals	7257	15237	13949	98293	86359
塑料及其制品	Plastic and Articles Thereof	2559	4317	4091	37082	54103
钢铁	Iron and Steel	2467	752	10949	11893	17403
铜及制品	Copper and Articles Thereof	2367	689	43343	169061	484480
铝及制品	Aluminium and Articles Thereof	2652	3627	3116	45295	43935
核反应堆、锅炉、机器、机械器具及其零件	Nuclear Reactors ,Boilers, Machinery and Mechanical Appliances; and Parts Thereof	12990	38050	134753	2017587	2021311
电机、电气设备及其零件；录音机及放声机、电视图象、声音的录制和重放设备及其零件、附件	Electrical Machinery and Equipment and Parts Thereof;Sound Recorders and Repreducers, Television Image and Sound Recordes and Repreducers,and Parts and Accessories of Such Articles	5911	23337	207937	3919650	5011437
车辆及其零件、附件，但铁道及电车道车辆除外	Vehicles Other Than Railway or Tramway Rolling-Stock, and Rarts and Accessories Thereof	1530	1387	3109	17521	19700
航空器、航天器及其零配件	Aircraft, Spacecraft and Parts Thereof	10443	8800	3620	43191	35164
光学、照相、电影、计量、检验、医疗或外科仪器及设备、精密仪器及设备；上述物品的零配件、附件	Optical,Photographic,Cinematographic,Measuring, Checking,Precision Medical or Surgical Instruments and Apparatus;Parts and Accesseories Thereof	3673	10424	37414	452559	542812

17-8 续表 continued

单位：万美元 (USD 10 000)

商品分类	HS Section and Division	2016*	2017*	2018*	2019*	2020*
无机化学品；贵金属、稀土金属、放射性元素及其同位素的有机及无机化合物	Inorganic Chemicals,Organic or Inorganic Compounds of Precious Metals,of Rare Earth Metals,of Radioactive Elements or of Isotopes	299328	246352	371885	346091	405611
有机化学品	Organic Chemicals	154656	123439	148022	114497	174149
塑料及其制品	Plastic and Articles Thereof	76182	103008	157809	198420	211050
钢铁	Iron and Steel	16093	16567	18717	21793	30309
铜及制品	Copper and Articles Thereof	224287	240188	571455	652623	603906
铝及制品	Aluminium and Articles Thereof	34384	32032	71631	100994	90818
核反应堆、锅炉、机器、机械器具及其零件	Nuclear Reactors ,Boilers, Machinery and Mechanical Appliances; and Parts Thereof	990108	926081	1056642	2881715	3286053
电机、电气设备及其零件；录音机及放声机、电视图象、声音的录制和重放设备及其零件、附件	Electrical Machinery and Equipment and Parts Thereof;Sound Recorders and Repreducers, Television Image and Sound Recordes and Repreducers,and Parts and Accessories of Such Articles	5272203	6510729	9406713	8561929	9033247
车辆及其零件、附件，但铁道及电车道车辆除外	Vehicles Other Than Railway or Tramway Rolling-Stock, and Rarts and Accessories Thereof	22697	26662	22430	23238	47976
航空器、航天器及其零配件	Aircraft, Spacecraft and Parts Thereof	31933	101247	31940	28326	24734
光学、照相、电影、计量、检验、医疗或外科仪器及设备、精密仪器及设备；上述物品的零配件、附件	Optical,Photographic,Cinematographic,Measuring, Checking,Precision Medical or Surgical Instruments and Apparatus;Parts and Accesseories Thereof	521411	307404	341141	580507	680636

注：本表数据来源于西安海关。2014年起数据计量单位由“万美元”更改为“万元”。本表数据为西安原口径数据。

17-9 按贸易方式分外贸出口总值(2020年)

Total Value of Exports in Foreign Trade by Type of Trade (2020)

单位：万元 (10 000 yuan)

指　标	Item	2020	2020年比2019年增长（%） Growth Rate in 2020 over 2019 (%)
出口总值	**Total Exports**	**17759794**	**2.6**
1.一般贸易	General Trade	4203287	11.2
2.国家间、国际组织无偿援助	Between Countries, International Organizations	6015	-13.7
和赠送的物资	Aid and Donated Materials		
3.其他捐赠物资	Other Donated Materials		
4.来料加工装配贸易	Assembly Processing Trade	6884339	-2.2
5.进料加工贸易	Processing With Imported Trade	4095282	14.2
6.对外承包工程出口货物	Exports Contracted Projects	45585	-47.5
7.租赁贸易	Lease Trade		
8.易货贸易	Barter		
9.出料加工贸易	Material Processing	168	81.2
10.保税监管场所进出境货物	Inward and Outward Goods of Free	287	46.6
（保税仓库进出境货物）	(Trade Storehouse)		
11.海关特殊监管区域物流货物	Re-export Goods of Free Trade Zone	2504154	-10.1
12.其他	Others	15114	-12.9

注：本表数据来源于西安海关。本表数据为西安原口径数据。

17-10 按贸易方式分外贸进口总值(2020年)

Total Value of Imports in Foreign Trade by Type of Trade (2020)

单位：万元 (10 000 yuan)

指 标	Item	2020	2020年比2019年增（%）Growth Rate in 2020 over 2019(%)
进口总值	**Total Imports**	**16978644**	**12.3**
1.一般贸易	General Trade	3239657	15.8
2.国家间、国际组织无偿援助和赠送的物资	Between Countries, Internationals Organization Aid and Donated Materials		
3.华侨、港澳台同胞、外籍华人捐赠物资	The overseas Chinese, Hong Kong, Macao, Taiwan,Chinese of foreign Donated Materials		
4.来料加工装配贸易	Assembly Processing Trade	6321808	-2.0
5.进料加工贸易	Processing With Imported Trade	3644059	12.6
6.来料加工装配进口的设备	Assembly Processing Trade Equipment		
7.租赁贸易	Lease Trade		
8.外商投资企业作为投资进口的设备、物品	Foreign-invested Enterprises as the Import Investment of Equipment, Goods		
9.出料加工贸易	Material Processing	700	109.8
10.易货贸易	Barter		
11.保税监管场所进出境货物（保税仓库进出境货物）	Inward and Outward Goods of Free (Trade Storehouse)	75905	-2.0
12.海关特殊监管区域物流货物（保税区仓储转口货物）	Re-export Goods of Free Trade Zone (Re-exports)	1568423	95.6
13.海关特殊监管区域进口设备（出口加工区进口设备）	Export Processing Zones Imported (Equipment)	2062032	24.7
14.其他	Other	61311	-45.6

注：本表数据来源于西安海关。本表数据为西安原口径数据。

17-11 主要年份旅游人数及收入

Number of Tourists and Tourism Earnings in Representative Years

年 份 Year	接待旅游者人数（万人次） Number of Tourists (10 000 person-times)	#国际旅游人数 Number of International Tourists	旅游总收入（万元） Total Tourism Earnings (10 000 yuan)	#国际旅游收入 Earning of International Tourists	国际旅游者在西安人均停留天数（天） Number of Days of Average International Tourists Staying in Xi'an(day)
1980	4.00	4.00	1757	1757	3.8
1985	21.15	21.15	7029	7029	2.2
1990	25.88	25.88	19628	19628	2.1
1995	791.35	41.35	440000	103818	2.0
1998	1105.80	47.98	560000	160244	2.6
1999	1260.40	55.41	830000	186282	2.5
2000	1567.00	65.03	1050000	224100	2.5
2001	1752.20	67.20	1130000	240700	2.4
2002	1984.13	74.13	1310000	260000	2.2
2003	1647.67	33.66	1064200	121200	2.5
2004	2149.03	65.03	1544000	273900	2.9
2005	2423.60	77.56	1785000	335380	2.9
2006	2738.70	86.73	2043000	378270	2.9
2007	3118.01	100.01	2372000	424263	2.9
2008	3232.20	63.20	2435200	287200	2.6
2009	3929.29	67.29	2974000	310500	2.9
2010	5285.18	84.18	4051800	424000	2.9
2011	6653.23	100.23	5301500	512800	2.9
2012	7978.35	115.35	6543900	598900	2.9
2013	10130.00	121.11	8114400	641600	2.9
2014	12000.00		9500000		
2015	13600.80		10736900		
2016	15012.56		12138100		
2017	18093.14		16333000		
2018	24738.75		25548100		
2019	30110.43		31460500		
2020	18417.41		18824200		

注：1.本表数据来源于市文化和旅游局。2014年以后市文化和旅游局未发布国际旅游统计数据。2017年及以后数据包含西咸新区。
2.1980-1994年因未开展国内旅游统计，故接待旅游者人数和旅游总收入为国际旅游统计。

17-12 主要年份旅行社及A级景点

Travel Agencies and Level-A Scenic Spots in Representative Years

项 目	Item	2005	2010	2013	2014	2015	2016	2017	2018	2019	2020
旅行社数（个）	Number of Travel Agencies (unit)	221	334	360	385	353	410	452	583	574	550
旅行社营业收入（亿元）	Revenue of Travel Agencies (100 million yuan)	17.82	31.22	57.93	45.70	59.54	66.68	79.39	93.93	103.14	34.89
旅游A级景点数（个）	Number of Level-A Scenic Spots(unit)	18	34	61	67	74	72	77	77	77	83
旅游A级景点年接待游客人次（万人次）	Number of Tourists Received at Level-A Scenic Spots (10 000 person-times)	930	2726	7163	7462	8553	10454	18120	24506	22596	10866

注：本表数据来源于市文化和旅游局。2017年及以后所有指标均不包含西咸新区，但2018年旅行社数、旅行社营业收入来源于第四次经济普查583家有营业收入的企业数据，包含西咸新区。

主要统计指标解释

进出口总额 指实际进出我国国境的货物总金额。包括对外贸易实际进出口货物，来料加工装配进出口货物，国家间、联合国及国际组织无偿援助物资和赠送品，华侨、港澳台同胞和外籍华人捐赠品，租赁期满归承租人所有的租赁货物，进料加工进出口货物，边境地方贸易及边境地区小额贸易进出口货物（边民互市贸易除外），中外合资企业、中外合作经营企业、外商独资经营企业进出口货物和公用物品，到、离岸价格在规定限额以上的进出口货样和广告品（无商业价值、无使用价值和免费提供出口的除外），从保税仓库提取在中国境内销售的进口货物，以及其他进出口货物。该指标可以观察一个国家在对外贸易方面的总规模。我国规定出口货物按离岸价格统计，进口货物按到岸价格统计。

商品经营单位所在地进、出口额 指在所在地海关注册登记的有进出口经营权的企业实际进、出口额。

商品目的地进口额和商品货源地出口额 目的地进口额指进口货物的消费、使用或最终抵运地的实际进口额；货源地出口额指出口货物的产地或原始发货地的实际出口额。

利用外资 指我国各级政府、部门、企业和其他经济组织通过对外借款、吸收外商直接投资以及用其他方式筹措的境外现汇、设备、技术等。

外商直接投资 指外国企业和经济组织或个人（包括华侨、港澳台胞以及我国在境外注册的企业）按我国有关政策、法规，用现汇、实物、技术等在我国境内开办外商独资企业、与我国境内的企业或经济组织共同举办中外合资经营企业、合作经营企业或合作开发资源的投资（包括外商投资收益的再投资），以及经政府有关部门批准的项目投资总额内企业从境外借入的资金。

旅游人数：

（1）入境旅游人数：指报告期内来我国观光、度假、探亲访友、就医疗养、购物、参加会议或从事经济、文化、体育、宗教活动的外国人、港澳台同胞、入境游客。统计时，外国人、港澳台同胞每入境一次统计1人次。

（2）出境人数：指中国（大陆）居民因公或因私出境前往其他国家、中国香港特别行政区、澳门特别行政区和台湾省观光、度假、探亲访友、就医疗养、购物、参加会议或从事经济、文化、体育、宗教活动的人数，即出境游客。统计时，按每出境一次统计1人次。

（3）国内旅游人数：指在报告期内在中国（大陆）观光游览、度假、探亲访友、就医疗养、购物、参加会议或从事经济、文化、体育、宗教活动的中国（大陆）居民人数，其出游的目的不是通过所从事的活动谋取报酬。统计时，国内游客按每出游一次统计1人次。

国际旅游（外汇）收入 指入境游客在中国（大陆）境内旅行、游览过程中用于交通、参观游览、住宿、餐饮、购物、娱乐等全部花费。

国内旅游收入 又称旅游总花费，指国内游客在国内旅行、游览过程中用于交通、参观游览、住宿、餐饮、购物、娱乐等全部花费。

国际旅行社 指经营业务范围包括入境旅游业务、出境旅游业务和国内旅游业务的旅行社。

国内旅行社 指经营范围仅限于国内旅游业务的旅行社。

星级饭店 指设备、设施、服务符合《旅游饭店星级的划分与评定》（GB/T14308—2010）标准，通过相关旅游管理部门评定，并取得星级饭店称号的饭店（含预备星级饭店）。

Explanatory Notes on Main Statistical Indicators

Total Imports and Exports at Customs refer to the real value of commodities imported and exported across the border of China. They include the actual imports and exports through foreign trade, imported and exported goods under the processing and assembling trades and materials, supplies and gifts as aid given gratis between governments and by the United Nations and other international organizations, and contributions donated by overseas Chinese, compatriots in Hong Kong and Macao and Chinese with foreign citizenship, leasing commodities owned by tenant at the expiration of leasing period, the imported and exported commodities processed with imported materials, commodities trading in border areas (excluding mutual exchange goods), the imported and exported commodities and articles for public use of the Sino-foreign joint ventures, cooperative enterprises and ventures with sole foreign investment. Also included is import or export of samples and advertising goods for which CIF or FOB value are beyond the permitted ceiling (excluding goods of no trading or use value and free commodities for export), imported goods sold in China from bonded warehouses and other imported or exported goods. The indicator of the total imports and exports at customs can be used to observe the total size of external trade in a country. In accordance with the stipulation of the Chinese government, imports are calculated at CIF, while exports are calculated at FOB.

Import Export Value by Location of China's Foreign Trade Managing Units refers to actual value of imports and exports carried out by corporations which have been registered by the local Customs house and are vested with right to run import export business.

Import Value of Commodities by Place of Destination and Export Value of Commodities by Place of Origin in China The former indicator refers to the value of import commodities of the places of their consumption, utilization or the places of their final destination. The latter indicator refers to the value of export commodities of the places of their origin or the places of the commodities dispatched.

Utilization of Foreign Capitals refers to remittance, equipment and technology financed from abroad, by loans, foreign direct investment and other forms undertaken by the Chinese governments at all levels, by various departments, enterprises and other economic units.

Foreign Direct Investment refers to the investments inside China by foreign enterprises and economic organizations or individuals (including overseas Chinese, compatriots from Hong Kong, Macao and Taiwan, and Chinese enterprises registered abroad), following the relevant policies and laws of China, for the establishment of ventures exclusively with foreign own investment, Sino-foreign joint ventures and cooperative enterprises or for co-operative exploration of resources with enterprises or economic organizations in China.

Number of Tourists

(1) Visitor arrivals refer to the number of foreigners,Chinese compatriots from Hong Kong, Macao and Taiwan Chinese (mainland) who come to China (mainland) for sight-seeing,vacation,visiting relatives, medical treatment, shopping, attending conference, or to engage in economic, cultural, sports and religious activities. In compiling statistics, each time of entering China is counted as one person-time.

(2) Number of Chinese residents going abroad refer to the number of Chinese (mainland) residents going to other countries, Hong Kong Special Administrative region, Macao Special Administrative region and Taiwan for on official or private purposes, for sight-seeing, vacation, visiting relatives, medical treatment, shopping, attending conference, or to engage in economic, cultural, sports and religious activities. In compiling statistics, each time of leaving is counted as one person-time.

(3) Number of domestic tourists refers to the number of Chinese (mainland) residents who travel within China (mainland) for sight-seeing, vacation, visiting relatives, medical treatment, shopping, attending conference, or to engage in economic, cultural, sports and religious activities. In compiling

statistics, each time of travelling is counted as one person-time.

Foreign Exchange Earnings from International Tourism refer to the total expenditure of foreigners, overseas Chinese,Chinese compatriots from Hong Kong,Macao and Taiwan during their stay in the mainland of China on transportation,sighting,accommodation, food,shopping and entertainment.

Income from Domestic Tourism refer to expenditure of domestic tourists on transportation,sighting, accommodation, food, shopping and entertainment while they travel.

International Travel Agencies refer to travel agencies engaged in tourism entering China, Chinese residents going abroad and domestic tourism.

Domestic Travel Agencies refer to travel agencies only engaged in domestic tourism.

Star-rated Hotels refer to hotels rated with stars as assessed by the relevant tourism authorities according to GB/T14308-2010 standard with reference to their infrastructure, facilities and service levels.

18 规模以上服务业

SERVICE INDUSTRY OBOVE DESIGNATED SIZE

资料整理：冯　乐　杜　晖
Data management：Feng Le　Du Hui
数据审核：刘栋婷
Data audit：Liu Dongting

第十八部分　规模以上服务业

一、简要说明

1.本章主要包括规模以上服务业（九个门类、四个中类）单位个数及主要经济指标，由西安市统计局服务业与社会科技统计处提供。

2.统计范围：辖区内年营业收入2000万元及以上服务业法人单位。包括：交通运输、仓储和邮政业，信息传输、软件和信息技术服务业，水利、环境和公共设施管理业三个门类和卫生行业大类。

辖区内年营业收入1000万元及以上服务业法人单位。包括：租赁和商务服务业，科学研究和技术服务业，教育三个门类，以及物业管理、房地产中介服务、房地产租赁经营和其他房地产业四个行业中类。

辖区内年营业收入500万元及以上服务业法人单位。包括：居民服务、修理和其他服务业，文化、体育和娱乐业两个门类，以及社会工作行业大类。

二、主要指标

规模以上服务业单位个数（个）	2222		
规模以上服务业资产总计（亿元）	12546.88	比上年增长	13.5%
规模以上服务业营业收入（亿元）	3301.50	比上年增长	7.1%
规模以上服务业利润总额（亿元）	205.86	比上年下降	2.7%

18 SERVICE INDUSTRY OBOVE DESIGNATED SIZE

I .Brief Introduction

1.The data in this chapter consists of the number of service units and main economic indicators of Service enterprises above designated size (Including mine categories, four Class), data in this chapter is provided by Tertiary Industry and Social Science&Technology Division of Xi'an Bureau of Statistics.

2.Scope of statistics:The annual operating income of the service enterprise within the jurisdiction is 20 million yuan or more. It includes transportation, storage and postal services, information transmission, software and information technology services, water conservancy, environment and public facilities management, and health services. The annual operating income of the service enterprise within the jurisdiction is 10 million yuan or more. It includes: leasing and business services, scientific research and technology services, three categories of education, and property management, real estate intermediary services, real estate leasing and other real estate industry.

The annual operating income within the jurisdiction is 5 million yuan or more. Including: residential services, repair and other services, culture, sports and entertainment two categories, and social work industry categories.

II. Major Indicators

		Increase over Preceding Year
Number of Units for services and Enterprises above the Designated Size(units)	2222	
Total Assets for services and Enterprises above the Designated Size(100 mil.yuan)	12546.88	13.5%
Operating Income for services and Enterprises above the Designated Size(100 mil.yuan)	3301.50	7.1%
The total Profit for services and Enterprises above the Designated Size(100 mil.yuan)	205.86	-2.7%

18-1 主要年份规模以上服务业主要经济指标

Major Economic Indicators for Services above the Designated Size in Representative Years

单位：万元 (10 000 yuan)

指　标	Item	2015	2016	2017	2018	2019	2020
企业单位数（个）	Number of Enterprises(unit)	1056	1229	1546	1670	2075	2222
资产总计	Total Assets	62321993.9	70706084.2	81172689.4	83589990.5	104196300.9	125468817.0
固定资产原价	Original Value of Fixed Assets	34083410.8	37690984.8	42493526.7	47715297.2	52484267.4	56646202.8
负债合计	Total Liabilities	38612455.8	44500949.3	50412896.1	49777084.0	61769819.9	75768947.6
所有者权益合计	Total Owners' Equities	23706613.0	26205716.2	30759793.3	33812906.5	42426481.0	49699869.4
营业收入	Business Revenue	15622838.8	17699509.4	21146457.1	25887537.8	30847961.6	33014968.7
营业成本	Business Cost	11094383.8	13037904.8	15282402.8	19661919.2	23565609.4	26159714.2
销售费用	Selling Expenses	1138387.7	979373.2	1206035.9	1258937.1	1361655.9	1433201.2
管理费用	Managenment Expenses	1595009.8	1806745.9	2104498.2	2485578.9	2354924.6	2435128.3
研发费用	R&D Expenses					660652.9	854836.1
财务费用	Financial Expenses	974310.3	1032444.2	1191706.4	1256296.0	1403795.5	1280074.4
投资收益	Investment Income	436577.4	382392.0	286218.3	223023.6	282996.3	694559.2
营业利润	Business Profits	1256825.3	1132716.0	1616118.6	1588474.9	1967982.6	1961738.3
利润总额	Total Profits	1559208.3	1422770.3	1701396.9	1582864.5	2052358.0	2058642.1
应付职工薪酬	Salary Payable	2823540.9	3362254.1	4228194.3	5114155.7	6346279.9	6856080.1
平均用工人数（人）	Annual Average Employed Persons(person)	335722	359745	406270	478344	532203	550624

18-2 规模以上服务业按登记注册类型分主要经济指标（2020年）

单位：万元

指标	Item	企业单位数（个）Number of Enterprises (unit)	资产总计 Total Assets	固定资产原价 Original Value of Fixed Assets
总计	**Total**	**2222**	**125468817.0**	**56646202.8**
按登记注册类型分组	**Grouped by Registration Type**			
内资	Domestic Funded Enterprises	2143	122614569.0	55956173.0
国有	State-owned Enterprises	73	3131869.2	898710.2
集体	Collective-owned Enterprises	15	101032.3	31177.3
股份合作	Corperative Enterprises	3	12699.1	2988.9
联营	Joint Ownership Enterprises			
有限责任公司	Limited Liability Corporrations	841	104808136.4	48120014.2
股份有限公司	Other Limited Liability Corporrations	51	5258381.7	4447337.8
私营	Other Limited Liability Corporrations	1144	9024124.6	2344391.1
其他	Other Enterprises	16	278325.7	111553.5
港澳台商投资	Enterprises with Funds from Hong Kong, Macao &Taiwan	32	1687975.5	314402.5
外商投资	Foreign Funded Enterprises	47	1166272.5	375627.3

18-2 续表1

单位：万元

指标	Item	管理费用 Management Expenses	研发费用 R&D Expenses	财务费用 Financial Expenses
总计	**Total**	**2435128.3**	**854836.1**	**1280074.4**
按登记注册类型分组	**Grouped by Registration Type**			
内资	Domestic Funded Enterprises	2351245.3	809500.1	1259014.3
国有	State-owned Enterprises	161202.1	10753.1	1682.5
集体	Collective-owned Enterprises	22387.0	443.2	-695.7
股份合作	Corperative Enterprises	1071.7	829.2	-138.9
联营	Joint Ownership Enterprises			
有限责任公司	Limited Liability Corporrations	1283340.2	601143.2	1143763.2
股份有限公司	Other Limited Liability Corporrations	132606.7	21321.8	36799.6
私营	Other Limited Liability Corporrations	718563.6	175009.6	70889.0
其他	Other Enterprises	32074.0		6714.6
港澳台商投资	Enterprises with Funds from Hong Kong, Macao &Taiwan	42376.9	16015.5	7463.2
外商投资	Foreign Funded Enterprises	41506.1	29320.5	13596.9

Main Economic Indicators for Services above the Designated Size grouped by Registration Type（2020）

（10 000 yuan)

负债合计 Total Liabilities	所有者权益合计 Total Owners' Equities	营业收入 Business Revenue	营业成本 Business Cost	销售费用 Selling Expenses
75768947.6	**49699869.4**	**33014968.7**	**26159714.2**	**1433201.2**
74371175.7	48243393.3	32293250.0	25668592.9	1403749.7
1820023.7	1311845.5	1213569.0	1049264.3	16652.9
78484.3	22548.0	90281.3	51954.5	12714.6
6645.1	6054.0	2101.5	390.3	140.6
64605278.0	40202858.4	21292479.0	17088029.2	898913.1
941342.1	4317039.6	2630774.9	2045210.0	119546.2
6713614.3	2310510.3	6836318.5	5266531.9	342017.9
205788.2	72537.5	227725.8	167212.7	13764.4
787881.2	900094.3	246198.5	153460.7	19283.5
609890.7	556381.8	475520.2	337660.6	10168.0

continued 1

（10 000 yuan)

投资收益 Investment Income	营业利润 Business Profits	利润总额 Total Profits	应付职工薪酬 Salary Payable	平均用工人数（人） Annual Average Employed Persons (person)
694559.2	**1961738.3**	**2058642.1**	**6856080.1**	**550624**
570013.9	1794309.5	1894429.5	6630505.0	537027
8509.1	-2156.6	25889.2	315263.6	28291
69.1	3347.7	3338.0	42476.4	6295
	-300.0	-205.0	1118.9	190
534354.3	1252107.0	1283028.1	4345012.0	281072
10610.3	268683.9	256510.3	364619.6	25697
16471.1	264428.2	313275.7	1474997.1	189267
	8199.3	12593.2	87017.4	6215
124526.2	125175.9	119575.3	41345.8	3572
19.1	42252.9	44637.3	184229.3	10025

18-3 规模以上服务业按规模分主要经济指标（2020年）

单位：万元

指标	Item	企业单位数（个）Number of Enterprises (unit)	资产总计 Total Assets	固定资产原价 Original Value of Fixed Assets
总计	**Total**	**2222**	**125468817.0**	**56646202.8**
按企业规模分组	**Grouped by Size of Enterprises**			
大型企业	Large-size	180	60134152.7	45921539.5
中型企业	Medium-size	437	18704681.9	5597729.0
小型企业	Small-size	1273	43871909.5	4371981.2
微型企业	Microenterprise	332	2758072.9	754953.1

18-3 续表1

单位：万元

指标	Item	管理费用 Managenment Expenses	研发费用 R&D Expenses	财务费用 Financial Expenses
总计	**Total**	**2435128.3**	**854836.1**	**1280074.4**
按企业规模分组	**Grouped by Size of Enterprises**			
大型企业	Large-size	1058523.3	559323.3	784383.1
中型企业	Medium-size	577883.5	178514.6	166021.3
小型企业	Small-size	725622.0	107610.1	297089.0
微型企业	Microenterprise	73099.5	9388.1	32581.0

Main Economic Indicators for Services above the Designated Size grouped by Size of Enterprises (2020)

(10 000 yuan)

负债合计 Total Liabilities	所有者权益合计 Total Owners' Equities	营业收入 Business Revenue	营业成本 Business Cost	销售费用 Selling Expenses
75768947.6	**49699869.4**	**33014968.7**	**26159714.2**	**1433201.2**
33499168.2	26634984.5	17668621.3	13931125.6	750074.5
11704865.4	6999816.5	6518022.5	4973865.2	445641.6
28569468.5	15302441.0	7717222.3	6263405.1	217170.4
1995445.5	762627.4	1111102.6	991318.3	20314.7

continued 1

(10 000 yuan)

投资收益 Investment Income	营业利润 Business Profits	利润总额 Total Profits	应付职工薪酬 Salary Payable	平均用工人数（人） Annual Average Employed Persons (person)
694559.2	**1961738.3**	**2058642.1**	**6856080.1**	**550624**
203572.3	1062988.0	1066457.4	4486961.6	274369
290996.2	533821.3	546877.0	1282761.0	133938
185284.2	378783.2	417226.1	1020814.4	135831
14706.5	-13854.2	28081.6	65543.1	6486

18-4 规模以上服务业按行业分主要经济指标（2020年）

单位：万元

指 标	Item	企业单位数（个）Number of Enterprises (unit)	资产总计 Total Assets	固定资产原价 Original Value of Fixed Assets
总计	**Total**	**2222**	**125468817.0**	**56646202.8**
按国民经济行业大类分组	**Grouped by sector categories**			
铁路运输业	Railway transport industry	3	4123166.8	4835543.6
道路运输业	The road transport industry	133	34350459.3	25574640.3
水上运输业	Water transportation			
航空运输业	The air transport industry	11	4437807.9	2033603.5
管道运输业	Pipeline transportation	1	59097.4	16781.9
多式联运和运输代理业	Handling and transport industry	42	288143.3	113438.4
装卸搬运和仓储业	Warehousing industry	35	1153114.8	207017.5
邮政业	The postal service	11	897959.4	565829.2
电信、广播电视和卫星传输服务	Telecommunication, broadcasting and satellite transmission services	23	8811948.6	13910451.6
互联网和相关服务	The Internet and related services	70	868416.4	50155.4
软件和信息技术服务业	Software and information technology services	240	4497204.1	756144.6
物业管理	Property management	186	1700462.8	287864.8
房地产中介服务	Real estate intermediary service	17	59295.2	6749.9
房地产租赁经营	Owned Real Estate Business Activities	67	3325563.7	713448.8
其他房地产业	Other Real Estate			
租赁业	Leasing industry	25	147082.4	63411.9
商务服务业	Business services	425	24357293.4	3145699.8
研究和试验发展	Research and development	32	1463915.3	419173.1
专业技术服务业	Professional and technical services	350	13725739.8	1104770.7
科技推广和应用服务业	Promotion and application of science and technology services	28	564310.5	190426.3
水利管理业	Water resources management industry	4	6332.8	1502.6
生态保护和环境治理业	Ecological protection and environmental control industries	7	169847.6	85153.8
公共设施管理业	Public facilities management industry	50	2692045.8	450354.2
土地管理业	Land Administration Industry	6	12344473.5	96869.3
居民服务业	Resident services	33	156407.6	88798.3
机动车、电子产品和日用产品修理业	Motor vehicles, electronics and household goods-repairing	21	46532.8	9825.2
其他服务业	Other service industries	23	57641.7	11257.7
教育	Education	24	253838.3	47802.8
卫生	Health	75	1566569.2	1028867.1
社会工作	Social work	1	1049.7	4.7
新闻出版业	Press and publishing industry	32	532512.7	89435.7
广播、电视、电影和影视录音制作业	Radio, television, film and video recordings	109	1181904.8	131799.5
文化艺术业	Culture and arts	67	794854.0	372572.6
体育	Physical education	9	41937.9	33424.5
娱乐业	The entertainment industry	62	791887.5	203383.5

Main Economic Indicators for Services above the Designated Size grouped by Industry（2020）

（10 000 yuan）

负债合计 Total Liabilities	所有者权益合计 Total Owners' Equities	营业收入 Business Revenue	营业成本 Business Cost	销售费用 Selling Expenses	管理费用 Managenment Expenses
75768947.6	**49699869.4**	**33014968.7**	**26159714.2**	**1433201.2**	**2435128.3**
2698075.0	1425091.8	740045.7	641640.6	134.7	6009.5
20572691.5	13777767.8	2510935.7	2163517.0	13513.2	166443.5
2080059.5	2357748.4	376285.0	445966.2	7549.0	47789.2
44457.4	14640.0	37224.9	36440.2		1776.1
169828.1	118315.2	609999.1	577908.3	3304.1	21033.1
847288.5	305826.3	306259.0	277307.9	16408.0	21462.2
616241.2	281718.2	1270712.8	1115257.0	7650.3	123787.3
2510914.6	6301034.0	4691317.6	3292962.3	452260.7	270680.8
548655.1	319761.3	1605605.5	1221114.1	196894.9	60284.4
2574768.7	1922435.4	4447046.4	3179014.7	189452.7	269983.4
1304283.9	396178.9	1201323.2	1013677.7	10268.2	129731.8
29846.9	29448.3	74131.2	34703.0	16346.5	9848.7
2595789.1	729774.6	313780.3	144294.6	17206.1	82973.8
120735.3	26347.1	104569.4	90653.0	3022.8	8156.5
16081494.8	8275798.6	4159982.2	3437088.1	145415.4	343467.1
515174.6	948740.7	625826.7	474975.8	7756.5	55438.4
8313619.4	5412120.4	6881195.6	5657862.5	126719.0	428273.3
327315.6	236994.9	117062.2	76147.7	5501.2	15329.7
5203.4	1129.4	13983.3	10235.2	65.6	2606.9
88162.3	81685.3	62371.2	51787.5	1151.2	4263.8
1747293.1	944752.7	414804.9	334915.2	12300.1	46796.0
8434207.5	3910266.0	333111.3	233381.3	11.8	14518.0
162908.6	-6501.0	72677.2	34968.6	16731.1	21128.3
24603.8	21929.0	37713.9	29057.4	3949.6	3673.2
32189.3	25452.4	69151.9	56646.9	2038.2	7248.3
145460.1	108378.2	227498.8	138560.5	19481.8	35399.8
1079779.0	486790.2	727510.8	577661.8	58749.0	112658.7
2310.0	-1260.3	834.1	466.6		282.3
251148.6	281364.1	337262.9	257291.0	25199.7	41367.3
714411.7	467493.1	196762.4	173943.3	22052.8	32873.8
450982.1	343871.9	134824.6	89809.7	32399.2	33894.8
40410.3	1527.6	9659.6	2657.3	5271.1	1949.9
638638.6	153248.9	303499.3	287801.2	14396.7	13998.4

18-4 续表

单位：万元

指 标	Item	研发费用 R&D Expenses	财务费用 Financial Expenses
总计	**Total**	**854836.1**	**1280074.4**
按国民经济行业大类分组	**Grouped by sector categories**		
铁路运输业	Railway transport industry	537.2	87625.5
道路运输业	The road transport industry	1672.7	641113.1
水上运输业	Water transportation		
航空运输业	The air transport industry		15663.7
管道运输业	Pipeline transportation	55.7	-94.2
多式联运和运输代理业	Handling and transport industry	0.2	2170.5
装卸搬运和仓储业	Warehousing industry		19386.5
邮政业	The postal service		3474.6
电信、广播电视和卫星传输服务	Telecommunication, broadcasting and satellite transmission services	7882.6	65195.8
互联网和相关服务	The Internet and related services	34129.3	6376.6
软件和信息技术服务业	Software and information technology services	558350.6	9041.6
物业管理	Property management	578.1	11188.4
房地产中介服务	Real estate intermediary service		-86.3
房地产租赁经营	Owned Real Estate Business Activities	117.9	53471.0
其他房地产业	Other Real Estate		
租赁业	Leasing industry	857.9	906.6
商务服务业	Business services	10794.1	196438.8
研究和试验发展	Research and development	47388.9	2035.2
专业技术服务业	Professional and technical services	182407.8	6835.8
科技推广和应用服务业	Promotion and application of science and technology services	5846.3	5831.6
水利管理业	Water resources management industry		2.4
生态保护和环境治理业	Ecological protection and environmental control industries	154.0	472.7
公共设施管理业	Public facilities management industry	104.3	13593.4
土地管理业	Land Administration Industry		91049.2
居民服务业	Resident services		386.4
机动车、电子产品和日用产品修理业	Motor vehicles, electronics and household goods-repairing		514.5
其他服务业	Other service industries	294.5	167.4
教育	Education	965.5	16.4
卫生	Health	278.4	26657.3
社会工作	Social work		1.1
新闻出版业	Press and publishing industry	176.8	-1372.2
广播、电视、电影和影视录音制作业	Radio, television, film and video recordings	481.8	8108.7
文化艺术业	Culture and arts	1495.1	4699.4
体育	Physical education		553.8
娱乐业	The entertainment industry	266.4	8649.1

continued

(10 000 yuan)

投资收益 Investment Income	营业利润 Business Profits	利润总额 Total Profits	应付职工薪酬 Salary Payable	平均用工人数（人） Annual Average Employed Persons (person)
694559.2	**1961738.3**	**2058642.1**	**6856080.1**	**550624**
	3455.3	-3021.9	5531.6	224
22812.9	-97471.8	-78293.9	597935.8	58546
1859.6	-134971.8	-130443.9	191725.0	10571
	-1901.7	-2034.8	9035.0	675
-43.8	6104.9	14924.8	32252.1	4312
3228.6	-1136.0	8362.4	21583.6	2901
261.3	15755.9	11914.1	353943.0	35683
5710.7	562208.3	529827.7	703893.4	40815
2226.2	86713.5	81118.2	135845.4	10445
2817.9	292647.2	307560.0	1852551.8	84666
6034.9	37325.6	66623.7	315435.6	52200
1116.1	13302.2	13513.2	27167.2	2259
24202.8	14091.7	8906.8	44306.5	3518
5.8	694.5	1366.9	11011.4	1423
341879.0	431048.2	447176.6	704336.4	99367
22113.1	65289.5	71519.8	155528.6	6695
102527.5	568045.0	580133.6	1031614.3	61486
1124.0	6887.4	8800.0	16294.3	1090
	1075.1	1210.4	1048.1	153
113.1	6223.7	6796.8	8161.9	961
1577.8	398.0	-665.4	88791.1	13092
64351.2	57751.5	54986.0	9175.1	380
48.5	-534.0	-178.5	21164.2	4561
-431.4	28.5	105.4	5479.6	1025
	2404.5	2336.4	29560.6	6400
6949.8	40651.9	44454.9	88826.7	6931
74219.9	23773.6	31020.1	252329.8	24491
	84.0	185.0	263.9	47
1155.0	15511.1	20306.2	53759.5	4430
383.1	-22926.2	-21245.2	22597.7	2696
7882.3	-5919.9	1257.9	42652.5	5467
	-342.0	267.0	2922.6	634
433.3	-24529.4	-20148.2	19355.8	2480

18-5 规模以上服务业按隶属关系分主要经济指标（2020年）

单位：万元

指标	Item	企业单位数（个）Number of Enterprises (unit)	资产总计 Total Assets	固定资产原价 Original Value of Fixed Assets
总计	**Total**	**2222**	**125468817.0**	**56646202.8**
按隶属关系分	**Grouped by affiliation**			
中央	Central	96	16868039.6	14087257.4
地方	Region	119	14070433.8	1234954.6
其他	Others	2007	94530343.6	41323990.8

18-5 续表

单位：万元

指标	Item	管理费用 Management Expenses	研发费用 R&D Expenses	财务费用 Financial Expenses
总计	**Total**	**2435128.3**	**854836.1**	**1280074.4**
按隶属关系分	**Grouped by affiliation**			
中央	Central	447053.4	149732.8	120943.0
地方	Region	139731.8	24600.9	27900.0
其他	Others	1848343.1	680502.4	1131231.4

Main Economic Indicators for Services above the Designated Size grouped by Affiliation（2020）

（10 000 yuan)

负债合计 Total Liabilities	所有者权益合计 Total Owners' Equities	营业收入 Business Revenue	营业成本 Business Cost	销售费用 Selling Expenses
75768947.6	**49699869.4**	**33014968.7**	**26159714.2**	**1433201.2**
8120671.5	8747368.1	9383377.9	7573467.2	369859.6
8297372.2	5773061.6	1292225.8	1043921.8	67473.2
59350903.9	35179439.7	22339365.0	17542325.2	995868.4

continued

（10 000 yuan)

投资收益 Investment Income	营业利润 Business Profits	利润总额 Total Profits	应付职工薪酬 Salary Payable	平均用工人数（人） Annual Average Employed Persons (person)
694559.2	**1961738.3**	**2058642.1**	**6856080.1**	**550624**
57833.4	732014.2	719066.4	1365246.9	78314
85512.5	90743.8	102938.5	244234.8	23671
551213.3	1138980.3	1236637.2	5246598.4	448639

18-6 分区县、开发区规模以上服务业主要经济指标（2020年）

单位：万元

区 县	Region	企业单位数（个） Number of Enterprises (unit)	资产总计 Total Assets	固定资产原价 Original Value of Fixed Assets
全 市	**Total**	**2222**	**125468817.0**	**56646202.8**
新城区	Xincheng	108	3092753.7	1764945.3
碑林区	Beilin	185	5361554.3	4321443.8
莲湖区	Lianhu	153	4204944.6	1098099.2
灞桥区	Baqiao	145	14085666.4	2231362.4
未央区	Weiyang	458	24773667.1	11314147.5
雁塔区	Yanta	784	53200179.8	32026472.9
阎良区	Yanliang	28	889325.3	67163.4
临潼区	Lintong	31	1837506.0	264983.7
长安区	Chang'an	145	10093216.3	766409.6
高陵区	Gaoling	41	545419.0	177326.5
鄠邑区	Huyi	16	130579.4	77258.7
蓝田县	Lantian	17	228191.6	112398.5
周至县	Zhouzhi	9	94949.8	60413.2
西咸新区	Xixian	102	6930863.7	2363778.1
#开发区	Development Zones			
高新区	Gaoxin	428	22290910.6	14920516.6
经开区	Jingkai	328	20609363.6	10619755.2
曲江新区	Qujiang	222	12022658.5	1562054.6
航空基地	Aviation Industry Base	12	822300.8	25815.7
航天基地	Aerospace Base	56	2433421.7	282827.7
浐灞生态区	Chanba Eco-District	64	1895906.1	293077.7
国际港务区	International Trade & Logistics Park	74	12279675.1	1848182.4

Major Economic Indicators for Services above the Designated Size by Region(2020)

(10 000 yuan)

负债合计 Total Liabilities	所有者权益合计 Total Owners' Equities	营业收入 Business Revenue	营业成本 Business Cost	销售费用 Selling Expenses
75768947.6	**49699869.4**	**33014968.7**	**26159714.2**	**1433201.2**
705200.4	2387553.3	1057713.8	649101.6	94867.3
3437691.4	1923862.9	2089563.2	1696903.2	122134.3
2362969.6	1841975.0	953201.6	792687.0	39557.6
8914790.2	5170876.2	2002774.9	1632812.8	31822.9
14767533.8	10006133.3	4219780.1	3732984.2	119406.3
32230666.1	20969513.7	18219462.5	14122019.2	852314.8
557435.3	331890.0	155211.3	130229.5	4383.9
1283488.8	554017.2	164294.9	108861.3	25711.8
6097182.4	3996033.9	1950215.5	1321559.8	105063.5
362868.1	182550.9	642630.6	567996.9	6664.1
103419.9	27159.5	108236.9	93622.4	6631.4
170336.8	57854.8	36642.9	21620.0	1852.6
95097.7	-147.9	20915.0	20241.6	1128.6
4680267.1	2250596.6	1394325.5	1269074.7	21662.1
11979110.1	10311800.5	13767677.7	10585505.7	775381.6
11414742.3	9194621.3	3640104.4	3318686.9	97305.5
8359234.6	3663423.9	1343282.2	1065127.9	76192.4
513615.8	308685.0	56908.2	48253.3	578.3
1231411.3	1202010.4	669159.1	548240.8	12453.1
1082004.6	813901.5	401475.4	295500.1	9369.1
7911990.5	4367684.6	1641983.0	1378980.3	19352.5

18-6 续表

单位：万元

区 县	Region	管理费用 Managenment Expenses	研发费用 R&D Expenses	财务费用 Financial Expenses
全 市	**Total**	**2435128.3**	**854836.1**	**1280074.4**
新城区	Xincheng	94585.4	2907.9	9937.5
碑林区	Beilin	176430.8	13669.4	63668.3
莲湖区	Lianhu	142382.1	1384.8	30208.1
灞桥区	Baqiao	135777.4	7885.8	88468.1
未央区	Weiyang	392286.9	51663.9	230363.9
雁塔区	Yanta	1160929.6	466255.3	738243.1
阎良区	Yanliang	20588.1		1742.0
临潼区	Lintong	16333.4	733.2	27680.6
长安区	Chang'an	145838.0	299445.3	48715.7
高陵区	Gaoling	48989.5	3776.0	3103.6
鄠邑区	Huyi	7698.6		1399.6
蓝田县	Lantian	10789.9	305.3	408.1
周至县	Zhouzhi	3641.7	1.4	1406.5
西咸新区	Xixian	78856.9	6807.8	34729.3
#开发区	Development Zones			
高新区	Gaoxin	824328.8	610801.6	114723.4
经开区	Jingkai	322522.7	50477.5	195611.1
曲江新区	Qujiang	171122.4	2949.0	179935.1
航空基地	Aviation Industry Base	8763.6		1725.4
航天基地	Aerospace Base	62767.8	27256.5	2723.2
浐灞生态区	Chanba Eco-District	49972.6	2094.0	10227.4
国际港务区	International Trade & Logistics Park	85350.6	6835.9	82555.1

continued

(10 000 yuan)

投资收益 Investment Income	营业利润 Business Profits	利润总额 Total Profits	应付职工薪酬 Salary Payable	平均用工人数（人） Annual Average Employed Persons (person)
694559.2	**1961738.3**	**2058642.1**	**6856080.1**	**550624**
-180.5	197955.7	189946.3	161262.3	17050
4389.3	14114.9	20688.8	352809.0	33731
18385.5	1361.0	36491.7	236423.7	29837
20794.1	112350.5	113066.5	105002.6	15081
101450.6	172413.7	191700.3	1205220.4	123642
418375.0	1289684.6	1295826.1	3791973.4	239112
937.2	1495.4	2610.3	35957.8	4165
240.9	-13910.6	-13088.0	30638.0	4201
133135.3	214080.4	225977.5	502697.1	36259
5800.2	4198.2	12967.3	136931.1	11219
0.7	-388.1	1989.5	18449.2	3788
	1330.4	1353.3	7372.4	1659
	-5673.5	-5541.5	6124.8	1292
-8769.1	-27274.3	-15346.0	265218.3	29588
215187.8	1060893.9	1055833.5	3248070.1	190215
93300.7	54830.7	70615.9	1087203.9	101968
167927.9	74255.9	77086.6	211242.0	21714
892.2	-128.9	778.1	11986.9	1617
127760.3	144812.0	150053.6	102541.4	9054
3858.0	38554.7	46103.9	85577.1	9646
17252.6	72949.3	66270.8	31693.2	4551

主要统计指标解释

国家统计局规模以上服务业单位统计标准：辖区内年营业收入2000万元及以上服务业法人单位。包括：交通运输、仓储和邮政业，信息传输、软件和信息技术服务业，水利、环境和公共设施管理业三个门类和卫生行业大类。

辖区内年营业收入1000万元及以上服务业法人单位。包括：租赁和商务服务业，科学研究和技术服务业，教育三个门类，以及物业管理、房地产中介服务、房地产租赁经营和其他房地产业四个行业中类。

辖区内年营业收入500万元及以上服务业法人单位。包括：居民服务、修理和其他服务业，文化、体育和娱乐业两个门类，以及社会工作行业大类。

固定资产原价 指固定资产的成本，包括企业在购置、自行建造、安装、改建、扩建、技术改造某项固定资产时所发生的全部支出总额。根据会计“固定资产”科目的期末借方余额填报。

资产总计 指企业过去的交易或者事项形成的、由企业拥有或者控制的、预期会给企业带来经济利益的资源。包括企业拥有的土地、办公楼、厂房、机器、运输工具、存货等实物资产和现金、存款、应收账款和预付账款等金融资产。资产一般按流动性（资产的变现或耗用时间长短）分为流动资产和非流动资产。其中流动资产可分为货币资金、交易性金融资产、应收票据、应收账款、预付款项、其他应收款、存货等；非流动资产可分为长期股权投资、固定资产、无形资产及其他非流动资产等。根据会计“资产负债表”中“资产总计”项目的期末余额数填报。

负债合计 指企业过去的交易或者事项形成的，预期会导致经济利益流出企业的现时义务。包括银行贷款、借款、应付账款、应付职工工资、应付职工福利费、应交税金等企业负有偿还责任的债务。根据会计“资产负债表”中“负债合计”项目的期末余额数填报。

负债一般按偿还期长短分为流动负债和非流动负债。根据会计资产负债表中“负债合计”项目的期末余额数填报。执行企业会计准则或《小企业会计准则》的企业：负债合计=流动负债合计+非流动负债合计；执行其他企业会计制度的企业负债包括流动负债和长期负债。

所有者权益合计 指企业资产扣除负债后由所有者享有的剩余权益。公司的所有者权益又称股东权益。包括实收资本、资本公积、盈余公积、未分配利润等。根据会计“资产负债表”中“所有者权益合计”项目的期末余额数填报。

营业收入 指企业从事销售商品、提供劳务和让渡资产使用权等生产经营活动形成的经济利益流入。营业收入包括“主营业务收入”和“其他业务收入”。根据会计“利润表”中“营业收入”项目的本年累计数填报。

营业成本 指企业从事销售商品、提供劳务和让渡资产使用权等生产经营活动发生的实际成本。“营业成本”应当与“营业收入”进行配比。包括“主营业务成本”和“其他业务成本”。根据会计“利润表”中“营业成本”项目的本年累计数填报。

销售费用 指企业在销售商品和材料、提供劳务的过程中发生的各种费用，包括保险费、包装费、展览费和广告费、商品维修费、预计产品质量保证损失、运输费、装卸费等以及为销售本企业商品而专设的销售机构（含销售网点、售后服务网点等）的职工薪酬、业务费、折旧费等经营费用。建筑业企业销售费用指企业从事施工生产活动过程中发生的各项费用，包括应由企业负担的运输费、装卸费、包装费、保险费、维修费、展览费、差旅费、广告费和其他经费。房地产企业销售费用指企业在从事主要经营业务过程中所发生的各项销售费用，包括转让、销售、结算和出租开发产品等。执行企业会计准则或《小企业会计准则》的企业,根据会计“利润表”中“销售费用”项目的本年累计数填报。执行其他企业会计制度的企业，根据会计“利润表”中“营业费用（或经营费用）”项目的本年累计数填报。

管理费用 指企业为组织和管理企业生产经营所发生的费用，包括企业在筹建期间内发生的开办费、董事会和行政管理部门在企业经营管理中发生的，或者应当由企业统一负担的公司经费等。为了与财政部《关于修订印发2019年度一般企业财务报表格式的通知》（财会〔2019〕6号）保持一致，“管理费用”不包含“研发费用”。执行企业会计准则的企业,根据会计“利润表”中“管理费用”项目的本年累计数填报。执行《小企业会计准则》的企业,应将会计“利润表”中“管理费用”项目本年累计数减“研究费用”项目本年累计数后填报。执行其他企业会计制度的企业以及未执行财政部《关于修订印发2019年度一般企业财务报表格式的通知》（财会〔2019〕6号）的企业，在会计“利润表”中“管理费用”项目的本年累计数的基础上，根据会计“管理费用”科目下的“研究费用”相关明细科目，将“研发费用”剔除后填报。

研发费用 指企业在新知识、新技术、新产品、新工艺等的研究与开发过程中发生的费用化支出，以及计入“管理费用”会计科目的企业自行开发无形资产的摊销。费用化支出主要包括研发活动的人工费用、直接投入费用、用于研发活动的仪器、设备的折旧费、用于研发活动的软件、专利权、非专利技术的摊销费用、新产品设计费、新工艺规程制定费以及其他研发活动相关费用。执行企业会计准则的企业,根据会计“利润表”中“研发费用”项目的本年累计数填报。执行《小企业会计准则》的企业,根据会计“利润表”中“研究费用”项目的本年累计数填报。执行其他企业会计制度的企业以及会计“利润表”未列示“研发费用”或“研究费用”的企业，根据会计“管理费用”科目下“研究费用”明细科目的本期发生额，以及“管理费用”科目下“无形资产摊销”明细科目的本期发生额分析填报。

财务费用 指企业为筹集生产经营所需资金等而发生的筹资费用，包括企业生产经营期间发生的利息支出（减利息收入）、汇兑损失（减汇兑收益）以及相关的手续费等。根据会计“利润表”中“财务费用”项目的本年累计数填报。

投资收益 指企业确认的投资收益或投资损失，反映企业以各种方式对外投资所取得的收益。根据会计“利润表”中“投资收益”项目的本年累计数填报。如为投资损失以“–”号记。

营业利润 指企业从事生产经营活动所取得的利润。执行《企业会计准则》或《小企业会计准则》的企业，营业利润为营业收入减去营业成本、税金及附加、销售费用、管理费用、财务费用、研发费用、资产减值损失、信用减值损失，再加上公允价值变动收益、资产处置收益、投资收益、净敞口套期收益和其他收益。执行其他企业会计制度的企业，营业利润为营业收入减去营业成本、税金及附加，加上其他业务利润后，再减去销售费用、管理费用、财务费用、研发费用后的金额，应符合以下逻辑关系：营业利润等于营业收入减去营业成本、税金及附加、销售费用、管理费用、财务费用、研发费用。根据会计“利润表”中“营业利润”项目的本年累计数填报。

利润总额 指企业在一定会计期间的经营成果，是生产经营过程中各种收入扣除各种耗费后的盈余，反映企业在报告期内实现的盈亏总额。利润总额为营业利润加上营业外收入，减去营业外支出后的金额，根据会计“利润表”中“利润总额”项目的本年累计数填报。

应付职工薪酬（本年贷方累计发生额） 指企业为获得职工提供的服务或解除劳动关系而给予的各种形式的报酬或补偿。包括职工工资、奖金、津贴和补贴，职工福利费，医疗保险费、养老保险费、失业保险费、工伤保险费和生育保险费等社会保险费，住房公积金，工会经费和职工教育经费，带薪缺勤，利润分享计划，非货币性福利，辞退福利和其他为获得职工提供的服务而给予的报酬或补偿。如果企业财务报告附注中包含“应付职工薪酬”项目，则根据其“应付职工薪酬列示”部分的合计项的本期增加额填报。或者，执行企业会计准则或《小企业会计准则》的企业，根据会计“应付职工薪酬”科目的本年贷方累计发生额填报；执行其他企业会计制度的企业，应将本年上述职工薪酬包含的项目归并填报。

“应付职工薪酬”应包含“劳务派遣人员薪酬”，但不得重复计入。如果企业财务报告或会计账簿中的“应付职工薪酬”不含“劳务派遣人员薪酬”，则应加“劳务派遣人员薪酬”后填报。如果“劳务派遣人员薪酬”已按类别拆分并分别计入“应付职工薪酬”会计科目下的工资、奖金、津贴和补贴、福利费等明细科目，则表明“应付职工薪酬”会计科目已包含“劳务派遣人员薪酬”，此时不应加“劳务派遣人员薪酬”。

平均用工人数 指报告期内（年度、月度）企业平均拥有的从事服务业活动的人员数。按“谁用工，谁统计”的原则实施统计，包括参加企业服务业活动的正式人员，劳务派遣人员和临时聘用人员。不包括在本企业领取工资、股息、红利、未参加服务业活动的人员。

Explanatory Notes on Main Statistical Indicators

Statistical standard of the services unit above the designated size of the National Bureau of Statistics: The legal entities of the area whoseannual revenues are10 million yuan and above, or at the end of the service sector whose employees are more than 50 people.Including: transportation, storage and postal services, information transmission, software and information technology services, leasing and business services, scientific research and technological services, water conservancy, environment and public facilities management industry, education, health and social work as well as property management and real estate services industries.The legal entitiesof the area whoseannual revenues are 5 million yuan and above, or at the end of the service sector whose employees are more than 50 people.Including: service, repair and other services, cultural, sports and entertainment.

Total assets: It refers to the resourcesformed by past transactions or events, that the enterprise owns or controls, is expected to bring economic benefits to the enterprise. Asset is classified into current assets and non-current assets by its liquidity (realization of assets or spent time). Current assets can be divided into currency, tradable financial assets, notes receivable, accounts receivable, prepayments, other receivables and inventory; and non-current assets can be classified as equity investments, fixed assets, intangible assets and other non-current assets. It depends on the "balance sheet" of "total assets" closing balance number of items.

Total liabilities: It refers tothe present obligations of the enterprise that formed by past transactions or events and are expected to lead to an outflow of economic benefits. Liability is divided into current and non-current liabilities according to the length of the repayment period. It depends onthe "balance sheets" in the "total" closing balance number of items.

Total owners' equity: It refers to the residual rights and interests enjoyed by the owner after deducting the liabilities of an enterprise. The owner of the company is also called the shareholder's right. It includes the paid in capital, capital reserves, surplus reserves, undistributed profit and so on. According to the accounting "balance sheet", "the owner's equity total", the final balance of the project is reported.

Business revenue: It refers to the total revenue recognized by the business and other business operations of the enterprise. Total operating income includes "main business income" and "other business income". It's reported according to the "business income" project of the "business income" in the accounting "profit statement".

Business cost: It refers to the total cost incurred by the business and other business of the enterprise. It includes a variety of costs of enterprises (units) in the reporting period to engage in sales of goods, services and other daily activities provided.It includes"the main business costs" and "other business costs". According to the "operating cost" of the "business cost" of the project in accordance with the accounting statement.

Selling expenses: It refers to the expenses of the enterprisein sales of goods and materials and providing services, including insurance, packing, exhibition fees and advertising fees, maintenance of commodity, expected to ensure product quality loss, transportation, loading and unloading charges and sales of the enterprise products and dedicated sales organizations (including sales network and after-sales service network) employee compensation, business expenses, depreciation charges and operating expenses. Construction enterprises selling expenses refers to expenses occurring in the process of production enterprises engaged in construction activities, including transportation fee shall be borne by the enterprise, handling, packing, insurance, maintenance, exhibition fees, poor travel costs, advertising costs and other expenses. Real estate enterprise sales cost refers to the business in the main business process of the sales costs, including transfer, sales, settlement and rental development products, etc.. According to the "sales expense" in accounting "profit statement", the amount of the item in this period of the project is reported. For business enterprises that didn't implement the 2006 accounting standard, according to the number of "operating expenses (or operating expenses)" of the project in accordance with the "profit statement".

Management expenses: It refers to the expenses for the organization and management of enterprise production and management of the enterprises, And the amortization of intangible assets developed by enterprises themselves included in the accounting subject of "management expenses". including costs in construction occurred during the start-up costs, the board of directors and administrative departments in enterprise management, or shall be made by the enterprise unified burden of company funds. According to the "management fee" in the accounting "profit table", the amount of this period of the project is reported. And the analysis and reporting of the current amount of the detailed account of "amortization of intangible assets" under the account of "management expenses".

Financial expenses: It refers to the costs of the enterprise to raise the production and business operation required capital and funding, including occurred during the production and operation of enterprises interest payments (a reduction in interest income), exchange loss (less exchange gains) and related fees. It is reported according to the amount of the "financial expense" in the project of "financial expense" in the accounting "profit statement".

Investment income: It refers to the enterprise confirming the investment income or investment losses, reflecting the foreign investment income of the enterprise in various ways. According to the "investment income" in the accounting "profit statement", the amount of this period of the project is reported. Such as investment losses to "-".

Operating profit: It refers to the profits made by the enterprises in the production and operation activities. For business enterprises that implemented the 2006 accounting standard, operating profit is revenues minus operating costs, business taxes and surcharges, sales, management costs, financial costs, asset impairment loss and plus fair value changes in income and investment income. Without executing the "accounting standards for business enterprises" enterprises, operating profit equals the main business income minus the cost of major business, main business tax and surcharges, and plus profit from other operations, then minus the cost of sales and management costs, financial costs. It is reported according to the number of "operating profit" items in the accounting "profit table".

Total profit: It refers to the business results of the enterprise in a certain accounting period, and it is the production and operation of various kinds of income after deducting the cost of earnings, reflecting the enterprise in the reporting period to achieve total profit and loss. the total profit is operating profit plus operating income, andminus operating expenses; Fill in according to the accumulated amount of "total profit" item in the accounting income statement this year.

Employee compensation: It refers tovarious forms of remuneration and other related expenses paid by the company for the services provided by the staff and workers. It includes wages, bonuses, allowances and subsidies, employee welfare benefit expenses, medical insurance, endowment insurance, unemployment insurance, work-related injury insurance premiums and maternity insurance fees social insurance, housing provident fund, the trade union funds and employee education funds, non-monetary benefits, for the solution in addition to give labor relations and workers compensation, and obtain a worker to provide other services related expenditure. For business enterprises that implemented the accounting standard, according to accounting subjects "to deal with workers' compensation" this year, the accumulated credits is filled; "Salary payable to employees" shall include "Salary of labor dispatch personnel", but shall not be included repeatedly. If the "salary payable to employees" in the financial report or accounting book of the enterprise does not include "salary of labor dispatch personnel", it should be filled in after adding "salary of labor dispatch personnel". If the "Salary of Labor Dispatchers" has been split by category and included in the detailed subjects such as wages, bonuses, allowances and subsidies, welfare funds, etc. under the accounting subject of "Salary Payable to Employees", it indicates that the accounting subject of "Salary Payable to Employees" already includes "Salary of Labor Dispatchers", and "Salary of Labor Dispatchers" should not be added at this time.

Average number of persons engaged in service activities: It refers to the number of persons engaged in the service industry in the reporting period (annual, monthly). The principles of statistics is implemented according to the principle that "who labor, who statistics," including the official personnel, labor sent contingent personnel and temporaryemployeeswho take part in the enterprise service activities. And it don't include employees who receive wages, dividends, bonusas well as not participate in the service activities of the enterprise.

19 金融业

FINANCIAL INTERMEDIATION

资料整理：孟　刚
Data management:Meng Gang
数据审核：边可为
Data audit:Bian Kewei

第十九部分　金融业

一、简要说明

本章资料包括金融、证券和保险业情况，由西安市统计局综合处根据人民银行西安分行营业管理部和市金融工作局提供资料整理。本部分银行、保险类为西安原口径数据，证券类含西咸新区。

二、主要指标

金融机构人民币（含外资）存款余额（亿元）	25730.51	比上年增长	11.5%
金融机构人民币（含外资）贷款余额（亿元）	25559.04	比上年增长	14.8%
保费收入（亿元）	550.43	比上年增长	5.3%

19　FINANCIAL INTERMEDIATION

Ⅰ.Brief Introduction

This chapter includes information of the financial, securities and insurance, compiled by Integration Division of the Xi'an Bureau of Statistics, according to data from Xi'an Branch Management Department of the People's Bank of China, Provincial Banking Bureau and Xi'an Financial Office. Data in this chapter is based on original range.

Ⅱ.Major Indicators

		Increase over Preceding Year
Deposits in Financial Institution(100 mil. yuan)	25730.51	11.5%
Loans in Financial Institutions(100 mil.yuan)	25559.04	14.8%
Premiums(100 mil. yuan)	550.43	5.3%

19-1 西安银行系统机构、人员数

Number of Institution and Employed Person in Finance System in Xi'an

机构名称	Name of Institution	2019		2020	
		机构数（个）Number of Institution (unit)	年末人数（人）Number of Staff and Workers (person)	机构数（个）Number of Institution (unit)	年末人数（人）Number of Staff and Workers (person)
合计	**Total**	**2106**	**38962**	**2111**	**39355**
1. 人民银行西安分行营业管理部	Management Department of the People's Bank of China Xi'an Branch	1	357	1	356
2. 国家开发银行	National Development Bank	1	211	1	221
3. 中国进出口银行	Export Import Bank of China	1	76	1	81
4. 中国工商银行	Industrial and Commercial Bank of China	181	4472	185	4292
5. 中国农业银行	Agricultural Bank of China	164	3093	165	3199
6. 中国银行	Bank of China	132	3335	131	3448
7. 中国建设银行	Construction Bank of China	203	4443	204	4508
8. 交通银行	Bank of Communication	59	1202	51	1206
9. 中国邮政储蓄银行	The Postal Savings Bank of China	268	982	267	955
10. 中国农业发展银行	Agricultural Development Bank of China	11	280	11	277
11. 中信银行	CITIC Bank	29	861	29	876
12. 中国光大银行	China Everbright Bank	42	943	41	935
13. 华夏银行	China Huaxia Bank	25	747	26	690
14. 广发银行	China Guangfa Bank	11	218	11	276
15. 平安银行	Pingan Bank	16	427	16	459
16. 招商银行	China Merchants Bank	55	1552	55	1587
17. 上海浦东发展银行	Pufa Bank	31	703	31	801
18. 兴业银行	Fujian Industrial Bank	56	819	62	820
19. 中国民生银行	China Minsheng Banking	22	1066	24	1107
20. 恒丰银行	Evergrowing Bank	17	467	17	475
21. 浙商银行	China Zheshang Bank	10	487	10	482
22. 渤海银行	China Bohai Bank	2	125	2	163
23. 北京银行	Bank of Beijing	25	799	26	808
24. 齐商银行	Qi Commercial Bank	8	214	7	194
25. 成都银行	Bank of Chengdu	6	173	6	186
26. 重庆银行	Bank of Chongqing	7	283	7	283
27. 宁夏银行	Bank of Ningxia	7	204	7	189
28. 昆仑银行	Bank of Kunlun	16	465	15	494
29. 西安银行	Bank of Xi'an	144	2581	145	2609
30. 长安银行	Bank of Changan	59	673	61	810
31. 农村商业银行	Rural Commercial Bank	406	5321	404	5246
其中：秦农银行	Qinnong Bank	298	4264	298	4245
32. 农村信用社	Rural Credit Cooperatives	67	810	67	780
33. 村镇银行	Village Bank	12	259	14	272
34. 香港汇丰银行	Huifeng Bank of Hong Kong	2	40	2	32
35. 香港东亚银行	Dongya Bank of Hong Kong	6	157	5	123
36. 新加坡星展银行	DBS Bank	1	15	1	13
37. 英国标准渣打银行	British Standard Chartered Bank	1	31	1	30
38. 韩亚银行	Hana Bank	1	40	1	43
39. 富邦华一银行	Fubon Bank	1	31	1	29

注：本表数据来源于人民银行西安分行营管部，本表为西安原口径数据（下同，除证券类）。

19-2 金融机构（含外资）本外币存贷款年末余额（2020年）

Deposits and Loans of Local Currency and Foreign Currency in Financial Institution (Including Foreign-Funded Institution)at Year-end (2020)

单位：万元 (10 000 yuan)

指 标	Item	2020	比年初增减额 Increase or Decrease Compared with The Beginning of The Year
一、各项存款	**All Deposits**	**260458660**	**27050306**
（一）境内存款	Domestic Deposits	260134731	27005213
1. 住户存款	Household Deposits	110170137	13637254
（1）活期存款	Demand Deposits	39900319	4405883
（2）定期及其他存款	Time and Other Deposits	70269818	9231370
2. 非金融企业存款	Non Financial Enterprises Deposits	99081148	9954134
（1）活期存款	Demand Deposits	47497754	1804509
（2）定期及其他存款	Time and Other Deposits	51583394	8149625
3. 机关团体存款	Institution Deposits	38844723	2480581
4. 财政性存款	Fiscal Deposits	1134093	-824777
5. 非银行业金融机构存款	Non Banking Financial Institution Deposits	10904631	1758021
（二）境外存款	Foreign Deposits	323929	45093
二、各项贷款	**All Loans**	**257928921**	**33562448**
（一）境内贷款	Domestic Loans	257721579	33545245
1. 住户贷款	Household loans	74862077	11726558
（1）短期贷款	Short-term Loans	8274369	816582
消费贷款	Consumer loans	5182743	266614
经营贷款	Business loans	3091626	549968
（2）中长期贷款	Medium-term and Long-term loans	66587709	10909976
消费贷款	Consumer loans	60745582	9434917
经营贷款	Business loans	5842126	1475059
2. 非金融企业及机关团体贷款	Non Financial Enterprises and Institution Loans	182857775	21818817
（1）短期贷款	Short-term Loans	34967397	3675113
（2）中长期贷款	Medium-term and Long-term loans	137801085	20660468
（3）票据融资	Bill Financing	9938327	-2512700
（4）融资租赁	Financial Leasing	207	-782
（5）各项垫款	Various Advance Funds	150759	-3283
3. 非银行业金融机构贷款	Non Banking Financial Institution Loans	1727	-130
（二）境外贷款	Foreign Loans	207342	17203

注：本表数据来源于人民银行西安分行营管部。

19-3　金融机构（不含外资）本外币存贷款年末余额（2020年）

Deposits and Loans Domestic Funded Financial Institution of Local Currency and Foreign Currency at Year-end（2020）

单位：万元　　　　(10 000 yuan)

指　标	Item	2020	比年初增减额 Increase or Decrease Compared with The Beginning of The Year
一、各项存款	**All Deposits**	**259012053**	**27505354**
（一）境内存款	Domestic Deposits	258717347	27461225
1. 住户存款	Household Deposits	110005772	13665621
（1）活期存款	Demand Deposits	39838993	4405492
（2）定期及其他存款	Time and Other Deposits	70166779	9260129
2. 非金融企业存款	Non Financial Enterprises Deposits	97828354	10381452
（1）活期存款	Demand Deposits	47313882	1849229
（2）定期及其他存款	Time and Other Deposits	50514472	8532222
3. 机关团体存款	Institution Deposits	38844498	2480908
4. 财政性存款	Fiscal Deposits	1134093	-824777
5. 非银行业金融机构存款	Non Banking Financial Institution Deposits	10904630	1758021
（二）境外存款	Foreign Deposits	294706	44129
二、各项贷款	**All Loans**	**256859772**	**33821015**
（一）境内贷款	Domestic Loans	256677719	33801778
1. 住户贷款	Household loans	74778612	11720216
（1）短期贷款	Short-term Loans	8274369	816992
消费贷款	Consumer loans	5182743	266614
经营贷款	Business loans	3091626	550378
（2）中长期贷款	Medium-term and Long-term loans	66504243	10903224
消费贷款	Consumer loans	60674437	9428675
经营贷款	Business loans	5829806	1474549
2. 非金融企业及机关团体贷款	Non Financial Enterprises and Institution Loans	181897381	22081692
（1）短期贷款	Short-term Loans	34692370	3845461
（2）中长期贷款	Medium-term and Long-term loans	137118764	20750640
（3）票据融资	Bill Financing	9935280	-2510344
（4）融资租赁	Financial Leasing	207	-782
（5）各项垫款	Various Advance Funds	150759	-3283
3. 非银行业金融机构贷款	Non Banking Financial Institution Loans	1727	-130
（二）境外贷款	Foreign Loans	182053	19237

注：本表数据来源于人民银行西安分行营管部。

19-4 主要年份金融机构（含外资）人民币存贷款年末余额

Deposits and Loans in Financial Institutions (Including Foreign-funded) in Representative Years

单位：亿元 (100million yuan)

年 份 Year	存款年末余额 Balance of Deposit at Year-end	非金融企业存款 Non Financial Enterprises Deposits	住户存款 Household Deposits	贷款年末余额 Balance of Loan at Year-end
1978	11.66		2.57	21.72
1980	17.02		4.22	23.08
1985	40.64		14.26	49.08
1990	146.17	31.10	77.09	152.77
1995	471.89	114.54	291.46	403.16
1996	619.98	199.85	394.02	477.97
1997	686.72	227.61	433.56	503.32
1998	799.54	245.44	499.68	597.34
1999	1014.27	347.49	586.40	786.20
2000	1335.63	540.19	675.83	972.51
2001	1629.72	674.49	800.86	1185.97
2002	2191.47	884.69	988.04	1598.42
2003	2665.87	1041.43	1210.56	1954.18
2004	3061.66	1159.98	1432.86	2052.33
2005	3599.70	1237.37	1716.76	2158.10
2006	4066.16	1374.91	1950.53	2344.77
2007	4582.71	1702.12	2002.38	2683.77
2008	5749.37	2213.67	2513.70	3275.12
2009	7522.08	3077.99	3084.20	4482.63
2010	8933.23	3556.78	3641.09	6482.28
2011	10430.27	5997.60	4155.65	7564.93
2012	12125.53	6927.84	4787.03	8635.22
2013	13763.19	7759.61	5357.05	10023.63
2014	15166.78	8604.03	5698.15	11668.14
2015	17796.38	7031.75	6571.18	13714.02
2016	19073.96	7788.07	7035.81	15282.65
2017	20047.62	8203.27	7497.30	16954.81
2018	20948.18	8125.23	8360.33	19729.82
2019	23066.85	8756.48	9553.29	22264.12
2020	25730.51	9713.23	10913.05	25559.04

注：本表数据来源于人民银行西安分行营管部，对部分历史年份数据进行了修订。

19-5 金融机构（含外资）人民币存贷款年末余额（2020年）

Year-end Balance of RMB Deposits and Loans in Financial Institutions (Including Foreign-funded) (2020)

单位：万元 (10 000 yuan)

指标	Item	2020	比年初增减额 Increase or Decrease Compared with The Beginning of The Year
一、各项存款	**All Deposits**	**257305137**	**26636605**
（一）境内存款	Domestic Deposits	257121085	26587674
1. 住户存款	Household Deposits	109130545	13597662
（1）活期存款	Demand Deposits	39309737	4336205
（2）定期及其他存款	Time and Other Deposits	69820808	9261457
2. 非金融企业存款	Non Financial Enterprises Deposits	97132315	9567552
（1）活期存款	Demand Deposits	46228201	1237407
（2）定期及其他存款	Time and Other Deposits	50904114	8330145
3. 机关团体存款	Institution Deposits	38825037	2490447
4. 财政性存款	Fiscal Deposits	1134093	-824777
5. 非银行业金融机构存款	Non Banking Financial Institution Deposits	10899097	1756790
（二）境外存款	Foreign Deposits	184051	48932
二、各项贷款	**All Loans**	**255590367**	**32949149**
（一）境内贷款	Domestic Loans	255584750	32949998
1. 住户贷款	Household loans	74860549	11728059
（1）短期贷款	Short-term Loans	8273001	818130
消费贷款	Consumer loans	5181375	268162
经营贷款	Business loans	3091626	549968
（2）中长期贷款	Medium-term and Long-term loans	66587548	10909928
消费贷款	Consumer loans	60745422	9434869
经营贷款	Business loans	5842126	1475059
2. 非金融企业及机关团体贷款	Non Financial Enterprises and Institution Loans	180722474	21222069
（1）短期贷款	Short-term Loans	33723916	3398453
（2）中长期贷款	Medium-term and Long-term loans	136909265	20339538
（3）票据融资	Bill Financing	9938327	-2512700
（4）融资租赁	Financial Leasing	207	-782
（5）各项垫款	Various Advance Funds	150759	-2439
3. 非银行业金融机构贷款	Non Banking Financial Institution Loans	1727	-130
（二）境外贷款	Foreign Loans	5617	-849

注：本表数据来源于人民银行西安分行营管部。

19-6 金融机构（不含外资）人民币存贷款年末余额（2020年）

Year-end Balance of RMB Deposits and Loans in Financial Institutions (Not Including Foreign-funded) (2020)

单位：万元 (10 000 yuan)

指　标	Item	2020	比年初增减额 Increase or Decrease Compared with The Beginning of The Year
一、各项存款	**All Deposits**	**256005261**	**27086416**
（一）境内存款	Domestic Deposits	255832547	27039907
1. 住户存款	Household Deposits	109009122	13620135
（1）活期存款	Demand Deposits	39270654	4337380
（2）定期及其他存款	Time and Other Deposits	69738467	9282755
2. 非金融企业存款	Non Financial Enterprises Deposits	95965425	9996986
（1）活期存款	Demand Deposits	46108444	1305810
（2）定期及其他存款	Time and Other Deposits	49856981	8691176
3. 机关团体存款	Institution Deposits	38824812	2490773
4. 财政性存款	Fiscal Deposits	1134093	-824777
5. 非银行业金融机构存款	Non Banking Financial Institution Deposits	10899096	1756790
（二）境外存款	Foreign Deposits	172714	46509
二、各项贷款	**All Loans**	**254567033**	**33214731**
（一）境内贷款	Domestic Loans	254561695	33215410
1. 住户贷款	Household loans	74777084	11721717
（1）短期贷款	Short-term Loans	8273001	818540
消费贷款	Consumer loans	5181375	268162
经营贷款	Business loans	3091626	550378
（2）中长期贷款	Medium-term and Long-term loans	66504082	10903176
消费贷款	Consumer loans	60674277	9428627
经营贷款	Business loans	5829806	1474549
2. 非金融企业及机关团体贷款	Non Financial Enterprises and Institution Loans	179782884	21493824
（1）短期贷款	Short-term Loans	33469695	3577679
（2）中长期贷款	Medium-term and Long-term loans	136226943	20429710
（3）票据融资	Bill Financing	9935280	-2510344
（4）融资租赁	Financial Leasing	207	-782
（5）各项垫款	Various Advance Funds	150759	-2439
3. 非银行业金融机构贷款	Non Banking Financial Institution Loans	1727	-130
（二）境外贷款	Foreign Loans	5338	-679

注：本表数据来源于人民银行西安分行营管部。

19-7 保险业务情况

Indicators of Insurance Business

单位：万元　　　　(10 000 yuan)

指　标	Item	2016	2017	2018	2019	2020
保费收入(万元)	**Premiums(10 000 yuan)**	**3458459**	**4211039**	**4785554**	**5228513**	**5504259**
一、财产险(万元)	**Property Insurance(10 000 yuan)**	**933181**	**1037060**	**1125618**	**1062003**	**1162414**
（一）财产保险	Property Insurance	833296	916524	959618	868183	928967
1. 机动车辆及第三者责任	Motor Vehicle and Outside Person Liability	738965	821186	862137	759314	795563
2. 企业财产险	Enterprise Property Insurance	64568	62226	65716	73996	85294
3. 货物运输险	Freight Transport Insurance	4814	5314	6777	7230	6749
4. 家庭财产险	Family Property Insurance	981	1385	1772	1436	3259
5. 建工及安工保险及其责任险	Construction and Installation Projects Insurance and Related Liability Insurance	18368	20001	17174	17067	27392
6. 其他	Others	5600	6412	6042	9140	10710
（二）责任保险	Liability Insurance	26922	32136	38508	54267	86279
（三）信用保险	Export Credit Insurance	17563	14733	10114	9128	10741
（四）保证保险	Guarantee Insurance	42665	60814	100393	112277	115323
（五）农业保险	Agriculture Insurance	12735	12853	16985	18148	21104
二、人身险(万元)	**Personnel Insurance(10 000 yuan)**	**2525278**	**3173979**	**3659936**	**4166510**	**4341845**
（一）人寿保险	Life Insurance	2158260	2625509	3023129	3313934	3402702
1. 普通寿险	General Life Insurance	1261138	1554807	1355990	1653013	1902890
2. 分红保险	Dividend Insurance	882110	1055099	1651416	1645508	1485230
3. 投资连接保险	Insurance Connection Insurance	236	217	212	280	326
4. 万能保险	Universal Insurance	14776	15386	15512	15133	14256
（二）意外伤害险	Unforeseen Injury Insurance	71888	84603	112382	145991	131819
（三）健康保险	Health Insurance	295130	463867	524426	706585	807325
赔款支出和各项给付(万元)	**Indemnity and Other Expenditure(10 000 yuan)**	**1159143**	**1187057**	**1308241**	**1414228**	**1577456**
一、财产险(万元)	**Property Insurance(10 000 yuan)**	**422765**	**489353**	**553641**	**617430**	**700304**
（一）财产保险	Property Insurance	393905	452892	497773	537006	574214
1. 机动车辆及第三者责任	Motor Vehicle and Outside Person Liability	359288	393011	459840	487263	526217
2. 企业财产险	Enterprise Property Insurance	22038	30811	20020	23175	21502
3. 家庭财产保险	Family Property Insurance	324	757	4565	3255	788
4. 货物运输保险	Freight Transport Insurance	1341	2427	1376	864	3828
5. 建工及安工保险及其责任险	Construction and Installation Projects Insurance and Related Liability Insurance	9741	12471	9663	8136	13154
6. 其他	Others	1173	13414	2309	14314	8725
（二）责任保险	Liability Insurance	11030	12703	14948	20710	35618
（三）信用保险	Export Credit Insurance	3287	3346	5273	3384	5602
（四）保证保险	Guarantee Insurance	10690	11597	23608	48247	70146
（五）农业保险	Agriculture Insurance	3853	8816	12039	8082	14723
二、人身险(万元)	**Personnel Insurance(10 000 yuan)**	**736378**	**697704**	**754600**	**796798**	**877152**
（一）人寿保险	Life Insurance	637444	557798	581062	565089	624946
1. 普通寿险	General Life Insurance	82635	136279	138591	136772	133902
2. 分红保险	Dividend Insurance	551206	418013	438997	424665	488409
3. 投资连接保险	Insurance Connection Insurance	485	162	35	4	72
4. 万能保险	Universal Insurance	3118	3344	3438	3647	2564
（二）意外伤害险	Unforeseen Injury Insurance	15577	19939	23621	30778	32710
（三）健康保险	Health Insurance	83357	119967	149917	200930	219496
退保金(万元)	**Withdrawal(10 000 yuan)**	**482983**	**682534**	**762277**	**617446**	**452376**
#人寿保险	Life Insurance	459733	659965	751597	588932	437378
1. 普通寿险	General Life Insurance	276544	524211	582955	368570	271586
2. 分红保险	Dividend Insurance	183191	135723	168632	220354	165781
3. 投资连接保险	Insurance Connection Insurance					
4. 万能保险	Universal Insurance	-2	31	11	7	11

注：本表数据来源于市金融工作局。

19-8 西安地区证券期货系统机构、人员数（2020年）

Number of Institution and Employed Person in Securities and Futures System in Xi'an (2020)

机构名称	Name of Institution	2019		2020	
		机构数（个）Number of Institution (unit)	年末人数（人）Number of Staff and Workers (person)	机构数（个）Number of Institution (unit)	年末人数（人）Number of Staff and Workers (person)
一、证券经营机构总数	**Number of Securities Operating Institutions**	**400**	**8688**	**399**	**8384**
1、证券公司机构总数	Number of Securities Companies	206	5093	238	5503
西部证券股份有限公司	Western Securities Company Ltd.	115	2375	111	2410
开源证券股份有限公司	KaiYuan Securities Company Ltd.	49	1932	83	2236
中邮证券有限责任公司	China Post Securities	42	786	44	857
2、外地驻我市证券机构总数	Number of Non-Local Securities Institutions In the City	194	3595	161	2881
二、期货公司机构总数	**Number of Futures Companies**	**33**	**551**	**30**	**513**
迈科期货股份有限公司	Maike Futures Company Ltd.	12	210	11	184
长安期货有限公司	ChangAn Company Ltd.	10	154	10	169
西部期货有限公司	Western Futures Brokerage Co., Ltd.	11	187	9	160

注：1.本表数据来源于市金融工作局。
2.证券公司包括三家公司及其在西安和外地的营业部。
3.中邮证券有限责任公司原为西安华弘证券经纪有限责任公司。

19-9 证券期货市场基本情况（2020年）

Basic Facts on Securities and Futures Markets（2020）

指　标	Item	2020
一、上市公司情况	**Listed Securities Companies**	
拥有境内上市股份公司（个）	Number of Domestic Listed Joint-Stock Companies(unit)	42
上市股份公司总股本（亿股）	Total Capital of Listed Share-holding Companies (100 millon shares)	648.05
#流通股(亿股)	Negotiable Shares(100 million shares)	544.51
总市值（亿元）	Total Market Capitalization(100 million yuan)	10794.33
本年度证券市场筹措资金（亿元）	Securities Market Financing this year(100 millon yuan)	216.60
二、证券经营机构情况	**Securities Trading Organizations**	
拥有证券公司（个）	Number of Securities Companies(unit)	3
证券经营机构（个）	Number of Securities Trading Institutions (unit)	399
投资者开户数（万户）	Number of Investors Who have Opened an Account(10 000 accounts)	442.74
证券交易总额（亿元）	Total Turnover(100 million yuan)	58526.64
三、期货市场情况	**Futures Market**	
拥有期货经纪公司（个）	Number of Futures Business Management Companies(unit)	3
期货营业部（个）	Futures Business Department(unit)	30
期货代理交易额（亿元）	Total Transaction Value in Futures Commissioning (100 million yuan)	62516.78
每个经纪公司平均拥有注册资金（亿元）	Average Registered Capital of Each Business Management Company(100 million yuan)	4.40

注：本表数据来源于市金融工作局，期货分支机构、代理交易额数据为西安本市和外地公司在西安市口径数据。

主 要 统 计 指 标 解 释

存款 指企业、机关、团体或居民根据资金必须收回的原则，把货币资金存入银行或其他信贷机构保管并取得一定利息的一种信用活动形式。根据存款对象或性质的不同可划分为企业存款、财政存款、机关团体存款、住户存款、信托及委托类存款、其他存款等科目。它是银行信贷资金的主要来源。

贷款 指银行或其他信贷机构根据资金必须归还的原则，按一定利率，为企业、个人等提供资金的一种信用活动形式。我国银行贷款分为短期贷款、中长期贷款、融资租赁、票据融资等。

保险金额 指保险人承担赔偿或者给付保险金责任的最高限额。

保费 指投保人为取得保险人在约定范围内所承担赔偿责任而支付给保险人的费用。

赔款 指保险人根据保险合同的规定，向被保险人支付的赔偿保险责任损失的金额。

给付 包括死伤医疗给付和满期给付。死伤医疗给付是指保险人根据人寿保险及长期健康保险合同的规定，因被保险人在保险期内发生保险责任范围内的保险事故支付给被保险人（或受益人）的金额。满期给付是指被保险人生存期满，保险人按人寿保险合同规定支付给被保险人的满期保险金额。

Explanatory Notes on Main Statistical Indicators

Deposit is a form of credit by which enterprises, institutions, organizations or households can put money into banks and other credit institutions for safekeeping and interest earning under the principle of free withdrawal. According to different depositors, deposits are divided into enterprise deposits, fiscal deposits, deposits of government agencies and organizations, savings deposits of rural and household deposits, agricultural savings deposits, entrusted deposits and other deposits. Deposits are major sources of the credit funds of banks.

Loan is a form of credit by which banks and other credit institutions provide funds at certain interest rate to enterprises and individuals in the light of the principle of unconditional repayment. Loans from Chinese banks include short-term loan, medium and long term loans, finance lease and other bill finance.

Amount Insured refers to the maximum that the insurant will get for the claim of the case insured.

Premium is the fee paid by the insurant to the insurer to obtain the obligation of compensation from the insurance within the agreed terms.

Settled Claim is the compensation paid by the insurer to the insurant in accordance with the insurance contract.

Payment includes payment for death, injury or medical treatment and payment at maturity. Payment for death, injury or medical treatment refers to the money paid to the insurant (or the beneficiary) in accordance with the life or health insurance contract when the insurant encounters accidents within the insured period covered in the contract. Payment at maturity refers to the payment to the insurant in accordance with the life insurance contract at the end of the insured period.

20 教育和科技

EDUCATION, SCIENCE AND TECHNOLOGY

资料整理：陈超毅　刘志杰　陈花娥
Data management: Chen Chaoyi Liu Zhijie Chen Huae
数据审核：刘栋婷
Data audit: Liu Dongting

第二十部分 教育和科技

一、简要说明

本章资料包括教育事业、科技事业基本情况，由西安市统计局服务业与社会科技统计处根据统计一套表资料和西安市教育局等有关部门提供资料整理。本章资料数据口径见表下备注。科技部分因数据来源较晚，故从2018年起错年使用。

二、主要指标

普通高等学校数（所）	63	与上年	持平
普通高等学校（本专科）在校学生（万人）	78.39	比上年增加	4.38
高等学校研究生在校人数（万人）	14.74	比上年增加	1.61

20 EDUCATION,SCIENCE AND TECHNOLOGY

Ⅰ.Brief Introduction

Data in this chapter consists of primarily data of educational undertakings, science and technology activities of Xi'an city, compiled by Tertiary Industry and Social & Science and Technology Division of the Xi'an Bureau of Statistics according to data from units of "One Sheet" and Xi'an Bureau of Education concerned. Field and range of data are Listed in the explanatory notes below the chart. Due to the late source of science and technology data. the information content provides the data of 2018.

Ⅱ Major Indicators

		Increase over Preceding Year
Number of Regular Institutions of Higher Education(unit)	63	essentially on a par with last year's
Student Enrollment of Regular Institutions of Higher Education (Universities and colleges) (10 000 persons)	78.39	4.38
Postgraduates Enrollment of Regular Institutions of Higher Education (10 000 persons)	14.74	1.61

20-1 主要年份各类普通教育基本情况

Basic Statistics on Regular Eduction in Representative Years

指 标	Item	2010	2013	2014	2015	2016	2017	2018	2019	2020
学校数（所）	**Number of Schools (units)**									
普通高等学校	Regular Institutions of Higher Educatior	50	63	63	63	63	63	63	63	63
普通中等专业学校	Regular Specialized Secondary Schools	28	22	22	20	20	16	15	15	15
普通中学	Regular Secondary School	436	418	421	422	422	448	456	469	495
小学	Primary Schools	1531	1291	1257	1234	1190	1125	1130	1145	1172
幼儿园	Kindergarten	1004	1295	1343	1417	1475	1605	1780	1839	1966
毕业生人数（万人）	**Graduates (10 000 persons)**									
普通高等学校	Regular Institutions of Higher Educatior	18.3	20.17	21.27	23.23	24.06	23.07	23.21	22.02	22.67
普通中等专业学校	Regular Specialized Secondary Schools	2.5	1.93	1.76	1.32	1.25	1.06	0.84	0.72	0.81
普通中学	Regular Secondary School	17.0	15.24	14.54	13.92	13.96	13.89	13.50	13.89	13.89
小学	Primary Schools	9.6	8.51	8.29	7.85	8.46	9.06	9.32	10.17	10.75
幼儿园	Kindergarten	5.4	8.42	8.90	10.01	9.81	10.79	11.41	11.85	12.25
招生数（万人）	**New Enrollment (10 000 persons)**									
普通高等学校	Regular Institutions of Higher Educatior	21.7	23.88	23.58	23.41	23.08	23.70	23.67	26.88	29.26
普通中等专业学校	Regular Specialized Secondary Schools	2.1	1.35	1.25	0.95	0.88	0.96	0.83	1.12	1.16
普通中学	Regular Secondary School	16.2	14.47	13.97	13.41	13.72	14.08	14.37	15.29	16.20
小学	Primary Schools	8.6	9.56	10.13	10.51	11.65	13.13	15.16	15.80	16.92
幼儿园	Kindergarten	8.4	11.00	9.55	11.96	13.65	13.98	13.03	12.86	15.46
在校学生数（万人）	**Total Enrollment (10 000 persons)**									
普通高等学校	Regular Institutions of Higher Educatior	73.3	83.83	85.42	84.83	83.10	83.02	82.44	87.14	93.13
普通中等专业学校	Regular Specialized Secondary Schools	6.8	4.66	4.07	3.47	3.11	2.74	2.48	2.79	3.02
普通中学	Regular Secondary School	48.9	43.73	42.57	41.37	40.70	41.74	42.46	43.56	45.68
小学	Primary Schools	51.6	51.95	53.79	56.62	59.79	66.68	73.09	78.98	85.20
幼儿园	Kindergarten	18.4	28.56	28.95	30.90	31.80	34.81	35.40	36.05	39.64
教职工数（人）	**Staff and Teachers (persons)**									
普通高等学校	Regular Institutions of Higher Educatior	72247	74993	74954	74857	73686	74218	75609	73688	75213
普通中等专业学校	Regular Specialized Secondary Schools	3249	2599	2315	1991	1917	1556	1529	1386	1474
普通中学	Regular Secondary School	39207	41003	40576	40689	41352	44546	45390	47037	49388
小学	Primary Schools	34118	31863	32162	32585	34646	38494	41122	44511	48838
幼儿园	Kindergarten	18710	31989	33062	36004	39753	44895	49604	52442	59605
专任教师（人）	**Number of Full-time Teachers (persons)**									
普通高等学校	Regular Institutions of Higher Educatior	42098	46436	46766	47768	47158	47917	49018	50236	51996
普通中等专业学校	Regular Specialized Secondary Schools	1845	1474	1346	1228	1210	998	958	918	970
普通中学	Regular Secondary School	31506	31419	32615	33014	33962	36565	37539	39143	41133
小学	Primary Schools	29944	29421	28395	28748	30941	34163	36878	39836	43423
幼儿园	Kindergarten	10638	16238	17337	19096	21395	23789	25823	26496	29948

注：1.本表数据来源于市教育局。
2.本表中普通高等学校毕业生、招生、在校生数含普通高等学校研究生及普通高等学校本、专科学生。
3.本表中小学的学校数是指独立小学个数，其在校生、教职工等指标均为普通初等教育；幼儿园的校数是指独立的幼儿园个数，其在校生、教职工等指标均为学前教育。（下表同）
4.本表中普通中学学生数据为普通中等教育口径，小学学生数为普通初等教育口径，幼儿园学生数为学前教育口径。
5.本表2017年及以后年份数据含西咸新区。

20-2 各级各类学校、教职工情况（2020年）

Situation of All Kinds of Schools and Staff Members at All Levels （2020）

指　标	Item	学校数（所）Number of Schools (units)	教职工数（人）Number of Staff and Teachers (persons)	专任教师数（人）Full-time Teachers (persons)
一、高等教育	**Higher education**	**75**	**77482**	**53228**
（一）研究生培养机构	Postgraduate training institutions	(43)		
1、普通高校	Institutions of Higher Schools	(22)		
2、科研机构	Scientific Research Institution	(21)		
（二）普通高等学校	Regular Institutions of Higher Schools	63	75213	51996
1、本科院校	Universities and Colleges of Undergraduate Course	44	66187	45497
其中：独立学院	Non-university Tertiary	9	4666	3148
2、专科院校	Higher Vocational Colleges	19	9026	6499
其中：高等职业学校	Higher Vocational College	17	7595	5672
（三）成人高等学校	Adult Higher Schools	12	2269	1232
二、中等职业教育	**Secondary Occupation Education**	**150**	**13739**	**10399**
（一）普通中等专业学校	Regular Specialized Secondary Schools	15	1474	970
（二）成人中等专业学校	Adult Secondary Specialized Schools	2	145	91
（三）职业高中学校	Vocational Hight Schools	57	4790	3421
其中：市属	Municipal schools	57	4790	3421
（四）技工学校	Technical Schools	76	7330	5917
其中：市属	Municipal schools	34	2661	2199
三、基础教育	**Elementary Education**	**3645**	**158312**	**114870**
（一）普通中等教育	Regular Institutions Education	495	49388	41133
1、高中	Senior High Schools	171	25332	21148
完全中学	Complete Secondary Schools	107	15437	13038
高级中学	Senior Secondary Schools	54	7634	6382
十二年一贯制学校	Twelve-year Consistency Schools	10	2261	1728
2、初中	Junior Middle Schools	324	24056	19985
初级中学	Junior Middle Schools	252	16081	13371
九年一贯制学校	Nine-year Consistency Schools	72	7975	6614
完全中学	Complete Secondary school	(107)		
十二年一贯制学校	Twelve-year Consistency schools	(10)		
附设普通初中班的学校	Senior Secondary Schools with Regular Junior Secondary Classes	(1)		
（二）普通初等教育	Regular Primary Education	1172	48838	43423
独立小学	Independent Primary Schools	1172	47517	42287
教学点	Teaching Points	(232)	1321	1136
九年一贯制学校	Nine-year Consistency schools	(72)		
十二年一贯制学校	Twelve-year Consistency schools	(10)		
附设小学班的学校	Schools with Primary Classes	(3)		
（三）特殊教育	Special Education Schools	11	438	333
特殊教育学校	Special Education Schools	11	438	333
附设特教班的学校	Schools with Special Edution Classes	(1)		
（四）工读学校	Reformatory Schools	1	43	33
（五）学前教育	Preschool Education	1966	59605	29948
幼儿园	Kindergarten	1966	59605	29948
附设幼儿班的学校	Schools with Nursery Classes	(50)		
另有：职业技术培训机构	Technique Training Institution	1889	18948	13192

注：1.本表数据来源于市教育局。
2.本表为西安市行政区划内各级各类学校全口径数据（不含军事院校、党校）。
3.技工学校数据由西安市人力资源和社会保障局提供。
4.按照事业统计主体校原则，完全中学、十二年一贯制学校的学校数计入普通高中，九年一贯制学校的校数计入普通初中。
5.教职工和专任教师数按照办学类型划分。
6.（）内数据不计入总计，下表同。
7.本表数据包含西咸新区。

20-3 各级各类教育学生情况（2020年）

Basic Facts on Education Student by School Type（2020）

单位：人 (person)

指 标	Item	毕业生数 Number of Graduates	招生数 New Enrollment	在校学生数 Total Enrollment	女生 Female Students
一、高等教育	**Higher education**	**493060**	**497002**	**1433557**	**661303**
（一）研究生	Postgraduates	33355	51726	148025	71409
1、高等学校	Institutions of Higher Schools	33157	51493	147358	71245
2、科研机构	Scientific Research Institution	198	233	667	164
（二）普通高等教育	Regular Institutions of Higher Schools	193579	241142	783893	367530
1、本科	Universities Course Schools	124323	146955	536815	266795
2、专科	Junior Colleges	69256	94187	247078	100735
（三）成人高等教育	Higher Vocational Colleges	64281	91808	191366	90482
其中：成人高等学校	Contains:Adult Higher Education	15244	21745	43985	18212
（四）网络本专科生	Network Undergraduate and clooege students	201845	112326	310273	131882
1、本科	Universities Course Schools	67730	71409	169601	75312
2、专科	Junior Colleges	134115	40917	140672	56570
二、中等职业教育	**Secondary Occupation Education**	**56973**	**74541**	**207474**	**38409**
1、普通中等专业学校	Regular Specialized Secondary Schools	8132	11625	30219	12946
2、成人中等专业学校	Adult Secondary Specialized Schools	102	101	326	157
3、职业高中学校	Vocational high Schools	16028	22359	58444	25306
其中：市属	Municipal schools	16028	22359	58444	25306
4、技工学校	Technical Schools	32711	40456	118485	
其中：市属	Municipal schools	8141	15972	39131	
三、基础教育	**Elementary Education**	**369335**	**486421**	**1708613**	**814525**
（一）普通中等教育	Regular Institutions Education	138885	161987	456788	216635
1、高中	Senior High Schools	51141	53275	154730	75661
完全中学	Complete Secondary Schools	25776	26460	77675	38130
高级中学	Senior Secondary Schools	23394	24819	71717	34962
十二年一贯制学校	Twelve-year Consistency schools	1971	1996	5338	2569
2、初中	Junior Middle Schools	87744	108712	302058	140974
初级中学	Junior Middle Schools	44956	51820	148036	69107
九年一贯制学校	Nine-year Consistency Schools	7475	12724	33769	15525
十二年一贯制学校	Twelve-year Consistency Schools	3781	3516	10448	4817
完全中学	Complete Secondary school	31532	40652	109805	51525
（二）普通初等教育	Regular Primary Education	107455	169248	852031	405061
独立小学	Pricmary Schools	98005	151757	767671	365367
九年一贯制学校	Nine-year Consistency schools	7417	15568	74106	35042
十二年一贯制学校	Twelve-year Consistency Schools	2033	1923	10254	4652
（三）特殊教育	Special Education Schools	508	589	3333	1278
1、特殊教育学校	Special Education Schools	188	165	1095	416
2、小学附设特教班	Primary Schools with Special Education Classes		1	3	
3、小学随班就读	Elementary Inclusive	185	178	1284	497
4、初中随班就读	Junior Mainstreaming	131	173	505	202
5、小学送教上门	Primary School Delivery	3	40	355	124
6、初中送教上门	Junior High School Delivery	1	32	91	39
（四）工读学校	Reformatory Schools	4	10	16	2
（五）学前教育	Preschool Education	122483	154587	396445	191549
1、独立幼儿园	Independent Kindergartens	122023	154293	395852	191248
2、附设幼儿园	Attached Kindergartens	460	294	593	301
另有：职业技术培训机构	Technique Training Institution	611811		520608	265455

注：1.本表数据来源于市教育局。
2.本表数据包含西咸新区。

20-4 主要年份普通高等学校和科研机构研究生情况

Basic Statistics of Postgraduates on Regular Institutions of Higher Education and Scientific Research Institution in Representative Years

单位：人 (person)

年 份 Year	毕业生数 Number of Graduates	高等学校 Higher Schools	招生数 New Enrollment	高等学校 Higher Schools	在校学生数 Total Enrollment	高等学校 Higher Schools
1978			232	232	232	232
1980			127	127	651	651
1985	754	754	2819	2819	4799	4799
1990	2051	2051	1662	1662	5275	5275
1995	1769	1769	2712	2712	7974	7974
2000	3236	3236	6924	6924	16620	16620
2001	3881	3770	9274	8966	22564	21855
2002	4103	3952	11282	10882	28446	27471
2003	5971	5765	14322	13882	36936	35790
2004	8384	8127	17310	16871	45402	44169
2005	10416	10127	18583	18106	52699	51310
2006	12914	12552	19581	19105	58433	56951
2007	15506	15124	20570	20167	64137	62801
2008	17234	16788	21892	21443	67296	65834
2009	19025	18574	24879	24400	72366	70908
2010	19526	19129	25971	25477	76993	75483
2011	20965	20605	26686	26256	81696	80332
2012	22963	22578	28065	27618	84712	83306
2013	24778	24385	28786	28333	87002	85570
2014	24092	23881	28636	28436	88518	87826
2015	25322	25104	29487	29293	91448	90790
2016	24779	24562	30263	30079	94720	94102
2017	25808	25616	36296	36084	104092	103458
2018	27276	27088	38582	38399	112250	111626
2019	28619	28448	42653	42439	131982	131325
2020	33355	33157	51726	51493	148025	147358

注：1.本表数据来源于市教育局。
2.本表2017年及以后年份数据包含西咸新区。

20-5 主要年份普通高等学校基本情况（本专科）

Basic Statistics on Regular Institution of Higher Education in Representative Years

单位：所、万人 (units,10 000 persons)

年份 Year	学校数 Number of Schools	毕业生数 Number of Graduates	招生数 New Enrollment	在校学生数 Total Enrollment	教职工数 Number of Staff and Teachers	专任教师数 Full-time Teachers
1978	21	0.60	1.31	2.88	2.24	0.87
1980	24	0.21	1.08	4.17	2.55	0.97
1985	28	1.17	2.28	6.49	3.40	1.28
1990	31	2.11	2.00	7.50	4.15	1.56
1995	32	2.87	3.13	10.07	4.21	1.59
2000	25	2.71	6.79	17.75	3.81	1.57
2001	32	3.31	8.31	23.24	4.30	1.75
2002	35	3.82	10.75	30.15	4.67	2.06
2003	37	5.89	12.21	36.42	4.92	2.21
2004	41	7.66	13.17	40.29	5.45	2.69
2005	44	10.08	14.68	47.79	5.73	2.95
2006	47	11.75	15.15	51.40	6.14	3.29
2007	48	14.33	16.96	56.03	6.56	3.67
2008	48	15.82	19.31	60.10	6.90	3.89
2009	49	15.04	18.84	63.22	7.08	4.06
2010	50	16.33	19.16	65.74	7.22	4.21
2011	61	17.68	20.52	68.52	7.27	4.27
2012	62	18.64	22.46	72.40	7.40	4.45
2013	63	17.73	21.05	75.27	7.50	4.64
2014	63	18.88	20.74	76.64	7.50	4.68
2015	63	20.72	20.49	75.75	7.49	4.78
2016	63	21.60	20.07	73.68	7.37	4.72
2017	63	20.50	20.10	72.68	7.42	4.79
2018	63	20.50	19.83	71.28	7.56	4.90
2019	63	19.18	22.63	74.01	7.37	5.02
2020	63	19.38	24.11	78.39	7.52	5.20

注：1.本表数据来源于市教育局。
2.本表2017年及以后年份数据包含西咸新区。

20-6 主要年份普通中等专业学校基本情况

Basic Statistics on Regular Specialized Secondary Schools in Representative Years

年份 Year	学校数（所）Number of Schools (units)	毕业生数（万人）Number of Graduates (10 000 persons)	招生数（万人）New Enrollment (10 000 persons)	在校学生数（万人）Total Enrollment (10 000 persons)	教职工数（人）Number of Staff and Teachers(person)	专任教师数（人）Full-time Teachers(person)
1978	19	0.19	0.45	0.82	3937	1110
1980	31	0.18	0.42	1.50	3895	1474
1985	37	0.43	0.76	1.70	6071	2363
1990	44	0.56	0.68	2.09	7136	2891
1995	46	0.97	1.37	3.74	5903	2533
2000	47	1.63	1.90	6.02	6964	3172
2001	47	1.70	1.58	5.63	5252	2467
2002	46	1.60	1.69	5.57	5170	2508
2003	34	1.62	1.80	5.28	4562	2302
2004	35	1.40	2.09	5.71	4676	2388
2005	32	1.44	2.26	6.16	3924	2130
2006	31	1.84	2.61	7.30	3621	2014
2007	30	2.03	2.91	7.97	3548	2011
2008	29	2.58	2.55	8.06	3278	1814
2009	28	2.70	2.15	7.44	2965	1720
2010	28	2.45	2.08	6.75	3249	1845
2011	24	2.34	1.96	6.11	2868	1723
2012	24	2.15	1.67	5.43	2733	1595
2013	22	1.93	1.35	4.66	2599	1474
2014	22	1.76	1.25	4.07	2315	1346
2015	20	1.32	0.95	3.47	1991	1228
2016	20	1.25	0.88	3.11	1917	1210
2017	16	1.06	0.96	2.74	1556	998
2018	15	0.84	0.83	2.48	1529	958
2019	15	0.72	1.12	2.79	1386	918
2020	15	0.81	1.16	3.02	1474	970

注：1.本表数据来源于市教育局。
2.本表2017年及以后年份数据包含西咸新区。

20–7 主要年份普通中等教育基本情况

Basic Situation of General Secondary Education in Major Years

年 份 Year	学校数（所） Number of Schools (units)	毕业生数（万人） Number of Graduates (10 000 persons)	招生数（万人） New Enrollment (10 000 persons)	在校学生数（万人） Total Enrollment (10 000 persons)	教职工数（人） Number of Staff and Teachers(person)	专任教师数（人） Full-time Teachers(person)
1978	962	10.85		44.16	27380	20660
1980	1002	12.33	14.03	44.08	29867	22530
1985	563	10.72	13.05	38.24	30063	22050
1990	518	9.11	10.49	30.03	30739	22386
1995	485	8.13	12.40	32.32	30423	21984
2000	466	12.01	17.88	48.31	34385	26230
2001	470	13.85	18.98	52.50	35442	27190
2002	467	15.76	19.68	55.36	36706	28335
2003	467	16.76	18.78	56.44	38252	29887
2004	461	18.01	18.85	56.54	39121	30600
2005	460	18.82	18.83	55.74	39456	31094
2006	457	18.04	18.61	56.11	39341	31203
2007	453	18.37	17.96	54.68	39171	31373
2008	442	17.99	17.16	52.83	39088	31425
2009	439	17.80	16.57	50.63	39002	31415
2010	436	17.01	16.15	48.89	39207	31506
2011	423	16.44	15.42	47.20	41135	31675
2012	419	15.64	14.98	45.33	41197	31526
2013	418	15.24	14.47	43.73	41003	31419
2014	421	14.54	13.97	42.57	40576	32615
2015	422	13.92	13.41	41.37	40689	33014
2016	422	13.96	13.72	40.70	41352	33962
2017	448	13.89	14.08	41.74	44546	36565
2018	456	13.50	14.37	42.46	45390	37539
2019	469	13.89	15.29	43.56	47037	39143
2020	495	13.89	16.20	45.68	49388	41133

注：1.本表数据来源于市教育局。

2.本表2017年及以后年份数据包含西咸新区。

20-8 各区县普通中等教育基本情况（2020年）

Basic Situation of Ordinary Secondary Education in Various Districts and Counties（2020）

单位：所、人 (unit, person)

区 县	Region	学校数 Number of Schools	毕业生数 Number of Graduates	高中 Senior	招生数 New Enrollment	高中 Senior	在校学生数 Total Enrollment	女生 Female Students	高中 Senior	教职工数 Number of Staff and Teachers	专任教师数 Full-time Teachers
合 计	**Total**	**495**	**138885**	**51141**	**161987**	**53275**	**456788**	**216635**	**154730**	**49388**	**36632**
新城区	Xincheng	24	10692	3790	11684	4075	32986	15777	11744	2634	2150
碑林区	Beilin	32	16305	6487	17198	6558	50083	22830	19299	4163	3393
莲湖区	Lianhu	20	10136	3502	10801	3210	31497	14989	10081	2434	2032
灞桥区	Baqiao	17	5635	1712	7486	2041	20518	9737	6023	2071	1644
未央区	Weiyang	21	6677	2007	8155	2088	24213	11544	6160	2600	1721
雁塔区	Yanta	34	11355	4324	12130	4197	34782	16403	12254	3820	2549
阎良区	Yanliang	12	3168	1142	3512	1100	9975	5051	3274	1036	931
临潼区	Lintong	33	8789	3552	8926	3181	26265	13000	9701	3444	2732
长安区	Chang'an	39	10078	3971	12008	4237	33660	16034	11897	3417	2868
高陵区	Gaoling	14	3203	1201	4166	1430	11658	5937	4105	1000	862
鄠邑区	Huyi	26	7041	3190	6213	2360	19345	9086	7762	2205	1835
蓝田县	Lantian	45	8521	3676	7908	3330	24154	11861	10176	3395	2547
周至县	Zhouzhi	35	8880	3696	7933	3735	24950	11221	10679	3022	2114
西咸新区	Xixian	52	9174	2451	12634	2954	33863	15566	7963	4948	3383
高新区	Gaoxin	50	8555	3128	12676	4190	32950	15589	11328	3870	2619
经开区	JingKai	13	4594	1769	7249	2459	18826	8980	6818	2441	1338
曲江新区	Qujiang	5	796	214	3075	500	6907	3393	1141	791	452
航空基地	Aviation Industry Base										
航天基地	Aerospace Base	3	1363	232	1939	397	4950	2355	930	454	392
浐灞生态区	Chanba Eco-District	12	2410	738	4119	733	9839	4706	2180	990	719
国际港务区	International Trade& Logistic Park	8	1513	359	2175	500	5367	2576	1215	653	351

注：1.本表数据来源于市教育局。
2.专任教师按办学层次统计，不含一贯制学校小学部专任教师数。

20-9 主要年份职业高中基本情况

Basic Statistics on Vocational Secondary Schools in Representative Years

单位：所、人 (unit, person)

年 份 Year	学校数 Number of Schools	毕业生数 Number of Graduates	招生数 New Enrollment	在校学生数 Total Enrollment	教职工数 Number of Staff and Teachers	专任教师数 Full-time Teachers
1985	40	1661	8346	17621	1375	868
1990	58	5936	8095	20151	2674	1574
1995	71	8976	12490	32673	2394	1877
2000	95	9949	13903	32188	3311	1997
2001	85	10300	15591	34336	3517	2113
2002	78	8659	17231	39428	3461	2192
2003	87	10755	17310	44033	4036	2458
2004	83	12177	17865	46358	4101	2515
2005	91	15092	20603	51766	4750	2892
2006	96	14887	21158	53828	5193	3126
2007	86	14881	24434	56012	4899	3064
2008	84	15813	30201	62963	4878	3008
2009	84	14691	31042	72388	5129	3179
2010	84	18100	30042	78244	5222	3178
2011	78	22493	27641	75108	4849	3173
2012	77	24048	24995	67969	4775	3148
2013	74	21243	23043	61968	4699	3085
2014	81	19156	19508	60024	4860	3186
2015	80	18565	15060	49092	3239	2214
2016	64	17773	14305	43576	3126	2275
2017	62	14325	17080	45145	3318	2405
2018	60	14064	17295	46380	3499	2584
2019	60	12559	19797	52553	3801	2685
2020	57	16028	22359	58444	4790	3421

注：1.本表数据来源于市教育局。
2.本表2017年及以后年份数据包含西咸新区。

20-10 各区县职业高中基本情况（2020年）

Basic Statistics on Vocational Secondary Schools by Region（2020）

单位：所、人 (unit, person)

区 县	Region	学校数 Number of Schools	毕业生数 Number of Graduates	招生数 New Enrollment	在校学生数 Total Enrollment	女生 Female Students	教职工数 Number of Staff and Teachers	专任教师数 Full-time Teachers
合 计	**Total**	**57**	**16028**	**22359**	**58444**	**25306**	**4790**	**3421**
新城区	Xincheng	4	812	2842	4041	2129	453	294
碑林区	Beilin	4	387	423	851	409	115	91
莲湖区	Lianhu	5	1273	1323	3577	1807	282	222
灞桥区	Baqiao	4	3459	3358	10508	3579	416	269
未央区	Weiyang	2	522	487	1372	767	142	95
雁塔区	Yanta	6	797	1032	3328	1617	382	294
阎良区	Yanliang	1	461	562	1461	655	165	126
临潼区	Lintong	4	875	1160	2988	1342	256	201
长安区	Chang'an	6	1904	2958	7673	3722	815	599
高陵区	Gaoling	1	323	534	1222	451	110	103
鄠邑区	Huyi	2	1065	1354	3884	1833	291	220
蓝田县	Lantian	3	775	1511	3026	1269	193	154
周至县	Zhouzhi	3	408	531	1381	578	83	61
西咸新区	Xixian	3	97	237	760	310	29	20
高新区	Gaoxin	3	2137	1949	5652	1810	440	209
经开区	JingKai	1	172	409	880	388	50	43
曲江新区	Qujiang							
航空基地	Aviation Industry Base	1	134	240	1154	668	108	66
航天基地	Aerospace Base	1		780	2870	1104	260	211
浐灞生态区	Chanba Eco-District	2	418	622	1709	793	179	130
国际港务区	International Trade& Logistic Park	1	9	47	107	75	21	13

注：本表数据来源于市教育局。

20-11 主要年份普通初等教育基本情况

Basic Situation of General Primary Education in Major Years

年 份 Year	学校数（所） Number of Schools (units)	毕业生数 （万人） Number of Graduates (10 000 persons)	招生数 （万人） New Enrollment (10 000 persons)	在校学生数 （万人） Total Enrollment (10 000 persons)	教职工数（人） Number of Staff and Teachers(person)	专任教师数 （人） Full-time Teachers(person)
1978	2667	13.07	14.10	74.03	29744	26428
1980	2337	11.91	12.57	73.36	31770	28360
1985	2337	11.21	9.57	62.16	31075	26430
1990	2343	8.67	10.85	61.87	33788	29090
1995	2360	9.93	14.09	79.36	35568	30270
2000	2323	13.83	11.51	77.81	35336	30215
2001	2277	14.20	11.07	74.51	34257	29281
2002	2137	13.89	10.13	70.78	34143	29428
2003	2084	12.97	9.28	66.78	34080	29531
2004	2016	12.37	9.12	63.75	33794	29367
2005	1980	11.92	8.47	60.47	33907	29674
2006	1929	11.53	9.16	59.33	34460	30018
2007	1872	11.38	8.67	56.83	34901	30533
2008	1781	10.58	8.33	54.66	34653	30382
2009	1666	9.96	7.84	52.52	34389	30334
2010	1531	9.61	8.64	51.56	34118	29944
2011	1424	8.92	8.77	51.39	32457	29900
2012	1322	8.88	8.88	50.85	32208	29651
2013	1291	8.51	9.56	51.95	31863	29421
2014	1257	8.29	10.13	53.79	32162	28395
2015	1234	7.85	10.51	56.62	32585	28748
2016	1190	8.46	11.65	59.79	34646	30941
2017	1125	9.06	13.13	66.68	38494	34163
2018	1130	9.32	15.16	73.09	41122	36878
2019	1145	10.17	15.80	78.98	44511	39836
2020	1172	10.75	16.92	85.20	48838	43423

注：1.本表数据来源于市教育局。
2.本表2017年及以后年份数据包含西咸新区。

20-12 各区县普通初等教育基本情况（2020年）

Basic Situation of General Primary Education in Various Districts and Counties（2020）

单位：所、人 (unit, person)

区 县	Region	学校数 Number of Schools	毕业生数 Number of Graduates	招生数 New Enrollment	在校学生数 Total Enrollment	女生 Female Students	教职工数 Number of Staff and Teachers	专任教师数 Full-time Teachers
合 计	**Total**	**1172**	**107455**	**169248**	**852031**	**405061**	**48838**	**43423**
新城区	Xincheng	35	6256	7076	38297	18013	2172	1980
碑林区	Beilin	35	6695	8519	43455	20463	2514	2170
莲湖区	Lianhu	48	8849	11187	58211	27754	2833	2573
灞桥区	Baqiao	43	4591	7201	37010	17550	1926	1784
未央区	Weiyang	46	8690	11840	64971	30840	3081	2813
雁塔区	Yanta	42	9752	13594	71216	33970	3589	3223
阎良区	Yanliang	22	2491	3128	16981	8249	997	943
临潼区	Lintong	105	6287	7273	42800	20622	3129	2596
长安区	Chang'an	105	7631	13111	63881	30275	4030	3563
高陵区	Gaoling	65	3310	4875	24832	12007	1693	1444
鄠邑区	Huyi	76	3744	4599	25105	11908	1856	1626
蓝田县	Lantian	83	4645	4404	27524	13220	2487	2241
周至县	Zhouzhi	110	4265	6087	35537	16548	2350	2068
西咸新区	Xixian	130	9753	18205	88176	42007	4849	4366
高新区	Gaoxin	106	7791	14517	68762	32628	3722	3269
经开区	JingKai	24	3466	9277	42052	19887	1681	1486
曲江新区	Qujiang	19	2099	6998	28138	13316	1718	1463
航空基地	Aviation Industry Base	1		367	1526	706	105	98
航天基地	Aerospace Base	11	1069	2890	11522	5501	734	671
浐灞生态区	Chanba Eco-District	42	4589	11716	50474	23998	2768	2498
国际港务区	International Trade& Logistic Park	24	1482	2384	11561	5599	604	548

注：本表数据来源于市教育局。

20–13 主要年份学前教育基本情况

Basic Conditions of Pre-school Education in Representative Years

年　份 Year	幼儿园（所） Number of Kindergartens (unit)	班数（个） Number of Class (unit)	在园幼儿数（万人） Student Enrollment (10 000 persons)	教职工数（人） Number of Staff and Teachers(person)	专任教师数（人） Full-time Teachers(person)
1978	191		4.44	3568	1315
1980	186		9.61	5525	2657
1985	310	3135	9.71	6887	2770
1990	256	3816	14.04	6123	2058
1995	257	4464	16.40	6173	2659
2000	367	4142	12.85	6346	2995
2001	366	4306	11.97	6224	3069
2002	378	4186	11.53	6541	3397
2003	610	4470	12.39	8959	4853
2004	660	4507	12.16	9870	5577
2005	737	4712	12.75	10528	5959
2006	863	5037	13.00	12335	7106
2007	830	5081	14.00	13468	7951
2008	905	5506	15.00	14932	8704
2009	896	5710	16.00	15928	9240
2010	1004	6420	18.00	18710	10638
2011	1122	8010	24.00	23680	12577
2012	1239	8729	27.10	27735	14293
2013	1295	9408	28.56	31989	16238
2014	1343	9782	28.95	33062	17337
2015	1417	10457	30.90	36004	19096
2016	1475	11090	31.80	39753	21395
2017	1605	12234	34.81	44895	23789
2018	1780	12970	35.39	49604	25823
2019	1839	13375	36.05	52442	26496
2020	1966	14612	39.64	59605	29948

注：1.本表数据来源于市教育局。
2.本表2017年及以后年份数据包含西咸新区。

20-14 主要年份特殊教育基本情况

Basic Statistics on Special Education in Representative Years

单位：所、人 (unit, person)

年 份 Year	学校数 Number of Schools	毕业生数 Number of Graduates	招生数 New Enrollment	在校学生数 Total Enrollment	教职工数 Number of Staff and Teachers	专任教师数 Full-time Teachers
1980	1	48	64	315	66	43
1985	2	14	36	318	94	59
1990	5	35	111	451	142	96
1995	5	27	147	1363	204	141
2000	5	269	145	1880	230	156
2001	5	237	209	1915	238	162
2002	5	216	148	1661	232	157
2003	5	156	161	1380	237	166
2004	5	137	142	1290	236	167
2005	5	184	182	1445	240	169
2006	6	171	143	1425	254	178
2007	6	169	114	1342	259	190
2008	6	83	96	1286	259	190
2009	7	311	202	1523	335	234
2010	8	214	402	1529	340	235
2011	8	280	222	1393	343	231
2012	8	197	220	1392	352	248
2013	8	194	212	1174	338	243
2014	8	172	222	1225	345	238
2015	8	168	338	1373	352	240
2016	8	214	327	1604	359	246
2017	9	237	774	2498	386	272
2018	9	352	461	2615	379	271
2019	10	435	541	2967	404	300
2020	11	508	589	3333	438	333

注：1.本表数据来源于市教育局。
2.包括盲、聋、哑、智力障碍者儿童教育。
3.本表2017年及以后年份数据包含西咸新区。

20-15 基础教育监测评价情况（2020年）

Monitoring and Evaluation of Basic Education（2020）

指　标	Item	2020
入学率（%）	Enrollment Rate(%)	
小学	Primary Schools	99.99
初中	Junior Middle Schools	99.87
巩固率（%）	The Consolidation Rate (%)	
小学（六年）	Primary Schools (six years)	101.26
初中（三年）	Junior Middle Schools (three years)	98.48
毕业率（%）	The Graduate Rate(%)	
小学	Primary school	99.69
初中	Junior middle school	99.13
专任教师学历合格率（%）	Qualified Rate Of Full-time Teacher Education (%)	
小学	Primary Schools	100.00
初中	Junior Middle Schools	100.00
高中	Senior Middle Schools	99.25
幼儿园	Kindergartens	99.54
小学教师专科以上学历达到率（%）	Rate of Primary School Teachers with College degree or Above (%)	99.66
初中教师本科以上学历达到率（%）	Rate of Junior Middle SchoolTeachers with Bachelor degree or Above (%)	95.71
高中教师研究生以上学历达到率（%）	Rate of Senior Middle School Teachers with Postgraduate degree or Above (%)	21.88

注：1.本表数据来源于市教育局。
2.本表数据计算入学率和小学巩固率不包含西咸新区的咸阳部分。

20-16　主要年份平均每万人口在校学生数及构成

单位：人、%

年　份 Year	平均每万人 高等学校在校学生 Per 10000 people on average Hight Education Students in the school	平均每万人 高中阶段在校学生 Per 10000 people on average Number of Senior high School Students in the school	平均每万人 初中在校学生 Per 10000 people on average Number of Junior Secondary School Students in the school	平均每万人 小学在校学生 Per 10000 people on average Number of Primary School Students in the school
1978	58			1486
1980	84			1434
1985	117			1124
1990	123			1016
1995	168			1224
2000	282			1131
2001	366			1072
2002	470			1007
2003	560			932
2004	618	463	517	879
2005	715	492	489	815
2006	760	534	484	788
2007	817	543	466	744
2008	863	571	444	708
2009	901	619	413	672
2010	939	635	361	660
2011	973	514	301	539
2012	986	471	278	518
2013	988	386	265	522
2014	983	352	256	532
2015	929	309	236	537
2016	865	288	224	513
2017	732	271	201	516
2018	741	260	209	566
2019	1044	277	215	600
2020	1106	279	233	657

注：1.本表数据来源于市教育局。
2.2011年起，表中三个比重指标数据参与计算的学生总数含普通教育、成人教育及网络教育数据。
3.2019年平均每万人高等学校在校学生包含全部高等教育在校生。
4.本表2017年及以后年份数据含西咸新区。
5.2020年，依据西安市常住人口数的修订，对2011年到2019年平均每万人在校学生数进行了修订。

The Average Number of Students in the School every 10000 Individuals in Representative Years

(persons,%)

平均每万人学前教育在校学生 Average Number of Pre-school Students per 10,000 people	普通高等学校在校学生占学生总数比重 Senior high School Students in the school in accounting for the proportion of the total number of students	中等学校在校学生占学生总数比重 Junior Secondary School students in the school in accounting for the proportion of the total number of students	小学在校学生占学生总数比重 Primary School students in the school in accounting for the proportion of the total number of students
	2.3	34.9	58.6
	3.1	33.2	55.3
	5.3	31.3	50.9
	6.7	25.1	51.7
	7.3	28.0	53.6
	11.5	34.8	46.0
	14.6	35.9	42.6
	18.2	36.4	39.0
	20.1	33.8	33.5
	22.2	35.2	31.6
	26.4	36.2	30.1
	27.7	37.1	28.7
	29.3	36.3	26.7
	30.8	36.1	25.2
	31.8	36.5	23.7
217	33.0	35.0	23.2
252	29.8	30.1	19.9
276	31.0	28.2	19.5
287	32.6	25.3	20.2
285	33.2	23.8	20.9
293	32.8	22.2	21.9
288	31.4	21.4	22.6
270	29.1	21.3	23.4
274	27.5	20.2	24.4
273	27.4	20.4	24.9
306	27.8	19.8	25.4

20-17 民办教育情况（2020年）

单位：所、人

指 标	Item	学校数 Number of Schools	毕业生数 Number of Graduates
一、民办高等教育(民办高校)	**Private higher Education (Institutions)**	**29**	**71369**
二、民办中等教育	**Private Secondary Education**	**103**	**41405**
民办普通高中	Ordinary High School	31	6733
民办普通中等专业学校	Civilian run ordinary secondary vocational school	1	534
民办职业高中	Vocational high school	35	10288
民办普通初中	Ordinary Junior middle school	36	22236
民办的附设中职班	Private primary school class	(10)	1614
三、民办普通小学	**Private Primary School**	**93**	**16933**
四、民办幼儿园	**Private kindergarten**	**944**	**85955**
另有：民办培训机构	Private Training Institutions	996	371878

注：1.本表数据来源于市教育局。
2.毕业生数中幼儿园为离园人数。
3.民办高等教育在校生为民办高校普通、成人本专科学生数。
4.聘请校外教师中，小学、中学、幼儿园为代课教师和兼任教师之和。
5.按照教育报表制度，民办的附设中职班教职工计入基础教育主体校教职工总数，专任教师为中职层次，故单独统计。
6.本表数据含西咸新区。

Private Education Situation（2020）

(unit, person)

招生数 New Enrollment	在校学生数 Total Enrollment	教职工数 Number of Teachers and Staff	专任教师 Full-time Teachers	聘请校外教师 Teachers hired from Outside Schools
93475	**274700**	**19872**	**13809**	
55387	**151184**	**14360**	**10971**	**94**
8338	23182	5614	4517	
1577	3075	241	175	
14705	39134	2841	1782	94
28340	80012	5664	4497	
2427	5781			
28491	**153764**	**7261**	**6135**	
61296	**195236**	**30475**	**14105**	**4**
	272992	13266	9394	2592

20-18　全市研究与试验发展（R&D）活动情况（2019年）

Scientific and Technological Activities in the Whole City （2019）

指　标	Item	2019
一、单位数（个）	**Number of Units(unit)**	**3936**
#有R&D活动单位数	The Number of R&D active units	892
二、R&D人员（人）	**Personnel Eagaged in R&D(person)**	**129558**
三、R&D人员折合全时当量（人年）	**R&D Stuff Equivalent to Full Time equivalent (person year)**	**92462**
四、R&D经费内部支出（万元）	**R&D Internal Expenditure(10 000 yuan)**	**4817559.4**

注：本表数据来源于省统计局反馈。

20-19　规模以上重点行业企业研究与试验发展（R&D）情况（2019年）

R&D Project Status of Key Enterprises above Designated Size（2019）

指　标	Item	2019
一、企业数（个）	**Number of Enterprises(unit)**	**3705**
工业	Industry	1634
非工业	Non-industry	2071
#有R&D活动的单位数	The number of R&D active units	716
工业	Industry	530
非工业	Non-industry	186
二、R&D人员（人）	**Personnel Eagaged in R&D (person)**	**53277**
工业	Industry	38570
非工业	Non-industry	14707
三、R&D人员折合全时当量（人年）	**R&D Stuff Equivalent to Full Time equivalent (person year)**	**38873**
工业	Industry	27917
非工业	Non-industry	10956
四、R&D经费内部支出（万元）	**R&D Internal Expenditure (10000 yuan)**	**2129970**
工业	Industry	1541612
非工业	Non-industry	588358

20-20 规模以上工业企业研究与试验发展（R&D）基本情况（2019年）

R&D Project Status of Industrial Enterprises above Designated Size（2019）

指 标	Item	企业数（个）Number of enterprises (unit)	有R&D活动的企业数 The Number of R&D enterprises
总计	**Total**	**1634**	**530**
按企业规模分	**Grouped by Size of Enterprises**		
大型企业	Large-size	69	45
中型企业	Medium-size	183	101
小型企业	Small-size	1307	375
微型企业	Microenterprise	75	9
按登记注册类型分	**Grouped by Registered Status**		
内资企业	Domestic Investment Enterprises	1520	490
国有企业	State-owned Enterprises	20	13
集体企业	Collective-owned Enterprise	4	
股份合作企业	Stock Cooperative Enterprises	4	1
联营企业	Affiliated Enterprise		
有限责任公司	Limited Liability Corporations	637	242
股份有限公司	Share-holding Corporation Ltd	123	79
私营企业	Private Enterprise	731	155
其他	Other Domestic Funded Enterprises	1	
港、澳、台商投资企业	Enterprises with Funds from Hong Kong, Macao And Taiwan	22	4
外商投资企业	Foreign Funded Enterprises	92	36
按国民经济行业分	**Grouped by Sector**		
采矿业	Mining	9	4
煤炭开采和洗选业	Mining and Washing of Coal		
石油和天然气开采业	Extraction of Petroleum and Natural Gas	1	1

20-20 续表1 continued 1

指 标	Item	企业数（个）Number of enterprises (unit)	有R&D活动的企业数 The Number of R&D enterprises
黑色金属矿采选业	Mining of Ferrous Metal Ores		
有色金属矿采选业	Mining of Non-ferrous Metal Ores		
非金属矿采选业	Mining and Processing of Nonmetal Ores		
开采专业及辅助性活动	Mining Professional and Auxiliary Activity	8	3
其他采矿业	Mining of other Ores		
制造业	Manufacturing Industry	1564	522
农副食品加工业	Processing of Food from Agriculture Products	46	4
食品制造业	Manufacture of Food	53	8
酒、饮料和精制茶制造业	Manufacture of Beverages	22	2
烟草制品业	Manufacture of Tobacco	2	1
纺织业	Manufacture of Textile	15	2
纺织服装、服饰业	Manufacture of Textile Wearing, Apparel	4	
皮革、毛皮、羽毛及其制品和制鞋业	Manufacture of Leather, Furs, Feather, Related Products and Footware	2	1
木材加工和木、竹、藤、棕、草制品业	Processing of Timber,Manufacture of Wood, Bamboo, Rattan, Palm and Straw Products	3	
家具制造业	Manufacture of Furniture	18	
造纸及纸制品业	Manufacture of Paper And Paper Products	24	
印刷和记录媒介复制业	Printing and Reproduction of Recording Media	32	7
文教、工美、体育和娱乐用品制造业	Education, Art, Sports And Entertainment Products Manufacturing	9	
石油、煤炭及其他燃料加工业	Processing of Petroleum,Coal and Other Fuels	6	2
化学原料和化学制品制造业	Manufacture of Raw Chemical Materials and Chemical Products	78	35
医药制造业	Manufacture of Medicines	66	33

20-20 续表2 continued 2

指 标	Item	企业数（个）Number of enterprises (unit)	有R&D活动的企业数 The Number of R&D enterprises
化学纤维制造业	Manufacture of Chemical Fiber	4	1
橡胶和塑料制品业	Manufacture of Rubber and Manufacture of Plastic	49	11
非金属矿物制品业	Manufacture of Non-metallic Mineral Products	185	20
黑色金属冶炼和压延加工业	Smelting and Pressing of Ferrous Metals	11	2
有色金属冶炼和压延加工业	Smelting and Pressing of Non-ferrous Metals	45	22
金属制品业	Manufacture of Metal Products	113	20
通用设备制造业	Manufacture of General Purpose Machinery	98	43
专用设备制造业	Manufacture of Special Equipment	146	63
汽车制造业	Manufacture of Motor Vehicle	67	21
铁路、船舶、航空航天和其他运输设备制造业	Railways, Ships, Aerospace And Other Transportation Equipment Manufacturing Industry	95	49
电气机械和器材制造业	Manufacture of Electric Equipment and Machinery	158	61
计算机、通信和其他电子设备制造业	Manufacture of Communication Equipment, Computers and Other Electronic Equipment	122	67
仪器仪表制造业	Manufacture of Measuring Instruments and Machinery	71	42
其他制造业	Other Manufacturing	7	3
废弃资源综合利用业	Comprehensive Utilization Of Waste Resources	4	
金属制品、机械和设备修理业	Metal Products, Machinery and Equipment Repair Industry	9	2
电力、热力、燃气及水生产供应业	Production and Distribution of Electricity, Heat,Gas and Water	61	4
电力、热力生产和供应业	Production and Supply of Electric Power and Heat Power	28	3
燃气生产和供应业	Production and Supply of Gas	18	1
水的生产和供应业	Production and Supply of Water	15	

20-21 规模以上工业企业研究与试验发展（R&D）人员和经费支出情况（2019年）

指标	Item	R&D人员（人）R&D personnel（person）	研究人员 Researchers
总计	**Total**	**38570**	**35811**
按企业规模分	**Grouped by Size of Enterprises**		
大型企业	Large-size	23177	21513
中型企业	Medium-size	7955	7431
小型企业	Small-size	7315	6745
微型企业	microenterprise	123	122
按登记注册类型分	**Grouped by Registion Status**		
内资企业	Domestic Investment Enterprises	35106	32493
国有企业	State-owned Enterprises	3362	3000
集体企业	Collective-owned Enterprises		
股份合作企业	Stock cooperative enterprises	7	7
联营企业	Affiliated companies		
有限责任公司	Limited Liability Corporations	23636	22056
股份有限公司	Share-holding Corperation Ltd.	4900	4458
私营企业	Private Enterprises	3201	2972
其他	Other Domestic Funded Enterprises		
港、澳、台商投资企业	Enterprises with Funds from Hong Kong,Macao and Taiwan	530	466
外商投资企业	Foreign Funded Enterprises	2934	2852
按国民经济行业分	**Grouped by Sector**		
采矿业	Mining	1300	1104
煤炭开采和洗选业	Mining and Washing of Coal		
石油和天然气开采业	Extraction of Petroleum and Natural Gas	1073	903
黑色金属矿采选业	Mining of Ferrous Metal Ores		
有色金属矿采选业	Mining of Non-ferrous Metal Ores		
非金属矿采选业	Mining and Processing of Nonmetal Ores		
开采专业及辅助性活动	Mining Professional and Auxiliary Activity	227	201
其他采矿业	Mining of other Ores		
制造业	Mannfacturing Industry	36874	34334
农副食品加工业	Processing of Food from Agricultural Products	31	28
食品制造业	Manufacture of Foods	98	96
酒、饮料和精制茶制造业	Manufacture of Beverages	35	29
烟草制品业	Manufacture of Tobacco	26	25
纺织业	Manufacture of Textile	65	57
纺织服装、服饰业	Manufacture of Textile Wearing Apparel		
皮革、毛皮、羽毛及其制品和制鞋业	Manufacture of Leather, Fur, Feather and Related Products and Footwear	97	66

R&D Personnel and Expenditure Conditions of Industrial Enterprises above Designated Size（2019）

R&D经费内部支出（万元） R&D Intramural Expenditure (10 000 yuan)	政府资金 Government funds	企业资金 Enterprise Funds	境外资金 Foreign Funds
1541612	**285918**	**1255534**	**3**
1023382	273891	749331	3
315874	8030	307844	
200982	3907	197075	
1374	90	1284	
1375597	285441	1089996	3
91706	27689	63896	
60		60	
1015369	249613	765717	3
145259	6400	138859	
123203	1739	121465	
8537	231	8306	
157478	246	157232	
42894	8143	34751	
34628	3759	30870	
8266	4385	3882	
1489761	277701	1211901	3
588	20	568	
1243	101	1141	
392		392	
1797		1797	
3661	200	3461	
1514		1514	

20-21 续表1

指标	Item	R&D人员（人）R&D personnel（person）	研究人员 Researchers
木材加工和木、竹、藤、棕、草制品业	Processing of Timber,Manufacture of Wood, Bamboo,Rattan,aplam and Straw Products		
家具制造业	Manufacture of Furniture		
造纸及纸制品业	Manufacture of Paper and Paper Products		
印刷和记录媒介复制业	Printing,Reproduction of Recording Media	203	162
文教、工美、体育和娱乐用品制造业	Manufacture of Articles For Culture, Education and Sport Activities		
石油、煤炭及其他燃料加工业	Processing of Petroleum, Coal and Other Fuels	10	8
化学原料及化学制品制造业	Manufacture of Raw Chemical Materials and Chemical Products	1465	1334
医药制造业	Manufacture of Medicines	1452	1353
化学纤维制造业	Manufacture of Chemical Fibers	57	53
橡胶和塑料制品业	Manufacture of Rubber and Manufacture of Plastics	400	330
非金属矿物制品业	Manufacture of Non-metallic Mineral Products	525	495
黑色金属冶炼和压延加工业	Smelting and Pressing of Ferrous Metals	15	14
有色金属冶炼和压延加工业	Smelting and Pressing of Non-ferrous Metals	1095	1030
金属制品业	Manufacture of Metal Products	927	843
通用设备制造业	Manufacture of General Purpose Machinery	827	761
专用设备制造业	Manufacture of Special Equipment	2993	2788
汽车制造业	Manufacture of Motor Vehicle	3866	3675
铁路、船舶、航空航天和其他运输设备制造业	Railways,Shipbuilding,Aerospace and Other Transportation Equipment Manufacturing Industry	9349	8638
电气机械和器材制造业	Manufacture of Electric Equipment and Machinery	3822	3565
计算机、通讯和其他电子设备制造业	Manufacture of Communication Equipment, Computers and other Electronic Equipment	6418	6157
仪器仪表制造业	Manufacture of Measuring Instruments and Machinery	3027	2764
其他制造业	Other Manufacturing	50	48
废弃资源综合利用业	Comprehensive Utilization Of Waste Resources		
金属制品、机械和设备修理业	Metal Products,Machinery and Equipment Repair Industry	21	15
电力、热力、燃气及水生产和供应业	Production and Distribution of Electricity,Heat,Gas and Water	396	373
电力、热力的生产和供应业	Production and Supply of Electric Power and Heat Power	304	288
燃气生产和供应业	Gas mining and supplying industry	92	85
水的生产和供应业	Production and Supply of Water		

continued 1

R&D经费内部支出（万元） R&D Intramural Expenditure (10 000 yuan)	政府资金 Government funds	企业资金 Enterprise Funds	境外资金 Foreign Funds
5386		5386	
250		250	
48543	5919	42625	
40639	305	40334	
673		673	
19706		19706	
20157	98	20059	
525		525	
34763	3075	31688	
35790	10780	24889	
17599	643	16956	
81855	6872	74983	
264550	2111	262439	
393390	227559	165794	1
160576	865	159711	1
292936	3745	289192	
61832	15410	46422	
827		827	
570		570	
8957	74	8882	
4539		4539	
4417	74	4343	

20-22 规模以上工业企业新产品开发、生产及销售情况（2019年）

指标	Item	新产品开发项目数（项） Number of new product development projects（item）
总计	**Total**	**4609**
按企业规模分	**Grouped by Size of Enterprises**	
大型企业	Large-size	1289
中型企业	Medium-size	1018
小型企业	Small-size	2263
微型企业	microenterprise	39
按登记注册类型分	**Grouped by Registion Status**	
内资企业	Domestic Investment Enterprises	4346
国有企业	State-owned Enterprises	281
集体企业	Collective-owned Enterprises	
股份合作企业	Stock cooperative enterprises	2
联营企业	Affiliated companies	
有限责任公司	Limited Liability Corporations	2389
股份有限公司	Share-holding Corperation Ltd.	688
私营企业	Private Enterprises	986
其他	Other Domestic Funded Enterprises	
港、澳、台商投资企业	Enterprises with Funds from Hong Kong,Macao and Taiwan	48
外商投资企业	Foreign Funded Enterprises	215
按国民经济行业分	**Grouped by Sector**	
采矿业	Mining	103
煤炭开采和洗选业	Mining and Washing of Coal	
石油和天然气开采业	Extraction of Petroleum and Natural Gas	
黑色金属矿采选业	Mining of Ferrous Metal Ores	
有色金属矿采选业	Mining of Non-ferrous Metal Ores	
非金属矿采选业	Mining and Processing of Nonmetal Ores	
开采专业及辅助性活动	Mining Professional and Auxiliary Activity	103
其他采矿业	Mining of other Ores	
制造业	Mannfacturing Industry	4478
农副食品加工业	Processing of Food from Agricultural Products	8
食品制造业	Manufacture of Foods	33
酒、饮料和精制茶制造业	Manufacture of Beverages	18
烟草制品业	Manufacture of Tobacco	6
纺织业	Manufacture of Textile	16
纺织服装、服饰业	Manufacture of Textile Wearing Apparel	
皮革、毛皮、羽毛及其制品和制鞋业	Manufacture of Leather, Fur, Feather and Related Products and Footwear	20

注：国家统计局未反馈新产品产值数据。

New Product Development, Production and Sales of Above-scale Industrial Enterprises（2019）

新产品开发经费支出（万元） New Product Development Expenditure （10 000 yuan）	新产品产值 （万元） New product output value （10 000 yuan）	新产品销售收入 （万元） Sales of new products （10 000 yuan）
1813016		**15506565**
1174303		11649194
350976		2434190
285798		1416934
1939		6246
1640384		14014438
112002		513849
159		1722
1220265		10922932
153973		1081925
153985		1494011
9959		1135741
162673		356386
24981		10905
		189
24981		10716
1779978		15493056
2933		891
5070		54078
2207		31613
699		206572
4406		7470
1514		7410

20-22 续表1

指标	Item	新产品开发项目数（项）Number of new product development projects（item）
木材加工和木、竹、藤、棕、草制品业	Processing of Timber,Manufacture of Wood, Bamboo,Rattan,aplam and Straw Products	
家具制造业	Manufacture of Furniture	
造纸及纸制品业	Manufacture of Paper and Paper Products	1
印刷和记录媒介复制业	Printing,Reproduction of Recording Media	38
文教、工美、体育和娱乐用品制造业	Manufacture of Articles For Culture, Education and Sport Activities	
石油、煤炭及其他燃料加工业	Processing of Petroleum,Coal and Other Fuels	2
化学原料及化学制品制造业	Manufacture of Raw Chemical Materials and Chemical Products	354
医药制造业	Manufacture of Medicines	193
化学纤维制造业	Manufacture of Chemical Fibers	14
橡胶和塑料制品业	Manufacture of Rubber and Manufacture of Plastics	66
非金属矿物制品业	Manufacture of Non-metallic Mineral Products	143
黑色金属冶炼和压延加工业	Smelting and Pressing of Ferrous Metals	3
有色金属冶炼和压延加工业	Smelting and Pressing of Non-ferrous Metals	192
金属制品业	Manufacture of Metal Products	165
通用设备制造业	Manufacture of General Purpose Machinery	254
专用设备制造业	Manufacture of Special Equipment	438
汽车制造业	Manufacture of Motor Vehicle	234
铁路、船舶、航空航天和其他运输设备制造业	Railways,Shipbuilding,Aerospace and Other Transportation Equipment Manufacturing Industry	568
电气机械和器材制造业	Manufacture of Electric Equipment and Machinery	778
计算机、通讯和其他电子设备制造业	Manufacture of Communication Equipment, Computers and other Electronic Equipment	612
仪器仪表制造业	Manufacture of Measuring Instruments and Machinery	306
其他制造业	Other Manufacturing	14
废弃资源综合利用业	Comprehensive Utilization Of Waste Resources	
金属制品、机械和设备修理业	Metal Products,Machinery and Equipment Repair Industry	2
电力、热力、燃气及水生产和供应业	Production and Distribution of Electricity,Heat,Gas and Water	28
电力、热力的生产和供应业	Production and Supply of Electric Power and Heat Power	16
燃气生产和供应业	Gas mining and supplying industry	10
水的生产和供应业	Production and Supply of Water	2

continued 1

新产品开发经费支出（万元） New Product Development Expenditure （10 000 yuan）	新产品产值 （万元） New product output value （10 000 yuan）	新产品销售收入 （万元） Sales of new products （10 000 yuan）
32		8
5752		67891
		500
250		65
56268		234787
42646		566116
1068		
15298		101372
23252		275352
622		294
34972		324429
50628		185438
49622		375296
86081		711626
280793		6717416
513083		2194661
173292		2431425
355140		645396
72297		337991
1752		14958
301		
8058		2604
2871		
4516		
670		2604

20–23 规模以上非工业重点行业企业研究与试验发展（R&D）基本情况（2019年）

R&D Project Status of Non-Industrial Key Enterprises above Designated Size（2019）

指标	Item	单位数（个）Number of Units (unit)	#有R&D活动单位数（个）#The Number of R&D active units (unit)
总计	**Total**	**2071**	**186**
按企业规模分	**Grouped by Size of Enterprises**		
大型企业	Large-size	190	68
中型企业	Medium-size	483	52
小型企业	Small-size	1102	64
微型企业	Microenterprise	296	2
按登记注册类型分	**Grouped by Registered Status**		
内资企业	Domestic Investment Enterprises	1999	179
港、澳、台商投资企业	Enterprises with Funds from Hong Kong, Macao And Taiwan	25	3
外商投资企业	Foreign Funded Enterprises	47	4
按国民经济行业分	**Grouped by Sector**		
建筑业	Construction	373	38
交通运输、仓储和邮政业	Traffic, Transport, Storage and Post	240	1
信息传输、软件和信息技术服务业	Information Transmission, Computer Services and Software	290	49
租赁和商务服务业	Leasing and Business Services	405	6
科学研究和技术服务业	Scientific Research, Technical Sevice	374	86
水利、环境和公共设施管理业	Management of Water Conservancy, Environment and Public Facilities	67	3
卫生和社会工作	Health, Social Security	69	
文化、体育和娱乐业	Culture, Sports and Entertainment	253	3

20-24 规模以上非工业重点行业企业研究与试验发展（R&D）人员和经费支出情况（2019年）

R&D Personnel and Expenditure of Non-Industrial Key Enterprises above Designated Size（2019）

指标	Item	R&D人员（人）R&D personnel（person）	#研究人员 #Researchers
总计	**Total**	**14707**	**13450**
按企业规模分	**Grouped by Size of Enterprises**		
大型企业	Large-size	12032	10977
中型企业	Medium-size	1509	1390
小型企业	Small-size	1159	1076
微型企业	Microenterprise	7	7
按登记注册类型分	**Grouped by Registered Status**		
内资企业	Domestic Investment Enterprises	14119	12876
港、澳、台商投资企业	Enterprises with Funds from Hong Kong, Macao And Taiwan	60	58
外商投资企业	Foreign Funded Enterprises	528	516
按国民经济行业分	**Grouped by Sector**		
建筑业	Construction	6236	5441
交通运输、仓储和邮政业	Traffic, Transport, Storage and Post	28	27
信息传输、软件和信息技术服务业	Information Transmission, Computer Services and Software	3705	3566
租赁和商务服务业	Leasing and Business Services	46	43
科学研究和技术服务业	Scientific Research, Technical Sevice	4640	4323
水利、环境和公共设施管理业	Management of Water Conservancy, Environment and Public Facilities	39	38
卫生和社会工作	Health, Social Security		
文化、体育和娱乐业	Culture, Sports and Entertainment	13	12

注：境外资金列数据均为0。

20-24 续表1 continued 1

指标	Item	R&D经费内部支出（万元） R&D Intramural Expenditure (10 000 yuan)	#政府资金 # Government funds
总计	**Total**	**588358**	**15035**
按企业规模分	**Grouped by Size of Enterprises**		
大型企业	Large-size	522905	13432
中型企业	Medium-size	17727	787
小型企业	Small-size	47366	816
微型企业	Microenterprise	360	
按登记注册类型分	**Grouped by Registered Status**		
内资企业	Domestic Investment Enterprises	557970	15035
港、澳、台商投资企业	Enterprises with Funds from Hong Kong, Macao And Taiwan	506	
外商投资企业	Foreign Funded Enterprises	29882	
按国民经济行业分	**Grouped by Sector**		
建筑业	Construction	233261	1374
交通运输、仓储和邮政业	Traffic, Transport, Storage and Post	169	10
信息传输、软件和信息技术服务业	Information Transmission, Computer Services and Software	235060	525
租赁和商务服务业	Leasing and Business Services	585	
科学研究和技术服务业	Scientific Research, Technical Sevice	118999	13116
水利、环境和公共设施管理业	Management of Water Conservancy, Environment and Public Facilities	162	10
卫生和社会工作	Health, Social Security		
文化、体育和娱乐业	Culture, Sports and Entertainment	122	

20-24 续表2 continued 2

指标	Item	#企业资金 # Enterprise Funds	#境外资金 # Foreign Funds
总计	**Total**	**573023**	
按企业规模分	**Grouped by Size of Enterprises**		
大型企业	Large-size	509173	
中型企业	Medium-size	16940	
小型企业	Small-size	46550	
微型企业	Microenterprise	360	
按登记注册类型分	**Grouped by Registered Status**		
内资企业	Domestic Investment Enterprises	542635	
港、澳、台商投资企业	Enterprises with Funds from Hong Kong, Macao And Taiwan	506	
外商投资企业	Foreign Funded Enterprises	29882	
按国民经济行业分	**Grouped by Sector**		
建筑业	Construction	231887	
交通运输、仓储和邮政业	Traffic, Transport, Storage and Post	159	
信息传输、软件和信息技术服务业	Information Transmission, Computer Services and Software	234535	
租赁和商务服务业	Leasing and Business Services	585	
科学研究和技术服务业	Scientific Research, Technical Sevice	105583	
水利、环境和公共设施管理业	Management of Water Conservancy, Environment and Public Facilities	152	
卫生和社会工作	Health, Social Security		
文化、体育和娱乐业	Culture, Sports and Entertainment	122	

20-25 主要年份知识产权情况

Intellectual Property Rights in Major Years

指 标	Item	2015	2016	2017	2018	2019	2020
一、专利申请合计数（件）	**Patents Application Accepted(piece)**	**60986**	**45417**	**81110**	**56408**	**72377**	**68353**
发明专利	Inventions	14024	18282	40439	24074	29297	31376
实用新型专利	Utility Models	15735	18087	22461	24313	28087	33406
外观专利	Designs	31227	9048	18210	8021	14993	3571
二、授权专利合计（件）	**Patents Application Granted(piece)**	**25103**	**37744**	**25042**	**31640**	**34123**	**45407**
发明专利	Inventions	5873	6565	7902	8025	9017	11067
实用新型专利	Utility Models	12030	12035	11595	17070	18937	29916
外观专利	Designs	7200	19144	5545	6545	6169	4424
三、注册商标（件）	**Registered Trade Mark(piece)**	**30527**	**23887**	**27060**	**43205**	**61692**	**58842**

注：1.本表数据由市场监管局提供，并对历史数据进行了重新修订。
2.本表数据为西安原口径数据。
3.专利申请合计数中2020年的数据为截止到2020年11月底的数据。

20-26 主要年份民事知识产权维权情况

Protection of Civil Intellectual Property Rights in Major Years

单位：件 (piece)

指 标	Item	2015	2016	2017	2018	2019	2020
1、专利纠纷	Patent controversies	130	95	112	449	233	157
2、商标纠纷	Trade mark controversies	277	353	404	892	744	1245
3、著作权纠纷	Copyright controversies	327	404	190	520	1852	1413
4、技术合同纠纷	Technological contract controversies	12	10	36	47	52	74
5、其他知识产权纠纷	Others IPR controversies	67	25	110	182	366	667

注：1.本表数据由市中级人民法院提供。
2.本表数据为西安原口径数据。

20-27 规模以上工业企业自主知识产权情况（2019年）

The Independent Intellectual Property Rights of Industrial Enterprises above Designated Size（2019）

指 标	Item	专利申请数（件）Number of Patent Applications (piece)	#发明专利 Invention of Patent	期末有效发明专利数（件）Number of Valid Invention Patents At the End of the Term (piece)
总计	**Total**	**8579**	**3969**	**13336**
按企业规模分	**Grouped by Size of Enterprises**			
大型企业	Large-size	3186	1675	5138
中型企业	Medium-size	1868	876	3938
小型企业	Small-size	3463	1397	4210
微型企业	Microenterprise	62	21	50
按登记注册类型分	**Grouped by Registered Status**			
内资企业	Domestic Investment Enterprises	8187	3818	12636
国有企业	State-owned Enterprises	589	407	1247
集体企业	Collective-owned Enterprise			
股份合作企业	Stock Cooperative Enterprises	8		5
联营企业	Affiliated Enterprise			
有限责任公司	Limited Liability Corporations	4805	2292	7663
股份有限公司	Share-holding Corporation Ltd	1272	598	2138
私营企业	Private Enterprise	1513	521	1583
其他	Other Domestic Funded Enterprises			
港、澳、台商投资企业	Enterprises with Funds from Hong Kong, Macao And Taiwan	163	50	66
外商投资企业	Foreign Funded Enterprises	229	101	634
按国民经济行业大类分	**Grouped by Sector**			
采矿业	Mining	322	175	818
煤炭开采和洗选业	Mining and Washing of Coal			
石油和天然气开采业	Extraction of Petroleum and Natural Gas	266	136	118
黑色金属矿采选业	Mining of Ferrous Metal Ores			
有色金属矿采选业	Mining of Non-ferrous Metal Ores			
非金属矿采选业	Mining and Processing of Nonmetal Ores			
开采专业及辅助性活动	Mining Professional and Auxiliary Activity	56	39	700
其他采矿业	Mining of other Ores			
制造业	Manufacturing Industry	8055	3684	12157
农副食品加工业	Processing of Food from Agriculture Products	3	1	
食品制造业	Manufacture of Food	38	2	39
酒、饮料和精制茶制造业	Manufacture of Beverages	29	4	67
烟草制品业	Manufacture of Tobacco	77	14	15
纺织业	Manufacture of Textile	16	15	18
纺织服装、服饰业	Manufacture of Textile Wearing, Apparel			
皮革、毛皮、羽毛及其制品和制鞋业	Manufacture of Leather, Furs, Feather, Related Products and Footware	18	4	5

20-27 续表1 continued 1

指　标	Item	专利申请数（件）Number of Patent Applications (piece)	#发明专利 Invention of Patent	期末有效发明专利数（件）Number of Valid Invention Patents At the End of the Term (piece)
木材加工和木、竹、藤、棕、草制品业	Processing of Timber,Manufacture of Wood, Bamboo, Rattan, Palm and Straw Products			
家具制造业	Manufacture of Furniture			
造纸及纸制品业	Manufacture of Paper And Paper Products	1	1	2
印刷和记录媒介复制业	Printing and Reproduction of Recording Media	26	9	143
文教、工美、体育和娱乐用品制造业	Education, Art, Sports And Entertainment Products Manufacturing	9	7	7
石油、煤炭及其他燃料加工业	Processing of Petroleum,Coking and Processing of Nuclear Fuel	1		
化学原料和化学制品制造业	Manufacture of Raw Chemical Materials and Chemical Products	433	323	781
医药制造业	Manufacture of Medicines	124	66	470
化学纤维制造业	Manufacture of Chemical Fiber	7	6	32
橡胶和塑料制品业	Manufacture of Rubber and Manufacture of Plastic	75	23	239
非金属矿物制品业	Manufacture of Non-metallic Mineral Products	211	61	284
黑色金属冶炼和压延加工业	Smelting and Pressing of Ferrous Metals	12	7	7
有色金属冶炼和压延加工业	Smelting and Pressing of Non-ferrous Metals	331	211	741
金属制品业	Manufacture of Metal Products	264	154	477
通用设备制造业	Manufacture of General Purpose Machinery	531	221	609
专用设备制造业	Manufacture of Special Equipment	1106	387	1391
汽车制造业	Manufacture of Motor Vehicle	737	234	361
铁路、船舶、航空航天和其他运输设备制造业	Railways, Ships, Aerospace And Other Transportation Equipment Manufacturing Industry	1305	843	2289
电气机械和器材制造业	Manufacture of Electric Equipment and Machinery	1141	433	1349
计算机、通信和其他电子设备制造业	Manufacture of Communication Equipment, Computers and Other Electronic Equipment	1009	413	1846
仪器仪表制造业	Manufacture of Measuring Instruments and Machinery	523	239	934
其他制造业	Other Manufacturing	17	4	46
废弃资源综合利用业	Comprehensive Utilization Of Waste Resources	3		3
金属制品、机械和设备修理业	Metal Products, Machinery and Equipment Repair Industry	8	2	2
电力、热力、燃气及水生产和供应业	Production and Distribution of Electricity, Heat,Gas and Water	202	110	361
电力、热力生产和供应业	Production and Supply of Electric Power and Heat Power	180	108	360
燃气生产和供应业	Production and Supply of Gas	14	1	
水的生产和供应业	Production and Supply of Water	8	1	1

20-28 规模以上非工业重点行业企业知识产权（2019年）

Intellectual Property Rights of Non-Industrial Key Enterprises above Designated Size（2019）

指 标	Item	专利申请数（件）Number of Patent Applications (piece)	#发明专利 Invention of Patent	有效发明专利数（件）Number of Valid Invention Patents At the End of the Term (piece)
总计	**Total**	**4017**	**1775**	**4812**
按企业规模分	**Grouped by Size of Enterprises**			
大型企业	Large-size	3105	1434	3711
中型企业	Medium-size	508	181	491
小型企业	Small-size	392	160	609
微型企业	Microenterprise	12		1
按登记注册类型分	**Grouped by Registered Status**			
内资企业	Domestic Investment Enterprises	3997	1774	4758
港、澳、台商投资企业	Enterprises with Funds from Hong Kong, Macao And Taiwan	13	1	14
外商投资企业	Foreign Funded Enterprises	7		40
按国民经济行业分	**Grouped by Sector**			
建筑业	Construction	1012	297	717
交通运输、仓储和邮政业	Traffic, Transport, Storage and Post	8	1	1
信息传输、软件和信息技术服务业	Information Transmission, Computer Services and Software	960	583	658
租赁和商务服务业	Leasing and Business Services	21	7	17
科学研究和技术服务业	Scientific Research, Technical Sevice	1994	883	3399
水利、环境和公共设施管理业	Management of Water Conservancy, Environment and Public Facilities	11	2	12
卫生和社会工作	Health, Social Security			
文化、体育和娱乐业	Culture, Sports and Entertainment	11	2	8

20-29　规模（限额）以上企业创新活动总体情况（2019年）

指　标	Item	企业数（个）Number of Enterprises (unit)	开展创新活动企业数（个）Number of Ubbovation Activity Enterprises (unit)
总计	**Total**	**5901**	**3024**
按企业规模分	**Grouped by Size of Enterprises**		
大型企业	Large-size	331	239
中型企业	Medium-size	1483	791
小型企业	Small-size	3471	1808
微型企业	Microenterprise	616	186
按登记注册类型分	**Grouped by Registered Status**		
内资企业	Domestic Investment Enterprises	5639	2880
港、澳、台商投资企业	Enterprises with Funds from Hong Kong, Macao And Taiwan	75	40
外商投资企业	Foreign Funded Enterprises	187	104
按行业分	**Grouped by Sector**		
采矿业	Mining	9	5
制造业	Manufactruring Industry	1564	1092
电力、热力、燃气及水生产和供应业	Production and Distribution of Electricity, Heat ,Gas and Water	61	32
建筑业	Construction	1028	415
批发和零售业	Wholesale and Retail Trades	1863	761
交通运输、仓储和邮政业	Traffic, Transport, Storage and Post	240	75
信息传输、软件和信息技术服务业	Information Transmission, Computer Services and Software	290	232
租赁和商务服务业	Leasing and Business Services	405	162
科学研究和技术服务业	Scientific Research, Technical Sevice	374	224
水利、环境和公共设施管理业	Management of Water Conservancy, Environment and Public Facilities	67	26

Basic Statistics on Enterprise Innovation Activities above Designated Size（2019）

#实现创新企业 Achieve Innovative Enterprise	#同时实现四种创新企业 Achieve Four Kinds of Innovative Enterprises At Same Time	#实现产品创新企业 Achieve Product Innovation Enterprises	#实现工艺创新企业 Achieve Process Innovation Enterprises	#实现组织创新企业 Achieve Organizational Innovation Enterprises	#实现营销创新企业 Achieve Marketing Innovation Enterprises
2898	**553**	**1095**	**1342**	**2283**	**1776**
231	72	134	166	185	128
761	138	261	336	600	472
1728	325	664	787	1359	1061
178	18	36	53	139	115
2770	527	1031	1273	2190	1698
36	4	15	15	24	27
92	22	49	54	69	51
5	1	3	3	5	2
1035	299	608	684	772	676
32		1	12	28	16
399	36	77	145	351	139
758	94	151	209	572	590
71	6	12	18	65	32
207	60	121	122	168	124
156	17	28	36	124	95
209	38	90	108	174	91
26	2	4	5	24	11

20-29 续表1

指 标	Item	开展创新活动企业 Ubbovation Activity Enterprises
总计	**Total**	**51.2**
按企业规模分	**Grouped by Size of Enterprises**	
大型企业	Large-size	72.2
中型企业	Medium-size	53.3
小型企业	Small-size	52.1
微型企业	Microenterprise	30.2
按登记注册类型分	**Grouped by Registered Status**	
内资企业	Domestic Investment Enterprises	51.1
港、澳、台商投资企业	Enterprises with Funds from Hong Kong, Macao And Taiwan	53.3
外商投资企业	Foreign Funded Enterprises	55.6
按行业分	**Grouped by Sector**	
采矿业	Mining	55.6
制造业	Manufactruring Industry	69.8
电力、热力、燃气及水生产和供应业	Production and Distribution of Electricity, Heat ,Gas and Water	52.5
建筑业	Construction	40.4
批发和零售业	Wholesale and Retail Trades	40.8
交通运输、仓储和邮政业	Traffic, Transport, Storage and Post	31.3
信息传输、软件和信息技术服务业	Information Transmission, Computer Services and Software	80.0
租赁和商务服务业	Leasing and Business Services	40.0
科学研究和技术服务业	Scientific Research, Technical Sevice	59.9
水利、环境和公共设施管理业	Management of Water Conservancy, Environment and Public Facilities	38.8

continued 1

在全部企业中占比（%） The Proportion in All Enterprises(%)					
#实现创新企业 Achieve Innovative Enterprise	#同时实现四种创新企业 Achieve Four Kinds of Innovative Enterprises At Same Time	#实现产品创新企业 Achieve Product Innovation Enterprises	#实现工艺创新企业 Achieve Process Innovation Enterprises	#实现组织创新企业 Achieve Organizational Innovation Enterprises	#实现营销创新企业 Achieve Marketing Innovation Enterprises
49.1	**9.4**	**18.6**	**22.7**	**38.7**	**30.1**
69.8	21.8	40.5	50.2	55.9	38.7
51.3	9.3	17.6	22.7	40.5	31.8
49.8	9.4	19.1	22.7	39.2	30.6
28.9	2.9	5.8	8.6	22.6	18.7
49.1	9.3	18.3	22.6	38.8	30.1
48.0	5.3	20.0	20.0	32.0	36.0
49.2	11.8	26.2	28.9	36.9	27.3
55.6	11.1	33.3	33.3	55.6	22.2
66.2	19.1	38.9	43.7	49.4	43.2
52.5		1.6	19.7	45.9	26.2
38.8	3.5	7.5	14.1	34.1	13.5
40.7	5.0	8.1	11.2	30.7	31.7
29.6	2.5	5.0	7.5	27.1	13.3
71.4	20.7	41.7	42.1	57.9	42.8
38.5	4.2	6.9	8.9	30.6	23.5
55.9	10.2	24.1	28.9	46.5	24.3
38.8	3.0	6.0	7.5	35.8	16.4

20-30 规模以上工业企业创新活动总体情况（2019年）

指 标	Item	企业数（个）Number of Enterprises (unit)	开展创新活动企业数（个）Number of Ubbovation Activity Enterprises (unit)
总计	**Total**	**1634**	**1129**
按企业规模分	**Grouped by Size of Enterprises**		
大型企业	Large-size	69	58
中型企业	Medium-size	183	162
小型企业	Small-size	1307	871
微型企业	Microenterprise	75	38
按登记注册类型分	**Grouped by Registered Status**		
内资企业	Domestic Investment Enterprises	1520	1056
港、澳、台商投资企业	Enterprises with Funds from Hong Kong, Macao And Taiwan	22	14
外商投资企业	Foreign Funded Enterprises	92	59
按行业分	**Grouped by Sector**		
采矿业	Mining	9	5
煤炭开采和洗选业	Mining and Washing of Coal		
石油和天然气开采业	Extraction of Petroleum and Natural Gas	1	1
黑色金属矿采选业	Mining of Ferrous Metal Ores		
有色金属矿采选业	Mining of Non-ferrous Metal Ores		
非金属矿采选业	Mining and Processing of Nonmetal Ores		
开采专业及辅助性活动	Mining Professional and Auxiliary Activity	8	4
其他采矿业	Mining of other Ores		
制造业	Manufacturing Industry	1564	1092
农副食品加工业	Processing of Food from Agriculture Products	46	24
食品制造业	Manufacture of Food	53	37
酒、饮料和精制茶制造业	Manufacture of Beverages	22	15
烟草制品业	Manufacture of Tobacco	2	1
纺织业	Manufacture of Textile	15	11
纺织服装、服饰业	Manufacture of Textile Wearing, Apparel	4	4
皮革、毛皮、羽毛及其制品和制鞋业	Manufacture of Leather, Furs, Feather, Related Products and Footware	2	2
木材加工和木、竹、藤、棕、草制品业	Processing of Timber,Manufacture of Wood, Bamboo, Rattan, Palm and Straw Products	3	2
家具制造业	Manufacture of Furniture	18	7
造纸和纸制品业	Manufacture of Paper And Paper Products	24	11
印刷和记录媒介复制业	Printing and Reproduction of Recording Media	32	20

Basic Statistics on Industrial Enterprise Innovation Activities above Designated Size（2019）

#实现创新企业 Achieve Innovative Enterprise	#同时实现四种创新企业 Achieve Four Kinds of Innovative Enterprises At Same Time	#实现产品创新企业 Achieve Product Innovation Enterprises	#实现工艺创新企业 Achieve Process Innovation Enterprises	#实现组织创新企业 Achieve Organizational Innovation Enterprises	#实现营销创新企业 Achieve Marketing Innovation Enterprises
1072	**300**	**612**	**699**	**805**	**694**
57	25	45	51	45	36
154	54	110	111	110	97
824	216	444	519	621	540
37	5	13	18	29	21
1004	282	567	654	757	655
13	1	6	5	7	9
55	17	39	40	41	30
5	1	3	3	5	2
1		1	1	1	
4	1	2	2	4	2
1035	299	608	684	772	676
23	2	7	9	13	19
37	9	16	16	28	32
14	2	4	5	8	12
1	1	1	1	1	1
11	2	6	7	6	10
3			3	3	3
2	1	2	2	2	1
2		1		1	1
7			3	6	5
11		2	3	6	5
16	3	6	10	11	8

20-30 续表1

指 标	Item	开展创新活动企业 Ubbovation Activity Enterprises
总计	**Total**	**69.1**
按企业规模分	**Grouped by Size of Enterprises**	
大型企业	Large-size	84.1
中型企业	Medium-size	88.5
小型企业	Small-size	66.6
微型企业	Microenterprise	50.7
按登记注册类型分	**Grouped by Registered Status**	
内资企业	Domestic Investment Enterprises	69.5
港、澳、台商投资企业	Enterprises with Funds from Hong Kong, Macao And Taiwan	63.6
外商投资企业	Foreign Funded Enterprises	64.1
按行业分	**Grouped by Sector**	
采矿业	Mining	55.6
煤炭开采和洗选业	Mining and Washing of Coal	
石油和天然气开采业	Extraction of Petroleum and Natural Gas	100.0
黑色金属矿采选业	Mining of Ferrous Metal Ores	
有色金属矿采选业	Mining of Non-ferrous Metal Ores	
非金属矿采选业	Mining and Processing of Nonmetal Ores	
开采专业及辅助性活动	Mining Professional and Auxiliary Activity	50.0
其他采矿业	Mining of other Ores	
制造业	Manufacturing Industry	69.8
农副食品加工业	Processing of Food from Agriculture Products	52.2
食品制造业	Manufacture of Food	69.8
酒、饮料和精制茶制造业	Manufacture of Beverages	68.2
烟草制品业	Manufacture of Tobacco	50.0
纺织业	Manufacture of Textile	73.3
纺织服装、服饰业	Manufacture of Textile Wearing, Apparel	100.0
皮革、毛皮、羽毛及其制品和制鞋业	Manufacture of Leather, Furs, Feather, Related Products and Footware	100.0
木材加工和木、竹、藤、棕、草制品业	Processing of Timber,Manufacture of Wood, Bamboo, Rattan, Palm and Straw Products	66.7
家具制造业	Manufacture of Furniture	38.9
造纸和纸制品业	Manufacture of Paper And Paper Products	45.8
印刷和记录媒介复制业	Printing and Reproduction of Recording Media	62.5

continued 1

在全部企业中占比（%） The Proportion in All Enterprises (%)					
#实现创新企业 Achieve Innovative Enterprise	#同时实现四种创新企业 Achieve Four Kinds of Innovative Enterprises At Same Time	#实现产品创新企业 Achieve Product Innovation Enterprises	#实现工艺创新企业 Achieve Process Innovation Enterprises	#实现组织创新企业 Achieve Organizational Innovation Enterprises	#实现营销创新企业 Achieve Marketing Innovation Enterprises
65.6	**18.4**	**37.5**	**42.8**	**49.3**	**42.5**
82.6	36.2	65.2	73.9	65.2	52.2
84.2	29.5	60.1	60.7	60.1	53.0
63.0	16.5	34.0	39.7	47.5	41.3
49.3	6.7	17.3	24.0	38.7	28.0
66.1	18.6	37.3	43.0	49.8	43.1
59.1	4.5	27.3	22.7	31.8	40.9
59.8	18.5	42.4	43.5	44.6	32.6
55.6	11.1	33.3	33.3	55.6	22.2
100.0		100.0	100.0	100.0	
50.0	12.5	25.0	25.0	50.0	25.0
66.2	19.1	38.9	43.7	49.4	43.2
50.0	4.3	15.2	19.6	28.3	41.3
69.8	17.0	30.2	30.2	52.8	60.4
63.6	9.1	18.2	22.7	36.4	54.5
50.0	50.0	50.0	50.0	50.0	50.0
73.3	13.3	40.0	46.7	40.0	66.7
75.0			75.0	75.0	75.0
100.0	50.0	100.0	100.0	100.0	50.0
66.7		33.3		33.3	33.3
38.9			16.7	33.3	27.8
45.8		8.3	12.5	25.0	20.8
50.0	9.4	18.8	31.3	34.4	25.0

20-30 续表2

指 标	Item	企业数（个） Number of Enterprises (unit)	开展创新活动企业数（个） Number of Ubbovation Activity Enterprises (unit)
文教、工美、体育和娱乐用品制造业	Education, Art, Sports And Entertainment Products Manufacturing	9	6
石油、煤炭及其他燃料加工业	Processing of Petroleum,Coking and Processing of Nuclear Fuel	6	3
化学原料和化学制品制造业	Manufacture of Raw Chemical Materials and Chemical Products	78	61
医药制造业	Manufacture of Medicines	66	54
化学纤维制造业	Manufacture of Chemical Fiber	4	2
橡胶和塑料制品业	Manufacture of Rubber and Manufacture of Plastic	49	27
非金属矿物制品业	Manufacture of Non-metallic Mineral Products	185	74
黑色金属冶炼和压延加工业	Smelting and Pressing of Ferrous Metals	11	4
有色金属冶炼和压延加工业	Smelting and Pressing of Non-ferrous Metals	45	35
金属制品业	Manufacture of Metal Products	113	52
通用设备制造业	Manufacture of General Purpose Machinery	98	77
专用设备制造业	Manufacture of Special Equipment	146	123
汽车制造业	Manufacture of Motor Vehicle	67	52
铁路、船舶、航空航天和其他运输设备制造业	Railways, Ships, Aerospace And Other Transportation Equipment Manufacturing Industry	95	77
电气机械和器材制造业	Manufacture of Electric Equipment and Machinery	158	122
计算机、通信和其他电子设备制造业	Manufacture of Communication Equipment, Computers and Other Electronic Equipment	122	108
仪器仪表制造业	Manufacture of Measuring Instruments and Machinery	71	66
其他制造业	Other Manufacturing	7	7
废弃资源综合利用业	Comprehensive Utilization Of Waste Resources	4	2
金属制品、机械和设备修理业	Metal Products, Machinery and Equipment Repair Industry	9	6
电力、热力、燃气及水生产和供应业	Production and Distribution of Electricity, Heat,Gas and Water	61	32
电力、热力生产和供应业	Production and Supply of Electric Power and Heat Power	28	16
燃气生产和供应业	Production and Supply of Gas	18	8
水的生产和供应业	Production and Supply of Water	15	8

continued 2

#实现创新企业 Achieve Innovative Enterprise	#同时实现四种创新企业 Achieve Four Kinds of Innovative Enterprises At Same Time	#实现产品创新企业 Achieve Product Innovation Enterprises	#实现工艺创新企业 Achieve Process Innovation Enterprises	#实现组织创新企业 Achieve Organizational Innovation Enterprises	#实现营销创新企业 Achieve Marketing Innovation Enterprises
5		2	2	2	5
3	1	2	2	3	1
57	14	36	39	41	33
53	14	27	36	40	41
2			1	1	1
26	3	12	16	14	19
72	12	17	33	56	46
4		1	2	3	1
35	10	27	31	24	17
50	12	17	30	42	30
71	26	40	52	60	50
118	44	83	78	94	86
49	17	34	37	38	30
73	20	53	55	55	34
110	34	67	71	80	73
103	39	85	83	74	60
62	31	56	46	49	45
7	2	4	6	7	5
2			1	1	1
6			4	3	1
32		1	12	28	16
16			7	14	7
8			3	8	5
8		1	2	6	4

20-30 续表3

指　标	Item	开展创新活动企业 Ubbovation Activity Enterprises
文教、工美、体育和娱乐用品制造业	Education, Art, Sports And Entertainment Products Manufacturing	66.7
石油、煤炭及其他燃料加工业	Processing of Petroleum,Coking and Processing of Nuclear Fuel	50.0
化学原料和化学制品制造业	Manufacture of Raw Chemical Materials and Chemical Products	78.2
医药制造业	Manufacture of Medicines	81.8
化学纤维制造业	Manufacture of Chemical Fiber	50.0
橡胶和塑料制品业	Manufacture of Rubber and Manufacture of Plastic	55.1
非金属矿物制品业	Manufacture of Non-metallic Mineral Products	40.0
黑色金属冶炼和压延加工业	Smelting and Pressing of Ferrous Metals	36.4
有色金属冶炼和压延加工业	Smelting and Pressing of Non-ferrous Metals	77.8
金属制品业	Manufacture of Metal Products	46.0
通用设备制造业	Manufacture of General Purpose Machinery	78.6
专用设备制造业	Manufacture of Special Equipment	84.2
汽车制造业	Manufacture of Motor Vehicle	77.6
铁路、船舶、航空航天和其他运输设备制造业	Railways, Ships, Aerospace And Other Transportation Equipment Manufacturing Industry	81.1
电气机械和器材制造业	Manufacture of Electric Equipment and Machinery	77.2
计算机、通信和其他电子设备制造业	Manufacture of Communication Equipment, Computers and Other Electronic Equipment	88.5
仪器仪表制造业	Manufacture of Measuring Instruments and Machinery	93.0
其他制造业	Other Manufacturing	100.0
废弃资源综合利用业	Comprehensive Utilization Of Waste Resources	50.0
金属制品、机械和设备修理业	Metal Products, Machinery and Equipment Repair Industry	66.7
电力、热力、燃气及水生产和供应业	Production and Distribution of Electricity, Heat,Gas and Water	52.5
电力、热力生产和供应业	Production and Supply of Electric Power and Heat Power	57.1
燃气生产和供应业	Production and Supply of Gas	44.4
水的生产和供应业	Production and Supply of Water	53.3

continued 3

在全部企业中占比（%） The Proportion in All Enterprises (%)					
#实现创新企业 Achieve Innovative Enterprise	#同时实现四种创新企业 Achieve Four Kinds of Innovative Enterprises At Same Time	#实现产品创新企业 Achieve Product Innovation Enterprises	#实现工艺创新企业 Achieve Process Innovation Enterprises	#实现组织创新企业 Achieve Organizational Innovation Enterprises	#实现营销创新企业 Achieve Marketing Innovation Enterprises
55.6		22.2	22.2	22.2	55.6
50.0	16.7	33.3	33.3	50.0	16.7
73.1	17.9	46.2	50.0	52.6	42.3
80.3	21.2	40.9	54.5	60.6	62.1
50.0			25.0	25.0	25.0
53.1	6.1	24.5	32.7	28.6	38.8
38.9	6.5	9.2	17.8	30.3	24.9
36.4		9.1	18.2	27.3	9.1
77.8	22.2	60.0	68.9	53.3	37.8
44.2	10.6	15.0	26.5	37.2	26.5
72.4	26.5	40.8	53.1	61.2	51.0
80.8	30.1	56.8	53.4	64.4	58.9
73.1	25.4	50.7	55.2	56.7	44.8
76.8	21.1	55.8	57.9	57.9	35.8
69.6	21.5	42.4	44.9	50.6	46.2
84.4	32.0	69.7	68.0	60.7	49.2
87.3	43.7	78.9	64.8	69.0	63.4
100.0	28.6	57.1	85.7	100.0	71.4
50.0			25.0	25.0	25.0
66.7			44.4	33.3	11.1
52.5		1.6	19.7	45.9	26.2
57.1			25.0	50.0	25.0
44.4			16.7	44.4	27.8
53.3		6.7	13.3	40.0	26.7

20-31　资质内建筑业企业创新活动总体情况（2019年）

指　标	Item	企业数（个） Number of Enterprises (unit)	开展创新活动企业数（个） Number of Ubbovation Activity Enterprises (unit)
总计	**Total**	**1028**	**415**
按企业规模分	**Grouped by Size of Enterprises**		
大型企业	Large-size	73	63
中型企业	Medium-size	375	165
小型企业	Small-size	485	168
微型企业	Microenterprise	95	19
按登记注册类型分	**Grouped by Registered Status**		
内资企业	Domestic Investment Enterprises	1024	414
港、澳、台商投资企业	Enterprises with Funds from Hong Kong, Macao And Taiwan	2	
外商投资企业	Foreign Funded Enterprises	2	1
按行业分	**Grouped by Sector**		
建筑业	Construction	1028	415
房屋建筑业	Construction of Building	400	143
土木工程建筑业	Civil Engineering	306	148
建筑安装业	Architectural Installation	137	60
建筑装饰、装修和其他建筑业	Architectural Decoration and Other Construction	185	64

Basic Statistics on Innovation Activities of Qualified Construction Enterprises above Designated Size（2019）

#实现 创新企业 Achieve Innovative Enterprise	#同时实现 四种创新企业 Achieve Four Kinds of Innovative Enterprises At Same Time	#实现产品 创新企业 Achieve Product Innovation Enterprises	#实现工艺 创新企业 Achieve Process Innovation Enterprises	#实现组织 创新企业 Achieve Organizational Innovation Enterprises	#实现营销 创新企业 Achieve Marketing Innovation Enterprises
399	**36**	**77**	**145**	**351**	**139**
61	14	27	51	49	27
159	13	25	52	139	60
162	9	24	39	148	47
17		1	3	15	5
398	36	77	145	350	139
1				1	
399	36	77	145	351	139
138	9	21	46	122	48
143	13	27	55	127	45
55	8	17	23	46	23
63	6	12	21	56	23

20-31 续表1

指 标	Item	开展创新活动企业 Ubbovation Activity Enterprises
总计	**Total**	**40.4**
按企业规模分	**Grouped by Size of Enterprises**	
大型企业	Large-size	86.3
中型企业	Medium-size	44.0
小型企业	Small-size	34.6
微型企业	Microenterprise	20.0
按登记注册类型分	**Grouped by Registered Status**	
内资企业	Domestic Investment Enterprises	40.4
港、澳、台商投资企业	Enterprises with Funds from Hong Kong, Macao And Taiwan	
外商投资企业	Foreign Funded Enterprises	50.0
按行业分	**Grouped by Sector**	
建筑业	Construction	40.4
房屋建筑业	Construction of Building	35.8
土木工程建筑业	Civil Engineering	48.4
建筑安装业	Architectural Installation	43.8
建筑装饰、装修和其他建筑业	Architectural Decoration and Other Construction	34.6

continued 1

在全部企业中占比（%） The Proportion in All Enterprises(%)					
#实现创新企业 Achieve Innovative Enterprise	#同时实现四种创新企业 Achieve Four Kinds of Innovative Enterprises At Same Time	#实现产品创新企业 Achieve Product Innovation Enterprises	#实现工艺创新企业 Achieve Process Innovation Enterprises	#实现组织创新企业 Achieve Organizational Innovation Enterprises	#实现营销创新企业 Achieve Marketing Innovation Enterprises
38.8	**3.5**	**7.5**	**14.1**	**34.1**	**13.5**
83.6	19.2	37.0	69.9	67.1	37.0
42.4	3.5	6.7	13.9	37.1	16.0
33.4	1.9	4.9	8.0	30.5	9.7
17.9		1.1	3.2	15.8	5.3
38.9	3.5	7.5	14.2	34.2	13.6
50.0				50.0	
38.8	3.5	7.5	14.1	34.1	13.5
34.5	2.3	5.3	11.5	30.5	12.0
46.7	4.2	8.8	18.0	41.5	14.7
40.1	5.8	12.4	16.8	33.6	16.8
34.1	3.2	6.5	11.4	30.3	12.4

20-32 规模（限额）以上服务业企业创新活动总体情况（2019年）

指 标	Item	企业数（个）Number of Enterprises (unit)	开展创新活动企业数（个）Number of Ubbovation Activity Enterprises (unit)
总计	**Total**	**3239**	**1480**
按企业规模分	**Grouped by Size of Enterprises**		
大型企业	Large-size	189	118
中型企业	Medium-size	925	464
小型企业	Small-size	1679	769
微型企业	Microenterprise	446	129
按登记注册类型分	**Grouped by Registered Status**		
内资企业	Domestic Investment Enterprises	3095	1410
港、澳、台商投资企业	Enterprises with Funds from Hong Kong, Macao And Taiwan	51	26
外商投资企业	Foreign Funded Enterprises	93	44
按行业分	**Grouped by Sector**		
批发和零售业	Wholesale and Retail Trades	1863	761
批发业	Wholesale Trade	952	368
零售业	Retail Trade	911	393
交通运输、仓储和邮政业	Traffic, Transport, Storage and Post	240	75
铁路运输业	Transport Via Railway	4	2
道路运输业	Transport Via Road	147	37
水上运输业	Water Transport		
航空运输业	Air Transport	12	5
管道运输业	Transport Via Pipeline	1	1
多式联运和运输代理业	Multimodal Transport and Transportation Agency	33	19
装卸搬运和仓储业	Loading,Unloading,Portage,Storge and Management of Land Industry	33	8

Basic Statistics on Service Enterprise Innovation Activities above Designated Size（2019）

#实现创新企业 Achieve Innovative Enterprise	#同时实现四种创新企业 Achieve Four Kinds of Innovative Enterprises At Same Time	#实现产品创新企业 Achieve Product Innovation Enterprises	#实现工艺创新企业 Achieve Process Innovation Enterprises	#实现组织创新企业 Achieve Organizational Innovation Enterprises	#实现营销创新企业 Achieve Marketing Innovation Enterprises
1427	**217**	**406**	**498**	**1127**	**943**
113	33	62	64	91	65
448	71	126	173	351	315
742	100	196	229	590	474
124	13	22	32	95	89
1368	209	387	474	1083	904
23	3	9	10	17	18
36	5	10	14	27	21
758	94	151	209	572	590
366	37	65	98	288	248
392	57	86	111	284	342
71	6	12	18	65	32
1		1			
35	4	6	8	32	16
5		1	2	4	2
1				1	
18	2	3	6	17	9
8			1	8	2

20-32 续表1

指　标	Item	开展创新活动企业 Ubbovation Activity Enterprises
总计	**Total**	**45.7**
按企业规模分	**Grouped by Size of Enterprises**	
大型企业	Large-size	62.4
中型企业	Medium-size	50.2
小型企业	Small-size	45.8
微型企业	Microenterprise	28.9
按登记注册类型分	**Grouped by Registered Status**	
内资企业	Domestic Investment Enterprises	45.6
港、澳、台商投资企业	Enterprises with Funds from Hong Kong, Macao And Taiwan	51.0
外商投资企业	Foreign Funded Enterprises	47.3
按行业分	**Grouped by Sector**	
批发和零售业	Wholesale and Retail Trades	40.8
批发业	Wholesale Trade	38.7
零售业	Retail Trade	43.1
交通运输、仓储和邮政业	Traffic, Transport, Storage and Post	31.3
铁路运输业	Transport Via Railway	50.0
道路运输业	Transport Via Road	25.2
水上运输业	Water Transport	
航空运输业	Air Transport	41.7
管道运输业	Transport Via Pipeline	100.0
多式联运和运输代理业	Multimodal Transport and Transportation Agency	57.6
装卸搬运和仓储业	Loading,Unloading,Portage,Storge and Management of Land Industry	24.2

continued 1

在全部企业中占比（%） The Proportion in All Enterprises(%)					
#实现创新企业 Achieve Innovative Enterprise	#同时实现四种创新企业 Achieve Four Kinds of Innovative Enterprises At Same Time	#实现产品创新企业 Achieve Product Innovation Enterprises	#实现工艺创新企业 Achieve Process Innovation Enterprises	#实现组织创新企业 Achieve Organizational Innovation Enterprises	#实现营销创新企业 Achieve Marketing Innovation Enterprises
44.1	**6.7**	**12.5**	**15.4**	**34.8**	**29.1**
59.8	17.5	32.8	33.9	48.1	34.4
48.4	7.7	13.6	18.7	37.9	34.1
44.2	6.0	11.7	13.6	35.1	28.2
27.8	2.9	4.9	7.2	21.3	20.0
44.2	6.8	12.5	15.3	35.0	29.2
45.1	5.9	17.6	19.6	33.3	35.3
38.7	5.4	10.8	15.1	29.0	22.6
40.7	5.0	8.1	11.2	30.7	31.7
38.4	3.9	6.8	10.3	30.3	26.1
43.0	6.3	9.4	12.2	31.2	37.5
29.6	2.5	5.0	7.5	27.1	13.3
25.0		25.0			
23.8	2.7	4.1	5.4	21.8	10.9
41.7		8.3	16.7	33.3	16.7
100.0				100.0	
54.5	6.1	9.1	18.2	51.5	27.3
24.2			3.0	24.2	6.1

20-32 续表2

指　标	Item	企业数（个）Number of Enterprises (unit)	开展创新活动企业数（个）Number of Ubbovation Activity Enterprises (unit)
邮政业	Post	10	3
信息传输、软件和信息技术服务业	Information Transmission, Computer Services and Software	290	232
电信、广播电视和卫星传输服务	Telecom & Other Information Transmission Services	23	13
互联网和相关服务	Internet and Relevant Services	52	37
软件和信息技术服务业	Software Industry	215	182
租赁和商务服务业	Leasing and Business Services	405	162
租赁业	Leasing	15	9
商务服务业	Business Services	390	153
科学研究和技术服务业	Scientific Research, Technical Sevice	374	224
研究和试验发展	Research and Experimental Development	31	26
专业技术服务业	Professional Technical Services	321	182
科技推广和应用服务业	Services of Science and Technology Exchanges and Promotion	22	16
水利、环境和公共设施管理业	Management of Water Conservancy, Environment and Public Facilities	67	26
水利管理业	Management of Water Conservancy	4	1
生态保护和环境治理业	Environmental Management	8	5
公共设施管理业	Management of Public Facilities	49	17
土地管理业	Lang management	6	3

continued 2

#实现创新企业 Achieve Innovative Enterprise	#同时实现四种创新企业 Achieve Four Kinds of Innovative Enterprises At Same Time	#实现产品创新企业 Achieve Product Innovation Enterprises	#实现工艺创新企业 Achieve Process Innovation Enterprises	#实现组织创新企业 Achieve Organizational Innovation Enterprises	#实现营销创新企业 Achieve Marketing Innovation Enterprises
3		1	1	3	3
207	60	121	122	168	124
12	4	6	6	11	8
35	9	19	19	27	21
160	47	96	97	130	95
156	17	28	36	124	95
9	1	1	3	9	4
147	16	27	33	115	91
209	38	90	108	174	91
24	2	11	12	17	9
169	31	69	89	143	72
16	5	10	7	14	10
26	2	4	5	24	11
1		1	1	1	
5	2	2	2	5	4
17		1	1	15	7
3			1	3	

20-32 续表3

指 标	Item	开展创新活动企业 Ubbovation Activity Enterprises
邮政业	Post	30.0
信息传输、软件和信息技术服务业	Information Transmission, Computer Services and Software	80.0
电信、广播电视和卫星传输服务	Telecom & Other Information Transmission Services	56.5
互联网和相关服务	Internet and Relevant Services	71.2
软件和信息技术服务业	Software Industry	84.7
租赁和商务服务业	Leasing and Business Services	40.0
租赁业	Leasing	60.0
商务服务业	Business Services	39.2
科学研究和技术服务业	Scientific Research, Technical Sevice	59.9
研究和试验发展	Research and Experimental Development	83.9
专业技术服务业	Professional Technical Services	56.7
科技推广和应用服务业	Services of Science and Technology Exchanges and Promotion	72.7
水利、环境和公共设施管理业	Management of Water Conservancy, Environment and Public Facilities	38.8
水利管理业	Management of Water Conservancy	25.0
生态保护和环境治理业	Environmental Management	62.5
公共设施管理业	Management of Public Facilities	34.7
土地管理业	Lang management	50.0

continued 3

在全部企业中占比（%） The Proportion in All Enterprises(%)					
#实现创新企业 Achieve Innovative Enterprise	#同时实现四种创新企业 Achieve Four Kinds of Innovative Enterprises At Same Time	#实现产品创新企业 Achieve Product Innovation Enterprises	#实现工艺创新企业 Achieve Process Innovation Enterprises	#实现组织创新企业 Achieve Organizational Innovation Enterprises	#实现营销创新企业 Achieve Marketing Innovation Enterprises
30.0		10.0	10.0	30.0	30.0
71.4	20.7	41.7	42.1	57.9	42.8
52.2	17.4	26.1	26.1	47.8	34.8
67.3	17.3	36.5	36.5	51.9	40.4
74.4	21.9	44.7	45.1	60.5	44.2
38.5	4.2	6.9	8.9	30.6	23.5
60.0	6.7	6.7	20.0	60.0	26.7
37.7	4.1	6.9	8.5	29.5	23.3
55.9	10.2	24.1	28.9	46.5	24.3
77.4	6.5	35.5	38.7	54.8	29.0
52.6	9.7	21.5	27.7	44.5	22.4
72.7	22.7	45.5	31.8	63.6	45.5
38.8	3.0	6.0	7.5	35.8	16.4
25.0		25.0	25.0	25.0	
62.5	25.0	25.0	25.0	62.5	50.0
34.7		2.0	2.0	30.6	14.3
50.0			16.7	50.0	

主要统计指标解释

普通高等学校 指按国家规定的设置标准和审批程序批准举办的，通过全国普通高等学校统一招生考试，招收高中毕业生为主要培养对象，实施高等学历教育的全日制大学、独立设置的学院和高等专科学校、高等职业学校及其他机构（独立学院和分校、大专班）。

大学、独立设置的学院主要实施本科层次以上教育。高等专科学校、高等职业学校实施专科层次教育。其他机构是承担国家普通招生计划任务不计校数的机构，包括独立学院、普通高等学校分校、大专班和批准筹建的普通高等学校等。独立学院指由普通本科高校按新机制、新模式举办的本科层次的二级学院，一些普通本科高校按公办机制和模式建立的二级学院，“分校”或其他类似的二级办学机构不属此范畴。

成人高等学校 指按照国家规定的设置标准和审批程序批准举办的，通过全国成人高等教育统一招生考试，招收具有高中毕业或同等学历的人员为主要培养对象，利用函授、业余、脱产等多种形式对其实施高等学历教育的学校。包括职工高等学校、农民高等学校、管理干部学院、教育学院、独立函授学院、广播电视大学、其他机构等。其他机构是承担国家成人招生计划任务不计校数的机构。

小学学龄儿童净入学率 指调查范围内已入小学学习的学龄儿童占校内外学龄儿童总数（包括弱智儿童，不包括盲聋哑儿童）的比重。计算公式为：

小学学龄儿童净入学率（%）=已入学的小学学龄儿童数/校内外小学学龄儿童总数×100%

研究与试验发展（R&D） 指在科学技术领域，为增加知识总量，以及运用这些知识去创造新的应用进行的系统的创造性的活动，包括基础研究、应用研究、试验发展三类活动。国际上通常采用R&D活动的规模和强度指标反映一国的科技实力和核心竞争力。

基础研究 指为了获得关于现象和可观察事实的基本原理的新知识（揭示客观事物的本质、运动规律，获得新发现、新学说）而进行的实验性或理论性研究，它不以任何专门或特定的应用或使用为目的。其成果以科学论文和科学著作为主要形式。用来反映知识的原始创新能力。

应用研究 指为获得新知识而进行的创造性研究，主要针对某一特定的目的或目标。应用研究是为了确定基础研究成果可能的用途，或是为达到预定的目标探索应采取的新方法（原理性）或新途径。其成果形式以科学论文、专著、原理性模型或发明专利为主。用来反映对基础研究成果应用途径的探索。

试验发展 指利用从基础研究、应用研究和实际经验所获得的现有知识，为产生新的产品、材料和装置，建立新的工艺、系统和服务，以及对已产生和建立的上述各项作实质性的改进而进行的系统性工作。其成果形式主要是专利、专有技术、具有新产品基本特征的产品原型或具有新装置基本特征的原始样机等。在社会科学领域，试验发展是指把通过基础研究、应用研究获得的知识转变成可以实施的计划（包括为进行检验和评估实施示范项目）的过程。人文科学领域没有对应的试验发展活动。主要反映将科研成果转化为技术和产品的能力，是科技推动经济社会发展的物化成果。

R&D人员 指参与研究与试验发展项目研究、管理和辅助工作的人员，包括项目（课题）组人员，企业科技行政管理人员和直接为项目（课题）活动提供服务的辅助人员。反映投入从事拥有自主知识产权的研究开发活动的人力规模。

R&D人员全时当量 指全时人员数加非全时人员按工作量折算为全时人员数的总和。例如：有两个全时人员和三个非全时人员（工作时间分别为20%、30%和70%），则全时当量为2+0.2+0.3+0.7=3.2人年。为国际上比较科技人力投入而制定的可比指标。

R&D经费内部支出 合计指调查单位用于内部开展R&D活动（基础研究、应用研究和试验发展）的实际支出。包括用于R&D项目（课题）活动的直接支出，以及间接用TR&D活动的管理费、服务费、与R&D有关的基本建设支出以及外协加工费等。不包括生产性活动支出、归还贷款支出以及与外单位合作或委托外单位进行R&D活动而转拨给对方的经费支出。

R&D经费内部支出中政府资金 指R&D经费内部支出中来自各级政府部门的各类资金，包括财政科学技术拨款、科学基金、教育等部门事业费以及政府部门预算外资金的实际支出。

R&D经费内部支出中企业资金 指R&D经费内部支出中来自本企业的自有资金和接受其他企业委托而获得的经费，以及科研院所、高校等事业单位从企业获得的资金的实际支出。

R&D项目（课题）数 指在当年立项并开展研究工作、以前年份立项仍继续进行研究的研发项目（课题）数，包括当年完成和年内研究：工作已告失败的研发项目（课题），但不包括委托外单位进行的研发项目（课题）数。

R&D项目（课题）人员全时当量 指实际参加研发项目（课题）活动人员折合的全时当量。

R&D项目（课题）经费内部支出 指调查单位内部在报告年度进行研发项目（课题）研究和试制等的实际支出。包括劳务费、其他日常支出、固定资产购建费、外协加工费等，不包括委托或与外单位合作进行项目（课题）研究而拨付给对方使用的经费。

新产品产值 指报告期企业生产的新产品的产值。新产品是指采用新技术原理、新设计构思研制、生产的全新产品，或在结构、材质、工艺等某一方面比原有产品有明显改进，从而显著提高了产品性能或扩大了使用功能的产品。新产品产值、新产品销售收入既包括经政府有关部门认定并在有效期内的新产品，也包括企业自行研制开发，未经政府有关部门认定，从投产之日起一年之内的新产品。

新产品销售收入 指报告期企业销售新产品实现的销售收入。

专利 是专利权的简称，是对发明人的发明创造经审查合格后，由专利局依据专利法授予发明人和设计人对该项发明创造享有的专有权。包括发明、实用新型和外观设计。反映拥有自主知识产权的科技和设计成果情况。

发明（专利） 指对产品、方法或者其改进所提出的新的技术方案。是国际通行的反映拥有自主知识产权技术的核心指标。

Explanatory Notes on Main Statistical Indicators

Regular Institutions of Higher Education refer to educational establishments set up according to the government evaluation and approval procedures, recruiting graduates from senior secondary schools as the main target by National Matriculation TEST. They include full-time universities, colleges, institutions of higher professional education, institutions of higher vocational education, institutions of higher vocational education and others (non-university tertiary, branch schools and undergraduate classes) .

Universities and colleges primarily provide undergraduate courses; institutions of higher professional education and institutions of higher vocational education primarily provide professional trainings; and others refer to educational establishments, which are responsible for enrolling higher education students under the State Plan but not enumerated in the total number of schools, including: branch schools of universities and colleges, and universities and colleges that have been approved and under plan for construction. Non-university tertiary refers to the regular undergraduate branch college which is running in new mechanism and mode, excluding the branch schools and other similar branches of educational institutions.

Institutions of Higher Education for Adults refer to educational establishments, set up in line with relevant rules approved by the government, enrolling staff and workers with senior secondary school or equivalent education, and providing higher education courses in many forms of correspondence, spare time, or full time for adults. Professionals thus trained receive a qualification equivalent to graduates studying regular courses at regular universities, colleges and professional colleges. Institutions of higher learning for adults include schools of higher education for staff and workers, schools of higher education for peasants, colleges for management cadres, pedagogical colleges, independent correspondence colleges, Radio and TV universities and other educational establishments. Other educational establishments have undertakings to enrol adult students but not enumerated in the schools under the State Plan.

Net Enrolment Ratio of Primary Schools refers to the proportion of school age children enrolled at schools to the total number of school age children both in and outside schools (including retarded children, but excluding blind, deaf and mute children) . The formula is:

$$\text{Net Enrolment Ratio Of Primary Schools} = \frac{\text{Total Primary School-age Children at Schools}}{\text{Total Primary School-age WnerdlihChether or Not Attending School}} \times 100\%$$

Research and Development (R&D) refers to systematic and creative activities in the field of science and technology aiming at increasing the knowledge and using the knowledge for new application. R&D includes 3 categories of activities: basic research, applied research and experimentation for development. The scale and intensity of R&D are widely used internationally to reflect the strength of S&T and the core competitiveness of a country in the world.

Basic Research refers to empirical or theoretical research aiming at obtaining new knowledge on the fundamental principles regarding phenomena or observable facts to reveal the intrinsic nature and underlying laws and to acquire new discoveries or new theories. Basic research takes no specific or designated application as the aim of the research. Results of basic research are mainly released or disseminated in the form of scientific papers or monographs. This indicator reflects the innovation capacity for original knowledge.

Applied Research refers to creative research aiming at obtaining new knowledge on a specific objective or target. Purpose of the applied research is to identify the possible uses of results from basic research, or to explore new (fundamental) methods or new approaches. Results of applied research are expressed in the form of scientific papers, monographs, fundamental models or invention patents. This indicator reflects the exploration of ways to apply the results of basic research.

Experiments and Development refer to systematic activities aiming at using the knowledge from basic and applied researches or from practical experience to develop new products, materials and equipment, to establish new production process, systems and services, or to make substantial improvement on the existing products, process or services. Results of experiment and development activities are embodied in patents, exclusive technology, and monotype of new products or equipment. In social sciences, experiment and development activities refer to the process of converting the knowledge from basic or applied researches into feasible programmes (including conduct of demonstration projects for assessment and evaluation) . There are no experiment and development activities in the science of humanities. This indicator reflects the capability of transferring the results of S&T into technique and products, and measures the realization of S&T in spearheading the economic and social development.

R&D Personnel refer to persons engaged in research, management and supporting activities of R&D, including persons in the project teams, persons engaged in the management of S&T activities of enterprises and supporting staff providing direct service to the research projects. This indicator reflects the size of personnel engaged in R&D activities with independent intellectual property.

Full-time Equivalent of R&D Personnel refers to the sum of the full-time persons and the full-time equivalent of part-time persons converted by workload. For instance, if there are 2 full-time persons and 3 part-time workers (20%, 30% and 70% of working hours respectively on R&D activities) , the full-time equivalent are 2+0.2+0.3+0.7=3.2 person-years. This is an internationally comparable indicator of S&T manpower input.

Total Internal Expenditure of Funds on R&D refers to the real expenditure of surveyed units on their own R&D activities (basic research, application study, test and development) including direct expenditure on R&D activities, indirect expenditure of management and services on R&D activities, expenditure on capital construction and material processing by others. Excluding the expenditure on production activities, return of loan, and fees transferred to cooperated and entrusted agencies on R&D activities.

Internal Expenditure of Government Funds refersto the expenditure of funds on R&D activities from government agencies at different levels, including appropriate funds on science and technology from financial departments, scientific funds, operating expenses from education departments and the real expenditure of extra budgetary funds from government agencies.

Internal Expenditure of Funds of Enterprises refers to the expenditure of funds on R&D activities from self-raised funds of enterprises and funds from other enterprises through entrustment, and the expenditure of funds of institutions, such as institution of scientific research and universities, from enterprises.

Number of R&D Projects (subjects) refers to the number of R&D projects (subjects) set up and implemented at the reference year, and the number of R&D projects (subjects) set up in former years and under implementation, including the projects (subjects) finished and failed at the reference year, excluding the projects (subjects) implemented by others through entrustment.

Full-time Equivalent of R&D Personnel refers to the full-time equivalent of persons actually engaged in R&D projects. (subjects)

Internal Expenditure of Funds on R&D Projects (subjects) refers to the real expenditure of internal funds of the surveyed units on research and test of R&D projects (subjects) at the reference year, including service fee, other daily expenditure, cost for capital goods, cost of external process; excluding expenditure of funds transferred to other cooperated and entrusted units of the projects.

Output Value of New Products refers to the output value of new products during the reporting period. The new products refer to brand new products produced with new technology and new design, or product that represent noticeable improvement in terms of structure, material, or production process for improving significantly the character of function of the older versions. The output value and sales income of the new products include those of new products certified by relevant government agencies within the period of certification, as well as new products designed and produced by enterprises within a year without certification by government agencies.

Sales Income of New Products refers to the real sales income of new products of the enterprises at the reporting period.

Patent is an abbreviation for the patent right and refers to the exclusive right of ownership by the inventors or designers for the creation or inventions, given from the patent offices after due process of assessment and approval in accordance with the Patent Law. Patents are granted for inventions, utility models and designs. This indicator reflects the achievements of S&T and design with independent intellectual property.

Patented Inventions refer to new technical proposals to the products or methods or their modifications. This is universal core indicator reflecting the technologies with independent intellectual property.

21 文化、体育、卫生、社会福利和其他

CULTURE,SPORTS,PUBLIC HEALTH,SOCIAL WELFARE INSTITUTIONS AND OTHER SOCIAL ACTIVITIES

资料整理：陈超毅　齐昆峰
Data management：Chen Chaoyi　Qi Kunfeng
数据审核：刘栋婷
Data audit：Liu Dongting

第二十一部分　文化、体育、卫生、社会福利和其他

一、简要说明

本章资料主要包括文化、体育、卫生、社保、公检法等方面的内容，由西安市统计局服务业与社会科技统计处根据统计一套表资料和市委宣传部、市文化和旅游局、卫健委、民政局、体育局、人社局、公安局、医保局、退役军人事务局、团市委、司法局、妇联、应急管理局、消防救援支队、法院、检察院等部门及机构提供资料整理。本章资料数据口径见表下注释。

二、主要指标

公共图书馆藏量（千册件）	7977	比上年减少	35
医院数（个）	359	与上年持平	
医院床位数（万张）	6.65	比上年减少	0.07

21　CULTURE,SPORTS,PUBLIC HEALTH,SOCIAL WELFARE INSTITUTIONS AND OTHER SOCIAL ACTIVITIES

Ⅰ.Brief Introduction

Data in this Chapter primarily consists of data of culture, sanitation,civiladministration, physicaleducation,familyplanning, CommunistYouth League, the Women's Federation, public security organs,procuratorial organs and people's court,compiled by Tertiary Industry and Social Science Technology Division of Xi'an Bureau of Statistics according to data from units of "One Sheet" and Xi'an Bureau of Cuture, health and Family Planning Commision, Bureau of CivialAdministration, Bureau of PE, the Women's Federation, Municipal Committee of Communist Youth League, Bureau of Public Security, Procuratorate, People's Court and other department concerned. The field and range of data in this chapter are listed in the explanatory notes below the chare.

Ⅱ.Major Indicators

		Increase over Preceding Year
Number of Collections in Libraries (1000 volume-times)	7977	-35
Number of Hospitals(units)	359	essentially on a par with lasst years
Numbers of Beds(10000 units)	6.65	-0.07

21-1 电影基本情况（2020年）

The Basic Situation of Film（2020）

指　标	Item	2020
全年上映本市生产的院线影片数量（个）	Number of Theatrical Films Produced In The Whole Year(unit)	3
电影发行放映管理机构（个）	Film Projection and Publication Administrating Institutions(unit)	2
电影发行放映管理机构从业人员（人）	Film Projection and Publication Administrating Institution Staff(person)	8
电影放映单位（个）	Unit of Film Shows(unit)	277
电影院	Cinema	125
放映队	File Projection Team	152
电影放映单位从业人员（人）	Staff of Unit of Film Shows(person)	2106
电影院	Cinema	1900
放映队	File Projection Team	206
电影放映场数（千场）	Number of Film Shows（1000 shows）	829.8
电影观众人数（千人次）	Number of Spectators(1000 person-times)	12634
电影票房收入（万元）	Box-office Receipts(10 000yuan)	35597
平均每一放映场次的观众人次（人次）	Average Audience of Each Projection(person-times)	13
平均每一放映场次的放映收入（元）	Average Income of Each Projcetion(yuan)	447

注：本表数据来源于市委宣传部及文化和旅游局。
本表数据含西咸新区。

21-2 图书馆基本情况（2020年）

The Basic Situation of Library（2020）

指 标	Item	2020
公共图书馆个数（个）	Number of Public Libraries(unit)	14
公共图书馆从业人员（人）	Public Library Practitioners (person)	452
公共图书馆藏量（千册件）	Public Library Reserves(1 000 volume-times)	7977
电子图书（千册）	E-books(1 000 volumes)	6434
阅览室坐席（个）	Number of Seatings in Reading Room(unit)	5480
书刊文献外借人次（千人次）	Number of Books and literature Borrowed by Readers (1 000 person-times)	399
书刊文献外借册次（千册件）	Volumes of Books and literature Lent to Readers(1 000 volume-times)	1270
图书流通人次（千人次）	Book Circulation Person-time (1 000 person-times)	1578
县以上公共图书馆购书经费（万元）	Book-purchase Fund of Public Library above the County Level(10 000 yuan)	1405
公共图书馆建筑面积（万平方米）	Building Area of Public Library (10 000 sq.m)	10.26

注：本表数据来源于市文化和旅游局。
本表数据含西咸新区。

21-3 艺术表演基本情况（2020年）

The Basic Situation of Art Performance（2020）

指 标	Item	2020
艺术表演团体机构数（个）	Number of Organization of Art Performance Troupes(unit)	18
艺术表演团体从业人员（人）	Art Performance Troupes Practitioners (person)	2473
艺术表演团体演出场次（场）	Number of Performances by Art Performance Troupes(show)	2000
#国内演出场次	Domestic Performance	1600
艺术表演观众人次（千人次）	Audience for the Art Performance(1 000 person-times)	2675
艺术表演团体本年创作首映剧目（个）	Art Performance Troupes Creative Premieres of the Year (unit)	18
艺术表演场馆数（个）	Number of Art Performance Places(unit)	14
艺术表演场馆从业人员（人）	Art Performance Place Practitioners (person)	327
艺术表演场馆坐席（个）	Art Performance Place Seatings(unit)	9995
艺术科研机构（个）	Art and Research Institutions(unit)	2
艺术科研机构从业人员（人）	Art and Research Institutions Practitioners(person)	54

注：本表数据来源于市文化和旅游局。
本表数据含西咸新区。

21-4 主要年份群众艺术馆、文化馆（站）活动情况

Basic Statistics on Activities of Mass Art Centers and Cultural Centers in Representative Years

指 标	Item	2010	2014	2015	2016	2017	2018	2019	2020
机构数（个）	Number of Insititutions (unit)	197	199	199	190	202	202	202	204
举办展览个数（个）	Number of Exhibitions (unit)	705	627	606	562	649	632	594	627
举办展览参观人次（千人次）	Number of Exhibition Visitors (1 000 person-times)		326	289	287	418	392	442	354
组织文艺活动次数（次）	Art Performances and Story-telling Sessions (times)	3729	3617	3811	4246	5498	6518	6589	5587
组织文艺活动参加人次（千人次）	Number of Culture Activities attendees (1 000 person-times)		1576	1574	1688	2631	3322	2476	1668
举办训练班班次（个）	Number of Training Courses (unit)	3018	1872	2126	1906	2597	3310	2608	2968
举办训练班结业人次（千人次）	Number of Certificate Trained Persons (1 000 person-times)	133	156	207	149	188	209	174	239
组织各类理论研讨和讲座次数（次）	Number of Theoretical Discussion and Seminars(times)		254	216	189	101	113	144	148
组织各类理论研讨和讲座参加人次（千人次）	Number of Persons in Theoretical and Seminars(1 000 person-times)		28	25	18	17	15	20	27
本年收入（千元）	Income of this year (1 000 yuan)	42937	89520	102567	103706	133378	116324	115525	111177
本年支出（千元）	Expenditure of this year (1 000 yuan)	45160	84827	100749	111942	141012	119354	123727	113812

注：本表数据来源于市文化和旅游局。
本表2017年及以后年份数据含西咸新区。

21-5 文物保护业基本情况（2020年）

Basic Statistics on Cultural Relics Protection（2020）

指 标	Item	机 构（个）Insititution (unit)	人 员（人）Personnel (person)	文物藏品 实际数量（件）Factual Number of Collections (piece)	一级品（件）Grade One (piece)	举办陈列展览次数(次) Times of exhibition (times)	参观人员（千人次）Number of Visitors (1000 person-times)
文物保护管理机构	Cultural Relics administrative Departments	30	592	11606	19		
其他文物机构	Other Agencies	3	63				
博物馆	Museums	133	5143	2124676	3888	250	12886
#免费开放馆	Museums Open Free	98	2191	2005571	2094	214	5940
文物科研机构	Scientific Research of Historical Relics Preservation	3	249	60703	186		

注：本表数据来源于市文化和旅游局。
本表数据2020年起含西咸新区数据。

21-6 主要年份广播电台及节目制作情况

Basic Statistics of Broadcasting Stations and Program Production in Representative Years

指　标	Item	2010	2014	2015	2016	2017	2018	2019	2020
省、地广播电台（座）	Broadcasting Stations at the Province and District Level(set)	2							
省、地广播电视台（座）	Broadcasting Station at Province and District Level(set)		2	2	2	2	2	1	4
县级广播电视台（座）	Number of Wire Broadcasting Stations and TV Relaying Stations(set)	6	6	6	6	6	6	8	6
中、短波转播发射台（座）	Medium and Short Wave Broadcast Transmitting Station (base)	55	57	13	13	13	13	13	13
节目套数（套）	Number of Programs(set)	18	20	20	20	20	20	25	19
全年播出时间（时）	Broadcasting Hours annually(hour)	124100	143873	137075	139159	132252	132596	131122	143283
广播节目综合人口覆盖率（%）	Broadcasts comprehensive population coverage（%）	99.40	99.49	99.55	99.62	99.65	100.00	99.99	100.00
制作广播节目（时）	Productions of Broadcasting(hour)	110639	104459	116603	119424	100169	117418	112202	126748
#新闻资讯类	News Programs	13786	13208	12208	7590	6362	6761	6719	9303
专题服务类	Special Subject Programs	24451	26884	21864	26957	26907	28463	29278	38530
综艺类	Variety Programs	37720	27148	37885	39735	25793	41535	39475	34605
广播剧类	Literature Programs	2406	3712	6674	3990	4680	5404	4378	4614
广告类	Advertisements	28339	18465	15777	18363	15968	13627	10584	14192
其他类	Service Programs	3937	15042	22195	22787	20459	21628	21768	25504

注：本表数据来源于市文化和旅游局。

中、短波转播发射台2014年之前统计口径为中短波、调频发射台及转播台。数据变化因指标含义变化所致。

本表2017年及以后年份数据含西咸新区。

21-7 主要年份电视台及节目制作情况

Basic Statistics of TV Stations and Production of TV Program in Representative Years

指　标	Item	2010	2014	2015	2016	2017	2018	2019	2020
调频电视转播发射台（座）	FM Television Relay Station (base)	10	11	48	48	47	48	43	39
无线电视节目（套）	Program Productions of Non-cable television Stations (set)	6	6	6	2	2	2	2	
有线电视节目（套）	Program Productions of cable television Stations (set)	16	16	16	20	20	21	20	
全年播出时间（时）	Broadcasting Hours annually(hour)	141856	143000	141839	140312	136960	128368	142289	121671
电视节目综合人口覆盖率（%）	TV shows comprehensive population coverage（%）	98.57	98.96	99.01	99.11	99.13	100	99.99	100
制作电视节目（时）	Earth Stations of Satellite TV(hour)	29626	35182	43563	54200	49001	45731	58427	30016
#新闻资讯类	News and Information Programs	8930	11797	11839	12891	10517	9387	14172	8358
专题服务类	Special Subject Programs	7762	8289	8073	9346	9769	10808	14581	10319
综艺类	Variety Programs	3942	5014	6242	7883	9080	8789	8728	4446
影视剧类	Literature Programs	1729	110	462	490	870	363	3482	461
广告类	Advertisement	3313	3491	7921	6198	6493	3981	6489	2620
其他类	Service Programs	3950	6479	9026	17390	12272	12403	10975	3812

注：本表数据来源于市文化和旅游局。

电视转播发射台2014年之前统计口径为发射台及转播台，数字变化因指标含义变化所致。影视剧及广告类节目2019年数据变化较大，是因统计口径变化所致。

本表2017年及以后年份数据含西咸新区。2020年全国广播电视统计信息网上直报系统取消无线电视节目、有线电视节目两项指标，因此无数据。

21-8 全市及各区县、开发区规模以上文化及相关产业法人单位数（2020年）

Number of Enterprises Culture and Related Industries above Designated Size by Region (2020)

单位：个 (unit)

区县、开发区	Region	法人单位数 Number of Enterprises	文化制造业 Culture Manufacture	文化批零业 Culture Whole and Retail Trade	文化服务业 Culture Service
西安市	**Total**	**729**	**42**	**97**	**590**
新城区	Xincheng	30		9	21
碑林区	Beilin	53		14	39
莲湖区	Lianhu	43	2	11	30
灞桥区	Baqiao	50	1	8	41
未央区	Weiyang	73	8	15	50
雁塔区	Yanta	327	6	26	295
阎良区	Yanliang	9		2	7
临潼区	Lintong	12		1	11
长安区	Chang'an	31	4	1	26
高陵区	Gaoling	14	6		8
鄠邑区	Huyi	15	5	4	6
蓝田县	Lantian	17	6	1	10
周至县	Zhouzhi	4		1	3
西咸新区	Xixian	51	4	4	43
在总计中：	**In Total:**				
高新区	Gaoxin	109	8	10	91
经开区	JingKai	49	7	10	32
曲江新区	Qujiang	196		9	187
航空基地	Aviation Industry Base	4		1	3
航天基地	Aerospace Base	8	1		7
浐灞生态区	Chanba Eco-District	51	4	4	43
国际港务区	International Trade&Logistic Park	21	1	6	14

21-9 全市及各区县、开发区规模以上文化制造业企业基本情况（2020年）

Basic Statistics on Culture and Related Industries above Designated Size by Region（2020）

单位：万元 (10 000yuan)

区县、开发区	Region	企业单位数（个） Number of Enterprises (unit)	年末从业人员（人） Engaged Persons at Year-end (person)	资产总计 Total Assets	营业收入 Total Revenue	营业利润 Operating Profit
西安市	**Total**	**42**	**7461**	**771734**	**662797**	**36301**
新城区	Xincheng					
碑林区	Beilin					
莲湖区	Lianhu	2	1881	275445	241875	19696
灞桥区	Baqiao	1	60	7204	7432	469
未央区	Weiyang	8	1425	100902	45048	-3343
雁塔区	Yanta	6	2276	250919	240022	15433
阎良区	Yanliang					
临潼区	Lintong					
长安区	Chang'an	4	449	35032	35801	3558
高陵区	Gaoling	6	471	19211	28727	-558
鄠邑区	Huyi	5	446	42900	37885	1359
蓝田县	Lantian	6	264	24306	8517	166
周至县	Zhouzhi					
西咸新区	Xixian	4	189	15816	17489	-480
在总计中：	**In Total:**					
高新区	Gaoxin	8	2536	277725	267254	17918
经开区	JingKai	7	1253	96693	40866	-3543
曲江新区	Qujiang					
航空基地	Aviation Industry Base					
航天基地	Aerospace Base	1	149	5582	6644	1067
浐灞生态区	Chanba Eco-District					
国际港务区	International Trade&Logistic Park	1	60	7204	7432	469

21-10 全市及各区县、开发区限额以上文化批零业企业基本情况（2020年）

Basic Statistics on Culture Whole and Retail Trade above Designated Size by Region (2020)

单位：万元 (10 000yuan)

区县、开发区	Region	企业单位数（个） Number of Enterprises (unit)	年末从业人员（人） Engaged Persons at Year-end (person)	资产总计 Total Assets	营业收入 Total Revenue	营业利润 Operating Profit
西安市	**Total**	**97**	**4856**	**801536**	**1017285**	**10861**
新城区	Xincheng	9	1077	171643	91334	743
碑林区	Beilin	14	361	77704	278533	-586
莲湖区	Lianhu	11	578	208777	314393	5420
灞桥区	Baqiao	8	221	91306	48783	-988
未央区	Weiyang	15	569	27248	79594	932
雁塔区	Yanta	26	1805	193740	163771	4742
阎良区	Yanliang	2	10	778	1572	81
临潼区	Lintong	1	39	1891	2164	-231
长安区	Chang'an	1	10	92	706	5
高陵区	Gaoling					
鄠邑区	Huyi	4	76	20037	25648	35
蓝田县	Lantian	1	5	161	734	26
周至县	Zhouzhi	1	19	625	784	111
西咸新区	Xixian	4	86	7535	9268	571
在总计中：	**In Total:**					
高新区	Gaoxin	10	392	91929	76399	1467
经开区	JingKai	10	529	17788	70148	856
曲江新区	Qujiang	9	941	38588	54958	3573
航空基地	Aviation Industry Base	1	5	401	783	49
航天基地	Aerospace Base					
浐灞生态区	Chanba Eco-District	2	64	4317	16409	368
国际港务区	International Trade&Logistic Park	6	160	86032	30715	-1351

21–11　全市及各区县、开发区规模以上文化服务业企业基本情况（2020年）

Basic Statistics on Culture Service above Designated Size by Region（2020）

单位：万元　　(10 000yuan)

区县、开发区	Region	企业单位数（个）Number of Enterprises (unit)	年末从业人员（人）Engaged Persons at Year-end (person)	资产总计 Total Assets	营业收入 Total Revenue	营业利润 Operating Profit
西安市	**Total**	**590**	**53417**	**13377802**	**4348829**	**191042**
新城区	Xincheng	21	861	75467	32718	-1832
碑林区	Beilin	39	4621	336855	191584	-12228
莲湖区	Lianhu	30	2292	233609	198278	3395
灞桥区	Baqiao	41	1870	971861	134065	9295
未央区	Weiyang	50	6127	1219004	494663	37956
雁塔区	Yanta	295	27912	9054185	2889650	166498
阎良区	Yanliang	7	171	20762	10039	833
临潼区	Lintong	11	2122	171201	37171	-12168
长安区	Chang'an	26	1826	199808	163594	4957
高陵区	Gaoling	8	153	14794	11145	1119
鄠邑区	Huyi	6	389	34537	7225	-488
蓝田县	Lantian	10	655	198013	22447	1077
周至县	Zhouzhi	3	175	42511	4204	-1931
西咸新区	Xixian	43	4243	805196	152046	-5441
在总计中：	**In Total:**					
高新区	Gaoxin	91	10719	1424296	1859434	141117
经开区	JingKai	32	5055	822433	430903	34244
曲江新区	Qujiang	187	16340	7345247	1054986	36012
航空基地	Aviation Industry Base	3	98	15336	8050	1037
航天基地	Aerospace Base	7	200	45572	31632	1274
浐灞生态区	Chanba Eco-District	21	1796	1097284	116022	17064
国际港务区	International Trade&Logistic Park	14	221	72656	28641	-3196

21-12 竞技体育情况（2020年）

The Situation of Competitive Sports (2020)

指　标	Item	2020
奥运会获得奖牌(枚)	Number of Medals Won in the Olympic Games(unit)	
金牌数	Gold	
银牌数	Silver	
铜牌数	Bronze	
全运会获得奖牌(枚)	Number of Medals Won in the National Games(unit)	
金牌数	Gold	
银牌数	Silver	
铜牌数	Bronze	
省运会获得奖牌(枚)	Number of Medals Won in the Provincial Games(unit)	
金牌数	Gold	
银牌数	Silver	
铜牌数	Bronze	
其他国际、国内赛事	Other International and Domestic Events	
金牌数(枚)	Gold(unit)	17
银牌数(枚)	Silver(unit)	18
体育传统项目学校(个)	Sports Traditional Project School(unit)	159
体育传统项目学校在校训练学生数(人)	Number of Students in the Sports Traditional Project School (person)	6560
高水平体育后备人才基地(个)	High Level Sports Reserve Base(unit)	7
省级示范性体校(个)	Provincial Demonstration Sports School(unit)	3
等级教练员人数(人)	Number of Graded Coaches (person)	69
国家级	National Level	1
高　级	Senior Level	19
一　级	One Level	25
二　级	Two Level	22
三　级	Three Level	2
二级运动员人数(人)	Second Grade Athletes (person)	311

注：本表数据来源于市体育局。
　　本表数据不含西咸新区。

21-13 群众体育情况（2020年）

The Situation of Mass Sports（2020）

指　标	Item	2020
全年承办的县级以上群众性体育赛事（个）	Mass Sports Events Held throughout the Year(unit)	600
国家级	National Level	3
省　级	Provincial Level	7
市　级	City Level	290
县　级	County Level	300
全年举办的社会体育指导员培训班（期）	Training Course for Social Sports Instructors Held throughout the Year （time）	22
社会体育指导员人数（名）	Social Sports Instructor（person）	27004
体育先进社区（个）	Advanced Sports Community(unit)	
#国家级	National Level	
省　级	Provincial Level	
群众体育先进单位（个）	Advanced Unit of Mass Sports(unit)	1
#国家级	National Level	
省　级	Provincial Level	1
晨晚健身站点（个）	Morning and Evening Fitness sites(unit)	1952
全民健身活动中心（个）	National Fitness Center(unit)	7
乡镇体育健身工程（个）	Township Sports Fitness Project(unit)	
村级农民体育健身工程（个）	Village Level Farmers' Sports Fitness Project(unit)	124
体育人口（万人）	Sports Population(10 000 person)	500

注：本表数据来源于市体育局。
　　本表数据不含西咸新区。

21-14 体育产业情况（2020年）

The Situation of Sport Industry (2020)

指　标	Item	2020
全市县级标准公共体育场地建设情况	Construction of Standard Public Sports Venues in the County Level	
已建场地个数（个）	Number of Built Sites(units)	10
在建场地个数（个）	Number of Sites in Construction(units)	2
全市全民健身设施建设情况	Construction of National Fitness Facilities in the City	
全民健身园区（个）	National Fitness Park(units)	29
多功能运动场（个）	Multifunction Playground(units)	63
户外营地（个）	Outdoor Camps(units)	
全民健身室内健身房（个）	Fitness Indoor Gymnasium(units)	20
健身步道（千米）	Fitness Footpath(km)	31.5
自行车专用道（千米）	Bicycle Special Road(km)	104
全市体育彩票销售情况	Sales of Sports Lottery in the City	
体育彩票销售网点数量（个）	Number of Sales Outlets of Sports Lottery (units)	1760
体育彩票销售网点数量占全省的比重（%）	Proportion of Sports Lottery Sales Outlets Accounts for the Proportion of the Whole Province（%）	35
本年体育彩票销售金额（万元）	Sales Amount of Sports Lottery in this Year (10 000 yuan)	187697
本年体育彩票销售金额占全省的比重（%）	Sales Amount of Sports Lottery in this year Accounts for the Proportion of the Whole Province（%）	41
全市体育产业单位数量（个）	Number of Sports Industrial Units in the City (units)	

注：本表数据来源于市体育局。
本表数据不含西咸新区。
2020年全市体育产业单位数量数据缺。

21-15 主要年份医疗卫生机构、床位、人员情况

Number of Health Care Institutions, Beds and Personnel in Health Care Institutions in Representative Years

年份 Year	医疗卫生机构数（个） Number of Health Care Institutions (unit)	医院数（个） Number of Health Care Hospital (unit)	医疗卫生机构床位数（张） Number of Health Care Bed (unit)	医院床位数（张） Number of Hospital Bed (unit)	卫生技术人员数（人） Number of Medical Technical Personnel (person)
2009	5284	261	36849	32371	52620
2010	5632	258	39407	34274	57756
2011	5554	268	41010	35976	61281
2012	5576	276	44239	39213	66899
2013	5503	281	47867	42753	71134
2014	5554	281	51065	45561	76005
2015	5802	295	54708	49830	81462
2016	5869	292	56332	51508	86258
2017	6376	329	63942	58219	94221
2018	6638	343	68981	63365	101477
2019	7011	359	72549	67238	112243
2020	7129	359	75007	66506	117656

注：本表数据来源于市卫健委。
本表2017年及以后年份数据含西咸新区。

21-16 医疗卫生机构、床位及人员情况（2020年）

卫生机构	Health Care Institutions	机构数（个）Number of Institutions (unit)	床位数（张）Number of Beds (unit)
总计	**Total**	**7129**	**75007**
一、医院	**Hospitals**	**359**	**66506**
综合医院	General Hospitals	212	48604
中医医院	Hospitals Specialized in Traditional Chinese Medicine	53	7271
中西医结合医院	Hospitals Integrating Traditional Chinese Medicine with Western Therapeutics in Practice	5	1006
民族医院	Nationalities Hospitals		
专科医院	Specialized Hospitals	86	9416
护理院	Nursing centers	3	209
二、基层医疗卫生机构	**Commuting Health Hare Service Centre**	**6668**	**3765**
社区卫生服务中心(站)	Community Health Care Center(Station)	262	1825
社区卫生服务中心	Community Health Care Center	126	1825
社区卫生服务站	Community Health Care Station	136	
卫生院	Health Center	117	1920
街道卫生院	Urban Health-center	2	108
乡镇卫生院	Rural Health-center	115	1812
村卫生室	Village Clinics	2961	
门诊部	Outpatient Department	377	20
诊所、卫生所、医务室	Clinic, Health Center, Infirmary	2951	
三、专业公共卫生机构	**College of Public Health Institutions**	**55**	**4506**
疾病预防控制中心	Center for Disease Control and Prevention	16	
专科疾病防治院（所、站）	Specialized Disease Prevention and Cure Center (Place, Station)	4	2749
健康教育所（站、中心）	Health Education Institute (Station, Center)	2	
妇幼保健院（所、站）	Maternal and Child Health Hospital (Place, Station)	14	1757
急救中心（站）	Emergency Center (Station)	2	
采供血机构	Blood Collection Agencies	1	
卫生监督所（中心）	Health Supervision Agencies (Center)	15	
计划生育技术服务机构	Institutions of Technical Service for Family Planning	1	
四、其他卫生机构	**Other Health Institution**	**47**	**230**
疗养院	Nursing Centres	1	230
卫生监督检验(监测、检测)所(站)	Health Supervision and Inspection Agencies(Station)		
医学科学研究机构	Medical Scientific Research Institutions	3	
医学在职培训机构	Medical Training Institutions	4	
临床检验中心（所、站）	Clinical Testing Center (Place, Station)	5	
统计信息中心	Statistical Information Center	2	
其他	Other	32	

注：本表数据来源于市卫健委。
本表人员合计中包括乡村医生2495人和卫生员134人，不含乡镇卫生院在村卫生室工作的执业（助理）医师、注册护士。
本表数据含西咸新区。

Number of Health Care Institutions, Beds and Personnel in Health Care Institutions (2020)

人员合计（人）Total Number of Employed Persons (person)	卫生技术人员 Medical Technical Personnel	执业（助理）医师数 Licensed (Assistant) Doctors	#执业医师 Chartered Doctors
142809	**117656**	**40714**	**36086**
96784	**80092**	**24904**	**23741**
74274	62233	19344	18512
9168	7420	2295	2162
1517	1220	396	388
11740	9146	2847	2661
85	73	22	18
34746	**29019**	**13359**	**10048**
7471	6243	1873	1482
6114	5039	1415	1104
1357	1204	458	378
4106	3443	906	617
267	237	73	45
3839	3206	833	572
4513	1884	1650	507
6038	5445	2509	2060
12618	12004	6421	5382
9198	**7034**	**2024**	**1925**
1143	890	419	384
2333	1813	414	410
75	30	4	2
4743	3668	1121	1067
129	75	56	55
141	86	8	6
601	452		
33	20	2	1
2081	**1511**	**427**	**372**
71	38	13	12
145	88	51	50
176	79	15	15
273	100	4	2
43			
1373	1206	344	293

21-16 续表1

卫生机构	Health Care Institutions	人员合计（人） 卫生技术人员 注册护士 Registered Nurses	药师（士） Junior Paramedics
总计	**Total**	**54329**	**4814**
一、医院	**Hospitals**	**40244**	**3195**
综合医院	General Hospitals	31535	2285
中医医院	Hospitals Specialized in Traditional Chinese Medicine	3343	471
中西医结合医院	Hospitals Integrating Traditional Chinese Medicine with Western Therapeutics in Practice	582	85
民族医院	Nationalities Hospitals		
专科医院	Specialized Hospitals	4743	349
护理院	Nursing centers	41	5
二、基层医疗卫生机构	**Commuting Health Hare Service Centre**	**10652**	**1377**
社区卫生服务中心(站)	Community Health Care Center(Station)	2456	440
社区卫生服务中心	Community Health Care Center	1928	356
社区卫生服务站	Community Health Care Station	528	84
卫生院	Health Center	1043	218
街道卫生院	Urban Health-center	103	13
乡镇卫生院	Rural Health-center	940	205
村卫生室	Village Clinics	234	
门诊部	Outpatient Department	2242	240
诊所、卫生所、医务室	Clinic, Health Center, Infirmary	4677	479
三、专业公共卫生机构	**College of Public Health Institutions**	**2856**	**228**
疾病预防控制中心	Center for Disease Control and Prevention	73	16
专科疾病防治院（所、站）	Specialized Disease Prevention and Cure Center (Place, Station)	1025	79
健康教育所（站、中心）	Health Education Institute (Station, Center)		
妇幼保健院（所、站）	Maternal and Child Health Hospital (Place, Station)	1714	124
急救中心（站）	Emergency Center (Station)	17	2
采供血机构	Blood Collection Agencies	26	6
卫生监督所（中心）	Health Supervision Agencies (Center)		
计划生育技术服务机构	Institutions of Technical Service for Family Planning	1	1
四、其他卫生机构	**Other Health Institution**	**577**	**14**
疗养院	Nursing Centres	15	5
卫生监督检验(监测、检测)所(站)	Health Supervision and Inspection Agencies(Station)		
医学科学研究机构	Medical Scientific Research Institutions	8	2
医学在职培训机构	Medical Training Institutions	13	2
临床检验中心（所、站）	Clinical Testing Center (Place, Station)	2	
统计信息中心	Statistical Information Center		
其他	Other	539	5

continued 1

Total Number of Employed Persons (person)				
Medical Technical Personnel		其他技术人员 Other Technical Personnel	管理人员 Administrative Personnel	工勤技能人员 Logistics Technical Workers
技师（士） Technicians	其他 Others			
6983	**10816**	**937**	**10526**	**11061**
4707	**7042**	**674**	**7892**	**8126**
3633	5436	481	5673	5887
428	883	99	783	866
88	69	4	181	112
554	653	89	1248	1257
4	1	1	7	4
1206	**2425**	**78**	**1395**	**1625**
502	972	47	573	608
433	907	38	466	571
69	65	9	107	37
339	937	26	294	343
15	33		8	22
324	904	26	286	321
264	190	5	312	276
101	326		216	398
742	**1184**	**103**	**988**	**1073**
221	161	39	109	105
153	142	8	322	190
	26	28	17	
352	357	13	378	684
		10	20	24
14	32	1	49	5
	452	1	87	61
2	14	3	6	4
328	**165**	**82**	**251**	**237**
4	1		14	19
18	9	21	20	16
3	46	51	39	7
91	3	2	62	109
			41	2
212	106	8	75	84

21-17 各区县医疗卫生机构、床位及人员情况（2020年）

Number of Health Care Institutions, Beds and Employed Persons in Health Care Institutions By Region (2020)

区 县	Region	机构（个）Number of Health Care Institutions (unit)	床位（张）Number of Beds (unit)	人员合计（人）Total Number of Employed Persons (person)	#卫生技术人员 Total Number of Medical Technical Personnel
合 计	**Total**	**7129**	**75007**	**142809**	**117656**
新城区	Xincheng	296	8114	16104	13436
碑林区	Beilin	452	9297	17986	15321
莲湖区	Lianhu	436	9175	16733	13708
灞桥区	Baqiao	431	3284	5973	5084
未央区	Weiyang	556	6832	14054	12153
雁塔区	Yanta	671	9289	21785	18113
阎良区	Yanliang	186	1935	3300	2669
临潼区	Lintong	515	3135	4726	3718
长安区	Chang'an	603	6950	10803	8687
高陵区	Gaoling	233	2979	3892	3223
鄠邑区	Huyi	433	3152	5434	4459
蓝田县	Lantian	585	2162	3199	2577
周至县	Zhouzhi	485	2285	4259	3079
西咸新区	Xixian	744	2804	5198	4031
高新区	Gaoxin	449	3526	8996	7115
国际港务区	International Trade&Logistic Park	54	88	367	283

注：本表数据来源于市卫健委。

21-18 各区县农村村级卫生组织情况（2020年）

Village Level Health Organization in the Rural Area by Region（2020）

区县	Region	村卫生室（个）Village Health Room（unit）	乡村医生和卫生员（人）Rural Doctors and Health Workers（person）	#乡村医生 Rural Doctors	#卫生员 Health Workers
全市	**Total**	**2961**	**2629**	**2495**	**134**
新城区	Xincheng				
碑林区	Beilin				
莲湖区	Lianhu				
灞桥区	Baqiao	149	129	128	1
未央区	Weiyang	45	28	28	
雁塔区	Yanta	21	25	24	1
阎良区	Yanliang	80	104	100	4
临潼区	Lintong	330	304	265	39
长安区	Chang'an	309	232	230	2
高陵区	Gaoling	122	159	155	4
鄠邑区	Huyi	322	190	187	3
蓝田县	Lantian	481	303	302	1
周至县	Zhouzhi	399	540	470	70
西咸新区	Xixian	470	387	385	2
高新区	Gaoxin	197	186	181	5
国际港务区	International Trade&Logistic Park	36	42	40	2

注：本表数据来源于市卫健委。

21–19 各区县社区卫生服务中心（站）情况（2020年）

Situations of Community Health Service Center（Station）by Region（2020）

区 县	Region	社区卫生服务中心（站）（个）Community Health Care Center(Station) (unit)	床位数（张）Number of Beds (unit)	人员数（人）Personnel Number (person)	卫生技术人员（人）Medical Technical Personnel (person)	执业（助理）医师 Licensed (Assistant) Doctors	注册护士 Registered Nurses
全 市	**Total**	**262**	**1825**	**7471**	**6243**	**1873**	**2456**
新城区	Xincheng	18	35	341	286	104	107
碑林区	Beilin	21		410	335	143	118
莲湖区	Lianhu	25	235	970	811	249	312
灞桥区	Baqiao	24	75	507	426	139	173
未央区	Weiyang	28	70	802	687	204	300
雁塔区	Yanta	45	140	1383	1206	356	527
阎良区	Yanliang	8	76	169	152	38	70
临潼区	Lintong	28	584	715	599	151	163
长安区	Chang'an	16	339	680	540	150	165
高陵区	Gaoling	8		53	49	11	22
鄠邑区	Huyi						
蓝田县	Lantian						
周至县	Zhouzhi	1		136	98	13	50
西咸新区	Xixian	21	38	403	322	103	144
高新区	Gaoxin	16	145	680	549	159	219
国际港务区	International Trade& Logistic Park	3	88	222	183	53	86

注：本表数据来源于市卫健委。

21-20 主要年份医疗卫生机构各类人员情况

Number of Personnel in Health Care Institutions in Representative Years

单位：人 (person)

指标	Item	2010	2014	2015	2016	2017	2018	2019	2020
人员合计	**Total**	**71230**	**95633**	**102684**	**107906**	**116939**	**125179**	**136333**	**142809**
卫生技术人员	Medical Technical Personnel	56579	76005	81462	86258	94221	101477	112243	117656
执业（助理）医师	Licensed (Assistant) Doctors	18763	24820	26626	27864	30820	33776	38469	40714
#执业医师	Chartered Doctors	16613	22145	23818	25023	27683	30322	34102	36086
注册护士	Registered Nurses	22640	32136	34819	37518	41603	46450	51882	54329
药师(士)	Junior Paramedics	3030	3709	3957	4075	4280	4423	4709	4814
技师（士）	Technicians	4589	4276	4690	5058	5593	6035	6633	6983
其他	Other	7557	11064	11370	11743	11925	10793	10550	10816
其他技术人员	Other Technical Personnel	1156	621	816	835	839	925	936	937
管理人员	Administrative Personnel	6416	7355	8248	8470	9003	9723	10229	10526
工勤技能人员	Logistics Technical Workers	7079	7944	8326	8913	9179	9707	9901	11061

注：本表数据来源于市卫健委。
本表2011年及以后合计栏数据含乡村医生和卫生员。
本表2017年及以后年份数据含西咸新区。

21-21 医疗卫生机构门诊、住院及病床使用情况（2020年）

指 标	Item	总诊疗人次数（人次） 总计 Total
总计	**Total**	**55614881**
一、医院	**Hospitals**	**33480359**
综合医院	General Hospitals	25684087
中医医院	Hospitals Specialized in Traditional Chinese Medicine	3260311
中西医结合医院	Hospitals Integrating Traditional Chinese Medicine with Western Therapeutics in Practice	292414
民族医院	Nationalities Hospitals	
专科医院	Specialized Hospitals	4228153
护理院	Nursing Centers	15394
二、基层医疗卫生机构	**Commuting Health Care Service Centre**	**19152342**
社区卫生服务中心（站）	Community Health Care Center(Station)	4184254
社区卫生服务中心	Community Health Care Center	3401877
社区卫生服务站	Community Health Care Station	782377
卫生院	Health Center	1870786
街道卫生院	Urban Health-center	180347
乡镇卫生院	Rural Health-center	1690439
村卫生室	Village Clinics	6282705
门诊部	Outpatient Department	1986968
诊所、卫生所、医务室	Clinic, Health Center, Infirmary	4827629
三、专业公共卫生机构	**College of Public Health Institutions**	**2957013**
专科疾病防治院（所、站）	Specialized Disease Prevention and Cure Center (Place, Station)	244992
妇幼保健院（所、站）	Maternal and Child Health Hospital (Place, Station)	2516171
急救中心（站）	Emergency Center(Station)	195850
四、其他卫生机构	**Other Health Institution**	**25167**
疗养院	Sanatorium	25167

注：本表数据来源于市卫健委。
本表数据含西咸新区。

Medical and Health Institutions Outpatient, Inpatient and Utilization of Beds（2020）

Total Number of Clinics (person time)				观察室 Observation Room	
门、急诊人次数合计 Total Number of People In Outpatient and Emergency Department	门诊人次数(人次) Number of Outpatients (person time)	急诊人次数小计(人次) The Number of Emergency Subtotal (person time)	死亡人数（人） Number of Deaths (person)	留观病例数(人次) Number of Patients Receiving (person times)	死亡人数（人） Number of Deaths (persons)
54999762	**51683056**	**3316706**	**3709**	**45951**	**55**
33274632	**30374442**	**2900190**	**3699**	**42755**	**55**
25610872	23127867	2483005	3478	39520	55
3182424	3074727	107697	75	255	
291047	269455	21592	55	689	
4174895	3886999	287896	91	2291	
15394	15394				
18779858	**18708778**	**71080**	**2**		
4037343	3975653	61690	2		
3268976	3209958	59018	2		
768367	765695	2672			
1860620	1851230	9390			
180347	179588	759			
1680273	1671642	8631			
6080786	6080786				
1985381	1985381				
4815728	4815728				
2920105	**2574823**	**345282**	**8**	**3196**	
239488	234514	4974	3		
2484767	2340309	144458	5	3196	
195850		195850			
25167	**25013**	**154**			
25167	25013	154			

21-21 续表1

指 标	Item	急诊死亡率（%）Emergency Mortality (%)	入院人数合计（人）Total Number of Admission Patients (person)
总计	**Total**	**0.11**	**2085858**
一、医院	**Hospitals**	**0.13**	**1953423**
综合医院	General Hospitals	0.14	1566402
中医医院	Hospitals Specialized in Traditional Chinese Medicine	0.07	163774
中西医结合医院	Hospitals Integrating Traditional Chinese Medicine with Western Therapeutics in Practice	0.25	20732
民族医院	Nationalities Hospitals		
专科医院	Specialized Hospitals	0.03	200582
护理院	Nursing Centers		1933
二、基层医疗卫生机构	**Commuting Health Care Service Centre**		**25690**
社区卫生服务中心（站）	Community Health Care Center(Station)		14566
社区卫生服务中心	Community Health Care Center		14566
社区卫生服务站	Community Health Care Station		
卫生院	Health Center		11124
街道卫生院	Urban Health-center		179
乡镇卫生院	Rural Health-center		10945
村卫生室	Village Clinics		
门诊部	Outpatient Department		
诊所、卫生所、医务室	Clinic, Health Center, Infirmary		
三、专业公共卫生机构	**College of Public Health Institutions**		**104245**
专科疾病防治院（所、站）	Specialized Disease Prevention and Cure Center (Place,Station)	0.06	26364
妇幼保健院（所、站）	Maternal and Child Health Hospital (Place, Station)		77881
急救中心（站）	Emergency Center(Station)		
四、其他卫生机构	**Other Health Institution**		**2500**
疗养院	Sanatorium		2500

continued 1

出院人数合计 (人) Total Number of Discharge Patients (person)	死亡人数 (人) Number of Hospital Csualty (person)	病床周转次数 (次) Nnumber of Bed Remover (times)	病床使用率 (%) Bed occupancy rate (%)	出院者平均住院 (天) Average Stay Days in Hospital (day)
2080434	**10086**	**28.4**	**64.52**	**8.3**
1948908	**9913**	**30.1**	**67.39**	**8.1**
1562100	9229	33.1	70.64	7.8
164911	334	23	60.12	9.8
20775	71	20.7	56.14	10
199200	254	21.7	58.69	9.6
1922	25	9.2	19.47	7.7
25461	**4**	**6.9**	**15.83**	**8.2**
14526	4	8.1	17.05	7.6
14526	4	8.1	17.05	7.6
10935		5.7	14.69	9.1
175		1.6	22.68	51.2
10760		5.9	14.21	8.4
103733	**169**	**23**	**65.66**	**10.3**
25856	139	9.4	66.82	25.3
77877	30	44.3	63.84	5.3
2332		**10.1**	**22.33**	**8**
2332		10.1	22.33	8

21-22 提供住宿的社会服务机构（2020年）

Social Welfare Insititutions Providing Accommodation（2020）

指 标	Item	机构数（个）Number of Institutions（unit）	年末职工人数（人）Number of Staff and Workers at the End of Year（person）	#女性 Female	床位数（张）Number of Beds（unit）	年末在院人数（人）Number of Persons Housed at the Year-end（person）
1、养老服务机构	Pension Service Institutions	168	3861	2158	28123	11877
2、儿童福利院	Baby Welfare Homes	2	77	49	565	551
3、社会福利医院	Social Welfare Hospitals	1	135	59	750	410
4、救助站	Rescue Station	8	102	30	472	92

注：本表数据来源于市民政局。
本表数据含西咸新区。

21-23 主要年份社会福利事业单位机构及人员情况

Number of Social Welfare Institutions and Personnel

单位：个、人 (unit, person)

指 标	Item	2010	2014	2015	2016	2017	2018	2019	2020
一、机构	**Insititutions**								
烈士纪念建筑物管理单位	Institutions Managing Memorial Buildings of Martyrs	2	2	2	2	2	2	2	2
救助类单位	Units Providing Assistance	8	9	9	9	9	9	9	8
殡仪服务单位	Funeral Service Units	22	26	26	25	27	25	26	25
殡仪馆	Funeral Homes	4	3	3	3	3	3	3	3
公墓	Cemeteries	14	16	16	16	19	18	19	19
殡葬管理单位	Funeral Management Units	4	7	7	6	5	4	4	3
二、人员	**Staff**								
烈士纪念建筑物管理单位	Institutions Managing Memorial Buildings of Martyrs	37	44	42	42	44	42	40	40
救助类单位	Units Providing Assistance	116	139	119	121	114	110	113	102
殡仪服务单位	Funeral Service Units	1371	1392	1510	1510	1518	1337	1282	1299
殡仪馆	Funeral Homes	375	470	497	481	484	458	476	461
公墓	Cemeteries	939	838	929	953	959	824	761	807
殡葬管理单位	Funeral Management Units	57	84	84	76	75	55	45	31

注：本表数据来源于市民政局及退役军人事务局。
本表2017年及以后年份数据含西咸新区。

21–24 社会保障基本情况（2020年）

Basic Situation of Social Security (2020)

单位：万人、万户 （10 000 persons、10 000 households）

指 标	Item	2020
基本养老保险参保人数	Number of Basic Old-age Insurance	768.98
1. 城镇企业职工养老保险参保人数	Number of Town Enterprise Worker Old-age Insurance	486.93
其中：离退休人员	Retired Personnel	70.75
2. 机关事业单位养老保险参保人数	Number of Institution Old-age Insurance	29.67
其中：离退休人员	Retired Personnel	10.59
3. 城乡居民养老保险参保人数	Number of Rural Residents Old-age Insurance	252.38
城乡基本医疗保险参保人数	Number of urban basic medical insurance	1062.64
失业保险参保人数	Number of unemployed insurance	240.75
生育保险参保人数	Number of Maternity insurance	283.8
工伤保险参保人数	Number of industrial injury insurance	280.19
城市居民最低生活保障户数	The Number of Minimum Living Guarantee for Urban Resident Households	1.44
城市居民最低生活保障人数	The Number of Minimum Living Guarantee for Urban Residents	2.10
农村居民最低生活保障户数	The Number of Minimum Living Guarantee for Rural Resident Households	3.05
农村居民最低生活保障人数	The Number of Minimum Living Guarantee for Rural Residents	8.25

注：本表数据来源于市人社局、市民政局及市医疗保障局。
本表中“基本养老保险参保人数”中的“机关事业单位养老参保人数”2019年含西咸新区数据，2020年不含西咸新区数据，另两个分项指标不含西咸新区数据。其他指标均含西咸新区数据。

21–25 全市及各区县优抚对象人员情况（2020年）

Statistics on Persons Enjoying Favoured Treatment by Region（2020）

单位：人 (person)

区 县	Region	伤残人员 Number of Disabled Veterans	烈军属人员 Number of Family Members of Martyrs and Soldiers	在乡复员军人 Demobilized Soldiers in Hometown	带病回乡退伍军人 Veterans Returning Home in Sick
合 计	**Total**	**5575**	**737**	**1816**	**1136**
新城区	Xincheng	607	32	4	2
碑林区	Beilin	656	34	6	2
莲湖区	Lianhu	765	46	18	9
灞桥区	Baqiao	265	35	67	91
未央区	Weiyang	282	43	63	15
雁塔区	Yanta	752	59	44	12
阎良区	Yanliang	118	36	113	59
临潼区	Lintong	295	76	356	179
长安区	Chang'an	332	33	119	31
高陵区	Gaoling	146	32	123	101
鄠邑区	Huyi	210	51	96	58
蓝田县	Lantian	249	52	169	156
周至县	Zhouzhi	307	112	213	135
西咸新区	Xixian	348	68	287	211
高新区	GaoXin	197	19	98	36
国际港务区	Interational Trade& Logistic Park	46	9	40	39

注：本表数据来源于市退役军人事务局。

21-26 全市及各区县计划生育和婚姻登记情况（2020年）

Conditions of Birth Control and Marriage Registration by Region（2020）

区 县	Region	计划生育率（%）Family Planning Rate(%)	结婚对数（对）Marriages (couple)	再婚人数（人）Remarriages (person)	离婚对数（对）Divorced Couple (couple)
合 计	**Total**	**99.2**	**75887**	**39593**	**41785**
新城区	Xincheng	99.9	3613	1875	2309
碑林区	Beilin	99.9	5916	2699	2948
莲湖区	Lianhu	99.9	5639	2961	3716
灞桥区	Baqiao	99.8	4408	2736	2104
未央区	Weiyang	99.9	7494	3771	4312
雁塔区	Yanta	99.8	8085	4476	5417
阎良区	Yanliang	99.8	1847	1147	1154
临潼区	Lintong	99.3	4399	2326	2397
长安区	Chang'an	99.6	6509	4079	4597
高陵区	Gaoling	99.0	2722	1853	1621
鄠邑区	Huyi	98.7	2958	1379	1688
蓝田县	Lantian	98.1	3986	1537	1542
周至县	Zhouzhi	97.8	3997	1610	1670
西咸新区	Xixian	99.0	6703	3696	3269
高新区	Gaoxin	99.4	6473	2632	2426
国际港务区	International Trade &Logistic Park	84.7	1138	816	615

注：本表数据来源于市卫健委、市民政局、市中级人民法院。
本表中计划生育率、节育率、结婚对数、再婚人数含西咸新区，离婚对数西咸包含不完全。

21-27 全市及各区县妇幼卫生保健情况（2020年）

Care Health Conditions of Women and Child by Region（2020）

区 县	Region	5岁以下儿童死亡率（‰） Mortality rate of Children under 5-year-old（‰）	新生儿死亡率（‰） Infant Mortality Ratio（‰）	婴儿死亡率（‰） Neonatal Mortality Ratio（‰）
合 计	**Total**	**1.98**	**0.89**	**1.45**
新城区	Xincheng	1.46	0.97	1.46
碑林区	Beilin	1.95	0.24	1.22
莲湖区	Lianhu	2.38	1.51	2.05
灞桥区	Baqiao	1.53	0.61	1.38
未央区	Weiyang	1.47	0.53	0.88
雁塔区	Yanta	1.10	0.34	0.75
阎良区	Yanliang	3.81	2.12	2.54
临潼区	Lintong	1.26	0.42	0.63
长安区	Chang'an	2.25	0.86	1.50
高陵区	Gaoling	3.17	1.36	2.27
鄠邑区	Huyi	4.61	2.71	3.80
蓝田县	Lantian	2.93	0.98	1.95
周至县	Zhouzhi	2.69	0.83	2.28
西咸新区	Xixian	1.55	0.78	1.07
高新区	Gaoxin	2.18	1.54	1.79
国际港务区	International Trade&Logistic Park	2.29	0.76	1.52

注：本表数据来源于市卫健委。

21-27 续表1 continued 1

区 县	Region	孕产妇死亡率（1/10万） Maternal Mortality Ratio (one in hundred thousandth)	产妇住院分娩比例(%) Proportion of maternal Hospital Births（%）
合 计	**Total**	**11.98**	**100.00**
新城区	Xincheng	97.42	100.00
碑林区	Beilin		100.00
莲湖区	Lianhu	10.80	100.00
灞桥区	Baqiao	15.30	100.00
未央区	Weiyang	17.65	100.00
雁塔区	Yanta		100.00
阎良区	Yanliang		100.00
临潼区	Lintong	41.94	99.98
长安区	Chang'an	10.73	100.00
高陵区	Gaoling		100.00
鄠邑区	Huyi		100.00
蓝田县	Lantian		100.00
周至县	Zhouzhi		100.00
西咸新区	Xixian	9.70	99.99
高新区	Gaoxin		99.99
国际港务区	International Trade&Logistic Park		100.00

21-28 主要年份律师、公证及调解情况

Basic Statistics on Lawyer, Notaries and Mediation in Representative Years

指　标	Item	2010	2014	2015	2016	2017	2018	2019	2020
一、律师工作	**Lawyers**								
律师事务所（个）	Number of Law Offices (unit)	95	122	149	176	200	224	254	282
律师（人）	Lawyers(person)	1202	1846	2198	2462	2836	3796	4220	4769
#专职	Full-time	1139	1738	2092	2337	2716	3476	3751	4222
兼职	Part-time	63	88	91	84	120	148	188	141
刑事诉讼辩护及代理（件）	The Criminal suit Defence andagents(suit)		3118	3524	3260	5872	5869	7481	7621
民事诉讼代理（件）	Civil Litigation Agent(suit)		9985	15308	16743	24593	28810	37116	40742
行政诉讼代理（件）	Administrative litigation(suit)		374	532	601	1584	1256	1720	2248
非诉讼法律事务（件）	Non-litigation legal affairs(suit)		2352	2780	2840	4981	3900	5864	7127
二、公证工作	**Notarization**								
公证处（个）	Number of Notary Offices (unit)	14	14	14	14	14	14	14	14
公证人员（人）	Notarial Personnel (person)	202	298	307	293	285	296	328	329
#公证员	Notaries	112	118	121	115	116	116	114	110
办理公证件数（件）	Number of Notarized Documents Issued (case)	106491	135413	135622	144662	150300	161932	122152	96125
国内	Domestic	72670	90171	86589	95194	96085	110311	75486	68848
涉外	Foreign-related	33410	44773	49033	49468	54215	51621	46666	27277
港澳台	Hong Kong. Macao and Taiwan related	411	469	373	512	641	1601	632	271
三、人民调解工作	**Number of People Mediations**								
已建调委会数（个）	Number of Mediation Committees (unit)	3911	4059	4052	4062	3903	3589	3411	3409
调解人员数（人）	Number of Mediators (person)	15717	15793	14838	14888	14295	14216	13895	13321
调解纠纷数（件）	Number of Civil Disputes Mediated (case)	22247	33641	31696	27455	48690	24868	22377	21209
#调解成功数	Number of Cases Successfully Mediated	22164	32537	30590	26426	47921	24364	21967	20830

注：本表数据来源于市司法局。
2015年开始司法统计将港澳台并入国内，表中2015年以后办理公证件数中港澳台所列数据为其中数，2014年及以前年份港澳台数据与国内、涉外数据为并列关系。
本表2017年及以后年份数据含西咸新区。

21-29 主要年份共青团组织情况

Basic Facts on Communist Youth League in Representative Years

单位：个、人　　(unit, person)

指 标	Item	2010	2014	2015	2016	2017	2018	2019	2020
一、基层团组织	Grass-root Youth League Organisations	7006	10152	10074	10530	10237	9438	10359	11879
二、共青团员	Youth League Members	308141	343121	331261	251706	201789	162527	166284	206018
三、专职团干部	Full-time Youth League Cadre	311	659	496	165	158	96	100	98

注：本表数据来源于共青团西安市委员会。
本表数据不含西咸新区。

21-30 妇联组织及工作情况（2020年）

The Basic Situation of Women's Federation（2020）

指 标	Item	2020
一、妇联组织	**Women's Organizations**	
市级妇联（个）	Municipal Women's Federation(unit)	1
街道妇联（个）	Street Women's Federation(unit)	139
社区妇联（个）	Community Women's Federation(unit)	1026
县（区）妇联（个）	County (district) Women's Federation(unit)	14
乡（镇）妇联（个）	Township (town) Women's Federation(unit)	49
村妇联	Village Women's Representative Conference	2115
二、妇联工作	**Women's Work**	
巾帼建功标兵（个）	Women Business Model(unit)	15
巾帼建功集体（个）	Group of Women Business Model(unit)	132
巾帼文明岗（个）	Women's Civilized Model Post(unit)	50
三八红旗手标兵（人）	Models of "March 8 Red-Banner Holders" (person)	11
三八红旗手（人）	March 8 Red-Banner Holders (person)	136
三八红旗集体（个）	March 8 Red-Banner Groups(unit)	87
五好家庭（户）	Five-virtue Family (household)	46
本级最美家庭（户）	The Best Family at the Present Level (household)	711
乡镇最美家庭（户）	The Best Family in the Town (household)	160
街道最美家庭（户）	The Best Family in the Street (household)	431
村最美家庭（户）	The Best Family in the Village (household)	559
社区最美家庭（户）	The Best Family in the Community (household)	504

注：本表数据来源于市妇联。
本表数据为西安原口径数据。

21–31 主要年份交通、火灾及安全生产情况

Transportation, Fire and Safety Production in Representative Years

指 标	Item	2010	2014	2015	2016	2017	2018	2019	2020
道路交通事故	**Road Accidents**								
事故数(起)	Number of Cases（case）	2323	1970	2392	2943	2858	3153	2973	2835
死亡人数（人）	Number of Deaths（person）	531	483	481	476	453	430	381	351
受伤人数（人）	Number of Injuries（person）	2520	1832	2318	3012	2856	3219	3156	2978
损失（万元）	Economic Loss（10 000yuan）	736.6	1264.0	1470.2	1653.7	1777.3	2190.9	1808.5	1737.5
火灾事故	**Fire Accidents**								
事故数(起)	Number of Cases (case)	1825	3199	2590	3434	2353	2066	1871	3034
死亡人数（人）	Number of Deaths (person)	13	17	20	16	8	26	18	27
受伤人数（人）	Number of Injuries (person)	7	5	7	7	2	37	2	2
损失（万元）	Economic Loss (10 000 yuan)	2224.2	4381.1	2401.5	1901.1	1659.1	1783.1	1886.6	2386.7
农机事故	**Farm Machinery Accidents**								
事故数(起)	Number of Cases (case)	5	24	47	4	2	4	1	2
死亡人数（人）	Number of Deaths (person)		1	1	1		2	1	1
工矿商贸事故	**Accidents in Industry, Mine,Business and Trade**								
事故数(起)	Number of Cases (case)	20	10	10	33	36	33	28	45
死亡人数（人）	Number of Deaths (person)	24	15	11	35	43	41	31	53

注：本表2019年及以后数据来源于市公安局、市应急管理局及市消防救援支队。2011年及以前年份数据均来自于市安监局；2012–2018年交通、火灾数据来自于市公安局，农机和工矿商贸数据来自市安监局。
2014年农机及工矿商贸事故发生起数统计口径变化，数据与以前年份不可比。
本表中交通火灾数据为西安原口径，农机和工矿商贸事故2017年及以后年份含西咸新区。

21–32 主要年份刑事案件情况

Data on Criminal Cases in Representative Years

指　标	Item	2010	2014	2015	2016	2017	2018	2019	2020
一、案件数情况	**Data on Number of Cases**								
立案数（起）	Number of Registered Cases(case)	48566	77051	108955	98056	79828	70332	69800	62738
破案数（起）	Number of Cleared up Cases(case)	18906	25830	28629	30730	33128	33616	36566	19540
破案率（%）	Percent of Cleared up Cases（%）	38.9	33.5	26.3	31.3	41.5	47.8	52.4	31.3
抓获作案成员(人)	Number of Criminals Caught(person)	13104	14184	12827	11982	12848	11153	15179	15196
二、查获犯罪集团情况	**Data on Hunted down and Seized Criminal Gangs**								
查获犯罪集团个数（个）	Number of Hunted down and Seized Criminal Gangs (unit)	186	359	153	119	97	75	46	15
查获犯罪集团人数（人）	Number of Members of Hunted down and Seized Criminal Gangs (person)	939	1508	680	492	418	359	254	62
涉及案件（起）	Number of Cases Involved(case)	1172	1111	291	242	303	180	199	19
三、涉枪案件情况	**Data on Cases with Guns Involved**								
立案数（起）	Number of Registered Cases(case)	16	13	9	21	22	13	14	13
破案数（起）	Number of Cleared up Cases(case)	11	8	6	17	17	7	10	4
破案率（%）	Percent of Cleared up Cases（%）	68.8	61.5	66.7	81.0	77.3	53.8	71.4	30.8

注：本表数据来源于市公安局。
　　本表数据为西安原口径数据。

21–33 主要年份治安案件情况

Data on Public Order Cases in Representative Years

指　标	Item	2010	2014	2015	2016	2017	2018	2019	2020
受理数（起）	Number of Accepted(case)	58968	108780	104553	109124	95821	92927	90250	77038
查处数（起）	Number of Investigated and Prosecuted(case)	57151	106811	100954	106999	93634	90563	88898	76345
查处率（%）	Percent of Investigated and Prosecuted Cases(%)	96.9	98.2	96.6	98.1	97.7	97.5	98.5	99.1
查处违法人数（人）	Number of Investigated and Prosecuted Laws breakers and Crime Committer(person)	45856	52922	40838	40126	34625	32185	31219	26155

注：本表数据来源于市公安局。
　　本表数据为西安原口径数据。

21-34 主要年份西安市人民检察院案件办理情况

Data on Acceptance of Cases of Xi'an People's Procuratorate

指 标	Item	2010	2014	2015	2016	2017	2018	2019	2020
一、审查逮捕案件受理件数（件）	**Examination and Arresting(case)**	**4229**	**6443**	**6545**	**7381**	**7184**	**7216**	**8345**	**5524**
二、逮捕各类案件人数（人）	**Arresting of Criminals of each kind(person)**	**6183**	**7534**	**6692**	**7763**	**7511**	**7162**	**9253**	**5523**
决定逮捕贪污贿赂犯罪嫌疑人（人）	Suspects of Corporation and Bribery to be Arrested (person)	51	64	100	26	27	56	29	
决定逮捕渎职、侵权犯罪嫌疑人（人）	Suspects of Misprision and Tortious to be Arrested (person)	2	18	4		22	2	5	1
批准逮捕刑事犯罪嫌疑人（人）	Suspects of Criminal to be Arrested (person)	6130	7452	6588	7737	7462	7104	9219	5522
三、刑事立案监督、侦查活动监督（件）	**Supervision of Acceptance of Criminal Cases and Investigation (case)**	**623**	**284**	**162**	**118**	**79**	**56**	**62**	**223**
四、审查起诉案件受理件数（件）	**Examination and Prosecution (case)**	**4662**	**7278**	**6922**	**8090**	**8933**	**9288**	**11107**	**9017**
五、起诉各类案件人数（人）	**Prosecution of Criminals of each kind(person)**	**5946**	**8399**	**8018**	**9445**	**10365**	**10193**	**11894**	**9981**
起诉贪污贿赂犯罪被告人（人）	Prosecution of Criminals of Corruption and Bribery to be Defendants(person)	163	123	153	154	179	101	102	87
起诉渎职、侵权犯罪被告人（人）	Prosecution of Misprision and Tortious to be Defendants (person)	22	44	17	39	38	12	8	8
起诉刑事犯罪被告人（人）	Prosecution of Criminal to be Defendants (person)	5761	8232	7848	9252	10148	10080	11784	9886

注：本表数据来源于市检察院。
本表数据为西安原口径数据。

21-35 西安市中级人民法院案件基本情况（2020年）

Law Cases Basic Data of Xi'an Intermediate People's Court（2020）

指 标	Item	全市结案（件）the whole City(case)	中级人民法院结案 the Intermediate People's Court	基层人民法院结案 the Basic People's Court
合 计	**Total**	**265811**	**31112**	**234699**
刑事	Criminal	9592	2423	7169
民事	Civil	164567	21612	142955
行政	Administration	1245	12	1233
执行	Execution	84730	5374	79356
其他类型	Other types	5677	1691	3986

注：本表数据来源于市中级人民法院。
本表数据为西安原口径数据。

主要统计指标解释

艺术表演团体 指由文化部门主办或实行行业管理（经文化行政部门审批并领取营业性演出许可证），专门从事表演艺术等活动的各类专业艺术表演团体，含民间职业剧团（不包括群众业余文艺表演团队）。

艺术表演场馆 指由文化部门主办或实行行业管理（向文化行政部门备案或领取合资（合作）演出场所许可证），有观众席、舞台、灯光设备，公开售票、专供文艺团体演出的文化活动场所。附属于文化部门机构内非独立核算的剧场、排演场，公开营业的也应单独统计。

图书馆 指各类图书馆的管理与服务（对文献和信息的搜集、整理、存储、利用和管理，向社会公众开放并提供科学、文化等各种知识普及教育）。包括公共图书馆和各类机构内部举办的或单独举办的图书馆的管理与服务。不包括部队系统以及文化馆（文化中心、群众艺术馆）、文化站内设的图书室。

群众文化活动 指开展群众文化活动的场所的管理和组织活动。包括文化馆（含综合性文化中心、群众艺术馆）、文化站、文化宫、少年宫等群众文化活动。在本制度中，目前暂不统计文化部门以外的文化宫和少年宫。

文化馆 （含综合性文化中心、群众艺术馆）、文化站：指专门从事群众文化活动的群众文化场馆。不包括临时抽调人员组成、没有编制的农村和街道文化工作队、服务站等。

广播节目综合人口覆盖率 根据国家广电总局制定的《广播电视人口覆盖率统计技术标准和方法》进行统计调查的，分别反映中央、省级、地市级、县级广播节目在本行政区域的综合覆盖情况，反应以无线方式传输的广播节目综合覆盖情况，综合反映广播公共服务覆盖的规模、能力、水平。

电视节目综合人口覆盖率 根据国家广电总局制定的《广播电视人口覆盖率统计技术标准和方法》进行统计调查的，分别反映中央、省级、地市级、县级电视节目在本行政区域的综合覆盖情况，反应以无线方式传输的电视节目综合覆盖情况，综合反映广播公共服务覆盖的规模、能力、水平。

博物馆 指为了研究、教育、欣赏的目的，收藏、保护、展示人类活动和自然环境的见证物，向公众开放，非盈利性、永久性社会服务机构，包括以博物馆（院）、纪念馆（舍）科技馆、陈列馆等专有名称开展活动的单位。

等级运动员人数 指经考核正式批准授予等级运动员称号的人数。运动员等级分为国际级运动健将、运动健将、一级运动员、二级运动员、三级运动员、少年级运动员。

等级裁判员人数 指经考核正式批准授予等级裁判员称号的人数。裁判员等级分为国际裁判、国家级裁判、一级裁判、二级裁判、三级裁判。

医疗卫生机构 指从卫生（卫生计生）行政部门取得《医疗机构执业许可证》、《计划生育技术服务许可证》或从民政、工商行政、机构编制管理部门取得法人单位登记证书，为社会提供医疗服务、公共卫生服务或从事医学科研和学在职培训等工作的单位。包括医院、基层医疗卫生机构、专业公共卫生机构、其他医疗卫生机构。

医院 包括综合医院、中医医院、中西医结合医院、民族医院、各类专科医院和护理院，不包括专科疾病防治院、妇幼保健院和疗养院，包括医学院校附属医院。

基层医疗卫生机构 包括社区卫生服务中心（站）、乡镇(街道)卫生院、村卫生室、门诊部、诊所(医务室)。

专业公共卫生机构 包括疾病预防控制中心、专科疾病防治机构、妇幼保健机构（含妇幼保健计划生育服务中心）、健康教育机构、急救中心（站）、采供血机构、卫生监督机构、取得《医疗机构执业许可证》或《计划生育技术服务许可证》的计划生育技术服务机构。

其他医疗卫生机构 包括疗养院、临床检验中心、医学科研机构、医学在职教育机构、卫生监督（监测、检测）机构、医学考试中心、农村改水中心、人才交流中心、统计信息中心等卫生事业单位。

卫生技术人员 包括执业医师、执业助理医师、注册护士、药师(士)、检验及影像技师(士)、卫生监督员和见习医(药、护、技)师(士)等卫生专业人员。不包括从事管理工作的卫生技术人员(如院长、副院长、党委书记等)。

执业(助理)医师 指《医师执业证》“级别”为“执业（助理）医师”且实际从事医疗、预防保健工作的人员，不包括实际从事管理工作的执业（助理）医师。执业（助理）医师类别分为临床、中医、口腔和公共卫生四类。

提供住宿的社会服务机构 包括养老服务机构、精神疾病服务机构、儿童福利机构以及其他提供住宿机构。

烈士纪念建筑物管理机构 指民政部门管理的、独立核算的褒扬烈士的陵园、纪念馆等单位的总称。

殡葬服务机构 指为殡葬服务的单位总称。殡仪馆（含火葬场）、公墓、独立核算的骨灰堂、殡葬管理机构等。

公证人员 指在国家公证机关依法办理公证事务的司法人员，包括公证员、助理公证员和在公证处工作的其他人员。

办理公证文书 指公证处在一定时期内办结的公证文书件数。公证文书按司法部规定或批准的格式制作，包括国内公证和涉外公证两部分。国内公证分为经济合同公证和民事法律关系公证两大类。

调解人员 指在人民调解委员会担负调解民间一般民事纠纷和轻微违法行为引起纠纷的工作人员，包括调解委员会的委员和调解小组的调解员。

Explanatory Notes on Main Statistical Indicators

Arts Performance Troupes refer to the various professional performing arts groups, which sponsored by the cultural sectors or guided by the cultural society (Receive commercial performance license approved by the cultural administration authority),including non-governmental troupes. (The mass amateur arts performance troupes are not included.)

Arts Performance Places refer to the various sites for cultural activities, which sponsored by the cultural sectors or guided by the cultural society (approved by the cultural market administration, or receive joint/cooperative venues permit), with the facility of auditorium, stage and lighting, and selling tickets in public, including the opera halls and rehearse sites, etc. which are affiliated to the culture sectors without independent financial accounts and open to the public.

Library refers to all types of library management and services(collection, collation, storage, use and management of literature and information, open and provide scientific, cultural and other literacy education to the public). Including the management and services of public libraries and the libraries internally or separately organized by various sectors. Excluding the libraries in troops system and cultural palaces (cultural centers, mass art centers),cultural stations.

Mass Culture Center refers to the management and organization of the places where mass culture activities hold. Including cultural palace (cultural center ,mass art center), cultural stations, cultural palaces ,youth palaces and other mass cultural activities. In this system ,cultural palaces and youth palaces beyond cultural sectors are not counted at present.

Cultural Palaces (Cultural Centers, Mass Art Centers),Cultural Stations refers to the mass cultural venues specialized in mass cultural activities. Excluding rural and street cultural teams, service stations which made up by temporary without authorized strength.

Radio Coverage of Population refers to the comprehensive coverage which respectively reflected central, province, city, prefecture and county radio programs by wireless in the administrative region, and comprehensively reflect the size, capacity, level of the public broadcasting services, according to Statistical Standard and Method on Television and Radio Coverage of Population established by the State Administration of Broadcasting ,Film and Television

Television Coverage of Population refers to the comprehensive coverage which respectively reflected central, province, city, prefecture and county television programs by wireless in the administrative region, and comprehensively reflect the size, capacity, level of the public broadcasting services, according to Statistical Standard and Method on Television and Radio Coverage of Population established by the State Administration of Broadcasting , Film and Television

Museum refers to the non-profit, permanent society service sectors which collect , protect , show human activities and the witnesses of natural environment , including the units that organize activities with the proper name such as museum, memorial hall , science and technology museum, exhibition hall, etc.

Number of Athletes in Grades refers to the number of athletes who have been given titles through examination. The titles of athletes include international masters of sports, masters of sports, first-grade, second-grade and third-grade sportsmen and young athletes.

Number of Referees in Grades refers to the number of referees who have been given titles after examination. They are classified as international referees, national referees and referees of the first, second and third grades.

Medical and health institutions are the organizations that have got the practice license of medical institution and family planning technical services license from health administrative departments or have obtained legal entity registration certificate from civil, industrial and commercial administration, organization management departments, to provide medical services, public health services or engaged in medical research and medical job training. It includes hospitals, primary medical and health institutions, professional public health institutions, and other medical and health institutions.

Hospitals include general hospital, hospital of traditional Chinese medicine, hospital of integrated traditional Chinese and Western Medicine, National Hospital, various specialist hospitals and nursing homes, excluding specialized disease prevention and treatment centers , Maternity and child care centers and sanatorium, including hospitals affiliated to medical colleges and universities.

Primary medical and health institutions include community health service centers (stations), township (street) health centers, village clinics, outpatient department, clinics.

Professional public health institutions include the center for disease control and prevention, specialized disease prevention and treatment centers, maternity and child care centers (including maternal and child health family planning service center), health education institutions, first aid agencies,collecting and supplying agencies, health supervision institutions, andfamily planning technical service institutions which have got the practice license of medical institution and family planning technical services license.

Other medical and health institutions include sanatorium, clinical inspection center, medical research institutions, medical in-service education institutions, health supervision institutions, medical examination center, Rural change water quality center, personnel exchange center, statistical information center and other health institutions.

Health technical personnel include practicing physician, practicing assistant doctors, registered nurses, pharmacists, inspection and imaging technicians, health supervisors and clerksand other health professionals. It does not include health technical personnel engaged in management work such as Dean, vice president, Secretary of the Party committee, etc.

Practicing physician(assistant) refers to the practitioner who is a practitioner (assistant) doctor and actually engaged in medical care and preventive health care, and does not include the practitioner (assistant) practitioner who is actually engaged in the management work. Practitioners (assistants) are classified into four categories: clinical, Chinese traditional, oral and public health.

Social services providing accommodation include pension services, psychiatric care services, child welfare institutions, and other lodging establishments.

Martyr memorial buildings management organization refers to the floorboard of cemetery, memorial and other units which are independent accounting and managedby civil affairs department to praise the Martyrs

Funeral service agencies refer to the units that serve funeral services. It includes Funeral home (including crematorium), cemetery, independent accounting ashes hall, funeral and interment management organization, etc.

Notary Personnel refers to judicial workers of the state notary offices handling notarization work according to law. They include notaries, assistant notaries, and other people working for notary offices.

Notarized Documents refer to the documents settled by notary offices in a year. The notary documents are drawn up in accordance with the regulations of the Ministry of Justice, including domestic documents and foreign-related documents. Domestic documents are divided into two major categories, documents on economic contracts and documents on civil legal relations.

Mediators refer to workers on peoples mediation committees responsible for mediating in civil disputes and cases of slight infraction of the law. They include members of the mediation committees and mediators of mediation groups.

22 企业调查

ENTERPRISES INVESTIGATION

资料整理：薛　燕
Data management：Xue Yan
数据审核：黄雪冰
Data audit：Huang Xuebing

第二十二部分　企业调查

一、简要说明

1.本章资料主要包括各行业企业景气调查指数和企业家信心指数等，由西安市统计局社会经济调查中心提供。

2.本章资料调查范围：包括规模以上工业、资质内建筑业、限额以上批发和零售业、限额以上住宿和餐饮业、房地产开发业和规模以上服务业。

3.调查方法：采用非全面调查的方法进行统计。

二、主要指标

企业景气指数（第四季度）	121.1
企业家信心指数（第四季度）	123.5

22 ENTERPRISES INVESTIGATION

Ⅰ.Brief Introduction

1.Data in this chapter consists prosperity survey indices of various industries and Entrepreneur Expectation Indicator, provided by Xi'an Municipal Bureau of Statics .

2. The field of investigation and statistics range. The data in this chapter consists of industrial enterprises above designated size, construction enterprises which possess qualification grades, wholesaletrades and retail trades enterprises above designated size, hotels and catering services enterprises above designated size, real estate industry and services above designated size.

3. Methodology on survey. The survey is conducted bynon-overall investigation.

Ⅱ.Major Indicators

Business Climate Index（Fourth Quarter）	121.1
Entrepreneur Expectation Indicator（Fourth Quarter）	123.5

22-1 企业景气指数（2020年）

Business Climate Index（2020）

指　　标	Item	一季度 First Quarter	二季度 Second Quarter	三季度 Third Quarter	四季度 Fourth Quarter
企业景气指数	**Business Climate Index**	**86.2**	**111.1**	**120.9**	**121.1**
按行业门类分	**Grouped by Sector**				
工业	Industry	107.0	131.9	137.4	137.0
建筑业	Construction	81.6	105.0	110.2	109.7
批发和零售业	Wholesale and Retail Sales	76.9	106.7	120.7	123.8
住宿和餐饮业	Hotels and Catering Services	27.2	68.3	114.8	85.7
房地产开发业	Real Estate Development	109.2	124.0	127.2	130.1
规模以上服务业	Services above the Designated Size	72.6	97.6	110.4	112.2

22-2 企业家信心指数（2020年）

Entrepreneur Expectation Indicator（2020）

指　　标	Item	一季度 First Quarter	二季度 Second Quarter	三季度 Third Quarter	四季度 Fourth Quarter
企业家信心指数	**Entrepreneur Expectation Indicator**	**90.8**	**113.7**	**123.0**	**123.5**
按行业门类分	**Grouped by Sector**				
工业	Industry	103.6	133.7	138.2	138.7
建筑业	Construction	91.2	110.3	113.4	113.7
批发和零售业	Wholesale and Retail Sales	82.0	104.8	120.7	124.4
住宿和餐饮业	Hotels and Catering Services	37.9	74.1	122.1	87.3
房地产开发业	Real Estate Development	112.0	126.2	130.1	132.1
规模以上服务业	Services above the Designated Size	81.7	101.0	113.2	115.1

主要统计指标解释

企业景气指数：是根据企业家对本企业综合生产经营情况所作的判断与预期（通常是对“良好”、“一般”、“不佳”的选择）而编制的指数，用以综合反映企业的生产经营状况。企业景气指数也称“企业综合生产经营景气指数”。

企业家信心指数：是根据企业家对企业外部市场经济环境与宏观政策的认识、看法判断和预期（通常是对“乐观”、“一般”、“不乐观”的选择）而编制的指数，用以综合反映企业家对宏观经济环境的感受与信心。企业家信心指数也称“宏观经济景气指数”。

景气指数的表示方式：景气指数的表示范围在0~200之间，其含义：100为景气指数的临界值，表明景气状况变化不大；100~200为景气区间，表明景气状况趋于上升或改善，越接近于200，状况越景气；0~100为不景气区间，表明经济状况趋于下降或恶化，越接近于0，状况越不景气。

Explanatory Notes on Main Statistical Indicators

Business Climate Index it is an index worked out according to the judgment and anticipation (normally a choice from good, ordinary, not good) of entrepreneurs made based on synthetic productive and operational situation of the enterprise. It is used to reflect synthetically the productive and operational situation of the enterprise. It is also referred to as synthetic and productive operational prosperity index of enterprise.

Confidence index of entrepreneur it is an index worked out according to the judgment and anticipation (normally a choice from optimistic , ordinary , not optimistic) of entrepreneurs made based on their understandings and views of the market and economic environment outside the enterprise and the macro policies. It is used to reflect synthetically the confidence and feelings of the entrepreneurs to the macro economic environment. It is also referred to as macro-economy prosperity index.

The way to express prosperity index the range of prosperity index is from 0 to 200; 100 is the critical value, and means economic situation didn't change largely; from 100 to 200 is the interval of prosperity; and from 0 to 100 is the interval of not prosperity, meaning economic situation is going down or worse, the closer to 0, the worse the economic situation.

中国统计出版社有限公司最新图书简目

(仅供参考,以实际出版为准)

统计资料

中国统计年鉴　中国统计摘要　中国第三产业统计年鉴
中国第三次全国农业普查综合资料　国际统计年鉴　金砖国家联合统计手册
中国-东盟国家统计手册　中国农村统计年鉴　中国县域统计年鉴
中国农产品价格调查年鉴　中国城市统计年鉴　中国价格统计年鉴
中国贸易外经统计年鉴　中国零售和餐饮连锁企业统计年鉴　中国商品交易市场统计年鉴
大中型批发零售和住宿餐饮企业统计年鉴　中国住户调查年鉴　中国工业统计年鉴
中国环境统计年鉴　中国能源统计年鉴　中国建筑业统计年鉴
中国房地产统计年鉴　中国投资领域统计年鉴　长江经济带发展统计年鉴
中国人口和就业统计年鉴　中国劳动统计年鉴　中国社会统计年鉴
中国科技统计年鉴　中国高技术产业统计年鉴　全国企业创新调查年鉴
中国文化及相关产业统计年鉴　中国妇女儿童状况统计资料　中国青年发展状况统计年鉴
中国基本单位统计年鉴　中国教育统计年鉴　中国教育经费统计年鉴
中国民族统计年鉴　中国残疾人事业统计年鉴　中国电力统计年鉴

省级综合统计年鉴系列

北京 天津 河北 山西 内蒙古 辽宁 吉林 黑龙江 上海 江苏 浙江 安徽 福建 江西 山东 河南 湖北 湖南
广东 广西 海南 重庆 四川 贵州 云南 西藏 陕西 甘肃 青海 宁夏 新疆 新疆生产建设兵团

市(县)级综合统计年鉴系列

滨海新区 石家庄 唐山 邯郸 邢台 保定 承德 沧州 衡水 太原 大同 晋城 晋中 长治 忻州 朔州 临汾 运城
阳泉 吕梁 呼和浩特 包头 鄂尔多斯 赤峰 大连 长春 四平 延吉 延边 哈尔滨 齐齐哈尔 黑龙江垦区 浦东新区
南京 无锡 徐州 常州 苏州 南通 淮安 盐城 扬州 镇江 宿迁 江阴 丹阳 海门 张家港 通州 如东 杭州 宁波
绍兴 台州 温州 金华 嘉兴 湖州 丽水 舟山 合肥 安庆 福州 厦门 漳州 宁德 龙岩 莆田 泉州 三明 南平 思明
南昌 上饶 抚州 赣州 九江 景德镇 宁都 济南 青岛 枣庄 潍坊 聊城 郑州 洛阳 三门峡 南阳 商丘 平顶山
信阳 济源 武汉 宜昌 十堰 荆州 荆门 咸宁 黄冈 长沙 广州 东莞 惠州 深圳 汕尾 珠海 南宁 桂林 柳州
防城港 贵港 梧州 玉林 钦州 海口 三亚 儋州 成都 贵阳 毕节 黔南 昆明 文山 德宏 西安 安康 延安 汉中
渭南 商洛 榆林 银川 兰州 庆阳 乌鲁木齐

调查年鉴系列

天津 内蒙古 上海 河南 湖北 湖南 广西 重庆 四川 云南 甘肃 宁夏 南宁 桂林 贵港 昆明

统计方法应用/实用手册

Python数据分析基础（第二版）　非参数统计（第五版）　现代金融投资统计分析（第四版）
国民经济核算初级教程（第二版）　国民经济核算教程（第五版）　概率统计基础
全国统计专业技术资格考试系列考试用书: 统计业务知识（第四版修订版）　统计业务知识学习指导与习题
全国统计专业技术资格考试系列考试用书: 统计相关知识（第四版）　统计相关知识学习指导与习题

统计通俗读物/统计科普图书

领导干部统计知识问答（第二版）　统计公文写作及会议办理实用手册　大数据在统计工作中的应用案例汇编
中国国民经济核算知识问答（修订版）　地区生产总值核算国际比较研究　新中国统计制度方法的发展与改革

重点图书

第七次全国人口普查年鉴　第四次全国经济普查地图集　中国经济普查年鉴2018
新编英汉汉英统计大词典　中国国民经济核算体系2016　国民经济行业分类注释
挑大学选专业2020—考研择校指南　挑大学选专业2020—高考志愿填报指南　中华医学统计百科全书